KU-270-758

MACROECONOMICS

Ninth Edition

RUDIGER DORNBUSCH

Late of Massachusetts Institute of Technology
Ford Professor of Economics and
International Management

◆

STANLEY FISCHER

Citigroup

◆

RICHARD STARTZ

University of Washington
Castor Professor of Economics

Boston   Burr Ridge, IL   Dubuque, IA   Madison, WI   New York   San Francisco   St. Louis
Bangkok   Bogotá   Caracas   Kuala Lumpur   Lisbon   London   Madrid   Mexico City
Milan   Montreal   New Delhi   Santiago   Seoul   Singapore   Sydney   Taipei   Toronto

MACROECONOMICS
International Edition 2004

Exclusive rights by McGraw-Hill Education (Asia), for manufacture and export. This book cannot be re-exported from the country to which it is sold by McGraw-Hill. The International Edition is not available in North America.

Published by McGraw-Hill/Irwin, a business unit of The McGraw-Hill Companies, Inc., 1221 Avenue of the Americas, New York, NY 10020. Copyright © 2004, 2001, 1998, 1994, 1990, 1987, 1984, 1981, 1978 by The McGraw-Hill Companies, Inc. All rights reserved. No part of this publication may be reproduced or distributed in any form or by any means, or stored in a database or retrieval system, without the prior written consent of The McGraw-Hill Companies, Inc., including, but not limited to, in any network or other electronic storage or transmission, or broadcast for distance learning.
Some ancillaries, including electronic and print components, may not be available to customers outside the United States.

10 09 08 07 06 05 04 03 02
20 09 08 07 06 05 04
CTF   BJE

Library of Congress Cataloging-in-Publication Data

Dornbusch, Rudiger.
    Macroeconomics / Rudiger Dornbusch, Stanley Fischer, Richard Startz.—9th ed.
        p.   cm.
    Includes index.
    ISBN 007-282340-2
    1.   Macroeconomics. I. Fischer, Stanley. II. Startz, Richard, 1952- III. Title.
HB172.5.D67 2004
    339—dc22   2003059968

When ordering this title, use ISBN 007-123237-0

Printed in Singapore

www.mhhe.com

About the Authors

RUDI DORNBUSCH (1942–2002) was Ford Professor of Economics and International Management at MIT. He did his undergraduate work in Switzerland and held a Ph.D. from the University of Chicago. He taught at Chicago, at Rochester, and from 1975 to 2002 at MIT. His research was primarily in international economics, with a major macroeconomic component. His special research interests included the behavior of exchange rates, high inflation and hyperinflation, and the problems and opportunities that high capital mobility pose for developing economies. He lectured extensively in Europe and in Latin America, where he took an active interest in problems of stabilization policy, and held visiting appointments in Brazil and Argentina. His writing includes *Open Economy Macroeconomics* and, with Stanley Fischer and Richard Schmalensee, *Economics.*

STANLEY FISCHER is vice chairman of Citigroup and president of Citigroup International. From 1994 to 2002 he was first deputy managing director of the International Monetary Fund. He was an undergraduate at the London School of Economics and has a Ph.D. from MIT. He taught at the University of Chicago while Rudi Dornbusch was a student there, starting a long friendship and collaboration. He was a member of the faculty of the MIT Economics Department from 1973 to 1998. From 1988 to 1990 he was chief economist at the World Bank. His main research interests are economic growth and development; international economics and macroeconomics, particularly inflation and its stabilization; and the economics of transition. www.iie.com/fischer

RICHARD STARTZ is Castor Professor of Economics at the University of Washington. He was an undergraduate at Yale University and received his Ph.D. from MIT, where he studied under Stanley Fischer and Rudi Dornbusch. He taught at the Wharton School of the University of Pennsylvania before moving on to the University of Washington, and he has taught, while on leave, at the University of California–San Diego, the Stanford Business School, and Princeton. His principal research areas are macroeconomics, econometrics, and the economics of race. In the area of macroeconomics, much of his work has concentrated on the microeconomic underpinnings of macroeconomic theory. His work on race is part of a long-standing collaboration with Shelly Lundberg. www.econ.washington.edu/user/startz

To Fine, Rhoda, and Shelly
and to the memory of
Rudi,
teacher/colleague/friend

Contents
in Brief

ix

CONTENTS

PART

3

FIRST MODELS 213

PART

4

PREFACE

The ninth edition of *Macroeconomics* is published 25 years after the first. We have been both amazed and flattered by the response our book has received over those years. Besides its use in the classrooms of many U.S. universities, it has been translated into many languages and used in many countries, from Canada to Argentina to Australia; all over Europe; in India, Indonesia, and Japan; and from China and Albania to Russia. Even before the Czech Republic gained independence from communism, an underground translation was secretly used in macroeconomics seminars at Charles University in Prague. There is no greater pleasure for teachers and textbook authors than to see their efforts succeed so concretely around the world.

We believe that the success of our textbook reflects the unique features it brings to the universe of undergraduate macroeconomics. These features can be summarized as follows:

- *"Compassionate Difficulty"* Through the years we have held the conviction that the best textbook is one written with an abiding respect for both student and instructor. What does this mean exactly? In practice it means that we explore more state-of-the-art research than is customary in undergraduate textbooks, allowing students a point of departure for deeper exploration of various topics and teachers the flexibility to emphasize topics in greater detail. At the same time, however, we have reduced the book's level of difficulty by providing straightforward explanations, emphasizing concepts over technique, and fitting difficult material into a larger framework so students can see its relevance. We also emphasize how empirical data can explain and test macroeconomic theory by providing numerous illustrations using real-world data.

- *Focus on Models* The best economists have a rich toolbox of simple models they can use to analyze various facets of the economy and know when to apply the right model to answer specific questions. We have consistently focused our textbook on the presentation of a series of simple models relevant to particular issues. We strive to help students understand the importance of a model-based approach to macroeconomic analysis as well as how the various models are connected. Our goal is to produce students who have the capacity to analyze current economic issues in the context of an economic frame of reference, namely, a set of macroeconomic models.

- *International Perspective*   It has always been important for students living in countries with highly open economies to understand the important links connecting foreign economies to their own. This is also becoming ever more true in the United States as international goods and financial markets become more intertwined. Recognizing this, we provide two detailed chapters discussing international linkages. The first, Chapter 12, provides a discussion of mainstream intermediate macroeconomic topics. The second, Chapter 19, gives advanced students the opportunity to explore modern theories of balance-of-payments crises, determinants of exchange rates, and the choice of exchange rate regimes. These chapters give instructors the flexibility to range from touching on a few international topics to a thorough discussion lasting several weeks.
- *Focus on Changing Times*   In preparing this edition we were surprised by how many issues have emerged and how many have become moot in just the three short years since the last edition of the textbook was published. We have strived to present updated data throughout the book, demonstrating key trends and thorough discussions of how such trends might be explained by traditional macroeconomic models.

PLANS OF ATTACK

A major goal in writing this textbook is to provide one that is comprehensive yet flexible enough to allow teachers to focus a class on their particular interests and time constraints. Our personal preference is to begin at the beginning and work through the entire book (which is, of course, why we organized the material in the way we did), but a number of approaches can be taken to give a different emphasis or simply to reduce the breadth of material covered. Examples of these approaches include

- *An Overview Course*   An overview course should contain what we feel is the core of the textbook: Chapters 1 and 2, which introduce the book and provide details on national income accounting; Chapter 5, which gives an overview of aggregate supply and demand; Chapter 6, which presents the aggregate supply curve in more detail; Chapter 7, which discusses the headline issues of inflation and unemployment; and Chapters 9, 10, and 11, which introduce the goods market, asset market, and some basics of monetary and fiscal policy. Beyond these core chapters the course can be shortened substantially by omitting chapters that focus on the microeconomic detail beneath macroeconomic theory—Chapters 13–17 and 20, for example, which supply such detail for consumption, investment, and money markets, respectively. And Chapters 8 and 18, which detail several current issues in policymaking, can be omitted or done only in part. In the United States, Chapters 4, 12, and 19, which present many basic issues of international interdependence and growth policy, might also be omitted (although probably everyone should do Sections 12-1 and 12-2).
- *A Traditional Aggregate Demand-Oriented Course*   For a Keynesian, short-run treatment of the course, the core chapters for the overview course should be emphasized and Chapter 8, which discusses policy, added. Chapter 18, which discusses big macroeconomic events, can be moved ahead of Chapter 13. Chapters 3 and 4,

on growth and policies to promote growth, can be moved to the end of the course. And for advanced students, the sections on New Keynesian economics in Chapter 20 might be included.

- *A Classical "Supply-Side" Course*   For a classical treatment of the course the core chapters for the overview course can be shortened by de-emphasizing the *IS-LM* material in Chapters 9–11. And in the early chapters greater emphasis might be given to Chapters 3 and 4 on long-run growth. The microeconomics of macroeconomic theory in Chapters 13–15 might also be emphasized, as might the discussion of hyperinflation in Chapter 18. Advanced students may wish to explore the sections on the random walk in GDP and on real business cycles in Chapter 20.

- *A Business School Course*   In addition to the core chapters for the overview course, a business school course should emphasize Chapters 16 and 17, which deal with the Federal Reserve and financial markets. And Chapters 3 and 4 on growth can be de-emphasized, while the advanced topics in Chapter 20 can be omitted. For students with an international perspective, Chapter 12 and parts of Chapter 19, especially the discussion of exchange rate determination, might be emphasized.

Throughout the book, we have labeled some material that is technically difficult as "optional." Many of the optional sections will be fun for students who enjoy a technical challenge, but the instructor should specify clearly which of these sections are required and which are truly optional.

ACKNOWLEDGMENTS

In the past we have acknowledged our debts to correspondents, colleagues, and students individually. There is no longer room to do that, but we have to depart from our new rule to thank Erika Gulyas for assistance diligent, unerring, and frequently inspired.

Our best efforts notwithstanding, small errors do creep into the text. We are ever grateful to our readers for drawing our attention to such so that they may be squashed. Particular thanks go to Catherine Langlois, Martha Olney, Edward Steinberg, and Jimmy Torrez.

In addition, the authors and McGraw-Hill would like to thank the following teachers for reviewing both this edition and the previous ones.

Current edition: Robert Burrus, University of North Carolina–Wilmington; E. Mine Cinar, Loyola University–Chicago; Loretta Fairchild, Nebraska Wesleyan University; Roy Gobin, Loyola University–Chicago; Jang-Tin Guo, University of California–Riverside; William Hamlen, SUNY–Buffalo; Robert Herren, North Dakota State University; Kangoh Lee, Towson State University; Ossma Mikhail, University of Central Florida; Michael Miller, DePaul University; Walter Padelford, Union University; and Robert Edward Wright, University of Sterling, United Kingdom.

Previous editions: Michael Ben-Gad, University of Houston; David Butler, University of Western Australia; E. Mine Cinar, Loyola University–Chicago; Monoranjan Dutta, Rutgers University; Michael Edelstein, Queens College–CUNY; James R. Gale, Michigan Technological University; Steven L. Green, Baylor University; Oscar Jornda, University of California–Davis; Garry MacDonald, Curtin University; Neil B. Niman, University of New Hampshire; Martha Olney, University of California–Berkeley; John

Prestage, Edith Cowan University; Willem Thorbecke, George Mason University; and Robert Windle, University of Maryland.

SUPPLEMENTARY MATERIAL

An *Instructor's Manual* and *Test Bank* to accompany the text have been prepared by Professor Juergen Fleck of Hollins University. The *Instructor's Manual* has been substantially updated and includes chapter summaries, learning objectives, solutions to the end-of-chapter problems, and many additional problems (and their solutions) that can be used for class discussion, homework assignments, or examination questions. The *Test Bank* has been expanded and now includes more than 1,000 questions. And there is also a computerized (Windows) test bank that has been provided by Brownstone's Diploma, sophisticated test-making software that ensures maximum flexibility in test development.

The *Study Guide,* by Arabinda Basistha of West Virginia University, has again been revised and brought up to date. It contains a wide range of questions, starting from the very easy and progressing in each chapter to material that will challenge the more advanced student. The *Study Guide* is a great help in studying, particularly since active learning is so important in mastering new material.

For this edition there will also be *transparency masters* and *PowerPoint* slides of all the graphs in the book, along with a *website* (www.mhhe.com/economics/dornbusch) that provides study aids for students and useful resources for teachers.

Stanley Fischer
Richard Startz

ONLINE LINKS FOR FURTHER EXPLORATION

www.economagic.com
Economagic: A comprehensive site of free, easily available economic time series data useful for economic research, in particular economic forecasting. This site gives easy access to large amounts of data, and includes built-in graphing facilities.

www.nber.org/cycles.html
Information on business cycle expansions and contractions determined by the National Bureau of Economic Research (NBER).

www.economist.com
Web page of the weekly news magazine *The Economist*.

www.aeaweb.org/RFE/EconFAQ.html
Bill Coffe's "Resources for Economist on the Internet."

www.bea.doc.gov/bea/dn/faweb
Interactive access to fixed assets tables from the Bureau of Economic Analysis.

http://books.nap.edu/catalog/6374.html
William D. Nordhaus and Edward C. Kokkelenberg (eds.), *Nature's Numbers: Expanding the National Economic Accounts to Include the Environment.*

http://research.stlouisfed.org/fred2
Federal Reserve Economic Data (FRED II) a database of over 1000 U.S. economic time series. With FRED II you can download data in Microsoft Excel and text formats and view charts of data series.

http://economics.sbs.ohio-state.edu/jhm/jhm.html
An up-to-date website on real and nominal interest rates.

www.bea.gov or www.bea.doc.gov
Bureau of Economic Analysis, an official source for U.S. national income accounts.

w3.access.gpo.gov/eop
The *Economic Report of the President,* including data tables and past issues.

www.statcan.ca/start.html or www.statcan.ca/start/_f.html
Statistics Canada, the source for Canadian data.

http://europa.eu.int/comm/eurostat/
European data at the Statistical Office of the European Union.

http://database.iadb.org
American (North and South) data provided by the Inter-American Development Bank.

www.worldbank.org/data
Data on developing countries at the World Bank website.

www.nber.org/databases/macrohistory/contents/index.html
Pre-World War II data for several countries at the NBER website.

http://emlab.berkeley.edu/users/chad/HallJones400.asc
Data on workers' productivity.

http://pwt.econ.upenn.edu
Penn World Tables.

www.phil.frb.org
Federal Reserve Bank of Philadelphia (for Livingston Survey data).

www.bls.gov
Bureau of Labor Statistics.

www.eia.doe.gov
Energy Information Administration.

www.gallup.com
Gallup Report.

www.cbo.gov
Congressional Budget Office (CBO).

www.wwws.princeton.edu/~pkrugman
Paul Krugman's website.

www.whitehouse.gov/news
Council of Economic Adviser.

www.federalreserve.gov/fomc
Minutes of the Federal Open Market Committee (FOMC) meetings.

www.nobel.se/economics/laureates/199/mundell-lecture.html
Video of Robert Mundell's Nobel Prize lecture.

www.frbsf.org/currency
A picture tour of the history of American currency.

www.federalreserve.gov/FOMC/default.htm
Federal Open Market Committee (FOMC).

http://faculty.washington.edu/karyiu/Asia/manuscri.htm
An excellent chronology of the Asian crises.

PART 1

Introduction and National Income Accounting

CHAPTER 1

Introduction

CHAPTER HIGHLIGHTS

- Each chapter starts off with "Chapter Highlights," giving you a guide to the chapter's most important points. In this chapter, we emphasize three linked models that collectively describe the macroeconomy.

- The very long run behavior of the economy is the domain of growth theory, which focuses on the growth of productive capacity.

- Over horizons of moderate length, the productive capacity of the economy can be treated as largely fixed. Output is thus determined by aggregate supply, and prices depend on both aggregate supply and aggregate demand. Large-scale inflation is always the result of changing aggregate demand.

- In the short run, the price level is essentially fixed and changes in aggregate demand generate changes in output, resulting in booms and recessions.

In the year 2000 in the United States, jobs were plentiful and times were good. In 1933 bread lines were the order of the day. A call at a pay phone cost 50 cents in 2003. A call in 1933 was a dime (if you were lucky enough to have a dime). Why are jobs plentiful in some years and scarce in others? What drives up prices over time? Macroeconomists answer these questions as they seek to understand the state of the economy—and seek methods to improve the economy for us all.

Macroeconomics is concerned with the behavior of the economy as a whole—with booms and recessions, the economy's total output of goods and services, the growth of output, the rates of inflation and unemployment, the balance of payments, and exchange rates. Macroeconomics deals with both long-run economic growth and the short-run fluctuations that constitute the business cycle.

Macroeconomics focuses on the economic behavior and policies that affect consumption and investment, the dollar and the trade balance, the determinants of changes in wages and prices, monetary and fiscal policies, the money stock, the federal budget, interest rates, and the national debt.

In brief, macroeconomics deals with the major economic issues and problems of the day. To understand these issues, we have to reduce the complicated details of the economy to manageable essentials. *Those essentials lie in the interactions among the goods, labor, and assets markets of the economy and in the interactions among national economies that trade with each other.*

In dealing with the essentials, we go beyond details of the behavior of individual economic units, such as households and firms, or the determination of prices in particular markets, which are the subject matter of microeconomics. In macroeconomics we deal with the market for goods as a whole, treating all the markets for different goods—such as the markets for agricultural products and for medical services—as a single market. Similarly, we deal with the labor market as a whole, abstracting from differences between the markets for, say, unskilled labor and doctors. We deal with the assets market as a whole, abstracting from differences between the markets for IBM shares and for Rembrandt paintings. The benefit of the abstraction is that it facilitates increased understanding of the vital interactions among the goods, labor, and assets markets. The cost of the abstraction is that omitted details sometimes matter.

It is only a short step from studying how the macroeconomy works to asking how to make it perform better. The fundamental questions are, *Can* the government and *should* the government intervene in the economy to improve its performance? The great macroeconomists have always enjoyed a keen interest in the application of macrotheory to policy. This was true in the case of John Maynard Keynes and is true of American leaders in the field, including members of the older Nobel laureate generation such as Milton Friedman of the University of Chicago and the Hoover Institution, Franco Modigliani and Robert Solow of MIT, and the late James Tobin of Yale University. The next generation's leaders, such as Robert Barro, Martin Feldstein, and N. Gregory Mankiw of Harvard University, Nobel laureate Robert Lucas of the University of Chicago, Olivier Blanchard of MIT, Ben Bernanke of Princeton, Robert Hall, Paul Romer, and John Taylor of Stanford University, and Thomas Sargent of NYU, despite being more—and in some cases altogether—skeptical about the wisdom of active government policies, also have strong views on policy issues.

Because macroeconomics is closely related to the economic problems of the day, it does not yield its greatest rewards to those whose primary interest is abstract. Macrotheory is a little untidy at the edges. But then the world is a little untidy around the edges. This book uses macroeconomics to illuminate economic events from the Great Depression through the beginning of the millennium. We refer continually to real-world events to elucidate the meaning and the relevance of the theoretical material.

There is a simple test for determining whether you understand the material in this book: Can you apply the material to understand current discussions about the national and international economy? Macroeconomics is an applied science. It is rarely beautiful, but it is overwhelmingly important to the well-being of nations and peoples.

1-1
MACROECONOMICS ENCAPSULATED IN THREE MODELS

Macroeconomics is very much about tying together facts and theories. We start with a few grand facts and then turn to models that help us explain these and other facts about the economy.

- Over a time span of decades, the U.S. economy grows rather reliably at 2 or 3 percent a year.
- In some decades, the overall price level has remained relatively steady. In the 1970s prices roughly doubled.
- In a bad year, the unemployment rate is twice what it is in a good year.

The study of macroeconomics is organized around three models that describe the world, each model having its greatest applicability in a different time frame. The *very long run* behavior of the economy is the domain of growth theory, which focuses on the growth of the economy's capacity to produce goods and services. The study of the very long run centers on the historical accumulation of capital and improvements in technology. In the model we label the *long-run,* we take a snapshot of the very long run model. At that moment, the capital stock and the level of technology can be taken to be relatively fixed, although we do allow for temporary shocks. Fixed capital and technology determine the productive capacity of the economy—we call this capacity "potential output." In the long-run, the supply of goods and services equals potential output. Prices and inflation over this horizon are determined by fluctuations in demand. In the *short run,* fluctuations in demand determine how much of the available capacity is used and thus the level of output and unemployment. In contrast to the long-run, in the short run prices are relatively fixed and output is variable. It is in the realm of the short-run model that we find the greatest role for macroeconomic policy.

Nearly all macroeconomists subscribe to these three models, but opinions differ as to the time frame in which each model is best applied. Everyone agrees that behavior over decades is best described by the growth theory model. There is less agreement over the applicable time scope for the long-run versus the short-run model.

This chapter is largely devoted to outlining the three models with a broad brush. The remainder of the text paints in the details.

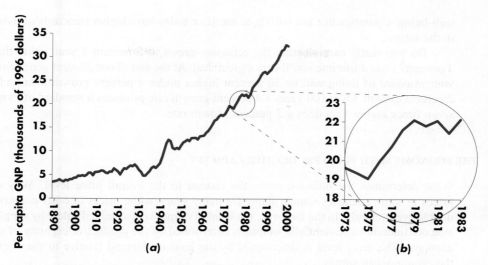

FIGURE 1-1   PER CAPITA GNP, 1890–2001 (THOUSANDS OF 1996 DOLLARS).

The diagram includes an exploded view of the period 1973–1983. (Note that the scales of the two panels differ.) (Source: U.S. Department of Commerce, Historical Statistics of the United States, Colonial Times to 1970; *and www.economagic.com.)*

VERY LONG RUN GROWTH

The very long run behavior of the economy is the domain of *growth theory.* Figure 1-1a illustrates the growth of income per person in the United States over more than a century. We see a fairly smooth growth curve, averaging 2 or 3 percent a year. In studying growth theory, we ask how the accumulation of inputs—investment in machinery, for example— and improvements in technology lead to an increased standard of living. We ignore recessions and booms and related short-run fluctuations in employment of people and other resources. We assume that labor, capital, raw materials, and so on are all fully employed.

How can a model that ignores fluctuations in the economy possibly tell us anything sensible? Fluctuations in the economy—the ups and downs of unemployment, for example—tend to average out over the years. Over very long periods, all that matters is how quickly the economy grows on average. Growth theory seeks to explain growth rates averaged over many years or decades. Why does one nation's economy grow at 2 percent a year while another nation's grows at 4 percent a year? Can we explain growth miracles such as the 8 percent annual growth in Japan in the early postwar period? What accounts for growth debacles such as Ghana's zero growth in the postwar period?

Chapters 3 and 4 examine the causes of economic growth and of differences in growth rates among nations. In industrialized countries, changes in the standard of living depend primarily on the development of new technology and the accumulation of capital—broadly defined. In developing countries, the development of a well-functioning infrastructure is more important than the development of new technology, because the latter can be imported. In all countries, the rate of saving is a key determinant of future well-being. Countries that are willing to sacrifice today have higher standards of living in the future.

Do you really care whether the economy grows at 2 percent a year rather than 4 percent? Over a lifetime you'll care a great deal: At the end of one 20-year generation, your standard of living will be 50 percent higher under 4 percent growth than under 2 percent growth. Over 100 years a 4 percent growth rate produces a standard of living *seven* times higher than does a 2 percent growth rate.

THE ECONOMY WITH FIXED PRODUCTIVE CAPACITY

What determines the inflation rate—the change in the overall price level? Why do prices in some countries remain stable for many years, while prices in other countries double every month? In the long-run, the level of output is determined solely by supply-side considerations. Essentially, output is determined by the productive capacity of the economy. The price level is determined by the level of demand relative to the output the economy can supply.

Figure 1-2 shows an *aggregate supply–aggregate demand* diagram with a vertical aggregate supply curve. It may be a little premature to ask you to work with this diagram, since we devote most of Chapters 5 and 6 to explaining it. Perhaps you should

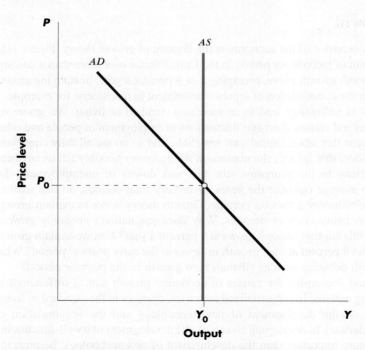

FIGURE 1-2   AGGREGATE DEMAND AND SUPPLY: THE LONG RUN.

BOX 1-1   Aggregate Supply and Aggregate Demand

- The *level of aggregate supply* is the amount of output the economy can produce given the resources and technology available.
- The *level of aggregate demand* is the total demand for goods to consume, for new investment, for goods purchased by the government, and for net goods to be exported abroad.

think of the diagram as a preview of coming attractions. For now we'll present the aggregate supply and aggregate demand schedules as the relationships between the overall price level in the economy and total output. **The *aggregate supply (AS) curve* depicts, for each given price level, the quantity of output firms are willing to supply.** The position of the aggregate supply curve depends on the productive capacity of the economy. **The *aggregate demand (AD) curve* presents, for each given price level, the level of output at which the goods markets and money markets are simultaneously in equilibrium.** The position of the aggregate demand curve depends on monetary and fiscal policy and the level of consumer confidence. The intersection of aggregate supply and aggregate demand determines price and quantity.[1]

In the long-run, the aggregate supply curve is vertical. (Economists argue over whether the long-run is a period of a few quarters or of a decade.) Output is pegged to the position where this supply curve hits the horizontal axis. The price level, in contrast, can take on any value.

Mentally shift the aggregate demand schedule to the left or right. You will see that the intersection of the two curves moves up and down (the price changes), rather than horizontally (output doesn't change). **It follows that *in the long-run* output is determined by aggregate supply alone and prices are determined by both aggregate supply and aggregate demand.** This is our first substantive finding.

The growth theory and long-run aggregate supply models are intimately linked: The position of the vertical aggregate supply curve in a given year equals the level of output for that year from the very long run model, as shown in Figure 1-3. Since economic growth over the very long run averages a few percent a year, we know that the aggregate supply curve typically moves to the right by a few percent a year.[2]

---

[1]You should be warned that the economics underlying the aggregate supply and aggregate demand schedules is very different from the economics of the ordinary, garden-variety supply and demand that you may remember from studying microeconomics.

[2]Sometimes there are shocks that temporarily disrupt the orderly rightward progression of the aggregate supply schedule. These shocks are rarely larger than a few percent of output.

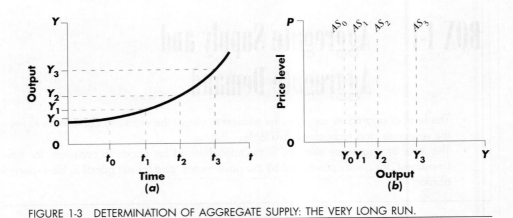

FIGURE 1-3   DETERMINATION OF AGGREGATE SUPPLY: THE VERY LONG RUN.

We are ready for our second conclusion: **Very high inflation rates—that is, episodes with rapid increases in the overall price level—are always due to changes in aggregate demand.** The reason is simple. Aggregate supply movements are on the order of a few percent; aggregate demand movements can be either small or large. So the only possible source of high inflation is large movements of aggregate demand sweeping across the vertical aggregate supply curve. In fact, as we will eventually learn, the only source of really high inflation rates is government-sanctioned increases in the money supply.[3]

Much of macroeconomics can be capsulized as the study of the position and slope of the aggregate supply and aggregate demand curves. You now know that in the long-run the position of the aggregate supply curve is determined by very long run economic growth and that the slope of aggregate supply is simply vertical.

THE SHORT RUN

Examine panel *(b)* in Figure 1-1. When we take a magnified look at the path of output, we see that it is not at all smooth. Short-run output fluctuations are large enough to matter a great deal. Accounting for short-run fluctuations in output is the domain of aggregate demand.[4]

The mechanical aggregate supply–aggregate demand distinction between the long-run and the short is straightforward. *In the short run, the aggregate supply curve is flat.* The short-run aggregate supply curve pegs the price level at the point where the supply curve hits the vertical axis. Output, in contrast, can take on any value. The underlying assumption is that the level of output does not affect prices in the short run. Figure 1-4 shows a horizontal short-run aggregate supply curve.

---

[3]Temporary price increases of 10 or 20 percent can be due to supply shocks—for example, the failure of the monsoon to arrive in an agricultural economy. However, ongoing double-digit annual price increases are due to printing too much money.

[4]Mostly. Supply shocks—the OPEC oil embargo is an example—sometimes matter too.

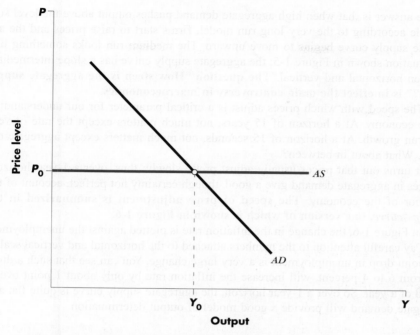

FIGURE 1-4   AGGREGATE DEMAND AND SUPPLY: THE SHORT RUN.

Repeat the exercise above and mentally shift the aggregate demand schedule to the left or right. You will see that the intersection of the two curves moves horizontally (output changes), rather than up and down (the price level doesn't change). It follows that *in the short run* output is determined by aggregate demand alone and prices are unaffected by the level of output. This is our third substantive finding.[5]

Much of this text is about aggregate demand alone. We study aggregate demand because in the short run aggregate demand determines output and therefore unemployment. When we study aggregate demand in isolation, we are not really ignoring aggregate supply; rather, we are assuming that the aggregate supply curve is horizontal, implying that the price level can be taken as given.

THE MEDIUM RUN

We need one more piece to complete our outline of how the economy works: How do we describe the transition between the short run and the long-run? In other words, what's the process that tilts the aggregate supply curve from horizontal to vertical? The

[5]As we said in the last footnote, "mostly." This is an example of what we mean when we say that applying a model requires judgment. There have certainly been historical periods when supply shocks outweighed demand shocks in the determination of output.

simple answer is that when high aggregate demand pushes output above the level sustainable according to the very long run model, firms start to raise prices and the aggregate supply curve begins to move upward. The medium run looks something like the situation shown in Figure 1-5; the aggregate supply curve has a slope intermediate between horizontal and vertical. **The question "How steep is the aggregate supply curve?" is in effect the main controversy in macroeconomics.**

The speed with which prices adjust is a critical parameter for our understanding of the economy. At a horizon of 15 years, not much matters except the rate of very long run growth. At a horizon of 15 seconds, not much matters except aggregate demand. What about in between?

It turns out that prices usually adjust pretty slowly; thus, over a 1-year horizon, changes in aggregate demand give a good, though certainly not perfect, account of the behavior of the economy. **The speed of price adjustment is summarized in the** *Phillips curve,* **one version of which is shown in Figure 1-6.**

In Figure 1-6, the change in the inflation rate is plotted against the unemployment rate. Pay careful attention to the numbers attached to the horizontal and vertical scales. A 2-point drop in unemployment is a very large change. You can see that such a drop, say, from 6 to 4 percent, will increase the inflation rate by only about 1 point over a period of a year. So over a 1-year horizon, the aggregate supply curve is quite flat and aggregate demand will provide a good model of output determination.

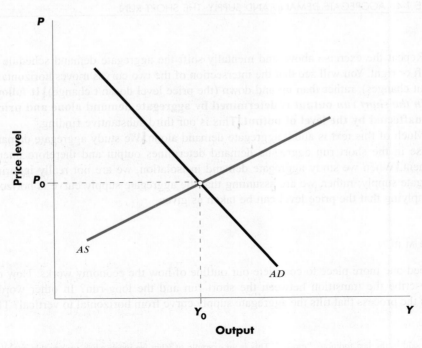

FIGURE 1-5   AGGREGATE DEMAND AND SUPPLY.

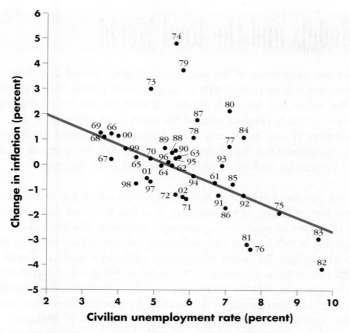

FIGURE 1-6   UNEMPLOYMENT AND THE CHANGE IN INFLATION, 1961–2002.
(*Source: Bureau of Labor Statistics.*)

1-2
TO REITERATE . . .

The remainder of the text just fills in the details.

More seriously, nearly everything you will learn about macroeconomics can be fitted into the growth theory, aggregate supply, and aggregate demand framework. This intellectual outline is so vital that it is worth the time to repeat parts of the previous section in slightly different words.

GROWTH AND GDP

The *growth rate* of the economy is the rate at which the gross domestic product (GDP) is increasing. On average, most economies grow by a few percentage points per year over long periods. For instance, U.S. real GDP grew at an average rate of 3.4 percent per year from 1960 to 2002. But this growth has certainly not been smooth, as Figure 1-1*b* confirms.

What causes GDP to grow over time? The first reason GDP changes is that the available amount of resources in the economy changes. The principal resources are

BOX 1-2   Models and the Real World

Models are simplified representations of the real world. A good model accurately explains the behaviors that are most important to us and omits details that are relatively unimportant. The notion that the earth revolves around the sun on an elliptical path and that the moon similarly revolves around the earth is an example of a model. The exact behavior of sun, earth, and moon is much more complicated, but this model enables us to understand the phases of the moon. For this purpose, it is a good model. Even though the real orbits are not simple ellipses, the model "works."

In economics, the complex behavior of millions of individuals, firms, and markets is represented by one, two, a dozen, a few hundred, or a few thousand mathematical relations in the form of graphs or equations or computer programs. The intellectual problem in model building is that humans can understand the interactions between, at most, only a handful of relations. So usable macrotheory relies on a toolbox of models, each consisting of two or three equations. A particular model is a tool based on a set of assumptions—for example, that the economy is at full employment—that are reasonable in some real-world circumstances. Understanding the macroeconomy requires a rich toolbox and the application of sound judgment regarding when to deploy a particular model. We cannot overemphasize this point: The only way to understand the very complicated world in which we live is to master a toolbox of simplifying models and to then make quite explicit decisions as to which model is best suited for analyzing a given problem.

As an illustration consider three very specific economic questions. (1) How will your grandchildren's standard of living compare to yours? (2) What caused the great inflation of the post–World War I German Weimar Republic (the inflation that contributed to Hitler's rise to power)? (3) Why did the U.S. unemployment rate, which had

capital and labor. The labor force, consisting of people either working or looking for work, grows over time and thus provides one source of increased production. The capital stock, including buildings and machines, likewise rises over time, providing another source of increased output. Increases in the availability of factors of production—the labor and capital used in the production of goods and services—thus account for part of the increase in GDP.

The second reason GDP changes is that the efficiency of factors of production may change. Efficiency improvements are called *productivity increases*. Over time, the same factors of production can produce more output. Productivity increases result from changes in knowledge, as people learn through experience to perform familiar tasks better.

Table 1-1 compares the growth rates of real per capita income in different countries. Studies of the sources of growth across countries and history seek to explain the reasons

been below 6 percent during parts of 1979, reach nearly 11 percent by the end of 1982? You can answer each of these questions by applying a model introduced in this chapter.

1. Over a time span a couple of generations long, we want a model of very long run growth. Nothing matters much except the development of new technology and the accumulation of capital (assuming you live in a developed economy). At growth rates between 2 and 4 percent, income will more than double and less than quintuple within two generations. Your grandchildren will certainly live much better than you do. They will certainly not be as rich as Bill Gates is today.

2. Huge inflations have one cause: great outward sweeps of the aggregate demand curve caused by the government's printing too much money. Small changes in the price level may have many contributing factors. But huge changes in prices are the domain of the long-run aggregate supply–aggregate demand model, in which a vertical aggregate supply curve remains relatively motionless while the aggregate demand curve moves outward.

3. Big changes over short time spans in the level of economic activity, and thus in unemployment, are explained by the short-run aggregate supply–aggregate demand model—with a horizontal aggregate supply curve. At the beginning of the 1980s the Federal Reserve clamped down on aggregate demand, driving the economy into a deep recession. The Fed's intention was to reduce inflation—eventually this is just what happened. But as the short-run model explains, over very short periods cutting back aggregate demand reduces output, increasing unemployment.

There's a flip side to knowing which model to use to answer a question: You also need to know which models to ignore. In thinking about growth over two generations, monetary policy is pretty much irrelevant. And in thinking about the great German inflation, technological change doesn't matter much. As you study macroeconomics you'll find that memorizing lists of equations is much less important than learning to match a model to the problem at hand.

TABLE 1-1	Per Capita Real Income Growth Rates, 1913–1998		
	(Average Annual Growth Rate, Percent)		
COUNTRY	GROWTH RATE	COUNTRY	GROWTH RATE
Argentina	.7	India	1.1
Brazil	2.3	Japan	3.4
China	2.4	Spain	2.0
France	2.1	United Kingdom	1.6
Ghana	.1	United States	1.7

Source: A. Maddison, "A Comparison of GDP Per Capita Income Levels in Developed and Developing Countries, 1700–1980," *Journal of Economic History,* March 1983, table 2, updated for 1981–1998 by the authors, from the World Bank, *At-a-Glance Tables, 1999.*

that a country like Brazil grew very rapidly (at least until the late 1980s) while Ghana, for example, has had very little growth. Ghana's income in 1980 was only 20 percent higher than in 1913, while Brazil's income had increased more than fivefold. Obviously, it would be well worth knowing what policies, if any, can raise a country's average growth rate over long periods of time.

THE BUSINESS CYCLE AND THE OUTPUT GAP

Inflation, growth, and unemployment are related through the *business cycle.* **The business cycle is the more or less regular pattern of expansion (recovery) and contraction (recession) in economic activity around the path of trend growth.** At a cyclical *peak,* economic activity is high relative to trend; at a cyclical *trough,* the low point in economic activity is reached. Inflation, growth, and unemployment all have clear cyclical patterns. For the moment we concentrate on measuring the behavior of output or GDP relative to trend over the business cycle.

The green line in Figure 1-7 shows the *trend path of real GDP.* **The trend path of GDP is the path GDP would take if factors of production were fully employed.** Over time, GDP changes for the two reasons we already noted. First, more resources become available: the size of the population increases, firms acquire machinery or build plants, land is improved for cultivation, the stock of knowledge increases as new goods and new methods of production are invented and introduced. This increased availability of resources allows the economy to produce more goods and services, resulting in a rising trend level of output.

But, second, factors are not fully employed all the time. Full employment of factors of production is an economic, not a physical, concept. Physically, labor is fully

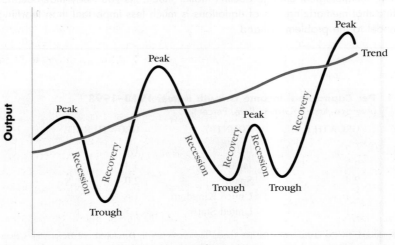

FIGURE 1-7 THE BUSINESS CYCLE.

employed if everyone is working 16 hours per day all year. In economic terms, there is full employment of labor when everyone who wants a job can find one within a reasonable amount of time. Because the economic definition is not precise, we typically define full employment of labor by some convention, for example, that labor is fully employed when the unemployment rate is 5.0 percent. Capital similarly is never fully employed in a physical sense; for example, office buildings or lecture rooms, which are part of the capital stock, are used only part of the day.

Output is not always at its trend level, that is, the level corresponding to (economic) full employment of the factors of production. Rather, output fluctuates around the trend level. During an *expansion* (or *recovery*) the *employment* of factors of production increases, and that is a source of increased production. Output can rise above trend because people work overtime and machinery is used for several shifts. Conversely, during a *recession* unemployment increases and less output is produced than could in fact be produced with the existing resources and technology. The wavy line in Figure 1-7 shows these cyclical departures of output from trend. Deviations of output from trend are referred to as the *output gap.*

The output gap measures the gap between actual output and the output the economy could produce at full employment given the existing resources. Full-employment output is also called *potential output.*

$$\text{Output gap} \equiv \text{actual output} - \text{potential output} \tag{1}$$

The output gap allows us to measure the size of the cyclical deviations of output from potential output or trend output (we use these terms interchangeably). Figure 1-8 shows actual and potential output for the United States; the shaded lines represent recessions.[6]

The figure shows that the output gap falls during a recession, such as in 1982. More resources become unemployed, and actual output falls below potential output. Conversely, during an expansion, most strikingly in the long expansion of the 1990s, actual output rises faster than potential output, and the output gap ultimately even becomes positive. A positive gap means that there is overemployment, overtime for workers, and more than the usual rate of utilization of machinery. It is worth noting that the gap is sometimes very sizable. For example, in 1982 it amounted to as much as 10 percent of output.

INFLATION AND THE BUSINESS CYCLE

Increases in *inflation* are positively related to the output gap. Expansionary aggregate demand policies tend to produce inflation, unless they occur when the economy is at high levels of unemployment. Protracted periods of low aggregate demand tend to reduce the inflation rate. Figure 1-9 shows one measure of inflation for the U.S. economy for the period since 1960. The inflation measure in the figure is the rate of change of the *consumer price index (CPI),* the cost of a given basket of goods representing the purchases of a typical urban consumer.

---

[6]Dating of the business cycle is done by the National Bureau of Economic Research (NBER, www.nber.org/cycles.html). The NBER is a private, nonprofit research organization based in Cambridge, Massachusetts.

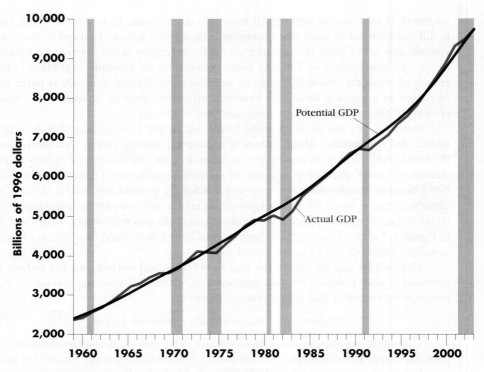

FIGURE 1-8   ACTUAL AND POTENTIAL OUTPUT, 1960–2002.
(*Source: Congressional Budget Office,* CBO's Method for Estimating Potential Output: An Update, *August 2001.*)

Figure 1-9 shows inflation, the *rate of increase* of prices. We can also look at the *level* of prices. All the inflation of the 1960s and 1970s adds up to a large increase in the price level. In the period 1960–2002, the price level more than sextupled. On average, a product that cost $1 in 1960 cost $6.16 by 2002. Most of that increase in prices took place after the early 1970s.

Inflation, like unemployment, is a major macroeconomic concern. However, the costs of inflation are much less obvious than those of unemployment. In the case of unemployment, potential output is going to waste, and it is therefore clear why the reduction of unemployment is desirable. In the case of inflation, there is no obvious loss of output. It is argued that inflation upsets familiar price relationships and reduces the efficiency of the price system. Whatever the reasons, policymakers have been willing to increase unemployment in an effort to reduce inflation—that is, to trade off some unemployment for less inflation.[7]

[7]For a very readable account of inflation, see Milton Friedman, "The Causes and Cures of Inflation," in his *Money Mischief* (New York: Harcourt Brace Jovanovich, 1992).

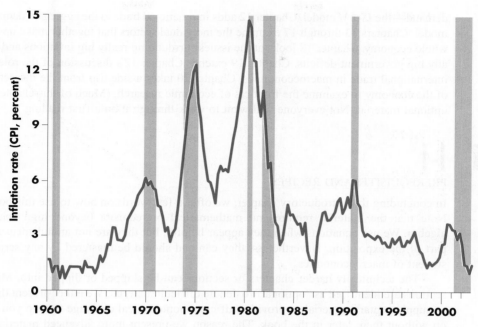

FIGURE 1-9   THE RATE OF INFLATION IN CONSUMER PRICES, 1960–2002.
(Source: Bureau of Labor Statistics.)

1-3

OUTLINE AND PREVIEW OF THE TEXT

We have sketched the major issues we shall discuss in this book. We now outline our approach to macroeconomics and the order in which the material will be presented. The key overall concepts, as already noted, are growth, aggregate supply, and aggregate demand. Growth depends on the accumulation of economic inputs and on improvements in technology. Aggregate supply depends primarily on growth but also on disturbances such as changes in the supply of oil. Aggregate demand is influenced by monetary policy, primarily via interest rates and expectations, and by fiscal policy.

The coverage starts in Chapter 2 with national income accounting, emphasizing data and relationships that are used repeatedly later in the book. The crucial long-run issue of growth is developed in Chapters 3 and 4. Chapter 5 introduces the aggregate supply–aggregate demand framework and discusses how aggregate supply and demand interact to determine both real GDP and the price level. Chapter 6 explores the aggregate supply curve in more detail. Chapter 7 looks further at the causes of, costs of, and tradeoffs between inflation and unemployment. Chapter 8 discusses the theory of policy—a discussion of the difficulties of going from macroeconomic theory to macroeconomic application. Chapters 9 through 11 present the underpinnings of aggregate demand—the *IS-LM* model. Chapter 12 adds international trade to the aggregate demand model. Chapters 13 through 17 examine the individual sectors that together make up the whole economy. Chapter 18 looks at the issues surrounding really big inflations and really big government deficits. Chapter 19 extends Chapter 12's discussion of the role of international trade in macroeconomics. Chapter 20 takes a side trip from the dissection of the economy to examine the frontiers of economic research. (Much of this chapter is optional material. Not everyone will want to work through it on a first reading.)

1-4

PREREQUISITES AND RECIPES

In concluding this introductory chapter, we offer a few words on how to use this book. Note that the material requires no mathematical prerequisite beyond high school algebra. We use equations when they appear helpful, but they are not an indispensable part of the exposition. Nevertheless, they can and should be mastered by any serious student of macroeconomics.

The technically harder chapters or sections can be skipped or dipped into. Many sections are identified as "optional" to denote difficult material. We either present them as supplementary material or provide sufficient nontechnical coverage to help you get on without them later in the book. The reason we present more advanced material is to afford complete and up-to-date coverage of the main ideas and techniques in macroeconomics.

The hard part of understanding our complex economy is trying to follow the interaction of several markets and many variables, as the direct and feedback effects in the economy constitute a quite formidable system. How can you ensure that you will progress efficiently and with some ease? The most important thing is to ask questions. Ask yourself, as you follow an argument: Why is it that this or that variable should affect, say, aggregate demand? What would happen if it did not? What is the critical link?

There is no substitute whatsoever for active learning. Are there simple rules for active study? The best way to study is to use pencil and paper and work through each argument by drawing diagrams, experimenting with flowcharts, writing out the logic of the argument, working out the problems at the end of each chapter, and underlining key ideas. Using the *Study Guide,* which contains summaries of each chapter and many practice problems, will also help in your studies. Another valuable approach is to take issue with an argument or position or to spell out the defense for a particular view on policy questions. Beyond that, if you get stuck, read on for half a page. If you are still stuck, go back five pages.

Macroeconomics is an applied art. Learn to link up textbook concepts with current events. We highly recommend publications such as the news magazine *The Economist,* www.economist.com. An excellent data source is www.economagic.com. But the online source of everything is Bill Goffe's "Resources for Economist on the Internet," www.aeaweb.org/RFE/EconFAQ.html. This website, with official sponsorship of the American Economic Association, lists and annotates over 1,000 sources of data, publications, research organizations, and even employers.

The publisher has arranged for textbook users to have subscriber privileges at the website www.economagic.com. A number of end-of-chapter problems use this resource, but economagic is also a place you can go to for data that you feel will help you to better understand (or disagree with!) the concepts in the text. As a first active-learning exercise, try to compute how much prices have risen since the year you were born. The following steps work this out under the assumption that today's date is December 2002 and that the author is 18 years old, neither of which is precisely accurate.

1. Point your web browser to www.economagic.com. Click on Subscriber Logon and then on "Level I Subscriber Login/Site License Entry."
2. Logon using the username and password provided bound into the textbook.
3. Click on Most Requested Series. Scroll down if necessary and click on "Consumer Price Index—All Urban Consumers."
4. Scroll down to find the December 2002 consumer price index, which is 181.60. (Things on the web, most especially data, get revised from time to time, so there is a chance the number you see will be different.) Scroll back to December 1984, where you'll find the consumer price index was 105.50.
5. A quick calculation shows that prices rose $100 \times (181.60 - 105.50)/105.50 = 72\%$ over this period.
6. Scroll back to the top of the page and push one of the chart buttons. By filling in some of the specification boxes below the chart you should be able to make a graph that looks something like this:

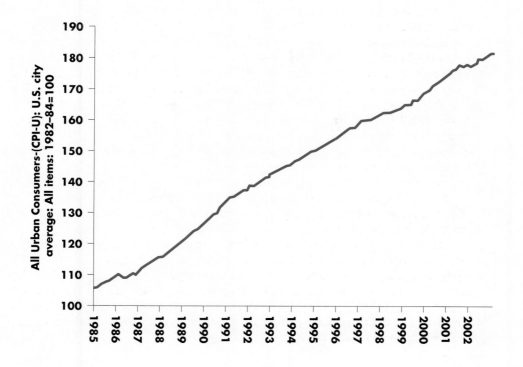

SUMMARY

1. Models are simplified depictions that attempt to capture just the essential elements of how the world works. We use a variety of models to focus on a variety of economic questions.

2. We use the concepts of growth theory, aggregate supply, and aggregate demand to focus our discussion.

3. Growth theory explains the very long run behavior of the economy through understanding how productive capacity grows.

4. In the long-run, productive capacity can be taken as given. Output depends on aggregate supply, and prices depend on both aggregate supply and aggregate demand.

5. In the short run, the price level is fixed and output is determined by the level of aggregate demand.

KEY TERMS

aggregate demand (*AD*) curve	consumer price index (CPI)	output gap
	growth rate	Phillips curve
aggregate supply– aggregate demand model	growth theory	potential output
	inflation	short run
aggregate supply (*AS*) curve	long-run	trend path of real GDP
business cycle	medium run	very long run

CHAPTER 2

National Income Accounting

CHAPTER HIGHLIGHTS

- Gross domestic product is the value of the goods and services produced within the country. In equilibrium, the amount of output produced equals the amount demanded.

- The production of output generates income for those who produce. The bulk of that income is received by labor and the owners of capital.

- Output is demanded for private consumption and investment, for government expenditure, and for international trade.

- The dollar value of gross domestic product depends on both physical production and the price level. Inflation is the change over time in the price level.

Good accounting turns data into information. We study national income accounting for two reasons. First, the national income accounts provide the formal *structure* for our macrotheory models. We divide output in two ways. On the production side, output is paid out to labor in the form of wages and to capital in the form of interest and dividends. On the demand side, output is consumed or invested for the future. The division of output into factor payments (wages, etc.) on the production side provides a framework for our study of growth and aggregate supply. The division of income into consumption, investment, and so on, on the demand side provides the framework for studying aggregate demand. The input and output, or demand and production, accountings are necessarily equal in equilibrium. In addition to looking at real output, the national income accounts include measures of the overall price level. This provides a basis for our discussions of inflation.

The second reason for studying national income accounts is to learn a few ballpark numbers that help characterize the economy. If we spread annual U.S. output equally across the population, would each person control $4,000, $40,000, or $400,000? Is a dollar today worth a 1947 penny, dime, or dollar? Is income paid mostly to labor or mostly to capital? While memorizing exact statistics is a waste of time, knowing rough magnitudes is vital for linking theory to the real world. And macroeconomics is very much about the world we live in.

We begin our study with the basic measure of output—*gross domestic product,* or *GDP*. **GDP is the value of all final goods and services produced in the country within a given period.** It includes the value of goods produced, such as houses and CDs, and the value of services, such as airplane rides and economists' lectures. The output of each of these is valued at its market price, and the values are added together to get GDP. In 2002 the value of GDP in the U.S. economy was about $10,400 billion, or something over $10 trillion. Since the U.S. population was about 287 million, *per capita GDP* (GDP per person) was roughly $36,000 per year (= $10,400 billion/287 million).

2-1
THE PRODUCTION OF OUTPUT AND PAYMENTS TO FACTORS OF PRODUCTION

The production side of the economy transforms inputs, such as labor and capital, into output, GDP. Inputs such as labor and capital are called *factors of production,* and the payments made to factors, such as wages and interest payments, are called *factor payments*. Imagine a student pie-baking economy with you as the entrepreneur. You hire several friends to roll dough, and you rent a kitchen from another friend. Your factor inputs are friends (labor) and kitchens (capital). Output is measured as the number of pies. With some experience, you could predict the number of pies that can be produced with a given number of friends and so many kitchens. You could express the relation as a mathematical formula called a *production function,* which is written in this case as

$$\text{Pies} = f(\text{friends, kitchens}) \tag{1}$$

We will, of course, be interested in a somewhat more general production function relating all the economy's production, GDP (Y) to inputs of labor (N) and capital (K), which we write as $Y = f(N,K)$. The production function will be a focal point for our study of growth in Chapters 3 and 4, where we will also elaborate on the role of technology and on the use of inputs other than labor and capital.

Once the pies are baked, it's time to make factor payments. Some of the pies you give to your friends as payment for their labor. These pies are wage income to your friends. You also need to set aside one slice from each pie (about 8 percent of the pie in the United States) to send to the government as a contribution for social security. This slice is also considered a payment to labor, since the payment is made on behalf of the worker. You should also take a pie for yourself as a fair return for your management skills. This pie, too, is a payment to labor. A few pies you leave for the kitchen owner. These are payments to capital. Any remaining pies are true profit.

All the factor payments, including profit, if any, add up to the total number of pies produced. We can express this as an equation:

$$\text{Pies} = \text{labor payments} + \text{capital payments} + \text{profit} \tag{2}$$

More generally, we might write that labor payments equal the wage rate (w) times the amount of labor used and that capital payments (the rent for the kitchen) equal the rental rate (r) times the amount of capital rented and write $Y = (w \times N) + (r \times K) + \text{profit}$.

Figure 2-1*a* shows the GDP pie broken down into factor payments plus a few complicating items.

GDP AND GNP

The first complication is that factor payments include receipts from abroad made as factor payments to domestically owned factors of production. Adding these payments to GDP gives *gross national product,* or *GNP*. For instance, part of U.S. GDP corresponds to the profits earned by Honda from its U.S. manufacturing operations. These profits are part of Japan's GNP, because they are the income of Japanese-owned capital. In the United States the difference between GDP and GNP is only about 1 percent and can be ignored for our purposes, but the difference can be more important in some other countries. For example, in the year 2000, in Ireland GDP was almost 15 percent higher than GNP, while in Switzerland GNP was about 6 percent higher than GDP.

GDP AND NDP

The second complication is quite important but also quite straightforward. Capital wears out, or *depreciates,* while it is being used to produce output. *Net domestic product (NDP)* **is equal to GDP minus depreciation.** NDP thus comes closer to measuring the net amount of goods produced in the country in a given period: It is the total value of production minus the value of the amount of capital used up in producing that output. *Depreciation* is typically about 11 percent of GDP, so NDP is usually about 89 percent of GDP.

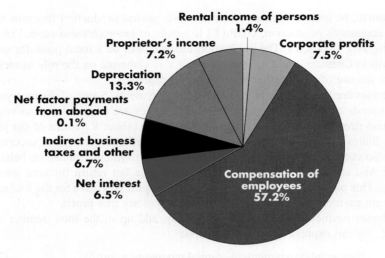

(a) Payments of factors of production

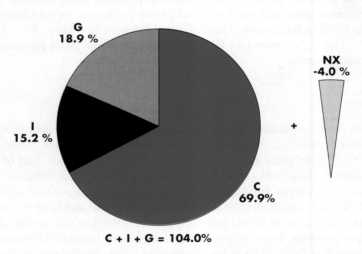

(b) Components of demand for output

FIGURE 2-1   COMPOSITION OF U.S. GDP IN 2002.

(Source: Bureau of Economic Analysis.)

NATIONAL INCOME

The third complication is that businesses pay indirect taxes (i.e., taxes on sales, property, and production) that must be subtracted from NDP before making factor payments. These payments are large, amounting to nearly 10 percent of NDP, so we need to mention them here. (Having done so, we won't mention them again.) What's left for making factor payments is *national income,* equaling about 80 percent of GDP.

You should remember that about three-fourths of factor payments are payments to labor. Most of the remainder goes to pay capital. Only a small amount goes for other factors of production or true profits. The same allocation is very roughly the case in most industrialized countries. (There are a small number of resource-extraction economies based on oil, copper, or guano where natural resources are a dominant factor of production.)

RECAP

From this section you should remember:

- GDP is the value of all final goods and services produced in the country within a given period.
- In the United States, per capita GDP is around $36,000 per year.
- GDP is the sum of all factor payments.
- Labor is the dominant factor of production.

 # 2-2

OUTLAYS AND COMPONENTS OF DEMAND

In this section we look at the demand for output, and we discuss the *components* of the aggregate demand for domestically produced goods and services, the different purposes for which GDP is demanded.

Total demand for domestic output is made up of four components: (1) consumption spending by households (*C*), (2) investment spending by businesses and households (*I*), (3) government (federal, state, and local) purchases of goods and services (*G*), and (4) foreign demand for our net exports (*NX*). These four categories account, definitionally, for all spending. **The fundamental *national income accounting identity* is**

$$Y \equiv C + I + G + NX \tag{3}$$

MEMORIZE THIS IDENTITY. You will use it repeatedly in this course and in organizing your thinking about the macroeconomy.

We now look more closely at each of the four components.

CONSUMPTION

Table 2-1 presents a breakdown of the demand for goods and services by components of demand. The table shows that the chief component of demand is *consumption spending* by the household sector. This includes spending on anything from food to golf lessons, but it also involves, as we shall see in discussing investment, consumer spending on durable goods such as automobiles—spending that might be regarded as investment rather than consumption.

TABLE 2-1   GDP and Components of Demand

	2002	
	$ BILLIONS	PERCENT
Personal consumption expenditures	7,301	69.9
Gross private domestic investment	1,586	15.2
Government purchases of goods and services	1,973	18.9
Net exports of goods and services	−418	−4.0
Gross domestic product	10,442	100.0

Source: Bureau of Economic Analysis.

Figure 2-2 shows the percentage of GDP accounted for by consumption in both Japan and the United States. Note that the consumption share is not constant by any means. Observe, too, that Japan consumes a far smaller share of its GDP than is the case in the United States. Given the share of government spending, higher consumption (or lower saving), as we will see in a moment, means either less investment or larger trade deficits.

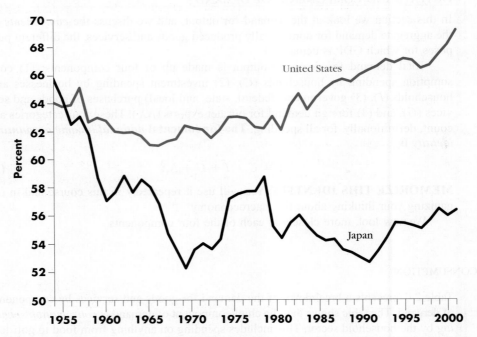

FIGURE 2-2   CONSUMPTION AS A SHARE OF GDP: UNITED STATES AND JAPAN, 1955–2001.
(*Source: International Financial Statistics CD-ROM, IMF.*)

GOVERNMENT

Next in size we have *government purchases* of goods and services. This component of GDP includes such items as national defense expenditures, costs of road paving by state and local governments, and salaries of government employees.

We draw attention to the use of certain words in connection with government spending. We refer to government spending on goods and services as *purchases* of goods and services. In addition, the government makes *transfer payments,* payments that are made to people without their providing a current service in exchange. Typical transfer payments are social security benefits and unemployment benefits. **Transfer payments are *not* counted as part of GDP because transfers are not part of current production.** We speak of *transfers plus purchases* as *government expenditure.* The federal government budget, on the order of $2,000 billion ($2.0 trillion), refers to federal government expenditure. Less than one-third of that sum is spent on federal government purchases of goods and services; most of it is used for transfers.

Total government spending, both items that are counted in GDP and items that are not, plays a large role in determining how the economy is split between the public sector and the private sector. In the United States federal, state, and local spending account for a little over a third of the economy, as can be seen in Figure 2-3.

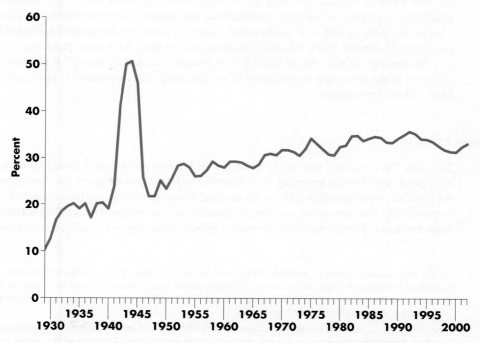

FIGURE 2-3   GOVERNMENT PURCHASES AND TRANSFER PAYMENTS AS A SHARE OF GDP.
(*Source: Bureau of Economic Analysis.*)

INVESTMENT

Gross private domestic investment requires some definitions. First, throughout this book, the term *investment* means additions to the physical stock of capital. As we use the term, investment does *not* include buying a bond or purchasing stock in General Motors. Investment includes housing construction, building of machinery, construction of factories and offices, and additions to a firm's inventories of goods.

If we think of investment more generally as any current activity that increases the economy's ability to produce output in the future, we would include not only physical investment but also what is known as investment in human capital. *Human capital* is the knowledge and ability to produce that is embodied in the labor force. Investment in education can be regarded as investment in human capital, but the official accounts treat personal educational expenditures as consumption and public educational expenditures as government spending.[1]

The classification of spending as consumption or investment is to a significant extent a matter of convention. From the economic point of view, there is little difference between a household's building up an inventory of peanut butter and a grocery store's doing the same. Nevertheless, in the national income accounts, the individual's purchase is treated as a personal consumption expenditure, whereas the store's purchase is treated as inventory investment. Although these borderline cases clearly exist, we can apply a simple rule of thumb: Investment is associated with the business sector's adding to the physical stock of capital, including inventories.[2] Officially, however, all household expenditures (except new housing construction) are counted as consumption spending. This is not quite so bad as it might seem, since the accounts do separate households' purchases of *durable goods* like cars and refrigerators from their other purchases.

In passing, we note that in Table 2-1 investment is listed as "gross." It is *gross investment* in the sense that depreciation is not deducted. *Net investment* is gross investment minus depreciation.

NET EXPORTS

The item "Net exports" appears in Table 2-1 to account for domestic spending on foreign goods and foreign spending on domestic goods. When foreigners purchase goods we produce, their spending adds to the demand for domestically produced goods. Correspondingly, that part of our spending that purchases foreign goods has to be subtracted from the demand for domestically produced goods. Accordingly, the difference between

---

[1]In the total incomes system of accounts (TISA), referred to in footnote 8 on page 36, the definition of investment is broadened to include investment in human capital, which means that total investment in that system is more than one-third of GDP. But in this book and in the official national income accounts, investment counts only additions to the physical capital stock.

[2]The GDP accounts record as investment *business sector* additions to the stock of capital. Some government spending, for instance, for roads or schools, also adds to the capital stock. Estimates of the capital stock owned by government are available in *Fixed Reproducible Tangible Wealth in the United States, 1925–97* (Washington, DC: U.S. Bureau of Economic Analysis, National Income and Wealth Division, 1999). For the most recent statistics, go to www.bea.doc.gov/bea/dn/faweb.

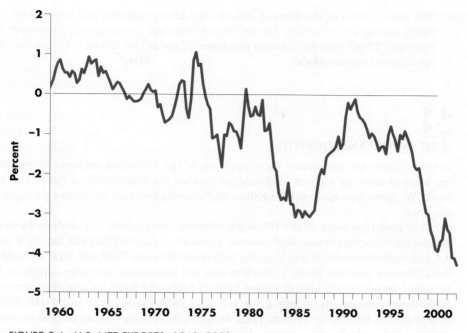

FIGURE 2-4   U.S. NET EXPORTS, 1960–2002.
(*Source: Bureau of Economic Analysis.*)

exports and imports, called *net exports,* is a component of the total demand for our goods. U.S. net exports have been negative since the 1980s, as shown in Figure 2-4, reflecting a high level of imports and a lower level of exports; note, though, that net exports have been close to zero in some years (trade has been nearly balanced) and very negative in others (the United States has had a large balance-of-trade deficit).

The role of net exports in accounting for GDP can be illustrated with an example. Assume that personal sector spending was higher by $2 billion. How much higher would GDP be? If we assume that government and investment spending remained unchanged, we might be tempted to say that GDP would have been $2 billion higher. That is correct if all the additional spending had fallen on domestic goods (e.g., cars built in Detroit). The other extreme, however, is that all the additional spending had fallen on imports (e.g., Jaguars imported from the U.K.). In that event, consumption would have been up $2 billion *and* net exports would have been down $2 billion, with *no* net effect on GDP.

RECAP

From this section you should remember:

• Demand for GDP is split into four components: consumption, investment, government, and net exports, according to the identity of the purchaser.
• $Y \equiv C + I + G + NX$.

- The relative sizes of the demand sectors vary across countries and across time, but rough numbers to remember for the United States are consumption, 70 percent; investment, 15 percent; government purchases of goods and services, 19 percent; and net exports, negative.

2-3

SOME IMPORTANT IDENTITIES

In this section we summarize the discussion of the preceding sections by presenting a set of national income relationships that we use extensively in the rest of the book. We introduce here some notation and conventions that we follow throughout the book.

For analytical work in the following chapters, we simplify our analysis by making assumptions that ensure that national income is equal to GDP. For the most part, we disregard depreciation and thus the difference between GDP and NDP as well as the difference between gross investment and net investment. We refer simply to investment spending. We also disregard indirect taxes and business transfer payments. With these conventions in mind, **we refer to national income and GDP interchangeably as income or output.** These simplifications have no serious consequences and are made only for convenience. Finally, just in the next subsection, we omit both the government and foreign sector.

A SIMPLE ECONOMY

We denote the value of output in our simple economy, which has neither a government nor foreign trade, by Y. Consumption is denoted by C and investment spending by I. The first key identity is that output produced equals output sold. What happens to unsold output? *We count the accumulation of inventories as part of investment* (as if the firms sold the goods to themselves to add to their inventories), and therefore all output is either consumed or invested. Output sold can be expressed in terms of the components of demand as the sum of consumption and investment spending. Accordingly, we can write

$$Y \equiv C + I \tag{4}$$

The next step is to establish a relation among *saving,* consumption, and GDP. How will income be allocated? Part will be spent on consumption, and part will be saved.[3] Thus we can write

$$Y \equiv S + C \tag{5}$$

---

[3]Decisions about saving are made by businesses as well as directly by consumers. It is convenient to ignore the existence of corporations and consolidate, or add together, the entire private sector.

where S denotes private sector saving. Identity (5) tells us that the whole of income is allocated to either consumption or saving. Next, identities (4) and (5) can be combined to read

$$C + I \equiv Y \equiv C + S \tag{6}$$

The left-hand side of identity (6) shows the components of demand, and the right-hand side shows the allocation of income. The identity emphasizes that output produced is equal to output sold. The value of output produced is equal to income received, and income received, in turn, is spent on goods or saved.

Identity (6) can be slightly reformulated to show the relation between saving and investment. Subtracting consumption from each part of identity (6), we have

$$I \equiv Y - C \equiv S \tag{7}$$

Identity (7) shows that in this simple economy *investment is identically equal to saving*.

One can think of what lies behind this relationship in a variety of ways. In a very simple economy, the only way the individual can save is by undertaking an act of physical investment—for example, by storing grain or building an irrigation channel. In a slightly more sophisticated economy, one could think of investors financing their investing by borrowing from individuals who save.

REINTRODUCING THE GOVERNMENT AND FOREIGN TRADE

We now reintroduce the government sector and the external sector.[4] We denote government purchases of goods and services by G and all taxes by TA. Transfers to the private sector (including interest on the public debt) are denoted by TR. Net exports (exports minus imports) are denoted by NX.

We return to the identity between output produced and sold, taking account now of all components of demand, including G and NX. Accordingly, we restate the fundamental identity:

$$Y \equiv C + I + G + NX \tag{8}$$

Next we turn to the derivation of the very important relation between output and disposable income. Now we have to recognize that part of income is spent on taxes and that the private sector receives net transfers (TR) in addition to national income. Disposable income (YD) is thus equal to income plus transfers less taxes:

$$YD \equiv Y + TR - TA \tag{9}$$

Disposable income, in turn, is allocated to consumption and saving:

$$YD \equiv C + S \tag{10}$$

---

[4]"Government" here means the federal government plus state and local governments.

Rearranging identity (9) and inserting for Y in identity (8), we have

$$YD - TR + TA \equiv C + I + G + NX \qquad (11)$$

Putting identity (10) into identity (11) yields

$$C + S - TR + TA \equiv C + I + G + NX \qquad (12)$$

With some rearrangement, we obtain

$$S - I \equiv (G + TR - TA) + NX \qquad (13)$$

SAVING, INVESTMENT, THE GOVERNMENT BUDGET, AND TRADE

Identity (13) cannot be overemphasized. The first set of terms on the right-hand side $(G + TR - TA)$ is the *government budget deficit (BD)*. $G + TR$ is equal to total government expenditure, consisting of government purchases of goods and services (G) plus government transfer payments (TR). TA is the amount of taxes received by the government. The difference $(G + TR - TA)$ is the excess of the government's spending over its receipts, or its budget deficit. (The budget deficit is a negative budget surplus, $BS = TA - (G + TR)$.) The second term on the right-hand side is the excess of exports over imports, or the *net exports of goods and services,* or net exports for short. NX is also called the *trade surplus.* When net exports are negative, we have a *trade deficit.*

Thus, identity (13) states that the excess of saving over investment $(S - I)$ in the private sector is equal to the government budget deficit plus the trade surplus. The identity suggests, correctly, that there are important relations among the excess of private saving over investment $(S - I)$, the government budget (BD), and the external sector (NX). For instance, if, for the private sector, saving is equal to investment, then the government's budget deficit (surplus) is reflected in an equal external deficit (surplus).

Table 2-2 shows the significance of identity (13). To fix ideas, suppose that private sector saving S is equal to $1,000 billion. In the first two rows we assume that exports are equal to imports, so the trade surplus is zero. In row 1, we assume the government budget is balanced. Investment accordingly has to equal $1,000 billion. In the next row we assume the government budget deficit is $150 billion. *Given the level of saving* of $1,000 billion and a zero trade balance, it has to be true that investment is now lower by $150 billion. Row 3 shows how this relationship is affected when there is a trade surplus.

TABLE 2-2 The Budget Deficit, Trade, Saving, and Investment
(Billions of Dollars)

SAVING (S)	INVESTMENT (I)	BUDGET DEFICIT (BD)	NET EXPORTS (NX)
1,000	1,000	0	0
1,000	850	150	0
1,000	900	0	100
1,000	950	150	−100

FIGURE 2-5   BUDGET AND TRADE SURPLUSES AS A PERCENTAGE OF GDP.
(Source: Bureau of Economic Analysis.)

Any sector that spends more than it receives in income has to borrow to pay for the excess spending. The private sector has three ways of disposing of its saving. It can make loans to the government, which thereby pays for the excess of its spending over the income it receives from taxes. Or the private sector can lend to foreigners, who are buying more from us than we are buying from them. They therefore are earning less from us than they need in order to pay for the goods they buy from us, and we have to lend to cover the difference. Or the private sector can lend to business firms, which use the funds for investment. In all three cases, households will be paid back later, receiving interest or dividends in addition to the amount they lent.

In the 1950s and 1960s, the U.S. budget balance and trade balance were usually in surplus, as Figure 2-5 shows. The story of the late 1970s through the mid-1990s was one of persistent government budget deficits and trade deficits. At the turn of the millennium, the budget had moved into surplus for the first time in many years, but the trade balance continued to be in deficit. By 2003 the budget balance appeared to be heading back toward significant deficit.

Figure 2-6 shows the federal debt, which is the accumulation of past deficits. Most federal debt has been the result of wars, but a considerable amount was added in the 1980s even though the United States was at peace.

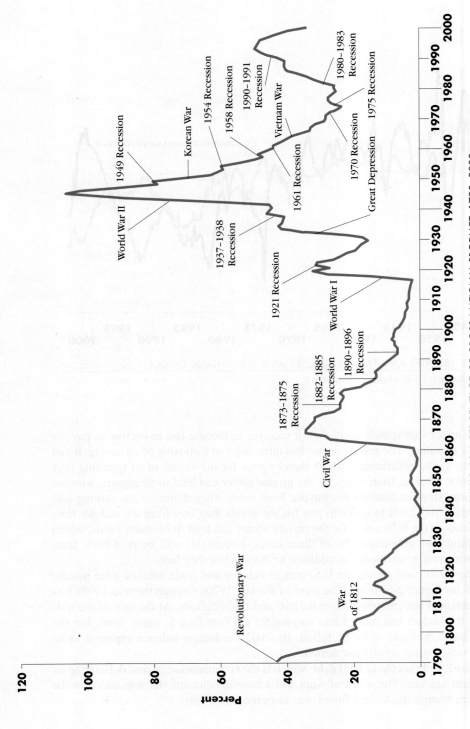

FIGURE 2-6 FEDERAL DEBT HELD BY THE PUBLIC AS A PERCENTAGE OF GROSS NATIONAL PRODUCT, 1790–2000.

(Source: Congressional Budget Office.)

2-4

MEASURING GROSS DOMESTIC PRODUCT

There are a number of subtleties in the calculation of GDP. There are also a number of nonsubtle problems. We start with the straightforward points.

FINAL GOODS AND VALUE ADDED

GDP is the value of *final goods and services* produced. The insistence on final goods and services is simply to make sure that we do not double-count. For example, we would not want to include the full price of an automobile in GDP and then also include as part of GDP the value of the tires that were bought by the automobile producer for use on the car. The components of the car that are bought by the manufacturers are called *intermediate goods,* and their value is not included in GDP. Similarly, the wheat that goes into a pie is an intermediate good. We count only the value of the pie as part of GDP; we do not count the value of the wheat sold to the miller and the value of the flour sold to the baker.

In practice, double counting is avoided by working with *value added.* At each stage of the manufacture of a good, only the value added to the good at that stage is counted as part of GDP. The value of the wheat produced by the farmer is counted as part of GDP. Then the value of the flour sold by the miller minus the cost of the wheat is the miller's value added. If we follow this process along, we will see that the sum of the value added at each stage of processing is equal to the final value of the bread sold.

CURRENT OUTPUT

GDP consists of the value of output *currently produced.* It thus excludes transactions in existing commodities, such as old masters or existing houses. We count the construction of new houses as part of GDP, but we do not add trade in existing houses. We do, however, count the value of realtors' fees in the sale of existing houses as part of GDP. The realtor provides a current service in bringing buyer and seller together, and that is appropriately part of current output.

PROBLEMS OF GDP MEASUREMENT

GDP data are, in practice, used not only as a measure of how much is being produced but also as a measure of the welfare of the residents of a country. Economists and politicians talk as if an increase in GDP means that people are better off. But GDP data are far from perfect measures of either economic output or welfare.[5] There are, specifically, three major problems:

- Some outputs are poorly measured because they are not traded in the market. If you bake homemade pie, the value of your labor isn't counted in official GDP statistics. If you buy a (no doubt inferior) pie, the baker's labor is counted. This means that the vastly increased participation of women in the labor force has increased official GDP numbers with no offsetting reduction for decreased production at home. (We officially measure the value of commercial day care, but taking care of your own kids is valued at zero.)

  Note, too, that government services aren't directly priced by the market. The official statistics assume that a dollar spent by the government is worth a dollar of value.[6] GDP is mismeasured to the extent that a dollar spent by the government produces output valued by the public at more or less than a dollar.

- Some activities measured as adding to GDP in fact represent the use of resources to avoid or contain "bads" such as crime or risks to national security. Similarly, the accounts do not subtract anything for environmental pollution and degradation. This issue is particularly important in developing countries. For instance, one study of Indonesia claims that properly accounting for environmental degradation would reduce the measured growth rate of the economy by 3 percent.[7]

- It is difficult to account correctly for improvements in the quality of goods. This has been the case particularly with computers, whose quality has improved dramatically while their price has fallen sharply. But it applies to almost all goods, such as cars, whose quality changes over time. The national income accountants attempt to adjust for improvements in quality, but the task is not easy, especially when new products and new models are being invented.

Attempts have been made to construct an *adjusted GNP* series that takes account of some of these difficulties, moving closer to a measure of welfare. The most comprehensive of these studies, by the late Robert Eisner of Northwestern University, estimates an adjusted GNP series in which the level of real GNP is about 50 percent higher than the official estimates.[8]

---

[5]See the articles by M. J. Boskin, B. R. Moulton, and W. D. Nordhaus under the heading "Getting the 21st Century GDP Right" in *American Economic Review,* May 2000.

[6]You probably have the immediate reaction that a dollar spent by the government on higher education is worth far more than a dollar spent on soft drinks—we hope.

[7]R. Repetto, W. Magrath, M. Wells, C. Beer, and F. Rossini, *Wasting Assets: Natural Resources in the National Income Accounts* (Washington, DC: World Resources Institute, June 1989). For a sophisticated look at accounting for the environment and natural resources, see William D. Nordhaus and Edward C. Kokkelenberg (eds.), *Nature's Numbers: Expanding the National Economic Accounts to Include the Environment* (Washington, DC: National Academy Press, 1999). You can read this book online at http://books.nap.edu/catalog/6374.html.

[8]Eisner presents his data in his book, *The Total Incomes System of Accounts* (Chicago: University of Chicago Press, 1989). In Appendix E, he reviews a variety of other attempts to adjust the standard accounts for major inadequacies. Eisner estimated an adjusted GNP rather than GDP series mainly because he did his work at the time when GNP was used as the basic measure of output.

BOX 2-1   Light and Truth

To shed light on just how much quality change can matter, William Nordhaus, of Yale University, has calculated how much better room lighting is now than in the past, based on estimates of energy requirements per lumen. The improvements—very few of which show up in the official statistics—are enormous. Today's electric light is about 25 times as efficient as Edison's first electric light was in 1883.

Unmeasured quality improvements are not new. Nordhaus calculates that 5 liters of sesame oil cost a Babylonian worker about 1/2 shekel (roughly 2 weeks' wages). Light equivalent to 2 candles burning for an hour cost a Babylonian about an hour's wages.*

*For other serious, but fun, comparisons, see William D. Nordhaus, "Do Real Output and Real Wage Measures Capture Reality? The History of Lighting Suggests Not," in Robert J. Gordon and Timothy F. Bresnahan (eds.), *The Economics of New Goods* (Chicago: University of Chicago Press, 1997), pp. 29–66.

2-5
INFLATION AND PRICE INDEXES

GDP would be easy to measure if all we consumed was pie. One year GDP would be 1,000 pies; the next year 1,005. Unfortunately, life is beer and skittles. You can't add a pint of beer to a game of skittles, but if the price of a pint is a dollar and a game of skittles costs 50 cents, you can say that a pint and a game adds $1.50 to GDP. Now suppose that next year all prices double: a pint and a game add $3 to GDP, but clearly nothing *real* has changed. While the dollar value of GDP has doubled, the amount of goods produced—which is what we care about—is unchanged.

Real GDP **measures changes in physical output in the economy between different time periods by valuing all goods produced in the two periods at the same prices, or in** *constant dollars.* Real GDP is now measured in the national income accounts at the prices of 1996.[9] This means that, in calculating real GDP, today's physical output is multiplied by the prices that prevailed in 1996 to obtain a measure of what today's output would have been worth had it been sold at the prices of 1996.

Nominal GDP **measures the value of output in a given period in the prices of that period, or, as it is sometimes put, in** *current dollars.*[10] Thus, 2004 nominal GDP

---

[9]The Bureau of Economic Analysis now produces "chain-weighted" estimates of real GDP. These estimates use 1996 prices but each year shift the weights given to various goods in measuring real GDP. See *Survey of Current Business,* January–February 1996.

[10]National income account data are regularly reported in the *Survey of Current Business (SCB)*. Historical data are available in the September issue of *SCB;* in the Commerce Department's *Business Statistics,* a biennial publication; and in the annual *Economic Report of the President.*

TABLE 2-3   Real and Nominal GDP, an Illustration

	1996 NOMINAL GDP	2004 NOMINAL GDP	2004 REAL GDP*
Beer	1 at $1.00 $1.00	2 at $2.00 $4.00	2 at $1.00 $2.00
Skittles	1 at $0.50 0.50	3 at $0.75 2.25	3 at $0.50 1.50
	$1.50	$6.25	$3.50

*Measured in 1996 prices.

measures the value of the goods produced in 2004 at the market prices prevailing in 2004, and 1929 nominal GDP measures the value of goods produced in 1929 at the market prices that prevailed in 1929. Nominal GDP changes from year to year for two reasons. First, the physical output of goods changes, and, second, market prices change. Changes in nominal GDP that result from price changes do not tell us anything about the performance of the economy in producing goods and services. That is why we use real rather than nominal GDP as the basic measure for comparing output in different years.

If all prices change in fixed proportion, say, every price doubles, then any reasonable price index will also change in that proportion. When some prices rise more than others, different price indexes will differ modestly according to how the different prices are weighted. Such differences are generally inconsequential for understanding macrotheory.

In Table 2-3 we present a simple example that illustrates the calculation of nominal and real GDP. The hypothetical outputs and prices of beer and skittles in 1996 and 2004 are shown in the first two columns of the table. Nominal GDP in 1996 was $1.50 and in 2004 was $6.25. However, much of the increase in nominal GDP is purely the result of the increase in prices and does not reflect an increase in physical output. When we calculate real GDP in 2004 by valuing 2004 output at the prices of 1996, we find that real GDP is $3.50. Since beer consumption doubled and skittle consumption tripled, we know that real GDP more than doubled and less than tripled. The fourfold increase in nominal GDP does not measure real value.

INFLATION AND PRICES

Inflation is the rate of change in prices, and the price level is the cumulation of past inflations. If P_{t-1} represents the price level last year and P_t represents today's price level, then the inflation rate over the past year can be written as

$$\pi \equiv \frac{P_t - P_{t-1}}{P_{t-1}} \tag{14}$$

where π stands for the inflation rate. Correspondingly, today's price level equals last year's price level adjusted for inflation:

$$P_t = P_{t-1} + (\pi \times P_{t-1}) \tag{15}$$

In the United States in the late nineties and early twenty-first century, the inflation rate was relatively low, around 2 or 3 percent per year, even though prices were much higher than they were 20 years earlier. High inflation rates in the 1970s had pushed up the price level. Once raised, the price level doesn't fall unless the inflation rate is negative—in other words, unless there is a *deflation*.

PRICE INDEXES

No single price index is perfect. The three main price indexes are the GDP deflator, the consumer price index, and the producer price index. Figure 2-7 shows the historical behavior of the GDP deflator, *p*, as well as the purchasing power of the dollar, $1/p$.

The GDP Deflator

The calculation of real GDP gives us a useful measure of inflation known as the *GDP deflator*. **The GDP deflator is the ratio of nominal GDP in a given year to real GDP of that year.** Since the GDP deflator is based on a calculation involving all the goods produced in the economy, it is a widely based price index that is frequently used to measure inflation. The deflator measures the change in prices that has occurred between the base year and the current year. Using the fictional example in Table 2-3, we

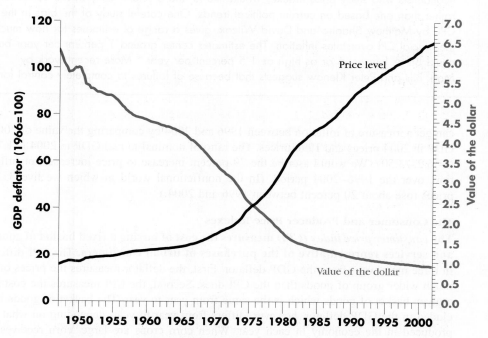

FIGURE 2-7   THE GDP DEFLATOR AND THE VALUE OF THE DOLLAR.
(*Source: Bureau of Economic Analysis.*)

40

BOX 2-2   Measuring Inflation: An "Academic" Exercise?

Price indexes are imperfect, in part because market baskets change and in part because quality changes are very hard to quantify. The resulting errors, on the order of a percent or so a year, have mostly been of interest to the economists who create and study price indexes. Recently, "correcting" price indexes has become a hot political topic. Many payments are "indexed to inflation," meaning that the nominal payment is adjusted for inflation to keep the real value constant. In the United States, social security is one such payment.

Because the U.S. social security system is in long-run financial danger, many politicians would like to reduce its costs. But the same politicians are loath to reduce benefits. Well, here's a clever solution: Suppose we announce that the official price index overstates inflation and legislate a "correction" of 1 percent per year. Then we can claim to be paying the same real benefits while spending 1 percent less the first year, 2 percent less the second year, and so forth.

Current price indexes probably overstate inflation. But as you can imagine, the economists who study price indexes would like to find a scientifically based correction rather than one based on current political trends. One careful study of the bias in the CPI, by Matthew Shapiro and David Wilcox, gives a range of estimates for how much the official CPI overstates inflation. The estimates center around 1 percent per year but could be as low as .6 or as high as 1.5 percent per year.* More recent work by Mark Bils and Peter Klenow suggests that because of failures to completely control for

can get a measure of inflation between 1996 and 2004 by comparing the value of 2004 GDP in 2004 prices and 1996 prices. The ratio of nominal to real GDP in 2004 is 1.79 (= 6.25/3.50). We would ascribe the 79 percent increase to price increases, or inflation, over the 1996–2004 period. (In the nonfictional world in which we live, U.S. prices rose about 20 percent between 1996 and 2004.)

The Consumer and Producer Price Indexes

The *consumer price index (CPI)* measures the cost of buying a fixed basket of goods and services representative of the purchases of urban consumers. The CPI differs in three main ways from the GDP deflator. First, the deflator measures the prices of a much wider group of goods than the CPI does. Second, the CPI measures the cost of a given basket of goods which is the same from year to year. The basket of goods included in the GDP deflator, however, differs from year to year, depending on what is produced in the economy in each year. When corn crops are large, corn receives a relatively large weight in the computation of the GDP deflator. By contrast, the CPI

quality improvements, measured inflation may have been overstated by as much as 2.2 percent per year between 1980 and 1996.**

The discussion of inflation mismeasurement is an example of how scientific work in economics has an immediate policy impact. To reduce the kind of criticism about political decision making hinted at above, in 1996 the Senate appointed a panel of blue-ribbon economists to review measurements of the CPI.[†] The panel reported that current CPI measurements overstate inflation by about 1.1 percent a year. As a dramatic example of how CPI measurement affects spending, the panel estimated that a 1 percent overestimate of cost-of-living increases would, between 1996 and 2008, increase the national debt by $1 trillion through overindexing of tax and benefit programs.

A 1 percent mismeasurement of the price level would matter less if the errors didn't build up year after year. Cumulative mismeasurement at the 1 percent annual level makes a very large difference. Leonard Nakamura gives a good example in terms of real wages.[‡] According to official statistics, between 1970 and 1995 the average real (measured in 1982 dollars) wage in the economy declined from about $8 an hour to just under $7.50. Correcting for a 1 percent annual bias in inflation would change this picture from a drop to an increase, from $8 to about $9.50 an hour.

*Matthew D. Shapiro and David W. Wilcox, "Mismeasurement in the Consumer Price Index: An Evaluation," NBER working paper, no. W5590, 1996.

**Mark Bils and Peter Klenow, "Quantifying Quality Growth," NBER working paper no. W7695, May 2000.

[†]Advisory Commission to Study the Consumer Price Index, "Final Report to the Senate Finance Committee," December 5, 1996. See also "Symposia: Measuring the CPI," *Journal of Economic Perspectives,* Winter 1998; Robert J. Gordon, "The Boskin Commission Report and Its Aftermath," NBER working paper no. W7759, June 2000; and, David E. Lebow and Jeremy B. Rudd, "Measurement Error in the Consumer Price Index: Where Do We Stand?" Board of Governors FEDS working paper no. 2001-61, December 2001.

[‡]Leonard Nakamura, "Measuring Inflation in a High-Tech Age," Federal Reserve Bank of Philadelphia *Business Review,* November–December 1995. See also, by the same author, "Is U.S. Economic Performance Really That Bad?" Federal Reserve Bank of Philadelphia working paper, April 1996.

---

measures the cost of a fixed basket of goods that does not vary over time. Third, the CPI directly includes prices of imports, whereas the deflator includes only prices of goods *produced* in the United States.[11]

The GDP deflator and the CPI differ in behavior from time to time. For example, at times when the price of imported oil rises rapidly, the CPI is likely to rise faster than the deflator. However, over long periods the two produce quite similar measures of inflation.

The *producer price index (PPI)* is the third price index that is widely used. Like the CPI, the PPI is a measure of the cost of a given basket of goods. However, it differs from the CPI in its coverage; the PPI includes, for example, raw materials and semi-finished goods. It differs, too, in that it is designed to measure prices at an early stage of the distribution system. Whereas the CPI measures prices where urban households

[11]Detailed discussion of the various price indexes can be found in the Bureau of Labor Statistics' *Handbook of Methods* and in the Commerce Department's biennial *Business Statistics.*

actually do their spending—that is, at the retail level—the PPI is constructed from prices at the level of the first significant commercial transaction.

   This makes the PPI a relatively flexible price index and one that frequently signals changes in the general price level, or the CPI, some time before they actually materialize. For this reason, the PPI and, more particularly, some of its subindexes, such as the index of "sensitive materials," serve as one of the business cycle indicators that are closely watched by policymakers. To return to the question posed at the beginning of the chapter, a dollar today buys—measured by the CPI—a bit more than what a dime would have bought in 1947.

2-6
UNEMPLOYMENT

The *unemployment rate* measures the fraction of the workforce that is out of work and looking for a job or expecting a recall from a layoff. Figure 2-8 shows unemployment rates for the United States and France. In the United States, 4 percent unemployment is very low and 9 percent is extremely high. Over the last half century, unemployment in France—and much of Europe—went from being well below U.S. unemployment to notably higher.

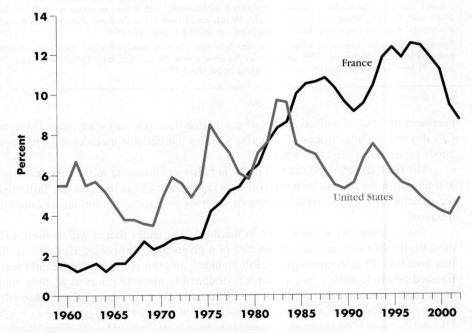

FIGURE 2-8   UNEMPLOYMENT RATES—UNITED STATES AND FRANCE.

(Source: Bureau of Labor Statistics.)

Because life is difficult for people without a job, and because it is more difficult to find a job when the unemployment rate is high, the unemployment rate is an important indicator of how well the economy is performing. Later in the book we will examine unemployment and its consequences in detail.

2-7
INTEREST RATES AND REAL INTEREST RATES

The interest rate states the rate of payment on a loan or other investment, over and above principal repayment, in terms of an annual percentage. If you have $1,000 in the bank and the bank pays you $50 in interest at the end of each year, then the annual interest rate is 5 percent. One of the simplifications we make in studying macroeconomics is to speak of "the" interest rate, when there are, of course, many interest rates. These rates differ according to the creditworthiness of the borrower, the length of the loan, and many other aspects of agreement between borrower and lender. (Some of the elements are discussed in Chapter 17.) Short-term U.S. Treasury bills are among the most heavily traded assets in the world. Figure 2-9 shows interest rates on 3-month Treasury bills.

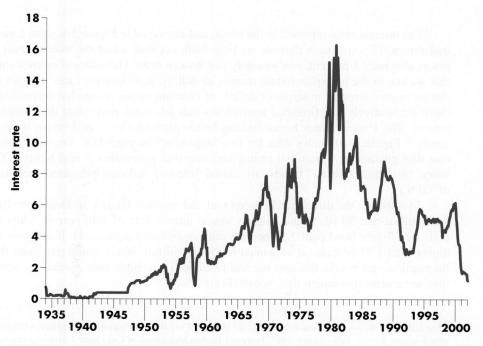

FIGURE 2-9   THREE-MONTH TREASURY BILL, SECONDARY MARKET.

(*Source: www.economagic.com.*)

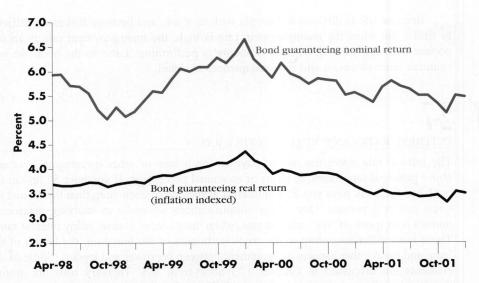

FIGURE 2-10   NOMINAL AND REAL INTEREST RATES FOR 30-YEAR TREASURY BONDS.
(Source: Federal Reserve Economic Data (FRED II), http://research.stlouisfed.org/fred2.*)*

The interest rates reported in the press, and displayed in Figure 2-9, state a nominal return. If you earn 5 percent on your bank account while the overall level of prices also rises 5 percent, you've really just broken even. The *nominal interest rates* that we see in the newspaper state returns in dollars. *Real interest rates* subtract inflation to give a return in terms of dollars of constant value. Somewhat surprisingly, there are relatively few financial instruments that guarantee real rather than nominal returns. The United States began issuing bonds guaranteeing a real return only recently.[12] Figure 2-10 shows data for two long-term (30-year) U.S. Treasury bonds, one that guarantees a nominal return and one that guarantees a real return. (The latter, "inflation indexed" bonds, are called Treasury inflation protected securities, or TIPS.)

To illustrate the difference between real and nominal returns, in December 2001 the nominal-rate 30-year bond paid an annual interest rate of 5.48 percent while the real-rate 30-year bond paid 3.53 percent *plus an inflation adjustment.* If inflation ran higher than 1.95 percent (at an annual rate) the real-rate bonds would pay more than the nominal-rate bonds. Because the real-rate bonds guarantee your purchasing power, they are a safer investment than nominal-rate bonds.

---

[12]See Jeffrey M. Wrase, "Inflation-Indexed Bonds: How Do They Work?" Federal Reserve Bank of Philadelphia *Business Review,* July–August 1997. Professor Huston McCulloch of Ohio State University maintains an up-to-date website on real and nominal interest rates at http://economics.sbs.ohio-state.edu/jhm/jhm.html.

BOX 2-3   Understanding Nominal versus Real Interest Rates in "Real Life"

When you invest money in bonds or an interest-bearing bank deposit, part of the return you receive (the *nominal* interest rate) is a real return (the *real* interest rate) and the remainder is an inflation adjustment to compensate for the fact that dollars will be worth less in the future. For example, if at the time of your birth your parents had deposited $1,927 in an account paying 5 percent interest, then in 18 years the account would have $4,636—which coincidentally is the cost of one year's in-state tuition at the University of Washington in 2003.

One never wants to discourage generous parents—but when you understand real versus nominal interest rates you know that the account isn't "really" paying 5 percent a year; part of the payment is just to offset inflation. If inflation is expected to average 3 percent, then the account is paying 2 percent a year after inflation is accounted for. Another way to say this is that if tuition costs rise at the rate of inflation, then while the account will have grown to $4,636, tuition will have risen to $7,892.

2-8
EXCHANGE RATES

In the United States, things monetary are measured in U.S. dollars. Canada uses Canadian dollars. Much of Europe uses the euro. The *exchange rate* is the price of foreign currency. For example, the exchange rate with the Japanese yen is about eight-tenths of a U.S. cent. The British pound is worth about US$1.56. Some countries allow their exchange rates to *float*, meaning the price is determined by supply and demand. Both Japan and Britain follow this policy, so their exchange rates fluctuate over time. Other countries *fix* the value of their exchange rate by offering to exchange their currency for dollars at a fixed rate. For example, the Bermuda dollar is always worth exactly one U.S. dollar and the Hong Kong dollar is set at US$0.13. In practice, many countries intervene to control their exchange rates at some times but not at others, so their exchange rates are neither purely fixed nor purely floating.

Whether a particular currency is worth more or less than a dollar has nothing to do with whether goods are more expensive in that country, as every tourist quickly learns. The Bermuda dollar is worth exactly one U.S. dollar, but even Bermuda onions are more expensive in Bermuda than in the United States. In contrast, there are about

10 Mexican pesos to the dollar, but for many goods you can buy more for 10 pesos in Mexico than you can for one dollar in the United States.

In later chapters we take a careful look at how exchange rates affect the economy and at how the economy helps determine exchange rates.

2-9

WHERE TO GRAB A LOOK AT THE DATA

One of the pleasures of the Internet is the ease with which you can find economic data. We repeat our earlier suggestion that to start looking for almost everything, the best site is "Resources for Economists on the Internet," www.aeaweb.org/RFE/EconFAQ.html. An excellent site for U.S. macroeconomic data, www.economagic.com has links to over 100,000 series and will plot data for you as well as provide easy downloads. The official source for U.S. national income accounts is the Bureau of Economic Analysis at www.bea.doc.gov. You can also find the *Survey of Current Business* online at this site. The *Economic Report of the President,* including data tables and past issues, is available at w3.access.gpo.gov/eop. The White House releases topical data at www.whitehouse.gov/fsbr/esbr.html.

Statistics Canada is the right place to look for Canadian data, www.statcan.ca/start.html (ou pour Statistique Canada, www.statcan.ca/start/_f.html). The Statistical Office of the European Union, http://europa.eu.int/comm/eurostat, is a good source for European data. American (North and South) data are provided by the Inter-American Development Bank at http://database.iadb.org. The World Bank is an excellent source of data on developing countries; see www.worldbank.org/data. The NBER provides a set of pre-World War II data for several countries at www.nber.org/databases/macrohistory/contents/index.html.

SUMMARY

1. GDP is the value of all final goods and services produced in the country within a given period.
2. On the production side, output is paid out as factor payments to labor and capital. On the demand side, output is consumed or invested by the private sector, used by the government, or exported.
3. $Y \equiv C + I + G + NX$.
4. $C + G + I + NX \equiv Y \equiv YD + (TA - TR) \equiv C + S + (TA - TR)$.
5. The excess of the private sector's saving over investment is equal to the sum of the budget deficit and net exports.
6. Nominal GDP measures the value of output in a given period in the prices of that period, that is, in current dollars.
7. Inflation is the rate of change in prices, and the price level is the cumulation of past inflations.
8. Nominal interest rates give the return on loans in current dollars. Real interest rates give the return in dollars of constant value.

9. The unemployment rate measures the fraction of the labor force that is out of work and looking for a job.

10. The exchange rate is the price of one country's currency in terms of another's.

KEY TERMS

adjusted GNP	gross domestic product	net domestic product (NDP)
consumer price index (CPI)	(GDP)	net exports
consumption spending	gross investment	net investment
deflation	gross national product	nominal GDP
depreciation	(GNP)	nominal interest rate
durable goods	gross private domestic	producer price index (PPI)
exchange rate	investment	production function
factor payments	human capital	real GDP
factors of production	inflation	real interest rate
final goods and services	intermediate goods	saving
GDP deflator	investment	transfer payments
government budget deficit	national income	unemployment rate
government expenditure	national income account	value added
government purchases	identity	

PROBLEMS

Conceptual

1. What would happen to GDP if the government hired unemployed workers, who had been receiving amount $TR in unemployment benefits, as government employees and now paid them $TR to do nothing? Explain.

2. In the national income accounts, what is the difference between
   a. A firm's buying an auto for an executive and the firm's paying the executive additional income to buy the automobile herself?
   b. Your hiring your spouse (who takes care of the house) rather than having him or her do the work without pay?
   c. Your deciding to buy an American car rather than a German car?

3. What is the difference between GDP and GNP? Is one a better measure of income/output than the other? Why?

4. What is NDP? Is it a better or worse measure of output than GDP? Explain.

5. Increases in real GDP are often interpreted as increases in welfare. What are some problems with this interpretation? Which do you think is the biggest problem with it, and why?

6. The CPI and PPI are both measures of the price level. How are they different, and when might you prefer one of these measures over the other?

7. What is the GDP deflator, and how does it differ from the consumer and producer price indexes? Under what circumstances might it be a more useful measure of price than the CPI and PPI?

8. If you woke up in the morning and found that nominal GDP had doubled overnight, what statistic would you need to check before you began to celebrate? Why?

9. Suppose you make a loan of $100 that will be repaid to you in 1 year. If the loan is denomi-
    nated in terms of a nominal interest rate, are you happy or sad if inflation is higher than ex-
    pected during the year? What if the loan instead had been denominated in terms of a real return?

Technical

1. In the text, we calculated the change in real GDP in the hypothetical economy of Table 2-3,
    using the prices of 1996. Calculate the change in real GDP between 1996 and 2004 using the
    same data but *the prices of 2004*. Your answer should demonstrate that the prices that are used
    to calculate real GDP do affect the calculated growth rate, but typically not by very much.
2. Show from national income accounting that
    a. An increase in taxes (while transfers remain constant) must imply a change in net ex-
        ports, government purchases, or the saving-investment balance.
    b. An increase in disposable personal income must imply an increase in consumption or
        an increase in saving.
    c. An increase in both consumption and saving must imply an increase in disposable income.
    [For both (b) and (c) assume there are no interest payments by households or transfer pay-
    ments to foreigners.]
3. The following is information from the national income accounts for a hypothetical country:

GDP	$6,000
Gross investment	800
Net investment	200
Consumption	4,000
Government purchases of goods and services	1,100
Government budget surplus	30

   What is
   a. NDP?   d. Disposable personal income?
   b. Net exports?   e. Personal saving?
   c. Government taxes minus transfers?
4. Assume that GDP is $6,000, personal disposable income is $5,100, and the government
    budget deficit is $200. Consumption is $3,800, and the trade deficit is $100.
    a. How large is saving (S)?
    b. How large is investment (I)?
    c. How large is government spending (G)?
5. If a country's labor is paid a total of $6 billion, its capital is paid a total of $2 billion, and
    profits are zero, what is the level of output? (*Hint:* see equation 2.)
6. Consider an economy that consists only of those who bake bread and those who produce its
    ingredients. Suppose that this economy's production is as follows: 1 million loaves of bread
    (sold at $2 each); 1.2 million pounds of flour (sold at $1 per pound); and 100,000 pounds
    each of yeast, sugar, and salt (all sold at $1 per pound). The flour, yeast, sugar, and salt are
    sold only to bakers, who use them exclusively for the purpose of making bread.
    a. What is the value of output in this economy (i.e., nominal GDP)?
    b. How much value is added to the flour, yeast, sugar, and salt when the bakers turn them
        into bread?

7. Suppose a country's CPI increased from 2.1 to 2.3 in the course of 1 year. Use this fact to compute the rate of inflation for that year. Why might the CPI overstate the rate of inflation?
8. Suppose you buy a $100 government bond that is due next year. How much nominal interest will you receive if inflation is 4 percent over the year and the bond promises a *real* return of 3 percent?

Empirical

1. Section 2.1 in this chapter deals with the relationship between the different components included in the National Income and Product Accounts (NIPA for short). Go to www.economagic.com. Under the heading "Browse by Source," choose the link to the Department of Commerce, BEA: National Accounts. Select the Current Annual option, and choose the data heading "Relation of Gross Domestic Product, Gross National Product, Net National Product, National Income, and Personal Income."

    Use the information provided there to fill in columns 1, 2, 3, and 5 in the following table, and calculate GNP and NNP based on the formulas given in the second row of the table. Do the values you found correspond to the numbers reported at www.economagic.com?

	GDP	INCOME RECEIPTS FROM ROW	INCOME PAYMENTS TO ROW	GNP	DEPRECIATION (CONSUMPTION OF FIXED CAPITAL)	NNP
	1	2	3	$4 = 1 + 2 - 3$	5	$6 = 4 - 5$
2000						
2001						
2002						

2. Check out the "Most Requested Series" website at www.economagic.com. How much was U.S. real GDP growth in the year 2002? What about the growth rate of U.S. population? Using these two pieces of information, what can you infer about the evolution of U.S. per capita real GDP in 2002?

PART 2

Growth, Aggregate
Supply and Demand,
and Policy

CHAPTER 3

Growth and Accumulation

CHAPTER HIGHLIGHTS

- Economic growth is due to growth in inputs, such as labor and capital, and to improvements in technology.

- Capital accumulates through saving and investment.

- The long-run level of output per person depends positively on the saving rate and negatively on the rate of population growth.

- The neoclassical growth model suggests that the standard of living in poor countries will eventually converge to the level in wealthy countries.

We have enormously higher incomes than did our great grandparents. People in industrialized nations are far wealthier than people living in less developed countries. In fact, Americans and many Europeans had higher incomes a century ago than people in poor countries do today. What accounts for these vast differences? What will determine our standard of living in the future? *Growth accounting* and *growth theory* answer these questions. Growth accounting explains what part of growth in total output is due to growth in different factors of production (capital, labor, etc.). Growth theory helps us understand how economic decisions determine the accumulation of factors of production, for example, how the rate of saving today affects the stock of capital in the future.

Figure 3-1 shows GDP for four countries over more than a century. The graph has four striking characteristics. First, the long-term growth record of the United States is remarkable, with average income increasing more than sixteenfold over the nineteenth and twentieth centuries. Second, Japan has gone from being a moderately poor country before World War II to being a wealthy country with a standard of living roughly equal to that of the United States. Third, Norwegian income has spurted in the last

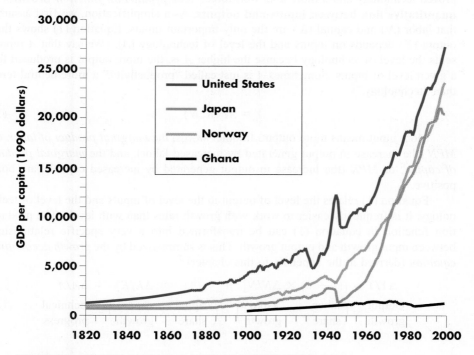

FIGURE 3-1   GDP PER CAPITA FOR FOUR COUNTRIES, 1820–1998.

The United States, Japan, and Norway have experienced growth in real GDP, while Ghana has had virtually zero growth. (Source: Angus Maddison, "Monitoring the World Economy 1820–1992," Paris: Organization for Economic Cooperation and Development, 1995; and "The World Economy: A Millenial Perspective," Paris: Organization for Economic Cooperation and Development, 2001.)

25 years. Fourth, Ghana was very poor 100 years ago and—growthless—sadly remains that way today.

Our goal in this chapter and the next is to explain Figure 3-1. Why is income in the United States so much higher today than it was a century ago? Why has Japan largely caught up with the United States, and why has Ghana not? We will learn that economic growth results from the accumulation of factors of production, particularly capital, and from increased productivity. In this chapter we see how these two factors account for economic growth and how saving rates and population growth determine capital accumulation. In the next chapter we turn to the question of why productivity increases.

3-1
GROWTH ACCOUNTING

In this section we use the production function to study two sources of growth. Output grows through increases in inputs and through increases in productivity due to improved technology and a more able workforce.[1] **The *production function* provides a quantitative link between inputs and outputs.** As a simplification, we first assume that labor (N) and capital (K) are the only important inputs. Equation (1) shows that output (Y) depends on inputs and the level of technology (A). (We say that A represents the level of technology because the higher A is, the more output is produced for a given level of inputs. Sometimes A is just called "productivity," a more neutral term than "technology.")

$$Y = AF(K, N) \qquad (1)$$

More input means more output. In other words, the *marginal product of labor,* or *MPN* (the increase in output generated by increased labor), and the *marginal product of capital,* or *MPK* (the increase in output generated by increased capital), are both positive.

Equation (1) relates the level of output to the level of inputs and the level of technology. It is frequently easier to work with growth rates than with levels. The production function in equation (1) can be transformed into a very specific relationship between input growth and output growth. This is summarized by the *growth accounting equation* (derived in the appendix to this chapter):[2]

$$\Delta Y/Y = [(1 - \theta) \times \Delta N/N] \quad + \quad (\theta \quad \times \Delta K/K) \quad + \quad \Delta A/A$$

$$\begin{array}{c} \text{Output} \\ \text{growth} \end{array} = \begin{pmatrix} \text{labor} \\ \text{share} \end{pmatrix} \times \begin{pmatrix} \text{labor} \\ \text{growth} \end{pmatrix} + \begin{pmatrix} \text{capital} \\ \text{share} \end{pmatrix} \times \begin{pmatrix} \text{capital} \\ \text{growth} \end{pmatrix} + \begin{array}{c} \text{technical} \\ \text{progress} \end{array} \qquad (2)$$

---

[1]For a sophisticated look at growth accounting, see Robert J. Barro, "Notes on Growth Accounting," *Journal of Economic Growth,* June 1999.

[2]The assumption of a competitive economy is required to move from equation (1) to equation (2). This assumption is discussed in the appendix. Box 3-1 begins an example using the Cobb-Douglas production function (the example continues in the appendix), but equation (2) in no way requires this specific production function.

BOX 3-1   The Cobb-Douglas Production Function

The generic formula for the production function is $Y = AF(K, N)$. If you prefer to follow the discussion with a specific formula, you can use the *Cobb-Douglas production function,* $Y = AK^\theta N^{1-\theta}$. At least for the United States, $\theta \approx .25$ makes the Cobb-Douglas function a very good approximation to the real economy, so the Cobb-Douglas function can be written as $Y = AK^{.25}N^{.75}$. Economists like the Cobb-Douglas functional form because it provides a relatively accurate description of the economy and is very easy to work with algebraically. For example, the marginal product of capital is

$$MPK = \theta AK^{\theta-1}N^{1-\theta} = \theta A(K/N)^{-(1-\theta)} = \theta Y/K$$

where $(1 - \theta)$ and θ are weights equal to labor's share of income and capital's share of income.[3]

Equation (2) summarizes the contributions of input growth and of improved productivity to the growth of output:

- Labor and capital each contribute an amount equal to their individual growth rates *multiplied by the share of that input in income.*
- The rate of improvement of technology, called *technical progress,* or the *growth of total factor productivity,* is the third term in equation (2).

The growth rate of total factor productivity is the amount by which output would increase as a result of improvements in methods of production, with all inputs unchanged. In other words, there is growth in total factor productivity when we get more output from the same factors of production.[4]

Example: Suppose capital's share of income is .25 and that of labor is .75. These values correspond approximately to the actual values for the U.S. economy. Furthermore, let labor force growth be 1.2 percent and growth of the capital stock be 3 percent, and suppose total factor productivity grows at the rate of 1.5 percent per annum. What is the growth rate of output? Applying equation (2), we obtain a growth rate of $\Delta Y/Y = (.75 \times 1.2$ percent$) + (.25 \times 3$ percent$) + 1.5$ percent $= 3.15$ percent.

An important point in equation (2) is that the growth rates of capital and labor are weighted by their respective income shares. Because labor's share is higher, a

---

[3]"Labor's share" means the fraction of total output that goes to compensate labor—in other words, wages, salaries, and so on, divided by GDP.

[4]There is a distinction between *labor productivity* and total factor productivity. Labor productivity is just the ratio of output to labor input, Y/N. Labor productivity certainly grows as a result of technical progress, but it also grows because of the accumulation of capital per worker.

1-percentage-point increase in labor raises output by more than a 1-percentage-point change in capital. Because the weights add to 1, if capital and labor *both* grow by an extra 1 percent, so does output.

This point—that growth in inputs is weighted by factor shares—turns out to be quite critical when we ask how much extra growth we get by raising the rate of growth of the capital stock, say, by implementing supply-side policies. Suppose that in the example above, capital growth had been twice as high—6 percent instead of 3 percent. Using equation (2), we find that output growth would increase from 3.15 to 3.9 percent, rising by less than a percentage point even though capital growth rose by an additional 3 percentage points.

ACCOUNTING FOR GROWTH IN PER CAPITA OUTPUT

Equation (2) describes growth in total output. But do we really care about total national income or about the income of an average person, *GDP per capita?* Switzerland is a "rich" country and India is a "poor" country even though aggregate Indian GDP is higher. Our notion of "standard of living" refers to individual well-being.

Per capita GDP is the ratio of GDP to population. In studying growth, it's traditional to use lowercase letters for per capita values, so we define $y \equiv Y/N$ and $k \equiv K/N$. The growth rate of GDP equals the growth rate of per capita GDP plus the growth rate of the population: $\Delta Y/Y = \Delta y/y + \Delta N/N$, and $\Delta K/K = \Delta k/k + \Delta N/N$. To translate the growth accounting equation into per capita terms, subtract population growth, $\Delta N/N$, from both sides of equation (2) and rearrange the terms:

$$\Delta Y/Y - \Delta N/N = \theta \times [\Delta K/K - \Delta N/N] + \Delta A/A \qquad (3)$$

Equation (3) is rewritten in per capita terms as:

$$\Delta y/y = \theta \times \Delta k/k + \Delta A/A \qquad (4)$$

The number of machines per worker, k, also called the *capital-labor ratio,* is a key determinant of the amount of output a worker can produce. Since θ is around .25, equation (4) suggests that a 1 percent increase in the amount of capital available to each worker increases per capita output by only about a quarter of 1 percent.

THE POSTWAR CONVERGENCE OF THE U.S. AND JAPANESE ECONOMIES

The process of one economy's catching up with another economy is called *convergence.* Since the end of World War II, the standard of living in Japan has basically caught up with that in the United States. How much of the remarkable postwar convergence between the United States and Japan can be explained by an accounting relation as simple as equation (4)? Table 3-1 presents the necessary data.

Figure 3-1 shows that the rate of Japanese catch-up with the United States was greater in the early than in the late postwar period, so we split the analysis into two periods, 1950–1973 and 1973–1992. We look first at the second period, in which the greater rate of capital accumulation in Japan accounts for much of the difference in output growth.

TABLE 3-1   Postwar Annual Growth Rates
(Percent)

	GDP PER CAPITA			CAPITAL (MACHINERY) PER CAPITA		
	UNITED STATES	JAPAN	DIFFERENCE	UNITED STATES	JAPAN	DIFFERENCE
1950–1973	2.42	8.01	5.59	2.48	6.92	4.44
1973–1992	1.38	3.03	1.65	2.89	6.38	3.49
1950–1992	1.95	5.73	3.78	2.66	6.67	4.01

Source: Angus Maddison, *Monitoring the World Economy 1820–1992* (Paris: Organization for Economic Cooperation and Development, 1995).

Between 1973 and 1992 (the second row of Table 3-1), Japan outpaced the United States in growth of GDP per capita by 1.65 percent per year. In just under 20 years, output in Japan grew 36 percent more than did output in the United States. What accounts for this achievement? Putting the numbers from Table 3-1 into equation (4), the difference of 3.49 percent per year in capital per capita growth ($\Delta k/k$) in the last column of Table 3-1 predicts a .87 percent ($.87 = \Delta y/y = \theta \times \Delta k/k = 0.25 \times 3.49$) GDP per capita growth differential. In other words, something as simple as equation (4) accounts for about half (.87 out of 1.65) of the observed difference in growth rates.

During the early postwar period, Japanese growth was an amazing 5.59 points higher than U.S. growth. We can show that this difference is too great to be explained by relative capital accumulation. Putting the data in the first row of Table 3-1 into equation (4) explains only 1.11 ($1.11 = \Delta y/y = \theta \times \Delta k/k = 0.25 \times 4.44$) points of the difference. This leaves 4.48 points to be explained by relative differences in technological change,[5] $\Delta A/A$. During the early postwar period, Japan actively imported technology from the West. Starting from a lower base level of technology, a huge amount of growth was possible through "technology catch-up." In the later postwar period, technology transfer became much more of a two-way street. Today, Japanese–American differences in $\Delta A/A$ are much less important than in the past.

Calculations such as these show that while capital accumulation is not the only determinant of GDP, it is a very important one. Therefore, we would like to know what determines the rate of capital accumulation. When we turn to growth theory later in the chapter, we examine how the saving rate determines capital growth.

3-2

EMPIRICAL ESTIMATES OF GROWTH

The calculations in the previous section showed the importance of capital accumulation for growth but also suggested that technical progress can be even more important. An early and famous study by Nobel Prize winner Robert Solow of MIT examined the

---

[5]As we will see below, improvements in human capital also play a role.

BOX 3-2   The Solow Residual

How is technical progress measured? By definition, changes in A account for all productivity changes not due to changes in factor inputs. Changes in A are sometimes called changes in *total factor productivity*, or *TFP*—a more neutral term than "technical progress." Since inputs and outputs are directly observable but A is not, economists measure $\Delta A/A$ by turning equation (2) inside out:

$$\Delta A/A = \Delta Y/Y - [(1 - \theta) \times \Delta N/N] - (\theta \times \Delta K/K)$$

and attributing everything left over to changes in *TFP*. Measured this way, changes in *TFP* are called the *Solow residual*.

period 1909–1949 in the United States, using a more sophisticated version of the calculations we just made.[6] Solow's surprising conclusion was that over 80 percent of the growth in output per labor hour over that period was due to technical progress.

Specifically, Solow estimated a U.S. GDP growth equation similar to equation (2) that identifies capital and labor growth along with technical progress as the sources of output growth. Between 1909 and 1949, the average annual growth of total GDP was 2.9 percent per year. Of that, Solow concluded that .32 percent was attributable to capital accumulation, 1.09 percent was due to increases in the input of labor, and the remaining 1.49 percent was due to technical progress. Per capita output grew at 1.81 percent per year, with 1.49 percentage points of that increase resulting from technical progress.

Solow found that the important determinants of GDP growth are technical progress, increased labor supply, and capital accumulation—in that order. The important determinants of growth in GDP per capita are technical progress and capital accumulation.

Increased population actually decreases GDP per capita even though it increases GDP. While this may sound confusing, both conclusions follow directly from equation (2). More workers means more output, but output increases less than proportionately. Equation (2) tells us that each percentage point of growth in the labor force leads to a $1 - \theta$ percentage-point increase in output, specifically, about three-quarters of a point. Because the increase is less than one for one, output grows less quickly than the number of workers and output per worker (GDP per capita) falls. There is another way to say all this: If you increase the number of workers without proportionately increasing the number of machines, the average worker will be less productive because she has less equipment to work with.

[6] R. Solow, "Technical Change and the Aggregate Production Function," *Review of Economics and Statistics,* August 1957.

FACTORS OTHER THAN CAPITAL AND LABOR

The production function and therefore equations (2) and (4) omit a long list of inputs other than capital and labor—in part because capital and labor are the most important inputs and in part just as a simplification. Of course, in specific times and in specific places inputs other than labor and capital matter a great deal. Two other important inputs are natural resources and human capital.

Natural Resources

Much of the early prosperity of the United States was due to the nation's abundant, fertile land. Between 1820 and 1870, the land area of the United States grew at 1.41 percent per year (contributing greatly to growth), although in modern times U.S. land growth has been negligible. The opening of the Russian east roughly coincided with the opening of the American west and similarly contributed to Russian economic growth.

For a more recent example of the occasional importance of natural resources, consider the recent sharp increase in Norwegian GDP (see Figure 3-1). Between 1970 and 1990, Norway's per capita GDP rose from 61 percent of U.S. per capita GDP to 77 percent. Much of this Norwegian growth spurt was due to the discovery and development of massive oil reserves.[7]

Human Capital

In industrialized countries, raw labor is less important than the skills and talents of workers. Society's stock of such skills is increased by investment in *human capital* through schooling, on-the-job training, and other means in the same way that physical investment leads to increased physical capital. (In poor countries, investments in health are a major contributor to human capital. In times of extreme poverty, the critical investment can be providing workers with enough calories to enable them to bring in the harvest.) Adding human capital, H, we can write the production function as

$$Y = AF(K, H, N) \tag{5}$$

The income share of human capital is large in industrialized countries. An influential article by Mankiw, Romer, and Weil suggests that the production function is consistent with factor shares of one-third each for physical capital, raw labor, and human capital.[8] Differential growth in these three factors can explain about 80 percent of the variation in GDP per capita across a wide sample of countries, emphasizing the critical role of factor accumulation in the growth process.

---

[7]Although possession of rich natural resources should contribute to a higher standard of living, some empirical evidence suggests that countries with more natural resources on average do *worse*. One explanation is that such countries squander their wealth. See Jeffrey D. Sachs and Andrew M. Warner, "The Big Push, Natural Resource Booms and Growth," *Journal of Development Economics,* 1999.

[8]N. G. Mankiw, D. Romer, and D. Weil, "A Contribution to the Empirics of Economic Growth," *Quarterly Journal of Economics,* May 1992.

According to the previous section, a large physical capital stock—the result of a high investment ratio—should lead to high GDP. Figure 3-2a plots (on a logarithmic scale) per capita GDP against investment (as a fraction of GDP) for a cross section of countries. It's apparent that high investment does lead to high income. But is there a

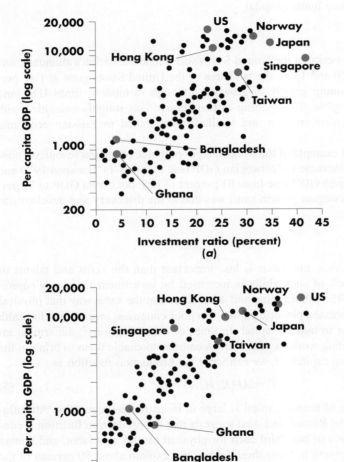

FIGURE 3-2 RELATIONSHIP OF (a) INVESTMENT RATIO AND (b) AVERAGE YEARS OF SCHOOLING TO GDP.

The higher the rate of investment—in physical or human capital—the higher the GDP. (*Source: Data taken from R. Barro and J. Lee, "International Comparisons of Educational Attainment,"* Journal of Monetary Economics, *1993.*)

similar relationship between human capital and output? Human capital is difficult to measure precisely, but average years of schooling can serve as a proxy for human capital. In Figure 3-2*b* we see that the evidence strongly supports the positive relationship between human capital and output. In the next chapter we will see that human capital, like physical capital, can continue to accumulate and therefore can be a contributor to permanent growth.

Any change in a major factor of production will affect output. GDP in some tropical countries depends greatly on the arrival of monsoons. Immigration boosts per capita output when skilled workers enter the country, a fact that has frequently benefited the United States. In contrast, immigration consisting of war refugees typically depresses per capita output in the short run. However, a factor of production adds to output growth only so long as the supply of the factor itself is growing. Such fluctuations in factor input may last for several years, but they rarely last for several decades (although the opening of the American west and the Russian east would be exceptions).

Short-run fluctuations in input factors—everything from monsoons to refugee flows—are sometimes quite important. Nonetheless, over great sweeps of history the two important factors are capital accumulation (physical and human) and technological progress. Our study of growth theory concentrates on these two factors.

3-3

GROWTH THEORY: THE NEOCLASSICAL MODEL

There have been two periods of intense work on growth theory, the first in the late 1950s and the 1960s and the second 30 years later, in the late 1980s and early 1990s. Research in the first period created *neoclassical growth theory*. Neoclassical growth theory focuses on capital accumulation and its link to savings decisions and the like. The best-known contributor is Robert Solow.[9] Endogenous growth theory, studied in the next chapter, focuses on the determinants of technological progress.

Neoclassical growth theory begins with a simplifying assumption. We start our analysis by pretending that there is no technological progress. This implies that the economy reaches a long-run level of output and capital called the *steady-state equilibrium*. The steady-state equilibrium for the economy is the combination of per capita GDP and per capita capital where the economy will remain at rest, that is, where per capita economic variables are no longer changing, $\Delta y = 0$ and $\Delta k = 0$.

Growth theory proceeds in three broad steps. First, we see how various economic variables determine the economy's steady state. Next, we study the transition from the economy's current position to this steady state. As a final step, we add technological progress to the model. (Perhaps this seems a bit roundabout. But this trick allows us to use simple graphs for the analysis and still get to the right answer.)

---

[9]R. Solow, "A Contribution to the Theory of Economic Growth," *Quarterly Journal of Economics,* February 1956. The collection of papers in Joseph Stiglitz and Hirofumi Uzawa (eds.), *Readings in the Theory of Economic Growth* (Cambridge, MA: MIT Press, 1969), contains many of the most important papers of that period.

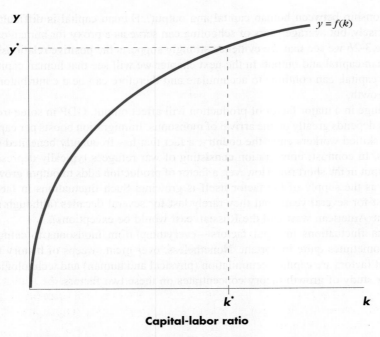

Capital-labor ratio

FIGURE 3-3   PER CAPITA PRODUCTION FUNCTION.

The production function $y = f(k)$ is the relationship between per capita output and the capital-labor ratio.

Figure 3-3 presents the production function in terms of GDP per capita graphed against the capital-labor ratio.[10] The production function in per capita terms is written

$$y = f(k) \tag{6}$$

Note the shape of the production function in Figure 3-3. As capital rises, output rises (the marginal product of capital is positive), but output rises less at high levels of capital

---

[10]The production function defined in equation (1) gave output as a function of both labor and capital. We wish to work in per capita variables. Divide both sides of the production function in (1) by N: $Y/N = AF(K, N)/N$. Next use the fact of constant returns to scale (discussed in the appendix to this chapter) to write $AF(K, N)/N = AF(K/N, N/N)$. Remembering that $K/N \equiv k$ (and since $N/N \equiv 1$), we write $AF(K/N, N/N) = AF(k, 1)$. To remind us that we are working in per capita terms, it is conventional to define $f(k) \equiv AF(k, 1)$.

The Cobb-Douglas in Per Capita Terms

Following through on the Cobb-Douglas example, we write

$$Y/N = AK^\theta N^{1-\theta}/N = AK^\theta N^{-\theta} N/N = A(K/N)^\theta \text{ or } y = f(k) = Ak^\theta$$

than at low levels (diminishing marginal product of capital). Each additional machine adds to production, but adds less than did the previous machine.[11] We will see below that *diminishing marginal product* is the key explanation of why the economy reaches a steady state rather than growing endlessly.

STEADY STATE

An economy is in a *steady state* when per capita income and capital are constant. The steady-state values of per capita income and capital,[12] denoted y^* and k^*, are those values where the investment required to provide capital for new workers and to replace machines that have worn out is just equal to the saving generated by the economy. If saving is greater than this investment requirement, then capital per worker rises over time and therefore output does as well. If saving is less than this investment requirement, then capital and output per worker fall. The steady-state values y^* and k^* are the levels of output and capital at which saving and required investment balance.

Once we have y^* and k^* as a point of reference, we can examine the transition path of the economy from an arbitrary point to the steady state. For example, if the economy starts with less capital than k^* and income below y^*, we examine how capital accumulation moves the economy over time toward y^* and k^*.

INVESTMENT AND SAVING

The investment required to maintain a given level, k, of capital per capita depends on population growth and the depreciation rate, the rate at which machines wear out. We assume first that the population grows at a constant rate $n \equiv \Delta N/N$. Therefore, the economy needs investment nk to provide capital for new workers. Second, we assume that depreciation is a constant d percent of the capital stock. Concretely, we might assume that depreciation is 10 percent per year, so every year 10 percent of the capital stock needs to be replaced to offset wear and tear. This adds dk to the requirement for new machinery. Thus, the investment required to maintain a constant level of capital per capita is $(n + d)k$.

Now we examine the link between saving and growth in capital. We are assuming there is no government sector and no foreign trade or capital flows. We also assume that saving is a constant fraction, s, of income, so per capita saving is sy. Since income equals production, we can also write $sy = sf(k)$.

---

[11]The diminishing curvature is the graphical equivalent of $\theta < 1$ in equation (2).

[12]For income *per head* and capital *per head* to remain unchanging even though population is growing, income and capital must grow at the same rate as population. As a symbol for the rate of population growth, we define $n \equiv \Delta N/N$, so in the steady state $\Delta Y/Y = \Delta N/N = \Delta K/K = n$.

BOX 3-3 Why Do Some Countries Produce So Much More Output per Worker than Others?

In an influential article (from which we've swiped the title for this box), Bob Hall and Chad Jones apply growth accounting to help us understand growth experiences across countries.* The first column in Table 1 gives output per worker relative to the United States. The next two columns show the contribution of physical capital and human capital in explaining output for a particular country relative to their contribution to output in the United States. The last column measures productivity, our A in equation (1), relative to the United States. For example, Canada's output per worker was 94.1 percent of output per worker in the United States; or, equivalently, Canada's output per worker was 5.9 percent below that of the United States. This difference is explained by Canada having 0.2 percent more physical capital per worker, 9.2 percent less human capital per worker, and 3.4 percent higher productivity.

Individual numbers in Table 1 need to be taken with a grain of salt both because international comparisons are notoriously difficult and because the underlying data are somewhat dated. For example, current measures of GDP per capita show China to be considerably better off than India. Imperfect data notwithstanding, three points stand out:

- The rich countries are *enormously* better off than the poor countries (column 1).
- Differences in physical and human capital explain much of the differences in output (columns 2 and 3).

The net change in capital per capita, Δk, is the excess of saving over required investment:

$$\Delta k = sy - (n + d)k \qquad (7)$$

The *steady state is defined by* $\Delta k = 0$ and occurs at the values of y^* and k^* satisfying

$$sy^* = sf(k^*) = (n + d)k^* \qquad (8)$$

Figure 3-4 presents a graphical solution for the steady state. With individuals saving a constant fraction of their income, the curve sy, which is a constant proportion of output, shows the level of saving at each capital-labor ratio. The straight line $(n + d)k$ shows the amount of investment that is needed at each capital-labor ratio to keep the capital-labor ratio constant by supplying machines both as replacements for those that have worn out and as additions for workers newly entering the labor force. Where the two lines intersect, at point C, saving and required investment balance with steady-state capital k^*. Steady-state income is read off the production function at point D.

- Productivity differences also account for a very large amount of the differences in output (column 4).

TABLE 1 Productivity Calculations: Ratios to U.S. Values

COUNTRY	OUTPUT PER WORKER	PHYSICAL CAPITAL PER WORKER	HUMAN CAPITAL PER WORKER	PRODUCTIVITY
United States	1.000	1.000	1.000	1.000
Canada	0.941	1.002	0.908	1.034
Australia	0.843	1.094	0.900	0.856
Italy	0.834	1.063	0.650	1.207
Netherlands	0.806	1.060	0.803	0.946
United Kingdom	0.727	0.891	0.808	1.011
Hong Kong	0.608	0.741	0.735	1.115
Singapore	0.606	1.031	0.545	1.078
Japan	0.587	1.119	0.797	0.658
Ireland	0.577	1.052	0.773	0.709
Indonesia	0.110	0.915	0.499	0.242
India	0.086	0.709	0.454	0.267
China	0.060	0.891	0.632	0.106
Ghana	0.052	0.516	0.465	0.218

*Robert E. Hall and Charles I. Jones, "Why Do Some Countries Produce So Much More Output per Worker than Others?" *Quarterly Journal of Economics*, February 1999, pp. 83–116. Data used in creating the table, and for many other countries, can be found at http://emlab.berkeley.edu/users/chad/HallJones400.asc.

THE GROWTH PROCESS

In Figure 3-4 we study the adjustment process that leads the economy from some initial capital-labor ratio over time to the steady state. The critical elements in this transition process are the rate of saving and investment compared with the rate of depreciation and population growth.

The key to understanding the neoclassical growth model is that when saving, sy, exceeds the investment requirement line, then k is increasing, as specified by equation (7). Accordingly, when sy exceeds $(n + d)k$, k must be increasing, and over time the economy is moving to the right in Figure 3-4. For instance, if the economy starts at capital-output ratio k_0, then with saving at A exceeding the investment needed to hold k constant at B, the horizontal arrow shows k increasing.

The adjustment process comes to a halt at point C. Here we have reached a capital-labor ratio, k^*, for which the saving associated with that capital-labor ratio exactly matches the investment requirement. Given the exact matching of actual and required

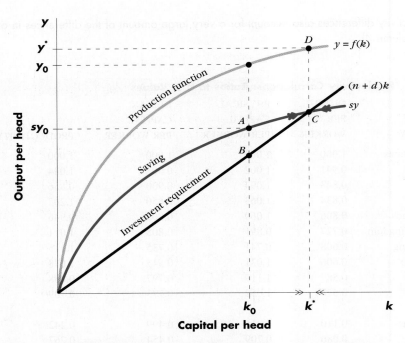

FIGURE 3-4   STEADY-STATE OUTPUT AND INVESTMENT.

investment, the capital-labor ratio neither rises nor falls. We have reached the steady state.

Note that this adjustment process leads to point C from any initial level of income. An important implication of neoclassical growth theory is that countries with equal saving rates, rates of population growth, and technology (that is, the same production function) should eventually converge to equal incomes, although the convergence process may be quite slow.

At that steady state, both k and y are constant. With per capita income constant, aggregate income is growing at the same rate as population, that is, at rate n. **It follows that the steady-state growth rate is not affected by the saving rate.** This is one of the key results of neoclassical growth theory.

AN INCREASE IN THE SAVING RATE

Why should the long-run growth rate be independent of the saving rate? Aren't we always being told that low American saving rates lead to low growth in the United States? Shouldn't it be true that an economy in which 10 percent of income is set aside for additions to the capital stock is one in which capital and therefore output grow faster than in an economy in which only 5 percent of income is saved? According to neoclassical growth theory, the saving rate does not affect the growth rate *in the long-run*.

In Figure 3-5 we show how an increase in the saving rate affects growth. In the short run, an increase in the saving rate raises the growth rate of output. **It does not affect the long-run growth rate of output, but it raises the long-run level of capital and output per head.**

In Figure 3-5, the economy is initially in steady-state equilibrium at point *C*, at which saving precisely matches the investment requirement. Now suppose people want to save a larger fraction of income, *s'* rather than *s*. This causes an upward shift of the saving schedule, to the dashed schedule.

At point *C*, at which we initially had a steady-state equilibrium, saving has now risen relative to the investment requirement; as a consequence, more is saved than is required to maintain capital per head constant. Enough is saved to allow the capital stock per head to increase. The capital stock per head, *k*, will keep rising until it reaches point *C'*. At *C'*, the higher amount of saving is just enough to maintain the higher stock of capital. At point *C'*, both capital per head and output per head have risen.

However, at point *C'*, the economy has returned to its steady-state growth rate of *n*. Thus, according to the neoclassical growth theory, an increase in the saving rate will

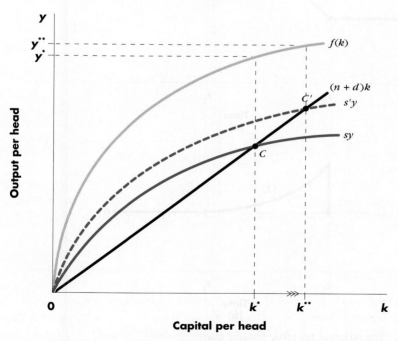

FIGURE 3-5   INCREASE IN SAVING RATE MOVES THE STEADY STATE.

If the saving rate increases, the steady-state capital-labor ratio increases.

in the long-run raise only the level of output and capital per head, and not the growth rate of output per head.

In the transition process, however, the higher saving rate increases the growth rate of output and the growth rate of output per head. This follows simply from the fact that the capital-labor ratio rises from $k*$ at the initial steady state to $k**$ in the new steady state. The only way to achieve an increase in the capital-labor ratio is for the capital stock to grow faster than the labor force (and depreciation).

Figure 3-6 summarizes the effects of an increase in the saving rate, paralleling the shift shown in Figure 3-5. Figure 3-6a shows the level of per capita output. Starting from an initial long-run equilibrium at time t_0, the increase in the saving rate causes saving and investment to increase, the stock of capital per head grows, and so does output per head. The process will continue at a diminishing rate. Figure 3-6b shows the growth rate of output, plotting the rate of change of the level of output in panel (a). The increase in the saving rate immediately raises the growth rate of output because it

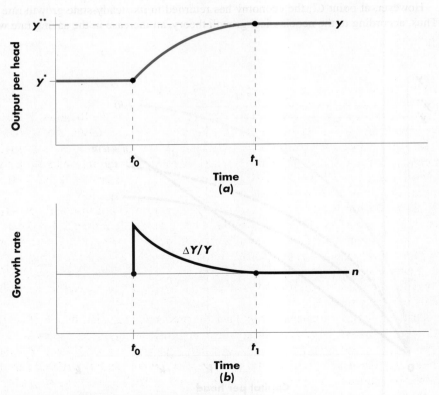

FIGURE 3-6   ADJUSTMENT TO NEW STEADY STATE.

Panels (a) and (b) show the adjustment of output and of the output growth rate following the increase in the saving rate depicted in Figure 3-5.

implies faster growth in capital and therefore in output. As capital accumulates, the growth rate decreases, falling back toward the level of population growth.

POPULATION GROWTH

The preceding discussion of saving and the influence of the saving rate on steady-state capital and output makes it easy to discuss the effects of increased population growth. An increase in the population growth rate affects the $(n + d)k$ line in the diagram, rotating it up and to the left. In the end-of-chapter problems we ask you to show the following results:

- An increase in the rate of population growth *reduces* the steady-state *level* of capital per head, k, and output per head, y.
- An increase in the rate of population growth *increases* the steady-state rate of growth of *aggregate* output.

The decline in output per head as a consequence of increased population growth points out the problem faced by many developing countries, as discussed in Chapter 4.

GROWTH WITH EXOGENOUS TECHNOLOGICAL CHANGE

Figure 3-2, and the analysis that followed, set $\Delta A/A = 0$ as a simplification. This simplification helped us understand steady-state behavior, but it eliminated the long-term-growth part of growth theory. In other words, the theory to this point says that GDP per capita is constant once the economy reaches its steady state. But we know that the economy grows. By allowing technology to improve over time, that is, $\Delta A/A > 0$, we reinstate growth in GDP per capita.

The production function in Figure 3-2 can be thought of as a snapshot of $y = Af(k)$ taken in a year in which A is normalized to 1. If technology improves at 1 percent per year, then a snapshot taken a year later will be $y = 1.01 f(k)$; 2 years later, $y = (1.01)^2 f(k)$; and so forth. In general, if the rate of growth is defined as $g = \Delta A/A$, then the production function rises at g percent per year, as shown in Figure 3-7. The savings function grows in a parallel fashion. As a result, in growth equilibrium y and k both grow over time.

The technology parameter A can enter the production function in any of several positions. For mathematical analysis, it is frequently assumed that technology is *labor-augmenting*, so the production function can be written $y = F(K, AN)$. ("Labor-augmenting" means that new technology increases the productivity of labor.) In this formulation, equation (4) is modified to $\Delta y/y = \theta \times \Delta k/k + (1 - \theta) \times \Delta A/A$. In growth equilibrium y and k both grow at the rate of technological progress, g. (Y and K both grow at the rate of technical progress plus the rate of population growth, $g + n$.) In this model, real wages also grow at rate g.

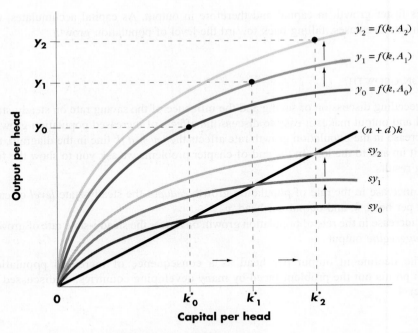

FIGURE 3-7 EXOGENOUS TECHNOLOGICAL CHANGE.

An exogenous increase in technology causes the production function and saving curve to rise. The result is a new steady-state point at a higher per capita output and higher capital-labor ratio. Thus, increases in technology over time result in growth of output over time.

We can estimate the rate of technical progress in the postwar United States using the data in Table 3-1 and the formula

$$g \approx (\Delta y/y - \theta \times \Delta k/k)/(1 - \theta) \qquad (4')$$

From the first line in Table 3-1 we can calculate $g \approx (2.42 - 0.25 \times 2.48)/(0.75) = 2.40$. Since growth in technology and in GDP and capital per capita all come out about the same, the data suggest that the United States had reached a growth steady state. (The numbers should all be equal to g.) The assumption that the economy was in a growth steady state works less well in the later postwar period, as capital growth is notably higher than GDP growth.

The second popular place to insert technology in the production function is, as it was at the beginning of the chapter, right out front, $Y = AF(K, N)$. Written this way, A is called *total factor productivity* because it augments all factors, not just labor. Here, equation (4) works as originally specified, so $g \approx (\Delta y/y - \theta \times \Delta k/k)$. [The difference between equations (4) and (4') is really just a difference in units of measurement.] Specified in this way, g is called the *Solow residual,* indicating that total factor productivity really measures all the changes in production that we can't account for by changes in input factors.

BOX 3-4   The Cobb-Douglas Production Function with Labor-Augmenting Technical Progress

Putting labor-augmenting technical progress into the Cobb-Douglas production function gives us the production function

$$Y = K^{\theta}(AN)^{1-\theta} = A^{1-\theta}K^{\theta}N^{1-\theta}$$

Note that the leading factor, A, now has an exponent of $1 - \theta$ instead of an implicit exponent of 1. This corresponds to the modification of equation (4) in the text to include $(1 - \theta) \times \Delta A/A$ in place of $\Delta A/A$.

Return again to Figure 3-1. We have used growth theory to explain the long upward trend in the standard of living in the United States (technical progress and the accumulation of physical and human capital); the convergence of Japanese and U.S. standards of living (transitional capital accumulation and technology transfer); and the Norwegian growth spurt (oil!).

RECAP

There are four key results of neoclassical growth theory:

- First, the growth rate of output in steady state is exogenous; in this case it is equal to the population growth rate, n. It is therefore independent of the saving rate, s.
- Second, although an increase in the saving rate does not affect the steady-state growth rate, it does increase the steady-state *level* of income by increasing the capital-output ratio.
- Third, when we allow for productivity growth, we can show that if there is a steady state, the steady-state growth rate of output remains exogenous. The steady-state rate of growth of per capita income is determined by the rate of technical progress. The steady-state growth rate of aggregate output is the sum of the rate of technical progress and the rate of population growth.
- The final prediction of neoclassical theory is that of *convergence:* If two countries have the same rate of population growth, the same saving rate, and access to the same production function, they will eventually reach the same level of income. In this framework, poor countries are poor because they have less capital, but if they save at the same rate as rich countries and have access to the same technology, they will eventually catch up.

Further, if countries have different saving rates, then according to this simple neoclassical theory, they will reach different *levels* of income in the steady state, but if their rates of technical progress and population growth are the same, their steady-state growth rates will be the same.

SUMMARY

1. Neoclassical growth theory accounts for growth in output as a function of growth in inputs, particularly capital and labor. The relative importance of each input depends on its factor share.
2. Labor is the most important input.
3. Long-run growth results from improvements in technology.
4. Absent technological improvement, output per person will eventually converge to a steady-state value. Steady-state output per person depends positively on the saving rate and negatively on the rate of population growth.

KEY TERMS

capital-labor ratio	growth accounting equation	production function
Cobb-Douglas production function	growth theory	Solow residual
convergence	human capital	steady state
diminishing marginal product	marginal product of capital (MPK)	steady-state equilibrium
GDP per capita	marginal product of labor (MPL)	total factor productivity
growth accounting	neoclassical growth theory	

PROBLEMS

Conceptual

1. What information does a production function provide?
2. Can the Solow growth model help to explain the phenomenon of convergence?
3. Consider a production function that omits the stock of natural resources. When, if ever, will this omission have serious consequences?
4. If, in the context of a standard production function, $Y = F(K, N)$, where K represents physical capital and N represents raw labor, we were to interpret the Solow residual ($\Delta A/A$) as "technological progress," we would be in error. What, besides technological progress, would this residual catch? How could you expand the model to eliminate this problem?
5. Figure 3-4 is a basic illustration of the Solow growth model. Interpret it, being careful to explain the meaning of the saving and investment requirement lines. Why does the steady state occur where they cross?
6. What factors determine the growth rate of steady-state per capita output? Are there other factors that could affect the growth rate of output in the *short run*?
7. Since the mid-1990s, the U.S. economy has undergone a surge in labor productivity, given by Y/N. What are some possible explanations given by equation (2) for this surge?

Technical

1. In a simple scenario with only two factors of production, suppose that capital's share of income is .4 and labor's share is .6 and that annual growth rates of capital and labor are 6 and 2 percent, respectively. Assume there is no technical change.
    a. At what rate does output grow?
    b. How long will it take for output to double?
    c. Now suppose technology grows at a rate of 2 percent. Recalculate your answers to (a) and (b).

2. Suppose output is growing at 3 percent per year and capital's and labor's shares of income are .3 and .7, respectively.
    a. If both labor and capital grow at 1 percent per year, what would the growth rate of total factor productivity have to be?
    b. What if both the labor and the capital stocks are fixed?

3. Suppose again that capital's and labor's shares of income are .3 and .7, respectively.
    a. What would be the effect (on output) of increasing the capital stock by 10 percent?
    b. What would be the effect of increasing the pool of labor by 10 percent?
    c. If the increase in labor is due entirely to population growth, will the resulting increase in output have an effect on people's welfare?
    d. What if the increase in labor is due, instead, to an influx of women into the workplace?

4. Suppose an earthquake destroys one-quarter of the capital stock. Discuss the adjustment process of the economy, and using Figure 3-5, show what happens to growth in the short run and in the long-run.

5. Suppose there is an increase in the population growth rate.
    a. Show graphically how this affects the growth rate of both output per capita and total output in the short and the long-run. (*Hint:* Use a diagram like Figure 3-5.)
    b. Chart the time paths of per capita income and the per capita capital stock following this change. (*Hint:* Use a diagram like Figure 3-6.)

6. Consider a production function of the form $Y = AF(K, N, Z)$, where Z is a measure of natural resources used in production. Assume this production function has constant returns to scale and diminishing returns in each factor.
    a. What will happen to output per head if capital and labor both grow but Z is fixed?
    b. Reconsider (a), but add technical progress (growth in A).
    c. In the 1970s there were fears that we were running out of natural resources and that this would limit growth. Discuss this view using your answers to (a) and (b).

7. Consider the following production function: $Y = K^{.5}(AN)^{.5}$, where both the population and the pool of labor are growing at a rate $n = .07$, the capital stock is depreciating at a rate $d = .03$, and A is normalized to 1.
    a. What are capital's and labor's shares of income?
    b. What is the form of this production function?
    c. Find the steady-state values of k and y when $s = .20$.
    d. At what rate is per capita output growing at the steady state? At what rate is total output growing? What if total factor productivity is increasing at a rate of 2 percent per year ($g = .02$)?

8. Suppose the level of technology is constant. Then it jumps to a new, higher constant level.
    a. How does this technological jump affect output per head, holding the capital-labor ratio constant?

   b. Show the new steady-state equilibrium. What has happened to per capita saving and the capital-labor ratio? What happens to output per capita?

   c. Chart the time path of the adjustment to the new steady state. Does the investment ratio rise during transition? If so, is this effect temporary?

9.* For a Cobb-Douglas production function $Y = AK^{\theta}N^{(1-\theta)}$, verify that $1 - \theta$ is labor's share of income. [*Hint:* Labor's share of income is the piece of income which results from that labor ($MPL \times N$) divided by total income.]

Empirical

1. Go to www.economagic.com and download the data for the U.S. population and total employment in educational services over the last decade (1992–2002). The easiest way to do this is to do two different searches. First, search for the keyword "population," and second search for the keyword "educational services." Once you have downloaded the data into a spreadsheet, calculate the average growth rate of U.S. population and total employment in educational services in the last decade (1992–2002). Everything else being constant, what could you infer about the average quality of U.S. workers? Would this have any implications on the perspectives for future growth in the United States?

2. Go to www.economagic.com and do a search for the keyword "information technology industries." Using the provided graphing possibilities, take a look at the evolution of the *value of shipments* for the information technology industries during the last decade. What event can be used to explain the increase in the value of information technology output during the 1990s?

APPENDIX

In this appendix we briefly show how the fundamental growth equation [equation (2) in this chapter] is obtained. We start with the production function $Y = AF(K, N)$ and ask how much output changes if labor changes by ΔN, capital changes by ΔK, and technology changes by ΔA. The change in output will be

$$\Delta Y = MPN \times \Delta N + MPK \times \Delta K + F(K, N) \times \Delta A \qquad (A1)$$

where MPN and MPK are the marginal products of labor and capital, respectively. Dividing both sides of the equation by $Y = AF(K, N)$ and simplifying yields

$$\frac{\Delta Y}{Y} = \frac{MPN}{Y}\Delta N + \frac{MPK}{Y}\Delta K + \frac{\Delta A}{A} \qquad (A2)$$

Now we multiply and divide the first term by N and the second term by K:

$$\frac{\Delta Y}{Y} = \left(\frac{MPN \times N}{Y}\right)\frac{\Delta N}{N} + \left(\frac{MPK \times K}{Y}\right)\frac{\Delta K}{K} + \frac{\Delta A}{A} \qquad (A3)$$

These transformations follow from rules of mathematics. To get the rest of the way to equation (2), we need to make a strong, but very reasonable, assumption: The economy is *competitive*.

In a competitive economy, factors are paid their marginal products. Thus, $MPN = w$, where w is the real wage. Total payment to labor is the wage rate times the amount of labor, $w \times N$;

---

*An asterisk denotes a more difficult problem.

BOX A3-1   Following Along with the Cobb-Douglas

The phrase "constant returns to scale" (CRTS) means that if all inputs increase in equal proportion, output increases in that same proportion. Mathematically, if we multiply both inputs by a constant, c, output will also be multiplied by c: $AF(cK, cN) = cAF(K, N) = cY$. CRTS is a believable assumption because of the *replication argument*: If one factory using X workers produces output Y, then two factories using X workers each should produce output $2Y$, three factories using X workers each should produce output $3Y$, and so forth. In addition to this attractive logical argument, empirical evidence also suggests that returns to scale are roughly constant.

To show that the Cobb-Douglas has constant returns to scale, multiply both K and N by c:

$$A(cK)^{\theta}(cN)^{1-\theta} = A(c^{\theta}K^{\theta})(c^{1-\theta}N^{1-\theta}) = c^{\theta}c^{1-\theta}AK^{\theta}N^{1-\theta} = c^{\theta+(1-\theta)}Y = cY$$

To show that capital's share is θ, multiply the marginal product of capital from Box 3-1 on page 55 (which is what a unit of capital gets paid in a competitive market) by the number of units of capital and divide by total output:

$$MPK \times K/Y = (\theta Y/K) \times K/Y = \theta$$

And yes, the exponent θ in the Cobb-Douglas is the same θ that appears in the growth accounting equation [equation (2)].

the total payment to labor as a fraction of all payments—which is to say, "labor's share"—is $MPN \times N/Y$. (The argument for capital is analogous.) Now substitute $1 - \theta \equiv$ labor's share for $MPN \times N/Y$ and $\theta \equiv$ capital's share for $MPK \times K/Y$ into equation (A3) to reach equation (2):

$$\Delta Y/Y = [(1 - \theta) \times \Delta N/N] + (\theta \times \Delta K/K) + \Delta A/A$$

$$\frac{\text{Output}}{\text{growth}} = \left(\frac{\text{labor}}{\text{share}} \times \frac{\text{labor}}{\text{growth}}\right) + \left(\frac{\text{capital}}{\text{share}} \times \frac{\text{capital}}{\text{growth}}\right) + \frac{\text{technical}}{\text{progress}}$$

CHAPTER 4

Growth and Policy

CHAPTER HIGHLIGHTS

- Rates of economic growth vary widely across countries and across time.

- Endogenous growth theory attempts to explain growth rates as functions of societal decisions, in particular saving rates.

- Income in poor countries appears to be converging toward income levels of rich countries, but at extraordinarily slow rates.

Can we grow faster? The previous chapter explained how GDP and GDP growth are determined by the saving rate, the rate of population growth, and the rate of technical progress. How do society's choices affect these parameters? In countries on the leading edge of technology, the advance of knowledge is a key determinant of growth. Invention of new technology is much less important for poorer countries, because poorer countries can grow by "borrowing" technology, as well as by investing in physical and human capital. In the first part of this chapter we look at how society's choices lead to technical progress—the subject called *endogenous growth theory.* Paul Romer and Robert Lucas are responsible for much of the early development of this concept.[1] In the second part of the chapter we turn to an examination of a variety of social policies affecting growth.[2]

4-1

GROWTH THEORY: ENDOGENOUS GROWTH

Neoclassical growth theory dominated economic thought for three decades because it does a good job of explaining much of what we observe in the world and because it is mathematically elegant. Nonetheless, by the late 1980s dissatisfaction with the theory had arisen on both theoretical and empirical grounds.[3] Neoclassical growth theory attributes long-run growth to technological progress but leaves unexplained the economic determinants of that technological progress. Empirical dissatisfaction developed over the prediction that economic growth and saving rates should be uncorrelated in the steady state. The data make it clear that saving rates and growth are positively correlated across countries.[4]

[1]Robert E. Lucas, Jr., "On the Mechanics of Economic Development," *Journal of Monetary Economics,* July 1988; Paul Romer, "Increasing Returns and Long-Run Growth," *Journal of Political Economy,* October 1986. The volume edited by Alwyn Young, *Readings in Endogenous Growth* (Cambridge, MA: MIT Press, 1993), contains many of the key papers.

[2]N. Gregory Mankiw provides an accessible overview of issues of growth in "The Growth of Nations," *Brookings Papers on Economic Activity, No. 1* (1995). The best state-of-the-art examination of the theory of growth is the graduate-level text by Robert J. Barro and Xavier Sala-i-Martin, *Economic Growth* (New York: McGraw-Hill, 1995). Jonathan Temple presents a thoughtful examination of the empirical evidence on growth in "The New Growth Evidence," *Journal of Economic Literature,* March 1999. Xavier Sala-i-Martin links empirical evidence and the intellectual development of new growth theory in a very readable article, "15 Years of New Growth Economics: What Have We Learnt?" Universitat Pompeu Fabra, Department of Economics and Business working paper no. 620, June 2002.

[3]For an especially readable discussion, see Paul Romer, "The Origins of Endogenous Growth," *Journal of Economic Perspectives,* Winter 1994. Two other excellent references are Mancur Olson, "Big Bills on the Sidewalk: Why Are Some Nations Rich and Others Poor?" *Journal of Economic Perspectives,* Spring 1996, and Bennett McCallum, "Neoclassical versus Endogenous Growth: An Overview," Federal Reserve Bank of Atlanta *Economic Quarterly,* Fall 1996. Empirical growth theory has been influenced remarkably by an amazing set of data put together by Alan Heston and Robert Summers of the University of Pennsylvania. You can find the data, called the Penn World Tables, online at http://pwt.econ.upenn.edu.

[4]More recent work raises questions as to whether this observation is really an important argument against the neoclassical model. Mankiw ("Growth of Nations") writes, "The inability of saving to affect steady-state growth . . . might appear inconsistent with the strong correlation between growth and saving across countries. But this correlation could reflect the transitional dynamics that arise as economies approach their steady states."

BOX 4-1   A Nobel Laureate's Words

I do not see how one can look at figures like these without seeing them as *possibilities*. Is there some action a government of India could take that would lead the Indian economy to grow like Indonesia's or Egypt's? If so, *what*, exactly? If not, what is it about the "nature of India" that makes it so? The consequences for human welfare involved in questions like these are simply staggering: Once one starts to think about them, it is hard to think about anything else.*

The opening quote was published in 1988. As you can see in Table 1, in the next ten years India succeeded in dramatically increasing its growth rate, although still not to the level of South Korea or China.

TABLE 1   GDP Per Capita

	1990 DOLLARS			AVERAGE ANNUAL GROWTH, %	
	1950	1988	1998	1950–1988	1988–1998
United States	9,561	22,499	27,331	1.8	2.0
Afghanistan	645	644	514	0.0	−2.2
Bangladesh	540	608	813	0.2	2.9
China	439	1,816	3,117	3.0	5.6
Egypt	718	2,001	2,128	2.2	0.6
Ghana	1,122	1,048	1,244	−0.1	1.7
India	619	1,216	1,746	1.4	3.7
Indonesia	840	2,196	3,070	2.0	3.4
Mexico	2,365	5,797	6,655	1.9	1.4
Somalia	1,057	1,067	883	0.0	−1.9
South Korea	770	7,621	12,152	4.9	4.8
Taiwan	936	9,714	15,012	5.0	4.4
Tanzania	377	549	553	0.8	0.1
Thailand	817	3,828	6,205	3.3	4.9
Former U.S.S.R.	2,834	7,032	3,893	1.9	−5.7

Source: Angus Maddison, *The World Economy: A Millennial Perspective* (Paris: Organization for Economic Cooperation and Development, 2001).

*Robert E. Lucas, Jr., "On the Mechanics of Economic Development," *Journal of Monetary Economics*, July 1988.

THE MECHANICS OF ENDOGENOUS GROWTH

The solution to both the theoretical and the empirical problems with neoclassical theory lies in modifying the production function in a way that allows for self-sustaining—*endogenous*—growth. In this section we look at the difference between endogenous growth and the previous chapter's neoclassical theory in a bit of a mechanical way. With the mechanical part under our belt, we flesh out the economics in the section following.

Figure 4-1*a* reproduces the basic Solow growth diagram from Chapter 3. You will remember that the steady state occurs at point *C*, where the saving and investment requirement lines cross. Anywhere the saving line is above the investment requirement line, the economy is growing because capital is being added. Starting at point *A*, for example, the economy moves, over time, to the right. How do we know that this process eventually comes to a halt (i.e., reaches a steady state)? Because of the *diminishing marginal product of capital,* the production function and the parallel saving curve eventually flatten out. Since the investment requirement line has a constant positive slope, the investment requirement line and saving curve are guaranteed to cross.

Contrast Figure 4-1*b*, where we have changed the assumed shape of the production function to show a *constant marginal product of capital.* The production function, like the parallel saving curve, is now a *straight line.* Since the saving curve no longer flattens out, saving is everywhere greater than required investment. The higher the saving rate, the bigger the gap of saving above required investment and the faster is growth.

The economy described in Figure 4-1*b* can be illustrated with a simple algebraic model leading to endogenous growth. Assume a production function with a constant marginal product of capital and with capital as the only factor. Specifically, let

$$Y = aK \tag{1}$$

That is, output is proportional to the capital stock. The marginal product of capital is simply the constant *a*.

Assume that the saving rate is constant at *s* and that there is neither population growth nor depreciation of capital. Then all saving goes to increase the capital stock. Accordingly,

$$\Delta K = sY = saK \tag{2}$$

or

$$\Delta K/K = sa$$

The growth rate of capital is proportional to the saving rate. Further, since output is proportional to capital, the growth rate of output is

$$\Delta Y/Y = sa \tag{3}$$

In this example, the higher the saving rate, the higher the growth rate of output.

THE DEEPER ECONOMICS OF ENDOGENOUS GROWTH

If a simple change to the assumed shape of the production function provides a satisfactory, albeit oversimplified, solution to the problems with neoclassical growth theory, what took 30 years to figure out? It turns out that eliminating diminishing marginal returns violates deep microeconomic principles. The changed assumption implies constant returns to scale for capital; in other words, a firm with twice as much machinery will produce twice as much output. But if doubling capital doubles output, then doubling all factors of production—that is, labor as well as capital—will more than double output. If there are constant returns to scale to capital alone, there will be

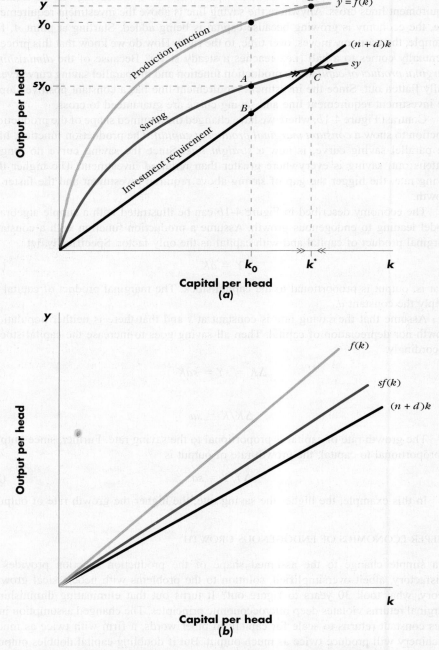

FIGURE 4-1 (a) SOLOW GROWTH MODEL VS. (b) ENDOGENOUS GROWTH.

increasing returns to scale to all factors taken together. This suggests that larger and larger firms are ever more efficient, so we should see a single firm come to dominate the entire economy. Since nothing remotely like this happens, we ought to rule out the possibility of increasing returns to scale to all factors and constant returns to a single factor, at least for a single firm.

Suppose, however, that an individual firm doesn't capture all the benefits of capital: Some of the benefits are *external* to the firm. In this case, when a firm increases capital, the firm's production rises but so does the productivity of other firms. As long as the *private* return has constant returns to all factors, there will be no tendency to monopolization.

Paul Romer's intellectual breakthrough was to partially separate private returns to capital from social returns.[5] Investment produces not only new machines but new ways of doing things as well—sometimes because of deliberate investment in research and sometimes because of serendipitous spin-offs. While firms do capture the production benefits of new machines, it is much harder to capture the benefits of new methods and new ideas because methods and ideas are easy to copy.

Endogenous growth theory hinges on the notion that there are substantial *external* returns to capital. Is this reasonable? If capital is physical machinery, probably not. After all, the benefits of a drill press are pretty much captured by the owner of the drill press. In contrast, consider the role of *human capital,* particularly investment knowledge. It is expensive to create a new drill press or a new idea. However, a copy of a drill press costs as much as the first one, while an idea can be copied at little or no expense. Since the contribution of new knowledge—new inventions and discoveries—is only partially captured by the creator, there can be substantial external benefits. Further, each new idea makes the next idea possible, so knowledge can grow indefinitely. Thus, economists think that investment in human capital in general and research and development specifically is the key to understanding long-run growth.

◆ O P T I O N A L ◆

We turn now to a more fully developed endogenous growth model, a model with labor as well as capital. The key assumption is that better technology is produced as a by-product of capital investment. Specifically, assume that technology is proportional to the level of capital per worker in the economy overall, $A = \alpha K/N = \alpha k$, and that technology is labor-augmenting, so the production function can be written as $Y = F(K, AN)$.[6] The growth equations are like those of Chapter 3, except that technology growth, instead of being exogenously specified, now depends on capital growth, $\Delta A/A = \Delta K/K - \Delta N/N$.

Working through the algebra requires two steps. First, we show that output and capital grow at equal rates, implying that y/k is a constant. Then we use this fact to work backward to the growth rates.

[5]See Romer, "Increasing Returns and Long-Run Growth."

[6]To be clear about notation, note that a is the marginal product of capital and that α governs the way capital and labor combine to produce technology, A.

The GDP growth equation from Chapter 3 was

$$\Delta y/y = \theta \times \Delta k/k + (1 - \theta) \times \Delta A/A$$

Now we substitute the technology growth formula, $\Delta A/A = \Delta K/K - \Delta N/N = \Delta k/k$, into the growth equation to show that output and capital grow at the same rate:

$$\Delta y/y = \theta \times \Delta k/k + (1 - \theta) \times \Delta k/k$$
$$\Delta y/y = \Delta k/k$$

Since the numerator and denominator of y/k grow at an equal rate, y/k is constant. We find this constant by dividing the production function by K and simplifying:

$$y/k = F(K, AN)/K = F(K/K, AN/K) = F(1, \alpha) \equiv a$$

From Chapter 3 we know that the equation for capital accumulation can be written $\Delta k/k = sy/k - (n + d)$. Making the substitution for y/k, we have

$$\Delta y/y = \Delta k/k = g = sy/k - (n + d) = sa - (n + d)$$

The growth rate of GDP per capita is $sa - (n + d)$. A high saving rate generates a high growth rate. High rates of population growth and depreciation lead to a low growth rate.

CONVERGENCE

The question of "convergence" centers on whether economies with different initial levels of output eventually grow to equal standards of living.

Neoclassical growth theory predicts *absolute convergence* for economies with equal rates of saving and population growth and with access to the same technology. In other words, they should all reach the same steady-state income. (If Figure 4-1a is the same for two economies, they eventually reach the same steady state even if one economy begins farther to the left.) *Conditional convergence* is predicted for economies with different rates of saving or population growth; that is, steady-state incomes will differ as predicted by the Solow growth diagram, but *growth rates* will eventually equalize.

Contrast conditional convergence with the prediction of endogenous growth theory that a high saving rate leads to a high growth rate. In a series of papers, Robert Barro has shown that while countries that invest more tend to grow faster, the impact of higher investment on growth seems to be transitory:[7] Countries with higher investment will end in a steady state with higher per capita income but not with a higher growth rate. This suggests that countries do converge *conditionally,* and thus endogenous growth theory is not very important for explaining international differences in

---

[7]See, for example, Robert Barro's "Economic Growth in a Cross Section of Countries," *Quarterly Journal of Economics,* May 1991, and his *Determinants of Economic Growth: A Cross-Country Empirical Study,* (Cambridge, MA: MIT Press, 1997).

BOX 4-2   One Idea Leads to the Next

Paul Samuelson, winner of the Nobel Prize in economics in 1970, wrote in his classic book *Foundations of Economic Analysis*,* "And most college graduates in physics know more than Isaac Newton: for as Newton himself said, a scientist sees further than his predecessors because he stands on the shoulders of earlier giants." The source of Samuelson's famous dictum is, "If I have seen further it is by standing on the shoulders of Giants" (Newton to Hooke, February 5, 1676).

*Cambridge, MA: Harvard University Press, 1947.

growth rates, although it may be quite important for explaining growth in countries on the leading edge of technology.

Barro's evidence suggests that conditional convergence is taking place at a rate of 2 percent per year. For instance, if India's income level is now 5 percent of that of the United States, in 35 years it would be approximately 10 percent of the U.S. level[8]—provided that the other variables that affect the level of income, such as the saving rate, are the same between the two countries. This convergence is very slow; it means that people in India today cannot look forward to catching up anytime soon with the United States merely by relying on the "natural" neoclassical force of convergence.

RECAP

- Endogenous growth theory relies on constant returns to scale to accumulable factors to generate ongoing growth.
- The microeconomics underlying endogenous growth theory emphasizes the difference between social and private returns when firms are unable to capture some of the benefits of investment.
- Current empirical evidence suggests that endogenous growth theory is not very important for explaining international differences in growth rates.

◆ O P T I O N A L ◆

GROWTH TRAPS AND TWO-SECTOR MODELS

Explaining high or low growth isn't the same as explaining *no* growth. Little or no growth is the most accurate description of Ghana since 1900—and of most of humankind for most of history. To explain a world with both no-growth and high-growth countries, we would like a model in which there is a possibility of both a no-growth,

---

[8]It takes 35 years for an economy growing at 2 percent to double its size. In this case the doubling is relative to another economy.

low-income equilibrium and a positive-growth, high-income equilibrium. In other words, something that combines elements of neoclassical and endogenous growth theories.

Suppose there are two kinds of investment opportunities: those with diminishing marginal product (as in the neoclassical growth model) at low income levels, and those with constant marginal product (as in the endogenous growth model) at higher income levels. The production function will begin with a curved section (as in Figure 4-1a) and end with an upward-sloping line (as in Figure 4-1b).

Figure 4-2 shows an example. This model has a "neoclassical growth equilibrium" at point A but acts like an endogenous growth model to the right of point B. At low income and capital, the capital requirement line strikes the saving line in the neoclassical region (point A), leading to a no-growth steady state. At high income and capital (past point B), the saving line is above the capital requirement line, leading to ongoing growth.

One remaining piece is omitted from Figure 4-2. With two outlets for investment, society must choose not only total investment but also the division between the two kinds. Societies that direct investment toward research and development will have ongoing growth. Societies that direct investment toward physical capital may have higher output in the short run at the cost of lower long-run growth.

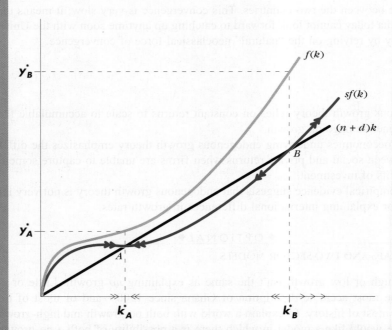

FIGURE 4-2   A CHOICE BETWEEN A STEADY STATE AND CONTINUED GROWTH.

A production function such as this could explain a world with both no-growth and high-growth countries.

4-2

GROWTH POLICY

The previous section focused on the determinants of the rate of technical progress, a problem of most interest to countries on the cutting edge of new technology. In this section we focus on the problems of population growth and the process by which some countries move from underdeveloped to developed status.

POPULATION GROWTH AND MALTHUS

One of the oldest ideas in economics is that population growth works against the achievement of high incomes.[9] The Solow growth model predicts that high population growth, n, means lower steady-state income because each worker will have less capital to work with. However, over a wide range of incomes, population growth itself depends on income. Extremely poor countries in modern times have very high birth rates and very high death rates, resulting in moderately high population growth. As incomes rise, death rates fall (especially through reductions in infant mortality) and population growth rises. At very high incomes, birth rates fall. Indeed, many of the wealthier countries in the world are approaching zero population growth (ZPG).

◆ OPTIONAL ◆

A simple version of a Solow model with endogenous population growth can be shown graphically. If we were to graph n against y, it would rise, fall, and then level off near zero. The slope of the investment requirement line depends on n, but since n is no longer constant, the investment requirement line becomes a curve. Modifying the investment requirement line on the Solow diagram to account for changing n gives a picture that looks something like Figure 4-3.

The investment requirement line with variable population growth in Figure 4-3, $[n(y) + d]k$, rises slowly, then sharply, and eventually flattens out. As shown, the investment requirement line crosses the saving curve at points A, B, and C. Point A is a

---

[9]For the original work by Malthus, see Thomas R. Malthus, "An Essay on the Principle of Population; or, A View of its Past and Present Effects on Human Happiness," 6th ed., first published in 1826, London, John Murray, Albermarle Street. Robert Lucas presents a very readable account of the interaction between technological growth and population in "The Industrial Revolution: Past and Future," University of Chicago working paper, February 1998. See also Oded Galor and David Weil, "From Malthusian Stagnation to Modern Growth," *American Economic Review,* May 1999. Growth, fertility, and economic inequality are tied together in Michael Kremer and Daniel Chen, "Income Distribution Dynamics with Endogenous Fertility," Harvard University working paper, 1999. (By the way, some of the origins of the paper lie in Chen's *undergraduate* senior thesis!) Growth, population, and intellectual property rights are tied together in Charles Jones, "Was an Industrial Revolution Inevitable? Economic Growth over the Very Long Run," *Advances in Macroeconomics* 1, no. 2 (2001).

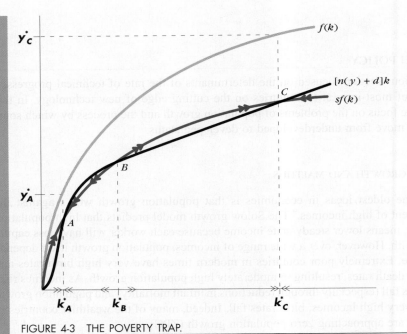

FIGURE 4-3.   THE POVERTY TRAP.

In this model with two steady-state equilibria, a high rate of population growth results in a low level of per capita income.

poverty trap with high population growth and low income. The equilibrium at *C* has low population growth and high income. Note the arrows showing the direction of movement toward the steady state. Points *A* and *C* are said to be *stable equilibria* because the economy moves toward these points. *B* is an *unstable equilibrium* since the economy tends to move away from *B*.

How can an economy escape from the low-level equilibrium? There are two possibilities. If a country can put on a "big push" that raises income past point *B*, the economy will continue on its own the rest of the way to the high-level point *C*. Alternatively, a nation can effectively eliminate the low-level trap by moving the saving curve up or the investment requirement line down so that they no longer touch at *A* and *B*. Raising productivity or raising the saving rate raises the saving line. Population control policies lower the investment requirement line.

Some governments are beginning to recognize the need to reduce population growth—in some countries, the government tries to persuade people to use contraceptives; in other countries, the government institutes policies that have even included forced sterilization. But it is often difficult to reduce the rate of population growth in very poor countries, where large families may serve as a social security system, since having children ensures that the parents are taken care of in their old age.

TABLE 4-1   Growth in the Asian Tigers
(Percent)

	HONG KONG (1966–1991)	SINGAPORE (1966–1990)	SOUTH KOREA (1966–1990)	TAIWAN (1966–1990)
GDP per capita growth	5.7	6.8	6.8	6.7
TFP growth	2.3	0.2	1.7	2.6
Δ % labor force participation	38 → 49	27 → 51	27 → 36	28 → 37
Δ % secondary education or higher	27.2 → 71.4	15.8 → 66.3	26.5 → 75.0	25.8 → 67.6

Source: Alwyn Young, "The Tyranny of Numbers: Confronting the Statistical Realities of the East Asian Growth Experience," *Quarterly Journal of Economics,* August 1995.

LESSONS FROM THE ASIAN TIGERS

Growth in Hong Kong, Singapore, South Korea, and Taiwan has been so remarkable that the four nations are sometimes called the "Asian Tigers." They have been held up as examples of effective development to the rest of the world. It has been argued—especially by some political leaders from these nations—that they have learned a special trick worthy of emulation. However, the best current evidence is that the principal "special trick" is old-fashioned hard work and sacrifice. In other words, these countries have not had remarkable increases in total factor productivity, *A*; they've saved and invested, put more people to work, and concentrated on education in order to raise human capital. What can we learn by examining the experience of the Asian Tigers?

Table 4-1 is taken from a very careful study of East Asian growth by Alwyn Young. All four countries have remarkably high growth, but their growth is mostly explained by increased input, not by higher productivity. Growth in total factor productivity, a measure of output per unit of input, is high, but not remarkable, in Hong Kong, South Korea, and Taiwan. Singapore's *TFP* growth is notably small. All four countries have had a drastic increase in the fraction of the population that works, largely due to increased labor force participation by women. Each country also greatly increased its human capital, moving educational attainment to levels close to those of the leading industrialized nations.

The Asian Tigers have several other characteristics in common. All four have relatively stable governments. The four share an outward-looking economic policy, encouraging their industries to export, compete, and learn to survive in the world market.

The near-zero productivity growth in Singapore is nonetheless noteworthy. In an influential article comparing Singapore and Hong Kong, Alwyn Young draws attention to the fact that Hong Kong has had an essentially laissez-faire, free-market government while Singapore's government maintains more control over the economy, with most of the economy's investments being indirectly directed by the government.[10] He argues

---

[10]A. Young, "A Tale of Two Cities: Factor Accumulation and Technical Change in Hong Kong and Singapore," *NBER Macroeconomics Annual,* 1992.

BOX 4-3   Is High Income Good? The Golden Rule

If this seems a strange question, remember that we're interested in high income insofar as it leads to high *consumption*. The higher the saving rate chosen by a society, the higher the steady-state capital and income. But the higher is *k*, the greater the investment required just to maintain the capital-labor ratio, as opposed to being used for current consumption. So too high a saving rate can lead to high income but low consumption.

Steady-state consumption, c^*, equals steady-state income, $y^* = f(k^*)$, minus steady-state investment, $(n + d)k^*$:

$$c^* = f(k^*) - (n + d)k^*$$

Steady-state consumption is maximized at the point where a marginal increase in capital produces just enough extra output to cover the increased investment requirement, $MPK(k^{**}) = (n + d)$. Capital k^{**}, the *golden-rule capital stock*, corresponds to the highest permanently sustainable level of consumption, the level at which we can "do unto future generations as we hope previous generations did unto us." Above the golden-rule level, we can cut back on saving and consume more both now and later. Below this level, we can increase future consumption only by making the choice to consume less today. The empirical evidence is that we are below the golden-rule level of saving.

that the government of Singapore has tried to force the pace of development, relying on foreign investment to bring in new technologies, but has moved on too rapidly to ever more sophisticated goods before local entrepreneurs and workers have mastered the current technology.

The fact remains that the Tigers have achieved something extraordinary in human history: They have been growing at rates that will transform them from being among the poorest of countries to having income levels that—already in Singapore, soon in the others—match those of the rich industrial countries. It is reassuring to see that this can be done the old-fashioned way, through saving, hard work, and competition.

THE TRULY POOR COUNTRIES

The growth line for Ghana (see Figure 3-1) and the nation's GDP data (see the table in Box 4-1) illustrate a striking problem. Compared with the rest of the world, Ghana has had very little economic growth! (Ghana is used as an example. The same holds true for a number of other countries.) Income is so low that much of the population lives at the border of subsistence.

Have we explained Ghana? In part yes. Saving in Ghana is quite low. According to the *World Development Indicators* CD-ROM, between 1960 and 1985 gross domestic savings in Ghana averaged 9.3 percent of GDP, as compared to 34.3 percent and

19.4 percent in Japan and the United States, respectively.[11] Population growth in Ghana, and other extremely poor countries, was also much higher than in Japan or the United States. So the effect of both saving and population growth is as theory would predict. The poorest countries are hard-pressed to invest in human capital. Many of the poorest countries also have hostile climates for foreign investment, either because of deliberate policies that attempt to encourage domestic production instead or simply because the economic and legal environment is uncertain and the nations are unwilling or unable to guarantee investors the ability to repatriate profits.

NATURAL RESOURCES: LIMITS TO GROWTH?

Production uses up natural resources, in particular energy. Is it true, as is sometimes alleged, that exponential growth in the economy will eventually use up the fixed stock of resources? Well yes, it is true in the limited sense that current theories suggest the universe will one day run down. However, this seems more of a concern for a course in astrophysics, or perhaps theology, than for a course in economics. Over any interesting horizon, the economy is protected from resource-depletion disasters by two factors. First, technical progress permits us to produce more using fewer resources. For example, the energy efficiency of room lighting has increased by a factor of 4,500 since Neolithic times.[12] Second, as specific resources come into short supply, their prices rise, leading producers to shift toward substitutes.

Environmental protection is important, however. Even here, technology can be directed to assist us. For example, the conversion of urban transportation systems from horses to internal combustion engines has eliminated most of the pollution associated with transportation.[13] As incomes rise and populations move away from the edge of survival, people and governments choose to spend more on protecting the environment. Unlike other consumption choices, environmental protection is often "bought" through political choices rather than in the marketplace. Because the benefits of environmental protection flow across property boundaries, there is greater reason for the government to intervene on environmental issues than there is with respect to purely private goods.

SOCIAL INFRASTRUCTURE AND OUTPUT

Our study of growth has identified a number of factors that help explain why some countries become rich while others do not, the accumulation of physical and human capital being primary examples. Two deep questions remain. The first is, Why do some countries have more capital than others? At one level the answer is that countries that save and invest more have more capital. But this answer suggests that we next ask, Why

---

[11]*World Development Indicators 2002,* CD-ROM, The World Bank.

[12]Actually, people in Neolithic times probably didn't have "rooms" per se. For a more recent benchmark, the energy efficiency of room lighting has improved by a factor of 20 since 1900. See William D. Nordhaus, "Do Real Output and Real Wage Measures Capture Reality? The History of Lighting Suggests Not," in Robert J. Gordon and Timothy F. Bresnahan (eds.), *The Economics of New Goods* (Chicago: University of Chicago Press, 1997), pp. 29–66.

[13]Think about it for a minute.

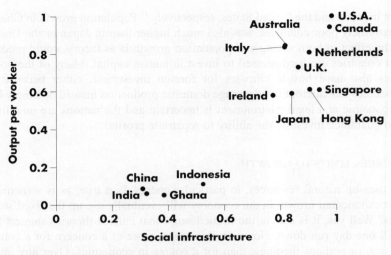

FIGURE 4-4   THE EFFECT OF SOCIAL INFRASTRUCTURE.

do some countries save and invest more than others? We are trying to determine whether, after accounting for identifiable factors of production, we can explain the remaining productivity differences. Table 1 in Box 3-3 shows that such unexplained productivity differences can account for a ratio of 4 or 5 to 1 in output between rich and poor countries. A number of macroeconomists are now investigating differences in *social infrastructure* as a potential answer to both questions.

In the United States or Ireland, you can open a small business and if it succeeds you keep most of the profits (although the government will take some of your gains in the form of taxes). You probably won't need to pay any bribes, the government will usually be able to protect you from being robbed, and the legal system is available to help enforce contracts and resolve disputes. In some other parts of the world, opening a business makes you a target for expropriation by other private parties, and maybe by the government as well. Unsurprisingly, people are more likely to be entrepreneurial and to save and invest in countries where they can reap the benefits.

All the things that go into making individuals and businesses productive—a good legal system, stable taxes, limits on government bureaucracy—are part of social infrastructure. Hall and Jones define social infrastructure as "the institutions and government policies that determine the economic environment."[14] Although social infrastructure is difficult to define precisely and even harder to measure, we use data put together by Hall and Jones in Figure 4-4 to show output per worker plotted against a measure of social infrastructure. The evidence supports the idea that social infrastructure does play an important role in determining output.[15]

[14]Robert E. Hall and Charles I. Jones, "Why Do Some Countries Produce So Much More Output per Worker than Others?" *Quarterly Journal of Economics,* February 1999, pp. 83–116.

[15]For an accessible, indeed delightful, read on this topic, see William Easterly, *The Elusive Quest for Growth: Economists' Adventures and Misadventures in the Tropics,* (Cambridge: MIT Press, 2002).

SUMMARY

1. Economic growth in the most developed countries depends on the rate of technological progress. According to endogenous growth models, technological progress depends on saving, particularly investment directed toward human capital.

2. International comparisons support conditional convergence. Adjusting for differences in saving and population growth rates, developing countries advance toward the income levels of the most industrialized countries.

3. There are extraordinarily different growth experiences in different countries. High saving, low population growth, outward-looking orientation, and a predictable economic environment are all important progrowth factors.

KEY TERMS

absolute convergence	golden-rule capital stock	stable equilibrium
conditional convergence	increasing returns to scale	unstable equilibrium
endogenous growth theory	social infrastructure	

PROBLEMS

Conceptual

1. What is endogenous growth? How do endogenous growth models differ from the neoclassical models of growth presented in Chapter 3?

2. Why doesn't the constant marginal product of capital assumed in this chapter's simple model of endogenous growth create a situation in which a single large firm dominates the economy, as traditional microeconomic reasoning would suggest?

3. How do the implications of an increase in saving with regard to both the level and the growth rate of output differ between the neoclassical growth model outlined in Chapter 3 and the basic endogenous growth model outlined in this chapter?

4. *(Optional)*
   a. What sorts of capital investment does this chapter suggest are most useful for explaining long-run equilibrium growth?
   b. Discuss the long-run growth potential of each of the following government programs:
      i. Investment tax credits
      ii. R&D subsidies and grants
      iii. Policies intended to increase saving
      iv. Increased funding for primary education

5. What is the difference between absolute and conditional convergence, as predicted by the neoclassical growth model? Which seems to be occurring, empirically?

6. Can endogenous growth theory help explain international differences in growth rates? If so, how? If not, what can it help explain?

7. Suppose a society can invest in two types of capital—physical and human. How can its choice regarding the distribution of investment affect its long-term growth potential?

8. a. Consider once more the neoclassical model with a steady-state level of per capita output. Suppose a society can choose its rate of population growth. How can this choice affect the steady-state per capita output? Could such a policy help the country avoid falling into a poverty trap?

    b. Now suppose we have an endogenous growth model. How will a lower population growth rate affect the society's long-term growth potential?

  9. What elements of neoclassical and endogenous growth models can help us explain the remarkable growth of the group of countries known as the Asian Tigers?

 10. Does growth in per capita output, among both more and less industrialized countries, have the potential to increase indefinitely? Explain.

Technical

(All optional)

  1. Consider a two-sector model of growth, with two kinds of investment opportunities—one with a diminishing marginal product and one with a constant marginal product. (*Hint:* See Figure 4-2.)

    a. What does the production function for this problem look like?

    b. Characterize the set of equilibria for this model. Does output in any of the equilibria have nonzero per capita growth?

    c. What can this model help us explain that strict endogenous and neoclassical growth models cannot?

  2. Now suppose we have a one-sector model with a variable rate of population growth. (*Hint:* See Figure 4-3.)

    a. What does the investment requirement line look like for this model?

    b. Characterize the set of equilibria, being sure to discuss their stability or lack thereof. Does output in any of these equilibria have nonzero per capita growth?

    c. Suppose your country is in a "poverty trap"—at the equilibrium with the very lowest level of output per person. What could the country do to move toward a point with higher income?

  3. ****Suppose you add a variable rate of population growth to a two-sector model of growth. (*Hint:* Combine Figures 4-2 and 4-3.)

    a. What do the production function, investment requirement line, and saving line look like?

    b. Characterize the set of equilibria for this model. Does output in any of the equilibria have nonzero per capita growth?

    c. Does the addition of the variable rate of population growth to this model help you explain anything that a simpler two-sector model with a fixed rate of growth, or a one-sector model with variable population growth, cannot?

  4. *Consider an economy whose production function is $Y = K^\theta(AN)^{1-\theta}$, with $A = 4\,K/N$. Suppose that it has a saving rate of .1, a population growth rate of .02, and an average depreciation rate of .03 and that $\theta = .5$.

    a. Reduce the production function to the form $y = ak$. What is a?

    b. What are the growth rates of output and capital in this model?

    c. Interpret a. What are we really saying when we assume that the labor-augmenting technology, A, is proportional to the level of capital per worker?

    d. What makes this an endogenous growth model?

  5. Consider an economy in which production is characterized by the neoclassical function $Y = K^{.5}N^{.5}$. Suppose, again, that it has a saving rate of .1, a population growth rate of .02, and an average depreciation rate of .03.

*One asterisk denotes a more difficult problem. Two asterisks means the problem is *really* hard.

    a. Write this production function in per capita form, and find the steady-state values of k and y.

    b. At the steady-state value of k, is there more or less capital than at the golden-rule level?

    c. Determine what saving rate would yield the golden-rule level of capital in this model.

    d. In the context of this neoclassical growth model, can a country have *too much* saving?

Empirical

1. The www.economagic.com website gives the possibility of browsing data by source. Under the heading "Bureau of Labor Statistics," choose the link "International Employment and Prices." Scroll down the page, until you get to data for the United Kingdom.

    a. Set up an EXCEL file in which you download the following four indicators for the United Kingdom for the period 1950–2001:

        Manufacturing Output Index

        Manufacturing Average Hours Index

        Manufacturing Employment Index

        Manufacturing Output per Hour Index

    These indexes give us the evolution of output, hours, and employment in the manufacturing sector. For example, if the manufacturing output index decreased from 113.3 in 2000 to 110.7 in 2001, one can conclude that manufacturing output fell by 2.3 percent in 2001 $[(110.7 - 113.3)/113.3 \times 100]$.

    b. What happened to manufacturing output, employment, and average hours worked by an employee in the period 1950–2001? What factors could lead to an increase in total manufacturing output, while employment and average hours worked fell considerably?

CHAPTER 5

Aggregate Supply and Demand

CHAPTER HIGHLIGHTS

- Output and prices are determined by aggregate supply and aggregate demand.

- In the short run, the aggregate supply curve is flat. In the long run, the aggregate supply curve is vertical.

- Changes in aggregate demand, the result of changes in fiscal and monetary policy as well as individual decisions about consumption and investment, change output in the short run and change prices in the long run.

Macroeconomics is concerned with the behavior of the economy as a whole—with booms and recessions, the economy's total output of goods and services, and the rates of inflation and unemployment. Having explored long-run economic growth in the preceding chapters, we turn to the short-run fluctuations that constitute the business cycle.

Business cycle swings are *big!* In the Great Depression in the 1930s, output fell by nearly 30 percent; between 1931 and 1940 the unemployment rate averaged 18.8 percent. The Great Depression was the defining event for a generation. Post-World War II recessions have been much milder, but they still dominated the political scene when they occurred.

Inflation rates vary widely. A dollar stuffed under your mattress in 1975 would have bought less than 30 cents' worth of goods in 2002. In contrast, during the Great Depression prices *dropped* by one-fourth.

The aggregate supply–aggregate demand model is the basic macroeconomic tool for studying output fluctuations and the determination of the price level and the inflation rate. We use this tool to understand why the economy deviates from a path of smooth growth over time and to explore the consequences of government policies intended to reduce unemployment, smooth output fluctuations, and maintain stable prices.

We focus in this chapter on the "big picture" view of the economy: Why do prices go up rapidly at some times and not at others? Why are jobs plentiful in some years and not in others? Shifts in the aggregate supply and aggregate demand schedules give us the tools to answer these questions. In this chapter we get some practice in using these tools. Chapters 3, 4, 6, and 7 provide underpinnings for the details of the aggregate supply schedule. Details of aggregate demand appear in Chapters 9 through 17. For now we'll work with simplified definitions of aggregate supply and demand in order to concentrate on why the slopes and positions of the curves matter. Aggregate supply and demand each describe a relation between the overall price level (think consumer price index or GDP deflator) and output (GDP). Taken together—an example appears in Figure 5-1—aggregate supply and demand can help us solve for the equilibrium levels of price and output in the economy. And when a change shifts either aggregate supply or demand, we can determine how price and output shift.

The *aggregate supply (AS) curve* **describes, for each given price level, the quantity of output firms are willing to supply.** The *AS* curve is upward-sloping because firms are willing to supply more output at higher prices. **The *aggregate demand (AD)* curve shows the combinations of the price level and level of output at which the goods and money markets are simultaneously in equilibrium.** The *AD* curve is downward-sloping because higher prices reduce the value of the money supply, which reduces the demand for output. The intersection of the *AD* and *AS* schedules at *E* in Figure 5-1 determines the equilibrium level of output, Y_0, and the equilibrium price level, P_0. Shifts in either schedule cause the price level and the level of output to change.

Before we go deeply into the factors underlying the aggregate demand and supply curves, we show how the curves will be used. Suppose that the Fed increases the money supply. What effects will that have on the price level and on output? In particular, does an increase in the money supply cause the price level to rise, thus producing inflation? Or does the level of output rise? Or do both output and the price level rise?

Figure 5-2 shows that an increase in the money supply shifts the aggregate demand curve, *AD*, to the right, to *AD′*. We will see later in this chapter why this should be so.

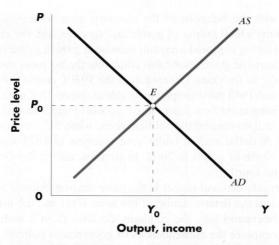

FIGURE 5-1   AGGREGATE SUPPLY AND DEMAND.

Their intersection at point E jointly determines the level of output, Y_0, and the price level, P_0.

The shift of the aggregate demand curve moves the equilibrium of the economy from E to E'. The price level rises from P_0 to P', and the level of output from Y_0 to Y'. Thus an increase in the money stock causes both the level of output and the price level to rise. It is clear from Figure 5-2 that the amount by which the price level rises depends on the slope of the aggregate supply curve as well as the extent to which the aggregate demand curve shifts and its slope. Much of the text is devoted to exploring the slope of the aggregate supply curve and the causes of shifts in the aggregate demand curve.

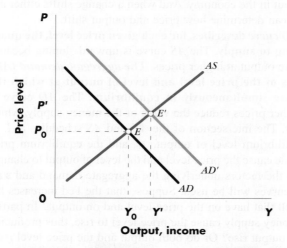

FIGURE 5-2   AN INCREASE IN THE NOMINAL MONEY STOCK SHIFTS AGGREGATE DEMAND TO THE RIGHT.

The equilibrium point moves from E to E'.

BOX 5-1   Aggregate Supply and Aggregate Demand—What's in a Name?

Figure 5-1 has the friendly, familiar appearance that you probably remember from your study of microeconomics. What's more, the mechanical workings of the model (demand shifts up . . . prices and quantities both rise . . . etc.) are the same as the workings of a microeconomic supply and demand diagram. However, the economics underlying the aggregate supply–aggregate demand diagram is unrelated to the microeconomic version. (It's too bad that our macroeconomic version wasn't given a different name.) In particular, "price" in microeconomics means the ratio at which two goods trade: I'll give you two bags of candy in exchange for one economics lecture, for example. In contrast, in macroeconomics "price" means the nominal price level, the cost of a basket of all the goods we buy measured in money terms.

One particular item from macroeconomics provides a special opportunity for confusion. In microeconomics, supply curves are relatively more elastic in the long run than in the short run, at least as a rough rule of thumb. The behavior of aggregate supply is just the opposite. The aggregate supply curve is vertical in the long run and horizontal in the short run. (We will, of course, discuss why this is so.)

Figure 5-3 shows the results of an adverse (upward and leftward) aggregate supply shock (the 1973 OPEC oil embargo is a classic example of such a shock). The leftward shift of the aggregate supply curve cuts output and raises prices.

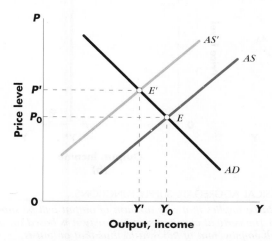

FIGURE 5-3   A LEFTWARD SHIFT OF AGGREGATE SUPPLY.

A shift to AS' moves the equilibrium point from E to E'.

5-1

THE AGGREGATE SUPPLY CURVE

The aggregate supply curve describes, for each given price level, the quantity of output firms are willing to supply. In the short run the *AS* curve is horizontal (the *Keynesian* aggregate supply curve); in the long run the *AS* curve is vertical (the *classical* aggregate supply curve). Figure 5-4 shows the two extreme cases. We begin by examining the long-run case.

THE CLASSICAL SUPPLY CURVE

The *classical aggregate supply curve* is vertical, indicating that the same amount of goods will be supplied whatever the price level. The classical supply curve is based on the assumption that the labor market is in equilibrium with full employment of the labor force. If the idea that the aggregate supply curve is vertical in the long run makes you uncomfortable, remember that the term "price level" here means overall prices. In a single market, manufacturers faced with high demand can raise the price for their products and go out and buy more materials, more labor, and so forth. This has the side effect of shifting factors of production away from lower demand sectors and into this particular market. But if high demand is economywide and all the factors of production are already at work, there isn't any way to increase overall production, and all that happens is that all prices increase (wages too, of course).

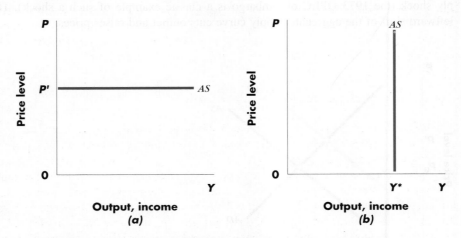

FIGURE 5-4   KEYNESIAN AND CLASSICAL AGGREGATE SUPPLY FUNCTIONS.

(a) The horizontal Keynesian AS curve implies that any amount of output will be supplied at the existing price level. (b) The vertical classical supply function is based on the assumption that there is always full employment of labor, and thus that output is always at the corresponding level, Y*.

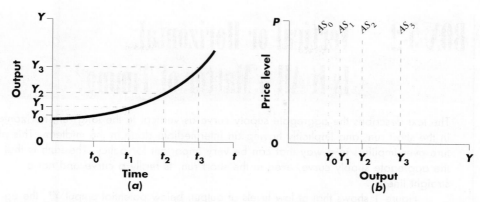

FIGURE 5-5   GROWTH OF OUTPUT OVER TIME, TRANSLATED INTO SHIFTS IN AGGREGATE SUPPLY.

We call the level of output corresponding to full employment of the labor force *potential GDP, Y**. Potential GDP grows over time as the economy accumulates resources and as technology improves, so the position of the classical aggregate supply curve moves to the right over time, as shown in Figure 5-5. In fact, the level of potential GDP in a particular year is determined largely as described by the growth theory models we have just studied.

It is important to note that while potential GDP changes each year, the changes *do not depend on the price level*. We say that potential GDP is "exogenous with respect to the price level"; what's more, changes in potential GDP over a short period are usually relatively small, a few percent a year. We can draw a single vertical line at potential GDP and call it "long-run aggregate supply" without needing to worry much about the rightward movement due to potential GDP growth.

THE KEYNESIAN AGGREGATE SUPPLY CURVE

The *Keynesian aggregate supply curve* is horizontal, indicating that firms will supply whatever amount of goods is demanded at the existing price level. The idea underlying the Keynesian aggregate supply curve is that because there is unemployment, firms can obtain as much labor as they want at the current wage. Their average costs of production therefore are assumed not to change as their output levels change. They are accordingly willing to supply as much as is demanded at the existing price level. The intellectual genesis of the Keynesian aggregate supply curve lay in the Great Depression, when it seemed that output could expand endlessly without increasing prices by putting idle capital and labor to work. Today, we've overlaid this notion with what we call "short-run price stickiness." In the short run, firms are reluctant to change prices (and wages) when demand shifts. Instead, at least for a little while, they increase or decrease output. As a result, the aggregate supply curve is quite flat in the short run.

BOX 5-2   Vertical or Horizontal: Is It All a Matter of Timing?

The text describes the aggregate supply curve as vertical in the long run, horizontal in the short run, and implicitly having an intermediate slope in the midterm. This picture oversimplifies in a way that can be very important for policy. The truth is that the aggregate supply curve, even in the short run, is really a curve and not a straight line.

Figure 1 shows that at low levels of output, below potential output Y*, the aggregate supply curve is quite flat. When output is below potential, there is very little tendency for prices of goods and factors (wages) to fall. Conversely, where output is above potential, the aggregate supply curve is steep and prices tend to rise continuously. The effects of changes in aggregate demand on output and prices therefore depend on the level of actual relative to potential output.

In a recession we are on the flat part of the aggregate supply curve, so demand management policies can be effective at boosting the economy without having much effect on the price level. However, as the economy approaches full employment, policymakers must be wary of too much stimulus to avoid running the aggregate demand curve up the vertical portion of the aggregate supply curve shown in the figure.

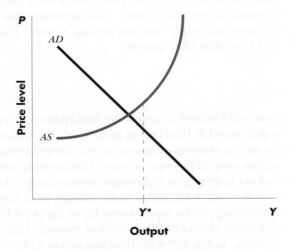

FIGURE 1 AGGREGATE DEMAND AND NONLINEAR AGGREGATE SUPPLY.

It is important to note that on a Keynesian aggregate supply curve, the price level *does not depend on GDP.* In most countries prices rise in most years; in other words, there is some ongoing, though perhaps small, inflation. For reasons we explore later, this price increase is associated with an upward shift of the aggregate supply curve—not a move along the curve. For the moment, we assume that we are in an economy with no expected inflation. The key point is that in the short run the price level is unaffected by current levels of GDP.

FRICTIONAL UNEMPLOYMENT AND THE NATURAL RATE OF UNEMPLOYMENT

Taken literally, the classical model implies that there is no unemployment. In equilibrium, everyone who wants to work is working. But there is always some unemployment. That level of unemployment is accounted for by labor market frictions, which occur because the labor market is always in a state of flux. Some people are moving and changing jobs; other people are looking for jobs for the first time; some firms are expanding and hiring new workers; others have lost business and have to reduce employment by firing workers. Because it takes time for an individual to find the right new job, there will always be some *frictional unemployment* as people search for jobs.

There is some amount of unemployment associated with the full-employment level of employment and the corresponding full-employment (or potential) level of output, Y^*. That amount of unemployment is called the *natural rate.* **The *natural rate of unemployment* is the rate of unemployment arising from normal labor market frictions that exist when the labor market is in equilibrium.** Current estimates are that the natural rate in the United States is about 5.5 percent, but an exact number has been frustratingly difficult to pin down.

5-2

THE AGGREGATE DEMAND CURVE

The aggregate demand curve shows the combinations of the price level and level of output at which the goods and money markets are simultaneously in equilibrium. Expansionary policies—such as increases in government spending, cuts in taxes, and increases in the money supply—move the aggregate demand curve to the right. Consumer and investor confidence also affects the aggregate demand curve. When confidence increases, the *AD* curve moves to the right. When confidence drops, the *AD* curve moves to the left.

The aggregate demand relation between output and prices is quite sophisticated. Indeed, Chapters 9, 10, and 11 are devoted to developing the *IS-LM* model, which is the underpinning of aggregate demand. Here we give a brief introduction.

The key to the aggregate demand relation between output and prices is that aggregate demand depends on the *real money supply.* The real money supply is the *value* of the

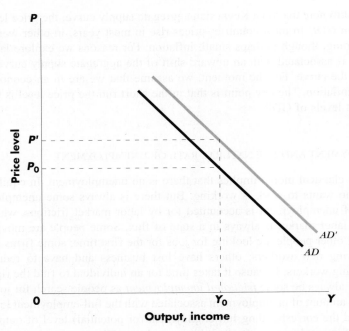

FIGURE 5-6   AN INCREASE IN THE MONEY SUPPLY SHIFTS AGGREGATE DEMAND UPWARD.
A 10 percent increase in the money supply shifts AD up by 10 percent.

money provided by the central bank (the Federal Reserve in the United States) and the banking system. If we write the number of dollars in the money supply (the *nominal money supply*) as $\overline{M}$ and the price level as P, we can write the real money supply as $\overline{M}/P$. When $\overline{M}/P$ rises, interest rates fall and investment rises, leading overall aggregate demand to rise. Analogously, lowering $\overline{M}/P$ lowers investment and overall aggregate demand.

For a given level of the nominal money supply, $\overline{M}$, high prices mean a low real money supply, $\overline{M}/P$. Quite simply, high prices mean that the *value* of the number of available dollars is low. As a result, a high price level means a low level of aggregate demand, and a low price level means a high level of aggregate demand. Thus, the aggregate demand curve in Figure 5-1 slopes down.[1]

The aggregate demand curve represents equilibrium in both the goods and money markets. Expansion from the goods markets—say, from increased consumer confidence or expansionary fiscal policy—moves the aggregate demand schedule up and to the right. Expansionary monetary policy similarly moves aggregate demand up and to the right. Figure 5-6 shows just such a shift in aggregate demand.

[1]Note that, strictly speaking, the aggregate demand curve should be drawn as a curve and not a straight line. We show it as a straight line for convenience.

Putting together the goods markets and money markets to derive the aggregate demand curve requires considerable detail—which we will supply in Chapter 10. It's much easier to understand the aggregate demand curve if we forget about the goods market for the moment. So we will! But you should maintain a mental reservation that we owe you another piece of the puzzle.

The *quantity theory of money* provides a simple way to get a handle on the aggregate demand curve, even if it does leave out some important elements. The total number of dollars spent in a year, *nominal GDP,* is $P \times Y$. We call the number of times per year a dollar turns over *velocity, V.* If the central bank provides M dollars, then

$$M \times V = P \times Y \tag{1}$$

For example, a money supply of \$5,200 billion (M) turning over 2 times a year (V) would support a nominal GDP of \$10,400 billion ($P \times Y$).

If we make one additional assumption—that V is constant—then equation (1) turns into an aggregate demand curve. With the money supply constant, any increase in Y must be offset by a decrease in P, and vice versa. The inverse relation between output and price gives the downward slope of AD. An increase in the money supply shifts AD upward for any given value of Y.

It is important for what follows to see that *an increase in the nominal money stock shifts the AD schedule up exactly in proportion to the increase in nominal money.* Why? Look at Figure 5-6 and at equation (1). Suppose that $\overline{M}_0$ leads to the AD curve shown in the figure and that the value P_0 corresponds to output Y_0. Now suppose $\overline{M}$ increases 10 percent to $\overline{M}'$ ($= 1.1 \times \overline{M}$). This shifts the aggregate demand curve up and to the right to AD'. The value of P corresponding to Y_0 must be exactly P' ($= 1.1 \times P_0$). At this value of P, the new *real* money supply equals the old real money supply ($\overline{M}'/P' = (1.1 \times \overline{M}_0)/(1.1 \times P_0) = \overline{M}_0/P_0$).

 # 5-3

AGGREGATE DEMAND POLICY UNDER ALTERNATIVE SUPPLY ASSUMPTIONS

In Figure 5-1 we showed how the aggregate supply and demand curves together determine the equilibrium level of income and prices in the economy. Now we use the aggregate demand and supply model to study the effects of aggregate demand policy in the two extreme supply cases—Keynesian and classical.

THE KEYNESIAN CASE

In Figure 5-7 we combine the aggregate demand schedule with the Keynesian aggregate supply schedule. The initial equilibrium is at point E, where AS and AD intersect. At that point the goods and assets markets are in equilibrium.

Consider an increase in aggregate demand—such as increased government spending, a cut in taxes, or an increase in the money supply—which shifts the AD

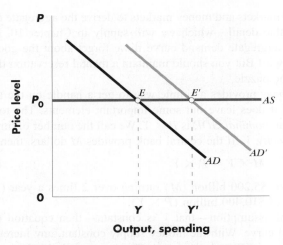

FIGURE 5-7   AGGREGATE DEMAND EXPANSION: THE KEYNESIAN CASE.
Given perfectly elastic supply, shifting AD to the right will increase output but leave the equilibrium price level unchanged.

schedule out and to the right, from AD to AD'. The new equilibrium is at point E', where output has increased. Because firms are willing to supply *any* amount of output at the level of prices P_0, there is no effect on prices. The only effect in Figure 5-7 is an increase in output and employment.

THE CLASSICAL CASE

In the classical case, the aggregate supply schedule is vertical at the full-employment level of output. Firms will supply the level of output Y^* whatever the price level. Under this supply assumption we obtain results very different from those reached using the Keynesian model. Now the price level is not given but, rather, depends on the interaction of supply and demand.

In Figure 5-8 we study the effect of an aggregate demand expansion under classical supply assumptions. The aggregate supply schedule is AS, with equilibrium initially at point E. Note that at point E there is full employment because, under the classical assumption, firms supply the full-employment level of output at any level of prices.

The expansion shifts the aggregate demand schedule from AD to AD'. At the initial level of prices, P_0, spending in the economy would rise to point E'. At price level P_0 the demand for goods has risen. But firms cannot obtain the labor to produce more output, and output supply cannot respond to the increased demand. As firms *try* to hire more workers, they bid up wages and their costs of production, so they must charge higher prices for their output. The increase in the demand for goods therefore leads only to higher prices, and not to higher output.

BOX 5-3   Keynesian and Classical— Short Run and Long

We have repeatedly used the terms "Keynesian" and "classical" to describe assumptions of a horizontal or vertical aggregate supply curve. Note that these are *not* alternative models providing alternative descriptions of the world. Both models are true: The Keynesian model holds in the short run, and the classical model holds in the long run. Economists do have contentious disagreements over the time horizons in which either model applies. Almost all economists (*almost* all) agree that the Keynesian model holds over a period of a few months or less and the classical model holds when the time frame is a decade or more. Unfortunately, the interesting time frame for policy relevance is several quarters to a few years. The speed with which prices adjust—that is, how long it takes the aggregate supply curve to rotate from horizontal to vertical—is an area of active research.

The increase in prices reduces the real money stock and leads to a reduction in spending. The economy moves up the *AD'* schedule until prices have risen enough, and the real money stock has fallen enough, to reduce spending to a level consistent

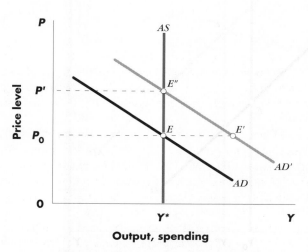

FIGURE 5-8   AGGREGATE DEMAND EXPANSION: THE CLASSICAL CASE.
Given perfectly inelastic supply, shifting AD to the right results in an increase in the price level but no change in output.

with full-employment output. That is the case at price level P'. At point E'' aggregate demand, at the higher level of government spending, is once again equal to aggregate supply.

5-4
SUPPLY-SIDE ECONOMICS

All economists are in favor of policies that move the aggregate supply curve to the right by increasing potential GDP. Such supply-side policies as removing unnecessary regulation, maintaining an efficient legal system, and encouraging technological progress are all desirable, although not always easy to implement. However, there is a group of politicians and pundits who use the term "supply-side economics" in reference to the idea that cutting tax rates will increase aggregate supply enormously—so much, in fact, that tax collections will rise, rather than fall. Even political allies of the supply-siders (George Bush [the father] before he was president, for instance) refer to this notion as "voodoo economics." We use the aggregate supply–aggregate demand diagram in Figure 5-9 to show what happens when tax rates are cut.

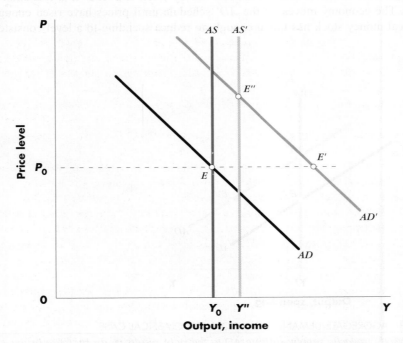

FIGURE 5-9   EFFECTS OF CUTTING TAX RATES ON AGGREGATE DEMAND AND SUPPLY.

BOX 5-4   Dynamic Scoring—Or Supply-Side Economics Revisited

When Congress considers tax cuts, the estimated effect of the tax cuts on the budget deficit plays a key role in the debate. Supply-siders have urged that the analysis of the deficit should include *dynamic scoring*.

The dynamic scoring argument is as follows: A cut in tax rates will increase economic growth through a supply-side stimulus. Given enough time, the resulting increase in output will increase the base upon which taxes are levied. The extra tax collections on this higher base will in part offset the increase in the deficit due to the cut in the tax rate. Accounting for this offset over a number of years following the policy change is called dynamic scoring.

The principle of dynamic scoring is hard to argue with, but many analysts disagree with its practical application. The first objection is that supply-side effects on increasing the tax base are very small, so that dynamic scoring cannot be very important. The second objection is that dynamic scoring is hard to do objectively, in particular because it requires analysts to take positions on how the Federal Reserve and future Congresses will change policies in reaction to current policy changes.

Cutting tax rates has effects on both aggregate supply and aggregate demand. The aggregate demand curve shifts right from AD to AD'. The shift is relatively large. The aggregate supply curve also shifts to the right, from AS to AS', because lower tax rates increase the incentive to work. However, economists have known for a very long time that the effect of such an incentive is quite small, so the rightward shift of potential GDP is small. The large shift in aggregate demand and small shift in aggregate supply are illustrated in Figure 5-9.

What should we expect to see? In the short run, the economy moves from E to E'. GDP does rise substantially. As a result, total tax revenues fall proportionately less than the fall in the tax rate.[2] However, this is purely an aggregate demand effect. In the long run, the economy moves to E''. GDP is higher, but only by a very small amount. As a result, total tax collections fall and the deficit rises. In addition, prices are permanently higher.

The United States experimented with supply-side economics in the 1981–1983 tax cuts. The results were just as predicted.

Not *all* supply-side policies are silly. In fact, *only* supply-side policies can permanently increase output. Important as they are, demand management policies are useful only for

---

[2]In principle, GDP *might* even rise so much that tax collections rise. In practice, it appears that the effect is not this strong.

short-term results. For this reason, many economists strongly favor supply-side policies—they just don't believe in exaggerating their effect. Many conservative economists favor cutting tax rates for the small, but real, incentive effect. However, these economists also believe in cutting government spending at the same time. Tax collections would fall, but so would government spending, so the effect on the deficit would be nearly neutral.

5-5

PUTTING AGGREGATE SUPPLY AND DEMAND TOGETHER IN THE LONG RUN

The long-run aggregate supply curve marches to the right over time at a fairly steady rate. Two percent annual growth is pretty low, and 4 percent is high. In contrast, movements in aggregate demand over long periods can be either large or small, depending mostly on movements in the money supply. Figure 5-10 shows a stylized set of aggregate supply and demand curves for the 1970s through 2000. Output rises as the curves shift to the right. The shift was somewhat greater in the 1990s than earlier, but not overwhelmingly so. In contrast, there were big vertical moves in aggregate demand between 1970 and 1980, so prices rose much more quickly in the 1970s than later.

Figure 5-10 shows that prices rise whenever aggregate demand moves out more than aggregate supply. Over long periods, output is essentially determined by aggregate supply and prices are determined by the movement of aggregate demand relative to the movement of aggregate supply.

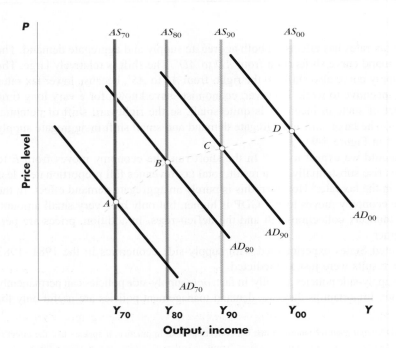

FIGURE 5-10   LONG-RUN SHIFTS IN *AD* AND *AS*.

SUMMARY

1. The aggregate supply and demand model is used to show the determination of the equilibrium levels of *both* output and prices.
2. The aggregate supply schedule, *AS*, shows at each level of prices the quantity of real output firms are willing to supply.
3. The Keynesian supply schedule is horizontal, implying that firms supply as many goods as are demanded at the existing price level. The classical supply schedule is vertical. It would apply in an economy that has full price and wage flexibility. In such a frictionless economy, employment and output are always at the full-employment level.
4. The aggregate demand schedule, *AD*, shows at each price level the level of output at which the goods and assets markets are in equilibrium. This is the quantity of output demanded at each price level. Along the *AD* schedule fiscal policy is given, as is the nominal quantity of money.
5. A fiscal expansion shifts the *AD* schedule outward and to the right. An increase in the nominal money stock shifts the *AD* curve up by the same proportion as the money stock increases.
6. Supply-side economics makes the claim that reducing tax rates generates very large increases in aggregate supply. In truth, tax cuts produce very small increases in aggregate supply and relatively large increases in aggregate demand.
7. Over long periods, output is essentially determined by aggregate supply and prices are determined by the movement of aggregate demand relative to the movement of aggregate supply.

KEY TERMS

aggregate demand (*AD*) curve	dynamic scoring	nominal GDP
aggregate supply (*AS*) curve	frictional unemployment	nominal money supply
classical aggregate supply curve	Keynesian aggregate supply curve	potential GDP
	natural rate of unemployment	quantity theory of money
		real money supply
		velocity

PROBLEMS

Conceptual

1. What do the aggregate supply and aggregate demand curves describe?
2. Explain why the classical supply curve is vertical. What are the mechanisms that ensure continued full employment of labor in the classical case?
3. What relationship is captured by the aggregate supply curve? Can you provide an intuitive justification for it?
4. How does the Keynesian aggregate supply curve differ from the classical one? Is one of these specifications more appropriate than the other? Explain, being careful to state the time horizon to which your answer applies.
5. The aggregate supply and demand model looks, and sounds, very similar to the standard supply and demand model of microeconomics. How, if at all, are these models related?

Technical

1. **a.** If the government were to reduce income taxes, how would the reduction affect output and the price level in the short run? In the long run? Show how the aggregate supply and demand curves would be affected, in both cases.

    b. What is supply-side economics? Is it likely to be effective, given your answer to (**a**)?

2. Suppose that the government increases spending from G to G' while simultaneously raising taxes in such a way that, at the initial level of output, the budget remains balanced.

    a. Show the effect of this change on the aggregate demand schedule.

    b. How does this affect output and the price level in the Keynesian case?

    c. How does this affect output and the price level in the classical case?

Empirical

1. The textbook identified the 1973 OPEC oil embargo as a classical example of an adverse supply shock. Go to www.economagic.com and do a search using two keywords: "consumer price index" and "energy." Choose the series "Consumer Price Index All Urban Consumers: Energy; 1982–84=100 NSA//cpiengns," and using the built-in graphing facilities create a graph for the period 1957–2003 (choose the option "Show recessions"). Besides the date 1973 given in the textbook, can you identify on the graph other probable dates when supply shocks (oil shocks) took place? Give an example.

2. In Section 5.1 of this chapter we stated that changes in potential GDP do not depend on the price level, or in other words, "potential GDP is exogenous with respect to the price level." The goal of this exercise is to give you a chance to convince yourself that this is the case.

    a. Go to www.economagic.com and download annual data for the period 1949–2002 for the following two variables: Real Potential Gross Domestic Product (potential RGDP) and Gross Domestic Product Implicit Price Deflator (the easiest way to do this is to do a search for the name of the variables, and then use the provided tools to transform the data from quarterly into annual—choose the option "Last Quarter of Year"). Copy the data into an EXCEL spreadsheet.

    b. Calculate the annual growth rate in potential RGDP and the annual inflation rate in GDP deflator. Create a scatterplot that has the growth rate of potential GDP on the Y axis and the annual inflation rate in the GDP deflator on the X axis. Can you visually identify any relationship between the two variables?

    *c. If you have taken a statistics class, use EXCEL or a statistical program in order to run the following regression:

    $$\text{Potential RGDP growth} = c + \beta \times \text{inflation in the GDP deflator} + \epsilon$$

    What do you find? Is the coefficient on the inflation rate statistically significant? Interpret your results.

*An asterisk denotes a more difficult problem.

CHAPTER 6

Aggregate Supply: Wages, Prices, and Unemployment

CHAPTER HIGHLIGHTS

- The aggregate supply curve describes the price adjustment mechanism of the economy.

- The Phillips curve links inflation and unemployment. The aggregate supply curve links prices and output. The Phillips curve and aggregate supply curve are alternative ways of looking at the same phenomena.

- According to the modern Phillips curve, inflation depends on expectations of inflation, as well as unemployment.

In this chapter we further develop the aggregate supply side of the economy. The aggregate supply curve describes the *price adjustment mechanism* of the economy. In the very short run, we know the aggregate supply curve is horizontal; and in the long run, we know the aggregate supply curve is vertical. In this chapter we examine the dynamic adjustment process that carries us from the short run to the long run.

We begin with an examination of the mechanics of the aggregate supply curve. We then look at some of the economics that underlie the mechanics. The price-output relation along the aggregate supply curve is built up from the links among wages, prices, employment, and output. The link between unemployment and inflation is called the *Phillips curve*. We translate between unemployment and output and also translate between inflation and price changes. Use of these translations makes it much easier to connect theory with the numbers reported on the evening news. When we hear that inflation has dropped below 2 percent (the metric used on the Phillips curve), we know immediately that price increases are pretty much under control. In contrast, when we hear that the CPI has hit 168.8 . . . well, that's a number that only a policy wonk could love.[1]

In the third section of this chapter we introduce the role of price expectations (into aggregate supply) or, equivalently, inflationary expectations (in the Phillips curve). Understanding the price expectations mechanism provides the explanation of *stagflation*—the simultaneous presence of high unemployment and high inflation. Having incorporated inflationary expectations into the model, we then take a look at the "rational expectations revolution"—the most important intellectual breakthrough in macroeconomics in the last quarter of the twentieth century. After these "big picture" topics, we turn to a more detailed examination of the slope of the aggregate supply curve and then take a look at how supply shocks—both good and bad—affect the economy.

Before we get down to business, some words of warning, and some of encouragement: The warning is that the theory of aggregate supply is one of the least settled areas in macroeconomics. We do not fully understand why wages and prices are slow to adjust, although we do have a number of reasonable theories. In practice the labor market seems to adjust slowly to changes in aggregate demand, the unemployment rate is clearly not always at the natural level, and output does change when aggregate demand changes. The words of encouragement are that although there is a variety of models of aggregate supply, the basic phenomenon that has to be explained—the apparent slow adjustment of output to changes in demand—is widely agreed on. All modern models, however different their starting points, tend to reach a similar result: that in the short run the aggregate supply curve is flat, but in the long run it is vertical.

6-1

THE AGGREGATE SUPPLY CURVE AND THE PRICE ADJUSTMENT MECHANISM

Figure 6-1*a* shows the flat short-run aggregate supply curve in black and the vertical long-run curve in green. It also illustrates an entire spectrum of intermediate-run curves. Think of the aggregate supply curve as rotating, counterclockwise, from horizontal to

[1]Note that economists use the term "policy wonk" as a compliment.

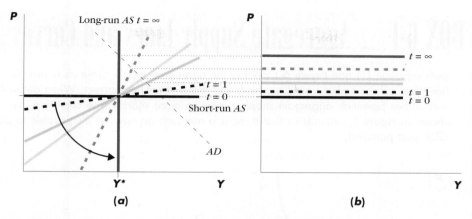

FIGURE 6-1   THE DYNAMIC RETURN TO LONG-RUN AGGREGATE SUPPLY.

vertical with the passage of time. The aggregate supply curve that applies at, say, a 1-year horizon is a black dashed line and medium-sloped. If aggregate demand is greater than potential output, Y^*, then this intermediate curve indicates that after a year's time prices will have risen enough to partially, but not completely, push GDP back down to potential output.

Figure 6-1a gives a useful, but static, picture of what is really a dynamic process. We focus on the aggregate supply curve as a description of the mechanism by which prices rise or fall over time. Equation (1) gives the aggregate supply curve:

$$P_{t+1} = P_t[1 + \lambda(Y - Y^*)] \tag{1}$$

where P_{t+1} is the price level next period, P_t is the price level today, and Y^* is potential output. Equation (1) embodies a very simple idea: If output is above potential output, prices will rise and be higher next period; if prices are below potential output, prices will fall and be lower next period.[2] What's more, prices will continue to rise or fall over time until output returns to potential output. Tomorrow's price level equals today's price level if, and only if, output equals potential output.[3] The difference between GDP and potential GDP, $Y - Y^*$, is called the *GDP gap,* or the *output gap.*

The upward-shifting horizontal lines in Figure 6-1b correspond to successive snap-shots of equation (1). We start with the horizontal black line at time $t = 0$. If output is above potential, then the price will be higher—that is, the aggregate supply curve will move up—by time $t = 1$, as shown by the black dashed line. According to equation (1),

[2]Sometimes equation (1) is written to show P_t adjusting from P_{t-1} rather than P_{t+1} adjusting from P_t. This alternative puts a little slope in even the shortest-run AS curve, where our version has the shortest-run curve horizontal. Nothing substantive rests on the difference.

[3]For the moment, we leave out the very important role of price expectations. If you look ahead in this chapter, you will see that including price expectations in the aggregate supply curve is necessary to explain inflation when the economy is at $Y = Y^*$.

BOX 6-1   Aggregate Supply Lines and Curves

Both equation (1) and Figure 6-1 portray the aggregate supply curve as a straight line. You will remember from Chapter 5 that this isn't entirely correct: When output is well above potential, aggregate supply curves up more sharply. The curvature, as shown in Figure 1, reminds us that there is a real limit on how far it's possible to push GDP past potential.

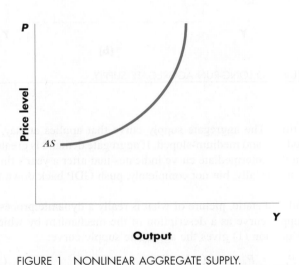

FIGURE 1   NONLINEAR AGGREGATE SUPPLY.

and as shown in Figure 6-1*b*, the price keeps moving up until output is no longer above potential output.

Note that Figure 6-1 *a* and *b* are alternative descriptions of the same process; (*a*) illustrates the dynamics of price movements, and (*b*) shows snapshots after a given amount of time has elapsed. For example, the black dashed schedule shows the cumulative effect of price movements after perhaps a year's time. Figure 6-2 is another way of looking at the adjustment process: plotting the equilibrium points from Figure 6-1 against elapsed time.

The *speed of price adjustment* is controlled by the parameter λ in equation (1). If λ is large, the aggregate supply curve moves quickly, or, equivalently, the counter-clockwise rotation in Figure 6-1*a* occurs over a relatively short time period. If λ is small, prices adjust only very slowly. Quite a bit of the disagreement among economists about the best course for macroeconomic policy centers on λ. If λ is large, the aggregate supply mechanism will return the economy to potential output relatively quickly; if λ is small, we might want to use aggregate demand policy to speed up the process.

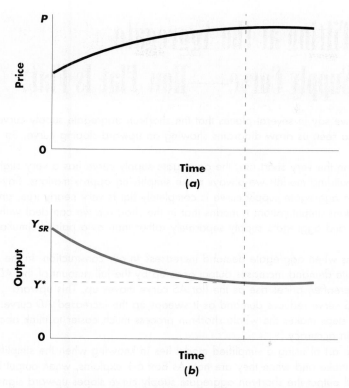

FIGURE 6-2   ADJUSTMENT PATHS OF PRICE LEVEL AND OUTPUT.

RECAP

We summarize the description of the aggregate supply schedule as follows:

- A relatively flat aggregate supply curve means that changes in output and employment have a small impact on prices, as shown in Figure 6-1a. Equivalently, we could
  say that the horizontal short-run AS curve shown in Figure 6-1b moves up slowly
  in response to increases in output or employment. The coefficient λ in equation (1)
  captures this output/price change linkage.
- The position of the short-run AS schedule depends on the level of prices. The schedule passes through the full-employment level of output, Y^*, at $P_{t+1} = P_t$. At higher
  output levels there is overemployment, and hence prices next period will be higher
  than those this period. Conversely, when unemployment is high, prices next period
  will be lower than those this period.
- The short-run AS schedule shifts over time. If output is maintained above the full-
  employment level, Y^*, prices will continue to rise over time.

BOX 6-2   Tilting at the Aggregate Supply Curve—How Flat Is Flat?

As you have seen, we say in several places that the short-run aggregate supply curve is flat. You have also seen us draw diagrams showing an upward sloping curve. So which is it?

In truth, even in the very short run, the aggregate supply curve has a very slight upward tilt. But in building models we always make simplifying approximations. Saying that the short-run aggregate supply curve is completely flat is very nearly true, and it buys us an important simplification: It means that in the short run we can deal with aggregate demand and aggregate supply separately rather than as a pair of simultaneous equations.

What happens when aggregate demand increases? In our construction, in the instant that aggregate demand increases output goes up by the full amount of the *AD* increase. *Shortly thereafter,* prices rise as the flat *AS* curve moves up. This upward movement of the *AS* curve reduces demand as it sweeps up the increased *AD* curve. Separating the two steps makes the whole short-run process much easier to think about with very little loss in accuracy.

Of course, the art of using a simplified model lies in knowing when the simplifications are safe to make and when they are not. As Box 6-1 explains, when output is well above potential output the short-run aggregate supply curve slopes upward significantly. In this situation the assumption of a horizontal short-run *AS* schedule is no longer tenable, and we really do need to use a positively sloped *AS* curve and solve for equilibrium using *AS* and *AD* curves simultaneously.

6-2
INFLATION AND UNEMPLOYMENT

Figure 6-3 shows the unemployment rate since 1960. With a quick glance one can see that the economy was in bad shape at the end of 1982. Contrast this with the low unemployment rate with which a healthy U.S. economy ended the century. In this section we discuss the Phillips curve, which gives the tradeoff between unemployment and inflation. Later in the chapter we give a more rigorous derivation, demonstrating the translation between the aggregate supply curve and the Phillips curve. (GDP connects to unemployment; potential GDP connects to the natural rate of unemployment; the price level connects to the inflation rate.) On an everyday basis it's much easier to work with figures for unemployment on the Phillips curve than with GDP numbers on the aggregate supply curve.

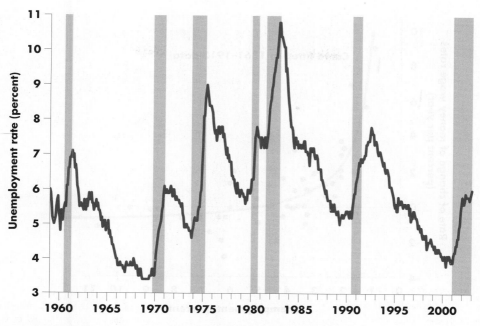

FIGURE 6-3   THE U.S. CIVILIAN UNEMPLOYMENT RATE, 1959–2002.
(Source: Bureau of Labor Statistics.)

THE PHILLIPS CURVE

In 1958 A. W. Phillips, then a professor at the London School of Economics, published a comprehensive study of wage behavior in the United Kingdom for the years 1861–1957.[4] The main finding is summarized in Figure 6-4, reproduced from his article: **The *Phillips curve* is an inverse relationship between the rate of unemployment and the rate of increase in money wages. The higher the rate of unemployment, the lower the rate of wage inflation. In other words, there is a tradeoff between wage inflation and unemployment.**

The Phillips curve shows that the rate of wage inflation decreases with the unemployment rate. Letting W_t be the wage this period, and W_{t+1} the wage next period, the rate of wage inflation, g_w, is defined as

$$g_w = \frac{W_{t+1} - W_t}{W_t} \tag{2}$$

[4]A. W. Phillips, "The Relation between Unemployment and the Rate of Change of Money Wages in the United Kingdom, 1861–1957," *Economica*, November 1958.

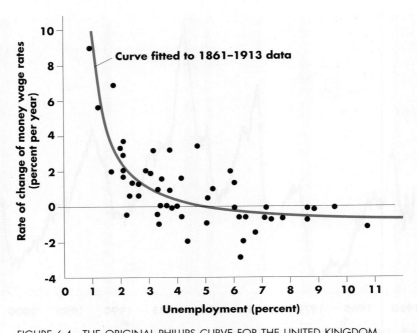

FIGURE 6-4   THE ORIGINAL PHILLIPS CURVE FOR THE UNITED KINGDOM.

(*Source: A. W. Phillips, "The Relation between Unemployment and the Rate of Change of Money Wages in the United Kingdom, 1861–1957,"* Economica, *November 1958.*)

With u^* representing the natural rate of unemployment,[5] we can write the simple Phillips curve as

$$g_w = -\epsilon(u - u^*) \tag{3}$$

where ϵ measures the responsiveness of wages to unemployment. This equation states that wages are falling when the unemployment rate exceeds the natural rate, that is, when $u > u^*$, and rising when unemployment is below the natural rate. The difference between unemployment and the natural rate, $u - u^*$, is called the *unemployment gap*.

Suppose the economy is in equilibrium with prices stable and unemployment at the natural rate. Now there is an increase in the money stock of, say, 10 percent. Prices and wages both have to rise by 10 percent for the economy to get back to equilibrium. But the Phillips curve shows that for wages to rise by an extra 10 percent, the unemployment rate will have to fall. That will cause the rate of wage increase to go up.

---

[5](1) You will see below that there is a close connection between the natural rate of unemployment, u^*, and potential output, Y^*. (2) Many economists prefer the term "nonaccelerating inflation rate of unemployment" (NAIRU) to the term "natural rate." See Laurence M. Ball and N. Gregory Mankiw, "The NAIRU in Theory and Practice," Harvard Institute Research working paper no. 1963, July 2002. See also Chap. 7, footnote 13 in this text.

Wages will start rising, prices too will rise, and eventually the economy will return to the full-employment level of output and unemployment. This point can be readily seen by rewriting equation (2), using the definition of the rate of wage inflation, in order to look at the level of wages today relative to the past level:

$$W_{t+1} = W_t[1 - \epsilon(u - u^*)] \qquad (3a)$$

For wages to rise above their previous level, unemployment must fall below the natural rate.

Although Phillips's own curve relates the rate of increase of wages or wage inflation to unemployment, as in equation (3) above, the term "Phillips curve" gradually came to be used to describe either the original Phillips curve *or* a curve relating the rate of increase of *prices*—the rate of inflation—to the unemployment rate. Figure 6-5 shows inflation and unemployment data for the United States during the 1960s that appear entirely consistent with the Phillips curve.

THE POLICY TRADEOFF

The Phillips curve rapidly became a cornerstone of macroeconomic policy analysis. It suggested that policymakers could choose different combinations of unemployment and inflation rates. For instance, they could have low unemployment as long as they put up with high inflation—say, the situation in the late 1960s in Figure 6-5. Or they could maintain low inflation by having high unemployment, as in the early 1960s.

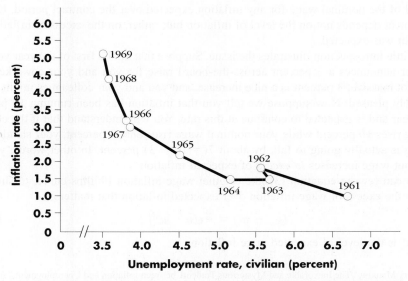

FIGURE 6-5   RELATIONSHIP OF INFLATION AND UNEMPLOYMENT: UNITED STATES, 1961–1969.
(Source: DRI/McGraw-Hill.)

You already know that the idea of a *permanent* unemployment-inflation tradeoff must be wrong because you know that the long-run aggregate supply curve is vertical. The piece of the puzzle that is missing in the simple Phillips curve is the role of price expectations. But the data in Figure 6-5 should leave you with two impressions that are clear and correct. First, there *is* a short-run tradeoff between unemployment and inflation. Second, the Phillips curve (and therefore the aggregate supply curve) really is quite flat in the short run. Applying ocular econometrics to Figure 6-5,[7] you should see that lowering unemployment by a full percentage point (which is a lot) increases the inflation rate in the short run by about half a point (a relatively modest amount). Note too that at very low unemployment rates the inflation/unemployment tradeoff becomes quite a bit steeper.

6-3

STAGFLATION, EXPECTED INFLATION, AND THE INFLATION-EXPECTATIONS-AUGMENTED PHILLIPS CURVE

The *simple* Phillips curve relationship fell apart after the 1960s, both in Britain and in the United States. Figure 6-6 shows the behavior of inflation and unemployment in the United States over the period since 1960. The data for the 1970s and 1980s do not fit the simple Phillips curve story.

Something is missing from the simple Phillips curve. That something is *expected,* or *anticipated, inflation.* When workers and firms bargain over wages, they are concerned with the real value of the wage, so both sides are more or less willing to adjust the level of the nominal wage for any inflation expected over the contract period. Unemployment depends not on the level of inflation but, rather, on the excess of inflation over what was expected.

A little introspection illustrates the issue. Suppose that on the first of the year your employer announces a 3 percent across-the-board raise for you and your coworkers. While not massive, 3 percent is a nice increase, and you and your colleagues might be reasonably pleased. Now suppose we tell you that inflation has been running 10 percent a year and is expected to continue at this rate. You will understand that if the cost of living rises 10 percent while your nominal wage rises only 3 percent, your standard of living is actually going to fall, by about $7(= 10 - 3)$ percent. In other words, you care about wage increases *in excess* of expected inflation.

We can rewrite equation (3), the original wage-inflation Phillips curve, to show that it is the excess of wage inflation over expected inflation that matters:

$$(g_w - \pi^e) = -\epsilon(u - u^*) \tag{4}$$

where π^e is the level of expected price inflation.

---

[6]N. Gregory Mankiw, "The Inexorable and Mysterious Tradeoff between Inflation and Unemployment," *Economic Journal* 111, May 2001.

[7]In other words, applying eyeball to data.

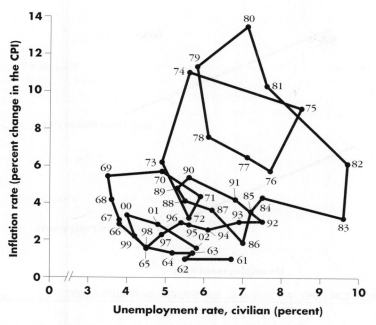

FIGURE 6-6   RELATIONSHIP OF INFLATION AND UNEMPLOYMENT: UNITED STATES, 1961–2002.

(Source: Bureau of Labor Statistics.)

Maintaining the assumption of a constant real wage, actual inflation, π, will equal wage inflation. Thus, the equation for the modern version of the Phillips curve, the *(inflation-) expectations-augmented Phillips curve,* is

$$\pi = \pi^e - \epsilon(u - u^*)\qquad(5)$$

Note two critical properties of the modern Phillips curve:

- Expected inflation is passed one for one into actual inflation.
- Unemployment is at the natural rate when actual inflation equals expected inflation.

We have now an additional factor determining the height of the short-run Phillips curve (and the corresponding short-run aggregate supply curve). Instead of intersecting the natural rate of unemployment at zero, the modern Phillips curve intersects the natural rate at the level of expected inflation. Figure 6-7 shows stylized Phillips curves for the early 1980s (when inflation had been running 6 to 8 percent) and the early oughts (when inflation had been running at about 2 percent).

Firms and workers adjust their expectations of inflation in light of the recent history of inflation.[8] The short-run Phillips curves in Figure 6-7 reflect the low level of

---

[8]How quickly firms and workers adjust and the extent to which they look to the future rather than to recent history are matters of some dispute.

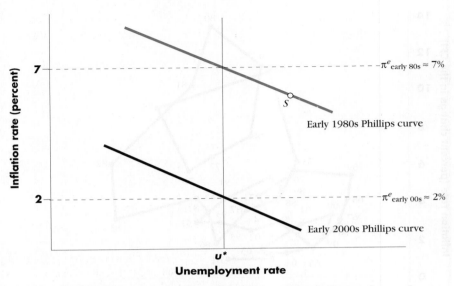

FIGURE 6-7   INFLATION EXPECTATIONS AND THE SHORT-RUN PHILLIPS CURVE.

inflation that was expected in the early oughts and the much higher level that was expected in the early 1980s. The curves have two properties you should note. First, the curves have the same short-run tradeoff between unemployment and inflation; that is to say, the *slopes are equal.* Second, in the early oughts full employment was compatible with roughly 2 percent annual inflation; in the early 1980s full employment was compatible with roughly 7 percent inflation.

The height of the short-run Phillips curve, the level of expected inflation, π^e, moves up and down over time in response to the changing expectations of firms and workers. *The role of expected inflation in moving the Phillips curve adds another automatic adjustment mechanism to the aggregate supply side of the economy.* When high aggregate demand moves the economy up and to the left along the short-run Phillips curve, inflation results. If the inflation persists, people come to expect inflation in the future (π^e rises) and the short-run Phillips curve moves up.

STAGFLATION

Stagflation **is a term coined to mean high unemployment ("stagnation") and high inflation.** For example, in 1982 unemployment was over 9 percent and inflation approximately 6 percent. Point S in Figure 6-7 is a stagflation point. It is easy to see how stagflation occurs.[9] Once the economy is on a short-run Phillips curve that includes

[9]For some reason, journalists delight in reporting that economists don't understand stagflation. This was probably true in the 1960s and early 1970s, before the role of inflation expectations was fully appreciated. The 1960s were a long time ago. As you see, stagflation is no longer a puzzle.

significant expected inflation, a recession will push actual inflation down below expected inflation (e.g., a movement to the right on the 1980s Phillips curve in Figure 6-7), but the absolute level of inflation will remain high. In other words, inflation will be lower than expected but well above zero.

DOES THE AUGMENTED PHILLIPS CURVE FIT THE DATA?

We have seen in Figure 6-6 that when we leave out expected inflation, the empirical relation between inflation and unemployment is a mess. We would like some *evidence* that adjusting for expected inflation gives us a reliable Phillips curve. Unlike inflation and unemployment, which are directly measurable and regularly reported by the official statistics agencies, expected inflation is an idea in the heads of everyone engaged in setting prices and wages. There can be no meaningful official measure of expected inflation, although there are surveys taken in which economic forecasters are asked what they expect inflation to be over the coming year.[10] Nonetheless, we get surprisingly good results from the naive assumption that people expect inflation this year to equal whatever inflation was last year—we assume $\pi_t^e = \pi_{t-1}$. So to check on the modern Phillips curve, we plot $\pi - \pi^e \approx \pi - \pi_{t-1} = -\epsilon(u - u^*)$ in Figure 6-8.

The figure shows that even this very simple model of expected inflation works quite well, although certainly not perfectly. What's more, the line through the data in Figure 6-8 gives us a number for the slope of the short-run Phillips curve. One extra point of unemployment reduces inflation by only about one-half of a percentage point; in other words, $\epsilon \approx .5$. One point of unemployment is a lot. One-half point of inflation is rather little. So the figure shows that the short-run Phillips curve (and the corresponding short-run aggregate supply curve) is quite flat, even though we know that the long-run Phillips curve (and the corresponding long-run aggregate supply curve) is vertical.

RECAP

Points to remember:

- The Phillips curve shows that output is at its full-employment level when actual inflation and expected inflation are equal.
- The modern Phillips curve states that inflation exceeds expected inflation when actual unemployment is below full employment.
- Stagflation occurs when there is a recession along a short-run Phillips curve based on high expected inflation.

---

[10]The classic survey data are described in Dean Croushore, "The Livingston Survey: Still Useful after All These Years," Federal Reserve Bank of Philadelphia *Business Review*, March–April 1997. You can find current and historical data by following links from www.phil.frb.org.

For a method of backing out inflationary expectations from nominal versus real interest rates, see Brian Sack, "Deriving Inflation Expectations from Nominal and Inflation-Indexed Treasury Yields," Board of Governors, FEDS working paper no. 2000-33, May 16, 2000.

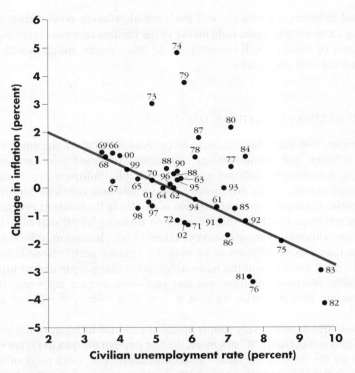

FIGURE 6-8   RELATIONSHIP OF CHANGES IN INFLATION AND UNEMPLOYMENT RATES.
(Source: Bureau of Labor Statistics.)

- Adjustments to expected inflation add a further automatic adjustment mechanism to the supply schedule and speed the progression from the short-run to the long-run aggregate supply curve.
- The short-run Phillips curve is quite flat.

6-4

THE RATIONAL EXPECTATIONS REVOLUTION

The theory of the expectations-augmented Phillips curve has a giant intellectual hole in it. We predict that actual inflation will rise above expected inflation when unemployment drops below the natural rate of unemployment. Well then, why doesn't everyone very quickly adjust their expectations to match the prediction? The Phillips curve relation depends precisely on people being wrong about inflation in a very predictable way. If people learn to use equation (5) to predict inflation, then expected inflation (on the right-hand side) should be set to whatever they forecast for actual inflation (on the left-hand side). But equation (5) says that if actual and expected inflation are equal, then unemployment must be at the natural rate! This is exactly consistent with the way we've described the long-run equilibrium of the economy. But the argument given here sounds like it should apply in the short run as well—arguing that aggregate demand policy (at least monetary policy) affects only inflation and not output or unemployment.

This argument just given doesn't sound very convincing—it pretty much requires economic agents to be omnipotent. The genius that Robert Lucas showed in bringing the idea of *rational expectations* into macroeconomics was to modify the argument by allowing for the role of mistakes.[11] Perhaps if we all knew that the monetary authority was going to increase the rate of growth of the money supply by 8 percent, we would all know that inflation would rise by 8 percent, both π and π^e would rise by 8 percent, and unemployment would remain unchanged. But perhaps the best guess the average person could reasonably make was that money growth would rise by 4 percent. We would have π^e rise by only 4 percent, actual inflation would rise by more than 4 percent, and unemployment would drop. Lucas argued that a good economics model should not rely on the public's making easily avoidable mistakes. So long as we are making predictions based on information available to the public, then the values we use for π^e should be the same as the values the model predicts for π. *While surprise shifts in money growth will change unemployment, predictable shifts won't.*

Good economic models assume that economic actors behave intelligently, and so the intellectual appeal of rational expectations is completely irresistible. But this appears to imply that only surprise changes in monetary policy affect output. The only really good argument against the notion that monetary policy is ineffective except when it surprises people lies in the data. When we observe the world we see that monetary policy does have real effects for significant periods. Why doesn't rational expectations explain how the world operates? We know some of the answers, but by no means all. One answer is that some prices simply can't be adjusted quickly. For example, labor contracts often set wages for 3 years in advance. Another piece of the answer is that even fully rational agents learn slowly. It has also been pointed out that the benefit of setting prices exactly right may be less than the cost of making the necessary price changes. In honesty, a very significant puzzle remains.

You can think of the argument over rational expectations as follows: The usual macro model takes the height of the Phillips curves in Figure 6-7 as being pegged in the short run by expected inflation, where expected inflation is set by recent historical experience. The rational expectations model, in contrast, has the short-run Phillips curve floating up and down in response to available information about the near future. Both models agree that if monetary growth were to be permanently increased, the Phillips curve would shift upward in the long run so that inflation would increase with no long-run change in unemployment. But the rational expectations model says that the upward shift is pretty much instantaneous, whereas the traditional model argues that the shift is only gradual. So this is very much the kind of argument over timing that we laid out at the beginning of the chapter.

---

[11]Robert E. Lucas, "Some International Evidence on Output-Inflation Tradeoffs," *American Economic Review*, June 1973. The general idea of rational expectations is credited to John Muth. Thomas Sargent, Neil Wallace, and Robert Barro also played major roles in bringing the idea into macroeconomics.

6-5

THE WAGE-UNEMPLOYMENT RELATIONSHIP: WHY ARE WAGES STICKY?

In the neoclassical theory of supply, wages adjust instantly to ensure that output is always at the full-employment level. But output is not always at the full-employment level, and the Phillips curve suggests that wages adjust slowly in response to changes in unemployment. The key question in the theory of aggregate supply is, Why does the nominal wage adjust slowly to shifts in demand? In other words, Why are wages *sticky?* **Wages are sticky, or wage adjustment is sluggish, when wages move slowly over time, rather than being fully and immediately flexible, so as to ensure full employment at every point in time.**

To clarify the assumptions that we make about *wage stickiness,* we translate the Phillips curve in equation (4) into a relationship between the rate of change of wages, g_w, and the level of employment. We denote the full-employment level of employment by N^* and the actual level of employment by N. We then define the unemployment rate as the fraction of the full-employment labor force, N^*, that is not employed:

$$u - u^* = \frac{N^* - N}{N^*} \tag{6}$$

Substituting equation (6) into (4), we obtain the Phillips curve relationship between the level of employment, expected inflation, and the rate of change in wages:

$$g_w - \pi^e = \frac{W_{t+1} - W_t}{W_t} - \pi^e = -\epsilon\left(\frac{N^* - N}{N^*}\right) \tag{3b}$$

Equation (3b), the wage-employment relation, WN, is illustrated in Figure 6-9. The wage next period (say, next quarter) is equal to the wage that prevailed this period but

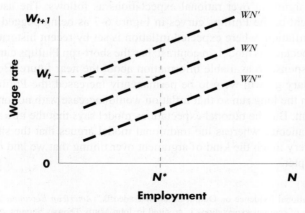

FIGURE 6-9   THE WAGE-EMPLOYMENT RELATION.

with an adjustment for the level of employment and expected inflation. At full employment ($N = N^*$), next period's wage is equal to this period's plus an adjustment for expected inflation. If employment is above the full-employment level, the wage next period increases above this period's wage by more than expected inflation. The extent to which the wage responds to employment depends on the parameter ϵ. If ϵ is large, unemployment has large effects on the wage and the *WN* line is steep.

The Phillips curve relationship also implies that the *WN* relationship shifts over time, as shown in Figure 6-9. If there is overemployment this period, the *WN* curve will shift upward next period to *WN′*. If there is less than full employment this period, the *WN* curve will shift downward next period to *WN″*. Thus, changes in aggregate demand that alter the rate of unemployment this period will have effects on wages in subsequent periods. The adjustment to a change in employment is dynamic; that is, it takes place over time.

WAGE AND PRICE STICKINESS

Although there are different approaches to macroeconomics, each school of thought has had to try to explain why there is a Phillips curve or, equivalently, the reasons for wage and price *stickiness*.[12] The explanations are not mutually exclusive, and we shall therefore briefly mention several of the leading approaches.

Imperfect Information—Market Clearing

Some economists have sought to explain the Phillips curve in a context in which markets clear: Wages are fully flexible but adjust slowly because expectations are temporarily wrong. In the 1960s, Milton Friedman and Edmund Phelps developed models in which, when nominal wages go up because prices have risen, workers mistakenly believe their real wage has risen and so are willing to work more.[13] Thus, in the short run, until workers realize that the higher nominal wage is merely a result of a higher price level, an increase in the nominal wage is associated with a higher level of output and less unemployment. In these models, the slow adjustment of wages arises from workers' slow reactions to or *imperfect information* about changes in prices.

Coordination Problems

The *coordination approach* to the Phillips curve focuses more on the process by which firms adjust their prices when demand changes than on wages.[14] Suppose there is an

---

[12]Recent empirical evidence on the extent to which wages are rigid appears in Joseph G. Altonji and Paul J. Devereux, "The Extent and Consequences of Downward Nominal Wage Rigidity," NBER working paper no. W7236, July 1999; and Mark Bils and Peter J. Klenow, "Some Evidence on the Importance of Sticky Prices," NBER working paper no. W9069, July 2002.

[13]Milton Friedman, "The Role of Monetary Policy," *American Economic Review,* March 1968; Edmund S. Phelps, "Phillips Curves, Expectations of Inflation, and Optimal Unemployment over Time," *Economica,* August 1967. See also Edmund Phelps, "A Review of Unemployment," *Journal of Economic Literature,* September 1992.

[14]See the papers under the heading "Coordination Failures" in N. Gregory Mankiw and David Romer (eds.), *New Keynesian Economics,* vol. 2 (Cambridge, MA: MIT Press, 1991).

increase in the money stock. Ultimately, as we know from Chapter 5, prices will go up in the same proportion as the money supply, and output will be unchanged. But if any one firm raises its price in proportion to the increase in the money stock, and no other firm does, then the single firm that has raised its price will lose business to the others. Of course, if all firms raised their prices in the same proportion, they would move immediately to the new equilibrium. But because the firms in an economy cannot get together to coordinate their price increases, each will raise prices slowly as the effects of the change in the money stock are felt through an increased demand for goods at the existing prices.

Coordination problems can also help explain why wages are sticky downward, that is, why they do not fall immediately when aggregate demand declines. Any firm cutting its wages while other firms do not will find its workers both annoyed and leaving the firm. If firms coordinated, they could all reduce wages together; but since they generally cannot coordinate, wages go down slowly as individual firms cut the nominal wages of their employees, probably with those firms whose profits have been hardest hit moving first.[15]

Efficiency Wages and Costs of Price Change

Efficiency wage theory focuses on the wage as a means of motivating labor. The amount of effort workers make on the job is related to how well the job pays relative to alternatives. Firms may want to pay wages above the market-clearing wage to ensure that employees work hard to avoid losing their good jobs.

Efficiency wage theory offers an explanation for slow changes in real wages but by itself does not explain why the average *nominal* wage is slow to change, although it does help explain the existence of unemployment. However, taken in combination with the fact that there are costs of changing prices, efficiency wage theory can generate some stickiness in nominal wages even if the costs of resetting prices are quite small.[16] Combining that stickiness with problems of coordinating, this theory can help account for nominal wage stickiness.

CONTRACTS AND LONG-TERM RELATIONSHIPS

In developing the explanation of wage stickiness, we build on the above theories and on one central element—the fact that the labor market involves long-term relations

---

[15]A very similar explanation for downward wage rigidity was presented by Keynes in his *General Theory* (New York: Macmillan, 1936). For some recent evidence, see Kenneth J. McLaughlin, "Are Nominal Wage Changes Skewed Away from Wage Cuts?" Federal Reserve Bank of St. Louis *Review,* May 1999.

[16]See George A. Akerlof and Janet L. Yellen, "A Near-Rational Model of the Business Cycle, with Wage and Price Inertia," *Quarterly Journal of Economics,* Supplement, 1985, and, edited by the same authors, *Efficiency Wage Models of the Labor Market* (New York: Cambridge University Press, 1986). See, too, "Costly Price Adjustment," in N. Gregory Mankiw and David Romer (eds.), *New Keynesian Economics,* vol. 1 (Cambridge, MA: MIT Press, 1991). For some empirical evidence, see Christopher Hanes, "Nominal Wage Rigidity and Industry Characteristics in the Downturns of 1893, 1929 and 1981," *American Economic Review,* December 2000.

between firms and workers. Most members of the labor force expect to continue in their current job for some time. Working conditions, including the wage, are renegotiated periodically, but not frequently, because it is costly to negotiate frequently. Even in cases where the wage is supposed to be set by market conditions, obtaining the information needed about alternative wages is costly. Typically, firms and workers reconsider wages and adjust them no more than once a year.[17]

Wages are usually set in nominal terms in economies with low rates of inflation.[18] Thus, the agreement is that the firm will pay the worker so many dollars per hour or per month for the next quarter or year. Most formal union labor contracts last 2 or 3 years and may fix nominal wages for the period of the contract. Frequently, labor contracts include separate wage rates for overtime hours; this implies that the wage rate paid by firms is higher when more hours are worked. That is one reason the *WN* curve in Figure 6-9 is positively sloped.

At any time, firms and workers will have agreed, explicitly or implicitly, on the wage schedule that is to be paid to currently employed workers. There will be some base wage that corresponds to a given number of hours of work per week and depends on the type of job, with perhaps a higher wage for overtime. The firm then sets the level of employment each period.

Now consider how wages adjust when the demand for labor shifts and firms increase the hours of work. In the short run, wages rise along the *WN* curve. With demand up, workers will press for an increase in the base wage at the next labor negotiation. However, it will take some time before all wages are renegotiated. Further, not all wages are negotiated simultaneously. Rather, wage-setting dates are *staggered;* that is, they overlap.[19] Assume that wages are set for half the labor force in January and for the other half in July. Suppose the money stock goes up in September. Prices will be slow to adjust because no wage will be adjusted until 3 months after the change in the money stock. And when the time comes to renegotiate half the contracts, in January, both the firms and the workers negotiating know that other wages will not change for the next 6 months.

Workers do not seek to adjust their base wage all the way to the level that will take the economy to the long-run equilibrium. If they did, their wages would be very high relative to other wages for the next 6 months, and firms would prefer to employ those workers whose wages have not yet risen. There is thus a danger of unemployment

---

[17]The frequency with which wages (and prices) are reset depends on the stability of the level of output and prices in the economy. In extreme conditions, such as hyperinflations, wages might be reset daily or weekly. The need to reset prices and wages frequently is one of the important costs of high and unstable rates of inflation.

[18]In economies with high inflation, wages are likely to be *indexed* to the price level; that is, they adjust automatically when the price level changes. Even in the United States, some long-term labor contracts contain indexing clauses under which the wage is increased to compensate for past price increases. The indexing clauses typically adjust wages once a quarter (or once a year) to compensate for price increases in the past quarter (or year).

[19]The adjustment process we present here is based on John Taylor, "Aggregate Dynamics and Staggered Contracts," *Journal of Political Economy,* February 1980.

to the January wage-setting workers if the renegotiated wages go too high. Wages are therefore adjusted only partway toward equilibrium.

Then in July, when the time comes to reset the other half of the wages, those too are not driven all the way to the equilibrium level because the January wages would then be relatively lower. So the July wages go above the January wages, but still only partway to the full-employment equilibrium base wage.

This process of *staggered price adjustment* keeps on going, with the supply curve rising from period to period as wages leapfrog each other while first one wage and then another is renegotiated. The position of the aggregate supply curve in any period will depend on where it was last period because each unit that is renegotiating wages has to consider the level of its wage relative to the wages that are not being reset. And the level of the wages that are not being reset is reflected in last period's wage rate.

During the adjustment process, firms will also be resetting prices as wages (and thus firms' costs) change. The process of wage and price adjustment continues until the economy is back at the full-employment equilibrium with the same real balances. The real-world adjustment process is more complicated than our January–July example because wages are not reset quite as regularly as that and, also, because both wage and price adjustment matter.[20] But the January–July example gives the essence of the adjustment process.

This account of slow wage and price adjustment raises at least two serious questions. First, why do firms and workers not adjust wages more frequently when clearly understandable disturbances affect the economy? If they did, perhaps they could adjust wages so as to maintain full employment. One line of research emphasizes that even comparatively small costs of resetting wages and prices can keep adjustment processes from operating quickly.[21] Further, the problems of coordinating wage and price adjustments so that wages and prices move back rapidly to equilibrium are formidable in a large economy in which there are many different forces affecting supply and demand in individual markets.

Second, when there is high unemployment, why do firms and unemployed workers not get together on wage cuts that create jobs for the unemployed? The main reason, addressed by efficiency wage theory, is that such practices are bad for the morale and therefore the productivity of those in the labor force who are on the job.[22]

To summarize, the combination of wages that are preset for a period of time and wage adjustments that are staggered generates the gradual wage, price, and output adjustment we observe in the real world. This accounts for the gradual vertical movement of the short-run aggregate supply curve.

[20]For an interesting study of the frequency of price adjustments (for newspapers), see Stephen G. Cecchetti, "Staggered Contracts and the Frequency of Price Adjustment," *Quarterly Journal of Economics,* Supplement, 1985.

[21]See the references in footnote 16.

[22]See Robert M. Solow, *The Labor Market as a Social Institution* (Cambridge, England: Basil Blackwell, 1990), for a discussion of the relation between pay and productivity.

INSIDER-OUTSIDER MODELS

Finally, we draw attention to an approach that emphasizes the implications for the wage behavior–unemployment link that result from this simple fact: The unemployed do not sit at the bargaining table.[23] While the unemployed would prefer firms to cut wages and create more jobs, firms effectively negotiate with the workers who have jobs, not with the people who are unemployed. That has an immediate implication. It is costly for firms to turn over their labor force—firing costs, hiring costs, training costs—and, as a result, *insiders* have an advantage over outsiders. More important, threatening insiders that they will be unemployed unless they accept wage cuts is not very effective. People who are threatened may have to give in, but they will respond poorly in terms of their morale, effort, and productivity. Far better to reach a deal with the insiders and pay them good wages even if there are unemployed workers who would be eager to work for less.

The *insider-outsider model* predicts that wages will not respond substantially to unemployment and thus offers another reason why we do not quickly return to full employment once the economy experiences recession.

PRICE STICKINESS SUMMARY

A good deal of modern work on the Phillips curve recognizes the existence of price stickiness without pinning down the underlying cause.[24] College tuition and professors' salaries rarely change more than once a year. Airfare quotes on the web can change minute by minute. A deep understanding of price stickiness is one of the areas where the gap between microeconomic explanation and macroeconomic effect is the greatest. This remains an area of intensely active research; meanwhile, there isn't any doubt about the empirical importance of price stickiness for understanding the Phillips curve.

6-6

FROM PHILLIPS CURVE TO THE AGGREGATE SUPPLY CURVE

Now we are ready to work back from the Phillips curve to the aggregate supply curve. The derivation will take four steps. First, we translate output to employment. Second, we link the prices firms charge to their costs. Third, we use the Phillips curve relationship between wages and employment. Fourth, we put the three components together to derive an upward-sloping aggregate supply curve.

---

[23]See Assar Lindbeck and Dennis J. Snower, "The Insider-Outsider Theory: A Survey," IZA discussion paper no. 534, July 2002.

[24]Guillermo A. Calvo, "Staggered Contracts in a Utility-Maximizing Framework," *Journal of Monetary Economics,* 1983, is a key, albeit highly technical, reference. For a new approach, see N. Gregory Mankiw and Ricardo Reis, "Sticky Information versus Sticky Prices: A Proposal to Replace the New Keynesian Phillips Curve," *Quarterly Journal of Economics,* November 2002.

OKUN'S LAW

In the short run, unemployment and output are pretty tightly linked. According to *Okun's law*, 1 extra point of unemployment costs 2 percent of GDP. (We'll return to this relation in the next chapter.) Equation (7) presents Okun's law formally:

$$\frac{Y - Y^*}{Y^*} = -\omega(u - u^*) \tag{7}$$

where $\omega \approx 2$.

COSTS AND PRICES

The second step in developing the theory of supply is to link firms' prices to their costs. Labor costs are the main component of total costs.[25] The guiding principle here is that a firm will supply output at a price that at least covers its costs. Of course, firms would like to charge more than cost, but competition from existing firms and firms that might enter the industry to capture some of the profits prevents prices from getting far out of line from costs.

We assume that firms base price on the labor cost of production. If each unit of labor produces a units of output, the labor cost of production per unit is W/a. For instance, if the wage is \$15 per hour and a is 3, the labor cost is \$5 per unit. **The ratio W/a is called the *unit labor cost*.** Firms set price as a *markup, z,* on labor costs:

$$P = \frac{(1 + z)W}{a} \tag{8}$$

The markup over labor costs covers the cost of other factors of production that firms use, such as capital and raw materials, and includes an allowance for the firms' normal profits. If competition in the industry is less than perfect, the markup will also include an element of monopoly profit.[26]

EMPLOYMENT AND WAGES AND THE AGGREGATE SUPPLY CURVE

The Phillips curve in equation (3b) gives wage increases as a function of expected price inflation and the gap between unemployment and the natural rate. Okun's law,

---

[25]We assume labor productivity is constant for simplicity, even though in practice it changes over the business cycle and over time. Productivity tends to grow over long periods, as workers become better trained and educated and are equipped with more capital. It also changes systematically during the business cycle. Productivity tends to fall before the start of a recession and to recover during the recession and at the beginning of the recovery.

[26]In a competitive industry, the price is determined by the market, rather than set by firms. That is quite consistent with equation (8), for if the industry were competitive, z would cover only the costs of other factors of production and normal profits, and the price would thus be equal to the competitive price. Equation (8) is slightly more general, because it allows also for price setting by firms in industries that are less fully competitive.

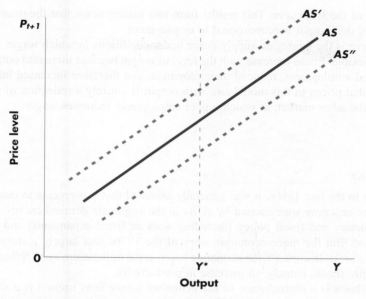

FIGURE 6-10   THE AGGREGATE SUPPLY CURVE.

The AS curve is derived from the WN curve, with the added assumptions that the markup is fixed and that output is proportional to employment.

equation (7), translates the unemployment gap to the GDP gap (actual GDP versus potential GDP), which is what we want for the aggregate supply curve. The price-cost relation in (8) tells us that the rate of wage inflation equals the rate of price inflation.[27] Putting these three equations together gives

$$P_{t+1} = P_{t+1}^e + P_t \frac{\epsilon}{\omega}\left(\frac{Y - Y^*}{Y^*}\right) \tag{9}$$

We often replace equation (9) with an approximate version, as shown in equation (10). Equation (10) is simpler but still emphasizes that the aggregate supply curve shows that next period's price level rises with price expectations and the GDP gap.

$$P_{t+1} = P_{t+1}^e[1 + \lambda(Y - Y^*)] \tag{10}$$

Figure 6-10 shows the aggregate supply curve implied by equation (10). The supply curve is upward-sloping. Like the *WN* curve on which it is based, the *AS* curve shifts over time. If output this period is above the full-employment level, Y^*, then next period the *AS* curve will shift up to *AS'*. If output this period is below the full-employment level, the *AS* curve next period will shift down to *AS"*. Thus, the properties of the *AS*

---

[27]In practice, wage and price inflation aren't always equal—both *a* and *z* change with technology and market conditions. But such changes are not an important part of the story of the aggregate supply curve.

curve are those of the *WN* curve. This results from two assumptions: that the markup is fixed at *z*, and that output is proportional to employment.

The *AS* curve is the aggregate supply curve under conditions in which wages are less than fully flexible. Prices increase with the level of output because increased output implies increased employment, reduced unemployment, and therefore increased labor costs. The fact that prices in this model rise with output is entirely a reflection of the adjustments in the labor market, in which higher employment increases wages.

6-7

SUPPLY SHOCKS

From the 1930s to the late 1960s, it was generally assumed that movements in output and prices in the economy were caused by shifts in the aggregate demand curve—by changes in monetary and fiscal policy (including wars as fiscal expansions) and investment demand. But the macroeconomic story of the 1970s was largely a story of negative *supply shocks*. In contrast, the economic boom at the millennium's end reflected a favorable supply shock, namely, an increase in productivity.

A supply shock is a disturbance to the economy whose first impact is a shift in the aggregate supply curve. In the 1970s, the aggregate supply curve was shifted by two major oil price shocks, which increased the cost of production and therefore increased the price at which firms were willing to supply output. In other words, the oil price shocks shifted the aggregate supply curve, in a way we shall soon show.

Figure 6-11 shows the real, or relative, price of oil.[28] The first OPEC shock, which doubled the real price of oil between 1971 and 1974, helped push the economy into the 1973–1975 recession, until then the worst recession of the post-World War II period. The second OPEC price increase, in 1979–1980, again doubled the price of oil and sharply accelerated inflation. The high inflation led, in 1980–1982, to a tough monetary policy to fight the inflation, with the result that the economy went into even deeper recession than in 1973–1975. After 1982 the relative price of oil fell throughout the 1980s, with a particularly sharp decline in 1985–1986. There was a brief oil price shock in the second half of 1990, as a result of the Iraqi invasion of Kuwait. That temporary shock played a part in worsening the recession of 1990–1991, though the recession is dated as having begun in July, before Kuwait was invaded.

The two oil price shock-related recessions of the 1970s leave no doubt that supply shocks matter.[29]

AN ADVERSE SUPPLY SHOCK

An *adverse supply shock* is one that shifts the aggregate supply curve up. Figure 6-12 shows the effects of such a shock—an increase in the price of oil. The *AS* curve shifts

---

[28]The real price of oil is calculated here as the U.S. average crude oil domestic first purchase price deflated by using gross domestic product implicit price deflators (chained 1996 dollars).

[29]For a less dramatic but more recent look at the impact of oil prices, see "Flaring Up?" *The Economist*, April 11, 2002.

outward by XX', and the equilibrium of the economy moves from A to E'. Immediate effect of the supply shock. Is that a rise in the price level and a reduction in the level of output. An adverse supply shock is doubly unfortunate: it causes a price increase and lower output.

There are two points to note about the impact of the supply shock. First, the shock shifts the AS curve up, because each unit of output now costs firms more to produce. Second, we are assuming that the supply shock does not affect the economy's potential output, which remains at Y^*.

What happens after the shock has hit? In Figure 6-12, the economy is at point E'. Because at E', the unemployment is at E', lower wages and thus the price level and the unemployment rate is at E' initial equilibrium E' is low because wages are now lower. The adjustment takes place along the AD' curve, with wages falling until the economy is back at full employment, with the new level of Y, such as it returns to the shock. But the nominal wage effect of the shock, now below the shock because the unemployment in the meantime has forced the wage down; the real level wage, too, is lower than it before the shock. The adverse supply shock reduced the real wage.

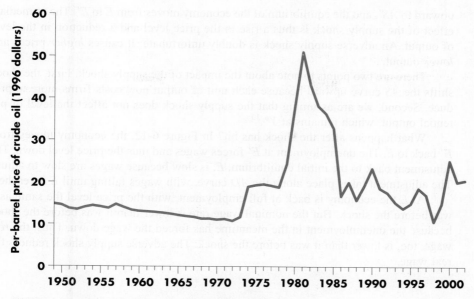

FIGURE 6-11   THE REAL PRICE OF OIL, 1959–2002.
(Source: Energy Information Administration, www.eia.doe.gov.)

Both fiscal and monetary policymakers responded when the first oil price shock hit the economy in the end of 1973. Macro-ec supply shocks were then a new phenomenon, and policymakers and policymakers knew what to anticipate. Could be done about them. But when the unemployment rate went above 6 percent at the end of 1974, both monetary and fiscal policy turned stimulatory. In 1975, 1976. These policies helped the economy recover from the recession more rapidly than it otherwise would have.

Why policymakers respond to an adverse supply shock with a stimulatory policy? To anticipate that unemployment would rise against at most 6 or 7 . if the accommodation. At the same time, to also off price increases such-cost-push inflation occurs. Higher wages, prices could have moved to E^* higher than E'. Prices would have risen more, too, offsetting the upward shift in the aggregate-supply curve.

The monetary and fiscal policies that shifted the curve to AD' in Figure 6-12 are known as accommodating policies. There was less disturbance that resulted in fall in the real wage. Policies is adjusted to make provide for accommodated to avoid the fall output of the economy shrinking.

So the question now is why accommodating policies were not undertaken in 1974 to 1975. The answer is that there is a tradeoff between the inflationary impact of a supply shock, and its recessionary effects. The more accommodation there is, the greater are the

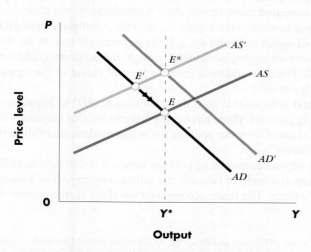

FIGURE 6-12   ADVERSE SUPPLY SHOCK RESULTING FROM AN INCREASE IN THE PRICE OF OIL.

upward to AS', and the equilibrium of the economy moves from E to E'. The immediate effect of the supply shock is thus a rise in the price level and a reduction in the level of output. An adverse supply shock is doubly unfortunate: It causes *higher* prices and *lower* output.

There are two points to note about the impact of the supply shock. First, the shock shifts the AS curve upward because each unit of output now costs firms more to produce. Second, we are assuming that the supply shock does not affect the level of potential output, which remains at $Y*$.[30]

What happens after the shock has hit? In Figure 6-12, the economy moves from E' back to E. The unemployment at E' forces wages and thus the price level down. The adjustment back to the initial equilibrium, E, is slow because wages are slow to adjust. The adjustment takes place along the AD curve, with wages falling until E is reached.

At E the economy is back at full employment, with the price level the same as it was before the shock. But the nominal wage rate is lower than it was before the shock because the unemployment in the meantime has forced the wage down. Thus, the *real* wage, too, is lower than it was before the shock: The adverse supply shock reduces the real wage.

ACCOMMODATION OF SUPPLY SHOCKS

Both fiscal and monetary policy barely responded when the first oil price shock hit the economy at the end of 1973. Because supply shocks were then a new phenomenon, neither economists nor policymakers knew what, if anything, could be done about them. But when the unemployment rate went above 8 percent at the end of 1974, both monetary and fiscal policy turned stimulatory in 1975–1976. These policies helped the economy recover from the recession more rapidly than it otherwise would have.

Why not always respond to an adverse supply shock with stimulatory policy? To answer that question, we look again at Figure 6-12. If the government had, at the time of the oil price increase, increased aggregate demand enough, the economy could have moved to $E*$ rather than E'. Prices would have risen by the full extent of the upward shift in the aggregate supply curve.

The monetary and fiscal policies that shift the AD curve to AD' in Figure 6-12 are known as *accommodating policies*. There has been a disturbance that requires a fall in the real wage. Policy is adjusted to make possible, or accommodate, that fall in the real wage *at the existing nominal wage.*

So the question now is why accommodating policies were not undertaken in 1973–1975. The answer is that there is a tradeoff between the inflationary impact of a supply shock and its recessionary effects. The more accommodation there is, the greater the

---

[30]The increase in the price of oil in the 1970s both shifted up the AS curve and reduced the level of potential output because firms reduced their use of oil and could not use capital as efficiently as before. For simplicity, we are assuming in Fig. 6-12 that the supply shock does not affect $Y*$. To test your understanding of Fig. 6-12, you should trace out the path of output and prices if the supply shock *both* shifts the AS' curve and reduces $Y*$ to, say, $Y*'$.

inflationary impact of the shock and the smaller the unemployment impact. The policy mix actually chosen resulted in an intermediate position—some inflation (quite a lot) and some unemployment.

In addition to weighing the relative costs of unemployment and inflation, policymakers faced with an aggregate supply shock need to decide whether the shock is *transitory* or *permanent.* Faced with a permanent supply shock, aggregate demand policy *cannot* keep output from eventually falling. Attempting to do so will only result in ever-higher prices. In principal, aggregate demand policy can be used to prevent the drop in output associated with a transitory supply shock—although getting the timing right can be tricky.

FAVORABLE SUPPLY SHOCKS

At the end of the millennium, economic times were good. Some part of this good fortune was clearly due to a burst of new technology, especially the advent of cheap computing. Figure 6-13 shows the drastic price drop for computation as the twentieth century came to a close.

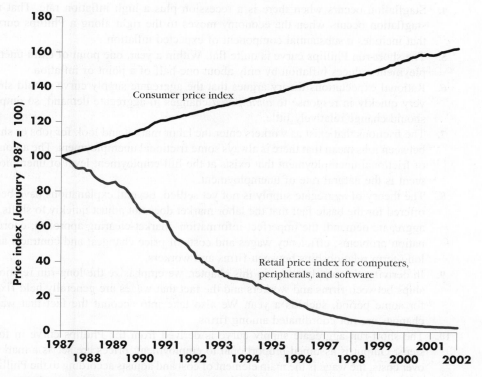

FIGURE 6-13   THE RELATIVE PRICE OF COMPUTING, 1987–2002.

(*Source: www.economagic.com.*)

A *favorable supply shock,* such as that caused by technological improvements, moves the short-run aggregate supply curve outward. It also typically increases potential GDP, moving the long-run aggregate supply curve to the right. Faced with such improvements, the central bank must ensure that the aggregate demand schedule moves to the right quickly enough to keep up with the permanent increase in aggregate supply while being vigilant with respect to any temporary overshooting. If the central bank gets it right, the economy experiences smooth growth with low inflation.

SUMMARY

1. The aggregate supply curve describes the price adjustment mechanism of the economy.
2. The labor market does not adjust quickly to disturbances. Rather, the adjustment process takes time. The Phillips curve shows that nominal wages change slowly in accordance with the level of employment. Wages tend to rise when employment is high and fall when employment is low.
3. Expectations of inflation are built into the Phillips curve. When actual inflation and expected inflation are equal, the economy is at the natural rate of unemployment. Expectations of inflation adjust over time to reflect the recent levels of inflation.
4. Stagflation occurs when there is a recession plus a high inflation rate. That is, stagflation occurs when the economy moves to the right along a Phillips curve that includes a substantial component of expected inflation.
5. The short-run Phillips curve is quite flat. Within a year, one point of extra unemployment reduces inflation by only about one-half of a point of inflation.
6. Rational expectations theory argues that the aggregate supply curve should shift very quickly in response to *anticipated* changes in aggregate demand, so output should change relatively little.
7. The frictions that exist as workers enter the labor market and look for jobs or shift between jobs mean that there is always some frictional unemployment. The amount of frictional unemployment that exists at the full-employment level of unemployment is the natural rate of unemployment.
8. The theory of aggregate supply is not yet settled. Several explanations have been offered for the basic fact that the labor market does not adjust quickly to shifts in aggregate demand: the imperfect-information–market-clearing approach; coordination problems; efficiency wages and costs of price changes; and contracts and long-term relationships between firms and workers.
9. In deriving the supply curve in this chapter, we emphasize the long-run relationships between firms and workers and the fact that wages are generally held fixed for some period, such as a year. We also take into account the fact that wage changes are not coordinated among firms.
10. The short-run aggregate supply curve is derived from the Phillips curve in four steps: Output is assumed proportional to employment; prices are set as a markup over costs; the wage is the main element of cost and adjusts according to the Phillips curve; and the Phillips curve relationship between the wage and unemployment is therefore transformed into a relationship between the price level and output.

11. The short-run aggregate supply curve shifts over time. If output is above (below) the full-employment level this period, the aggregate supply curve shifts up (down) next period.

12. A shift in the aggregate demand curve increases the price level and output. The increase in output and employment increases wages somewhat in the current period. The full impact of changes in aggregate demand on prices occurs only over the course of time. High levels of employment generate increases in wages that feed into higher prices. As wages adjust, the aggregate supply curve shifts until the economy returns to equilibrium.

13. The aggregate supply curve is derived from the underlying assumptions that wages (and prices) are not adjusted continuously and that they are not all adjusted together. The positive slope of the aggregate supply curve is a result of some wages being adjusted in response to market conditions and of previously agreed-on overtime rates coming into effect as employment changes. The slow movement of the supply curve over time is a result of the slow and uncoordinated process by which wages and prices are adjusted.

14. Materials prices (oil price, for example), along with wages, are determinants of costs and prices. Changes in materials prices are passed on as changes in prices and, therefore, as changes in real wages. Materials price changes have been an important source of aggregate supply shocks.

15. Supply shocks pose a difficult problem for macroeconomic policy. They can be accommodated through an expansionary aggregate demand policy, with increased prices but stable output. Alternatively, they can be offset, through a deflationary aggregate demand policy, with prices remaining stable but with lower output.

16. Favorable supply shocks appear to explain rapid growth at the end of the twentieth century. Wise aggregate demand policy in the presence of favorable supply shocks can provide rapid growth with low inflation.

KEY TERMS

accommodating policies	insider-outsider model	speed of price adjustment
adverse supply shock	Okun's law	stagflation
coordination approach	output gap	staggered price adjustment
efficiency wage theory	Phillips curve	supply shocks
expectations-augmented	price adjustment	unemployment gap
Phillips curve	mechanism	unit labor cost
favorable supply shock	price stickiness	wage stickiness
imperfect information	rational expectations	

PROBLEMS

Conceptual

1. Explain how the aggregate supply and Phillips curves are related to each other. Can any information be derived from one that cannot be derived from the other?

2. How do short- and long-term Phillips curves differ? (*Hint:* In the long run, we return to a classical world.)

3. This chapter has discussed a number of different models that can be used to justify the existence of sticky wages, and hence the ability of aggregate demand to affect output. What are they? What are their similarities and differences? Which of these models do you find the most plausible?

4. **a.** What is stagflation?
    b. Describe a situation that could produce it. Could the situation you've described be avoided? Should it be avoided?

5. Explain how the ability of inflation expectations to shift the Phillips curve helps the economy to adjust, automatically, to aggregate supply and demand shocks.

6. Discuss the main differences between the original expectations-augmented Phillips curve discussed in Section 6-3 and the one built on rational expectations discussed in Section 6-4.

Technical

1. Analyze the effects of a reduction in the nominal money stock on the price level, on output, and on the real money stock when the aggregate supply curve is positively sloped and wages adjust slowly over time.

2. Suppose the Federal Reserve adopts a policy of complete transparency; that is, suppose it announces beforehand how it will change the money supply. According to rational expectations theory, how will this policy affect the Fed's ability to move the real economy (e.g., the unemployment rate)?

3. **a.** Show, in an aggregate supply and demand framework, the long- and short-run effects of a decline in the real price of materials (a favorable supply shock).
    b. Describe the adjustment process, assuming that output began at its natural (full-employment) level.

Empirical

1. Section 6-3 emphasized how the Phillips curve (sans inflationary expectations) broke down in the United States. You might ask yourselves, But does it hold in other countries? The goal of this exercise is to give you the chance to experiment with the data and try to find a country for which the Phillips curve might still hold.

    In order to do this, go to www.economagic.com and choose the option "Browse by source." Under the heading "Bureau of Labor Statistics," choose the link "International Employment and Prices." Scroll down the page and choose a country for which you find listed both the Consumer Price Index and the unemployment rate. Download annual data for these two indicators into an EXCEL file. Calculate the inflation rate in the CPI and create a scatterplot that has the unemployment rate on the X axis and the inflation rate on the Y axis. Does your graph look anything like a Phillips curve? Try to do the same for another country. If you find a country for which it works, please let us know.

2. Section 6-3 investigates whether the expectations-augmented Phillips curve fits the data better. In doing this it assumes that next period's expected inflation rate is given by the inflation rate observed today ($\pi_{t+1}^e = \pi_t$). In this exercise you are asked to investigate whether the fit improves if one uses economic forecaster's measures of inflation expectations.
    a. Go to www.economagic.com and choose the "Most Requested Series" link. Under Consumer Price Index, choose and download into an EXCEL file "Annual Inflation (Dec–Dec)"

for the period 1978–2002. Also download annual unemployment rate (μ_t) data for the same period (on www.economagic.com use the built-in options to transform the data from monthly to annual by choosing the option "Annual Averages").

b. Now do a search for "University of Michigan Inflation Expectation." (Transform the monthly data into annual by using the option "Last Month of Year".) Copy the annual data into your EXCEL file.

c. Compute the difference between inflation and expected inflation ($\pi_t - \pi_t^e$). In computing the difference be careful about the dating of the variables. The University of Michigan inflation expectation variables gives the expected inflation over the following year. For example, the 1978 observation is equal to 7.3. This means that inflation during 1979 is expected to be equal to 7.3 percent.

d. Create a scatterplot that has the difference between inflation and expected inflation on the Y axis and the unemployment rate on the X axis. Visually compare the graph you obtained with Figure 6-8 in the chapter. Which one looks more like a Phillips curve?

*e. If you have taken a statistics class use EXCEL or a statistical program in order to run the following regression:

$$\pi_t - \pi_t^e = c + \beta \times \mu_t + \epsilon_t$$

What is the implied slope of the Phillips curve? Is it statistically significant? Interpret your results.

---

*An asterisk denotes a more difficult problem.

CHAPTER 7

The Anatomy of Inflation and Unemployment

CHAPTER HIGHLIGHTS

- The costs of unemployment, mainly forgone output, are very large.

- The cost of anticipated inflation is very small, at least at the moderate levels experienced in industrial countries.

- The cost of unanticipated inflation, which can be quite large, is mainly distributional. There are big winners and big losers.

- Unemployment rates, both the natural rate and the rate of cyclical unemployment, vary widely among different groups and countries.

The Gallup organization regularly conducts opinion polls asking, What is the most important problem facing the country? Possible answers include drugs, crime, pollution, and the threat of nuclear war. In 1981, with the inflation rate in double digits, a majority of those polled named inflation as the most important problem facing the country. In 2002, neither inflation nor unemployment was regarded as a major issue. As Table 7-1 shows, when inflation or unemployment (or both) is high, it is seen as *the* national issue, but when either is low, it practically disappears from the list of concerns.

We've concentrated so far on how various economic factors determine output and prices, unemployment, and inflation. Now we turn to the innards of unemployment and inflation. Both inflation and unemployment should be avoided as much as possible. But since short-run tradeoffs between inflation and unemployment exist, it is also important to get a better understanding of the relative economic costs of inflation and unemployment. This information provides the input for policymakers' evaluation of the tradeoffs.

In an ideal world, policymakers would pick the lowest-cost combination of unemployment and inflation. But how do policymakers deal with the tradeoff in practice?

TABLE 7-1   The Most Important Problem Facing the Country?

	INFLATION		UNEMPLOYMENT	
	RATE, %	NUMBER-ONE PROBLEM, % OF RESPONDENTS	RATE, %	NUMBER-ONE PROBLEM, % OF RESPONDENTS
1981	10.4	73	7.5	8
1982	6.2	49	9.6	28
1983	3.2	18	9.5	53
1984	4.4	10	7.5	28
1985	3.6	7	7.2	24
1986	1.9	4	7.0	23
1987	3.7	5	6.2	13
1988	4.1	—*	5.5	9
1989	4.8	3	5.3	6
1990	5.4	—	5.5	3
1991	4.2	—	6.8	23
1992	2.8	—	7.4	25
1993	3.1	—	7.1	13
1994	2.5	2	6.6	11
1995	2.8	2	5.5	9
1996	2.7	—	5.6	5
1997	2.2	1	4.9	8
1998	1.3	1	4.5	5
1999	2.1	—	4.2	5
2000	3.4	2	4.0	2
2001	2.9	2	4.8	6
2002	2.4	1	5.8	8

*— indicates less than 1 percent.

Source: *Gallup Report,* various issues; www.gallup.com; and Bureau of Labor Statistics.

BOX 7-1   The Sacrifice Ratio— An International Perspective

In the short run, governments can reduce inflation only at the cost of increased unemployment and reduced output. **The *sacrifice ratio* is the percentage of output lost for each 1 point reduction in the inflation rate.** The sacrifice ratio varies depending on the time, place, and methods used to reduce inflation. Nonetheless, it is useful to have a ballpark estimate for making choices about policy. Table 1 provides estimates for a number of countries. Be warned that there is a great deal of uncertainty about the sacrifice ratio even for the United States. Reasonable estimates range from 1 to 10.*

TABLE 1   Estimated Average Sacrifice Ratios

COUNTRY	RATIO, %
Australia	1.00
Canada	1.50
France	.75
Germany	2.92
Italy	1.74
Japan	.93
Switzerland	1.57
United Kingdom	.79
United States	2.39

Source: Laurence Ball, "How Costly Is Disinflation? The Historical Evidence," *Business Review,* Federal Reserve Bank of Philadelphia, November–December 1993.

*Stephan G. Cecchetti and Robert W. Rich, "Structural Estimates of the U.S. Sacrifice Ratio," Federal Reserve Bank of New York staff report, March 1999.

One answer is given by the theory of the political business cycle, described at the end of this chapter. According to this theory, policymakers try to make the inflation and unemployment results come out just right at the time of elections. Of course, the inflation (or the recession to stop it) will come later, after the election.

This chapter focuses on the details of the costs of unemployment and inflation. Before diving into the details, we remind you of the "big picture" costs for moderate inflation rates:

- **There are two main costs of unemployment: lost production and undesirable effects on the distribution of income.**
- **The costs of anticipated inflation are small. The costs of unanticipated inflation are probably small on net, but unanticipated inflation may cause significant redistributions of wealth within the economy.**

7-1

UNEMPLOYMENT

The largest single cost of unemployment is lost production.[1] People who can't work don't produce—high unemployment makes the social pie smaller.[2] The cost of lost output is very high: A recession can easily cost 3 to 5 percent of GDP, amounting to losses measured in hundreds of billions of dollars. As noted in Chapter 6, the late Arthur Okun codified an empirical relation between unemployment and output over the business cycle. *Okun's law* states that **1 extra point of unemployment costs 2 percent of GDP.** Figure 7-1 plots real GDP growth against the change in unemployment, showing that Okun's law gives an excellent account of the unemployment-output relation in the United States.

The costs of unemployment are borne very unevenly. There are large *distributional consequences.* In other words, the costs of a recession are borne disproportionately by those individuals who lose their jobs.[3] For example, college students who have the bad

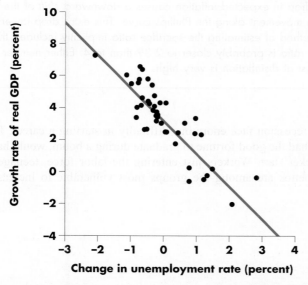

FIGURE 7-1   OKUN'S LAW: THE RELATION BETWEEN UNEMPLOYMENT AND GDP GROWTH.
(Source: Bureau of Labor Statistics and Bureau of Economic Analysis.)

---

[1]But see, as well, William Darity and Arthur Goldsmith, "Social Psychology, Unemployment and Macroeconomics," *Journal of Economic Perspectives,* Winter 1996.

[2]The unemployed do receive increased leisure, which ought to be counted as an offsetting benefit. When unemployment is *involuntary,* the value of leisure is less than the value of work.

[3]There is an old, rather pointed, joke about this: Person 1: "What's the difference between a 'recession' and a 'depression'?" Person 2: "A 'recession' is when you lose your job. A 'depression' is when I lose *my* job."

BOX 7-2   Okun's Law, the Short-Run Phillips Curve, and the Sacrifice Ratio

We've presented several ballpark numbers that bear directly on measuring the short-run tradeoff between output and inflation. How well do they fit together? In Chapter 6 we put a number to the slope of the short-run Phillips curve. We concluded that 1 extra point of unemployment reduces inflation by .5 point—holding inflation expectations constant. Turning this around, a 1-point reduction in inflation costs 2 points of unemployment. According to Okun's law, 2 points of unemployment cost 4 percent of output. Thus the implied sacrifice ratio is about 4, somewhat higher than Ball's estimate of 2.39.

Part of the difference reflects the fact that these rough estimates are just that— rough. But Ball's estimate of the sacrifice ratio includes an important element omitted when we paste together the Phillips curve and Okun's law. During a disinflation, expected inflation falls. The drop in expected inflation causes a downward *shift* of the Phillips curve on top of the movement *along* the Phillips curve. This extra drop lowers the sacrifice ratio. Ball's method of estimating the sacrifice ratio implicitly included this extra kick. So the sacrifice ratio is probably closer to 2.39 than to 4. Either number indicates that the output cost of disinflation is very high.

luck to graduate during a recession face enormous difficulty in starting a career. The same students, if they had had the good fortune to graduate during a boom, would have gotten off to a much quicker start. Workers just entering the labor force, teenagers, and residents of urban ghettos are among the groups most vulnerable to increased unemployment.

7-2
INFLATION

The costs of extremely high inflation are easy to see. Money lubricates the economy. In countries where prices double every month, money stops being a useful medium of exchange, and sometimes output drops dramatically. But at the low, single-digit levels of inflation typical in the United States, the costs of inflation are more difficult to identify. *Unexpected* inflation has an easily seen distributional cost: Debtors benefit by repaying in cheaper dollars, and creditors suffer by being repaid in cheaper dollars. Economists have a hard time understanding why low levels of more-or-less predictable inflation are more than a minor nuisance. However, economists aside, it is clear that the public has a very strong dislike of inflation that policymakers ignore at their own peril.

7-3

THE ANATOMY OF UNEMPLOYMENT

Research on the U.S. labor market has revealed five key characteristics of unemployment:

- There are large variations in unemployment rates across groups defined by age, race, or experience.
- There is high turnover in the labor market. Flows into and out of employment and unemployment are high relative to the numbers of employed or unemployed.
- A significant part of this turnover is cyclical: Layoffs and separations are high during recessions, and voluntary quits are high during booms.
- Most people who become unemployed in any given month remain unemployed for only a short time.
- Much of U.S. unemployment consists of people who will be unemployed for quite a long time.

These facts are critical to understanding what unemployment means and what can or should be done about it.[4]

The starting point for a discussion of unemployment is Table 7-2. The working-age (16 or older) population of the United States in 2002 was 218 million people, of whom 66.6 percent were in the *labor force*. The size of the labor force is determined from surveys. The labor force consists of people who respond that they are unemployed as well as those who say they are employed. An *unemployed person* in these surveys is defined as one who is out of work *and* who (1) has actively looked for work during the previous 4 weeks or (2) is waiting to be recalled to a job after having been laid off. The condition of having looked for a job in the past 4 weeks tests that the person is *actively* interested in working.[5]

Similarly, an *employed person* is defined as one who, during the reference week (the week including the 12th of the month), (*a*) did any work at all (at least 1 hour) as a paid employee, worked in his or her own business, profession, or on his or her own farm, or worked 15 hours or more as an unpaid worker in an enterprise operated by a member of the family, or (*b*) was not working but who had a job or business from which he or she was temporarily absent because of vacation, illness, bad weather, child care problems, maternity or paternity leave, a labor-management dispute, job training, or other family or personal reasons, whether or not he or she was paid for the time off or was seeking another job. Even if a worker has more than

---

[4]For reviews, see Kevin Murphy and Robert Topel, "The Evolution of Unemployment in the United States," *NBER Macroeconomics Annual,* 1987; and Chinhui Juhn, Kevin Murphy, and Robert Topel, "Why Has the Natural Rate of Unemployment Increased over Time?" *Brookings Papers on Economic Activity* 2 (1991).

[5]Those who are of working age but not in the labor force are not counted as unemployed. "Out of the labor force" includes retired persons, homemakers, and full-time students. It also includes *discouraged workers—* people who would like to work but have given up looking. For an interesting paper on discouraged workers, see Kerstin Johansson, "Labor Market Programs, the Discouraged-Worker Effect, and Labor Force Participation," *Institute for Labour Market Policy Evaluation,* working paper, 2002, 9.

TABLE 7-2 U.S. Labor Force and Unemployment, 2002
(Millions of Persons 16 Years and Over)

Working-age population	217.6
Labor force	144.9
Employed	136.5
Unemployed	8.4
Not in labor force	72.7

Source: Bureau of Labor Statistics.

one job, he or she is only counted as one employed person. Persons for whom the only activity was work around their own house (painting, repairing, or own home housework) or volunteer work (i.e., for charitable organizations) are not considered employed.

THE UNEMPLOYMENT POOL

At any point in time there is a given number, or pool, of unemployed people, and there are flows in and out of the *unemployment pool*. A person may become unemployed for one of four reasons:

1. He or she may be a new entrant into the labor force—someone looking for work for the first time—or may be a reentrant—someone returning to the labor force after not having looked for work for more than 4 weeks.
2. The person may quit a job in order to look for other employment and may register as unemployed while searching.
3. The person may be laid off. The definition of *layoff* is a suspension without pay lasting or expected to last more than 7 consecutive days, initiated by the employer "without prejudice to the worker."[6]
4. The worker may lose a job, either by being fired or because the firm closes down.

There are essentially three ways of moving out of the unemployment pool:

1. A person may be hired into a new job.
2. Someone laid off may be recalled to his or her employer.
3. An unemployed person may stop looking for a job and thus, by definition, leave the labor force.

The concept of the unemployment pool gives a good way of thinking about changes in unemployment. Unemployment is rising when more people are entering the pool than leaving. Thus, other things equal, increases in quits and layoffs increase unemployment, as does an increase in the flow of new entrants into the labor market. Job loss accounts for about half of new unemployment. Voluntary separations, new entrants, and reentrants into the labor force together account for the other half.

---

[6]The qualification means that the worker was not fired but, rather, will return to the old job if demand for the firm's product recovers. Until the 1990–1991 recession, over 75 percent of laid-off workers in manufacturing typically returned to jobs with their original employers. The proportion in 1990–1991 was much lower.

The contemporaneous link between unemployment and output embodied in Okun's law and Figure 7-1 is an accurate first approximation, but the dynamics of the output-unemployment link are somewhat more complicated. Consider the typical adjustment pattern of labor use during a recession. Employers first adjust hours per worker—for example, by cutting overtime—and only then trim their workforce. Next, layoffs and firings increase, increasing the flow into unemployment. But, at the same time, quits decrease, as workers sensibly decide to hold on to their current job. During a prolonged recession, many of the unemployed become discouraged and leave the labor force, making the *reported* unemployment rate lower than it would otherwise be. As a result of all these effects, unemployment changes usually lag behind output changes.

VARIATION IN UNEMPLOYMENT ACROSS GROUPS

At any point in time there is a given aggregate level of unemployment or, expressed as a fraction of the labor force, an unemployment rate. For example, in December 2002, the unemployment rate was 6.0 percent. But this aggregate number conceals wide variations across various segments of the population. Figure 7-2 shows the unemployment rates for several groups. Teenagers have much higher unemployment rates than do older workers. Black unemployment is typically double the rate of white unemployment. Female unemployment was higher than male unemployment up through the late 1970s, but today the unemployment rate for women is about the same as—or perhaps a bit lower than—the rate for men.

The variation of unemployment rates across different groups in the labor force can be examined using the relationship between the overall unemployment rate, u, and the unemployment rates, u_i, of groups within the labor force. The overall rate is a weighted average of the unemployment rates of the groups:

$$u = w_1 u_1 + w_2 u_2 + \cdots + w_n u_n \qquad (1)$$

The w_i weights are the fraction of the civilian labor force that falls within a specific group, say, black teenagers.

Equation (1) shows that the overall unemployment rate can change for two reasons: (1) The unemployment rate changes for all groups; or (2) the weights shift toward a group with higher- (or lower-) than-average unemployment.[7] For example, the number of teenagers relative to the number of older workers began rising in the late 1990s and continues to rise in the early years of the twenty-first century. Since teenagers have above-average unemployment, we would expect the national unemployment rate to rise even if neither the unemployment rate for teenagers nor that for older workers changed.

CYCLICAL AND FRICTIONAL UNEMPLOYMENT

There is an important distinction between cyclical and frictional unemployment. *Fric-tional unemployment* is the unemployment that exists when the economy is at full

---

[7]See, for example, Robert Shimer, "Why Is the U.S. Unemployment Rate so Much Lower?" *NBER Macro-economics Annual,* 1998.

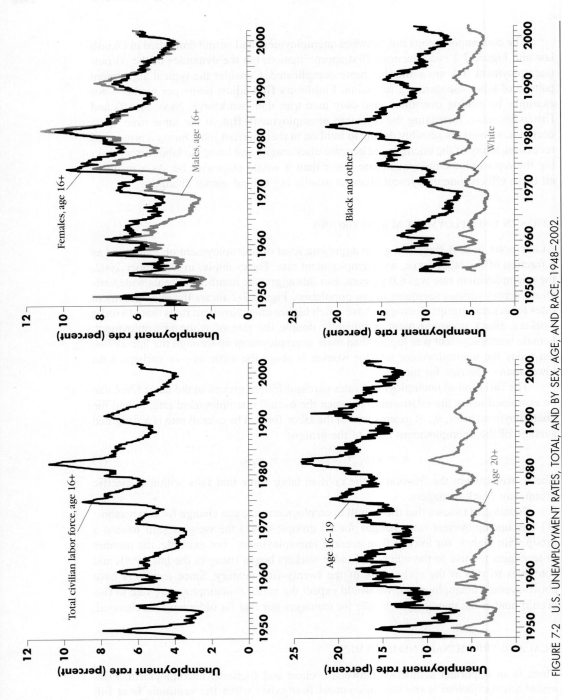

FIGURE 7-2 U.S. UNEMPLOYMENT RATES, TOTAL, AND BY SEX, AGE, AND RACE, 1948–2002.

Note the different scales in panels (a) and (b) versus (c) and (d). (Source: Bureau of Labor Economics.)

TABLE 7-3   Labor Turnover Rates in Manufacturing, 2002
(Per 100 Employees; Average of Monthly Data)

ACCESSIONS	SEPARATIONS			
HIRES	QUITS	LAYOFFS*	OTHER	TOTAL
3.3	1.8	1.2	0.2	3.2

*Includes involuntary separations.

Source: Bureau of Labor Statistics, Job Openings and Labor Turnover Survey.

employment. Frictional unemployment results from the structure of the labor market—from the nature of jobs in the economy and from the social habits and labor market institutions (e.g., unemployment benefits) that affect the behavior of workers and firms. The frictional unemployment rate is the same as the natural unemployment rate, which we discuss in more detail below. *Cyclical unemployment* is unemployment in excess of frictional unemployment: It occurs when output is below its full-employment level.

With this preliminary discussion in mind, we now turn to a closer examination of unemployment.

LABOR MARKET FLOWS

Labor market turnover, flows into and out of unemployment and employment and between jobs, is large.[8] Table 7-3 shows the average of monthly flows in 2002 into and out of employment. These data show the movement, or turnover, in the labor market by splitting net employment changes into their different components.

Table 7-3 presents a remarkable picture of the movement in the labor force. In 2002, in each month, manufacturing companies on average added 3.3 names to their payrolls per 100 employees and, at the same time, removed on average 3.2 names from their payrolls per 100 employees. These data show that people are taking *and* leaving jobs.

DURATION OF UNEMPLOYMENT

A second way of looking at flows into and out of unemployment is to consider the duration of spells of unemployment. A *spell of unemployment* is a period in which an individual remains continuously unemployed. The duration of unemployment is the average length of time a person remains unemployed.

By looking at the duration of unemployment, we get an idea of whether unemployment is typically short-term, with people moving quickly into and between jobs,

---

[8]The important papers in this area include Robert E. Hall, "Why Is the Unemployment Rate So High at Full Employment?" *Brookings Papers on Economic Activity* 3 (1970); and George Akerlof, Andrew Rose, and Janet Yellen, "Job Switching, Job Satisfaction and the U.S. Labor Market," *Brookings Papers on Economic Activity* 2 (1988).

TABLE 7-4 Unemployment by Duration

LENGTH OF UNEMPLOYMENT, WEEKS	PERCENT OF UNEMPLOYED	
	2000	2002
Less than 5	44.9	34.5
5–14	31.9	30.8
15–26	11.8	16.3
27 and over	11.4	18.4
Mean number of weeks	12.6 wk.	16.6 wk.
Unemployment rate	4.0	5.7

Source: Bureau of Labor Statistics.

and whether long-term unemployment is a major problem. Table 7-4 shows data on the duration of unemployment for 2000 and 2002, years of low and then considerably increased unemployment. Historically, the duration of unemployment was high when the unemployment rate was high.[9] A quick glance at the figures in Box 7-4 shows what appears to be a permanent shift toward long-term unemployment. For a given stage of the business cycle, the length of unemployment spells has increased by about 1 month.

7-4
FULL EMPLOYMENT

The notion of full employment—or the natural, or frictional, rate of unemployment—plays a central role in macroeconomics and also in macroeconomic policy. We start by discussing the theory of the natural rate, and then turn to examine estimates of the rate.

DETERMINANTS OF THE NATURAL RATE

The determinants of the natural rate of unemployment, u^*, can be thought of in terms of the *duration* and *frequency* of unemployment. The duration of unemployment depends on cyclical factors and, in addition, on the following structural characteristics of the labor market:

*   The organization of the labor market, including the presence or absence of employment agencies, youth employment services, and the like.
*   The demographic makeup of the labor force.
*   The ability and desire of the unemployed to keep looking for a better job, which depends in part on the availability of unemployment benefits.

[9]Michael Baker, in "Unemployment Duration: Compositional Effects and Cyclical Variability," *American Economic Review*, March 1992, shows that historically the duration of unemployment for all labor market groups tended to increase when unemployment went up.

The last point deserves special notice. A person may quit a job to have more time to look for a new and better one. We refer to this kind of unemployment as *search unemployment*. If all jobs are the same, an unemployed person will take the first one offered. If some jobs are better than others, it is worthwhile searching and waiting for a good one. The higher the unemployment benefits, the more likely people are to keep searching for a better job, and the more likely they are to quit their current job to try to find a better one. Thus, an increase in unemployment benefits will increase the natural rate of unemployment.

The behavior of workers who have been laid off is also important when considering the duration of unemployment. Typically, a worker who has been laid off returns to his or her original job and does not search much for another job. The reason is quite simple: A worker who has been with a firm for a long time has special expertise in the way that firm works and may have built up seniority rights, including a pension. Hence, such an individual is unlikely to find a better-paying job by searching. The best course of action may be to wait to be recalled, particularly if the individual is eligible for unemployment benefits while waiting. However, as discussed in Box 7-3, this return-to-original-job pattern appears to have broken down in the early 1990s.

FREQUENCY OF UNEMPLOYMENT

The *frequency of unemployment* is the average number of times, per period, that workers become unemployed. There are two basic determinants of the frequency of unemployment. The first is the variability of the demand for labor across different firms in the economy. Even when aggregate demand is constant, some firms are growing and some are contracting. The contracting firms lose labor, and the growing firms hire more labor—so turnover and the frequency of unemployment is greater. The greater the variability of the demand for labor across different firms, the higher the unemployment rate. The second determinant is the rate at which new workers enter the labor force, since new potential workers start out as unemployed. The more rapidly new workers enter the labor force—that is, the faster the growth rate of the labor force—the higher the natural rate of unemployment.

The three factors affecting duration and the two factors affecting frequency of unemployment are the basic determinants of the natural rate of unemployment. These factors obviously change over time. The structure of the labor market and the labor force can change. The variability of the demand for labor by differing firms can shift. As Edmund Phelps has noted, the natural rate is *not* "an intertemporal constant, something like the speed of light, independent of everything under the sun."[10]

ESTIMATES OF THE NATURAL RATE OF UNEMPLOYMENT

Estimates of the natural rate keep changing, from about 4 percent in the 1960s to 6 percent in the early 1980s to 5.2 percent in the late 1990s. The estimates are made pragmatically, using as a benchmark some period when the labor market was thought to be in equilibrium.

[10]See E. S. Phelps, "Economic Policy and Unemployment in the Sixties," *Public Interest,* Winter 1974.

BOX 7-3   Downsizing, Unemployment Duration, and the Recovery of the 1990s

One possible explanation for the increase in unemployment duration is the wave of corporate "downsizing" that swept the United States in the early 1990s. In a typical recovery, unemployed workers return to their old jobs or find similar work at other firms. After the 1991–1992 recession, many jobs, particularly many management jobs, were permanently eliminated. As a consequence, unemployed workers had to undertake much lengthier searches and were unemployed for long periods.

Figure 1 shows that the average duration of unemployment remained high through the first half of the 1990s. This further illustrates the uneven distributional consequences of unemployment. In 2000, relatively few workers were unemployed, but those who were had been jobless for a long time.

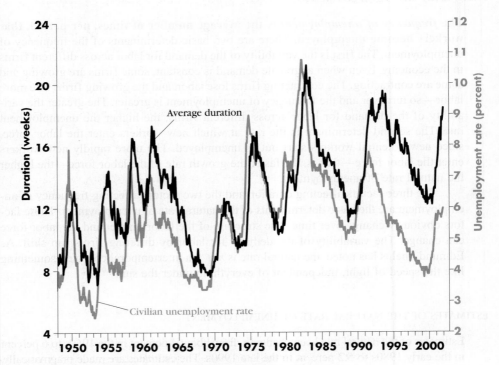

FIGURE 1   UNEMPLOYMENT RATES AND DURATION, 1948–2002.
(Source: Bureau of Labor Statistics.)

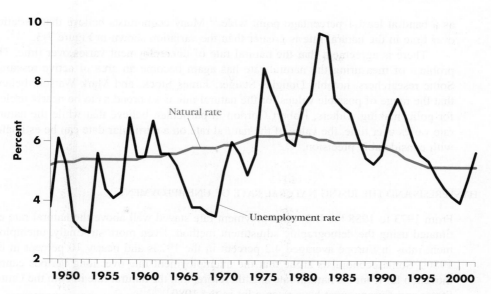

FIGURE 7-3   THE NATURAL AND ACTUAL RATES OF UNEMPLOYMENT, 1948–2002.
(Source: Congressional Budget Office and Bureau of Labor Statistics.)

The basis for the estimate is an equation for the natural rate (which we denote u^*) that is very similar to equation (1):

$$u^* = w_1u_1^* + w_2u_2^* + \cdots + w_nu_n^* \qquad (2)$$

Equation (2) says that the natural rate is the weighted average of the natural rates of unemployment of the subgroups in the labor force. The estimate usually starts from a period like the mid-1950s, when the overall unemployment rate was 4 percent. It is then adjusted for changes in the composition of the labor force (i.e., the w weights) and for changes in the natural rates for the different groups (i.e., the u^* for each group).

The first set of adjustments, for the changing composition of the labor force, takes into account such changes as the increasing share of teenagers, for whom the natural rate of unemployment appears to be higher, in the labor force. These adjustments increase the natural rate, but very little.[11] The second set of adjustments tries in a variety of ways to take account of changes in the fundamental determinants of the natural rate, such as unemployment benefits.

The Congressional Budget Office (CBO) provides an official full-employment–unemployment rate estimate. Graphs of the CBO estimate of the natural rate and the actual unemployment rate are provided in Figure 7-3. It is important to recognize that the full-employment rate, u^*, is nothing but a benchmark and should properly be viewed

[11]See, for example, the demographic adjustments in Brian Motley, "Has There Been a Change in the Natural Rate of Unemployment?" Federal Reserve Bank of San Francisco *Economic Review*, Winter 1990.

as a band at least 1 percentage point wide.[12] Many economists believe that variation over time in the natural rate is greater than the variation shown in Figure 7-3.

There is agreement that the natural rate of unemployment varies over time. The problem of measuring the natural rate has again become an area of active research. Some researchers, notably Douglas Staiger, James Stock, and Mark Watson, believe that the range of possible values for the natural rate is so broad as to be nearly useless for policymaking. Others, Robert Gordon in particular, believe that while the natural rate varies over time, the value of the natural rate on a particular date can be estimated with considerable precision.[13]

HYSTERESIS AND THE RISING NATURAL RATE OF UNEMPLOYMENT

From 1973 to 1988 the U.S. unemployment rate stayed well above the natural rate estimated using the demographic adjustment method. Even more strikingly, unemployment rates in Europe averaged 4.2 percent in the 1970s and nearly 10 percent in the 1980s. Some economists argue that the unemployment rate over long periods cannot move too far from the natural rate and, therefore, that the natural rate in both the United States and Europe must have risen a lot in the 1980s.

One possible explanation is that extended periods of high unemployment raise the natural rate, a phenomenon known as *unemployment hysteresis*.[14] There are various ways in which this could happen. The unemployed might become accustomed to not working. They might find out about unemployment benefits, how to obtain them, and how to spend the day doing odd jobs. Or the unemployed may become discouraged and apply less than full effort to locating a job.

The problem may be reinforced by the actions of potential employers. For instance, they may believe that the longer a person has been unemployed, the more likely it is that the person lacks either the energy or the qualifications to work. Long unemployment spells thus *signal* to firms the possibility (not the certainty) that the worker is undesirable, and, accordingly, firms shy away from hiring such workers. Hence, the higher the unemployment rate (and therefore the longer the unemployment spells), the more unbreakable the vicious circle lengthening unemployment spells.

---

[12]The CBO estimate is actually an important alternative estimate of the natural rate of unemployment: the *nonaccelerating inflation rate of unemployment* (NAIRU). This terrible terminology arises from the use of a Phillips curve like $\pi = \pi_{-1} + \epsilon(u - u^*)$, where π_{-1} may represent the expected inflation rate. It is then possible to get an estimate of u^*—the natural rate, or NAIRU—by looking for the unemployment rate at which inflation is neither accelerating nor decelerating (i.e., where $\pi = \pi_{-1}$).

[13]The Winter 1997 *Journal of Economic Perspectives* has a careful discussion of the controversy; see in particular Robert J. Gordon, "The Time-Varying NAIRU and Its Implications for Economic Policy"; see also, Douglas Staiger, James H. Stock, and Mark W. Watson, "Prices, Wages and the U.S. NAIRU in the 1990s," in Alan B. Krueger and Robert M. Solow (eds.), *The Roaring Nineties: Can Full Employment Be Sustained?* (New York: Russell Sage Foundation, 2002); and Athanasios Orphanides and John C. Williams, "Robust Monetary Policy Rules with Unknown Natural Rates," *Brookings Papers on Economic Activity* 2 (2002).

[14]See James Tobin, "Stabilization Policy Ten Years After," *Brookings Papers on Economic Activity* 1 (1980); and Olivier Blanchard and Lawrence Summers, "Hysteresis in the Unemployment Rate," *NBER Macroeconomics Annual,* 1986.

REDUCING THE NATURAL RATE OF UNEMPLOYMENT

Discussion of methods for reducing the natural rate of unemployment tends to focus on the high unemployment rates of teenagers and on the very high proportion of total unemployment accounted for by the long-term unemployed.

We start with teenage unemployment. Teenagers enter and leave the labor force in part because the jobs they hold are not particularly attractive. To improve jobs, the emphasis in some European countries, especially Germany, is to provide technical training for teenagers and thus make holding on to a job more rewarding. The European apprenticeship system, in which young people receive on-the-job training, is also widely credited not only with providing serious jobs for the young but also with making youths productive workers for the long term.

Teenagers' wages (on average) are closer to the minimum wage than are those of more experienced workers. Many teenagers earn the minimum wage, and some would earn less if that were permissible. Accordingly, reducing the minimum wage might be one way of reducing the teenage unemployment rate. However, programs allowing "subminimum" wages for teenagers appear to mitigate the negative unemployment effect of minimum wage laws.[15]

UNEMPLOYMENT BENEFITS

We come next to the implication of unemployment benefits for unemployment. A key concept is the *replacement ratio*. **The replacement ratio is the ratio of after-tax income while unemployed to after-tax income while employed.**

Unemployment benefits increase the rate of unemployment in two ways. First, unemployment benefits allow longer job search. The higher the replacement ratio, the less urgent it is for an unemployed person to take a job. Feldstein and Poterba have shown that high replacement ratios significantly affect the *reservation wage,* the wage at which a person receiving unemployment benefits is willing to take a new job.[16]

The issue of the effects of unemployment benefits on unemployment is particularly lively in Europe. Many observers argue that high levels of European unemployment result from the very high replacement ratios there. Patrick Minford states: "The picture presented is a grim one from the point of view of incentives to participate in employment. The replacement ratios are such that, should a person 'work the system,' incentives to have a job are, on the whole, rather small for a family man."[17]

---

[15]See David Neumark and William Wascher, "Employment Effects of Minimum and Subminimum Wages: Panel Data on State Minimum Wage Laws," *Industrial and Labor Relations Review,* October 1992, 46, no. 1, pp. 55–81; and Sabrina Wulff Pabilonia, "The Effects of Federal and State Minimum Wages upon Teen Employment and Earnings," Bureau of Labor Statistics working paper, May 2002.

[16]Martin Feldstein and James Poterba, "Unemployment Insurance and Reservation Wages," *Journal of Public Economics,* February–March 1984.

[17]Patrick Minford, *Unemployment, Causes and Cures* (Oxford: Basil Blackwell, 1985), p. 39.

BOX 7-4   Unemployment in International Perspective

In the early postwar period—indeed, through the 1960s—European unemployment was typically far less than unemployment in the United States. But this is no longer the case, as can be seen in Table 1 and Figure 1. European unemployment in the

TABLE 1   Unemployment Rates and Long-Term Unemployed, Selected Countries, 1990, 1995, and 2001

	UNEMPLOYMENT RATE**, PERCENT			UNEMPLOYED MORE THAN 1 YEAR, PERCENT OF TOTAL UNEMPLOYMENT**		
	1990	1995	2001	1990	1995	2001
North America						
Canada	8.1	9.4	7.2	7.2	14.1	9.5
United States	5.6	5.6	4.8	5.5	9.7	6.1
Japan	2.1	3.1	5.0	19.1	18.1	26.6
Central and Western Europe						
Belgium	6.6	9.7	6.6	68.7	62.4	51.7
France	8.6	11.4	8.6	38.0	42.3	37.6
Germany*	4.8	8.2	7.9	46.8	48.7	n.a.
Ireland	13.4	12.3	3.8	66.0	61.4	n.a.
Netherlands	5.9	6.6	2.4	49.3	46.8	n.a.
United Kingdom	6.9	8.5	5.0	34.4	43.6	27.7
Southern Europe						
Italy	8.9	11.5	9.5	69.8	63.6	63.4
Spain	16.1	22.7	13.0	54.0	56.9	44.0
Nordic countries						
Finland	3.2	15.2	9.1	9.2	37.6	26.2
Norway	5.3	5.0	3.6	20.4	24.1	4.9
Sweden	1.7	8.8	5.1	12.1	27.8	22.3
Australia	6.7	8.2	6.7	21.6	30.8	21.5

*For 1990, unemployment rates are for Western Germany only.

**The unemployment measure and unemployment rate attempts to standardize across countries and so may differ from official statistics. For further discussion and an earlier version of this table, see R. Ehrenberg and J. Smith, *Modern Labor Economics,* 6th ed. (Reading, MA: Addison-Wesley, 1997).

Source: OECD, *Employment Outlook,* 1999 and 2002, tables A and G.

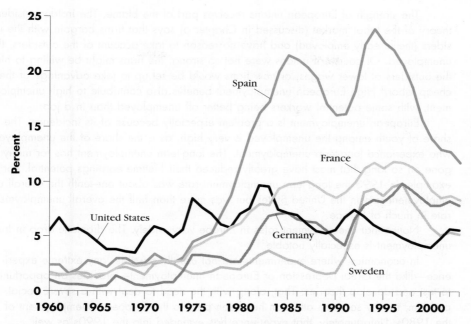

FIGURE 1   UNEMPLOYMENT RATES FOR SELECTED EUROPEAN COUNTRIES AND THE UNITED STATES, 1960–2003.

(Source: European Commission, Directorate General for Economic and Financial Affairs.)

1980s averaged more than twice its 1970s level, which in turn was almost twice the 1960s level and was still very high by historical standards in the new millennium.

With the European unemployment rate averaging more than 9 percent for a decade, it became a prime public issue and topic of academic research.* Many reasons have been advanced for the continuation of high unemployment, among them high unemployment benefits and the hysteresis theory discussed in the text.

Other prominent explanations include the *inflexibility* of European labor markets, specifically the downward inflexibility of real wages and the high firing costs imposed by law. The argument is that firms were reluctant to hire workers because it would be so expensive to fire them if necessary later.†

*An extensive study of the European labor market appears in *The OECD Jobs Study: Evidence and Explanations* (Paris: OECD, 1995). See also Olivier J. Blanchard and Justin Wolfers, "The Role of Shocks and Institutions in the Rise of European Unemployment: The Aggregate Evidence," MIT working paper, March 1999.

†See Edmond Malinvaud, *Mass Unemployment* (Oxford: Basil Blackwell, 1988); and Charles Bean, Richard Layard, and Stephen Nickell (eds.), *Unemployment* (Oxford: Basil Blackwell, 1987).

The strength of European unions receives part of the blame. The insider-outsider theory of the labor market (discussed in Chapter 6) says that firms bargain with the insiders (the already employed) and have no reason to take account of the outsiders, the unemployed. Of course, if unions were not so strong, the firms might be willing to hire the outsiders at lower wages, or new firms would be set up to take advantage of the cheap labor.[‡] High European unemployment benefits also contribute to high unemployment, with some potential workers being better off unemployed than in a job.

European unemployment is a problem especially because of its incidence. The share of youth among the unemployed is very high, as is the share of the unemployed who experience long-term unemployment. The long-term unemployment has for many gone on so long that most have greatly reduced their lifetime earnings potential. For example, in 1993 the long-term unemployment rate was about one-tenth the overall unemployment rate in the United States but was more than half the overall unemployment rate in much of Europe.

Notice that unemployment rates in Europe vary widely. The dramatic drop in Irish unemployment is especially notable.

In economics, where experiments are not usually possible, any extreme experience—like the Great Depression or European unemployment—provides an opportunity to test and develop theories. That, along with the need to deal with a severe social problem, is why so much attention has been paid to the European unemployment of the 1980s. Unfortunately, that experience has extended into the 1990s as well.

[‡]See Assar Lindbeck and Dennis Snower, *The Insider-Outsider Theory* (Cambridge, MA: MIT Press, 1989). For a recent discussion of the linkages between the economics and the politics of European unemployment, see Gilles Saint-Paul, "Exploring the Political Economy of Labour Market Institutions," *Economic Policy*, October 1996.

The second channel is *employment stability*. With unemployment insurance, the consequences of being in and out of jobs are less severe.[18] Accordingly, it is argued, workers and firms do not find it as much in their interest to create highly stable employment, and firms are more willing to lay off workers temporarily than to attempt to keep them on the job. The employment stability effect is mitigated by *experience rating*. The unemployment insurance tax is raised on firms whose employees have high unemployment rates, giving firms an incentive toward more stable employment. However, experience rating does not make firms bear the entire cost of unemployment insurance, so the mitigation is only partial.

In addition to changes in real unemployment, unemployment benefits raise the *measured* unemployment rate through *reporting effects*. To collect unemployment ben-

[18]Randall Wright argues that European insurance compensates for short work hours rather than just total unemployment, as is the case in the United States and Canada. He concludes that the European system results in less variability of employment, though higher variability in hours per worker. See his "The Labor Market Implications of Unemployment Insurance and Short-Time Compensation," Federal Reserve Bank of Minneapolis *Quarterly Review*, Summer 1991.

efits, people have to be "in the labor force," looking for work even if they do not really want a job. They therefore get counted as unemployed. One estimate suggests that reporting effects raise the unemployment rate by about half a percentage point.

There seems to be little doubt that unemployment compensation does add to the natural rate of unemployment.[19] This does not imply, though, that unemployment compensation should be abolished. Unemployment insurance may increase economic efficiency by subsidizing the job search process, which results in improved worker-employer matches. Of greater importance, there is considerable randomness in who becomes unemployed and who does not, and fairness argues for sharing the burden of unemployment. In designing unemployment benefits, there is a tradeoff between reducing the distress suffered by the unemployed and the likelihood that higher benefits raise the natural rate.[20]

7-5

THE COSTS OF UNEMPLOYMENT

The unemployed as individuals suffer both from their income loss while unemployed and from the related social problems that long periods of unemployment cause. Society on the whole loses from unemployment because total output is below its potential level.

This section provides some estimates of the costs of forgone output resulting from unemployment, and it clarifies some of the issues connected with the costs of unemployment and the potential benefits from reducing unemployment. We emphasize the costs of cyclical unemployment, which is associated with short-run deviations of the unemployment rate from the natural rate.

THE COSTS OF CYCLICAL UNEMPLOYMENT

A first measure of the costs of cyclical unemployment is the output lost because the economy is not at full employment. We can obtain an estimate of this loss by using Okun's law, illustrated in Figure 7-1.

According to Okun's law, the economy loses about 2 percent of output for each 1 percent that the unemployment rate exceeds the natural rate. Consider the 2001–2002

---

[19]Among the most convincing evidence is the finding that unemployment spells tend to end, with the worker going back to a job, at precisely the time that unemployment benefits run out (typically after 26 or 39 weeks of unemployment). See Lawrence Katz and Bruce Meyer, "Unemployment Insurance, Recall Expectations, and Unemployment Outcomes," *Quarterly Journal of Economics,* November 1990.

[20]This tradeoff was at the center of an argument between Congress and the Reagan and Bush administrations during recent recessions: Congress generally voted to extend the payment of unemployment benefits by 3 months, in order to help the unemployed, while the administration sometimes argued that this would raise unemployment.

mild recession. Using the CBO estimate that the natural rate of unemployment was equal to 5.2 percent, and noting that the actual unemployment rate was 5.7 percent, we conclude that the recession caused a loss of 1.0 percent of GDP in 2001–2002. That amounts to about $100 billion.

These very large costs invite the question of why policymakers should tolerate such high unemployment.

Distributional Impact of Unemployment

While the Okun's law estimate provides the basic measure of the overall costs of cyclical unemployment, the distributional impact of unemployment also has to be taken into account. Typically a 1-percentage-point increase in the overall unemployment rate is accompanied by a 2-percentage-point increase in the unemployment rate among blacks (see Figure 7-2). In general, unemployment hits poorer people harder than it hits the rich, and this aspect should increase concern about the problem.

The Okun's law estimate encompasses *all* the lost income, including that of all individuals who lose their jobs. That total loss could, in principle, be distributed among different people in the economy in many different ways. For instance, one could imagine that the unemployed would continue to receive benefit payments totaling close to what their income had been while employed, with the benefit payments financed through taxes on working individuals. In that case, the unemployed would not suffer an income loss from being unemployed, but society would still lose from the reduction in total output. The unemployment compensation system partially, but by no means fully, spreads the burden of unemployment.

Other Costs and Benefits

Are there any other costs of unemployment or, for that matter, any offsetting benefits? A possible offsetting benefit occurs because the unemployed, by not working, have more leisure. However, the value that can be placed on that leisure is small. In the first place, much of it is unwanted leisure.

Second, because people pay taxes on their wages, society in general receives a benefit in the form of tax revenue when workers are employed. When a worker loses a job, society at large and the worker share the cost of lost output—society loses tax revenue and the worker loses her take-home pay. This is an additional reason that the benefit of increased leisure provides only a partial offset to the Okun's law estimate of the cost of cyclical unemployment.

7-6

THE COSTS OF INFLATION

There is no direct loss of output from inflation, as there is from unemployment. In considering the costs of inflation, it is important to distinguish between inflation that is *perfectly anticipated,* and taken into account in economic transactions, and *imperfectly anticipated,* or unexpected, inflation. We start with perfectly anticipated inflation.

PERFECTLY ANTICIPATED INFLATION

Suppose that an economy has been experiencing a given rate of inflation, say, 5 percent, for a long time and that everyone correctly anticipates that the rate of inflation will continue to be 5 percent. In such an economy, all contracts would build in the expected 5 percent inflation.

Borrowers and lenders would know and agree that the dollars in which a loan is repaid will be worth less than the dollars given up by the lender when making the loan. Nominal interest rates would be raised 5 percent to compensate for the inflation. Long-term labor contracts would increase wages at 5 percent per year to take account of the inflation and would then build in whatever changes in real wages are agreed to. Long-term leases would take account of the inflation. In brief, any contracts in which the passage of time is involved would take the 5 percent inflation into account. In that category we include the tax laws, which we are assuming would be indexed. The tax brackets themselves would be increased at the rate of 5 percent per year.[21]

In such an economy, inflation has no real costs—except for two qualifications. The first qualification arises because no interest is paid on currency—notes and coins—not least because it is very difficult to do so. This means that the costs of holding currency rise along with the inflation rate.

The cost to the individual of holding currency is the interest forgone by not holding an interest-bearing asset.[22] When the inflation rate rises, the nominal interest rate rises, the interest lost by holding currency increases, and the cost of holding currency therefore increases. Accordingly, the demand for currency falls. Individuals have to make do with less currency, making more trips to the bank to cash smaller checks than they did before. The costs of these trips to the bank are often described as the "shoe-leather" costs of inflation. They are related to the amount by which the demand for currency is reduced by an increase in the anticipated inflation rate, and they are estimated to be small. One estimate is that reducing inflation in the United States from 10 percent (a very high number by historical standards) to zero would, in the long run, be equivalent to increasing output by 1 percent.[23]

The second qualification is the *menu costs* of inflation. These arise from the fact that with inflation—as opposed to price stability—people have to devote real resources to marking up prices and changing pay telephones and vending machines as well as cash registers. Those costs are there, but one cannot get too excited about them.

We should add that we are assuming here reasonable inflation rates, say, in the single or low double digits, that are low enough not to disrupt the payments system.

---

[21]The taxation of interest would have to be on the *real* (after-inflation) return on assets for the tax system to be properly indexed.

[22]Note that cash holders are effectively making an interest-free loan to the government. The direct effect of higher interest rates is a transfer of revenue from the private to the public sector. This is sometimes called an "inflation tax."

[23]See Robert E. Lucas, Jr., "Inflation and Welfare," *Econometrica,* March 2000.

At such low to moderate inflation rates, the costs of fully anticipated inflation are small.[24]

The notion that the costs of fully anticipated inflation are small does not square well with the strong aversion to inflation reflected in policymaking and politics. The most important reason for that aversion is that the inflationary experience of the United States is one of varying, imperfectly anticipated inflation, the costs of which are substantially different from those discussed in this section.

IMPERFECTLY ANTICIPATED INFLATION

The idyllic scenario of full adjustment to inflation does not describe economies in the real world. Modern economies include a variety of institutional features representing different degrees of adjustment to inflation. Economies with long inflationary histories, such as those of Brazil and Israel in the 1970s and 1980s, made substantial adjustments to inflation through the use of indexing. Those in which inflation has been episodic, such as the U.S. economy, have not.

Unanticipated Inflation and Efficient Decision Making

Most contracts are written in nominal terms. If you've agreed to make a set dollar payment at some future date and inflation is unexpectedly high, you pay in cheaper dollars and come out ahead on the deal. Of course, if inflation is lower than expected, you take a loss. Either way, someone wins and someone loses. This means that the possibility of unanticipated inflation introduces an extra element of risk. Such extra risk eliminates some of what would otherwise be attractive exchanges among both businesses and consumers. This is a clear cost associated with unanticipated inflation, though one that is quite hard to measure.

Wealth Redistribution through Inflation

One important effect of inflation is a change in the real value of assets fixed in nominal terms. Between 1972 and 2002, the price level in the United States rose almost fivefold, cutting the purchasing power of all claims or assets fixed in money terms to one-fifth their initial value.[25] Thus, someone who bought a 30-year government bond in 1972 and expected to receive principal of, say, $100 in constant purchasing power at the 2002

---

[24]There is clear cross-country evidence that high rates of inflation are associated with low rates of sustained growth. The negative link is not due to costs of inflation per se. Rather, "The inflation rate serves as an indicator of the overall ability of the government to manage the economy. Since there are no good arguments for very high rates of inflation, a government that is producing high inflation is a government that has lost control." (Stanley Fischer, "Macroeconomic Factors in Growth," *Journal of Monetary Economics,* December 1993.) See also V. V. Chari, Larry E. Jones, and Rodolfo E. Manuelli, "Inflation, Growth, and Financial Intermediation"; Michael Bruno and William Easterly, "Inflation and Growth: In Search of a Stable Relationship"; and Robert J. Barro, "Inflation and Growth," all in Federal Reserve Bank of St. Louis *Review,* May–June 1996; and M. Bruno, "Does Inflation Really Lower Growth," *Finance and Development,* September 1995.

[25]Remember from Chap. 2 that measured inflation probably overstates true inflation. A rough guess might be that prices over this period rose to 3.5, rather than to 5, times their original level.

BOX 7-5   Surely, Anticipated Inflation Isn't Really Costless?

It mainly is, but the view of the average citizen seems to be closer to "5 percent inflation costs me 5 percent." Probably the misperception arises from a viewpoint something like the following: We understand that in a 5 percent anticipated inflation nominal prices and nominal wages both rise 5 percent and so real wages are unchanged. Workers, however, see the 5 percent wage increase and attribute it to their own hard work, to the bargaining power of their unions, or to the success of their companies. The increase in prices is seen as eroding these "earned" gains.*

While students of economics understand that the increases in nominal wages and prices are linked consequences of the inflation rate, it is hard to convince the general public of this view.

*For a very readable discussion of this issue see Alan Blinder, *Hard Heads, Soft Hearts: Tough Minded Economics for a Just Society* (Reading, MA: Addison-Wesley, 1987).

maturity date actually wound up with a $100 principal that had a purchasing power of $20 in 1972 dollars. Similarly, a worker who retired on a fixed dollar pension in 1972 finds that his or her income will buy only about one-fifth of what it did at retirement. The near quintupling of the price level has—if it was unanticipated—transferred wealth from the creditors or holders of bonds to the borrowers and from pensioners to firms.

This redistribution effect operates with respect to all assets fixed in nominal terms, in particular, money, bonds, savings accounts, insurance contracts, and some pensions. It implies that *realized real interest rates* are lower than nominal interest rates on assets, and even possibly negative. Obviously, it is an extremely important effect, since it can wipe out the purchasing power of a lifetime's saving that is supposed to finance retirement consumption. Table 7-5 shows real returns on various assets. We note that currency earns negative real returns whenever inflation is positive.

TABLE 7-5   Real Asset Returns
(Percent per Year)

	1960–1969	1970–1979	1980–1989	1990–1999
Currency	−2.3	−7.1	−5.6	−2.9
Treasury bills	1.6	−0.8	3.3	2.5
Bonds	2.3	0.4	5.0	4.1

Source: Haver Analytics Macroeconomic Database.

BOX 7-6   Unanticipated Inflation in the Short and Long Run

Does unanticipated inflation matter much? At the low levels of inflation common in most countries, a little unanticipated inflation just isn't that big a deal in the short run. (The answer is different in times and places with extremely high inflation rates. See Section 18-4 on hyperinflations.) Suppose you underestimate inflation by 3 percent. You'll find that a year from now cash, and other assets with fixed nominal value, is worth 3 cents on the dollar less than you anticipated. Of course, you also get to repay any nominal debts you owe in slightly cheaper dollars. When inflation is running be-tween 1 and 4 percent, as it has for the last decade in the United States, it's hard to be off in your inflation guess over the coming year by more than 3 percent.

But suppose you sign a contract with fixed nominal payments for 30 years and underestimate inflation by 3 percent per year for the life of the contract. A dollar at the end of the 30 years would be worth only 41 cents. Now that's a difference one really cares about. In the United States, many home mortgages have long-term fixed nominal payments, so homeowners gain substantially from long-term unanticipated in-flation, and some pension plans have fixed payments—pensioners can really be hurt by unanticipated long-term inflation.

Table 7-6 shows the asset and liability positions by sector in the U.S. economy. The *net* nominal creditor status of a sector is just equal to nominal assets less nominal liabilities. Under this definition, the household sector is a debtor in nominal terms. Unanticipated inflation therefore increases the real value of households' net nominal position, by a small amount.

In 2001 the total value of household and nonprofit organizations' nominal net li-abilities was about $1.4 trillion. An increase of 1 percentage point in the price level would lower the real value of net position by $14 billion. **A change in the price level brings about a major *redistribution of wealth* between individuals and sectors of one economy. In particular, with government as the major net nominal debtor, the main redistribution is between the government sector and the private sector.**

We must go beyond Table 7-6 in two respects. First, the table does not tell us to what extent inflation was anticipated when the contracts behind the figures in the table were drawn up. Inflation might have been correctly anticipated, so the wealth transfers occurring as a result of the inflation would not cause any surprises or upset.

Second, the gains and losses from the redistributions of wealth among sectors and individuals that takes place as a result of unanticipated inflation basically cancel out over the economy as a whole. When the government gains from inflation, the private sector pays lower taxes. When the corporate sector gains from inflation, owners of cor-porations benefit at the expense of others. If we really did not care about redistributing wealth among individuals, the costs of unanticipated inflation would be negligible. In-

TABLE 7-6   Net Nominal Creditor Status, Year-End 2001
(Billions of Dollars)

| | ASSETS | | | LIABILITIES, |
| | TANGIBLE | FINANCIAL | | NOMINAL |
		NOMINAL	REAL	
Households and nonprofit organizations	16,266.0	6,679.5	24,993.2	8,055.6
Farm sector	1,173.3	57.1		196.5
Nonfarm noncorporate business	5,281.6	1,504.1		2,809.5
Nonfarm nonfinancial corporate business	9,112.4	9,089.1		9,622.0
Commercial banks	310.2	6,159.7		6,016.6
General government (net)*				4,224.4

*Financial liabilities.

Source: Board of Governors of the Federal Reserve System, *Flow of Funds Accounts of the United States,* 1995–2001, and *Assets and Liabilities of Commercial Banks in The United States,* January 2002; Organization for Economic Cooperation and Development, *OECD Economic Outlook* no. 71, June 2002, Annex Table 34; and United States Department of Agriculture, *Balance Sheet of the U.S. Farming Sector,* 1997–2002.

cluded in the individuals of the previous sentence are those belonging to different generations, since the current owners of the national debt might be harmed by inflation—to the benefit of future taxpayers.

Who gains and who loses from unanticipated inflation? There is a popular belief that the old are more vulnerable to inflation than the young in that the old own more nominal assets. Offsetting this, however, is the fact that social security benefits are indexed, so a substantial part of the wealth of retirees is protected from unanticipated inflation. Common political rhetoric also states that the poor are especially vulnerable to unanticipated inflation. There appears to be little evidence supporting this view for the United States,[26] although for other countries there is considerable evidence that inflation hurts the poor.[27]

Inflation redistributes *wealth* between debtors and creditors. It could also redistribute *income.* A popular line of argument has always been that inflation benefits capitalists or recipients of profit income at the expense of wage earners. Unanticipated inflation, it is argued, means that prices rise faster than wages and therefore allow profits to expand. For the United States in the post-World War II period, there is no persuasive evidence to this effect. There is evidence that the real return on common stocks—that is, the real value of dividends and capital gains on equity—is reduced by unanticipated inflation. Thus, equity holders are hurt by unanticipated inflation.[28]

[26]See Rebecca Blank and Alan Blinder, "Macroeconomics, Income Distribution and Poverty," in Sheldon Danziger and Daniel Weinberg (eds.), *Fighting Poverty* (Cambridge, MA: Harvard University Press, 1986).

[27]See William Easterly and Stanley Fischer, "Inflation and the Poor," World Bank policy research working paper no. 2335, May 2000.

[28]See Charles R. Nelson, "Inflation and Rates of Return on Common Stocks," *Journal of Finance,* May 1976, for one of the earliest articles with this result—which has stood up to repeated testing. See also Franco Modigliani and Richard Cohn, "Inflation, Rational Valuation and the Market," *Financial Analysts Journal,* March–April 1979, for a controversial view of the reasons inflation affects the stock market.

The last important distributional effect of inflation concerns the real value of tax liabilities. A failure to index the tax structure implies that inflation moves the public into higher tax brackets and thus raises the real value of its tax payments or reduces real disposable income. Absent indexed tax brackets, inflation is effectively the same as a congressionally voted increase in tax schedules. Tax brackets in the United States have been indexed since 1985.[29]

The fact that unanticipated inflation serves mainly to redistribute wealth has led to some questioning of the reasons for public concern over inflation. The gainers, it seems, do not shout as loudly as the losers. Since some of the gainers (future taxpayers) have yet to be born, this is hardly surprising. There is also a notion that the average wage earner misperceives the connection between the nominal wage and price-level increases (see Box 7-5).

7-7

INFLATION AND INDEXATION: INFLATION-PROOFING THE ECONOMY

In this section we look briefly at two kinds of contracts that are especially affected by inflation: long-term loan contracts and wage contracts. We then discuss the possibility of reducing people's vulnerability to inflation by *indexation,* which ties the terms of contracts to the behavior of the price level.

INFLATION AND INTEREST RATES

There are many long-term nominal loan contracts, including 20-year government bonds and 25- or 30-year mortgages. For example, a firm may sell 20-year bonds in the capital markets at an interest rate of 8 percent per year. Whether the *real* (after-inflation) interest rate on the bonds turns out to be high or low depends on what the inflation rate will be over the next 20 years. The rate of inflation is thus of great importance to long-term lenders and borrowers, and this is especially true in housing.

Inflation and Housing

The typical U.S. or Canadian household buys a home by borrowing from a bank or a savings and loan institution. The interaction of inflation and taxes has a big impact on the real cost of borrowing. Traditionally, U.S. mortgages—this is the term for the home loan—set a fixed nominal interest rate for a duration of 25 or 30 years. The interest payments are deductible in calculating U.S. federal income taxes,[30] thereby reducing

---

[29]Inflation also affects the real rate of taxation of interest and other asset returns when taxes are not adjusted for inflation. U.S. tax laws do not adjust the taxation of asset returns for inflation. For example, suppose the interest rate is 6 percent while inflation is 5 percent. On a $100 investment, a taxpayer in the 33 percent tax bracket receives $6 in interest and pays $2 in taxes, leaving a total of $104—which is worth only about $99 after adjusting for inflation.

[30]In an interesting difference between two fairly similar tax codes, interest payments on home mortgages are not deductible in Canada.

the effective interest cost of the loan. For instance, suppose the marginal tax rate is 30 percent; then the nominal interest cost is 70 percent of the actual mortgage rate.[31]

Now consider the economics of investing in a home, for example, for someone buying a home in 1963 and financing it with a 25-year fixed-interest mortgage. The mortgage rate in 1963 was 5.9 percent, and the rate of inflation over the next 25 years averaged 5.4 percent. Thus, the pretax actual real interest cost of borrowing was .5 percent. In addition, the home buyer could deduct the interest paid on the mortgage from his or her taxable income. At an interest rate of 5.9 percent and a tax rate of 30 percent, the tax reduction was worth 1.77 percent a year (30 percent of 5.9 percent), so the after-tax real cost of borrowing was *minus* 1.3 percent—not a bad deal! But of course inflation could have turned out to be lower than expected, and then the borrower would have done worse than expected and the lender would have made, rather than lost, money.

Uncertainty about the outlook for inflation was one of the reasons a new financial instrument made its appearance: the *adjustable rate mortgage (ARM)*, which is a particular example of a *floating rate loan*. This is a long-term loan with an interest rate that is periodically (every year, for example) adjusted in line with prevailing short-term interest rates. To the extent that nominal interest rates roughly reflect inflation trends, adjustable rate mortgages reduce the effects of inflation on the long-term real costs of financing home purchases. Both adjustable rate and long-term fixed-interest mortgages are now in use in the United States. Interestingly, mortgage loans in Canada have been variants of ARMs for many years.

Indexed Debt

In countries where inflation rates are high and uncertain, long-term borrowing using nominal debt becomes impossible: Lenders are simply too uncertain about the real value of the repayments they will receive. In such countries, governments typically issue *indexed debt*. **A bond is indexed (to the price level) when either the interest or the principal or both are adjusted for inflation.**[32]

The holder of an indexed bond will typically receive interest equal to the stated real interest rate (e.g., 3 percent) plus whatever the inflation rate turns out to be. Thus, if inflation is 18 percent, the bondholder receives 21 percent; if inflation is 50 percent, the *ex post* nominal interest payment is 53 percent. That way the bondholder is compensated for inflation.

Many economists have argued that governments should issue indexed debt so that citizens can hold at least one asset with a safe real return. It used to be that governments in high-inflation countries, such as Brazil, Argentina, and Israel, issued such debt, and they did it because they could not otherwise borrow.

Among low-inflation countries, the UK government has been issuing indexed bonds since 1979. The U.S. Treasury began issuing indexed debt in 1997, hoping that the value of "inflation insurance" would lower the real interest rate the government pays. Of course, since social security payments in many countries are effectively indexed, the citizens of those countries do hold an asset that protects them against

---

[31]A table of worked-out examples appears in Chap. 14.

[32]It is also common to index debt to the value of a foreign currency, frequently the U.S. dollar.

inflation. However, the stream of social security payments is not an asset they can buy and sell.

We will consider the arguments for and against indexation below.

INDEXATION OF WAGES

Formal labor contracts sometimes include automatic *cost-of-living adjustment (COLA)* provisions. COLA provisions link increases in money wages to increases in the price level. COLA clauses are designed to allow workers to recover, wholly or in part, purchasing power lost through price increases since the signing of the labor contract.

This form of indexation is a quite common feature of labor markets in many countries. Indexation strikes a balance between the advantages of long-term wage contracts and the interests of workers and firms in not having *real* wages get too far out of line.

Because wage bargaining is time-consuming and difficult, wages are not negotiated once a week or once a month but, rather, in the form of 1- or 3-year contracts. But since prices will change over the term of these contracts, some adjustment has to be made for inflation. Broadly, there are two possibilities. One is to index wages to the CPI or the GDP deflator and, through periodic (say, quarterly) reviews, to increase wages by the increase in prices over the period. The other is to schedule periodic, pre-announced wage increases based on the expected rate of price increase. If inflation were known with certainty, the two methods would produce the same result. But since inflation can differ from expectations, there will be discrepancies.

We should expect to find indexation, rather than preannounced wage increases, when uncertainty about inflation is high. Inflation is more uncertain when the inflation rate is high than when it is low, and therefore wage indexation is more prevalent in high-inflation than low-inflation countries.

In the U.S. economy, more than 50 percent of workers who were covered in major collective bargaining agreements in the mid-1980s had contract provisions for automatic cost-of-living adjustments. These provisions were much more common after 1973, when inflation became higher and more variable, than they were before. They have again declined as inflation has stayed low. However, while COLA clauses are an important part of many collective bargaining contracts, relatively few American workers are covered because of the decline in unionization. By 1995, for example, only about 22 percent of workers included in major collective bargaining agreements were covered by COLA provisions.

Supply Shocks and Wage Indexation

Suppose real materials prices increase, and firms pass these cost increases on as higher prices of final goods. Consumer prices will rise, and under a system of wage indexation, wages will rise. This leads to further price, materials-cost, and wage increases. Indexation here feeds an inflation spiral that would be avoided under a system of prefixed wage increases, because then real wages could fall as a consequence of higher materials prices.

The example makes it clear that we must distinguish two possibilities in considering the effects of wage indexing: demand shocks and supply shocks. In the case of a demand shock, there is a "pure" inflation disturbance, and firms can afford to pay the same real wages and therefore will not be adversely affected in real terms by 100 percent indexation. In the case of an adverse supply shock, however, real wages must fall, and full indexation prevents that happening.

Wage indexation thus greatly complicates the adjustment of an economy to supply shocks. In the 1970s and 1980s, the U.S. economy adjusted more easily to the oil shocks than did countries in Europe, where full indexation is more common. The limited extent of wage indexing in the United States helped bring this easier adjustment about.[33]

WHY NOT INDEX?

Economists have often argued that governments should adopt indexation on a broad scale, indexing bonds, the tax system, and everything else they control. That way, inflation would be much easier to live with, and most of the costs of unanticipated inflation would disappear. Governments, by contrast, have been very reluctant to index.

There are three good reasons. First, as we see in the case of wage indexation, indexing makes it harder for the economy to adjust to shocks whenever changes in relative prices are needed. Second, indexing is in practice complicated, adding another layer of calculation to most contracts. Third, governments are scared that by making inflation easier to live with, indexation will weaken the political will to fight inflation, lead to higher inflation, and possibly make the economy worse off since indexation can never deal perfectly with the consequences of inflation.[34]

This last argument is one of political business cycle theory, the subject we discuss in the last section of the chapter.

 # 7-8

IS A LITTLE INFLATION GOOD FOR THE ECONOMY?

Nominal wage cuts are rare. More than 25 years ago, James Tobin argued that a small amount of inflation is good for the economy—and reduces the natural rate of unemployment—because it provides a necessary mechanism for lowering real wages without cutting nominal wages.[35] The idea has been revived in an influential article by George A. Akerlof, William T. Dickens, and George L. Perry.[36]

The argument is as follows: In a changing world, some real wages need to go up and some need to go down in order to achieve economic efficiency and low unemployment. It is easy to raise real wages by simply raising nominal wages faster than

[33]See Michael Bruno and Jeffrey Sachs, *The Economics of Worldwide Stagflation* (Cambridge, MA: Harvard University Press, 1985).

[34]Indexation cannot be perfect because there are lags in measuring the price level and making payments.

[35]See James Tobin, "Inflation and Unemployment" (American Economic Association presidential address), *American Economic Review,* March 1972.

[36]See G. A. Akerlof, W. T. Dickens, and G. L. Perry, "The Macroeconomics of Low Inflation," *Brookings Papers on Economic Activity* 1 (1996).

inflation. To cut real wages, firms must hold nominal wage increases below the rate of inflation. For example, at a 10 percent inflation rate, a 3 percent real wage cut can be accomplished by holding the nominal wage increase to 7 percent. But at zero inflation, firms would have to cut paychecks by 3 percent.

Except when a firm is known to be in dire straits, workers are extraordinarily resistant to cuts in nominal pay. Such cuts are therefore very costly to firms. The recommendation, then, is to maintain inflation at something like 3 percent so that the real wage adjustment can be achieved without nominal pay cuts.

Nominal pay cuts have been relatively rare.[37] It is certainly true that workers and firms *say* they have a strong dislike for nominal pay cuts.[38] It is argued, on the other hand, that in an environment of steady zero inflation, workers and firms would come to regard a 3 percent nominal cut in the same way they had previously viewed a 7 percent nominal wage increase during a 10 percent inflation.

The idea that positive inflation has a significant benefit is very controversial.[39] The very existence of this controversy is a departure from the traditional view that zero is the best inflation target.

7-9
POLITICAL BUSINESS CYCLE THEORY

While the best of all worlds is one with neither inflation nor excess unemployment, that world is not available. In the short run, policymakers frequently have to decide how hard to fight an inflationary shock, knowing that the less they accommodate it, the more unemployment they will have. In the long run, policymakers have to decide whether to aim for a very low, or even zero, inflation rate or be willing to live with positive inflation.

Political business cycle theory **studies the interactions between economic policy decisions and political considerations.** The best-known prediction of the theory is that the business cycle mirrors the timetable of the election cycle.

We now review the building blocks of this theory.[40] We have already discussed the first, the tradeoffs from which a policymaker can choose. There are two more building blocks: how voters rate the issue (of inflation versus unemployment), and the optimal timing for influencing election results.

---

[37]See David Card and Dean Hyslop, "Does Inflation 'Grease the Wheels of the Labor Market'?" NBER working paper no. W5538, April 1996, for some evidence on the frequency of wage cuts.

[38]It is interesting to note that many universities have regulations that effectively forbid nominal wage cuts for individual faculty, although across-the-board cuts sometimes occur.

[39]William Poole presents a cogent rebuttal in "Is Inflation Too Low?" Federal Reserve Bank of St. Louis *Review,* July–August 1999.

[40]For a survey, see Alberto Alesina, "Macroeconomics and Politics," *NBER Macroeconomics Annual,* 1988; and William Nordhaus, "Alternative Approaches to the Political Business Cycle," *Brookings Papers on Economic Activity* 2 (1989). For a critical view, see K. Alec Chrystal and David A. Peel, "What Can Economics Learn from Political Science, and Vice Versa," *American Economic Review,* May 1986.

Rating the Issues

Table 7-1 showed results of Gallup opinion polls. We noted there that voters worry about inflation and unemployment when they are high. More careful study of the polls reveals a further important lesson: Voters worry about both the *level* and the *rate of change* of the inflation and unemployment rates. *Rising* unemployment increases the public's concern over unemployment. Concern over inflation depends on the expectation of rising inflation as well as on the level of inflation. These facts influence the types of policies politicians will choose.

Timing

The policymaker wants to be sure that at election time the economy is pointed in the right direction in order to garner maximum voter approval. The inflation rate and unemployment rate should be falling if possible—and should not be too high, if that can be managed. The problem is how to use the period from inauguration to election to bring the economy to just the right position.

The political business cycle hypothesis suggests the following: Politicians use restrictive policies early in an administration, raising unemployment to reduce inflation. The need for restraint can often be blamed on a previous administration. But as the election approaches, expansion takes over to ensure that falling unemployment brings voter approval even while the level of unemployment still checks inflation. According to this hypothesis, there should be a systematic cycle in unemployment, rising in the first part of a presidential term and declining in the second.

The empirical evidence on the political business cycle remains mixed.[41] The U.S. data do not show as clear a pattern over the 4-year presidential cycle as the theory would lead us to expect. Every now and then, though, as in 1969–1972, 1981–1984, and in 1988, the model seems to work to perfection.

In any event, there are factors that work against the political business cycle. In general, we know that the ability of the government to fine-tune the economy is limited. There are also difficulties specific to the implementation of politically motivated manipulations. One is that the president cannot use the business cycle fully because of midterm congressional elections. The second is that a president cannot indulge too openly in staging recessions and recoveries timed solely with a view to the election. There are risks to being caught in cynical manipulation of macroeconomic policies. Third, large macroshocks—oil shocks and wars—may on occasion overshadow the election cycle. Fourth, the executive does not control the full range of instruments. Specifically, the Fed is in large part independent and therefore need not accommodate an attempt to move the economy in an election cycle. In fact, though, the Fed has not always spoiled the game. At least on one occasion, in 1972, the Fed very obviously provided expansion just at the right time.[42] Fifth, if expectations are rational, monetary

---

[41]See Ray Fair, "Econometrics and Presidential Elections," *Journal of Economic Perspectives,* Summer 1996; and Allan Drazen, "The Political Business Cycle after 25 Years," as well as comments by Alberto Alesina and Carl Walsh in *NBER Macroeconomics Annual 2000.*

[42]See Chap. 16 for a more extensive discussion of central bank independence.

BOX 7-7   The Misery Index

The public dislikes both unemployment and inflation. One attempt to measure the political effect of unemployment and inflation is called the *misery index*, which is simply the sum of unemployment and inflation:

$$\text{Misery index} = u + \pi$$

One version of political business cycle theory suggests that the party in power will do well if the misery index is low or falling and will do poorly if the misery index is high or rising. Figure 1 shows the misery index in the United States, as well as the percentage of the presidential vote received by the candidate of the incumbent party.

The data behind Figure 1 show a weak negative relation between the change in the misery index and the fortunes of the incumbent's party. But as you can gather from the figure, the evidence for the relation is hardly overwhelming. In part, this is because so many other factors also drive voters' decisions. In addition, voters probably do not weigh unemployment and inflation equally—as the misery index does implicitly.

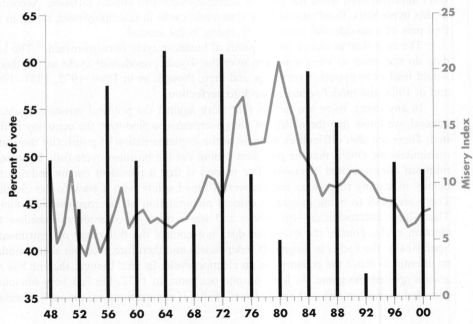

FIGURE 1   THE MISERY INDEX AND THE PERCENTAGE OF THE PRESIDENTIAL VOTE TO THE INCUMBENT.

(Source: Bureau of Labor Statistics and Statistical Abstract of the United States, 2001.)

policy expansions staged just for the elections will have only small real effects and will mainly produce inflation.

Thus, we should not be surprised that the electoral cycle is not completely regular. Nonetheless, the hypothesis should not be dismissed. No doubt, every administration would like to have the economy strongly expanding, with declining inflation, at election time. Some are skilled or lucky, and they are reelected. Others are less skilled, or unlucky, and they lose the election.

SUMMARY

1. The anatomy of unemployment in the United States reveals frequent short spells of unemployment. Nonetheless, a substantial fraction of U.S. unemployment is accounted for by those who are unemployed for a large portion of time.

2. There are significant differences in unemployment rates across age groups and race. Unemployment among black teenagers is highest, and that among white adults is lowest. The young and minorities have significantly higher unemployment rates than middle-aged whites.

3. The concept of the natural, or frictional, rate of unemployment singles out the part of unemployment that would exist even at full employment. This unemployment arises from the natural frictions of the labor market, as people move between jobs. The natural rate is hard to measure, but the consensus is to estimate it at about 5.5 percent, up from the 4 percent of the mid-1950s.

4. Policies to reduce the natural rate of unemployment involve structural labor market policies. Disincentives to employment and training, such as minimum wages, and incentives to extended job search, such as high unemployment benefits, tend to raise the natural rate. It is also possible that unemployment displays hysteresis, with extended periods of high unemployment raising the natural rate.

5. The costs of unemployment are the psychological and financial distress of the unemployed, as well as the loss of output. In addition, higher unemployment tends to hit the poorer members of society disproportionately.

6. The economy can adjust to perfectly anticipated inflation by moving to a system of indexed taxes and to nominal interest rates that reflect the expected rate of inflation. If inflation were perfectly anticipated and adjusted to, the only costs of inflation would be shoe-leather and menu costs.

7. Imperfectly anticipated inflation has important redistributive effects among sectors. Unanticipated inflation benefits monetary debtors and hurts monetary creditors. The government gains real tax revenue, and the real value of government debt declines.

8. In the U.S. housing market, unanticipated increases in inflation, combined with the tax deductibility of interest, made housing a particularly good investment during the 1960–1980 period.

9. In the U.S. economy, indexation is neither very widespread nor complete. The absence of strong indexation probably eased the adjustment to supply shocks.

10. While very high inflation rates are bad, there is some evidence that a small positive inflation rate lubricates the economy by reducing real wage rigidity.

11. The political business cycle hypothesis emphasizes the economy's direction of change. For incumbents to win an election, the unemployment rate should be falling and the inflation rate not worsening.

KEY TERMS

adjustable rate mortgage (ARM)	indexed debt	replacement ratio
	labor force	reporting effects
cost-of-living adjustment (COLA)	labor market turnover	reservation wage
	layoff	sacrifice ratio
cyclical unemployment	menu costs	search unemployment
distributional consequences	misery index	spell of unemployment
employment stability	Okun's law	unemployed person
experience rating	perfectly/imperfectly anticipated inflation	unemployment hysteresis
frequency of unemployment		unemployment pool
frictional unemployment	political business cycle theory	
indexation		

PROBLEMS

Conceptual

1. Discuss strategies whereby the government (federal, state, or local) could reduce unemployment in or among (a) depressed industries, (b) unskilled workers, (c) depressed geographical regions, (d) teenagers. Include comments on the type of unemployment you would expect to see in these various groups, as well as on the relative duration of unemployment spells that should exist among these groups.

2. Discuss how the following changes would affect the natural (or frictional) rate of unemployment:
   a. Elimination of unions.
   b. Increased participation of teenagers in the labor market.
   c. Larger fluctuations in the level of aggregate demand.
   d. Increase in unemployment benefits.
   e. Elimination of minimum wages.
   f. Larger fluctuations in the composition of aggregate demand.

3. Discuss the differences in the unemployment patterns of adults and teenagers. What does this imply about the types of jobs (on average) that the groups are seeking?

4. A reduction in minimum wages during the summer months would reduce the cost of labor to firms, but it would also reduce the wage that minimum-wage earners receive.
   a. Who would benefit from this measure?
   b. Who would lose?
   c. Would you support this program?

5. Some people say that since inflation can be reduced in the long run without an increase in unemployment, we should reduce inflation to zero. Others believe that a steady rate of inflation at, say, 3 percent, should be our goal. What are the pros and cons of these two arguments? What, in your opinion, are good long-run goals for reducing inflation and unemployment?

6. Define the sacrifice ratio. At what horizons is it not zero? Explain.

7. State Okun's law. How does it help us evaluate the cost (to society) of unemployment?

8. What costs are associated with perfectly anticipated inflation? Do these costs change as the rate of inflation changes?

9. What costs are associated with imperfectly anticipated inflation? Discuss them carefully. Who loses, and who gains, when inflation is higher than we expect?

10. Should the United States index its wages and prices? Detail the pros and cons of such a plan. How would your answer differ if you expected that the nation would face a period of extremely high inflation (say, 300 percent)?

Technical

1. The following information is to be used for calculations of the unemployment rate: Suppose there are two major groups, adults and teenagers, with adults divided into men and women. Teenagers account for 10 percent of the labor force; adults account for 90 percent. Women make up 35 percent of the adult labor force. Suppose also that the unemployment rates for these groups are as follows: teenagers, 19 percent; men, 7 percent; women, 6 percent.

   a. Calculate the aggregate unemployment rate.

   b. What if the share of teenagers in the labor force increases from 10 to 15 percent. How will this affect the aggregate unemployment rate?

Empirical

1. Use www.economagic.com or the *Economic Report of the President* to find unemployment data for the years 1992, 1997, and 2002. Use four labor force groups: males, and females, in each case 17 to 19 years of age, versus 20 years of age or over. Assuming that the labor force shares of these four groups are as given in the table below, what would 1992 and 2002 unemployment have been if the unemployment rates of the four groups had been at their 1997 level? Interpret the result.

Labor Force Shares by Demographic Groups
(In Percent)

	16–19 YEARS OLD		20 YEARS AND OVER	
	MALE	FEMALE	MALE	FEMALE
1992	2.5	2.3	51.9	43.3
1997	2.6	2.5	51.2	43.7
2002	2.4	2.4	50.9	44.3

2. Use www.economagic.com or the *Economic Report of the President* to find data on the duration of unemployment in 1997 and 2002. Compare the distribution of unemployment by duration over these years. What relationship, if any, do you find?

3. Section 7-1 introduces Okun's law—1 extra point of unemployment costs 2 percent of GDP— and illustrates the concept by the unemployment-output relation in the United States (Figure 7-1). After reading the chapter, you might ask yourself: But does this hold in other countries

as well? In this exercise we are going to investigate the unemployment-output relationship for Australia (if you are interested, you might repeat this exercise for other countries as well) and see whether Okun's law fits it.

a.   Go to www.economagic.com and download data for Australian unemployment rate and RGDP over the period 1960–2001 into an EXCEL file. The easiest way to do this is to do two searches. First, search for "Australia" and "GDP." Choose the variable "GDP Expenditure: GDP (AUS$ million, Average 1997/98 prices, SA): Australia,"[1] transform the series into annual data by choosing the option "annual averages," and copy it into an EXCEL file. Second, do a search for "Australia" and "unemployment." Choose the variable "Australia: Unemployment Rate; NSA" and copy it into the EXCEL file.

b.   Calculate the annual growth rate of RGDP ($[RGDP_t - RGDP_{t-1}]/RGDP_{t-1} \times 100$) and the change in the unemployment rate ($u_t - u_{t-1}$). Create a scatterplot that has the change in the unemployment rate on the X axis and the growth rate of RGDP on the Y axis. What is the relationship between unemployment and output in Australia? Visually, on average by how much would an increase of 1 percentage point in the unemployment rate affect output?

*c.   If you have taken a statistics class, use EXCEL or a statistical program in order to run the following regression:

$$RGDP \text{ growth} = c + \beta \times \text{change in unemployment rate} + \epsilon$$

What is the implied slope? What does it mean? Is it statistically significant? Can you set up a test to see if it is different from the usually cited number of 2 percent?

4.   One of the determinants of the natural rate of unemployment is the ability and desire of the unemployed to keep looking for a better job. A possible proxy of this concept would be the average number of search methods used by somebody in need of a job. We investigated variations in unemployment rates by different demographic groups (age, sex, race). Before taking a look at the data, ask yourselves the following questions and write down your hypothesized answers for them.

a.   Over the last 30 years, do you think that people started using more or fewer methods of searching for a job?

b.   Do you think that men or women use more job search methods?

c.   Do you think that teenagers (16–19), young workers (25–34), or mature workers (35–44) use more job search methods?

d.   Do you think that white or black people use more job search methods?

e.   At any moment in time the people who are looking for a job can be divided in four different groups: people who lost their job, people who quit their job in order to find a better one, people who just entered the labor force and are in search of their first job, and people who reentered the labor force after a break (they had once had a job). Try to order these groups in terms of their desire of finding a new job, as proxied by the average number of search methods used.

[1]Since the name of the variable says "Average 1997/98 prices," it means that we have a measure of GDP at constant prices. Thus, it is RGDP.

*An asterisk denotes a more difficult problem.

Now that you have certain expectations in your mind, let us take a look at the data and see whether you are right or not. Go to www.economagic.com. Under "Browse by Source," "Bureau of Labor Statistics" choose "US Civilian Labor Force: 22,000+ series." Scroll down the page and choose "Average number of search methods used." Either by using the charting options on the website or by copying the data into an EXCEL file, create five graphs:

Overall average number of search methods used.

Average number of search methods used by sex (female vs. male).

Average number of search methods used by race (white vs. black).

Average number of search methods used by age (16–19, 25–34, 35–44).

Average number of search methods used by reason for search (job losers, job leavers, new entrants to labor force, and reentrants to labor force).

Were your answers right? Can the difference in average number of search methods used by black and white people explain the difference in unemployment rates between these two groups?

CHAPTER 8

Policy

CHAPTER HIGHLIGHTS

- Uncertainty about the economy places limits on the reach of successful policy.

- Our imperfect knowledge of the economy sometimes argues for a go-slow approach in the application of economic policy.

- Choice of policy targets should be influenced by the limits of our knowledge as well as by the extent of our knowledge.

- Democracies face the difficult problem of structuring policymaking bodies so as to avoid temptation toward an inflationary bias.

This chapter is about policy.

But isn't *everything* in the text either an explanation of macroeconomic outcomes or a study of how we might use policy to change those outcomes? Yes, but while elsewhere in the text we focus on our knowledge of the macroeconomy, in this chapter we ask how wise policymaking can be guided by an understanding of the limits of our knowledge. Policymakers ought to take heed of our uncertainty about the best target for the economy. Once a target is chosen, policymakers need to remember that we are unsure of the exact magnitude and timing of the effects of policy actions. Finally, policymakers must account for the effects that policies have on the public's expectations of the future.

In this chapter we look at how timing issues and specific kinds of uncertainty suggest particular ways of formulating policy. We begin by looking at lags in policymaking and policy implementation. Decisions cannot be made instantaneously, and even after a policy decision is made, implementation can take time. Further, the effect of policy may work its way through the economy slowly and with uncertain speed. New policies change the expectations of economic agents. The changed expectations themselves affect the economy but are hard to predict and hard to measure. For all these reasons, plus ongoing uncertainty about the "right" model for the economy, predictions of what a policy will do are uncertain. This argues for a degree of caution in choosing a policy. In addition to these general points, this chapter emphasizes some of the practical issues in policymaking.

This is the "whoa, not so fast" chapter, in the sense that we explore the limitations of macroeconomic policy. Acknowledging the limits of policy is very different from attempting to avoid policy altogether. *A large country does not have the option of* not *having a macroeconomic policy.* The choices of government spending, of taxation, and of the money supply *will* affect the economy. So in deciding on their budgets and on monetary policy, governments need to consider how best to affect the economy—or at least, how to avoid some common mistakes.

 ## 8-1

POLICY: WORKING BACKWARD

In explaining the macroeconomy, we start with an observed shock or proposed policy change; work through the details of the relations underlying aggregate supply and aggregate demand; ask how the *AS* and *AD* curves shift; and then, taking into account the slopes of the *AS* and *AD* curves, calculate output and the price level. Although policymakers use the same tools, they have to run the exercise in reverse. Policymakers begin by asking where output and the price level (or, if you prefer, unemployment and inflation) should be. Then the policymakers ask how much they need to shift *AS* or *AD* to hit those targets. The final calculation is to ask how large a policy change is required to move *AS* or *AD* the necessary distance. Box 8-1 works out an example of this sort of policy formulation.

BOX 8-1   A Policy Exercise—Ah, if Only It Were This Easy

You are in charge of the economy—at least until the end of this box. Right now the economy stands at 5.5 percent unemployment. Your task is to use monetary policy to move the economy to full employment.

STEP-BY-STEP

1. "Full employment" is 4 percent unemployment. How do we know? That's what the law says in the United States. So our target is to reduce unemployment by 1.5 percentage points.
2. According to Okun's law (see Chapter 7), a 1.5 point reduction in unemployment requires a 3 percent increase in output.
3. If you believe that aggregate demand can be completely described by the quantity theory, then a 1 percent increase in the money supply increases nominal GDP by 1 percent. If you also believe that prices are completely fixed in the short run, an increase in nominal GDP translates completely into an increase in real GDP. So each 1 percent increase in the money supply causes a 1 percent increase in real GDP.
4. Our monetary policy answer is to increase the money supply by 3 percent.

INCH-BY-INCH

1. Is this policy easily implemented? We will see in later chapters that the central bank lacks perfect control over the money supply, as it has to work through the banking system. So perhaps you cannot simply, by fiat, increase the money supply by 3 percent (an implementation practicality).

We turn now to look at some of the implications of uncertainty for policymaking as well as some of the practicalities faced in the policymaking process.[1]

8-2
LAGS IN THE EFFECTS OF POLICY

Suppose that the economy is at full employment and has been affected by an aggregate demand disturbance that will reduce the equilibrium level of income below full employment. Suppose further that there was no advance warning of this disturbance

---

[1]The president of the Federal Reserve Bank of St. Louis, William Poole, presents a hands-on view of these issues in "A Policymaker Confronts Uncertainty," *Federal Reserve Bank of St. Louis Review,* September–October 1998. See also Frederic Mishkin, "What Should Central Banks Do?" Federal Reserve Bank of St. Louis *Review,* November–December 2000.

2. Does the quantity theory link from money to output really work instantaneously? Does it take 10 seconds? 10 weeks? 10 months? (Policy lags matter, and timing is uncertain.)

3. Does money growth really translate proportionately into output growth?* In other words, is the "multiplier" of output on money growth 1.0? (There is multiplier uncertainty.)†

4. Are prices really fixed over the policy horizon? On learning of our proposed policy change, will economic agents raise their expectations of inflation? (What is the reaction to our policy?)

5. You didn't really believe full employment is 4 percent unemployment just because federal law says so, did you? (Target uncertainty.)

SLOWLY I TURN

In the face of uncertainty we should conduct a risk analysis. What can go wrong if we start with the 3 percent increase in the money supply computed above and then just keep increasing the money supply until unemployment hits 4 percent?

If we're persistent we *can* get unemployment down to 4 percent. That's true even if full employment is 5 percent or higher. The hitch is that we can move unemployment below the natural rate—but only temporarily. In the process we pump up the money supply enough to cause inflation. And the inflation may not show up until several quarters *after* our policy move. And if we continue to pump up the money supply, we will generate ever higher prices.

Having the wisdom to abandon an unattainable target is difficult for politicians and technocrats alike.

---

*Of course not. If life were so simple, macroeconomics texts would be a lot shorter.

†In general, "multiplier" means the effect of one variable on another. For example, if a one unit change in money leads to a one unit change in output the multiplier is one.

---

and that, consequently, no policy actions were taken in anticipation of its occurrence. Policymakers now have to decide *whether to respond at all* and *how* to respond to the disturbance.

The first concern is to distinguish whether the disturbance is *permanent,* or at least very persistent, or *transitory* and thus short-lived. Suppose the disturbance is only transitory, such as a one-period reduction in consumption spending. When the disturbance is transitory, so that consumption rapidly reverts to its initial level, the best policy may be to do nothing at all. Provided suppliers or producers do not mistakenly interpret the transitory decrease in demand as permanent, they will absorb it by production and inventory changes rather than by capacity adjustments. The disturbance will affect income in this period but will have very little permanent effect. Since today's policy actions take time to have an effect, today's actions would be hitting an economy that would otherwise have been close to full employment, and they would tend to move the economy *away* from the full-employment level. Thus, if a disturbance is temporary and has no long-lived effects and policy operates with a lag, the best policy is to do nothing.

Figure 8-1 illustrates the main issue. Assume that an aggregate demand disturbance reduces output below potential, starting at time t_0. Without active policy intervention, output declines for a while but then recovers and reaches the full-employment level again at time t_2. Consider next the path of GDP under an active stabilization policy, but one that works with the disadvantage of lags. Thus expansionary policy might be initiated at time t_1 and start taking effect some time after. Output now tends to recover faster as a consequence of the expansion but, because of poor dosage and/or timing, actually overshoots the full-employment level. By time t_3, restrictive policy is initiated, and some time after, output starts turning down toward full employment and may well continue cycling for a while. In this example, "stabilization" policy may actually *destabilize* the economy.

One of the main difficulties of policymaking is establishing whether or not a disturbance is temporary. It was clear enough in the case of World War II that a high level of defense expenditures would be required for some years. However, in the case of the OPEC oil embargo of 1973–1974, it was not at all clear how long the embargo would last or whether the high prices for oil that were established in late 1973 would persist. At the time, there were many who argued that the oil cartel would not survive and that oil prices would soon fall—that is, that the disturbance was temporary. "Soon" turned out to be 12 years.

Let us suppose, however, that it is known that the disturbance will have effects that will last for several quarters and that the level of income will, without intervention, be below the full-employment level for some time. What lags do policymakers encounter?

We now consider the steps required before action can be taken after a disturbance has occurred, and then we examine the process by which that policy action affects the economy. There are delays, or lags, at every stage, and these can be divided into two stages: an *inside lag,* which is the time period it takes to undertake a policy

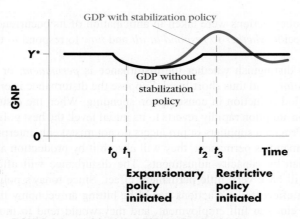

FIGURE 8-1   LAGS AND DESTABILIZING POLICY.

action—such as a tax cut or an increase in the money supply—and an *outside lag,* which describes the timing of the effects of the policy action on the economy. The inside lag, in turn, is divided into recognition, decision, and action lags.

THE RECOGNITION LAG

The *recognition lag* is the period that elapses between the time a disturbance occurs and the time the policymakers recognize that action is required. This lag could, in principle, be *negative* if the disturbance can be predicted and appropriate policy actions considered *before* it even occurs. For example, we know that seasonal factors affect behavior. Thus, it is known that at Christmas the demand for money is high. Rather than allow this to exert a restrictive effect on the economy, the Fed will accommodate this seasonal demand by an expansion in the supply of money.

In general, however, the recognition lag is positive, so time elapses between the disturbance and the recognition that active policy is required. In a classic work, Kareken and Solow studied the history of policymaking and concluded that on average the recognition lag is about 5 months.[2] The lag was found to be somewhat shorter when the required policy was expansionary and somewhat longer when restrictive policy was required. The speed with which tax cuts follow sharp increases in unemployment was clearly evident when the Bush administration took office in 2001.

THE DECISION AND ACTION LAGS

The *decision lag*—the delay between the recognition of the need for action and the policy decision—differs between monetary and fiscal policy.[3] The Federal Reserve System's Open Market Committee meets frequently to discuss and decide on policy. Thus, once the need for a policy action has been recognized, the decision lag for monetary policy is short. Further, the *action lag*—the lag between the policy decision and its implementation—for monetary policy is also short. The major monetary policy actions can be undertaken almost as soon as a decision has been made. Thus, under the existing arrangements of the Federal Reserve System, the decision lag for monetary policy is short and the action lag practically zero.

However, fiscal policy actions are less rapid. Once the need for a fiscal policy action has been recognized, the administration has to prepare legislation for that action. Next, the legislation has to be considered and approved by both houses of Congress before the policy change can be made. That may be a lengthy process. Even after the legislation has been approved, the policy change has still to be put into effect. If the

[2] See John Kareken and Robert Solow, "Lags in Monetary Policy," in *Stabilization Policies,* prepared for the Commission on Money and Credit (Englewood Cliffs, NJ: Prentice Hall, 1963). With regard to monetary policy, see Charles A.E. Goodhart, "Monetary Transmission Lags and the Formulation of the Policy Decision on Interest Rates," Federal Reserve Bank of St. Louis *Review,* July–August 2001.

[3] Monetary policy, actions by the Federal Reserve to change the money supply on interest rates, and fiscal policy, changes in government spending and tax programs, are discussed in detail in Chaps. 9–11.

BOX 8-2   How Fast Can the Fed Move in an Emergency?

New York City is the financial center of the United States and much of the world. Much of the computing and communications facilities for the financial system—and many of the people who keep it running—were located in or near the World Trade Center. The Federal Reserve Bank of New York, which conducts most of the actual financial operations required to implement monetary policy in the United States, is located two blocks from the World Trade Center. When the United States was attacked on September 11, 2001, there was a risk that the financial system could have been brought to its knees.

Within minutes of the attack, security personnel moved New York Fed employees into the inner core of the building and reversed the ventilation system to keep smoke out. Fed officials around the country were in immediate contact with major financial intermediaries to collect information about developments in the financial system. On the day of the attack and over the next few days, the Fed pumped reserves into the financial system—30 billion dollars more on September 12 than on the same day of the preceding week. And the Fed made huge temporary loans to financial institutions—45.5 billion dollars on September 12—nearly 50 times the loans made the previous Wednesday.

Cooperation between the Fed and the private sector in the hours and days immediately following the attack guaranteed that the financial system would have all the liquidity it needed to meet the crisis. The September 11 attacks were the worst on U.S. soil since the Civil War. Because of quick and resolute Fed action, the financial system survived with hardly a ripple.

fiscal policy takes the form of a change in tax rates, it may be some time before the change in tax rates begins to be reflected in paychecks—that is, there may be an action lag. On occasion, though, as in early 1975 when taxes were reduced, the fiscal decision lag may be short; in 1975 it was about 2 months.

AUTOMATIC STABILIZERS

The existence of the inside lag in policymaking focuses attention on the use of automatic stabilizers. An *automatic stabilizer* **is any mechanism in the economy that automatically—that is, without case-by-case government intervention—reduces the amount by which output changes in response to a shock to the economy.** One of the major benefits of automatic stabilizers is that their inside lag is zero. The most important automatic stabilizer is the income tax. It stabilizes the economy by reducing the multiplier effects of any disturbance to aggregate demand. The multiplier for the

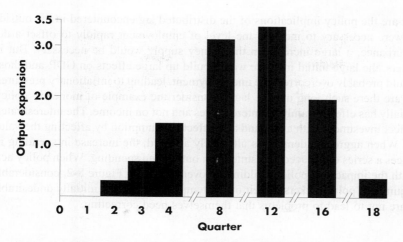

FIGURE 8-2   MONETARY POLICY MULTIPLIER FROM THE DRI MODEL.

effects of changes in autonomous spending on GDP is inversely related to the income tax rate, as we will see in Chapter 9. Unemployment compensation is another automatic stabilizer. When workers become unemployed and reduce their consumption, that reduction in consumption demand tends to have multiplier effects on output. Those multiplier effects are reduced when a worker receives unemployment compensation because disposable income is reduced by less than the loss in earnings.

Although built-in stabilizers have desirable effects, they cannot be carried too far without also affecting the overall performance of the economy. The multiplier could be reduced to 1 by increasing the tax rate to 100 percent, and that would appear to be a stabilizing influence on the economy. But with 100 percent marginal tax rates, who would want to work? There are limits on the extent to which automatic stabilizers are desirable.[4]

THE OUTSIDE LAG

The inside lag of policy is a *discrete lag*—so many months—from recognition to decision and implementation. The outside lag is generally a *distributed lag:* Once the policy action has been taken, its effects on the economy are spread over time. There may be a small immediate effect of a policy action, but other effects occur later.

The idea that policy operates on aggregate demand and income with a distributed lag is illustrated by the dynamic multiplier in Figure 8-2. There we show the effects over time of a once-and-for-all 1 percent increase in the money supply in period zero. The impact is initially very small, but it continues to increase over a long period of time. The lags of monetary policy are represented by the fact that any significant impact of money on spending and output takes several quarters and builds up only gradually.

[4]For a discussion of the history of automatic stabilizers, see Herbert Stein, *The Fiscal Revolution in America: Policy in Pursuit of Reality* (Washington DC: American Enterprise Institute for Public Policy Research, 1996).

What are the policy implications of the distributed lag encountered in the outside lag? If it were necessary to increase the level of employment rapidly to offset a demand disturbance, a large increase in the money supply would be necessary. But in later quarters, the large initial increase would build up large effects on GDP, and those effects would probably overcorrect the unemployment, leading to inflationary pressures.

Why are there such long outside lags? Consider the example of monetary policy, which initially has effects mainly on interest rates and not on income. The interest rates, in turn, affect investment with a lag, and also affect consumption by affecting the value of wealth. When aggregate demand is ultimately affected, the increase in spending itself produces a series of induced adjustments in output and spending. When policy acts slowly, with the impacts of policy building up over time as in Figure 8-2, considerable skill is required of policymakers if their own attempts to correct an initially undesirable situation are not to lead to problems that themselves need correcting.

MONETARY VERSUS FISCAL POLICY LAGS

Fiscal policy and, certainly, changes in government spending—which act directly on aggregate demand—affect income more rapidly than monetary policy. However, while fiscal policy has a shorter outside lag, it has a considerably longer inside lag. The long inside lag makes fiscal policy less useful for stabilization and means that fiscal policy tends to be used relatively infrequently to try to stabilize the economy.

Our analysis of lags indicates one difficulty in undertaking stabilizing short-term policy actions: It takes time to set the policies in action, and then the policies themselves take time to affect the economy. But that is not the only difficulty. Further difficulties arise because policymakers cannot be certain about the size and the timing of the effects of policy actions.

GRADUALIST VERSUS COLD-TURKEY POLICIES

Faced with a given policy objective—for example, to reduce inflation—a policymaker must choose between gradualist and cold-turkey policies. Gradualist policies move the economy slowly toward the target, while cold-turkey policies are those that try to hit the target as quickly as possible. Cold-turkey policies generate a "shock effect," which can be bad if the shock is disruptive but good if dramatic action adds to the policymaker's credibility. Gradualist policies, in contrast, have the advantage of allowing for the incorporation of new information as the policy plays out.

8-3

EXPECTATIONS AND REACTIONS

Uncertainty about the effects of policies on the economy arise because policymakers do not know the precise values of multipliers. The government is always uncertain about how the economy will react to policy changes. In practice, governments work with econometric models of the economy in estimating the effects of policy changes. **An *econometric model* is a statistical description of the economy or some part of it.**

Government uncertainty about the effects of policy arises partly because the government does not know the true model of the economy and partly because it does not know what expectations firms and consumers have. In this section we concentrate on the role of expectations.

REACTION UNCERTAINTIES

Suppose that in early 2010, because of weakness in the economy, the government decides to cut taxes. The tax cut is meant to be strictly temporary—a brief shot in the arm to get the economy moving and nothing more.

In figuring out how big a tax cut is needed, the government has to guess how the public will react to a temporary tax cut. One possible answer is that since the tax cut will be temporary, it will not affect long-term income very much and thus not affect spending by much. That suggests that to be useful, a temporary tax cut would have to be large. Alternatively, perhaps consumers will believe that the tax cut will last much longer than the government says—after all, the public knows that raising taxes is difficult. In this case the marginal propensity to spend out of a tax cut announced as temporary would be larger. A smaller tax cut would be enough to raise spending a lot. If the government is wrong in its guess about consumers' reactions, it could destabilize rather than stabilize the economy.

CHANGES IN POLICY REGIME

A special problem emerges when the government changes the way it has traditionally responded to disturbances. For example, a government that has typically cut taxes in recessions and now no longer does so (e.g., because the deficit is large) may find that the cut had been expected and that there is an extra drop in demand when consumers realize taxes will not be cut this time.

It is particularly important to consider the effects of a given policy action itself on expectations, since it is possible that a new type of policy will affect the way in which expectations are formed.[5] Suppose that the Federal Reserve System announced that from now on its policy would be aimed *solely* at maintaining price stability and that in response to any price-level increase it would reduce the money supply (and vice versa). If people believed the announcement, they would not base expectations of money growth and inflation on the past behavior of the inflation rate.

However, people are not likely to fully believe such an announcement immediately. The policymakers are likely to lack full *credibility*. **Policymakers have credibility when their announcements are believed by economic agents.** Typically, policymakers

---

[5]The interactions of policy and expectations have been the focus of the rational expectations approach to macroeconomics, introduced in Chap. 6. For a very early statement, see Thomas J. Sargent and Neil Wallace, "Rational Expectations and the Theory of Economic Policy," *Journal of Monetary Economics,* April 1976.

BOX 8-3   How Good Are Macroeconomic Forecasts?

In business and finance and in government, knowing what will happen in the economy next quarter and next year is critical as an ingredient for planning, for portfolio selection, and for policymaking. The demand for forecasts is met by a broad group of professional forecasters. The methods used range from informal, almost back-of-the-envelope, calculations to sophisticated macroeconometric models where literally thousands of equations representing the economy are the basis of the outlook.*

How good are the forecasts? Table 1 shows the forecasts and the actual results from three sources. The first is the Congressional Budget Office (CBO), which uses macroeconometric models as the background for revenue and outlay projections. The second is the administration forecasts. The third source is the Blue Chip forecast, a consensus of private forecasters. The projections in the table are obviously sometimes off—the forecasters missed low growth in 1990–1991 and high growth in 1995–2000. From 1993 through 1995, in contrast, the forecasts were right on target.

How can forecasters go wrong? They may not predict disturbances (the Gulf war, for example); they may misread the current state of the economy and hence base their forecasts on a wrong picture of the present situation; and they may misjudge the

*To learn about a large-scale econometric model, see F. Brayton and P. A. Tinsley, "A Guide to FRB/US: A Macroeconomic Model of the United States," Board of Governors of the Federal Reserve System, October 1996.

have to earn credibility, by behaving consistently over long periods, so that people learn to believe what they say.[6]

Earning credibility is likely to be costly. Consider what happens if the Fed announces it will keep inflation low and is not believed. Then the expected inflation rate is above the actual inflation rate, and—as the Phillips curve shows—a recession follows. Only over time, as the new policies are understood, is credibility earned.

As an example, credibility issues are always a problem when governments promise to keep exchange rates fixed. In the 1980s, governments in the European Monetary System of quasi-fixed exchange rates announced that they would no longer respond to increases in wages and prices with devaluations. Initially, the policymakers lacked credibility, and inflation stayed high. But eventually, by holding fast, and with the aid of recessions, policymakers gained credibility and inflation came down. Then in 1992, under the macroeconomic impact of German unification, major devaluations were forced on reluctant governments, and their credibility was seriously dented.

[6]See Alan S. Blinder, "Central Bank Credibility: Why Do We Care? How Do We Build It?" *American Economic Review,* December 2000.

timing or vigor of the government's monetary and fiscal responses to booms or recessions. The fact is that forecasting has not reached perfection, particularly at major turning points in the economy, as illustrated in the table.[†]

TABLE 1	How Accurate Are Macroeconomic Forecasts? Actual versus Forecast 2-Year Average Growth Rates for Real Output			
	ACTUAL	CBO	ADMINISTRATION	BLUE CHIP
1976–1977	5.2	6.2	5.9	—
1986–1987	3.2	3.1	3.7	3.0
1990–1991	0.7	2.0	2.8	1.9
1993–1994	3.3	2.9	2.9	3.0
1994–1995	3.3	2.8	2.9	2.8
1995–1996	3.1	2.4	2.6	2.6
1996–1997	4.0	1.9	2.2	2.1
1997–1998	4.4	2.1	2.1	2.2
1998–1999	4.2	2.3	2.2	2.4
1999–2000	3.9	2.0	2.2	2.3
2000–2001	2.0	3.2	3.0	3.3

Source: *CBO's Economic Forecasting Record*, Table 2, A Supplement to *The Budget and Economic Outlook: Fiscal Years 2003–2012*, Congressional Budget Office, February 2002.

[†]Stephen K. McNees, "How Large Are Economic Forecast Errors?" *New England Economic Review*, July–August 1992, provides detailed examination of the historical record of forecasters and identifies what they are good at and what they seemingly do not do so well. Also, Christopher A. Sims, "The Role of Models and Probabilities in the Monetary Policy Process," *Brookings Papers on Economic Activity*, 2 (2002).

8-4

UNCERTAINTY AND ECONOMIC POLICY

Uncertainty about the expectations of firms and consumers is one reason that policymakers can go wrong in using active stabilization policy. Another reason is that it is difficult to forecast disturbances, such as changes in the price of oil, that might disturb the economy before policy takes effect.

A third reason is that economists and therefore policymakers do not know enough about the true structure of the economy. We distinguish between uncertainty about the correct model of the economy and uncertainty about the precise values of the parameters or coefficients within a given model of the economy, even though the distinction is not watertight.

First, there is considerable disagreement and therefore uncertainty about the correct model of the economy, as evidenced by the large number of macroeconometric models. Reasonable economists can and do differ about what theory and empirical evidence suggest are the correct behavioral functions of the economy. Generally, each economist will have reasons for favoring one particular form and will use that form.

But, being reasonable, the economist will recognize that the particular formulation being used may not be the correct one and will thus regard its predictions as subject to a margin of error. In turn, policymakers will know that there are different predictions about the effects of a given policy, and they will want to consider the range of predictions that are being made in deciding on policy.

Second, even within a given model there is uncertainty about the values of parameters and multipliers. The statistical evidence does allow us to say something about the likely range of parameters or multipliers, so we can at least get some idea of the type of errors that could result from a particular policy action.[7]

Uncertainty about the size of the effects that will result from any particular policy action—whether because of uncertainty about expectations or about the structure of the economy—is known as *multiplier uncertainty*. For instance, our best estimate of the multiplier of an increase in government spending might be 1.2. If GDP has to be increased by $60 billion, we would increase government spending by $50 billion. But the statistical evidence might be better interpreted as saying only that we can be quite confident that the multiplier is between .9 and 1.5. In that case, when we increase government spending by $50 billion, we expect GDP to rise by some amount between $45 and $75 billion.

How should a policymaker react in the face of these uncertainties? The more precisely policymakers are informed about the relevant parameters, the more activist the policy can afford to be. Conversely, if there is a considerable range of error in the estimate of the relevant parameters—in our example, the multiplier—then policy should be more modest. With poor information, very active policy runs a large danger of introducing unnecessary fluctuations in the economy.

THE POLICY PORTFOLIO UNDER UNCERTAINTY

Consider the choice between monetary policy and fiscal policy when both monetary and fiscal policy multipliers are uncertain. The best procedure is to employ a *portfolio of policy instruments*—use a weaker dose of both monetary and fiscal policies. The reason for practicing *diversification* in this way is that there is at least a chance that the errors in estimating one multiplier will be offset by the errors in estimating the other.[8] With good luck, errors in setting policy will partially cancel one another. Even if we are unlucky, we are no worse off than if we had relied fully on one instrument.[9]

---

[7]We are discussing here confidence intervals about estimates of parameters; see Robert Pindyck and Daniel Rubinfeld, *Econometric Models and Economic Forecasts* (New York: McGraw-Hill, 1997), for further discussion.

[8]If you have studied finance, you will be familiar with the notion of picking a *portfolio* of investments in order to reduce risk through *diversification*. The choice of words here is no coincidence—the principles of choosing a policy portfolio are the same as those involved in choosing an investment portfolio.

[9]The practice of coordinating monetary and fiscal policies has an interesting downside for macroeconomists. We are, of course, very interested in separating the effects of one type of policy from those of another. But if two policies are generally used in concert, it is very difficult to use historical data to know which policy was responsible for the observed results.

◆ O P T I O N A L ◆

MULTIPLIER UNCERTAINTY AND POLICY: A FORMAL ANALYSIS

Multipliers measure the quantitative effect of policy. The argument that the less certain we are about the size of a multiplier, the more cautious we should be in application of the associated policy instrument is intuitively plausible. This intuition was first given formal expression by William Brainard.[10] We present a simplified version here.

Suppose that our entire knowledge of the effect of monetary policy on the economy can be boiled down to one equation:

$$Y = \beta M \tag{1}$$

where Y is output, M is the money stock, and β is the monetary policy multiplier. Y^* is the target for output. Because we may not be able to hit the target precisely, we need a rule for evaluating the success of policy that measures the damage done when we miss the target. While we hope that Y will hit Y^* exactly, we recognize there will generally be some gap between actual and target outcomes, $Y - Y^*$. We "keep score"; that is, we measure the damage attributable to a "miss" with the *loss function:*

$$L = \tfrac{1}{2}(Y - Y^*)^2 \tag{2}$$

Note that this loss function puts a much larger penalty on large losses than on small losses. We evaluate the success of a policy choice, M, by substituting βM for the realized value of output, Y, in equation (2). The *marginal loss function, ML(M)*, measures the change in the loss function from a small change in the policy instrument M. As is usual in economics, one way to think about minimizing losses is to set the marginal loss to zero. The marginal loss function corresponding to equations (1) and (2) is given by[11]

$$ML(M) = (\beta M - Y^*) \times \beta \tag{3}$$

We now work out an example, first when the multiplier is known and then when it is uncertain. Suppose that our target is $Y^* = 3$ and that we somehow know the multiplier is exactly $\beta = \overline{\beta} = 1$. The appropriate policy is obviously to set $M = 3$, but to carry out the formal analysis, we set the marginal loss equal to zero in equation (4) and solve for the optimal policy in equation (5):

$$ML(M) = 0 = (Y - Y^*) \times \overline{\beta} = (\overline{\beta}M - Y^*) \times \overline{\beta} \tag{4}$$

$$M = \frac{Y^*}{\overline{\beta}} \tag{5}$$

So we choose $M = 3/1 = 3$; observe $Y = 1 \times 3 = 3 = Y^*$; hit the target exactly; and according to the rating from equation (2), achieve a perfect, zero-loss, score.

Now, suppose instead that β is either .5 or 1.5, with a 50 percent chance for either value. The average value of β remains $\overline{\beta} = (0.5 + 1.5)/2 = 1.0$, just as in the previous example; the difference is that we have introduced uncertainty. Suppose basing

[10]William Brainard, "Uncertainty and the Effectiveness of Policy," *American Economic Review*, May 1967.

[11]If you are comfortable with calculus, you will see that all we are doing is substituting equation (1) into equation (2) and then taking the derivative with respect to M.

policy on this average value, we again set policy at $M = 3$. (This is called the *certainty-equivalence policy*.) If β is actually .5, we will undershoot the target; if β equals 1.5, we will overshoot. However, we can do a little better by shading in the direction of undershooting rather than overshooting, because a low value of β means that the marginal impact of the policy is lower.

We can work out the optimal choice for M in this case by weighting the marginal loss function with equal chances for each value of β. The weighted marginal loss function is

$$ML(M) = 0 = 50\% \times [(0.5M - Y^*) \times 0.5] + 50\% \times [(1.5M - Y^*) \times 1.5] \quad (6)$$

$$M = \frac{Y^*}{1.25} \quad (7)$$

Equation (7) tells us to set M to 2.4 instead of 3—we are more conservative in our use of policy than we would be under certainty equivalence. Thus Brainard's analysis affirms our intuition that uncertainty should lead to caution.

8-5

TARGETS, INSTRUMENTS, AND INDICATORS: A TAXONOMY

Economic variables play a variety of roles in policy discussions. It is useful to divide variables into *targets, instruments,* and *indicators.*[12]

Targets—Targets are identified goals of policy. While the ultimate target is "the good of society," we focus more specifically on output and prices, unemployment and inflation. Targets are usefully subdivided into *ultimate targets* and *intermediate targets.* An example of an ultimate target is "to achieve zero inflation." As part of overall economic policy, a particular policymaking unit may be assigned the task of hitting a particular intermediate target. For example, the central bank may be instructed to aim for 2 percent annual growth of the money stock. Even though money growth per se is not an ultimate economic goal, targeting money growth may be the appropriate task (intermediate target) to assign to the central bank.

Instruments—Instruments are the tools the policymaker manipulates directly. For example, a central bank might have an exchange-rate target. Its instrument would be the purchase or sale of foreign exchange.

Indicators—Indicators are economic variables that signal us as to whether we are getting closer to our desired targets. As an example, increases in interest rates (an indicator) sometimes signal that the market anticipates increased future inflation (a target). So indicators provide information feedback that allows a policymaker to adjust the instruments in order to do a better job of hitting the target.

[12]See Benjamin M. Friedman, "Targets, Instruments, and Indicators of Monetary Policy," *Journal of Monetary Economics,* October 1975.

Most economists agree that the best way to reach ultimate targets is for policy-makers to use indicators to provide additional information in computing the best adjustments to the available instruments.

The categorization of variables into target, instrument, or indicator is sometimes situational. For example, in some years central banks have treated interest rates as intermediate targets. In other years central banks have used interest rates as indicators of the success of money supply policy. Indeed, policymakers often face a choice of whether to use a particular policy tool as an instrument, destroying its value as an indicator, or to keep the tool as an indicator and forgo its use as a direct instrument.

8-6
ACTIVIST POLICY

We look at two questions in this section. First, Should policymakers actively try to off-set shocks? In particular, Should they attempt to fine-tune the economy or should they limit themselves to respond only to major shocks? If our answers lean toward activism, we then ask whether responses should be precommitted to specified rules, or whether policymakers should exercise case-by-case discretion.

The list of difficulties in the way of successful policymaking that we have outlined may have raised the question, Why should one believe that policy can do *anything* to reduce fluctuations in the economy?[13]

Indeed, Milton Friedman and others argued that there should be no use of active countercyclical monetary policy and that monetary policy should be confined to making the money supply grow at a constant rate. The precise value of the constant rate of money growth, Friedman suggests, is less important than the fact that monetary growth should be constant and that policy should *not* respond to disturbances. At various times, he has suggested growth rates for money of 2 or 4 or 5 percent. As Friedman has expressed it, "By setting itself a steady course and keeping to it, the monetary authority could make a major contribution to promoting economic stability. By making that course one of steady but moderate growth in the quantity of money, it would make a major contribution to avoidance of either inflation or deflation of prices."[14] Friedman thus advocates a simple monetary rule in which the Fed does not respond to the condition of the economy. Policies that respond to the current or predicted state of the economy are called *activist policies*. Interestingly, Friedman does make an exception to this rule in the face of extreme disturbances.

In discussing the desirability of activist monetary and fiscal policy, we want to distinguish between policy actions taken in response to major disturbances to the economy and *fine tuning,* in which policy variables are continually adjusted in response to small disturbances in the economy. We see no case for arguing that monetary and fiscal

---

[13]An excellent discussion of the issues is found in Steven Sheffrin, *The Making of Economic Policy* (Oxford, England: Basil Blackwell, 1989).

[14]Milton Friedman, "The Role of Monetary Policy," *American Economic Review,* March 1968. See also his book, *A Program for Monetary Stability* (New York: Fordham University Press, 1959).

BOX 8-4   Fine Tuning and Monetary Policy in the 1980s and 1990s

At the same time as the analytic arguments against fine tuning and discretionary policy were being refined in the 1980s and 1990s, the Fed, under the chairmanship first of Paul Volcker (1979–1987) and then Alan Greenspan (1987–present), was in one of the most successful periods of implementation of monetary policy in its history—and the policies were clearly discretionary.

What happened? Through the 1970s, inflation had been rising from business cycle to business cycle; in each cycle, the peak inflation rate was higher than it had been in the previous cycle. Paul Volcker's priority as chairman was to bring inflation under control. That goal was achieved, albeit at the cost of the recession of 1981–1982, during which the unemployment rate hit the highest level of the post-World War II period, 10.8 percent.

When Alan Greenspan took over in August 1987, the inflation rate was 4.6 percent and the economy was fundamentally at full employment. Two months later, the new chairman of the Fed was faced with a potentially massive crisis, when the stock market crashed on October 19, 1987. The Fed rose to the challenge by providing enough liquidity to make sure there was no financial panic.

Perhaps partly as a result of that injection of liquidity, inflationary pressures continued to rise through the end of the decade, and the Fed accordingly tightened monetary policy by raising interest rates. Eventually, in July 1990, a recession began. However, the recession was shallow, with unemployment rising to a maximum of only 7.7 percent. Once the recession was clearly recognized, the Fed cut interest rates, slowly and repeatedly. The recession ended in March 1991, and the recovery continued as inflation declined.

By the end of 1994, the economy was back at full employment, but inflation stayed low. And during the following 2 years the Fed succeeded in keeping both inflation and unemployment low.

There can be no doubt that in the 1990s active and discretionary Fed policy, a fine-tuning policy, helped keep the economy operating better than at any time in the

policy should not be used actively in the face of major disturbances to the economy. Most of the considerations of the previous sections of this chapter indicate some uncertainty about the effects of policy, but sometimes there can be no doubt about which direction policy should take.

For instance, an administration coming to power in 1933 should not have worried about the uncertainties associated with expansionary policy that we have outlined. The economy does not move from 25 percent unemployment to full employment in a short time. Thus, expansionary measures, such as a rapid growth of the money supply,

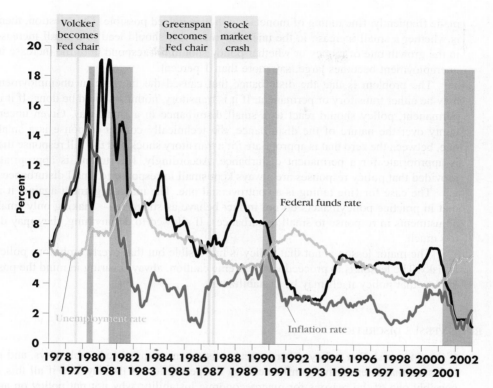

FIGURE 1   INFLATION, UNEMPLOYMENT, AND THE FEDERAL FUNDS INTEREST RATE, 1978–2002.

(Source: Bureau of Labor Statistics and Federal Reserve Economic Data at Federal Reserve Bank of St. Louis.)

previous 30 years. Of course, the Fed was not perfect, and in particular it has been criticized for cutting interest rates too slowly during the 1990–1991 recession and for raising rates too slowly as the economy boomed at the end of the last century. But, on balance, the Fed has done an excellent job.

increased government expenditures, tax reductions, or all three, would have been appropriate policy since there was no chance that the economy would have overshot into a boom. Similarly, contractionary policies for private demand are called for in wartime. In the event of large disturbances in the future, activist monetary or fiscal policy, or both, should once again be used.

Fine tuning presents more complicated issues. In the case of fiscal policy, the long inside lags make discretionary fine tuning virtually impossible, though automatic stabilizers are in fact fine-tuning all the time. But with monetary policy decisions being made frequently, fine tuning of monetary policy is indeed possible. The question, then, is whether a small increase in the unemployment rate should lead to a small increase in the growth rate of money or whether policy should not respond until the increase in unemployment becomes large, say more than 1 percent.

The problem is that the disturbance that caused the increase in unemployment may be either transitory or permanent. If it is transitory, nothing should be done. If it is permanent, policy should react to a small disturbance in a small way. Given uncertainty over the nature of the disturbance, the technically correct response is a small one, between the zero that is appropriate for a transitory shock and the full response that is appropriate for a permanent disturbance. Accordingly, fine tuning is appropriate provided that policy responses are always kept small in response to small disturbances.

The case for fine tuning is a controversial one. The major argument against it is that in practice policymakers do not in fact behave as suggested—making only small adjustments in response to small disturbances. If allowed to do anything, they may do too much.

The major lesson is not that policy is impossible but that overly ambitious policy is risky. The lesson is to proceed with extreme caution, always bearing in mind the possibility that policy itself may be destabilizing.

RULES VERSUS DISCRETION

If there is a risk that policymakers react to disturbances in unpredictable ways, and in a dosage that is excessively influenced by the perception of the day, and if all this is possibly one of the reasons for macroeconomic instability, why not put policy on automatic pilot? This is the issue of *rules versus discretion*. Should the monetary authority and also the fiscal authority conduct policy in accordance with preannounced rules that describe precisely how their policy variables will be determined in all future situations, or should they be allowed to use their discretion in determining the values of the policy variables at different times?

One example of a rule is the constant-growth-rate rule, say at 4 percent, for monetary policy. The rule is that no matter what happens, the money supply will be kept growing at 4 percent. Another example would be a rule stating that the money supply growth rate will be increased by 2 percent per year for every 1 percent unemployment in excess of an estimate of the natural rate, say 5.5 percent. Algebraically, such a rule would be expressed as

$$\frac{\Delta M}{M} = 4.0 + 2(u - 5.5) \tag{8}$$

where the growth rate of money $\Delta M/M$ is an annual percentage rate, and u is the percentage unemployment rate.[15]

[15]Engineering students will recognize this as an argument between open-loop (set a path in advance) and closed-loop (use feedback) control systems.

BOX 8-5   Fiscal Policy and Fine Tuning— the Side Effects

Fiscal policy can be an inappropriate tool with which to tune the economy because of its side effects. Presumably the best tax rate is one that pays for the government while introducing minimal distortions in private decisions. Presumably the level of unemployment compensation is set so as to balance fairness to the unemployed against lost incentives to work. There is little reason that such choices will coincidentally be just the right ones to move the economy out of a recession.

So even if purely macroeconomic considerations argue for the use of fiscal rather than monetary policy, the existence of side effects limits the availability of fiscal policy for short-run stabilization.

The activist monetary rule of equation (8) implies that at 5.5 percent unemployment, monetary growth is 4 percent. If unemployment rises above 5.5 percent, monetary growth is *automatically* increased. Thus, with 7.5 percent unemployment, monetary growth would be 8 percent, using equation (8). Conversely, if unemployment dropped below 5.5 percent, monetary growth would be lowered below 4 percent. The rule therefore gears the amount of monetary stimulus to an indicator of the business cycle. By linking monetary growth to the unemployment rate, an activist, anticyclical monetary policy is achieved, but this is done without any discretion.

The issue of rules versus discretion has been clouded by the fact that most proponents of rules have been nonactivists, whose preferred monetary rule is a constant-growth-rate rule. Consequently, the argument has tended to center on whether activist policy is desirable or not. The fundamental point to recognize is that we can design *activist rules*. We can design rules that have countercyclical features without, at the same time, leaving any discretion about their actions to policymakers. The point is made by equation (8), which is an activist rule because it expands money growth when unemployment is high and reduces it when unemployment is low. The equation leaves no room for policy discretion and in this respect is a rule.

Given that both the economy and our knowledge of it are changing over time, there is no economic case for stating permanent policy rules that would tie the hands of the monetary and fiscal authorities permanently.[16] Two practical issues, then, arise in the rules-versus-discretion debate. The first is where the authority to change the rule is located. At one extreme, the growth rate of money could be prescribed by the Constitution. At the other it is left to the Fed or the "Fisc" (the equivalent fiscal policymaking

---

[16]For evidence on this point, see John B. Taylor, "Discretion versus Policy Rules in Practice," *Carnegie-Rochester Conference Series on Public Policy,* December 1993.

BOX 8-6   Taylor's Rule

The best known example of an activist rule is Taylor's rule, named for its discoverer/inventor John B. Taylor of Stanford University (and later, undersecretary of the Treasury). Taylor's rule tells the monetary authority how to set interest rates in response to economic activity. Specifically, Taylor's rule is

$$i_t = 2 + \pi_t + 0.5 \times (\pi_t - \pi_t^*) + 0.5 \times \left(100 \times \frac{Y_t - Y_t^*}{Y_t^*}\right)$$

where π_t^* is the target inflation rate, and the constant "2" aproximates the long-run average real interest rate. For example, to hit a 2 percent inflation target at full-employment, the Fed would set the nominal interest rate to be 4 percent. As a second example, if inflation is running at 5 percent with a 2 percent target while GDP is 1 percent above potential, Taylor's rule would tell the Fed to set the nominal interest rate at 9 percent $(2 + 5 + 0.5 \times [5 - 2] + 0.5 \times 1)$.

The rule states that when inflation goes up 1 point above the target, the Fed should counteract the increase by raising interest rates by 1.5 points. When the GDP gap rises 1 percent, interest rates are raised by ½ percent. Taylor argued that this rule is both a pretty good rough rule and pretty close to what the Fed actually did.*

Taylor's rule illustrates a critical characteristic of any good policy rule: *negative feedback*. (Positive feedback is best illustrated by putting a live microphone in front of a loudspeaker.) Remember that the nominal interest rate, i, equals the real interest rate plus inflation. By increasing nominal interests by more than the increase in inflation, Taylor's rule increases real interest rates—cooling off the economy—when inflation increases.

*John B. Taylor, "Discretion versus Policy Rules in Practice," *Carnegie-Rochester Conference Series on Public Policy*, 1993. For a good discussion, see John P. Judd and Glenn D. Rudebusch, "Taylor's Rule and the Fed: 1970–1997," *Federal Reserve Bank of San Francisco Review*, 1998.

body). In each case policy can be changed, but changing the Constitution takes longer than it takes the Fed to change its policy. In the tradeoff between certainty about future policy and flexibility of policy, activists place a premium on flexibility, and those in favor of rules that are difficult to change place a premium on the fact that the Fed has often made mistakes in the past. Because the financial system responds very quickly to shocks and is so interconnected, we believe it essential that the Fed have considerable discretion and thus flexibility to respond to disturbances. But that is far from a universal judgment.

The second issue is whether the policymakers should announce in advance the policies they will be following for the foreseeable future. Such announcements are in principle desirable because they help private individuals to forecast future policy. In fact, the chairperson of the Fed is required to announce to Congress the Fed's monetary targets. In practice, however, these announcements have not been a great help because the Fed does not stick to its targets. If the Fed is able to keep output close to potential and inflation low by departing from announced policy, it helps private individuals forecast the variables in which they are really interested—their future incomes and, in the case of firms, the demand for their goods—rather than those, like the money supply, that they need know only as an intermediate step in forecasting.

8-7

WHICH TARGET?—A PRACTICAL APPLICATION

Suppose the primary goal of policy is to keep GDP close to potential GDP and the secondary goal is to achieve a low inflation rate. In this section we consider a series of possible targeting approaches. If we had perfect information, any approach would be suitable. Information is, of course, quite imperfect. For each possible target, we ask what can go wrong.

REAL GDP TARGETING

If we hit potential GDP just right, then *real GDP targeting* is optimal. We achieve our primary goal bang on. Since the Phillips curve has the natural rate of unemployment equal to actual unemployment when actual and anticipated inflation are equal, hitting potential GDP is consistent with low actual and anticipated inflation.

Now suppose we guess too high as to the growth rate of potential GDP. For example, we think potential GDP can grow at 4 percent per year when in fact it grows at only 2 percent. In the short run we will pump up actual GDP growth, hitting 4 percent growth. But this pushes GDP above potential, causing inflation to accelerate. The longer we persist, the faster inflation accelerates. Nor will we be able to maintain the 4 percent growth permanently.

NOMINAL GDP TARGETING

We might adopt a plan to grow *nominal* GDP at 4 percent.[17] If we start at potential GDP and it happens that potential GDP grows at 4 percent, then we hit both primary and secondary targets just right. However, if we start well below potential, then we forgo the chance to move real GDP quickly.

Suppose again that potential GDP really grows at only 2 percent annually. In the long run, 4 percent nominal GDP growth will split into 2 percent real growth and 2 percent inflation. This isn't perfect, but 2 percent long-run inflation sure beats unlimited inflation, which can occur under real GDP targeting.

---

[17]See Michael D. Bradley and Dennis W. Jansen, "Understanding Nominal GNP Targeting," Federal Reserve Bank of St. Louis *Review,* November–December 1989. See also Jeffrey A. Frankel with Menzie Chinn, "The Stabilizing Properties of a Nominal GNP Rule in an Open Economy," *Journal of Money, Credit, and Banking,* May 1995, for an extension of the analysis to the open economy.

BOX 8-7   Output versus Inflation Targeting: The "Oops" Theory of Picking a Target

For policymakers—just as for the rest of us—there is a natural tendency to target the desired outcome. For the last 20 years, opinion polls have suggested that unemployment, and thus output, are viewed by the population as more important than inflation rates, implying that policymakers should focus on targeting output rather than inflation. But a wise policymaker asks about what can go wrong with a certain policy.

Consider the major pitfall of output targeting. As a policymaker, if you overestimate potential GDP, or equivalently underestimate the natural rate of unemployment, you'll be continually overstimulating the economy, leading to higher and higher inflation rates. While you may hit your output target in the short run, in the long run the Phillips curve will move up and inflation will accelerate . . . and accelerate and accelerate. Eventually, you'll end up with *very* high inflation rates. Even if you know the right level of output, political pressures—from lobbyists or various interest groups—can tend to make you overstimulate.

Suppose you target inflation. Eventually, expected inflation will adjust to the target level and the movement of the Phillips curve will get the economy back to the right level of output. And because you are targeting inflation directly, there is no way for inflation to reach runaway levels. But "eventually" might be a while, since inflation targeters forswear the use of policy to mitigate recessions.

Errors in output targeting can lead to explosive inflation. Use of inflation targeting leaves recession untreated. In balancing these risks, a number of countries have decided to go with inflation targeting, while the United States continues to look at both output and inflation targets.

INFLATION TARGETING

At the opposite end of the spectrum from real GDP targeting is *inflation targeting*.[18] While policymakers may not be able to hit an inflation target exactly, they can certainly

[18]Stanley Fischer, "Why Are Central Banks Pursuing Long-Run Price Stability?" *Achieving Price Stability* (Federal Reserve Bank of Kansas City, 1996), and, by the same author, "Modern Central Banking," in *The Future of Central Banking: The Tercentenary Symposium of the Bank of England* (Cambridge, England: Cambridge University Press, 1994). See also Robert G. King and Alexander L. Wolman, "Inflation Targeting in a St. Louis Model of the 21st Century," Federal Reserve Bank of St. Louis *Review,* May–June 1996; William T. Gavin, "The FOMC in 1995: A Step Closer to Inflation Targeting?" Federal Reserve Bank of St. Louis *Review,* September–October 1996; Ben S. Bernanke et al., "Missing the Mark: The Truth about Inflation Targeting," *Foreign-Affairs,* September–October 1999; Lars O. E. Svensson, "Inflation Targeting: Should It Be Modeled as an Instrument Rule or a Targeting Rule?" NBER working paper no. W8925, December 2001; and Laurence H. Meyer, "Inflation Targets and Inflation Targeting," Federal Reserve Bank of St. Louis *Review,* November–December 2001.

come close. By giving up on the primary goal entirely, policymakers are in a position to do quite well on their secondary goal. Adopted first in New Zealand, inflation targeting is now the rule in Australia, Brazil, Canada, the Czech Republic, Chile, Finland, Iceland, Norway, Sweden, Switzerland, and the United Kingdom.

In the spectrum from focusing entirely on output to entirely on prices, note that real GDP targeting is the best option for hitting our primary goal but also holds the greatest risk of a big miss on our secondary goal. Not surprisingly, economists who think that the macroeconomy is largely self-correcting (i.e., those who think the Phillips curve is vertical over a fairly short time horizon) prefer nominal targets. Why risk high inflation if real GDP will largely take care of itself? Economists who believe that a flat Phillips curve persists for some time think the benefit of hitting output and unemployment goals outweighs the risk of inflation.

 ## 8-8

DYNAMIC INCONSISTENCY AND RULES VERSUS DISCRETION

The case for modest, activist, discretionary policy seems clear. Why then do countries, such as the United States, that follow such procedures sometimes seem to have a bias toward too much inflation? After all, once the inflation-expectations-augmented Phillips curve is understood we would hope policymakers would keep inflation low on average, which would also keep expected inflation low. Since there is no long-run tradeoff between unemployment and inflation, there is no unemployment-reducing benefit from keeping inflation high.

Is there any way to restructure stabilization policy to avoid this inflationary bias? The answer to these questions is found in an examination of the idea of *dynamic inconsistency*. Essentially, the argument is that policymakers who have discretion will be tempted to take short-run actions that are inconsistent with the economy's best long-run interests.[19] What's more, this is the natural outcome with rational, well-intentioned policymakers. In fact, the analysis of dynamic inconsistency begins with the assumption that the policymaker shares the public's dislike of both inflation and unemployment.

The key to understanding dynamic inconsistency lies in remembering that there is a short-run tradeoff between inflation and unemployment given by the short-run Phillips curve but there is no long-run tradeoff because of the adjustment of inflationary expectations. The best long-run position for the economy is full employment with zero (or at least low) inflation. However, a policymaker who announces a

[19]The basic reference is Finn Kydland and Edward Prescott, "Rules Rather than Discretion: The Inconsistency of Optimal Plans," *Journal of Political Economy,* June 1977. This is very difficult reading. See also V. V. Chari, "Time Consistency and Optimal Policy Design," Federal Reserve Bank of Minneapolis *Quarterly Review,* Fall 1988. See also Robert J. Barro and David B. Gordon, "A Positive Theory of Monetary Policy in a Natural Rate Model," *Journal of Political Economy,* August 1983, and "Rules, Discretion and Reputation in a Model of Monetary Policy," *Journal of Monetary Economics,* July 1983.

full-employment–zero-inflation policy will immediately be led to "cheat" by seeking lower unemployment and slightly higher inflation. It is this split between announced and executed plans that gives rise to the name "dynamic inconsistency."

One can model the interaction between policymaker and the economy as occurring in three sequential steps:

1. The policymaker announces a policy, say 0 percent inflation.
2. Economic decision makers choose a level of anticipated inflation consistent with the announced policy, implying the economy will be positioned on the short-run Phillips curve at full employment.
3. The policymaker implements the best possible policy. Since the short-run Phillips curve is now fixed, the policymaker can reduce unemployment at the expense of a little inflation. This policy is *optimal,* although it is *inconsistent* with the policy announced in step 1.

We use Figure 8-3 to illustrate the interactions between the policymaker and economic decision makers. The figure shows the Phillips curve tradeoff between unemployment and inflation. Everyone, policymaker and public, prefers to be at point *A,*

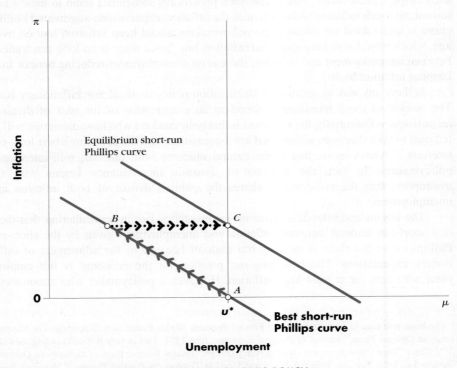

FIGURE 8-3   THE PHILLIPS CURVE AND ECONOMIC POLICY.

with full employment and zero inflation. At point *A*, the policymaker promises and the public expects zero inflation, so the economy operates on the lower short-run Phillips curve. Suppose, through good fortune, that the economy reached the preferred point, *A*. What will the policymaker do? At zero inflation, everyone, policymaker and public, is willing to accept a small amount of increased inflation in order to reduce unemployment. So the right thing for the policymaker to do is to increase inflation a little in order to reduce unemployment, sliding up and to the left along the lower short-run Phillips curve. The policymaker will push the economy to point *B*, where inflation is just high enough so that the marginal loss from more inflation equals the marginal benefit from lower unemployment.

At point *B*, inflation is greater than anticipated. Decision makers will come to anticipate higher inflation, and the short-run Phillips curve will move up to the equilibrium Phillips curve. Eventually, the economy reaches equilibrium at point *C*, at full employment but with positive inflation. (At point *C*, the marginal loss from inflation is high enough that the policymaker is unwilling to increase inflation further to reduce unemployment; that is, there is no temptation to move further to the left along the equilibrium Phillips curve.)

In equilibrium, the economy ends up with high inflation at point *C*, even though everyone prefers point *A*. The policymaker will gladly promise to return to zero inflation and stay at point *A*; but the promise isn't *credible,* because if the economy returned to point *A*, *everyone* would again agree to inflate back to *B*. It would be better if the policymaker kept her promises, but as soon as low-inflation promises are believed, it is then in everyone's best interest to "cheat."

How can the temptation to engage in dynamic inconsistency be avoided, or at least minimized? First, a forward-looking policymaker will realize the value of maintaining a *reputation* for consistency. The difficulty is that there will always be outside pressures pushing for a short-run inflationary bias. Second, the government can choose a policymaker whose personal tastes are more anti-inflationary than those of the public at large, so that the policymaker will lean against inflationary pressures. Third, the policymaker can be given a contract with payments that reward low inflation. Fourth, low-inflation "rules" can be adopted to prevent the policymaker from making the discretionary choices that lead to dynamic inconsistency. All these ideas have merit and all have been used to some extent. The problem remains that in a democracy there is always a temptation to lower unemployment at the cost of higher inflation "just this one time."

THE INDEPENDENCE OF THE CENTRAL BANK

One solution to the problem of dynamic inconsistency is to require that the central bank follow a monetary rule, for instance, to increase the money supply at a low, constant rate. However, because the monetary rule may be wrong and because there are good reasons for monetary policy to respond to some shocks, such as a supply shock, no country has adopted a rigid form of rule.

BOX 8-8   Central Bank Independence and Democracy—without Further Comment

I know there's the myth of the autonomous Fed . . . [short laugh] and when you go up for confirmation some Senator may ask you about your friendship with the President. Appearances are going to be important, so you can call Ehrlichman to get messages to me, and he'll call you.

—*Richard Nixon to about-to-be Fed chairman Arthur Burns*

Source: Cited in J. Bradford De Long, "America's Only Peacetime Inflation: The 1970s," NBER Historical Paper 84, May 1996, referencing John Ehrlichman, *Witness to Power* (New York: Simon & Schuster, 1982).

Another solution to the inflationary bias of discretionary policy is to set up a central bank that is independent of the electoral cycle and that has a clear mandate to fight inflation. The Fed is in principle independent of the administration, though it does report to Congress.[20] In Germany, the central bank, the Bundesbank, was fiercely independent and a fierce inflation fighter. As twelve European countries, including Germany, have given up their currencies and created a new currency, the euro, the Bundesbank no longer makes monetary policy. That is done by the European Central Bank, which is very independent. There is strong empirical evidence showing that the more independent the central bank, the lower the inflation rate in a country.[21]

The question of the optimal degree of independence of the central bank is a complicated one. There *are* short-run tradeoffs, and there is always a question of just how fast a central bank should try to reduce inflation. Thus, central banks end up exercising judgment, which ultimately depends on their evaluation of what the public's real interests are. But there is no way of knowing what those interests are without some democratic input. Whenever the Fed shows its independence, typically by refusing to expand as fast as the administration or Congress wants, there are calls to clip its wings. This is one way the Fed gets the message.

[20]See Alan S. Blinder, "Central Banking in a Democracy," Federal Reserve Bank of Atlanta *Economic Quarterly*, Fall 1996.

[21]Vittorio Grilli, Donato Masciandaro, and Guido Tabellini, in "Political and Monetary Institutions and Public Financial Policies in the Industrial Countries," *Economic Policy*, October 1991, show this result as well as results on the relationship between institutions and fiscal policy.

DYNAMIC INCONSISTENCY—A FORMAL APPROACH

In this section we present an algebraic version of the model of dynamic inconsistency illustrated in Figure 8-3. We assume that the policymaker chooses the level of inflation, although in practice the policymaker actually chooses monetary or fiscal policy and inflation is a result rather than a direct choice. The choice of inflation leads to the unemployment rate given by the short-run Phillips curve in equation (9):

$$\pi = \pi^e - \epsilon(u - u^*) \tag{9}$$

The policymaker, and the public, prefers low unemployment and zero inflation. We "keep score" by specifying a loss function for the policymaker in equation (10):

$$L = a(u - u^*) + \pi^2 \tag{10}$$

The loss function in equation (10) says that high unemployment is bad and that any deviation from zero inflation is bad. The higher the coefficient a, the greater the relative weight given to lowering unemployment.

The three steps in the "game" played by the policymaker are as follows: (1) The policymaker chooses and announces an inflation policy (point A in Figure 8-3); (2) "the economy" picks anticipated policy, π^e (point B); (3) the policymaker implements an actual policy, π, that minimizes the loss function in equation (10) (point C). In step 2, the decision makers look forward, guessing what the policymaker will do in step 3. In step 1, the policymaker is also looking forward, guessing what the economy will do in step 2 as it looks toward step 3. **So early choices by the policymaker must anticipate later stages, which themselves depend on the choices made earlier. Decision makers work out their choices by starting at the end and working backward. This choice method is a simple example of** *dynamic programming.*

The final score is calculated by inserting the actual policy, π, and anticipated inflation, π^e, into the loss function using the Phillips curve relation to compute the deviation of unemployment from the natural rate. The final "score" is

$$L(\pi) = a\left[-\frac{1}{\epsilon}(\pi - \pi^e)\right] + \pi^2 \tag{11}$$

The policymaker minimizes the loss in equation (11) by setting the marginal loss function in (12) equal to zero, giving the black line in Figure 8-3:

$$ML(\pi) = -\frac{a}{\epsilon} + 2\pi = 0 \tag{12}$$

So the optimal policy is

$$\pi = \frac{a}{2\epsilon} \tag{13}$$

Note that the result in equation (13) holds for *any* level value of π^e.

Everyone desires zero inflation, but in the last stage of the game it always pays for the policymaker to choose a positive inflation rate. In fact, since anticipated inflation equals $a/2\epsilon$, if the policymaker chooses in the last step to set inflation below $a/2\epsilon$, a recession will result. The problem is that society has no way to *commit* to zero inflation.

Note, in equation (13), that a loss function weighted heavily against unemployment—one with a high a—results in more inflation. This perverse result occurs because a high a increases the incentive in the last step to raise inflation to lower unemployment. But if society can cede power to a policymaker who cares less about unemployment, one with a lower a, lower inflation will result.

SUMMARY

1. The potential need for stabilizing policy actions arises from economic disturbances. Some of these disturbances, such as changes in money demand, consumption spending, or investment demand, arise from within the private sector. Others, such as wars, may arise for noneconomic reasons.

2. Wise policymakers work with what we know about the economy while also recognizing the limits of our knowledge. Good policy design includes an assessment of the risks associated with unforeseen errors.

3. The three key difficulties of stabilization policy are that (*a*) policy works with lags; (*b*) the outcome of policy depends very much on private sector expectations, which are difficult to predict and may react to policy; and (*c*) there is uncertainty about both the structure of the economy and the shocks that hit the economy.

4. When forming economic policy, policymakers must choose between sudden policy changes and gradual changes. Sudden policy changes may enhance the policymakers' credibility but are based on limited information. Gradual changes allow policymakers to incorporate new information as the economy moves toward its target.

5. For the purposes of policy, economic variables can be classified as targets (identified goals of policy), instruments (the tools of policy), and indicators (economic variables that signal whether we are getting close to our policy targets).

6. There are clearly occasions on which active monetary and fiscal policy actions should be taken to stabilize the economy. These are situations in which the economy has been affected by major disturbances.

7. Fine tuning—continuous attempts to stabilize the economy in the face of small disturbances—is more controversial. If fine tuning is undertaken, it calls for small policy responses in an attempt to moderate the economy's fluctuations, rather than to remove them entirely. A very active policy in response to small disturbances is likely to destabilize the economy.

8. In the rules-versus-discretion debate, it is important to recognize that activist rules are possible. The two important issues in the debate are how difficult it should be to change policy and whether policy should be announced as far ahead as possible. There is a tradeoff between the certainty about future policy that comes from rules and the flexibility of the policymakers in responding to shocks.

9. Central bank independence is one avenue democracies use to add to the credibility of policy and to help mitigate the problem of dynamic inconsistency.

KEY TERMS

action lag
activist policies
activist rules
automatic stabilizer
certainty-equivalence policy
credibility
decision lag
discrete lag
distributed lag
dynamic inconsistency

dynamic programming
econometric model
fine tuning
indicators
inflation targeting
inside lag
instruments
loss function
marginal loss function
multiplier uncertainty

outside lag
portfolio of policy
  instruments
  (diversification)
real GDP targeting
recognition lag
rules versus discretion
targets

PROBLEMS

Conceptual

1.* Suppose there was a small, negative shock to demand. You—a policymaker—have a stack of papers in front of you detailing the magnitude of the shock and its devastating effects on the people of your country. You are tempted to use an active policy to offset these effects. Your advisers have estimated its impact on the economy, in both the long and short runs. What questions should you ask yourself before committing to this course of action? Why?

2. **a.** What is an inside lag?
   b. We can divide inside lags into three smaller, sequential lags. What are these, and in what order do they occur?
   c. Which has the smaller inside lag—fiscal or monetary policy? Why?
   d. What is the inside lag for automatic stabilizers?

3. **a.** What is an outside lag?
   b. Why does it generally take the form of a distributed lag?
   c. Which has the smaller outside lag—fiscal or monetary policy?

4. Which would you recommend be used to offset the effect of a temporary shock to output—fiscal or monetary policy? Why?

5. **a.** What is an econometric model?
   b. How might one be used?
   c. There is always some uncertainty with respect to predictions based on such models. Why? What is the source of this uncertainty?

6. Evaluate the argument that monetary policy should be determined by a rule rather than discretion. How about fiscal policy?

7. Evaluate the arguments for a constant-growth-rate rule for money.

8. What is dynamic inconsistency? Explain intuitively how it might arise in the case of the short-run tradeoff between inflation and unemployment.

9. How does nominal GDP targeting differ from real GDP targeting? Why is real GDP targeting the riskier of the two strategies?

*An asterisk denotes a more difficult problem.

Technical

1. Suppose that GDP is $40 billion below its potential level. It is expected that next-period GDP will be $20 billion below potential and that two periods from now it will be back at its potential level. You are told that the multiplier for government spending is 2 and that the effects of the increased government spending are immediate. What policy actions can be taken to put GDP back on target each period?

2. The basic facts about the path of GDP are as in problem 1. But there is now a one-period outside lag for government spending. Decisions to spend today are translated into actual spending only tomorrow. The multiplier for government spending is still 2 in the period that the spending takes place.

    a. What is the best that can be done to keep GDP as close to target as possible each period?
    b. Compare the path of GDP in this question with the path in problem 1 after policy actions have been taken.

3. Life has become yet more complicated. Government spending works with a distributed lag. Now when $1 billion is spent today, GDP increases by $1 billion this period and $1.5 billion next period.

    a. What happens to the path of GDP if government spending rises enough this period to put GDP back to its potential level this period?
    b. Suppose fiscal policy actions are taken to put GDP at its potential level this period. What fiscal policy will be needed to put GDP on target next period?
    c. Explain why the government has to be so active in keeping GDP on target in this case.

4. Suppose that you knew that the multiplier for government spending was between 1 and 2.5 but that its effects ended in the period in which spending was increased. How would you run fiscal policy if GDP would, without policy, behave as in problem 1?

5.* Suppose that, as the chair of the Fed, you decided to "put policy on automatic pilot" and require that monetary policy follow an established rule. When might each of the following two rules be appropriate? (*a*) Maintain a constant interest rate. (*b*) Maintain a constant money supply.

Empirical

1. Check the *Federal Reserve Bulletin* (www.federalreserve.gov/fomc), where the forecasts of the Federal Reserve Board are presented twice a year following the February and July monetary policy report to Congress.

    a. How well did the Fed anticipate the economic performance of 2002?
    b. Explain why economic forecasts are not totally accurate.

2. Box 8-6 presents Taylor's rule, specifically,

$$i_t = 2 + \pi_t + 0.5 \times (\pi_t - \pi_t^*) + 0.5 \times \left(100 \times \frac{Y_t - Y_t^*}{Y_t^*} \right)$$

The purpose of this exercise is to see whether this simple rule can explain the evolution of interest rates in the United States over the last 40 years or so. We will assume that the target inflation rate π_t^* is equal to 2 percent.

Option a. Pick a few years, for example 1978, 1988, 2001, and 2002. Go to www.economagic.com and get data for potential RGDP, actual RGDP, annual inflation rate, and the Fed funds rate (short-term interest rate controlled by the Fed). Calculate the output gap ($gap = [RGDP_{actual} - RGDP_{potential}]/RGDP_{potential} \times 100$). Once you have the output gap, calculate the interest rate implied by Taylor's rule by plugging in the numbers into the equation given above. Compare the value you obtained with the observed Fed funds rate for the given years. Are the numbers close?

Option b. If you know how to use EXCEL, go to www.economagic.com, and download annual data for the period 1960–2002, for potential RGDP, actual RGDP, annual inflation, and the Fed funds rate. Setting up the appropriate formula in EXCEL, calculate the output gap and the interest rate implied by Taylor's rule. Create a graph that includes both the actual short-term interest rate (the Fed funds rate) and the value implied by Taylor's rule. Is there a period for which Taylor's rule seems to fit the data particularly well?

PART 3

First Models

CHAPTER 9

Income and Spending

CHAPTER HIGHLIGHTS

- In the most basic model of aggregate demand, spending determines output and income, but output and income also determine spending. In particular, consumption depends on income, but increased consumption increases aggregate demand and therefore output.

- Increases in autonomous spending increase output more than one for one. In other words, there is a multiplier effect.

- The size of the multiplier depends on the marginal propensity to consume and on tax rates.

- Increases in government spending increase aggregate demand and therefore tax collections. But tax collections rise by less than the increase in government spending, so increased government spending increases the budget deficit.

One of the central questions in macroeconomics is why output fluctuates around its potential level. Growth is highly uneven. In business cycle booms and recessions, output rises and falls relative to the trend of potential output. Over the last 30 years there have been five recessions, in which output declined relative to trend—even falling in some years, including 1991—and then recoveries, in which output rose relative to trend.

This chapter offers a first theory of these fluctuations in real output relative to trend. The cornerstone of this model is the mutual interaction between output and spending: Spending determines output and income, but output and income also determine spending.

The *Keynesian* model of income determination that we develop in this chapter is very simple; it will be elaborated in later chapters. The central simplification is that we assume for the time being that prices do not change at all and that firms are willing to sell *any* amount of output at the given level of prices. Thus, the aggregate supply curve, shown in Chapter 7, is assumed to be entirely flat. This chapter develops the theory of the aggregate demand schedule.

The key finding in this chapter is that because of the feedback between spending and output, increases in autonomous spending—increased government purchases, for example—generate further increases in aggregate demand. Other chapters introduce dynamic links between spending and output and allow for offsetting effects due to changes in prices and interest rates, but these more sophisticated models of the economy can be seen as elaborations of this chapter's model.

 ## 9-1

AGGREGATE DEMAND AND EQUILIBRIUM OUTPUT

Aggregate demand **is the total amount of goods demanded in the economy.** Distinguishing among goods demanded for consumption (C), for investment (I), by the government (G), and as net exports (NX), aggregate demand (AD) is determined by

$$AD = C + I + G + NX \tag{1}$$

Output **is at its** *equilibrium level* **when the quantity of output produced is equal to the quantity demanded.** Thus, an economy is at equilibrium output when

$$Y = AD = C + I + G + NX \tag{2}$$

When aggregate demand—the amount people want to buy—is not equal to output, there is unplanned inventory investment or disinvestment. We summarize this as

$$IU = Y - AD \tag{3}$$

where IU is unplanned additions to inventory. If output is greater than aggregate demand, there is unplanned inventory investment, $IU > 0$. As excess inventory accumulates, firms cut back on production until output and aggregate demand are again in equilibrium. Conversely, if output is below aggregate demand, inventories are drawn down until equilibrium is restored.

9-2

THE CONSUMPTION FUNCTION AND AGGREGATE DEMAND

With the concept of equilibrium output firmly defined, we now focus on the determinants of aggregate demand, and particularly on consumption demand. We focus on consumption in part because the consumption sector is so large and in part because it is easy to see the link between consumption and income. For simplicity, we omit the government and foreign trade, therefore setting both G and NX equal to zero.

In practice, the demand for consumption goods is not constant but, rather, increases with income: Families with higher incomes consume more than families with lower incomes, and countries where income is higher have higher levels of total consumption. **The relationship between consumption and income is described by the** *consumption function.*

THE CONSUMPTION FUNCTION

We assume that consumption demand increases with the level of income:

$$C = \overline{C} + cY \qquad \overline{C} > 0 \qquad 0 < c < 1 \qquad (4)$$

This consumption function is shown by the green line in Figure 9-1. The variable $\overline{C}$, the *intercept,* represents the level of consumption when income is zero.[1] For every dollar increase in income, the level of consumption increases by $c. For example, if c is .90, then for every $1 increase in income, consumption rises by 90 cents. The *slope* of the consumption function is c. Along the consumption function the level of consumption rises with income. Box 9-1 shows that this relationship holds in practice.

The coefficient c is sufficiently important to have a special name, the *marginal propensity to consume.* **The marginal propensity to consume is the increase in consumption per unit increase in income.** In our case, the marginal propensity to consume is less than 1, which implies that out of a dollar increase in income, only a fraction, c, is spent on consumption.

CONSUMPTION AND SAVING

What happens to the rest of the dollar of income, the fraction $(1 - c)$, that is not spent on consumption? If it is not spent, it must be saved. Income is either spent or saved;

---

[1]Two points need to be made about the consumption function, equation (4). First, individuals' consumption demands are related to the amount of income they have available to spend, that is, their disposable income (YD), rather than just to the level of output. However, in this section, where we are ignoring the role of government and foreign trade, disposable income is equal to the level of income and output. Second, the real role of the intercept is to represent factors affecting consumption other than income—ownership of assets, such as stocks, bonds, and houses.

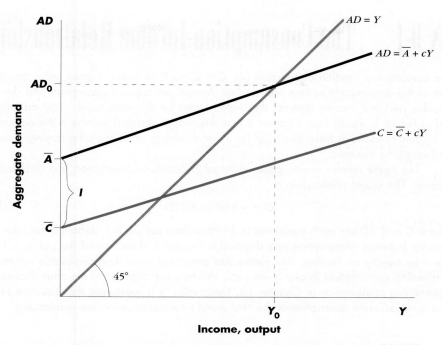

FIGURE 9-1 THE CONSUMPTION FUNCTION AND AGGREGATE DEMAND.

there are no other uses to which it can be put. It follows that any theory that explains consumption is equivalently explaining the behavior of saving.

More formally, look at equation (5), which states that income not spent on consumption is saved:

$$S \equiv Y - C \tag{5}$$

Equation (5) tells us that, by definition, *saving is equal to income minus consumption.*

The consumption function in equation (4), together with equation (5), which we call the *budget constraint,* implies a savings function. The savings function relates the level of saving to the level of income. Substituting the consumption function in equation (4) into the budget constraint in equation (5) yields the savings function:

$$S \equiv Y - C = Y - \overline{C} - cY = -\overline{C} + (1 - c)Y \tag{6}$$

From equation (6), we see that saving is an increasing function of the level of income because the *marginal propensity to save, $s = 1 - c$,* is positive.

In other words, saving increases as income rises. For instance, suppose the marginal propensity to consume, c, is .9, meaning that 90 cents out of each extra dollar of income is consumed. Then the marginal propensity to save, s, is .10, meaning that the remaining 10 cents of each extra dollar of income is saved.

BOX 9-1   The Consumption-Income Relationship

The consumption function of equation (4), $C = \overline{C} + cY$, provides a good initial description of the consumption-income relationship. Annual per capita consumption and disposable personal income data for the United States for the years since 1960 are plotted in Figure 1. Recall from Chapter 2 that disposable personal income is the amount of income households have available for either spending or saving after paying taxes and receiving transfers.

The figure reveals a very close relationship between consumption and disposable income. The actual relationship is

$$C = -818 + .95YD$$

where C and YD are each measured in 1996 dollars per person. Although the relationship between consumption and disposable income is close, not all the points in Figure 1 lie exactly on the line. This means that something other than disposable income is affecting consumption in any given year. We turn our attention to the other factors determining consumption in Chapter 13. Meanwhile, it is reassuring that equation (4) is a quite accurate description of the real world's consumption-income relationship.

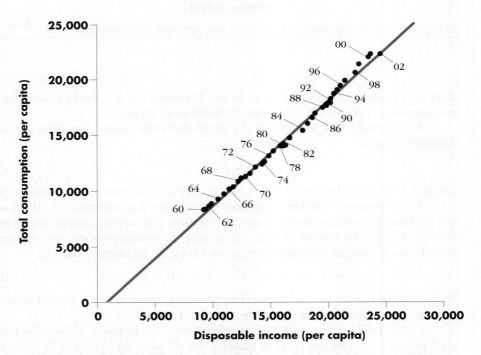

FIGURE 1   RELATIONSHIP BETWEEN CONSUMPTION AND DISPOSABLE INCOME.

(Source: Bureau of Economic Analysis.)

CONSUMPTION, AGGREGATE DEMAND, AND AUTONOMOUS SPENDING

We have specified one component of aggregate demand, consumption demand, and its link to income. Now we add investment, government spending and taxes, and foreign trade to our model, but we assume for the moment that each is *autonomous,* that is, determined outside the model and specifically assumed to be independent of income. Later chapters consider investment, the government, and foreign trade in detail. Here we just assume that investment is $\overline{I}$, government spending is $\overline{G}$, taxes are $\overline{TA}$, transfers are $\overline{TR}$, and net exports are $\overline{NX}$. Consumption now depends on *disposable income,*

$$YD = Y - TA + TR \tag{7}$$
$$C = \overline{C} + cYD = \overline{C} + c(Y + TR - TA) \tag{8}$$

Aggregate demand is the sum of the consumption function, investment, government spending, and net exports. Continuing to assume that the government sector and foreign trade are exogenous,

$$
\begin{aligned}
AD &= C + I + G + NX \\
&= \overline{C} + c(Y - \overline{TA} + \overline{TR}) + \overline{I} + \overline{G} + \overline{NX} \\
&= [\overline{C} - c(\overline{TA} - \overline{TR}) + \overline{I} + \overline{G} + \overline{NX}] + cY \\
&= \overline{A} + cY
\end{aligned}
\tag{9}
$$

The aggregate demand function, equation (9), is shown in Figure 9-2. Part of aggregate demand, $\overline{A} \equiv \overline{C} - c(\overline{TA} - \overline{TR}) + \overline{I} + \overline{G} + \overline{NX}$, is independent of the level of income, or autonomous. But *aggregate demand also depends on the level of income.* It increases with the level of income because consumption demand increases with income. The aggregate demand schedule is obtained by adding (vertically) the demands for consumption, investment, government spending, and net exports at each level of income. At the income level Y_0 in Figure 9-2, the level of aggregate demand is AD_0.

EQUILIBRIUM INCOME AND OUTPUT

The next step is to use the aggregate demand function, AD, from Figure 9-2 and equation (9) to determine the equilibrium levels of output and income.

Recall the basic point of this chapter: The equilibrium level of income is such that aggregate demand equals output (which in turn equals income). The 45° line, $AD = Y$, in Figure 9-2 shows points at which output and aggregate demand are equal. Only at point E in Figure 9-2, and at the corresponding equilibrium levels of income and output (Y_0), does aggregate demand exactly equal output.[2] At that level of output and income, planned spending precisely matches production.

The arrows in Figure 9-2 indicate how the economy reaches equilibrium. At any income level below Y_0, firms find that demand exceeds output and inventories are declining, and they therefore increase production. Conversely, for output levels above Y_0, firms find inventories piling up and therefore cut production. As the arrows show, this

[2]We frequently use the subscript 0 to denote the equilibrium level of a variable.

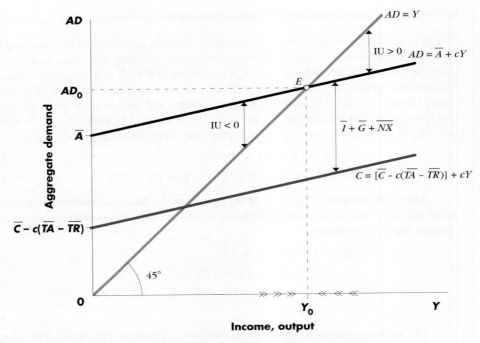

FIGURE 9-2   DETERMINATION OF EQUILIBRIUM INCOME AND OUTPUT.

process leads to the output level Y_0, at which current production exactly matches planned aggregate spending and unintended inventory changes (IU) are therefore equal to zero.

THE FORMULA FOR EQUILIBRIUM OUTPUT

The determination of equilibrium output in Figure 9-2 can also be expressed algebraically by using equation (9) and the equilibrium condition in the goods market, which is that output is equal to aggregate demand:

$$Y = AD \tag{10}$$

The level of aggregate demand, AD, is specified in equation (9). Substituting for AD in equation (10), we have the equilibrium condition:

$$Y = \overline{A} + cY \tag{11}$$

Since we have Y on both sides of the equilibrium condition in equation (11), we can collect the terms and solve for the equilibrium level of income and output, denoted by Y_0:

$$Y_0 = \frac{1}{1 - c}\overline{A} \tag{12}$$

Figure 9-2 sheds light on equation (11). The position of the aggregate demand schedule is characterized by its slope, c (the marginal propensity to consume), and intercept, $\bar{A}$ (autonomous spending). Given the intercept, a steeper aggregate demand function—as would be implied by a higher marginal propensity to consume—implies a higher level of equilibrium income. Similarly, for a given marginal propensity to consume, a higher level of autonomous spending—in terms of Figure 9-2, a larger intercept—implies a higher equilibrium level of income. These results, suggested by Figure 9-2, are easily verified using equation (12), the formula for the equilibrium level of income.

Thus, **the equilibrium level of output is higher the larger the marginal propensity to consume, c, and the higher the level of autonomous spending, $\bar{A}$.**

Equation (12) shows the *level* of output as a function of the marginal propensity to consume and autonomous spending. Frequently, we are interested in knowing how a change in some component of autonomous spending would *change* output. Starting from equation (12), we can relate changes in output to changes in autonomous spending through

$$\Delta Y = \frac{1}{1-c} \Delta \bar{A} \tag{13}$$

For example, if the marginal propensity to consume is .9, then $1/(1-c) = 10$, so a $1 billion increase in government spending increases output by $10 billion, since the recipients of the increased government spending increase their own spending, the recipients of that spending increase theirs, and so on. (We investigate the underpinnings of equation (13) more thoroughly in Section 9-3.) Note that we can compute the change in output without specifying the level of output either before or after the change.

SAVING AND INVESTMENT

There is a useful alternative formulation of the equilibrium condition that aggregate demand is equal to output. *In equilibrium, planned investment equals saving.* This condition applies only to an economy in which there is no government and no foreign trade.

To understand this relationship, return to Figure 9-2. Without government and foreign trade, the vertical distance between the aggregate demand and consumption schedules in the figure is equal to planned investment spending, $\bar{I}$. Note also that the vertical distance between the consumption schedule and the 45° line measures saving $(S = Y - C)$ at each level of income.

The equilibrium level of income is found where AD crosses the 45° line, at E. Accordingly, at the equilibrium level of income, and only at that level, the two vertical distances are equal. Thus, at the equilibrium level of income, saving equals (planned) investment. By contrast, above the equilibrium level of income, Y_0, saving (the distance between the 45° line and the consumption schedule) exceeds planned investment, while below Y_0, planned investment exceeds saving.

The equality between saving and investment can be seen directly from national income accounting. Since income is either spent or saved, $Y = C + S$. Without government and foreign trade, aggregate demand equals consumption plus investment, $Y = C + I$. Putting the two together, we have $C + S = C + I$, or $S = I$.

If we include government and foreign trade in the analysis, we get a more complete picture relating investment to saving and also to net exports. Now income can either be spent, saved, or paid in taxes, so $Y = C + S + TA - TR$ and complete aggregate demand is $Y = C + I + G + NX$. Therefore,

$$C + I + G + NX = C + S + TA - TR$$
$$I = S + (TA - TR - G) - NX \quad\quad (14)$$

That is, investment equals private savings (S) plus the government budget surplus ($TA - TR - G$) minus net exports (NX) or plus net imports, if you prefer.

Rather than using algebra, some people prefer to think of equation (14) in terms of a "corn economy": Investment is the leftover corn that will be planted for next year's crop. The sources of corn investment are corn saved by individuals, any corn left over from government tax collections net of government spending, and any net corn imported from abroad.

9-3

THE MULTIPLIER

In this section we develop an answer to the following question: By how much does a $1 increase in autonomous spending raise the equilibrium level of income? There appears to be a simple answer. Since, in equilibrium, income equals aggregate demand, it would seem that a $1 increase in (autonomous) demand or spending should raise equilibrium income by $1. That answer is wrong. Let us now see why.

Suppose first that output increased by $1 to match the increased level of autonomous spending. This increase in output and income would in turn give rise to further *induced* spending as consumption rises because the level of income has risen. How much of the initial $1 increase in income would be spent on consumption? Out of an additional dollar of income, a fraction c is consumed. Assume, then, that production increases further to meet this induced expenditure, that is, that output and thus income increase by $1 + c$. That will still leave us with an excess demand, because the expansion in production and income by $1 + c$ will give rise to further induced spending. This story could clearly take a long time to tell. Does the process have an end?

In Table 9-1 we lay out the steps in the chain more carefully. The first round starts off with an increase in autonomous spending, $\Delta \overline{A}$. Next, we allow an expansion in production to meet exactly that increase in demand. Production accordingly expands by $\Delta \overline{A}$. This increase in production gives rise to an equal increase in income and, therefore, via the marginal propensity to consume, c, gives rise in the second round to increased expenditures of size $c\Delta \overline{A}$. Assume again that production expands to meet this increase in spending. The production adjustment this time is $c\Delta \overline{A}$, and so is the increase in income. This gives rise to a third round of induced spending equal to the marginal propensity to consume times the increase in income, $c(c\Delta \overline{A}) = c^2 \Delta \overline{A}$. Since the marginal propensity to consume, c, is less than 1, the term c^2 is less than c,

TABLE 9-1   The Multiplier

ROUND	INCREASE IN DEMAND THIS ROUND	INCREASE IN PRODUCTION THIS ROUND	TOTAL INCREASE IN INCOME (ALL ROUNDS)
1	$\Delta \overline{A}$	$\Delta \overline{A}$	$\Delta \overline{A}$
2	$c\Delta \overline{A}$	$c\Delta \overline{A}$	$(1 + c)\Delta \overline{A}$
3	$c^2\Delta \overline{A}$	$c^2\Delta \overline{A}$	$(1 + c + c^2)\Delta \overline{A}$
4	$c^3\Delta \overline{A}$	$c^3\Delta \overline{A}$	$(1 + c + c^2 + c^3)\Delta \overline{A}$
. . .	. . .	. . .	. . .
. . .	. . .	. . .	. . .
. . .	. . .	. . .	$\dfrac{1}{1 - c}\Delta \overline{A}$

and therefore induced expenditures in the third round are smaller than those in the second round.

If we write out the successive rounds of increased spending, starting with the initial increase in autonomous demand, we obtain

$$\Delta AD = \Delta \overline{A} + c\Delta \overline{A} + c^2\Delta \overline{A} + c^3\Delta \overline{A} + \ldots$$
$$= \Delta \overline{A}(1 + c + c^2 + c^3 + \ldots) \tag{15}$$

For a value of $c < 1$, the successive terms in the series become progressively smaller. In fact, we are dealing with a geometric series, so the equation simplifies to

$$\Delta AD = \frac{1}{1 - c}\Delta \overline{A} = \Delta Y_0 \tag{16}$$

From equation (16), therefore, we find that the cumulative change in aggregate spending is equal to a multiple of the increase in autonomous spending—just as we deduced from equation (12). The multiple $1/(1 - c)$ is called the *multiplier*.[3] The multiplier is the amount by which equilibrium output changes when autonomous aggregate demand increases by 1 unit.

The concept of the multiplier is sufficiently important to create new notation. The general definition of the multiplier is $\Delta Y/\Delta \overline{A}$, the change in equilibrium output when autonomous demand increases by 1 unit. In this specific case, omitting the government sector and foreign trade, we define the multiplier as α, where

$$\alpha \equiv \frac{1}{1 - c} \tag{17}$$

[3]Table 9-1 and equation (16) derive the multiplier using the mathematics of geometric series. If you are familiar with calculus, you will realize that the multiplier is nothing other than the derivative of the equilibrium level of income, Y_0, in equation (12) with respect to autonomous spending. Use calculus on equation (12) to check the statements in the text.

Inspection of the multiplier in equation (17) shows that the larger the marginal propensity to consume, the larger the multiplier. For a marginal propensity to consume of .6, the multiplier is 2.5; for a marginal propensity to consume of .8, the multiplier is 5. This is because a high marginal propensity to consume implies that a larger fraction of an additional dollar of income will be consumed, and thus added to aggregate demand, thereby causing a larger induced increase in demand.

Why focus on the multiplier? The reason is that we are developing an explanation of fluctuations in output. The multiplier suggests that output changes when autonomous spending (including investment) changes *and* that the change in output can be larger than the change in autonomous spending. The multiplier is the formal way of describing a commonsense idea: If the economy for some reason—for example, a loss in confidence that reduces investment spending—experiences a shock that reduces income, people whose incomes have gone down will spend less, thereby driving equilibrium income down even further. The multiplier is therefore potentially part of the explanation of why output fluctuates.[4]

THE MULTIPLIER IN PICTURES

Figure 9-3 provides a graphical interpretation of the effects of an increase in autonomous spending on the equilibrium level of income. The initial equilibrium is at point E, with an income level Y_0. Now autonomous spending increases from $\overline{A}$ to $\overline{A}'$. This is represented by a parallel upward shift of the aggregate demand schedule to AD'. The upward shift means that now, at each level of income, aggregate demand is higher by an amount $\Delta \overline{A} \equiv \overline{A}' - \overline{A}$.

Aggregate demand now exceeds the initial level of output, Y_0. Consequently, inventories begin to run down. Firms will respond to the increase in demand and declining inventories by expanding production, say, to income level Y'. This expansion in production gives rise to induced expenditure, increasing aggregate demand to level A_G. At the same time, the expansion reduces the gap between aggregate demand and output to the vertical distance FG. The gap between demand and output is reduced because the marginal propensity to consume is less than 1.

Thus, with marginal propensity to consume less than unity, a sufficient expansion in output will restore the balance between aggregate demand and output. In Figure 9-3 the new equilibrium is indicated by point E', and the corresponding level of income is Y_0'. The change in income required is therefore $\Delta Y_0 = Y_0' - Y_0$.

The magnitude of the income change required to restore equilibrium depends on two factors. The larger the increase in autonomous spending, represented in Figure 9-3

---

[4]Two warnings: (1) The multiplier is necessarily greater than 1 in this very simplified model of the determination of income, but as we shall see in the discussion of "crowding out" in Chap. 10, there may be circumstances in which it is less than 1. (2) The term "multiplier" is used more generally in economics to mean the effect on some endogenous variable (a variable whose level is explained by the theory being studied) of a unit change in an exogenous variable (a variable whose level is not determined within the theory being examined). For instance, one can talk of the multiplier for a change in the money supply on the level of unemployment. However, the classic use of the term is as we are using it here—the effects of a change in autonomous spending on equilibrium output.

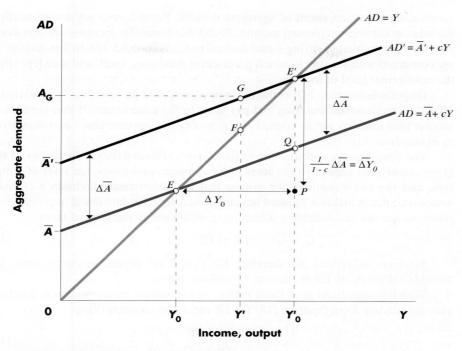

FIGURE 9-3   DERIVATION OF THE MULTIPLIER.

by the parallel shift in the aggregate demand schedule, the larger the income change. Furthermore, the larger the marginal propensity to consume—that is, the steeper the aggregate demand schedule—the larger the income change.

RECAP

There are three points to remember from this discussion of the multiplier:

- An increase in autonomous spending raises the equilibrium level of income.
- The increase in income is a multiple of the increase in autonomous spending.
- The larger the marginal propensity to consume, the larger the multiplier arising from the relation between consumption and income.

9-4

THE GOVERNMENT SECTOR

Whenever there is a recession, people expect and demand that the government do something about it. What can the government do? The government directly affects the level of equilibrium income in two separate ways. First, government purchases of goods and services, G, are a component of aggregate demand. Second, taxes and transfers affect the relation between output and income, Y, and the *disposable income*—income available for consumption or saving—that accrues to the household, YD. In this section we are concerned with the way in which government purchases, taxes, and transfers affect the equilibrium level of income.

Disposable income (YD) is the net income available for spending by households after they receive transfers from and pay taxes to the government. It thus consists of income plus transfers minus taxes, $Y + TR - TA$. The consumption function is given as in equation (8).

The final step is a specification of *fiscal policy*. **Fiscal policy is the policy of the government with regard to the level of government purchases, the level of transfers, and the tax structure.** We assume that the government purchases a constant amount, $\overline{G}$; that it makes a constant amount of transfers, $\overline{TR}$; and that it imposes a *proportional income tax,* collecting a fraction, t, of income in the form of taxes:

$$G = \overline{G} \qquad TR = \overline{TR} \qquad TA = tY \tag{18}$$

Since tax collections, and therefore YD, C, and AD, depend on the tax rate t, the multiplier depends on the tax rate as we will see below.

With this specification of fiscal policy, we can rewrite the consumption function, after substituting from equation (18) for TR and TA in equation (8), as

$$\begin{aligned} C &= \overline{C} + c(Y + \overline{TR} - tY) \\ &= \overline{C} + c\overline{TR} + c(1 - t)Y \end{aligned} \tag{19}$$

Note in equation (19) that the presence of transfers raises autonomous consumption spending by the marginal propensity to consume out of disposable income, c, times the amount of transfers.[5] Income taxes, by contrast, lower consumption spending at each level of income. That reduction arises because households' consumption is related to *disposable* income rather than income itself, and income taxes reduce disposable income relative to the level of income.

While the marginal propensity to consume out of disposable income remains c, the marginal propensity to consume out of income is now $c(1 - t)$, where $1 - t$ is the fraction of income left after taxes. For example, if the marginal propensity to consume, c, is .8 and the tax rate is .25, the marginal propensity to consume out of income, $c(1 - t)$, is .6 $[= .8 \times (1 - .25)]$.

Combining the aggregate demand identity with equations (18) and (19), we have

$$\begin{aligned} AD &= C + I + G + NX \\ &= [\overline{C} + c\overline{TR} + c(1 - t)Y] + \overline{I} + \overline{G} + \overline{NX} \\ &= (\overline{C} + c\overline{TR} + \overline{I} + \overline{G} + \overline{NX}) + c(1 - t)Y \\ &= \overline{A} + c(1 - t)Y \end{aligned} \tag{20}$$

---

[5]We are assuming no taxes are paid on transfers from the government. As a matter of fact, taxes are paid on some transfers, such as interest payments on the government debt, and not paid on other transfers, such as welfare benefits.

The slope of the AD schedule is flatter because households now have to pay part of every dollar of income in taxes and are left with only $1 - t$ of that dollar. Thus, as equation (20) shows, the marginal propensity to consume out of income is now $c(1 - t)$ instead of c.

EQUILIBRIUM INCOME

We are now set to study income determination when the government is included. We return to the equilibrium condition for the goods market, $Y = AD$, and using equation (19), write the equilibrium condition as

$$Y = \overline{A} + c(1 - t)Y$$

We can solve this equation for Y_0, the equilibrium level of income, by collecting terms in Y:

$$Y[1 - c(1 - t)] = \overline{A}$$

$$Y_0 = \frac{1}{1 - c(1 - t)}(\overline{C} + c\overline{TR} + \overline{I} + \overline{G} + \overline{NX})$$ (21)

$$Y_0 = \frac{\overline{A}}{1 - c(1 - t)}$$

In comparing equation (21) with equation (12), we see that the government sector makes a substantial difference. It raises autonomous spending by the amount of government purchases, $\overline{G}$, and by the amount of induced spending out of net transfers, $c\overline{TR}$; in addition, the presence of the income tax lowers the multiplier.

INCOME TAXES AND THE MULTIPLIER

Income taxes lower the multiplier, as can be seen from equation (21). If the marginal propensity to consume is .8 and taxes are zero, the multiplier is 5; with the same marginal propensity to consume and a tax rate of .25, the multiplier is cut in half, to $1/[1 - .8(1 - .25)] = 2.5$. Income taxes reduce the multiplier because they reduce the induced increase of consumption out of changes in income. The inclusion of taxes flattens the aggregate demand curve and hence reduces the multiplier.

INCOME TAXES AS AUTOMATIC STABILIZERS

The proportional income tax is one example of the important concept of *automatic stabilizers.* **As you remember, an automatic stabilizer is any mechanism in the economy that automatically—that is, without case-by-case government intervention—reduces the amount by which output changes in response to a change in autonomous demand.**
One explanation of the business cycle is that it is caused by shifts in autonomous demand, especially investment. Sometimes, it is argued, investors are optimistic and investment is high—and so, therefore, is output. But sometimes they are pessimistic, and so both investment and output are low.

Swings in investment demand have a smaller effect on output when automatic stabilizers—such as a proportional income tax, which reduces the multiplier—are in place. This means that in the presence of automatic stabilizers we should expect output to fluctuate less than it would without them.

The proportional income tax is not the only automatic stabilizer.[6] Unemployment benefits enable the unemployed to continue consuming even though they do not have a job, so TR rises when Y falls. This means that demand falls less when someone becomes unemployed and receives benefits than it would if there were no benefits. This, too, makes the multiplier smaller and output more stable. Higher unemployment benefits and income tax rates in the post-World War II period are reasons that the business cycle fluctuations have been less extreme since 1945 than they were earlier.[7]

EFFECTS OF A CHANGE IN FISCAL POLICY

We now consider the effects of changes in fiscal policy on the equilibrium level of income. Consider first a change in government purchases. This case is illustrated in Figure 9-4, where the initial level of income is Y_0. An increase in government purchases is a change in autonomous spending; therefore, the increase shifts the aggregate demand schedule upward by an amount equal to the increase in government purchases. At the initial level of output and income, the demand for goods exceeds output and, accordingly, firms expand production until the new equilibrium, at point E', is reached.

By how much does income expand? Recall that the change in equilibrium income will equal the change in aggregate demand, or

$$\Delta Y_0 = \Delta \overline{G} + c(1 - t)\Delta Y_0$$

where the remaining terms ($\overline{C}$, $\overline{TR}$, $\overline{I}$, and $\overline{NX}$) are constant by assumption. Thus, the change in equilibrium income is

$$\Delta Y_0 = \frac{1}{1 - c(1 - t)}\Delta \overline{G} = \alpha_G \Delta \overline{G} \qquad (22)$$

where we have introduced the notation α_G to denote the multiplier in the presence of income taxes:

$$\alpha_G \equiv \frac{1}{1 - c(1 - t)} \qquad (23)$$

Thus, a \$1 increase in government purchases will lead to an increase in income in excess of a dollar. With a marginal propensity to consume of $c = .8$ and an income

[6]Automatic stabilizers are discussed by T. Holloway, "The Economy and the Federal Budget: Guide to Automatic Stabilizers," *Survey of Current Business,* July 1984. For a more recent article on automatic stabilizers, see A. Auerbach and D. Feenberg, "The Significance of Federal Taxes as Automatic Stabilizers," *Journal of Economic Perspectives,* Summer 2000.

[7]For a (dissenting) discussion regarding whether U.S. business cycles have become more stable, see C. Romer, "Changes in Business Cycles: Evidence and Explanations," *Journal of Economic Perspectives,* Spring 1999.

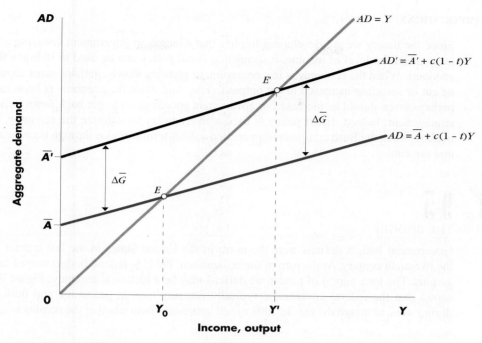

FIGURE 9-4   THE EFFECTS OF AN INCREASE IN GOVERNMENT PURCHASES.

tax rate of $t = .25$, we would have a multiplier of 2.5: A \$1 increase in government spending raises equilibrium income by \$2.50.

Suppose that instead of raising government spending on goods and services, $\overline{G}$, the government increases transfer payments, $\overline{TR}$. Autonomous spending, $\overline{A}$, will increase by only $c\Delta\overline{TR}$, so output will rise by $\alpha_G \times c\Delta\overline{TR}$. The multiplier for transfer payments is smaller than that for government spending—by a factor c—because part of any increase in $\overline{TR}$ is saved.

If the government raises marginal tax rates, two things happen. The direct effect is that aggregate demand will be reduced since the increased taxes reduce disposable income and therefore consumption. In addition, the multiplier will be smaller, so shocks will have a smaller effect on aggregate demand.

RECAP

- Government purchases and transfer payments act like increases in autonomous spending in their effects on income.
- A proportional income tax reduces the proportion of each extra dollar of output that is received as disposable income by consumers, and thus it has the same effects on income as a reduction in the propensity to consume.
- A proportional income tax is an automatic stabilizer.
- A reduction in transfers lowers output.

IMPLICATIONS

Since the theory we are developing implies that changes in government spending and taxes affect the level of income, it seems that fiscal policy can be used to stabilize the economy. When the economy is in a recession, or growing slowly, perhaps taxes should be cut or spending increased to get output to rise. And when the economy is booming, perhaps taxes should be increased or government spending cut to get back down to full employment. Indeed, fiscal policy is used actively to try to stabilize the economy, as in 2001, when the Bush administration created a short-term stimulus through tax refunds and tax cuts.

9-5
THE BUDGET

Government budget deficits were the norm in the United States in the last quarter of the twentieth century. At the turn of the millennium, the U.S. federal budget moved into surplus. The long period of peacetime deficits may be a historical anomaly; Figure 9-5 shows that the federal government typically ran surpluses in peacetime and deficits during wars, although the cuts in 2001 raised questions about whether the surplus would

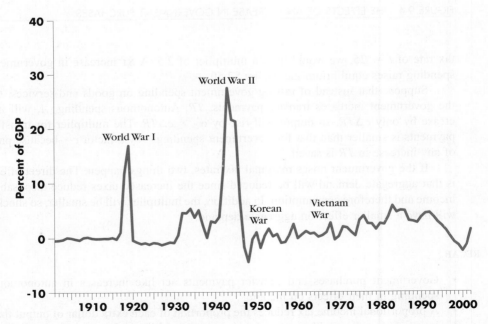

FIGURE 9-5   U.S. GOVERNMENT BUDGET DEFICIT AS A PERCENTAGE OF GDP, 1901–2002.
(*Source: www.economagic.com; and* Historical Statistics of the United States, Colonial Times to 1957.)

persist. Canada and the United Kingdom have also recently turned from budget deficit to budget surplus.[8]

The budget surplus on which the media and politicians focus is the federal budget surplus, which in 2000 was $206 billion, or around 2.1 percent of GDP.[9] "Government" in the national income accounts consists of all levels of government—federal, state, and local. State and local governments tend to run small (less than 1 percent of GDP) surpluses in boom years and small deficits in recession years. In 2000, the state and local surplus was $18.0 billion, about 0.2 percent of GDP.

Is there a reason for concern over a budget deficit? The fear is that the government's borrowing makes it difficult for private firms to borrow and invest and thus slows the economy's growth. Full understanding of this concern has to wait until later chapters, but this section serves as an introduction, dealing with the government budget, its effects on output, and the effects of output on the budget.

The first important concept is the *budget surplus,* denoted by *BS*. **The budget surplus is the excess of the government's revenues, taxes, over its total expenditures, consisting of purchases of goods and services and transfer payments:**

$$BS \equiv TA - \overline{G} - \overline{TR} \tag{24}$$

A negative budget surplus, an excess of expenditure over revenues, is a *budget deficit.*

Substituting in equation (24) the assumption of a proportional income tax that yields tax revenues $TA = tY$ gives us

$$BS = tY - \overline{G} - \overline{TR} \tag{24a}$$

Figure 9-6 plots the budget surplus as a function of the level of income for given $\overline{G}$, $\overline{TR}$, and income tax rate, t. At low levels of income, the budget is in deficit (the surplus is negative) because government spending, $\overline{G} + \overline{TR}$, exceeds income tax collection. At high levels of income, by contrast, the budget shows a surplus, since income tax collection exceeds expenditures in the form of government purchases and transfers.

Figure 9-6 shows that the budget deficit depends not only on the government's policy choices, reflected in the tax rate (t), purchases ($\overline{G}$), and transfers ($\overline{TR}$), but also on anything else that shifts the level of income. For instance, suppose there is an increase in investment demand that increases the level of output. Then the budget deficit will fall or the surplus will increase because tax revenues have risen. But the government has done nothing that changed the deficit.

We should, accordingly, not be surprised to see budget deficits in recessions, periods when the government's tax receipts are low. And in practice, transfer payments,

---

[8]Other countries with recent budget surpluses include Bahrain (2.2 percent of GDP in 2000), Denmark (1.59 percent of GDP in 2000), and Singapore (10 percent of GDP in 2000).

[9]The federal budget in the United States is officially divided into "on-budget" and "off-budget" items. When we use the terms "budget deficit" or "surplus" in the text, we're referring to the "unified budget," the sum of on- and off-budget items. The off-budget budget surplus is pretty much the current surplus in the social security program. At the beginning of the twenty-first century, almost all of the unified budget surplus came from the off-budget side. A note on budget measurement: while most of us think in terms of a calendar year, the U.S. federal government uses a fiscal year beginning in October of the previous year for budget calculations.

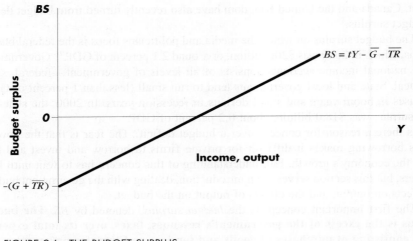

FIGURE 9-6   THE BUDGET SURPLUS.

through unemployment benefits, also increase during recessions, even though we are taking $\overline{TR}$, as autonomous in our model.

EFFECTS OF GOVERNMENT PURCHASES AND TAX CHANGES ON THE BUDGET SURPLUS

Next we show how changes in fiscal policy affect the budget. In particular, we want to find out whether an increase in government purchases must reduce the budget surplus. At first sight, this appears obvious, because increased government purchases, from equation (24), are reflected in a reduced surplus or an increased deficit. On further thought, however, the increased government purchases will cause an increase (multiplied) in income and therefore increased income tax collection. This raises the interesting possibility that tax collection might increase by more than government purchases.

A brief calculation shows that the first guess is right: Increased government purchases reduce the budget surplus. From equation (22) we see that the change in income due to increased government purchases is equal to $\Delta Y_0 \equiv \alpha_G \Delta \overline{G}$. A fraction of that increase in income is collected in the form of taxes, so tax revenue increases by $t\alpha_G \Delta \overline{G}$. The change in the budget surplus, using equation (23) to substitute for α_G, is therefore

$$\begin{aligned}
\Delta BS &= \Delta TA - \Delta \overline{G} \\
&= t\alpha_G \Delta \overline{G} - \Delta \overline{G} \\
&= \left[\frac{t}{1 - c(1 - t)} - 1 \right] \Delta \overline{G} \\
&= -\frac{(1 - c)(1 - t)}{1 - c(1 - t)} \Delta \overline{G}
\end{aligned} \qquad (25)$$

which is unambiguously negative.

We have therefore shown that an increase in government purchases will reduce the budget surplus, although in this model by considerably less than the increase in purchases. For instance, for $c = .8$ and $t = .25$, a \$1 increase in government purchases will create a \$0.375 reduction in the surplus.

In the same way, we can consider the effects of an increase in the tax rate on the budget surplus. We know that the increase in the tax rate will reduce the level of income. It might thus appear that an increase in the tax rate, keeping the level of government spending constant, could reduce the budget surplus. In fact, an increase in the tax rate increases the budget surplus, despite the reduction in income that it causes, as you are asked to show in the problem set at the end of this chapter.[10]

We signal here another interesting result known as the *balanced budget multiplier.* Suppose government spending and taxes are raised in equal amounts and thus in the new equilibrium the budget surplus is unchanged. By how much will output rise? The answer is that for this special experiment the multiplier is equal to 1—output rises by the increase in government spending and no more.

9-6
THE FULL-EMPLOYMENT BUDGET SURPLUS

The final topic to be treated here is the concept of the full-employment budget surplus.[11] Recall that increases in taxes add to the surplus and that increases in government expenditures reduce the surplus. Increases in taxes have been shown to reduce the level of income; increases in government purchases and transfers, to increase the level of income. It thus seems that the budget surplus is a convenient, simple measure of the overall effects of fiscal policy on the economy. For instance, when the budget is in deficit, we would say that fiscal policy is expansionary, tending to increase GDP.

However, the budget surplus by itself suffers from a serious defect as a measure of the direction of fiscal policy. The defect is that the surplus can change because of changes in autonomous private spending—as can be seen in Figure 9-4. Thus, an increase in the budget deficit does not necessarily mean that the government has changed its policy in an attempt to increase the level of income.

Since we frequently want to measure the way in which fiscal policy is being used to affect the level of income, we require some measure of policy that is independent of the particular position of the business cycle—boom or recession—in which we may find ourselves. Such a measure is provided by the *full-employment budget surplus,* which we denote by *BS**. **The full-employment budget surplus measures the budget**

[10]The theory that tax rate cuts would increase government revenue (or tax rate increases reduce government revenue) is associated with Arthur Laffer, formerly at the University of Chicago and University of Southern California. Laffer's argument, however, did not depend on the aggregate demand effects of tax cuts but, rather, on the possibility that a tax cut would lead people to work more. This is a strand in supply-side economics, which we examined in Chap. 5.

[11]The concept has a long history; it was first used by E. Cary Brown, "Fiscal Policy in the Thirties: A Reappraisal," *American Economic Review,* December 1956.

surplus at the full-employment level of income or at potential output. Using Y^* to denote the full-employment level of income, we can write

$$BS^* = tY^* - \overline{G} - \overline{TR} \qquad (26)$$

There are other names for the full-employment surplus. Among them are the *cyclically adjusted surplus* (or deficit), the *high-employment surplus,* the *standardized budget surplus,* and the *structural surplus.* These new names all refer to the same concept as the full-employment surplus, but they avoid implying that there is a unique level of full-employment output that the economy has not yet reached. They suggest, reasonably, that the concept is merely a convenient measuring rod that fixes a given level of employment as the reference point.

To see the difference between the actual and the full-employment budgets, we subtract the actual budget surplus in equation (24*a*) from the full-employment budget surplus in equation (26) to obtain

$$BS^* - BS = t(Y^* - Y) \qquad (27)$$

The only difference arises from income tax collection.[12] Specifically, if output is below full employment, the full-employment surplus exceeds the actual surplus. Conversely, if actual output exceeds full-employment (or potential) output, the full-employment surplus is less than the actual surplus. The difference between the actual and the full-employment budget is the *cyclical* component of the budget. In a recession the cyclical component tends to show a deficit, and in a boom there may even be a surplus.

We next look at the full-employment budget deficit shown in Figure 9-7. Public concern about the deficit mounted in the 1980s. For many economists, the behavior of the deficit during the high-unemployment years 1982 and 1983 was not especially worrisome. The actual budget is usually in deficit during recessions. But the shift toward deficit of the full-employment budget was regarded as an entirely different matter.

Two final words of warning: First, there is no certainty as to the true full-employment level of output. Various assumptions about the level of unemployment that corresponds to full employment are possible. The usual assumptions now are that full employment means an unemployment rate of about 5 to 5.5 percent, although when the actual unemployment rate was higher, there were some estimates as high as 7 percent. Estimates of the full-employment deficit or surplus will differ depending on the assumptions made about the economy at full employment.

Second, the high-employment surplus is not a perfect measure of the thrust of fiscal policy. There are several reasons for this: A change in spending with a matching increase in taxes, leaving the deficit unchanged, will raise income; expectations about future fiscal policy changes can affect current income; and in general, because fiscal

---

[12]In practice, transfer payments, such as welfare and unemployment benefits, are also affected by the state of the economy, so *TR* also depends on the level of income. But the major cause of differences between the actual surplus and the full-employment surplus is taxes. Automatic movements in taxes caused by a change in income are about five times the size of automatic movements in spending. (See T. M. Holloway and J. C. Wakefield, "Sources of Change in the Federal Government Deficit, 1970–86," *Survey of Current Business,* May 1985.)

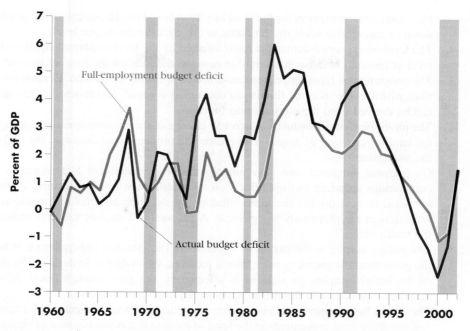

FIGURE 9-7   ACTUAL AND FULL-EMPLOYMENT BUDGET DEFICIT.
(*Source: Congressional Budget Office, www.cbo.gov.*)

policy involves the setting of a number of variables—the tax rate, transfers, and government purchases—it is difficult to describe the thrust of fiscal policy perfectly with a single number. But the high-employment surplus is nevertheless a useful guide to the direction of fiscal policy.[13]

SUMMARY

1. Output is at its equilibrium level when the aggregate demand for goods is equal to the level of output.
2. Aggregate demand consists of planned spending by households on consumption, by firms on investment goods, and by government on its purchases of goods and services and also includes net exports.
3. When output is at its equilibrium level, there are no unintended changes in inventories and all economic units are making precisely the purchases they had planned

[13]For further discussion of the full-employment deficit and alternative measures of fiscal policy, see Congressional Budget Office, *The Economic Outlook,* February 1984, appendix B; and Darrel Cohen, *A Comparison of Fiscal Measures Using Reduced Form Techniques,* Board of Governors of the Federal Reserve System, 1989. Early each year the Congressional Budget Office publishes *The Economic and Budget Outlook,* which contains an analysis of current fiscal policy and estimates of the full-employment budget. Much information about the budget and budget surplus is available online at www.cbo.gov.

to. An adjustment process for the level of output based on the accumulation or run-down of inventories leads the economy to the equilibrium output level.

4. The level of aggregate demand is itself affected by the level of output (equal to the level of income) because consumption demand depends on the level of income.

5. The consumption function relates consumption spending to income. Consumption rises with income. Income that is not consumed is saved, so the savings function can be derived from the consumption function.

6. The multiplier is the amount by which a $1 change in autonomous spending changes the equilibrium level of output. The greater the propensity to consume, the higher the multiplier.

7. Government purchases and government transfer payments act like increases in autonomous spending in their effects on the equilibrium level of income. A proportional income tax has the same effect on the equilibrium level of income as a reduction in the propensity to consume. A proportional income tax thus reduces the multiplier.

8. The budget surplus is the excess of government receipts over expenditures. When the government is spending more than it receives, the budget is in deficit. The size of the budget surplus (or deficit) is affected by the government's fiscal policy variables—government purchases, transfer payments, and tax rates.

9. The actual budget surplus is also affected by changes in tax collection and transfers resulting from movements in the level of income that occur because of changes in private autonomous spending. The full-employment (high-employment) budget surplus is used as a measure of the active use of fiscal policy. The full-employment surplus measures the budget surplus that would exist if output were at its potential (full-employment) level.

KEY TERMS

aggregate demand	consumption function	marginal propensity to
automatic stabilizer	disposable income	consume
balanced budget multiplier	equilibrium level of output	marginal propensity to save
budget constraint	fiscal policy	multiplier
budget deficit	full-employment budget	
budget surplus	surplus	

PROBLEMS

Conceptual

1. We call the model of income determination developed in this chapter a *Keynesian* one. What makes it Keynesian, as opposed to classical?

2. What is an autonomous variable? What components of aggregate demand have we specified, in this chapter, as being autonomous?

3. Using your knowledge of the amount of time required for the many components of the federal government to agree upon and implement changes in policy (i.e., tax codes, the welfare system), can you think of any problems with using fiscal policy to stabilize the economy?

4. Why do we call mechanisms such as proportional income taxes and the welfare system *automatic stabilizers*? Choose one of these mechanisms and explain carefully how and why it affects fluctuations in output.

5. What is the full-employment budget surplus, and why might it be a more useful measure than the actual, or unadjusted, budget surplus? The text provides other names for this measure, such as *cyclically adjusted surplus* and *structural surplus*. Why might we prefer to use these other terms?

Technical

1. Here we investigate a particular example of the model studied in Sections 9-2 and 9-3 with no government. Suppose the consumption function is given by $C = 100 + .8Y$, while investment is given by $I = 50$.
   a. What is the equilibrium level of income in this case?
   b. What is the level of saving in equilibrium?
   c. If, for some reason, output is at the level of 800, what will the level of involuntary inventory accumulation be?
   d. If I rises to 100 (we discuss what determines I in later chapters), what will the effect be on the equilibrium income?
   e. What is the value of the multiplier, α, here?
   f. Draw a diagram indicating the equilibria in both (a) and (d).

2. Suppose the consumption behavior in problem 1 changes so that $C = 100 + .9Y$, while I remains at 50.
   a. Is the equilibrium level of income higher or lower than it was in problem 1(a)? Calculate the new equilibrium level, Y', to verify this.
   b. Now suppose investment increases to $I = 100$, just as in problem 1(d). What is the new equilibrium income?
   c. Does this change in investment spending have more or less of an effect on Y than it did in problem 1? Why?
   d. Draw a diagram indicating the change in equilibrium income in this case.

3. Now we look at the role taxes play in determining equilibrium income. Suppose we have an economy of the type in Sections 9-4 and 9-5, described by the following functions:

$$C = 50 + .8YD$$
$$\bar{I} = 70$$
$$\bar{G} = 200$$
$$\overline{TR} = 100$$
$$t = .20$$

   a. Calculate the equilibrium level of income and the multiplier in this model.
   b. Calculate also the budget surplus, *BS*.
   c. Suppose that t increases to .25. What is the new equilibrium income? The new multiplier?
   d. Calculate the change in the budget surplus. Would you expect the change in the surplus to be more or less if $c = .9$ rather than .8?
   e. Can you explain why the multiplier is 1 when $t = 1$?

4. Suppose the economy is operating at equilibrium, with $Y_0 = 1,000$. If the government undertakes a fiscal change whereby the tax rate, t, increases by .05 and government spending increases by 50, will the budget surplus go up or down? Why?

5. Suppose Congress decides to reduce transfer payments (such as welfare) but to increase government purchases of goods and services by an equal amount. That is, it undertakes a change in fiscal policy such that $\Delta G = -\Delta TR$.

   a. Would you expect equilibrium income to rise or fall as a result of this change? Why? Check your answer with the following example: Suppose that, initially, $c = .8$, $t = .25$, and $Y_0 = 600$. Now let $\Delta G = 10$ and $\Delta TR = -10$.

   b. Find the change in equilibrium income, ΔY_0.

   c. What is the change in the budget surplus, ΔBS? Why has BS changed?

Empirical

1. Section 9-2 analyses the consumption function, and Box 9-1 shows that the consumption function holds in practice for the United States. In this exercise you will derive a consumption function for Australia.

   a. Go to www.economagic.com. Under "Browse by Source," choose "Australia," and download data for
   - Real Gross Domestic Income (found under the heading "Gross Domestic Product").
   - Private Spending: Household Consumption (found under the heading "Gross Domestic Product: Expenditure Components").

   b. Create a scatterplot that has Real Gross Domestic Income on the X axis and Household Consumption on the Y axis. What is the relationship between consumption and income in Australia? Visually, on average by how much would an increase of AU$10 billion in income affect consumption? Using your answer, compute the marginal propensity to consume for Australia.

   *c. If you have taken a statistics class, use EXCEL or a statistical program in order to run the following regression:

$$C = \overline{C} + cY + \epsilon$$

   What is the implied slope? What does it mean? Is it statistically significant?

*An asterisk denotes a more difficult problem.

CHAPTER 10

Money, Interest, and Income

CHAPTER HIGHLIGHTS

- The model we introduce in this chapter, the *IS-LM* model, is the core of short-run macroeconomics.

- The *IS* curve describes the combinations of income and interest rates at which the goods market is in equilibrium.

- The *LM* curve describes the combinations of income and interest rates at which the money market is in equilibrium.

- Together, the *IS* and *LM* curves give aggregate demand.

- Increases in government spending raise output and interest rates.

- Increases in the money supply raise output and lower interest rates.

Money plays a central role in the determination of income and employment. Interest rates are a significant determinant of aggregate spending, and the Federal Reserve, which controls money growth and interest rates, is the first institution to be blamed when the economy gets into trouble. However, the stock of money, interest rates, and the Federal Reserve seem to have no place in the model of income determination developed in Chapter 9.

This chapter introduces money and monetary policy and builds an explicit framework of analysis within which to study the interaction of goods markets and assets markets. This new framework leads to an understanding of the determination of interest rates and of their role in the business cycle and introduces an avenue by which monetary policy affects output. Figure 10-1 shows the interest rate on Treasury bills. The interest rate on Treasury bills represents the payment received by someone who lends to the U.S. government. An interest rate of 5 percent means that someone who lends $100 to the government for 1 year will receive 5 percent, or $5, in interest. Figure 10-1 shows that interest rates are typically, but not always, high just before a

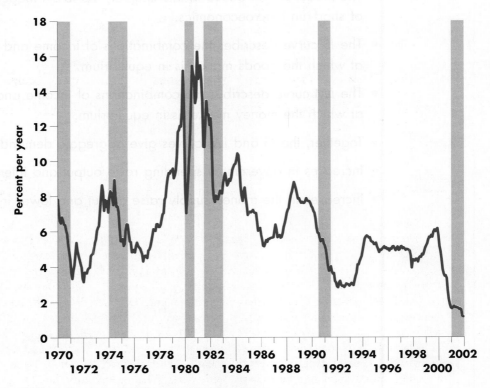

FIGURE 10-1   THE INTEREST RATE ON TREASURY BILLS.
(Source: www.economagic.com.)

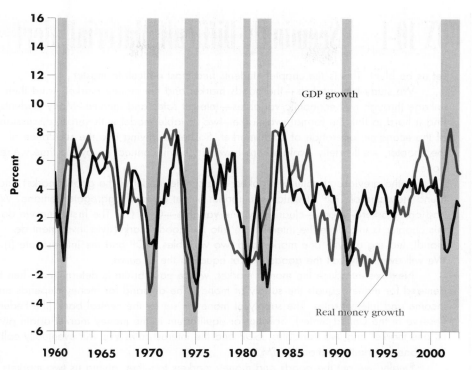

FIGURE 10-2   GDP GROWTH (QUARTERLY) AND REAL MONEY GROWTH (OVER PREVIOUS YEAR).
(Source: Bureau of Economic Analysis and Federal Reserve Economic Data.)

recession, drop during the recession, and rise during the recovery. Figure 10-2 shows money growth and output growth. There is a strong, but not absolute, link between money growth and output growth. This chapter explores the link from money to interest rates to output.

The model we introduce in this chapter, the *IS-LM* model, is the core of short-run macroeconomics. It maintains the spirit and, indeed, many details of the model of the previous chapter. The model is broadened, though, by introducing the interest rate as an additional determinant of aggregate demand. In Chapter 9, autonomous spending and fiscal policy were the chief determinants of aggregate demand. Now we add the interest rate as a determinant of investment and therefore aggregate demand. We then have to ask what determines the interest rate. That question extends our model to include the money market and forces us to study the interaction of goods and money markets. The Federal Reserve enters the picture through its role in setting the supply of money. Interest rates and income are jointly determined by equilibrium in the goods and money markets. As in the previous chapter, we maintain the assumption that the price level does not respond when aggregate demand shifts.

BOX 10-1   Seemingly Difficult Material Alert

Let us be blunt. This is *the* chapter students find most difficult to master.

We study two markets—the goods market and the money market—and their linkage through two economic variables—interest rates and income. Many students find it hard to link the formal two-market–two-variable model with verbal discussion of the economic operation of each market. So before diving into the substance of the chapter, we'll briefly explain here how things will connect up by the time we're done.

In the previous chapter we looked at a simple model of the goods market and found the value of GDP at which equilibrium output equaled aggregate demand. We had one market—goods—cleared by one variable—GDP (Y). The first thing we do in this chapter is introduce the interest rate into the goods market (via investment demand), leaving us with one market and two variables, GDP and the interest rate (i). We will eventually call the goods market equation the *IS curve*.

Next we introduce the money market, where equilibrium is determined when the demand for money equals the supply of money. The demand for money depends on income and interest rates. The supply of money is set by the central bank (the Federal Reserve in the United States). Solving for equilibrium in the money market again gives us one market and two variables, GDP and the interest rate. We will eventually call the money market equation the *LM curve*.

Finally, we put the goods and money markets together, giving us two markets (goods and money) and two variables (GDP and the interest rate). **The IS-LM model finds the values of GDP and the interest rate which simultaneously clear the goods and money markets.**

As we put all this together, be certain to keep a mental marker on whether we are talking about just the goods market, just the money market, or the linkage of the two. (Use different-color highlighters if it helps.) If you can do this, you should find the chapter not too difficult after all.

Understanding the money market and interest rates is important for three reasons:

1. Monetary policy works through the money market to affect output and employment.
2. The analysis qualifies the conclusions of Chapter 9. Consider Figure 10-3, which lays out the logical structure of the model. So far, we have looked at the box labeled "Goods market." By adding the assets markets, we provide a fuller analysis of the effect of fiscal policy, and we introduce monetary policy. We shall see, for instance, that an expansionary fiscal policy generally raises interest rates, thereby dampening its expansionary impact. Indeed, under certain conditions, the increase in interest rates may be sufficient to offset *fully* the expansionary effects of fiscal policy.

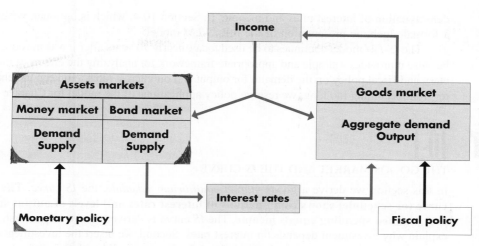

FIGURE 10-3   THE STRUCTURE OF THE *IS-LM* MODEL.

The IS-LM model emphasizes the interaction between the goods and assets markets. Spending, interest rates, and income are determined jointly by equilibrium in the goods and assets markets.

3. Interest rate changes have an important side effect. The *composition* of aggregate demand between investment and consumption spending depends on the interest rate. Higher interest rates dampen aggregate demand mainly by reducing investment. Thus, an expansionary fiscal policy tends to raise consumption through the multiplier but tends to reduce investment because it increases interest rates. Because the rate of investment affects the growth of the economy, this side effect of fiscal expansion is a sensitive and important issue in policymaking.

OUTLINE OF THE CHAPTER

We use Figure 10-3 once more to lay out the structure of this chapter. We start in Section 10-1 with a discussion of the link between interest rates and aggregate demand. We use the model of Chapter 9 directly, augmented to include the interest rate as a determinant of aggregate demand. We derive a key relationship—the *IS* curve—that shows combinations of interest rates and levels of income at which the goods markets clear. In Section 10-2 we turn to the assets markets, particularly the money market. We show that the demand for money depends on interest rates and income and that there are combinations of interest rates and income levels—the *LM* curve—at which the money market clears.[1] In Section 10-3 we combine the two schedules to study the joint

---

[1]The terms *IS* and *LM* are shorthand representations, respectively, of the relationships investment (*I*) equals saving (*S*)—the goods market equilibrium—and money demand (*L*) equals money supply (*M*)—the money market equilibrium. The classic article that introduced this model is J. R. Hicks, "Mr. Keynes and the Classics: A Suggested Interpretation," *Econometrica*, April 1937, pp. 147–59.

determination of interest rates and income. In Section 10-4, which is optional, we give a formal algebraic presentation of the full *IS-LM* model.

The *IS-LM* model continues to be used today, nearly 70 years after it was introduced, because it provides a simple and appropriate framework for analyzing the effects of monetary and fiscal policy on the demand for output and on interest rates.[2] To keep the chapter from becoming too long, we reserve policy applications of the model for Chapter 11.

10-1

THE GOODS MARKET AND THE *IS* CURVE

In this section we derive a *goods market equilibrium schedule,* the *IS curve.* **The *IS* curve (or schedule) shows combinations of interest rates and levels of output such that planned spending equals income.** The *IS* curve is derived in two steps. First, we explain why investment depends on interest rates. Second, we insert the investment demand function in the aggregate demand identity—just as we did with the consumption function in the last chapter—and find the combinations of income and interest rates that keep the goods market in equilibrium.

THE INVESTMENT DEMAND SCHEDULE

So far, investment spending (*I*) has been treated as *entirely* exogenous—some number like $1,000 billion, determined altogether outside the model of income determination. Now, as we make our macromodel more complete by introducing interest rates as a part of the model, investment spending, too, becomes endogenous. The desired or planned rate of investment is lower the higher the interest rate.

A simple argument shows why. Investment is spending on additions to the firm's capital, such as machines or buildings. Typically, firms borrow to purchase investment goods. The higher the interest rate for such borrowing, the lower the profits that firms can expect to make by borrowing to buy new machines or buildings, and therefore the less they will be willing to borrow and invest. Conversely, firms will want to borrow and invest more when interest rates are lower.

INVESTMENT•AND THE INTEREST RATE

We specify an investment spending function of the form[3]

$$I = \bar{I} - bi \qquad b > 0 \tag{1}$$

---

[2]For a modern perspective on the usefulness of the *IS-LM* model, see Bennett T. McCallum and Edward Nelson, "An Optimizing *IS-LM* Specification for Monetary Policy and Business Cycle Analysis," *Journal of Money, Credit, and Banking,* August 1999. See also Jordí Gali, "How Well Does the IS/LM Model Fit Postwar U.S. Data?" *Quarterly Journal of Economics,* May 1992.

[3]Here and in other places in the book, we specify linear (straight-line) versions of behavioral functions. We use the linear form to simplify both the algebra and the diagrams. The linearity assumption is not misleading as long as we confine ourselves to talking about small changes in the economy.

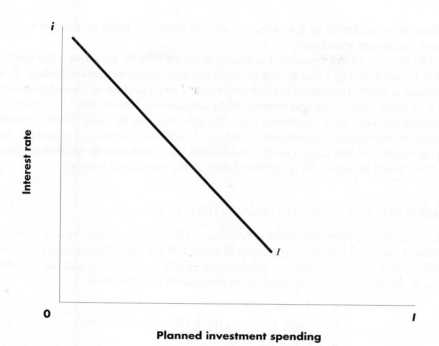

FIGURE 10-4   THE INVESTMENT SCHEDULE.

The investment schedule shows the planned level of investment spending at each rate of interest.

where i is the rate of interest and the coefficient b measures the responsiveness of investment spending to the interest rate. $\overline{I}$ now denotes autonomous investment spending, that is, investment spending that is independent of both income and the rate of interest.[4] Equation (1) states that the lower the interest rate, the higher is planned investment. If b is large, then a relatively small increase in the interest rate generates a large drop in investment spending.[5]

Figure 10-4, the investment schedule of equation (1), shows for each level of the interest rate the amount that firms plan to spend on investment. The schedule is negatively sloped to reflect the assumption that a reduction in the interest rate increases the

[4]In Chap. 9, investment spending was defined as autonomous with respect to income. Now that the interest rate appears in the model, we have to extend the definition of "autonomous" to mean independent of both the interest rate and income. To conserve notation, we continue to use $\overline{I}$ to denote autonomous investment, but we recognize that the definition has broadened. In fact, investment responds positively when income increases, for reasons discussed in Chap. 14. Here, we omit the responsiveness of investment to income as a simplification.

[5]The units of measurement of b depend on the units of measurement of interest rate, i. If investment is measured in billions and the interest rate is written as numbers like 5 or 10—so "percent per year" is implicit in the interest rate number—then b might be a number like 10. If the same interest rate were written instead as 0.05 or 0.10, then the equivalent value of b would be a number like 1,000.

profitability of additions to the capital stock and therefore leads to a larger rate of planned investment spending.

The position of the investment schedule is determined by the slope—the coefficient b in equation (1)—and by the level of autonomous investment spending, $\bar{I}$. If investment is highly responsive to the interest rate, a small decline in interest rates will lead to a large increase in investment, so the schedule is almost flat. Conversely, if investment responds little to interest rates, the schedule will be more nearly vertical. Changes in autonomous investment spending, $\bar{I}$, shift the investment schedule. An increase in $\bar{I}$ means that at each level of the interest rate, firms plan to invest at a higher rate. This would be shown by a rightward shift of the investment schedule.

THE INTEREST RATE AND AGGREGATE DEMAND: THE *IS* CURVE

We now modify the aggregate demand function of Chapter 9 to reflect the new planned investment spending schedule. Aggregate demand still consists of the demand for consumption, investment, government spending on goods and services, and net exports, only now investment spending depends on the interest rate. We have

$$
\begin{aligned}
AD &\equiv C + I + G + NX \\
&= [\bar{C} + c\overline{TR} + c(1 - t)Y] + (\bar{I} - bi) + \bar{G} + \overline{NX} \qquad (2) \\
&= \bar{A} + c(1 - t)Y - bi
\end{aligned}
$$

where

$$
\bar{A} \equiv \bar{C} + c\overline{TR} + \bar{I} + \bar{G} + \overline{NX} \qquad (3)
$$

From equation (2) we see that an increase in the interest rate reduces aggregate demand for a given level of income because a higher interest rate reduces investment spending. Note that $\bar{A}$, which is the part of aggregate demand unaffected by either the level of income or the interest rate, does include part of investment spending, namely, $\bar{I}$. As noted earlier, $\bar{I}$ is the *autonomous* component of investment spending, which is independent of the interest rate (and income).

At any given level of the interest rate, we can still proceed as in Chapter 9 to determine the equilibrium level of income and output. As the interest rate changes, however, the equilibrium level of income changes. We derive the *IS* curve using Figure 10-5.

For a given level of the interest rate, say, i_1, the last term of equation (2) is a constant (bi_1), and we can, in Figure 10-5a, draw the aggregate demand function of Chapter 9, this time with an intercept, $\bar{A} - bi_1$. The equilibrium level of income obtained in the usual manner is Y_1 at point E_1. Since that equilibrium level of income was derived for a given level of the interest rate (i_1), we plot that pair (i_1, Y_1) in the bottom panel as point E_1. This gives us one point, E_1, on the *IS* curve—that is, one combination of interest rate and income which clears the goods market.

Consider next a lower interest rate, i_2. Investment spending is higher when the interest rate falls. In terms of Figure 10-5a, that implies an upward shift of the aggregate demand schedule. The curve shifts upward because the intercept, $\bar{A} - bi$, has increased. Given the increase in aggregate demand, the equilibrium shifts to point E_2, with an

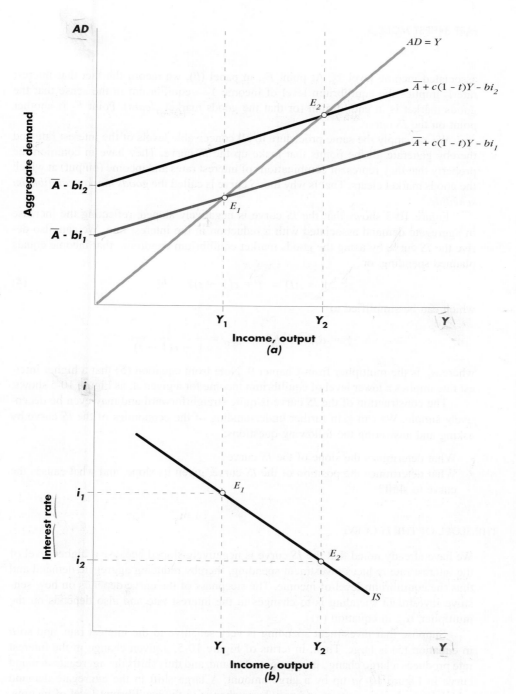

FIGURE 10-5   DERIVATION OF THE *IS* CURVE.

At a particular interest rate, equilibrium in panel (a) determines the income level. A decrease in the interest rate raises aggregate demand. The IS curve shows the resulting negative relationship between interest rates and income.

associated income level Y_2. At point E_2, in panel (b), we record the fact that interest rate i_2 implies the equilibrium level of income Y_2—equilibrium in the sense that the goods market is in equilibrium (or that the goods market *clears*). Point E_2 is another point on the *IS* curve.

We can apply the same procedure to all conceivable levels of the interest rate and thereby generate all the points that make up the *IS* curve. They have in common the property that they represent combinations of interest rates and income (output) at which the goods market clears. That is why the *IS* curve is called the *goods market equilibrium schedule*.

Figure 10-5 shows that the *IS* curve is negatively sloped, reflecting the increase in aggregate demand associated with a reduction in the interest rate. We can also derive the *IS* curve by using the goods market equilibrium condition, that income equals planned spending, or

$$Y = AD = \overline{A} + c(1 - t)Y - bi \tag{4}$$

which can be simplified to

$$Y = \alpha_G(\overline{A} - bi) \qquad \alpha_G = \frac{1}{1 - c(1 - t)} \tag{5}$$

where α_G is the multiplier from Chapter 9. Note from equation (5) that a higher interest rate implies a lower level of equilibrium income for a given $\overline{A}$, as Figure 10-5 shows.

The construction of the *IS* curve is quite straightforward and may even be deceptively simple. We can gain further understanding of the economics of the *IS* curve by asking and answering the following questions:

- What determines the slope of the *IS* curve?
- What determines the position of the *IS* curve, given its slope, and what causes the curve to shift?

THE SLOPE OF THE *IS* CURVE

We have already noted that the *IS* curve is negatively sloped because a higher level of the interest rate reduces investment spending, thereby reducing aggregate demand and thus the equilibrium level of income. The steepness of the curve depends on how sensitive investment spending is to changes in the interest rate and also depends on the multiplier, α_G, in equation (5).

Suppose that investment spending is very sensitive to the interest rate, and so b in equation (5) is large. Then, in terms of Figure 10-5, a given change in the interest rate produces a large change in aggregate demand, and thus shifts the aggregate demand curve in Figure 10-5a up by a large amount. A large shift in the aggregate demand schedule produces a correspondingly large change in the equilibrium level of income. If a given change in the interest rate produces a large change in income, the *IS* curve is very flat. This is the case if investment is very sensitive to the interest rate, that is, if b is large. Correspondingly, if b is small and investment spending is not very sensitive to the interest rate, the *IS* curve is relatively steep.

The Role of the Multiplier

Consider next the effects of the multiplier, α_G, on the steepness of the *IS* curve. Figure 10-6 shows aggregate demand curves corresponding to different multipliers. The coefficient c on the solid black aggregate demand curves is smaller than the corresponding coefficient c' on the dashed black aggregate demand curves. The multiplier is accordingly larger on the dashed aggregate demand curves. The initial levels of income, Y_1 and Y'_1, correspond to the interest rate i_1 in panel (*b*).

A given reduction in the interest rate, to i_2, raises the intercept of the aggregate demand curves by the same vertical distance, as shown in panel (*a*). However, the implied change in income is very different. On the dashed curve, income rises to Y'_2, while it rises only to Y_2 on the solid line. The change in equilibrium income corresponding to a given change in the interest rate is accordingly larger as the aggregate demand curve is steeper; that is, the larger the multiplier, the greater the rise in income. As we see from panel (*b*), the larger the multiplier, the flatter the *IS* curve. Equivalently, the larger the multiplier, the larger the change in income produced by a given change in the interest rate.

We have thus seen that **the smaller the sensitivity of investment spending to the interest rate and the smaller the multiplier, the steeper the *IS* curve.** This conclusion is confirmed using equation (5). We can turn equation (5) around to express the interest rate as a function of the level of income:

$$ i = \frac{\overline{A}}{b} - \frac{Y}{\alpha_G b} \tag{5a} $$

Thus, for a given change in Y, the associated change in i will be larger in size as b is smaller and as α_G is smaller.

Given that the slope of the *IS* curve depends on the multiplier, fiscal policy can affect that slope. The multiplier, α_G, is affected by the tax rate: An increase in the tax rate reduces the multiplier. Accordingly, the higher the tax rate, the steeper the *IS* curve.[6]

THE POSITION OF THE *IS* CURVE

Figure 10-7 shows two different *IS* curves, the lighter one of which lies to the right and above the darker *IS* curve. What might cause the *IS* curve to be at *IS'* rather than at *IS*? The answer is an increase in the level of autonomous spending.

In Figure 10-7*a* we show an initial aggregate demand curve drawn for a level of autonomous spending $\overline{A}$ and for an interest rate i_1. Corresponding to the initial aggregate demand curve is the point E_1 on the *IS* curve in Figure 10-7*b*. Now, at the same interest rate, let the level of autonomous spending increase to $\overline{A}'$. The increase in autonomous spending increases the equilibrium level of income at the interest rate i_1. The point E_2 in panel (*b*) is thus a point on the new goods market equilibrium schedule, *IS'*. Since E_1 was an arbitrary point on the initial *IS* curve, we can perform the exercise for all

---

[6]In the problem set at the end of this chapter we ask you to relate this fact to the discussion of automatic stabilizers in Chap. 9.

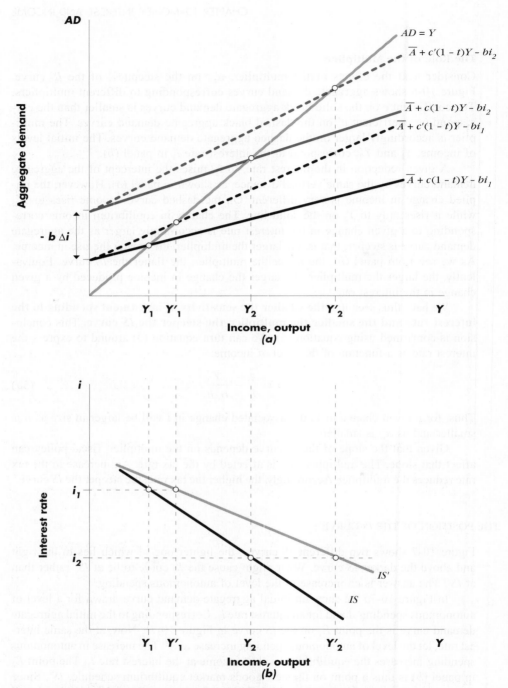

FIGURE 10-6   EFFECT OF THE MULTIPLIER ON THE SLOPE OF THE *IS* CURVE.

A higher marginal propensity to spend results in a steeper aggregate demand curve and, consequently, a flatter IS curve.

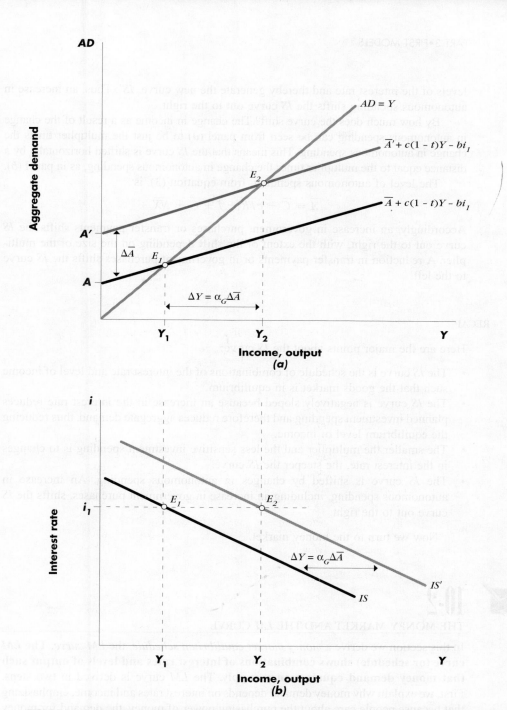

FIGURE 10-7   A SHIFT IN THE *IS* CURVE CAUSED BY A CHANGE IN AUTONOMOUS SPENDING.

An increase in autonomous spending increases aggregate demand and increases the income level at a given interest rate. This is represented by a rightward shift of the IS curve.

levels of the interest rate and thereby generate the new curve, *IS'*. Thus, an increase in autonomous spending shifts the *IS* curve out to the right.

By how much does the curve shift? The change in income as a result of the change in autonomous spending can be seen from panel (*a*) to be just the multiplier times the change in autonomous spending. This means that the *IS* curve is shifted horizontally by a distance equal to the multiplier times the change in autonomous spending, as in panel (*b*).

The level of autonomous spending, from equation (3), is

$$\overline{A} \equiv \overline{C} + c\overline{TR} + \overline{I} + \overline{G} + \overline{NX}$$

Accordingly, an increase in government purchases or transfer payments shifts the *IS* curve out to the right, with the extent of the shift depending on the size of the multiplier. A reduction in transfer payments or in government purchases shifts the *IS* curve to the left.

RECAP

Here are the major points about the *IS* curve:

- The *IS* curve is the schedule of combinations of the interest rate and level of income such that the goods market is in equilibrium.
- The *IS* curve is negatively sloped because an increase in the interest rate reduces planned investment spending and therefore reduces aggregate demand, thus reducing the equilibrium level of income.
- The smaller the multiplier and the less sensitive investment spending is to changes in the interest rate, the steeper the *IS* curve.
- The *IS* curve is shifted by changes in autonomous spending. An increase in autonomous spending, including an increase in government purchases, shifts the *IS* curve out to the right.

Now we turn to the money market.

10-2

THE MONEY MARKET AND THE *LM* CURVE

In this section we derive a *money market equilibrium schedule,* the *LM curve.* **The *LM* curve (or schedule) shows combinations of interest rates and levels of output such that money demand equals money supply.** The *LM* curve is derived in two steps. First, we explain why money demand depends on interest rates and income, emphasizing that because people care about the purchasing power of money, the demand for money is a theory of *real* rather than *nominal* demand. Second, we equate money demand with money supply—set by the central bank—and find the combinations of income and interest rates that keep the money market in equilibrium.

BOX 10-2   Real and Nominal Money Demand

At this stage we have to reinforce the crucial distinction between *real* and *nominal* variables. The nominal demand for money is the individual's demand for a given number of dollars. Similarly, the nominal demand for bonds is the demand for a given number of dollars' worth of bonds. The real demand for money is the demand for money expressed in terms of the number of units of goods that money will buy: It is equal to the nominal demand for money divided by the price level. If the nominal demand for money is $100 and the price level is $2 per good—meaning that the representative basket of goods cost $2—the real demand for money is 50 goods. If the price level later doubles to $4 per good and the demand for nominal money likewise doubles to $200, the real demand for money is unchanged at 50 goods.

Real money balances—real balances, for short—are the quantity of nominal money divided by the price level. The real demand for money is called the *demand for real balances*.

THE DEMAND FOR MONEY

We turn now to the money market and initially concentrate on the demand for real balances.[7] The demand for money is a demand for *real money balances* because people hold money for what it will buy. The higher the price level, the more nominal balances a person has to hold to be able to purchase a given quantity of goods. If the price level doubles, an individual has to hold twice as many nominal balances in order to be able to buy the same amount of goods.

The *demand for real balances* depends on the level of real income and the interest rate. It depends on the level of real income because individuals hold money to pay for their purchases, which, in turn, depend on income. The demand for money depends also on the cost of holding money. The cost of holding money is the interest that is forgone by holding money rather than other assets. The higher the interest rate, the more costly it is to hold money and, accordingly, the less cash will be held at each level of income.[8] Individuals can economize on their holdings of cash when the interest rate rises by being more careful in managing their money and by making transfers from money to bonds whenever their money holdings become large. If the interest rate is 1 percent, there is very little benefit from holding bonds rather than money. However,

---

[7]The demand for money is examined in depth in Chap. 15; here we present the arguments underlying the demand for money only briefly.

[8]Some types of money, including most bank deposits, earn interest, but at a lower rate than bonds. Several sizable parts of money holding—including currency—earn no interest; so, overall, money earns less interest than other assets. Thus, there is an interest cost to holding money.

when the interest rate is 10 percent, it is worth some effort not to hold more money than is needed to finance day-to-day transactions.

On these simple grounds, then, the demand for real balances increases with the level of real income and decreases with the interest rate. The demand for real balances, which we denote as L, is accordingly expressed as

$$L = kY - hi \qquad k, h > 0 \qquad (6)$$

The parameters k and h reflect the sensitivity of the demand for real balances to the level of income and the interest rate, respectively. A \$5 increase in real income raises money demand by $k \times 5$ real dollars. An increase in the interest rate of 1 percentage point reduces real money demand by h real dollars.

The demand function for real balances, equation (6), implies that for a given level of income, the quantity demanded is a decreasing function of the rate of interest. Such a demand curve is shown in Figure 10-8 for a level of income Y_1. The higher the level of income, the larger the demand for real balances and, therefore, the farther to the right the demand curve. The demand curve for a higher level of real income, Y_2, is also shown in Figure 10-8.

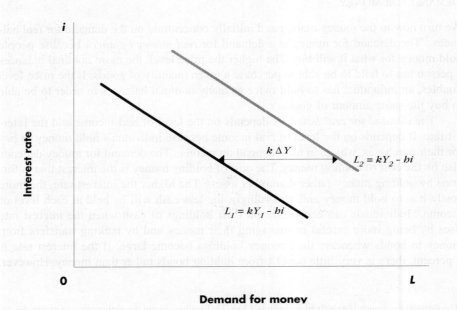

Demand for money

FIGURE 10-8   DEMAND FOR REAL BALANCES AS A FUNCTION OF THE INTEREST RATE AND REAL INCOME.

The higher the rate of interest, the lower the quantity of real balances demanded, given the level of income. An increase in income raises the demand for money, as shown by the rightward shift in the money demand schedule.

THE SUPPLY OF MONEY, MONEY MARKET EQUILIBRIUM, AND THE *LM* CURVE

To study equilibrium in the money market, we have to say how the supply of money is determined. The nominal quantity of money, M, is controlled by the Federal Reserve System ("the Fed") in the United States. The *central bank* has other names in other countries, and, of course, through much of history the nominal quantity of money was determined by gold discoveries or similar events. We take the nominal quantity of money as given at the level $\overline{M}$. We assume the price level is constant at the level $\overline{P}$, so the real money supply is at the level $\overline{M}/\overline{P}$.[9]

In Figure 10-9 we show combinations of interest rates and income levels such that the demand for real balances exactly matches the available supply. Starting with the level of income, Y_1, the corresponding demand curve for real balances, L_1, is shown in Figure 10-9*b*. It is drawn, as in Figure 10-8, as a decreasing function of the interest rate. The existing supply of real balances, $\overline{M}/\overline{P}$, is shown by the vertical line, since it is given and therefore is independent of the interest rate. At interest rate i_1, the demand for real balances equals the supply. Therefore, point E_1 is an equilibrium point in the money market. That point is recorded in Figure 10-9*a* as a point on the money market equilibrium schedule, or the *LM* curve.

Consider next the effect of an increase in income to Y_2. In Figure 10-9*b* the higher level of income causes the demand for real balances to be higher at each level of the interest rate, so the demand curve for real balances shifts up and to the right, to L_2. The interest rate increases to i_2 to maintain equilibrium in the money market at that higher level of income. Accordingly, the new equilibrium point is E_2. In Figure 10-9*a* we record point E_2 as a point of equilibrium in the money market. Performing the same exercise for all income levels, we generate a series of points that can be linked to give us the *LM* schedule.

The *LM* schedule, or *money market equilibrium schedule,* shows all combinations of interest rates and levels of income such that the demand for real balances is equal to the supply. Along the *LM* schedule, the money market is in equilibrium.

The *LM* curve is positively sloped. An increase in the interest rate reduces the demand for real balances. To maintain the demand for real balances equal to the fixed supply, the level of income has to rise. Accordingly, money market equilibrium implies that an increase in the interest rate is accompanied by an increase in the level of income.

The *LM* curve can be obtained directly by combining the demand curve for real balances, equation (6), and the fixed supply of real balances. For the money market to be in equilibrium, demand has to equal supply, or

$$\frac{\overline{M}}{\overline{P}} = kY - hi \qquad (7)$$

Solving for the interest rate,

$$i = \frac{1}{h}\left(kY - \frac{\overline{M}}{\overline{P}}\right) \qquad (7a)$$

The relationship (7*a*) is the *LM* curve.

[9]Since, for the present, we are holding constant the money supply and price level, we denote that fact by a bar.

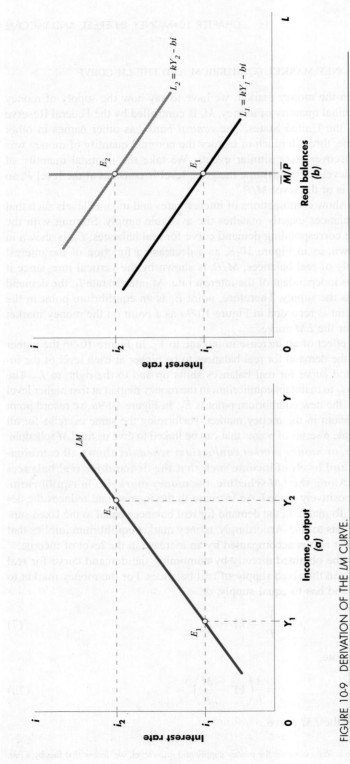

FIGURE 10-9 DERIVATION OF THE LM CURVE.

Panel (b) shows the money market. The supply of real balances is the vertical line $\overline{M}/P$. L_1 and L_2 represent money demand at different levels of income (Y_1 and Y_2).

Next we ask the same questions about the properties of the *LM* schedule that we asked about the *IS* curve.

THE SLOPE OF THE *LM* CURVE

The greater the responsiveness of the demand for money to income, as measured by k, and the lower the responsiveness of the demand for money to the interest rate, h, the steeper the *LM* curve will be. This point can be established by experimenting with Figure 10-9. It can also be confirmed by examining equation ($7a$), where a given change in income, ΔY, has a larger effect on the interest rate, i, the larger is k and the smaller is h. If the demand for money is relatively insensitive to the interest rate and thus h is close to zero, the *LM* curve is nearly vertical. If the demand for money is very sensitive to the interest rate and thus h is large, the *LM* curve is close to horizontal. In that case, a small change in the interest rate must be accompanied by a large change in the level of income in order to maintain money market equilibrium.

THE POSITION OF THE *LM* CURVE

The real money supply is held constant along the *LM* curve. It follows that a change in the real money supply will shift the *LM* curve. In Figure 10-10 we show the effect of an increase in the real money supply. Panel (b) shows the demand for real money balances for a level of income Y_1. With the initial real money supply, $\overline{M/P}$, the equilibrium is at point E_1, with the interest rate i_1. The corresponding point on the *LM* schedule is E_1.

Now the real money supply increases to $\overline{M'/P}$, which we represent by a rightward shift of the money supply schedule. To restore money market equilibrium at the income level Y_1, the interest rate has to decline to i_2. The new equilibrium is, therefore, at point E_2. This implies that in Figure 10-10a, the *LM* schedule shifts to the right and down to *LM'*. At each level of income the equilibrium interest rate has to be lower to induce people to hold the larger real quantity of money. Alternatively, at each level of the interest rate the level of income has to be higher to raise the transactions demand for money and thereby absorb the higher real money supply. These points can be noted, too, from inspection of the money market equilibrium condition in equation (7).

RECAP

The following are the major points about the *LM* curve:

- The *LM* curve is the schedule of combinations of interest rates and levels of income such that the money market is in equilibrium.
- The *LM* curve is positively sloped. Given the fixed money supply, an increase in the level of income, which increases the quantity of money demanded, has to be

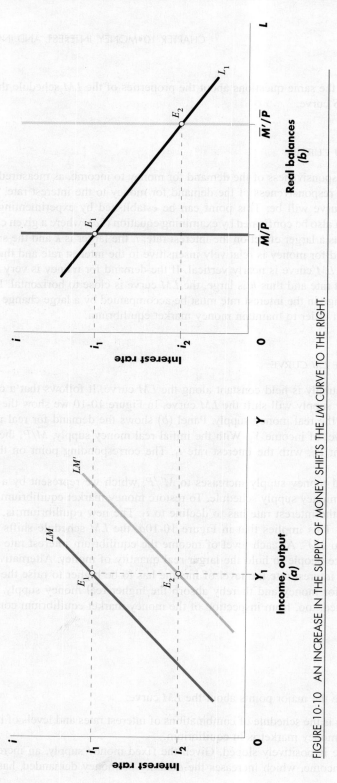

Income, output
(a)

Real balances
(b)

FIGURE 10-10   AN INCREASE IN THE SUPPLY OF MONEY SHIFTS THE *LM* CURVE TO THE RIGHT.

accompanied by an increase in the interest rate. This reduces the quantity of money demanded and thereby maintains money market equilibrium.

- The *LM* curve is steeper when the demand for money responds strongly to income and weakly to interest rates.
- The *LM* curve is shifted by changes in the money supply. An increase in the money supply shifts the *LM* curve to the right.

We are now ready to discuss the joint equilibrium of the goods and assets markets. That is to say, we can now discuss how output and interest rates are determined.

10-3

EQUILIBRIUM IN THE GOODS AND MONEY MARKETS

The *IS* and *LM* schedules summarize the conditions that have to be satisfied in order for the goods and money markets, respectively, to be in equilibrium. The task now is to determine how these markets are brought into *simultaneous* equilibrium. For simultaneous equilibrium, interest rates and income levels have to be such that both the goods market *and* the money market are in equilibrium. This condition is satisfied at point E in Figure 10-11. The equilibrium interest rate is therefore i_0 and the equilibrium level

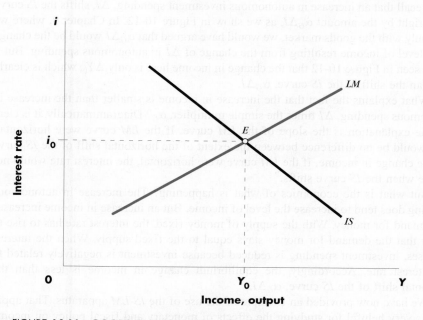

FIGURE 10-11   GOODS AND MONEY MARKET EQUILIBRIUM.

At point E, interest rates and income levels are such that the public holds the existing money stock and planned spending equals output.

of income is Y_0, given the exogenous variables, in particular, the real money supply and fiscal policy.[10] At point E, both the goods market and the money market are in equilibrium.

Figure 10-11 summarizes our analysis: The interest rate and the *level* of output are determined by the interaction of the money (LM) and goods (IS) markets.

It is worth stepping back now to review our assumptions and the meaning of the equilibrium at E. The major assumption is that the price level is constant and that firms are willing to supply whatever amount of output is demanded at that price level. Thus, we assume that the level of output Y_0 in Figure 10-11 will be willingly supplied by firms at the price level $\bar{P}$. We repeat that this assumption is one that is temporarily needed for the development of the analysis; it corresponds to the assumption of a flat, short-run aggregate supply curve.

CHANGES IN THE EQUILIBRIUM LEVELS OF INCOME AND THE INTEREST RATE

The equilibrium levels of income and the interest rate change when either the IS or the LM curve shifts. Figure 10-12, for example, shows the effects of an increase in the rate of autonomous investment on the equilibrium levels of income and the interest rate. Such an increase raises autonomous spending, $\bar{A}$, and therefore shifts the IS curve to the right. That results in a rise in the level of income and an increase in the interest rate at point E'.

Recall that an increase in autonomous investment spending, $\Delta \bar{I}$, shifts the IS curve to the right by the amount $\alpha_G \Delta \bar{I}$, as we show in Figure 10-12. In Chapter 9, where we dealt only with the goods market, we would have argued that $\alpha_G \Delta \bar{I}$ would be the change in the level of income resulting from the change of $\Delta \bar{I}$ in autonomous spending. But it can be seen in Figure 10-12 that the change in income here is only ΔY_0, which is clearly less than the shift in the IS curve, $\alpha_G \Delta \bar{I}$.

What explains the fact that the increase in income is smaller than the increase in autonomous spending, $\Delta \bar{I}$ times the simple multiplier, α_G? Diagrammatically, it is clear that the explanation is the slope of the LM curve. If the LM curve were horizontal, there would be no difference between the extent of the horizontal shift of the IS curve and the change in income. If the LM curve were horizontal, the interest rate would not change when the IS curve shifts.

But what is the economics of what is happening? The increase in autonomous spending does tend to increase the level of income. But an increase in income increases the demand for money. With the supply of money fixed, the interest rate has to rise to ensure that the demand for money stays equal to the fixed supply. When the interest rate rises, investment spending is reduced because investment is negatively related to the interest rate. Accordingly, the equilibrium change in income is less than the horizontal shift of the IS curve, $\alpha_G \Delta \bar{I}$.

We have now provided an example of the use of the IS-LM apparatus. That apparatus is very helpful for studying the effects of monetary and fiscal policy on income

---

[10] In general, exogenous variables are those whose values are not determined within the system being studied.

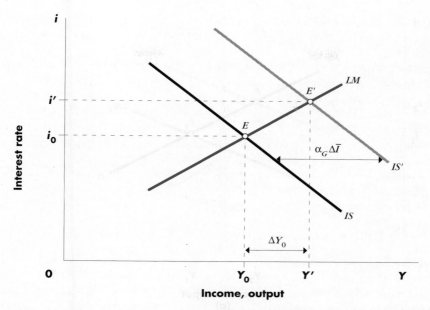

FIGURE 10-12   AN INCREASE IN AUTONOMOUS SPENDING SHIFTS THE *IS* CURVE TO THE RIGHT.

The equilibrium interest rate and level of income both rise.

and the interest rate, and we use it to do so in Chapter 11. To anticipate what is coming, you might want to experiment with how equilibrium income and interest rates change when expansionary fiscal policy moves the *IS* curve to the right or expansionary monetary policy moves the *LM* curve to the right.

10-4

DERIVING THE AGGREGATE DEMAND SCHEDULE

In earlier chapters we used the aggregate demand–aggregate supply apparatus. Here we derive the *aggregate demand schedule*. **The aggregate demand schedule maps out the *IS-LM* equilibrium holding autonomous spending and the nominal money supply constant and allowing prices to vary.** In other words, in learning to use the *IS-LM* model, you've already learned everything about deriving the aggregate demand schedule. Put simply, a higher price level means a lower *real* money supply, an *LM* curve shifted to the left, and lower aggregate demand.

Suppose the price level in the economy is P_1. Panel (*a*) of Figure 10-13 shows the *IS-LM* equilibrium. Note that the real money supply, which determines the position of the LM_1 curve, is $\overline{M}/P_1$. The intersection of the *IS* and LM_1 curves gives the level of aggregate demand corresponding to price P_1 and is so marked in the lower panel.

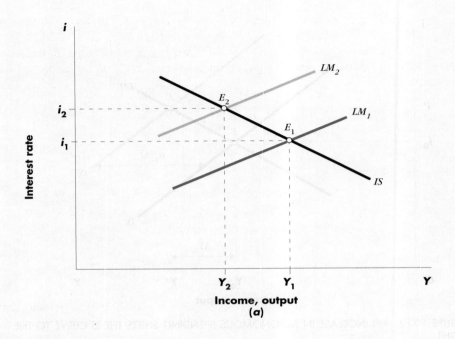

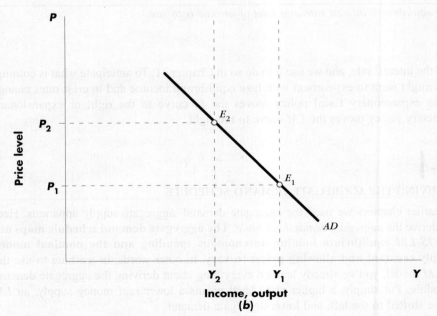

FIGURE 10-13   DERIVATION OF THE AGGREGATE DEMAND SCHEDULE.

Suppose, instead, that the price is higher, say P_2. The curve LM_2 shows the LM curve based on the real money supply $\overline{M}/P_2$. LM_2 is to the left of LM_1 since $\overline{M}/P_2 < \overline{M}/P_1$. Point E_2 shows the corresponding point on the aggregate demand curve. Repeat this operation for a variety of price levels, and connect the points to derive the aggregate demand schedule.

◆ OPTIONAL ◆

10-5

A FORMAL TREATMENT OF THE *IS-LM* MODEL

Our exposition so far has been verbal and graphical. We now round off the analysis with a more formal, algebraic, treatment of the *IS-LM* model.

EQUILIBRIUM INCOME AND THE INTEREST RATE

The intersection of the *IS* and *LM* schedules determines equilibrium income and the equilibrium interest rate. We now derive expressions for these equilibrium values by using the equations of the *IS* and *LM* schedules. Recall from earlier in the chapter that the goods market equilibrium equation is

$$IS \text{ schedule:} \quad Y = \alpha_G(\overline{A} - bi) \tag{5}$$

and that the equation for the money market equilibrium is

$$LM \text{ schedule:} \quad i = \frac{1}{h}\left(kY - \frac{\overline{M}}{P}\right) \tag{7a}$$

The intersection of the *IS* and *LM* schedules in the diagrams corresponds to a situation in which both the *IS* and the *LM* equations hold: The *same* interest rate and income levels ensure equilibrium in both the goods *and* the money market. In terms of the equations, that means we can substitute the interest rate from the *LM* equation (7a) into the *IS* equation (5):

$$Y = \alpha_G\left[\overline{A} - \frac{b}{h}\left(kY - \frac{\overline{M}}{P}\right)\right]$$

Collecting terms and solving for the equilibrium level of income, we obtain

$$Y = \frac{h\alpha_G}{h + kb\alpha_G}\overline{A} + \frac{b\alpha_G}{h + kb\alpha_G}\frac{\overline{M}}{P} \tag{8}$$

or equivalently

$$Y = \gamma\overline{A} + \gamma\frac{b}{h}\frac{\overline{M}}{P} \tag{8a}$$

where $\gamma = \alpha_G/(1 + k\alpha_G b/h)$.[11] Equation (8) shows that the equilibrium level of income depends on two exogenous variables: (1) autonomous spending ($\bar{A}$), including autonomous consumption and investment ($\bar{C}$ and $\bar{I}$) and fiscal policy parameters (G, TR), and (2) the real money stock ($\overline{M/P}$). Equilibrium income is higher the higher the level of autonomous spending, $\bar{A}$, and the higher the stock of real balances.

Equation (8) is the aggregate demand schedule. It summarizes the *IS-LM* relation, relating Y and P for given levels of $\bar{A}$ and $\overline{M}$. Since P is in the denominator, the aggregate demand curve slopes downward.

The equilibrium rate of interest, i, is obtained by substituting the equilibrium income level, Y_0, from equation (8) into the equation of the *LM* schedule (7a):

$$i = \frac{k\alpha_G}{h + kb\alpha_G}\bar{A} - \frac{1}{h + kb\alpha_G}\frac{\overline{M}}{P} \tag{9}$$

or equivalently

$$i = \frac{k}{h}\gamma\bar{A} - \frac{1}{h\alpha_G}\gamma\frac{\overline{M}}{P} \tag{9a}$$

Equation (9) shows that the equilibrium interest rate depends on the parameters of fiscal policy captured in the multiplier and the term $\bar{A}$ and on the real money stock. A higher real money stock implies a lower equilibrium interest rate.

For policy questions we are interested in the precise relation between changes in fiscal policy or changes in the real money stock and the resulting changes in equilibrium income. Monetary and fiscal policy *multipliers* provide the relevant information.

THE FISCAL POLICY MULTIPLIER

The *fiscal policy multiplier* shows how much an increase in government spending changes the equilibrium level of income, holding the real money supply constant. Examine equation (8) and consider the effect of an increase in government spending on income. The increase in government spending, $\Delta\bar{G}$, is a change in autonomous spending, so $\Delta\bar{A} = \Delta\bar{G}$. The effect of the change in $\bar{G}$ is given by

$$\frac{\Delta Y}{\Delta\bar{G}} = \gamma \qquad \gamma = \frac{h\alpha_G}{h + kb\alpha_G} \tag{10}$$

The expression γ is the fiscal or government spending multiplier once interest rate adjustment is taken into account. Consider how this multiplier, γ, differs from the simpler expression α_G that applied under constant interest rates. Inspection shows that γ is less than α_G since $1/(1 + k\alpha_G b/h)$ is less than 1. This represents the dampening effect of increased interest rates associated with a fiscal expansion in the *IS-LM* model.

We note that the expression in equation (10) is almost zero if h is very small and that it is equal to α_G if h approaches infinity. This corresponds, respectively, to vertical

[11]Equations (8) and (8a) are two different ways to write the same formula. Work with whichever one you find more convenient in a particular situation.

and horizontal *LM* schedules. Similarly, a large value of either b or k serves to reduce the effect of government spending on income. Why? A high value of k implies a large increase in money demand as income rises and hence a large increase in interest rates required to maintain money market equilibrium. In combination with a high b, this implies a large reduction in private aggregate demand.

THE MONETARY POLICY MULTIPLIER

The *monetary policy multiplier* **shows how much an increase in the real money supply increases the equilibrium level of income, keeping fiscal policy unchanged.** Using equation (8) to examine the effects of an increase in the real money supply on income, we have

$$\frac{\Delta Y}{\Delta (M/P)} = \frac{b}{h}\gamma = \frac{b\alpha_G}{h + kb\alpha_G} \tag{11}$$

The smaller h and k and the larger b and α_G, the more expansionary the effect of an increase in real balances on the equilibrium level of income. Large b and α_G correspond to a very flat *IS* schedule.

SUMMARY

1. The *IS-LM* model presented in this chapter is the basic model of aggregate demand that incorporates the money market as well as the goods market. It lays particular stress on the channels through which monetary and fiscal policy affect the economy.

2. The *IS* curve shows combinations of interest rates and levels of income such that the goods market is in equilibrium. Increases in the interest rate reduce aggregate demand by reducing investment spending. Thus, at higher interest rates, the level of income at which the goods market is in equilibrium is lower: The *IS* curve slopes downward.

3. The demand for money is a demand for *real* balances. The demand for real balances increases with income and decreases with the interest rate, the cost of holding money rather than other assets. With an exogenously fixed supply of real balances, the *LM* curve, representing money market equilibrium, is upward-sloping.

4. The interest rate and level of output are jointly determined by simultaneous equilibrium of the goods and money markets. This occurs at the point of intersection of the *IS* and *LM* curves.

5. Monetary policy affects the economy first by affecting the interest rate and then by affecting aggregate demand. An increase in the money supply reduces the interest rate, increases investment spending and aggregate demand, and thus increases equilibrium output.

6. The *IS* and *LM* curves together determine the aggregate demand schedule.

7. Changes in monetary and fiscal policy affect the economy through the monetary and fiscal policy multipliers.

KEY TERMS

aggregate demand	goods market equilibrium	monetary policy multiplier
schedule	schedule	money market equilibrium
central bank	*IS* curve	schedule
demand for real balances	*IS-LM* model	real money balances
fiscal policy multiplier	*LM* curve	

PROBLEMS

Conceptual

1. How does the *IS-LM* model developed in this chapter relate to the model of aggregate demand developed in Chapter 9?

2. **a.** Explain in words how and why the multiplier α_G and the interest sensitivity of aggregate demand affect the slope of the *IS* curve.

   b. Explain why the slope of the *IS* curve is a factor in determining the working of monetary policy.

3. Explain in words how and why the income and interest sensitivities of the demand for real balances affect the slope of the *LM* curve.

4. **a.** Why does a horizontal *LM* curve imply that fiscal policy has the same effects on the economy as those derived in Chapter 9?

   b. What is happening in this case in terms of Figure 10-3?

   c. Under what circumstances might the *LM* curve be horizontal?

5. It is possible that the interest rate might affect consumption spending. An increase in the interest rate could, in principle, lead to increases in saving and therefore a reduction in consumption, given the level of income. Suppose that consumption is, in fact, reduced by an increase in the interest rate. How will the *IS* curve be affected?

6.* Between January and December 1991, while the U.S. economy was falling deeper into its recession, the interest rate on Treasury bills fell from 6.3 to 4.1 percent. Use the *IS-LM* model to explain this pattern of declining output and interest rates. Which curve must have shifted? Can you think of a reason—historically valid or simply imagined—that this shift might have occurred?

Technical

1. The following equations describe an economy. (Think of C, I, G, etc., as being measured in billions and i as a percentage; a 5 percent interest rate implies $i = 5$.)

$$C = 0.8(1 - t)Y \tag{P1}$$

$$t = 0.25 \tag{P2}$$

$$I = 900 - 50i \tag{P3}$$

$$\overline{G} = 800 \tag{P4}$$

$$L = 0.25Y - 62.5i \tag{P5}$$

$$\overline{M/P} = 500 \tag{P6}$$

*An asterisk denotes a more difficult problem.

    a. What is the equation that describes the *IS* curve?

    b. What is the general definition of the *IS* curve?

    c. What is the equation that describes the *LM* curve?

    d. What is the general definition of the *LM* curve?

    e. What are the equilibrium levels of income and the interest rate?

2. Continue with the same equations.

    a. What is the value of α_G which corresponds to the simple multiplier (with taxes) of Chapter 9?

    b. By how much does an increase in government spending of $\Delta \overline{G}$ increase the level of income in this model, which includes the money market?

    c. By how much does a change in government spending of $\Delta \overline{G}$ affect the equilibrium interest rate?

    d. Explain the difference between your answers to parts **(a)** and **(b)**.

3. **a.** How does an increase in the tax rate affect the *IS* curve?

    b. How does the increase affect the equilibrium level of income?

    c. How does the increase affect the equilibrium interest rate?

4.* **a.** Show that a given change in the money stock has a larger effect on output the less interest-sensitive is the demand for money. Use the formal analysis of Section 10-5.

    b. How does the response of the interest rate to a change in the money stock depend on the interest sensitivity of money demand?

5. Discuss, using the *IS-LM* model, what happens to interest rates as prices change along a given *AD* schedule.

6. Show, using *IS* and *LM* curves, why money has no effect on output in the classical supply case.

7. Suppose there is a decline in the demand for money. At each output level and interest rate the public now wants to hold lower real balances.

    a. In the Keynesian case, what happens to equilibrium output and to prices?

    b. In the classical case, what is the effect on output and on prices?

Empirical

1. In the introduction to this chapter it was illustrated how interest rates on U.S. Treasury bills are typically high just before a recession, drop during the recession, and rise during the recovery. Go to www.economagic.com and check out whether this statement is true for Canada as well. Do a search for "Canadian Treasury bills." Choose the 3-month Treasury bills and, using the built-in graphing facilities, make a graph that shows Canadian interest rates since 1950 (choose the option "Show recessions"). What can you conclude?

2. By the end of this chapter you learned that increases in interest rates reduce aggregate demand. Is this true in practice? Let us take a look at how interest rates are related to the growth rate of the U.S. economy. Go to www.economagic.com and choose "Most Requested Series." Select the following two variables: (*a*) Real Gross Domestic Product, Annual percentage changes; and (*b*) Bank Prime Loan Rate (transform the monthly observations into annual data by choosing the option "annual averages"). Use the built-in graphing facilities to plot these two series on the same graph. What can you say by examining the graph? On average, do the two variables evolve in opposite directions?

CHAPTER 11

Monetary and Fiscal Policy

CHAPTER HIGHLIGHTS

- Both fiscal and monetary policy can be used to stabilize the economy.

- The effect of fiscal policy is reduced by crowding out: Increased government spending increases interest rates, reducing investment and partially offsetting the initial expansion in aggregate demand.

- As illustrative polar cases: In the case of the liquidity trap the *LM* curve is horizontal, fiscal policy has its maximum strength, and monetary policy is ineffective. In the classical case the *LM* curve is vertical, fiscal policy has no effect on output, and monetary policy has its maximum strength.

America's longest expansion on record came to an end in March 2001. Figure 11-1 shows the transition from high growth of the economy to drops in GDP. The Federal Reserve responded to the weakening economy by lowering its key interest rate, the federal funds rate, from 6.5 percent to a record low 1.75. The president and Congress enacted major tax cuts in 2001, which also worked in the direction of stimulating the economy. By late 2002 the economy, although still weak, seemed to be pulling out of recession.

In this chapter we use the *IS-LM* model developed in Chapter 10 to show how monetary policy and fiscal policy work. These are the two main macroeconomic policy tools the government can call on to try to keep the economy growing at a reasonable rate, with low inflation. They are also the policy tools the government uses to try to shorten recessions, as in 1991 and 2001, and to prevent booms from getting out of hand. Fiscal policy has its initial impact in the goods market, and monetary policy has its initial impact mainly in the assets markets. But because the goods and assets markets are closely interconnected, both monetary and fiscal policies have effects on both the level of output and interest rates.

Figure 11-2 will refresh your memory of our basic framework. The *IS* curve represents equilibrium in the goods market. The *LM* curve represents equilibrium in the money market. The intersection of the two curves determines output and interest rates

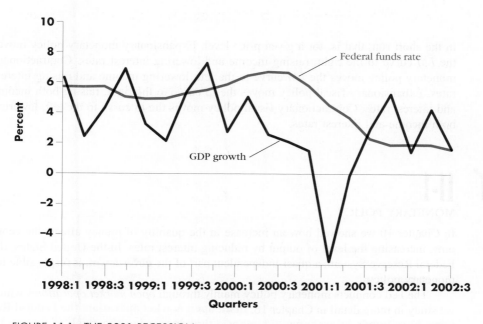

FIGURE 11-1 THE 2001 RECESSION.

The recession began in the spring of 2001. Very sharp drops in interest rates were aimed at limiting the depth and length of the recession. (Source: www.economagic.com.)

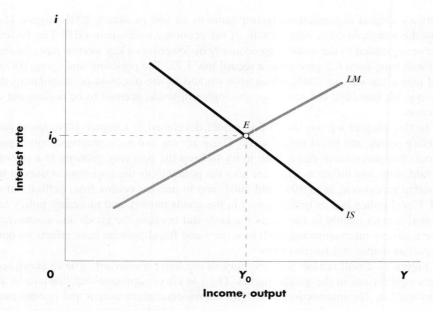

FIGURE 11-2   *IS-LM* EQUILIBRIUM.

in the short run, that is, for a given price level. Expansionary monetary policy moves the *LM* curve to the right, raising income and lowering interest rates. Contractionary monetary policy moves the *LM* curve to the left, lowering income and raising interest rates. Expansionary fiscal policy moves the *IS* curve to the right, raising both income and interest rates. Contractionary fiscal policy moves the *IS* curve to the left, lowering both income and interest rates.

11-1

MONETARY POLICY

In Chapter 10 we showed how an increase in the quantity of money affects the economy, increasing the level of output by reducing interest rates. In the United States, the Federal Reserve System, a quasi-independent part of the government, is responsible for monetary policy.

The Fed conducts monetary policy mainly through *open market operations,* which we study in more detail in Chapter 16. **In an open market operation, the Federal Reserve buys bonds in exchange for money, thus increasing the stock of money, or it sells bonds in exchange for money paid by the purchasers of the bonds, thus reducing the money stock.**

We take here the case of an open market purchase of bonds. The Fed pays for the bonds it buys with money *that it can create*. One can usefully think of the Fed as "printing" money with which to buy bonds, even though that is not strictly accurate, as we shall see in Chapter 16. When the Fed buys bonds, it reduces the quantity of bonds available in the market and thereby tends to increase their price, or lower their yield— only at a lower interest rate will the public be prepared to hold a smaller fraction of its wealth in the form of bonds and a larger fraction in the form of money.

Figure 11-3 shows graphically how an open market purchase works. The initial equilibrium at point E is on the initial LM schedule that corresponds to a real money supply, $\overline{M}/\overline{P}$. Now consider an open market purchase by the Fed. This increases the nominal quantity of money and, given the price level, the real quantity of money. As a consequence, the LM schedule will shift to LM'. The new equilibrium will be at point E', with a lower interest rate and a higher level of income. The equilibrium level of income rises because the open market purchase reduces the interest rate and thereby increases investment spending.

By experimenting with Figure 11-3, you will be able to show that the steeper the LM schedule, the larger the change in income. If money demand is very sensitive to the interest rate (corresponding to a relatively flat LM curve), a given change in the money stock can be absorbed in the assets markets with only a small change in the interest rate. The effects of an open market purchase on investment spending would then be small. By contrast, if the demand for money is not very sensitive to the interest rate

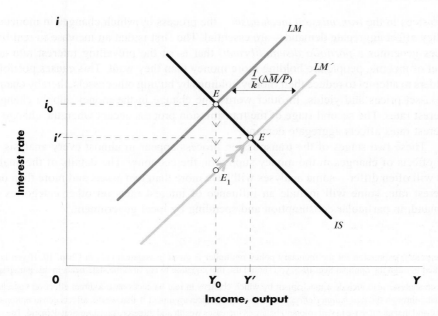

FIGURE 11-3   MONETARY POLICY.

An increase in the real money stock shifts the LM curve to the right.

(corresponding to a relatively steep *LM* curve), a given change in the money supply will cause a large change in the interest rate and have a big effect on investment demand. Similarly, if the demand for money is very sensitive to income, a given increase in the money stock can be absorbed with a relatively small change in income and the monetary multiplier will be smaller.[1]

Consider next the process of adjustment to the monetary expansion. At the initial equilibrium point, *E*, the increase in the money supply creates an excess supply of money to which the public adjusts by trying to buy other assets. In the process, asset prices increase and yields decline. Because money and asset markets adjust rapidly, we move immediately to point E_1, where the money market clears and where the public is willing to hold the larger real quantity of money because the interest rate has declined sufficiently. At point E_1, however, there is an excess demand for goods. The decline in the interest rate, given the initial income level Y_0, has raised aggregate demand and is causing inventories to run down. In response, output expands and we start moving up the *LM'* schedule. Why does the interest rate rise during the adjustment process? Because the increase in output raises the demand for money, and the greater demand for money has to be checked by higher interest rates.

Thus, the increase in the money stock first causes interest rates to fall as the public adjusts its portfolio and then—as a result of the decline in interest rates—increases aggregate demand.

THE TRANSMISSION MECHANISM

Two steps in the *transmission mechanism*—the process by which changes in monetary policy affect aggregate demand—are essential. The first is that an increase in real balances generates a *portfolio disequilibrium;* that is, at the prevailing interest rate and level of income, people are holding more money than they want. This causes portfolio holders to attempt to reduce their money holdings by buying other assets, thereby changing asset prices and yields. In other words, the change in the money supply changes interest rates. The second stage of the transmission process occurs when the change in interest rates affects aggregate demand.

These two stages of the transmission process appear in almost every analysis of the effects of changes in the money supply on the economy. The details of the analyses will often differ—some analyses will have more than two assets and more than one interest rate; some will include an influence of interest rates on other categories of demand, in particular consumption and spending by local government.[2]

---

[1]The precise expression for the monetary policy multiplier is given in equation (11) in Chap. 10. If you have worked through the optional Sec. 10-5, you should use that equation to confirm the statements in this paragraph.

[2]Some analyses also include a mechanism by which changes in real balances have a direct effect on aggregate demand through the *real balance effect.* The real-balance-effect argument is that wealth affects consumption demand and that an increase in real (money) balances increases wealth and therefore consumption demand. The real balance effect is not very important empirically, because the relevant real balances are only a small part of wealth. The classic work on the topic is Don Patinkin, *Money, Interest and Prices* (New York: Harper & Row, 1965).

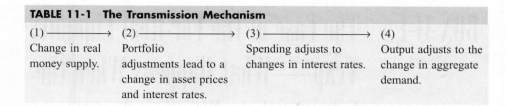

TABLE 11-1   The Transmission Mechanism

(1) →	(2) →	(3) →	(4)
Change in real money supply.	Portfolio adjustments lead to a change in asset prices and interest rates.	Spending adjusts to changes in interest rates.	Output adjusts to the change in aggregate demand.

Table 11-1 provides a summary of the stages in the transmission mechanism. There are two critical links between the change in real balances (i.e., the real money stock) and the ultimate effect on income. First, the change in real balances, by bringing about portfolio disequilibrium, must lead to a change in interest rates. Second, that change in interest rates must change aggregate demand. Through these two linkages, changes in the real money stock affect the level of output in the economy. But that outcome immediately implies the following: If portfolio imbalances do not lead to significant changes in interest rates, for whatever reason, or if spending does not respond to changes in interest rates, the link between money and output does not exist.[3] We now study these linkages in more detail.

THE LIQUIDITY TRAP

In discussing the effects of monetary policy on the economy, two extreme cases have received much attention. The first is the *liquidity trap,* a situation in which the public is prepared, at a given interest rate, to hold whatever amount of money is supplied. This implies that the *LM* curve is horizontal and that changes in the quantity of money do not shift it. In that case, monetary policy carried out through open market operations has no effect on either the interest rate or the level of income. In the liquidity trap, monetary policy is powerless to affect the interest rate.

The possibility of a liquidity trap at low interest rates is a notion that grew out of the theories of the great English economist John Maynard Keynes. Keynes himself did state, though, that he was not aware of there ever having been such a situation.[4] The liquidity trap is rarely relevant to policymakers, with the exception of a special case discussed in Box 11-1. But the liquidity trap is a useful expositional device for understanding the consequences of a relatively flat *LM* curve.

---

[3]We refer to the responsiveness of aggregate demand—rather than investment spending—to the interest rate because consumption demand may also respond to the interest rate. Higher interest rates may lead to more saving and less consumption at a given level of income. Empirically, it has been difficult to isolate such an interest rate effect on consumption (at least for consumption of nondurables and services).

[4]J. M. Keynes, *The General Theory of Employment, Interest and Money* (New York: Macmillan, 1936), p. 207. Some economists, most notably Paul Krugman of Princeton, have suggested that Japan's economy at the turn of the century was in a liquidity trap. See "Japan's Trap" and "Further Notes on Japan's Liquidity Trap" on Krugman's website (www.wws.princeton.edu/~pkrugman).

BOX 11-1 The Case of the For-Real Liquidity Trap—What Happens When the Interest Rate Hits Zero?

No amount of printing money will push the nominal interest rate below zero! Suppose you could borrow at minus 5 percent. You could borrow $100 today, pay back $95 in a year, and pocket the difference. The demand for money would be infinite!

Once the interest rate hits zero, there is nothing further that a central bank can do with *conventional* monetary policy to stimulate the economy because monetary policy cannot reduce interest rates any further. Figure 1 shows that this is pretty much what happened in Japan in the late 1990s and in the early years of the twenty-first century. Interest rates went from a few percent, down to around .5 percent, and then effectively to zero.

The inability to use conventional monetary policy to stimulate the economy in a liquidity trap had long been mostly important as an illustrative example for textbook writers. But in Japan the zero interest rate liquidity trap became a very real policy issue.

UNDERNEATH THE ZERO INTEREST RATE LOWER BOUND

You will remember that the nominal interest rate has two parts: the real interest rate and expected inflation. As a practical matter, an economy hits a zero interest rate bound when it experiences significant *deflation*. (Deflation means that prices are dropping or, equivalently, that the inflation rate is negative.) One way for policymakers to avoid the zero interest rate liquidity trap is to pump out enough money to keep inflation slightly positive.

Could the United States experience a zero interest rate liquidity trap? Unlikely, but not impossible. But should it occur, Federal Reserve policymakers are prepared to use

BANKS' RELUCTANCE TO LEND?

In 1991 a different possibility arose to suggest that sometimes monetary policy actions by the Fed might have only a very limited impact on the economy. In step (3) in Table 11-1, investment spending should increase in response to lower interest rates. However, in 1991, as interest rates declined, banks were reluctant to increase their lending.

The underlying reason was that many banks had made bad loans at the end of the 1980s, especially to finance real estate deals. When the real estate market collapsed in 1990 and 1991, banks faced the prospect that a significant portion of their existing

unconventional monetary policy, such as buying long-term bonds and other assets, to pump money into the economy. To quote Federal Reserve Board governor Ben Bernanke,

> To stimulate aggregate spending when short-term interest rates have reached zero, the Fed must expand the scale of its asset purchases or, possibly, expand the menu of assets that it buys. . . . [T]he chances of a serious deflation in the United States appear remote indeed, in large part because of our economy's underlying strengths but also because of the determination of the Federal Reserve and other U.S. policymakers to act preemptively against deflationary pressures.

> —Speech before the National Economists Club,
> Washington, D.C., November 21, 2002

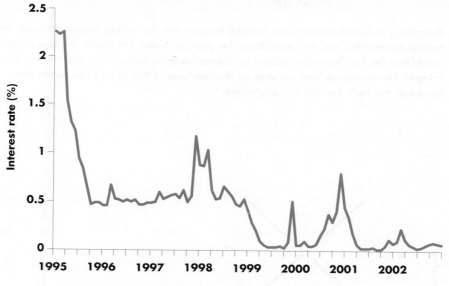

FIGURE 1   JAPANESE INTEREST RATES.
(*Source: www.economagic.com.*)

borrowers could not repay in full. Not surprisingly, banks showed little enthusiasm to lend more to new, perhaps risky, borrowers. Rather, they preferred to lend to the government, by buying securities such as Treasury bills. Lending to the U.S. government is as safe as any loan can be, because the U.S. government always pays its debts.[5]

[5]In 1995 the United States came close to suspending debt repayment while the president and Congress played a game of chicken over the federal budget. In the end, no payments were actually missed. (For readers unfamiliar with American slang, "chicken" is a game in which two male adolescents with more hormones than intelligence drive cars head-on at one another at high speed. The first one to turn aside is said to "chicken out"—to show cowardice. If neither turns aside, the results are much like the results of the U.S. government's failing to pay its debt.)

BOX 11-2   Q: Does the Federal Reserve Set the Interest Rate, or Does It Set the Money Supply?

A: Yes.

According to our discussion, the Federal Reserve sets the money supply, through open market operations, and this pins down the position of the *LM* curve. But one frequently reads that the Fed has either raised or lowered interest rates. How are the two connected? The answer is that, as long as the positions of the *IS* and *LM* curves are known to the Fed, the two are equivalent.*

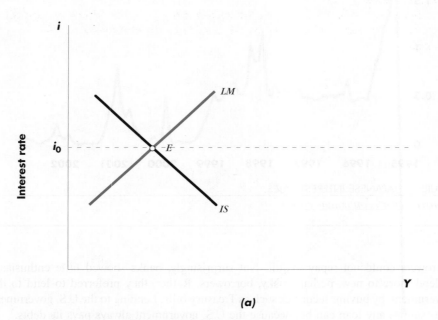

(a)

FIGURE 1   PEGGING THE INTEREST RATE.

*In practice the positions of the *IS* and *LM* curves are not known with absolute precision, and in the short run the difference between setting interest rates and setting the money supply is quite important. We investigate this question in detail in Chap. 16.

Suppose the Fed wishes to set the interest rate at a level i_0 and that the *IS* curve is positioned as shown in panel (*a*) of Figure 1. Rather than picking a value for the money supply and drawing a corresponding *LM* curve, you can draw an *LM* curve through point *E*—guaranteeing that the interest rate target i_0 is hit—and then work backward to find the money supply that will produce the *LM* curve drawn through *E*.

Suppose that, as illustrated in panel (*b*), the *IS* curve has shifted to the right. To keep the interest rate "pegged" at i_0, you would move the *LM* curve right to *LM'* and recompute the required money supply. So when the Fed pegs the interest rate, it is really adjusting the money supply to keep the *LM* intersecting the *IS* at the desired interest target.

At least in the short run, the Fed can peg the interest rate very effectively without actually carrying out calculations about the *IS-LM* equilibrium. Suppose the Fed wishes to peg the interest rate between 5.9 and 6 percent. The Fed, operating through its New York branch, offers to buy any amount of bonds at interest rates above 6 percent (promising unlimited open market purchases) and sell any amount at rates below 5.9 (promising unlimited open market sales). If interest rates start to veer above 6 percent, the Fed effectively increases the money stock, pushing interest rates back down. (And vice versa below 5.9 percent.)

Note that the Fed is *not* setting the interest rate by any sort of law or regulation. "Pegging the interest rate" is really just the use of open market operations on autopilot.

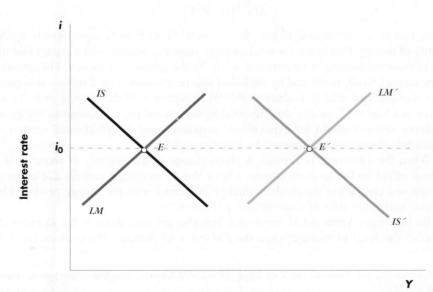

(b)

If banks will not lend to firms, an important part of the transmission mechanism between a Fed open market purchase and an increase in aggregate demand and output is put out of action. Careful study suggested that banks were lending less to private firms than usual for this stage of the business cycle.[6] However, many argued that further open market operations, leading to further cuts in interest rates, would get the economy moving again. That is, they were arguing that if a given dose of Fed medicine had less effect on bank lending than usual, the dose should be increased. They appear to have been right, and by 1992 bank lending was picking up.

THE CLASSICAL CASE

The polar opposite of the horizontal *LM* curve—which implies that monetary policy cannot affect the level of income—is the vertical *LM* curve. The *LM* curve is vertical when the demand for money is entirely unresponsive to the interest rate.

Recall from Chapter 10 [equation (7)] that the *LM* curve is described by

$$\frac{\overline{M}}{P} = kY - hi \tag{1}$$

If h is zero, then corresponding to a given real money supply, $\overline{M}/P$, there is a unique level of income, which implies that the *LM* curve is vertical at that level of income. (Sneak a look ahead at Figure 11-5.)

The vertical *LM* curve is called the *classical case*. Rewriting equation (1), with h set equal to zero and with P moved to the right-hand side, we obtain

$$\overline{M} = k(\overline{P} \times Y) \tag{2}$$

We see that the classical case implies that nominal GDP, $P \times Y$, depends only on the quantity of money. This is the classical *quantity theory of money*, which argues that the level of nominal income is determined solely by the quantity of money. The quantity theory was originally motivated by the belief that people would hold money in a quantity proportional to total transactions, $P \times Y$, irrespective of the interest rate. As we will see in Chapter 15, money does respond to the interest rate; nonetheless, the quantity theory remains useful for expositional purposes—and a sophisticated version of the quantity theory is still espoused by monetarists.[7]

When the *LM* curve is vertical, a given change in the quantity of money has a maximal effect on the level of income. Check this by moving a vertical *LM* curve to the right and comparing the resultant change in income with the change produced by a similar horizontal shift of a nonvertical *LM* curve.

By drawing a vertical *LM* curve, you can also see that shifts in the *IS* curve do not affect the level of income when the *LM* curve is vertical. Thus, when the LM

---

[6]See, for example, Ben Bernanke and Cara Lown, "The Credit Crunch," *Brookings Papers on Economic Activity* 2 (1991).

[7]In earlier chapters we wrote the quantity theory as $M \times V = P \times Y$, where V is the velocity of money. The expression here is equivalent if you think of k as defined by $k \equiv 1/V$.

curve is vertical, monetary policy has a maximal effect on the level of income, and fiscal policy has no effect on income. The vertical *LM* curve, implying the comparative effectiveness of monetary over fiscal policy, is sometimes associated with the view that "only money matters" for the determination of output. Since the *LM* curve is vertical only when the demand for money does not depend on the interest rate, the interest sensitivity of the demand for money turns out to be an important issue in determining the effectiveness of alternative policies. The evidence, to be reviewed in Chapter 15, is that the interest rate does affect the demand for money.

11-2

FISCAL POLICY AND CROWDING OUT

This section shows how changes in fiscal policy shift the *IS* curve, the curve that describes equilibrium in the goods market. Recall that the *IS* curve slopes downward because a decrease in the interest rate increases investment spending, thereby increasing aggregate demand and the level of output at which the goods market is in equilibrium. Recall also that changes in fiscal policy shift the *IS* curve. Specifically, a fiscal expansion shifts the *IS* curve to the right.

The equation of the *IS* curve, derived in Chapter 10, is repeated here for convenience:

$$Y = \alpha_G(\overline{A} - bi) \qquad \alpha_G = \frac{1}{1 - c(1 - t)} \tag{3}$$

Note that $\overline{G}$, the level of government spending, is a component of autonomous spending, $\overline{A}$, in equation (3). The income tax rate, t, is part of the multiplier. Thus, both government spending and the tax rate affect the *IS* schedule.

AN INCREASE IN GOVERNMENT SPENDING

We now show, in Figure 11-4, how a fiscal expansion raises equilibrium income and the interest rate. At unchanged interest rates, higher levels of government spending increase the level of aggregate demand. To meet the increased demand for goods, output must rise. In Figure 11-4, we show the effect of a shift in the *IS* schedule. At each level of the interest rate, equilibrium income must rise by α_G times the increase in government spending. For example, if government spending rises by 100 and the multiplier is 2, equilibrium income must increase by 200 at each level of the interest rate. Thus the *IS* schedule shifts to the right by 200.

If the economy is initially in equilibrium at point E and government spending rises by 100, we would move to point E'' *if the interest rate stayed constant*. At E'' the goods market is in equilibrium in that planned spending equals output. But the money market is no longer in equilibrium. Income has increased, and therefore the quantity of money demanded is higher. Because there is an excess demand for real balances, the

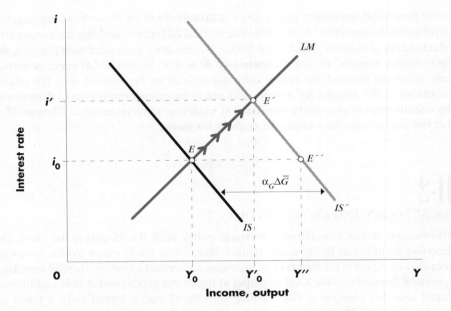

FIGURE 11-4   EFFECTS OF AN INCREASE IN GOVERNMENT SPENDING.
Increased government spending increases aggregate demand, shifting the IS curve to the right.

interest rate rises. Firms' planned investment spending declines at higher interest rates, and thus aggregate demand falls off.

What is the complete adjustment, taking into account the expansionary effect of higher government spending and the dampening effects of the higher interest rate on private spending? Figure 11-4 shows that only at point E' do both the goods *and* money markets clear. Only at point E' is planned spending equal to income and, at the same time, the quantity of real balances demanded equal to the given real money stock. Point E' is therefore the new equilibrium point.

CROWDING OUT

Comparing E' to the initial equilibrium at E, we see that increased government spending raises both income and the interest rate. But another important comparison is between points E' and E'', the equilibrium in the goods market at unchanged interest rates. Point E'' corresponds to the equilibrium we studied in Chapter 9, when we neglected the impact of interest rates on the economy. In comparing E'' and E', it becomes clear that the adjustment of interest rates and their impact on aggregate demand dampen the expansionary effect of increased government spending. Income, instead of increasing to level Y'', rises only to Y'_0.

The reason that income rises only to Y_0' rather than to Y'' is that the rise in the interest rate from i_0 to i' reduces the level of investment spending. We say that the increase in government spending crowds out investment spending. *Crowding out occurs when expansionary fiscal policy causes interest rates to rise, thereby reducing private spending, particularly investment.*

What factors determine how much crowding out takes place? In other words, what determines the extent to which interest rate adjustments dampen the output expansion induced by increased government spending? By drawing for yourself different *IS* and *LM* schedules, you will be able to show the following:

- Income increases more, and interest rates increase less, the flatter the *LM* schedule.
- Income increases less, and interest rates increase less, the flatter the *IS* schedule.
- Income and interest rates increase more the larger the multiplier, α_G, and thus the larger the horizontal shift of the *IS* schedule.

In each case the extent of crowding out is greater the more the interest rate increases when government spending rises.

To illustrate these conclusions, we turn to the two extreme cases we discussed in connection with monetary policy, the liquidity trap and the classical case.

THE LIQUIDITY TRAP

If the economy is in the liquidity trap, and thus the *LM* curve is horizontal, an increase in government spending has its full multiplier effect on the equilibrium level of income. There is no change in the interest rate associated with the change in government spending, and thus no investment spending is cut off. There is therefore no dampening of the effects of increased government spending on income.

You should draw your own *IS-LM* diagrams to confirm that if the *LM* curve is horizontal, monetary policy has no impact on the equilibrium of the economy and fiscal policy has a maximal effect. Less dramatically, if the demand for money is very sensitive to the interest rate, and thus the *LM* curve is almost horizontal, fiscal policy changes have a relatively large effect on output and monetary policy changes have little effect on the equilibrium level of output.

THE CLASSICAL CASE AND CROWDING OUT

If the *LM* curve is vertical, an increase in government spending has *no* effect on the equilibrium level of income and increases only the interest rate. This case, already noted when we discussed monetary policy, is shown in Figure 11-5a, where an increase in government spending shifts the *IS* curve to *IS'* but has no effect on income. If the demand for money is not related to the interest rate, as a vertical *LM* curve implies, there is a unique level of income at which the money market is in equilibrium.

Thus, with a vertical *LM* curve, an increase in government spending cannot change the equilibrium level of income and raises only the equilibrium interest rate. But if

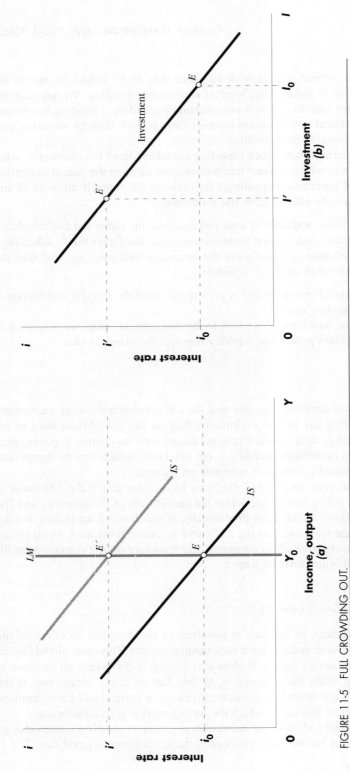

FIGURE 11-5 FULL CROWDING OUT.

With a vertical LM schedule, a fiscal expansion shifting out the IS schedule raises interest rates, not income. Government spending displaces, or crowds out, private spending, dollar for dollar.

government spending is higher and output is unchanged, there must be an offsetting reduction in private spending. In this case, the increase in interest rates crowds out an amount of private (particularly investment) spending equal to the increase in government spending. Thus, there is full crowding out if the *LM* curve is vertical.[8]

In Figure 11-5 we show the crowding out in panel (*b*), where the investment schedule of Figure 10-4 is drawn. The fiscal expansion raises the equilibrium interest rate from i_0 to i' in panel (*a*). In panel (*b*), as a consequence, investment spending declines from the level I_0 to I'.

Is Crowding Out Important?

How seriously must we take the possibility of crowding out? Here three points must be made. The first point is also an important warning. In this chapter, as in the two preceding, we are assuming an economy with prices given, in which output is below the full-employment level. In these conditions, when fiscal expansion increases demand, firms can increase the level of output by hiring more workers. But in fully employed economies, crowding out occurs through a different mechanism. In such conditions an increase in demand will lead to an increase in the price level (moving upward along the aggregate supply curve). The increase in price reduces *real* balances. (An increase in $\overline{P}$ reduces the ratio $\overline{M}/P$.) This reduction in the real money supply moves the *LM* curve to the left, raising interest rates until the initial increase in aggregate demand is fully crowded out.

The second point, however, is that in an economy with unemployed resources there will *not* be full crowding out because the *LM* schedule is not, in fact, vertical. A fiscal expansion will raise interest rates, but income will also rise. Crowding out is therefore a matter of degree. The increase in aggregate demand raises income, and with the rise in income, the level of saving rises. This expansion in saving, in turn, makes it possible to finance a larger budget deficit without *completely* displacing private spending.

The third point is that with unemployment, and thus a possibility for output to expand, interest rates need not rise at all when government spending rises, and there need not be any crowding out. This is true because the monetary authorities can *accommodate* the fiscal expansion by an increase in the money supply. **Monetary policy is accommodating when, in the course of a fiscal expansion, the money supply is increased in order to prevent interest rates from increasing.** *Monetary accommodation* **is also referred to as** *monetizing budget deficits,* **meaning that the Federal Reserve prints money to buy the bonds with which the government pays for its deficit.** When the Fed accommodates a fiscal expansion, both the *IS* and the *LM* schedules shift to the right, as in Figure 11-6. Output will clearly increase, but interest rates need not rise. Accordingly, there need not be any adverse effects on investment.

---

[8]Note that, in principle, consumption spending could be reduced by an increase in the interest rate, so both investment and consumption would be crowded out. Further, as we will see in Chap. 12, fiscal expansion can also crowd out net exports.

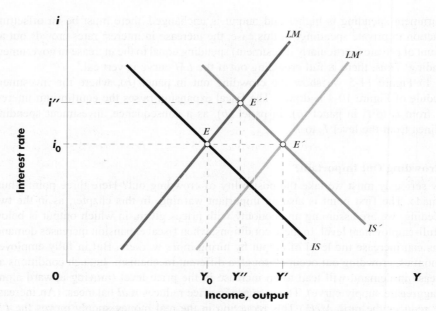

FIGURE 11-6   MONETARY ACCOMMODATION OF FISCAL EXPANSION.

11-3

THE COMPOSITION OF OUTPUT AND THE POLICY MIX

Table 11-2 summarizes our analysis of the effects of expansionary monetary and fiscal policy on output and the interest rate, provided the economy is not in a liquidity trap or in the classical case. Outside of these special cases, it is apparent that policymakers can, in practice, use either monetary or fiscal policy to affect the level of income.

What difference does it make whether monetary or fiscal policy is used to control output? The choice between monetary and fiscal policies as tools of stabilization policy is an important and controversial topic. One basis for decision is the flexibility and speed with which these policies can be implemented and take effect.

Here we do not discuss speed and flexibility; rather, we look at what those policies do to the components of aggregate demand, that is, to investment, consumption, and government spending, respectively. In that respect, there is a sharp difference between monetary policy and fiscal policy.[9] Monetary policy operates by stimulating interest-responsive components of aggregate demand, primarily investment spending. There is strong evidence that the earliest effect of monetary policy is on residential construction.

Fiscal policy, by contrast, operates in a manner that depends on precisely what goods the government buys or what taxes and transfers it changes. Choices include

[9]The two types of policy differ also in their impact on exports, as we shall see in Chap. 12.

TABLE 11-2   Policy Effects on Income and Interest Rates

POLICY	EQUILIBRIUM INCOME	EQUILIBRIUM INTEREST RATES
Monetary expansion	+	−
Fiscal expansion	+	+

government purchases of goods and services such as defense spending or a reduction in the corporate profits tax, sales taxes, or social security contributions. Each policy affects the level of aggregate demand and causes an expansion in output, but the composition of the increase in output depends on the specific policy. An increase in government spending raises consumption spending along with government purchases. An income tax cut has a direct effect on consumption spending. An investment subsidy, discussed below, increases investment spending. All expansionary fiscal policies will raise the interest rate if the quantity of money is unchanged.

AN INVESTMENT SUBSIDY

Both an income tax cut and an increase in government spending raise the interest rate and reduce investment spending. However, it is possible for the government to raise investment spending through an *investment subsidy,* as shown in Figure 11-7. In the United States, the government has sometimes subsidized investment through an *investment tax credit,* whereby a firm's tax payments are reduced when it increases its investment spending. For instance, President Clinton proposed an investment tax credit in his 1993 fiscal package.

When the government subsidizes investment, it essentially pays part of the cost of each firm's investment. An investment subsidy shifts the investment schedule in panel (*a*) of Figure 11-7. At each interest rate, firms now plan to invest more. With investment spending higher, aggregate demand increases.

In panel (*b*), the *IS* schedule shifts by the amount of the multiplier times the increase in autonomous investment brought about by the subsidy. The new equilibrium is at point E', where goods and money markets are again in balance. But note now that although interest rates have risen, we see, in panel (*a*), that investment is higher. Investment is at the level I'_0, up from I_0. The interest rate increase dampens but does not reverse the impact of the investment subsidy. This is an example in which both consumption, induced by higher income, and investment rise as a consequence of expansionary fiscal policy.

Table 11-3 summarizes the impacts of different types of fiscal policy on the composition of output, as well as on output and the interest rate.

THE POLICY MIX

In Figure 11-8 we show the policy problem of reaching full-employment output, Y^*, for an economy that is initially at point E, with unemployment. Should we choose a fiscal expansion, moving to point E_1 with higher income and higher interest rates? Or should we choose a monetary expansion, leading to full employment with lower interest

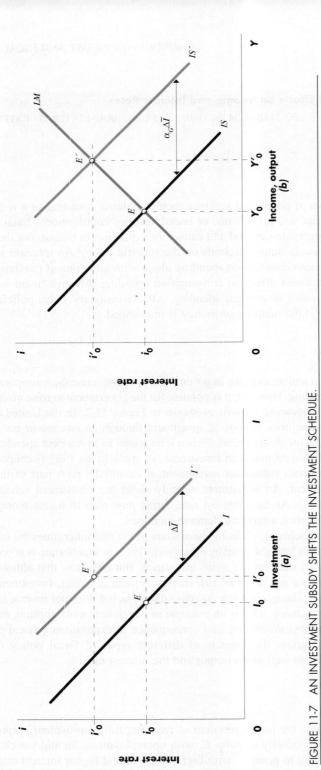

FIGURE 11-7   AN INVESTMENT SUBSIDY SHIFTS THE INVESTMENT SCHEDULE.

TABLE 11-3 Alternative Fiscal Policies

	INTEREST RATE	CONSUMPTION	INVESTMENT	GDP
Income tax cut	+	+	−	+
Government spending	+	+	−	+
Investment subsidy	+	+	+	+

rates at point E_2? Or should we pick a policy mix of fiscal expansion and accommodating monetary policy, leading to an intermediate position?

Once we recognize that all the policies raise output but differ significantly in their impact on different sectors of the economy, we open up a problem of political economy. Given the decision to expand aggregate demand, who should get the primary benefit? Should the expansion take place through a decline in interest rates and increased investment spending, or should it take place through a cut in taxes and increased personal spending, or should it take the form of an increase in the size of government?

Questions of speed and predictability of policies apart, the issues have been settled by political preferences. Conservatives will argue for a tax cut anytime. They will favor stabilization policies that cut taxes in a recession and cut government spending in a boom. Over time, given enough cycles, the government sector becomes very small, as a conservative would want it to be. The counterpart view belongs to those who believe that there is a broad scope for government spending on education, the environment, job training and rehabilitation, and the like, and who, accordingly, favor expansionary

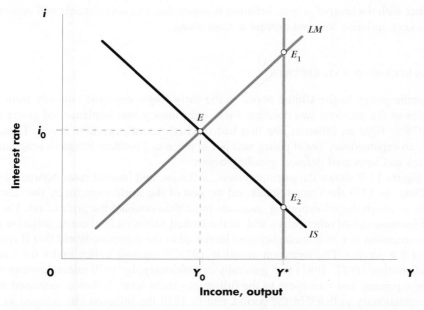

FIGURE 11-8 EXPANSIONARY POLICIES AND THE COMPOSITION OF OUTPUT.

policies in the form of increased government spending and higher taxes to curb a boom. Growth-minded people and the construction lobby argue for expansionary policies that operate through low interest rates or investment subsidies.

The recognition that monetary and fiscal policy changes have different effects on the composition of output is important. It suggests that policymakers can choose a *policy mix*—a combination of monetary and fiscal policies—that will not only get the economy to full employment but also make a contribution to solving other policy problems. We now discuss the policy mix in action.

11-4

THE POLICY MIX IN ACTION

In this section we review the U.S. monetary-fiscal policy mix of the 1980s, the economic debate over how to deal with the U.S. recession in 1990 and 1991, the behavior of monetary policy during the long expansion of the late 1990 and the subsequent recession of 2001, and the policy decisions made in Germany in the early 1990s as the country struggled with the macroeconomic consequences of the reunification of East and West Germany.

This section serves not only to discuss the issue of the policy mix in the real world but also to reintroduce the problem of inflation. The assumption that the price level is fixed is a useful expositional simplification for the theory of this chapter, but of course the real world is more complex. Remember that policies that reduce aggregate demand, such as reducing the growth rate of money or government spending, tend to reduce the inflation rate along with the level of output. An expansionary policy increases inflation together with the level of output. Inflation is unpopular, and governments will generally try to keep inflation low and prevent it from rising.

THE 1980S RECESSION AND RECOVERY

Economic policy in the United States in the early 1980s departed radically from the policies of the previous two decades. First, tight money was implemented at the end of 1979 to fight an inflation rate that had reached record peacetime levels. Then, in 1981, an expansionary fiscal policy was put in place as President Reagan's program of tax cuts and increased defense spending began.

Figure 11-9 shows the unemployment, inflation, and interest rates between 1972 and 2002. In 1973 the United States and the rest of the world were hit by the first oil shock, in which the oil-exporting countries more than doubled the price of oil. The oil price increase raised other prices and, in the United States, helped create inflation and also a recession in which unemployment increased to the then post-World War II record rate of 8.9 percent. The recession ended in 1975. Economic policy under the Carter administration (1977–1981) was generally expansionary; by 1979 unemployment was below 6 percent and thus close to the full-employment level. Inflation increased with the expansionary policies of the period, and in 1979 the inflation rate jumped as the second oil shock hit and the price of oil doubled.

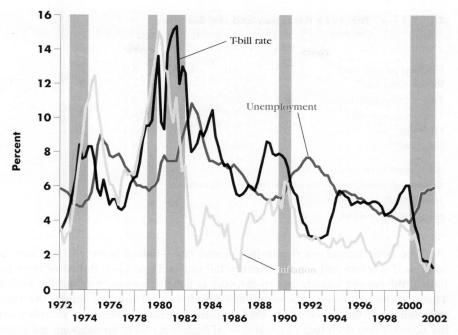

FIGURE 11-9   INFLATION, UNEMPLOYMENT, AND THE INTEREST RATE.
(*Source: www.economagic.com.*)

The rising inflation was extremely unpopular, and it was clear that some policy changes had to be made. In October 1979 the Fed acted, turning monetary policy in a highly restrictive direction. The monetary squeeze was tightened in the first half of 1980, at which point the economy went into a minirecession. After a brief recovery, 1982 brought the deepest recession since the Great Depression.

The reason for the sharp decline in activity was tight money. Because inflation was still above 10 percent and the money stock was growing at only 5.1 percent in 1981, the real money supply was falling. Interest rates continued to climb (see Table 11-4). Not surprisingly, investment, especially construction, collapsed. The economy was dragged into a deep recession with a trough in December 1982.

Table 11-4 also shows the second component of the early 1980s policy mix: The full-employment deficit increased rapidly from 1981 to 1984. The 1981 tax bill cut tax rates for individuals, with the cuts coming into effect over the next 3 years, and increased investment subsidies for corporations. The full-employment deficits in those years are the largest in peacetime U.S. history.

With a policy mix of easy fiscal and tight monetary policies, the analysis of Figure 11-8 tells us to expect a rise in the interest rate. With investment subsidies increased, Figure 11-7 tells us to look for the possibility that investment increases along with the interest rate.

TABLE 11-4   The 1982 Recession and the Recovery
(Percent)

	1980	1981	1982	1983	1984
Nominal interest rate*	11.5	14.0	10.7	8.6	9.6
Real interest rate†	2.0	4.0	4.5	4.5	5.2
Full-employment deficit	0.4	0.0	1.1	2.1	3.0
Unemployment rate	7.0	7.5	9.5	9.5	7.4
GDP gap	6.4	7.1	11.6	10.4	6.2
Inflation‡	9.5	10.0	6.2	4.1	4.4

*Three-month Treasury bill rate.

†Three-month Treasury bill rate less inflation rate of the GDP deflator.

‡GDP deflator.

Source: DRI/McGraw-Hill.

The first element—a rise in the interest rate—indeed occurred. That may be a surprise if you look only at the Treasury bill rate in Table 11-4. But when there is inflation, the correct interest rate to consider is not the *nominal* rate but the *real* rate. **The *real interest rate* is the nominal (stated) rate of interest minus the rate of inflation.** Over the period 1981–1984, the real interest rate increased sharply even as the nominal rate declined. The real cost of borrowing went up although the nominal cost went down. Investment spending responded to both the increased interest rates and the recession, falling 13 percent between 1981 and 1982, and the investment subsidies and prospects of recovery, increasing 49 percent between 1982 and 1984.

The unemployment rate peaked at over 11 percent in the last quarter of 1982 and then steadily declined under the impact of the huge fiscal expansion. Further fiscal expansion in 1984 and 1985 pushed the recovery of the economy forward, and the expansion continued throughout the 1980s.

THE RECESSION OF 1990–1991

The policy mix in the early 1980s featured highly expansionary fiscal policy and tight money. The tight money succeeded in reducing the inflation of the late 1970s and very early 1980s, at the expense of a serious recession. Expansionary fiscal policy then drove a recovery during which real interest rates increased sharply.

The recovery and expansion continued through the 1980s. By the end of 1988, the economy was close to full employment, and the inflation rate was nearing 5 percent. Fearing a continuing increase in inflation, the Fed tightened monetary policy, sharply raising the Treasury bill rate throughout 1988 and into 1989. Despite this, by early 1989 the unemployment rate touched its low for the decade, 5 percent.

The Fed kept nominal interest rates high—though declining—through 1989 (see Figure 11-9), and for a while it seemed to have put just the right amount of pressure on the brakes. The growth of real GDP slowed through 1989, inflation declined a bit, and unemployment slowly rose.

But by the middle of 1990, it was clear that the economy was heading for a recession. The recession was later determined to have begun in July 1990.[10] By the time the 1982–1990 recovery ended, it was the longest peacetime expansion on record.

The recession started before the Iraqi invasion of Kuwait in August. The price of oil jumped when Iraq invaded, and for a time the Fed was faced with the quandary of deciding whether to keep monetary policy tight by holding interest rates up, in order to fight inflation, or pursue an expansionary policy, in order to fight the recession. It compromised, letting interest rates fall slowly, but not much. The oil price rise turned out to be quite short-lived, and by the end of the year it was clear that the recession was the big problem.[11]

It was also clear that it was up to the Fed to fight the recession, because fiscal policy was immobilized. Why? First, the budget deficit (see Table 11-5) was already large, and was expected to rise, and no one was enthusiastic about increasing it. And second, for the political economy reasons we mentioned earlier, the Bush administration and the Democratic Congress fundamentally disagreed on the type of fiscal policy changes that should be made.

From the end of 1990, the Fed began to cut interest rates aggressively. The economy showed signs of recovering in the second quarter of 1991 but faltered in the fourth quarter (see Table 11-5). The political and economic talk turned to the possibility of a double-dip recession. The Fed, fearing that Congress and the president would agree on a fiscal policy change that would raise the budget deficit even more, cut the interest rate very sharply at the end of 1991, pushing it lower than it had been since 1972. In retrospect, this was sufficient to ward off a recession.

By spring of 1991, a recovery, very moderate by past standards, had begun. And the Fed's aggressive action had probably helped prevent an expansionary fiscal policy change. Nonetheless, with the benefit of hindsight, it is clear that the Fed should have moved much more rapidly to cut interest rates during the early part of 1991. Of course, there is a bias in the way we evaluate policymakers. The Fed played an active part in helping to keep the expansion going as long as it did during the 1980s, but we focus on the recession. The Fed rarely receives credit for doing things right, but it certainly gets the blame for its mistakes. As the recovery continued through the mid-1990s with modest but positive growth and with low inflation, the Fed began to receive greater appreciation on Wall Street and in Washington.

---

[10]The dates of peaks and troughs in the business cycle are determined *after the fact* by a committee of economists at the National Bureau of Economic Research in Cambridge, Massachusetts. They delay their decisions to be sure that enough evidence is in to distinguish a genuine change in the business cycle from a mere temporary blip. See Robert E. Hall, "The Business Cycle Dating Process," *NBER Reporter,* Winter 1991–92; and Victor Zarnovitz, *Business Cycles: Theory, History, Indicators and Forecasting* (Chicago: University of Chicago Press, 1991).

[11]Stephen McNees, "The 1990–91 Recession in Historical Perspective," Federal Reserve Bank of Boston *New England Economic Review,* January–February 1992, presents comparative data on this and earlier recessions.

TABLE 11-5   The 1990–1991 Recession
(Percent)

| | YEAR AND QUARTER | | | | | | |
| | 1990 | | 1991 | | | | 1992 |
	3	4	1	2	3	4	1
GDP growth	−1.6	−3.9	−3.0	1.7	1.2	0.6	2.7
Inflation rate*	4.7	3.9	5.3	3.5	2.4	2.4	3.1
Unemployment rate	5.6	6.0	6.5	6.8	6.8	7.0	7.2
Treasury bill rate	7.5	7.0	6.0	5.6	5.4	4.5	3.9
Budget deficit/GDP	2.6	3.5	2.6	3.7	3.7	4.2	4.9
Full-employment deficit, GDP†	0.0	0.5	1.0	1.8	1.8	2.4	3.0

*GDP deflator.

†Calculated by DRI/McGraw-Hill.

Source: DRI/McGraw-Hill.

THE LONGEST PEACETIME EXPANSION—THE 1990S

Coming out of the 1990–1991 recession the U.S. economy entered its longest peacetime expansion. Inflation and unemployment both fell; GDP grew relatively rapidly; and the stock market boomed. The expansion was credited to two sources: rapid technological growth (potential GDP and the aggregate supply curve moved out quickly) and prudent aggregate demand management by the Federal Reserve. The Fed—personified by its chair Alan Greenspan—deftly manipulated interest rates to allow the economic boom to continue while holding inflation under control. Notably, the Fed uses many of the same tools you've already learned about in framing its policy. As an example, the Fed explained its February 2000 decision to raise interest rates by saying:

> [The Fed] remains concerned that over time increases in demand will continue to exceed the growth in potential supply, even after taking account of the pronounced rise in productivity growth. Such trends could foster inflationary imbalances that would undermine the economy's record economic expansion.
>
> Against the background of its long-run goals of price stability and sustainable economic growth and of the information currently available, the committee believes the risks are weighted mainly toward conditions that may generate heightened inflation pressures in the foreseeable future.[12]

THE RECESSION OF 2001

The expansion of the Roaring Nineties ended in March 2001 as GDP growth turned negative. The Fed responded by dropping interest rates, and concomitantly increasing money growth, drastically. Indeed, the Fed began dropping interest rates as the economy

[12]Minutes of the Federal Open Market Committee, February 2, 2000.

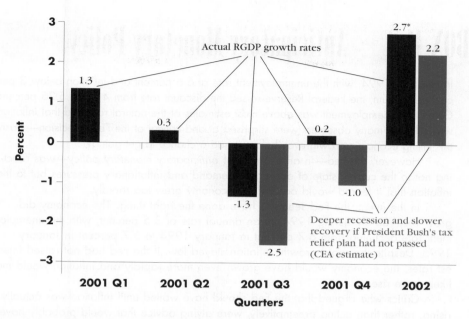

FIGURE 11-10 REAL GDP GROWTH AND PRESIDENT BUSH'S TAX RELIEF.

Growth rate is measured from the fourth quarter of 2001 to the fourth quarter of 2002. (Source: Council of Economic Advisers, www.whitehouse.gov/news.)

slowed before the economy actually entered the recession. President Bush, newly in office, wanted to decrease taxes as part of long-term policy. The recession added the argument of the need for short-term stimulus. The President's Council of Economic Advisers estimates that the tax cuts added about 1.2 percentage points to GDP growth in the short run, as shown in Figure 11-10.

THE GERMAN POLICY MIX, 1990–1992

When East Germany and West Germany were reunited in 1990, the West German government accepted the obligation to attempt to raise living standards in the eastern part of Germany rapidly. This required an immediate increase in government spending, for East German infrastructure, and for transfer payments to the residents of the former East Germany.

For political reasons, the German government did not want to raise taxes much. In effect, the government decided to run a loose fiscal policy, reflected in the increase in the budget deficit seen in Table 11-6. If aggregate demand and inflation were to be kept in check, it was up to the German central bank, the Bundesbank.

The Bundesbank was widely regarded as the most anti-inflationary of all central banks,[13] and it was certainly not going to accommodate the increase in government

[13]Since the creation of the European Central Bank in 1998, which makes monetary policy for the eleven-nation euro area, the Bundesbank no longer makes monetary policy decisions.

BOX 11-3   Anticipatory Monetary Policy

In February 1994, with the unemployment rate at 6.6 percent and inflation below 3 percent per annum, the Federal Reserve raised the discount rate from 4.75 to 5.25 percent. Given that unemployment was above most estimates of the natural rate and that inflation was still low, many observers were surprised at and critical of the Fed's decision—wasn't this killing economic growth even before it had a chance to get going?

However, the Fed—in an example of *anticipatory monetary policy*—was reacting not to the current state of aggregate demand and inflationary pressures but to the inflation that it feared would occur if the economy grew too rapidly.

In the event, the Fed seems to have done the right thing. The economy did grow very rapidly during 1994, at an annual rate of 3.5 percent, with the unemployment rate declining from 6.7 percent in January 1994 to 5.7 percent in January 1995. Despite the rapid growth, inflation stayed low. If the Fed had not raised interest rates, the economy would have grown even more rapidly and inflation would most likely have risen.

Critics who argued that the Fed should have waited until inflation was actually rising, rather than acting preemptively, were giving advice that would probably have forced the Fed to raise interest rates more in 1995 than it did in 1994—because inflation in 1995 would have been higher than it actually was.

The Fed found itself once again looking forward in the second half of 1999.* With the economy booming—but inflation very, very low—the Fed chose to raise interest rates hoping to gently rein in the economy. The Fed raised the federal funds rate, the interest rate it controls most directly, a quarter point on June 30. As the economy continued to boom, the Fed raised interest rates an additional quarter point on August 24, November 16, and February 2, 2000. By the beginning of 2001, the economy appeared to be weakening and the Fed started a series of interest rate cuts hoping to soften the downturn.

The bottom line: It pays to look ahead when setting monetary policy.

*You can find minutes of Fed policy meetings at www.federalreserve.gov/fomc.

spending. Accordingly, it kept money tight and allowed interest rates in Germany to rise to levels that had not been seen in that country for a decade. While the German nominal interest rate of 9.2 percent in 1991 does not look especially high, it is worth noting that the real interest rate in Germany in 1991 was well above that in the United States.[14]

The Bundesbank kept money tight through 1992, all the time expressing great unhappiness about the government's loose fiscal policy and the inflation that it had unleashed.

[14]In the end-of-chapter problems, we ask you to calculate the real interest rates in Germany and the United States in 1991. This can be done using Tables 11-5 and 11-6.

TABLE 11-6 Macroeconomic Consequences of German Unification
(Percent)

	1989	1990	1991	1992
GDP growth	3.8	4.5	0.9	1.8
Inflation rate	2.6	3.4	5.1	5.3
Budget deficit/GDP	−0.2	+1.7	+2.8	+3.2
Nominal interest rate	7.1	8.5	9.2	9.2

Source: International Monetary Fund.

In many countries, the German inflation rate in 1991 and 1992, under 5 percent, would be regarded as a miracle of low inflation. But in Germany, where the desire for low inflation is part of the national consensus, inflation at that rate is a matter for real concern.[15]

The German policy mix of the early 1990s was like that of the United States in the early 1980s: easy fiscal policy and tight monetary policy. The consequences in both countries were also similar: high interest rates and a deficit in the current account of the balance of payments.

In the next chapter we add international trade to our basic model. We will see there that the inclusion of foreign trade modifies but does not fundamentally alter the analysis of the impacts of monetary and fiscal policy on the economy. We will also see that the combination of tight monetary policy and easy fiscal policy tends to produce a deficit in the balance of payments.

SUMMARY

1. Monetary policy affects the economy, first, by affecting the interest rate and then by affecting aggregate demand. An increase in the money supply reduces the interest rate, increases investment spending and aggregate demand, and thus increases equilibrium output.
2. There are two extreme cases in the operation of monetary policy. In the classical case the demand for real balances is independent of the rate of interest. In that case monetary policy is highly effective. The other extreme is the liquidity trap, the case in which the public is willing to hold *any* amount of real balances at the going interest rate. In that case changes in the supply of real balances have no impact on interest rates and therefore do not affect aggregate demand and output.
3. Taking into account the effects of fiscal policy on the interest rate modifies the multiplier results of Chapter 9. Fiscal expansion, except in extreme circumstances, still leads to an income expansion. However, the rise in interest rates that comes about through the increase in money demand caused by higher income dampens the expansion.
4. Fiscal policy is more effective the smaller the induced changes in interest rates and the smaller the response of investment to these interest rate changes.

[15]Runaway German inflation after World War I contributed to Hitler's rise to power.

5. The two extreme cases, the liquidity trap and the classical case, are useful to show what determines the magnitude of monetary and fiscal policy multipliers. In the liquidity trap, monetary policy has no effect on the economy, whereas fiscal policy has its full multiplier effect on output and no effect on interest rates. In the classical case, changes in the money stock change income, but fiscal policy has no effect on income—it affects only the interest rate. In this case, there is complete crowding out of private spending by government spending.

6. A fiscal expansion, because it leads to higher interest rates, displaces, or crowds out, some private investment. The extent of crowding out is a sensitive issue in assessing the usefulness and desirability of fiscal policy as a tool of stabilization policy.

7. The question of the monetary-fiscal policy mix arises because expansionary monetary policy reduces the interest rate while expansionary fiscal policy increases the interest rate. Accordingly, expansionary fiscal policy increases output while reducing the level of investment; expansionary monetary policy increases output and the level of investment.

8. Governments have to choose the mix in accordance with their objectives for economic growth, or increasing consumption, or from the viewpoint of their beliefs about the desirable size of the government.

KEY TERMS

anticipatory monetary policy	investment tax credit	policy mix
classical case	liquidity trap	portfolio disequilibrium
crowding out	monetary accommodation	quantity theory of money
deflation	monetizing budget deficits	real interest rate
investment subsidy	open market operations	transmission mechanism

PROBLEMS

Conceptual

1. In the text we describe the effect of an open market purchase by the Fed.
   a. Define an open market sale by the Fed.
   b. Show the impact of an open market sale on the interest rate and output. Show both the immediate and the longer-term impacts.

2. Discuss the circumstances under which the monetary and fiscal policy multipliers are each, in turn, equal to zero. Explain in words why this can happen and how likely you think this is.

3. What is a liquidity trap? If the economy was stuck in one, would you advise the use of monetary or fiscal policy?

4. What is crowding out, and when would you expect it to occur? In the face of substantial crowding out, which will be more successful—fiscal or monetary policy?

5. What would the *LM* curve look like in a classical world? If this really were the *LM* curve that we thought best characterized the economy, would we lean toward the use of fiscal policy or monetary policy? (You may assume your goal is to affect output.)

6. What happens when the Fed monetizes a budget deficit? Is this something it should *always* try to do? (*Hint:* Outline the benefits and costs of such a policy over time.)

7. "We can have the GDP path we want equally well with a tight fiscal policy and an easier monetary policy, or the reverse, within fairly broad limits. The real basis for choice lies in many subsidiary targets, besides real GDP and inflation, that are differentially affected by fiscal and monetary policies." What are some of the subsidiary targets referred to in the quote? How would they be affected by alternative policy combinations?

Technical

1. The economy is at full employment. Now the government wants to change the composition of demand toward investment and away from consumption without, however, allowing aggregate demand to go beyond full employment. What is the required policy mix? Use an *IS-LM* diagram to show your policy proposal.

2. Suppose the government cuts income taxes. Show in the *IS-LM* model the impact of the tax cut under two assumptions: (*a*) The government keeps interest rates constant through an accommodating monetary policy. (*b*) The money stock remains unchanged. Explain the difference in results.

3. Consider two alternative programs for contraction. One is the removal of an investment subsidy; the other is a rise in income tax rates. Use the *IS-LM* model and the investment schedule, as shown in Figure 11-7, to discuss the impact of these alternative policies on income, interest rates, and investment.

4. In Figure 11-8 the economy can move to full employment by an expansion in either money or the full-employment deficit. Which policy leads to E_1 and which to E_2? How would you expect the choice to be made? Who would most strongly favor moving to E_1? versus E_2? What policy would correspond to "balanced growth"?

Empirical

1. Box 1-1 investigates the case of the liquidity trap in Japan, showing that interest rates have been virtually zero repeatedly in the late 1990s. Did these low interest rates manage to stimulate economic growth rates? Go to www.economagic.com. Under "Browse by Source," choose the link "Bank of Japan and Economic Planning Agency of Japan." Choose the heading "Japanese GDP at Constant Prices SA," and select "GDE (=GDP); SA." Using the built-in facilities, transform this series, selecting quarter-to-quarter percentage changes. Graph this series for the period since 1995. Compare the graph you obtained with Figure 1 in Box 11-1. Did the low interest rates encourage growth?

2. Figure 11-1 illustrates the Federal Reserve's response to the 2001 recession in the United States. How do central banks in other countries respond to recessions? Let us take a look at growth rates in the EU in the last few years and the reaction of the European Central Bank (ECB). Go to www.economagic.com. Under "Browse by Source," choose the link "Central Bank of Europe." Under the heading "EU GDP and Components at Constant Prices," choose the variable GDP. Similarly, under the heading "Money Market Interest Rates," choose EU 3-month deposit rate. Using the built-in facilities, transform the GDP series, selecting quarter-to-quarter at annual rates percentage changes. Create a graph for the period 1998–2003, showing GDP growth rates and the interest rate. Was the EU in a recession in 2001? How did the ECB react to the real economy? Did it start lowering interest rates when growth turned negative, or did it take preemptive action?

CHAPTER 12

International Linkages

CHAPTER HIGHLIGHTS

- Economies are linked internationally through trade in goods and through financial markets. The exchange rate is the price of a foreign currency in terms of the dollar. A high exchange rate—a weak dollar—reduces imports and increases exports, stimulating aggregate demand.

- Under fixed exchange rates, central banks buy and sell foreign currency to peg the exchange rate. Under floating exchange rates, the market determines the value of one currency in terms of another.

- If a country wishes to maintain a fixed exchange rate in the presence of a balance of payments deficit, the central bank must buy back domestic currency, using its reserves of foreign currency and gold or borrowing reserves from abroad. If the balance of payments deficit persists long enough for the country to run out of reserves, it must allow the value of its currency to fall.

- In the very long run, exchange rates adjust so as to equalize the real cost of goods across countries.

- With perfect capital mobility and fixed exchange rates, fiscal policy is powerful. With perfect capital mobility and floating exchange rates, monetary policy is powerful.

At the beginning of the twenty-first century, national economies are becoming more closely interrelated, and the notion of *globalization*—that we are moving toward a single global economy—is increasingly accepted. Economic influences from abroad already have powerful effects on the U.S. economy. And U.S. economic policies have even more substantial effects on foreign economies.

Whether the U.S. economy grows or moves into recession makes a big difference to Mexico or even to Japan, and whether other industrial countries shift to fiscal stimulus or stringency makes a difference to the U.S. economy. A tightening of U.S. monetary policy that raises domestic interest rates both affects interest rates worldwide and changes the value of the dollar relative to other currencies, and thus affects U.S. competitiveness and worldwide trade and GDP.

In this chapter we present the key linkages among *open economies*—economies that trade with others—and introduce some first pieces of analysis. We present more details on international aspects of macroeconomics in Chapter 19.

Any economy is linked to the rest of the world through two broad channels: trade (in goods and services) and finance. The *trade* linkage means that some of a country's production is exported to foreign countries, while some goods that are consumed or invested at home are produced abroad and imported. In 2002, U.S. exports of goods and services amounted to 11.2 percent of GDP, while imports were equal to 16.4 percent of GDP. Compared with other countries, the United States engages in relatively little international trade—it is a relatively closed economy. At the other extreme is the Netherlands—a very open economy—whose imports and exports each amount to about 60 percent of GDP.

Trade linkages are nonetheless important for the United States. Spending on imports escapes from the circular flow of income, in the sense that part of the income spent by U.S. residents is not spent on domestically produced goods; by contrast, exports appear as an increase in the demand for domestically produced goods. Thus, the basic *IS-LM* model of income determination must be amended to include international effects.

In addition, the prices of U.S. goods relative to those of our competitors have direct impacts on demand, output, and employment. A decline in the dollar prices of our competitors, relative to the prices at which U.S. firms sell, shifts demand away from U.S. goods toward goods produced abroad. Our imports rise and exports fall. This is precisely what happened in the United States between 1980 and 1985, when the value of the dollar increased to record levels relative to foreign currencies, imports became cheap, and foreigners found U.S. goods very expensive. Conversely, when the value of the dollar declines relative to other currencies, U.S.-produced goods become relatively cheaper, demand here and abroad shifts toward our goods, exports rise, and imports decline.

There are also strong international links in the area of *finance*. The *daily* turnover in the foreign exchange market is equal to $1.5 trillion, which is about 15 percent of *annual* U.S. GDP. U.S. residents, whether households, banks, or corporations, can hold U.S. assets such as Treasury bills or corporate bonds, or they can hold assets in foreign countries, say, in Canada or Germany. Most U.S. households hold almost exclusively U.S. assets, but that is certainly not true for banks or large corporations. Portfolio managers shop around the world for the most attractive yields, and they may well conclude that German government bonds, yen bonds issued by the Japanese government, or Brazilian government bonds offer a better yield—all things considered—than U.S. bonds.

As international investors shift their assets around the world, they link asset markets here and abroad, and thereby affect income, exchange rates, and the ability of monetary policy to affect interest rates. We show in this chapter how the *IS-LM* analysis has to be modified to take international trade and finance linkages into account. The first step is to discuss exchange rates and the balance of payments.

12-1
THE BALANCE OF PAYMENTS AND EXCHANGE RATES

The *balance of payments* is the record of the transactions of the residents of a country with the rest of the world. There are two main accounts in the balance of payments: the current account and the capital account. Table 12-1 shows recent data for the United States.

The simple rule for balance-of-payments accounting is that any transaction that gives rise to a payment by a country's residents is a deficit item in that country's balance of payments. Thus, for the United States, imports of cars, gifts to foreigners, a purchase of land in Spain, or a deposit in a bank in Switzerland—all are deficit items. Examples of surplus items, by contrast, would be U.S. sales of airplanes abroad, payments by foreigners for U.S. licenses to use American technology, pensions from abroad received by U.S. residents, and foreign purchases of U.S. assets.

The *current account* records trade in goods and services, as well as transfer payments. Services include freight, royalty payments, and interest payments. Services also include *net investment income,* the interest and profits on our assets abroad less the income foreigners earn on assets they own in the United States. Transfer payments consist of remittances, gifts, and grants. The *trade balance* simply records trade in goods. Adding trade in services and net transfers to the trade balance, we arrive at the current account balance.

TABLE 12-1	The U.S. Balance of Payments (Billions of Dollars)					
	1997	1998	1999	2000	2001	2002
Current account balance	−128.4	−203.8	−292.9	−410.3	−393.4	−503.4
Goods and services balance	−107.8	−166.9	−262.2	−378.7	−358.3	−435.5
Capital account balance	128.4	203.8	292.9	410.3	393.4	503.4
U.S. official reserve assets, net*	−1.0	−6.8	8.7	−0.3	−4.9	−3.7
Net private capital flows†	129.4	210.6	284.1	410.6	398.3	507.1
Balance of payments deficit	−1.0	−6.8	8.7	−0.3	−4.9	−3.7

*A positive number for net U.S. official reserve assets indicates a decrease in official reserves.

†Including statistical discrepancy.

Source: Bureau of Economic Analysis.

The current account is in *surplus* if exports exceed imports plus net transfers to foreigners, that is, if receipts from trade in goods and services and transfers exceed payments on this account.

The *capital account* records purchases and sales of assets, such as stocks, bonds, and land. There is a U.S. capital account surplus—also called a net capital inflow—when our receipts from the sale of stocks, bonds, land, bank deposits, and other assets exceed our payments for our own purchases of foreign assets.

EXTERNAL ACCOUNTS MUST BALANCE

The central point of international payments is very simple: Individuals and firms have to pay for what they buy abroad. If a person spends more than her income, her deficit needs to be financed by selling assets or by borrowing. Similarly, if a country runs a deficit in its current account, spending more abroad than it receives from sales to the rest of the world, the deficit needs to be financed by selling assets or by borrowing abroad. This selling or borrowing implies that the country is running a capital account surplus. Thus, any current account deficit is of necessity *financed* by an offsetting capital inflow:

$$\text{Current account} + \text{capital account} = 0 \tag{1}$$

Equation (1) makes a drastic point: If a country has no assets to sell, if it has no foreign currency reserves to use up, and if nobody will lend to it, the country *has* to achieve balance in its current account, however painful and difficult that may be.

It is often useful to split the capital account into two separate parts: (1) the transactions of the country's private sector and (2) official reserve transactions, which correspond to the central bank's activities. A current account deficit can be financed by private residents selling off assets abroad or borrowing abroad. Alternatively, or as well, a current account deficit can be financed by the government, which runs down its reserves of foreign exchange,[1] selling foreign currency in the foreign exchange market. Conversely, when there is a surplus, the private sector may use the foreign exchange revenues it receives to pay off debt or buy assets abroad; alternatively, the central bank can buy the (net) foreign currency earned by the private sector and add that currency to its reserves.

The increase in official reserves is also called the overall *balance-of-payments surplus*. We can summarize our discussion in the following statement:

$$\text{Balance-of-payments surplus} = \text{increase in official exchange reserves}$$

$$= \text{current account surplus} + \text{net private capital inflow}[2]$$

$$\tag{1a}$$

---

[1] All governments hold some amounts of foreign currency and of other assets such as gold. These are the country's *official reserves*.

[2] The term "net private capital inflow" is not entirely correct. Included here are also official capital flows unrelated to the exchange market operations. For example, the purchase of a new embassy building in Kiev would be an official capital account transaction, which would be put into the category "net private capital inflow." For our purposes, the broad distinctions are enough.

If both the current account and the private capital account are in deficit, then the overall balance of payments is in deficit; that is, the central bank is losing reserves. When one account is in surplus and the other is in deficit to precisely the same extent, the overall balance of payments is zero—neither in surplus nor in deficit.[3]

As Table 12-1 shows, the U.S. current account was in deficit during 1997–2002 (as it has been since 1982). In all years there was a net inflow of capital into the United States. In some years, the capital inflow was sufficient to cover the current account deficit. In other years, the United States had to run down its official reserves in order to make up for the difference.

FIXED EXCHANGE RATES

Let us first remind you that an exchange rate is the price of one currency in terms of another. As an example, in August 1999 you could buy 1 Irish punt for $1.38 in U.S. currency. So the *nominal exchange rate* was $e = 1.38$. A 6-inch Subway Club sandwich in Dublin cost 2.39 punts, the equivalent of $1.38 \times 2.39 = \$3.30$.[4] The same sandwich cost that week $3.09 in Seattle, so a really thrifty American tourist ought to have gotten takeout before going to Ireland and saved the difference as a down payment on a glass of Guinness.

We focus now on how central banks, through their official transactions, finance, or provide the means of paying for, balance-of-payments surpluses and deficits. At this point we distinguish between fixed and floating exchange rate systems.

In a *fixed exchange rate system* foreign central banks stand ready to buy and sell their currencies at a fixed price in terms of dollars. The major countries had fixed exchange rates against one another from the end of World War II until 1973. Today, some countries fix their exchange rates, but others don't.

In the 1960s, for example, the German central bank, the Bundesbank, would buy or sell any amount of dollars at 4 deutsche marks (DM) per U.S. dollar. The French central bank, the Banque de France, stood ready to buy or sell any amount of dollars at 4.90 French francs (FF) per U.S. dollar. The fact that the central banks were prepared to buy or sell *any* amount of dollars at these fixed prices, or exchange rates, meant that market prices would indeed be equal to the fixed rates. Why? Because nobody who wanted to buy U.S. dollars would pay more than 4.90 francs per dollar when francs could be purchased at that price from the Banque de France. Conversely, nobody would part with dollars in exchange for francs for less than 4.90 francs per dollar if the Banque de France, through the commercial banking system, was prepared to buy dollars at that price.[5]

---

[3]Balance-of-payments data are poor. Changes in official reserves are generally accurately reported, trade flow data are reasonably good, data on service flows are poor, and capital flow data are extremely poor. For example, in the second quarter of 2002, there was a statistical discrepancy of positive $54 billion—followed the next quarter by a statistical discrepancy of negative $43 billion!

[4]Perhaps we should explain that Subway is a franchise sandwich operation ubiquitous in the United States. The Subway location in Ireland in Dublin is on Nassau just off Grafton Street.

[5]Would the Bundesbank and the Banque de France also have to set a mark-franc exchange rate? Not really, because if there are 4.90 francs to the dollar and 4 marks to the dollar there must be $1.225 (= 4.90/4)$ francs to the mark.

Intervention

Foreign central banks hold *reserves*—inventories of dollars, other currencies, and gold that they can sell for dollars—to sell when they want to or have to intervene in the foreign exchange market. *Intervention is the buying or selling of foreign exchange by the central bank.*

What determines the amount of intervention that a central bank has to do in a fixed exchange rate system? We already have the answer to that question. The balance of payments measures the amount of foreign exchange intervention needed from the central banks. For example, if the United States were running a deficit in the balance of payments vis-à-vis Japan, and thus the demand for yen in exchange for dollars exceeded the supply of yen in exchange for dollars from Japanese, the Bank of Japan would buy the excess dollars, paying for them with yen.[6]

Fixed exchange rates thus operate like any other price support scheme, such as those in agricultural markets. Given market demand and supply, the price fixer has to make up the excess demand or take up the excess supply. In order to be able to ensure that the price (exchange rate) stays fixed, it is obviously necessary to hold an inventory of foreign currencies, or foreign exchange, that can be provided in exchange for the domestic currency.

As long as the central bank has the necessary reserves, it can continue to intervene in the foreign exchange markets to keep the exchange rate constant. **However, if a country persistently runs deficits in the balance of payments, the central bank eventually will run out of reserves of foreign exchange and will be unable to continue its intervention.**

Before that point is reached, the central bank is likely to decide that it can no longer maintain the exchange rate, and it will devalue the currency. In 1967, for instance, the British devalued the pound from $2.80 per pound to $2.40 per pound. That meant it became cheaper for Americans and other foreigners to buy British pounds, and the devaluation thus affected the balance of payments by making British goods relatively cheaper for foreigners to buy.

FLEXIBLE EXCHANGE RATES

Under fixed exchange rates, the central banks have to provide whatever amounts of foreign currency are needed to finance payments imbalances. **In a *flexible (floating) exchange rate system,* by contrast, the central banks allow the exchange rate to adjust to equate the supply and demand for foreign currency.** If the exchange rate of the dollar against the yen were .81 cents per yen and Japanese exports to the United States increased, thus requiring Americans to pay more yen to Japanese exporters, the Bank of Japan could simply stand aside and let the exchange rate adjust. In this

---

[6]Which central bank in fact intervenes in the foreign exchange market in the fixed rate system? If there was an excess supply of dollars and an excess demand for yen, either the Bank of Japan could buy dollars in exchange for yen or the Fed could sell yen in exchange for dollars. In practice, during the fixed rate period, each foreign central bank undertook to *peg* (fix) its exchange rate vis-à-vis the dollar, and most foreign exchange intervention was undertaken by the foreign central banks. The Fed was nonetheless involved in the management of the exchange rate system, since it frequently made dollar loans to foreign central banks that were in danger of running out of dollars.

BOX 12-1   The Euro

Western Europe has gone through 5 decades of increasing economic integration, from inconvertible currencies, trade quotas, and prohibitive tariffs at the end of World War II to unrestricted free trade within borders, total mobility of labor across borders, and indeed the abolition of internal borders, along with common passports, a European Parliament, and a central economic authority in Brussels. Lots of decisions remain at the national level, but it is impressive just how much Europe has moved from segmented national economies to an integrated political and economic area.

This process of economic and political integration has led to the European Union (EU). A controversial crowning piece of that economic agenda has been the creation of a monetary union, the *European Monetary Union (EMU)* and its new common money, the *euro*. This new currency started in January 1999 with exchange rates immutably fixed and was completed in January 2002 with the introduction of the actual currency—coins and notes. No more lira, deutsche marks, francs, or pesetas—just euros with the symbol € denoting the new money.

The new money was highly controversial for one simple reason: For much of the postwar period, Germany had a good money—low inflation—and most other

particular case, the exchange rate could move from .81 cents per yen to a level such as .85 cents per yen, making Japanese goods more expensive in terms of dollars and thus reducing the demand for them by Americans. Later in this chapter we shall examine the way in which changes in exchange rates under floating rates affect the balance of payments. The terms *flexible rates* and *floating rates* are used interchangeably.

FLOATING, CLEAN AND DIRTY

In a system of *clean floating*, central banks stand aside completely and allow exchange rates to be freely determined in the foreign exchange markets. Since the

European economies, France or Italy in particular, did not. No surprise then that Germans worried about their money. The key issue was the creation of a *convergence* process in which countries would have to reach specific targets (the "Maastricht criteria," named after the Dutch town where the agreements were reached). These qualifying hurdles were, specifically, 2 or less percent inflation, no restrictions on capital flows and no devaluation in the preceding 2 years, a budget deficit of less than 2 percent of GDP, and a debt ratio below 60 percent of GDP or at least committed to falling to that level over time. Convergence has happened—as evidenced by the fact that Italian interest rates, debts and deficits notwithstanding, have fallen to German levels!

Even though the European Central Bank (ECB) and the euro are up and running, questions remain about whether it was really a good idea to give up national monies and exchange rates. The key question is this: Can the various European economies adjust to shocks by movements in wages and prices? If not, exchange rates should be doing the job, but they are now gone. Suppose, for example, that demand shifts from Italian products (Fiats) to those of Germany (Mercedes and BMW). There would be unemployment in Italy and a boom in Germany. If German wages rise and Italian wages fall, that will help restore full employment in both regions. If the wage does not fall in Italy but only rises in Germany, that helps the German labor market but creates an inflation problem for the euro area. It does little to restore Italian full employment. Before the euro, Italian currency depreciation would have been the right answer—but with common money that option is gone. The answer to this issue, in practice, is twofold. First, Europe gave up the exchange rate as a policy tool quite a while ago, long before the new money. Second, whatever the difficulty, this is a political integration project, and that is what political integration is all about.

One of the important questions of the next few years is just how the euro area will expand. Will Great Britain decide to join? Will the new members of the European Union (Poland, Hungary, the Czech Republic, and more) soon also be part of the European Monetary Union? The answer is surely that a decade from now the euro will be used, one way or another, in a much larger part of the world map than just western Europe. Europe has taken a huge step toward creating a money that is on a par with the dollar.

---

central banks do not intervene in the foreign exchange markets in such a system, official reserve transactions are, accordingly, zero. That means the balance of payments is zero in a system of clean floating: The exchange rate adjusts to make the current and capital accounts sum to zero.

In practice, the flexible rate system, in effect since 1973, has not been one of clean floating. Instead, the system has been one of *managed,* or *dirty, floating.* **Under managed floating, central banks intervene to buy and sell foreign currencies in attempts to influence exchange rates.** Official reserve transactions are, accordingly, not equal to zero under managed floating. The reasons for central bank intervention under floating rates are discussed in Chapter 19.

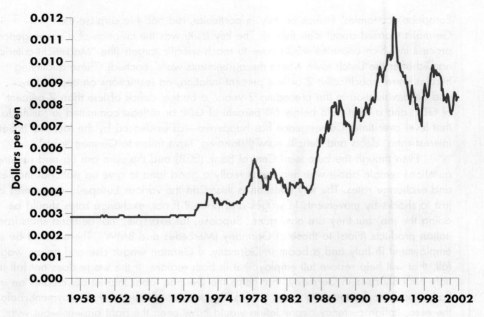

FIGURE 12-1   THE DOLLAR-YEN EXCHANGE RATE, 1957–2002.

(Source: Haver Analytics Macroeconomic Database and Federal Reserve Economic Data.)

TERMINOLOGY

Exchange rate language can be very confusing. In particular, the terms "deprecia-tion," "appreciation," "devaluation," and "revaluation" recur in any discussion of in-ternational trade and finance. Because the exchange rate is the price of one currency in terms of another, it can be quoted two ways, for example, either 124 yen per dollar or .81 cents per yen. The foreign exchange markets generally settle on one way of quoting each rate. For example, the yen is typically quoted in yen per dollar, the British pound in dollars per pound. In academic economics the convention is that the exchange rate is a price in terms of domestic currency. For example, a quote for the dollar-pound exchange rate is given in dollars per pound, say, $1.56 per pound—just as a quart of milk might cost $1.56. **So if the exchange rate falls, the domestic currency is worth *more*; it costs fewer dollars to buy a unit of the foreign currency.**[7]

Figure 12-1 shows the dollar-yen exchange rate since 1957. The vertical axis shows the exchange rate measured as the price of yen in U.S. dollars. Note that we show two subperiods: the fixed rate period, throughout the 1960s and lasting until 1972, and the flexible rate regime.

[7]Of course, this is only a convention, and in some countries, including Britain, economic theory uses the other convention (just like driving on the left side of the road).

A *devaluation* **takes place when the price of foreign currencies under a fixed rate regime is increased by official action.** A devaluation thus means that foreigners pay less for the devalued currency and that residents of the devaluing country pay more for foreign currencies. The opposite of a devaluation is a *revaluation.*

A change in the price of foreign exchange under flexible exchange rates is referred to as *currency depreciation* or *appreciation.* **A currency *depreciates* when, under floating rates, it becomes less expensive in terms of foreign currencies.** For instance, if the exchange rate of the pound sterling changes from $1.56 per pound to $1.50 per pound, the pound is depreciating. By contrast, a currency *appreciates* when it becomes more expensive in terms of foreign money.

For example, in Figure 12-1 we see that in 1995–1996 the yen was depreciating, meaning that it took fewer and fewer dollars to buy yen. By contrast, in 1998–1999 the yen was appreciating. Although the terms "devaluation/revaluation" and "depreciation/appreciation" are used in fixed and flexible rate regimes, respectively, there is no economic difference. These terms describe the *direction* in which an exchange rate moves.

RECAP

- The balance-of-payments accounts are a record of the transactions of the economy with other economies. The capital account describes transactions in assets, while the current account covers transactions in goods and services, as well as transfers.
- Any payment to foreigners is a deficit item in the balance of payments. Any payment from foreigners is a surplus item. The balance-of-payments deficit (or surplus) is the sum of the deficits (or surpluses) on current and capital accounts.
- Under fixed exchange rates, central banks stand ready to meet all demands for foreign currencies at a fixed price in terms of the domestic currency. They *finance* the excess demands for, or supplies of, foreign currency (i.e., the balance-of-payments deficits or surpluses, respectively) at the pegged (fixed) exchange rate by running down, or adding to, their reserves of foreign currency.
- Under flexible exchange rates, the demands for and supplies of foreign currency are equated through movements in exchange rates. Under clean floating, there is no central bank intervention and the balance of payments is zero. But central banks sometimes intervene in a floating rate system, engaging in so-called dirty floating.

 12-2

THE EXCHANGE RATE IN THE LONG RUN

A government or central bank can peg the value of its currency, that is, fix the exchange rate, for a period of time. But in the long run, the exchange rate between a pair of countries is determined by the relative purchasing power of currency within each country. For example, if a hot dog costs 25 Danish kroner (DKr) at a *polsevogn*[8] in Copenhagen

[8]"Sausage wagon."

and $2.50 from a street vendor in Philadelphia, one might reasonably expect that the dollar-krone exchange rate would be $0.10. This illustrates the theory of *purchasing power parity,* or *PPP.* **Two currencies are at purchasing power parity when a unit of domestic currency can buy the same basket of goods at home or abroad.** The relative purchasing power of two currencies is measured by the *real exchange rate.*

The real exchange rate is the ratio of foreign to domestic prices, measured in the same currency. It measures a country's competitiveness in international trade. The real exchange rate, R, is defined as

$$R = \frac{eP_f}{P} \qquad (2)$$

where P and P_f are the price levels here and abroad, respectively, and e is the dollar price of foreign exchange. Note that since P_f represents foreign prices, for example, prices measured in Danish kroner, and the exchange rate is measured as so many dollars per Danish kroner, the numerator expresses prices abroad measured in dollars; with the domestic price level, measured in this case in dollars, in the denominator, the real exchange rate expresses prices abroad relative to those at home.

If the real exchange rate equals 1, currencies are at purchasing power parity. If the U.S. real exchange rate rises above 1 that means that goods abroad are more expensive than goods in the United States. Other things equal, this implies that people—both in the United States and abroad—are likely to switch some of their spending to goods produced in the United States. This is often described as an increase in the competitiveness of our products. As long as R is greater than 1, we expect the relative demand for domestically produced goods to rise. Eventually, this should either drive up domestic prices or drive down the exchange rate, moving us closer to purchasing power parity.

Market forces prevent the exchange rate from moving *too* far from PPP or from remaining away from PPP indefinitely. However, pressures to move to PPP work only slowly. In the mid-1990s, the dollar-krone exchange rate was closer to 18 cents than to 10 cents and the real cost of hot dogs was nearly twice as much in Copenhagen as in Philadelphia. There are several reasons for slow movement toward PPP. The first reason is that market baskets differ across countries. Americans and Danes do not consume the same bundle of goods.[9] The second reason for slow movement toward PPP is that there are many barriers to the movement of goods between countries.[10] Some are natural barriers—transportation costs are one obvious extra cost—while others, tariffs for example, are imposed by governments. Sometimes movement of final goods isn't enough: Workers and capital would have to move. It isn't likely that Americans would commute to Denmark to sell hot dogs. Third, and probably of greatest importance, many goods—land is the classic example—are "nontraded" and cannot move.

[9] Hot dogs in Copenhagen are served on high-quality rolls—what Americans would call "French bread." Franks in Philadelphia are served on soft white buns, which Americans think of as the proper container for a hot dog but which most Danes wouldn't appreciate. Contrariwise, Danish *polse* are served with a white sauce instead of with mustard and sauerkraut as in Philadelphia.

[10] See Charles Engel and John Rogers, "How Wide Is the Border?" *American Economic Review,* December 1996.

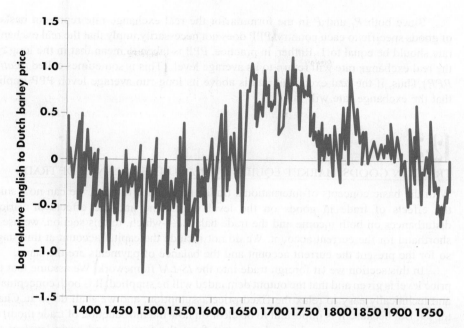

FIGURE 12-2   LOG RELATIVE ENGLISH TO DUTCH BARLEY PRICES, 1367–1985..

(Source: Kenneth A. Froot, Michael Kim, and Kenneth Rogoff, "The Law of One Price over 700 Years," NBER working paper no. W5132, 1996.)

Measured by Subway sandwiches in the example in the previous section, the Irish punt was below purchasing power parity with the U.S. dollar in August 1999. By March 2003, a Subway Club in Dublin cost 3.39 euros and 3.59 dollars in Seattle. The euro/dollar exchange rate was 1.07, so the U.S. dollar cost of a sandwich bought in Dublin had risen to $1.07 \times 3.39 = \$3.63$. In other words, in March 2003 the cost of a Subway Club was effectively the same in Seattle and Dublin. (Note that in the interim Ireland had joined the European Monetary Union and switched its currency from the punt to the euro.)

Figure 12-2 shows the cost of barley in England relative to that in Holland over a *really* long span of time. Barley is a relatively homogenous commodity that is reasonably transportable. You can see in Figure 12-2 that the real barley exchange rate tended toward equalization. But you can also see that there have been long periods of substantial deviation from equality. The best current estimate, for modern times, is that it takes about 4 years to reduce deviations from PPP by half.[11] So while PPP holds in the long run, over a period of months and even years, it is only one of the determinants of the exchange rate.

[11] J. Frankel and A. Rose, "A Panel Project on Purchasing Power Parity," *Journal of International Economics,* February 1996; and Charles Engel, "Long-Run PPP May Not Hold After All," *Journal of International Economics,* August 2000.

Since both P_f and P in the formula for the real exchange rate represent baskets of goods specific to each country, PPP does not necessarily imply that the real exchange rate should be equal to 1. Rather, in practice, PPP is taken to mean that in the long run the real exchange rate will return to its average level. (This is sometimes called *relative PPP.*) Thus, if the real exchange rate is above its long-run average level, PPP implies that the exchange rate will fall.

12-3

TRADE IN GOODS, MARKET EQUILIBRIUM, AND THE BALANCE OF TRADE

With the basic concepts of international trade and finance in hand, we can now study the effects of trade in goods on the level of income and the effects of various disturbances on both income and the trade balance—which, in this section, we use as shorthand for the current account. We do not include the capital account at this stage, so for the present the current account and the balance of payments are the same.

In this section we fit foreign trade into the *IS-LM* framework. We assume that the price level is given and that the output demanded will be supplied. It is both conceptually and technically easy to relax the fixed-price assumption, and we shall do so in Chapter 19. But because it is important to be clear on how the introduction of trade modifies the analysis of aggregate demand, we start from the familiar and basic level of the *IS-LM* model.

DOMESTIC SPENDING AND SPENDING ON DOMESTIC GOODS

In an open economy, part of domestic output is sold to foreigners (exports) and part of spending by domestic residents purchases foreign goods (imports). We have to modify the *IS* curve accordingly.

The most important change is that domestic spending no longer determines domestic output. Instead, *spending on domestic goods* determines domestic output. Some spending by domestic residents is on imports, for instance, purchases of imported beer. Demand for domestic goods, by contrast, includes exports or foreign demand along with part of spending by domestic residents.

The effect of external transactions on the demand for domestic output was examined in Chapter 2. Define A to be spending *by* domestic residents; then:

$$\text{Spending by domestic residents} = A = C + I + G \tag{3}$$

$$\begin{aligned}\text{Spending on domestic goods} = A + NX &= (C + I + G) + (X - Q) \\ &= (C + I + G) + NX\end{aligned} \tag{4}$$

where X is the level of exports, Q is imports, and $NX \equiv X - Q$ is the trade (goods and services) surplus. Spending on domestic goods is total spending by domestic residents less their spending on imports *plus* foreign demand or exports. Since exports minus imports is the trade surplus, or net exports (NX), spending on domestic goods is spending by domestic residents plus the trade surplus.

With this clarification we can return to our model of income determination. We will assume that domestic spending depends on the interest rate and income, so

$$A = A(Y, i) \tag{5}$$

NET EXPORTS

Net exports, or the excess of exports over imports, depend on our income, which affects import spending; on foreign income, Y_f, which affects foreign demand for our exports; and on the real exchange rate, R. A rise in R or a real depreciation improves our trade balance as demand shifts from goods produced abroad to those produced at home:[12]

$$NX = X(Y_f, R) - Q(Y, R) = NX(Y, Y_f, R) \tag{6}$$

We can immediately state three important results:

- A rise in foreign income, other things being equal, improves the home country's trade balance and therefore raises the home country's aggregate demand.
- A real depreciation by the home country improves the trade balance and therefore increases aggregate demand.
- A rise in home income raises import spending and hence worsens the trade balance.

GOODS MARKET EQUILIBRIUM

The increase in import demand caused by a $1 increase in income is called the *marginal propensity to import*. **The marginal propensity to import measures the fraction of an extra dollar of income spent on imports.** The fact that part of income will be spent on imports (rather than on domestic goods) implies that the IS curve will be steeper than it would be in a closed economy. For a given reduction in interest rates it takes a smaller increase in output and income to restore goods market equilibrium.

The open economy IS curve includes net exports as a component of aggregate demand. Therefore, the level of competitiveness, as measured by the real exchange rate R, affects the IS curve. A real depreciation increases the demand for domestic goods, shifting the IS curve out and to the right. Likewise, an increase in foreign income and, with it, an increase in foreign spending on our goods will increase net exports or demand for our goods. Thus, we have

$$IS \text{ curve:} \quad Y = A(Y, i) + NX(Y, Y_f, R) \tag{7}$$

---

[12]Note two points about net exports in equation (6). First, we measure net exports in terms of domestic output. To do so, we must measure imports (Q) in terms of their value in our currency. Second, we *assume* that a real appreciation worsens the trade balance and a real depreciation (a rise in R) improves the trade balance. This is a matter of assumption since there are opposing effects of changes in volume and in price. We return to this point in Chap. 19.

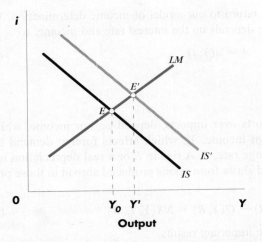

FIGURE 12-3   THE EFFECT OF A RISE IN FOREIGN INCOME.

Since the equilibrium level of income will now depend on both foreign income and the real exchange rate, we have to ask how disturbances in foreign income, or real exchange rate changes, affect the equilibrium level of income.

Figure 12-3 shows the effect of a rise in foreign income. The higher foreign spending on our goods raises demand and hence, at unchanged interest rates, requires an increase in output. This is shown by the rightward shift of the IS schedule. The full effect of an increase in foreign demand thus is an increase in interest rates and an increase in domestic output and employment. It is easy to go through the opposite change. A weakening of foreign economies reduces their imports and hence pulls down domestic demand. Equilibrium income at home would fall as would our interest rates.

Figure 12-3 can also help explain the effect of a real depreciation. As we saw, a real depreciation raises net exports at each level of income and hence shifts the IS schedule up and to the right. A real depreciation therefore leads to a rise in our equilibrium income.

Table 12-2 summarizes the effects of different disturbances on the equilibrium levels of income and net exports. Each of these examples can be worked out using the IS schedule in conjunction with the net export schedule.

TABLE 12-2 Effects of Disturbance on Income and Net Exports			
	INCREASE IN HOME SPENDING	INCREASE IN FOREIGN INCOME	REAL DEPRECIATION
Income	+	+	+
Net exports	−	+	+

TABLE 12-3 Effects of a 10 Percent Dollar Depreciation

IMPACT ON	YEAR 1	YEAR 2
Real GDP, %	0.5	0.6
CPI, %	0.4	1.3
Current account, $ billions	15	38

Source: Federal Reserve, unpublished model-based simulation.

REPERCUSSION EFFECTS

In an interdependent world, our policy changes affect other countries as well as ourselves, and then feed back on our economy. When we increase government spending, our income rises; part of the increase in income will be spent on imports, which means that income will rise abroad, too. The increase in foreign income will then raise foreign demand for our goods, which in turn adds to the domestic income expansion brought about by higher government spending, and so on.

These *repercussion effects* can be important in practice. When the United States expands, it tends, like a locomotive, to pull the rest of the world into an expansion. Likewise, if the rest of the world expands, we share in the expansion.

Repercussion effects also arise in response to exchange rate changes. In Table 12-3 we show empirical estimates of the impact of changes in real exchange rates on U.S. real GDP. The table reports the effect of a 10 percent dollar depreciation against all other currencies. The U.S. level of output expands strongly; abroad, by contrast, real GDP falls. The reason is that the increase in U.S. net exports raises income at home while lowering demand and output abroad.

Note that whereas an expansionary fiscal policy increases both our GDP and that of other countries, a depreciation of our exchange rate increases our income while reducing foreign incomes.

12-4
CAPITAL MOBILITY

One of the striking facts about the international economy is the high degree of integration, or linkage, among financial, or capital, markets—the markets in which bonds and stocks are traded. In most industrial countries today there are no restrictions on holding assets abroad. U.S. residents, or residents in Germany or the United Kingdom, can hold their wealth either at home or abroad. They therefore search around the world for the highest return (adjusted for risk), thereby linking together yields in capital markets in different countries. For example, if interest rates in New York rose relative to those in Canada, investors would turn to lending in New York, while borrowers would turn to Toronto. With lending up in New York and borrowing up in Toronto, yields would quickly fall into line.

In the simplest world, in which exchange rates are fixed forever, taxes are the same everywhere, and foreign asset holders never face political risks (nationalization, restrictions on transfer of assets, default risk by foreign governments), we would expect all asset holders to pick the asset that has the highest return. That would force asset returns into strict equality everywhere in the world capital markets because no country could borrow for less.

In reality, though, none of these three conditions exists. There are tax differences among countries; exchange rates can change, perhaps significantly, and thus affect the payoff in dollars of a foreign investment; and, finally, countries sometimes put up obstacles to capital outflows or simply find themselves unable to pay. These are some of the reasons that interest rates are not equal across countries.

However, interest rate differentials among major industrialized countries, adjusted to eliminate the risk of exchange rate changes, are quite small in practice. Consider the case of the United States and Canada. Once interest rates are measured on a "covered" basis, so that the exchange risk is eliminated, they should be exactly the same.[13] In fact the differential is very small, averaging less than .5 percent, a result primarily of tax differences. We take this evidence to support the view that capital is very highly mobile across borders, as we assume henceforth.

Our working assumption from now on involves *perfect capital mobility*. **Capital is perfectly mobile internationally when investors can purchase assets in any country they choose, quickly, with low transaction costs, and in unlimited amounts.** When capital is perfectly mobile, asset holders are willing and able to move large amounts of funds across borders in search of the highest return or lowest borrowing cost.

The high degree of capital market integration implies that any one country's interest rates cannot get too far out of line without bringing about capital flows that tend to restore yields to the world level. To return to the previous example, if Canadian yields fell relative to U.S. yields, there would be a capital outflow from Canada because lenders would take their funds out of Canada and borrowers would try to raise funds in Canada. From the point of view of the balance of payments, this implies that a relative decline in interest rates—a decline in our rates relative to those abroad—will tend to worsen the balance of payments because of the capital outflow resulting from lending abroad by U.S. residents.

The recognition that interest rates affect capital flows and the balance of payments has important implications for stabilization policy. First, because monetary and fiscal policies affect interest rates, the policies have an effect on the capital account and therefore on the balance of payments. The effects of monetary and fiscal policies on

---

[13]Cover, or protection, against the risk of exchange rate changes can be obtained by buying a futures contract, which promises (of course, at a cost) to pay a given amount of one currency in exchange for a specified amount of another currency at a given future date. There are, in practice, simpler ways of obtaining foreign exchange risk cover, but the essential mechanism is the same.

the balance of payments are *not* limited to the trade balance effects discussed above but extend to the capital account. The second implication is that the way in which monetary and fiscal policies work in affecting the domestic economy and the balance of payments changes when there are international capital flows.

THE BALANCE OF PAYMENTS AND CAPITAL FLOWS

We introduce the role of capital flows within a framework in which we assume that the home country faces a given price of imports and a given export demand. In addition, we assume that the world rate of interest, i_f (i.e., the rate of interest in foreign capital markets), is given. Moreover, with perfect capital mobility, capital flows into the home country at an unlimited[14] rate if our interest rate is above that abroad (from now on, until further notice, we assume that exchange risk is absent). Conversely, if our rate is below that abroad, capital outflows will be unlimited.

Next we look at the balance of payments. The balance-of-payments surplus, *BP*, is equal to the trade surplus, *NX*, plus the capital account surplus, *CF*:

$$BP = NX(Y, Y_f, R) + CF(i - i_f) \qquad (8)$$

Equation (8) shows the trade balance as a function of domestic and foreign income and the real exchange rate, and it shows the capital account as depending on the *interest differential*.[15] An increase in income worsens the trade balance, and an increase in the interest rate above the world level pulls in capital from abroad and thus improves the capital account. It follows that when income increases, even the tiniest increase in interest rates is enough to maintain an overall balance-of-payments equilibrium. The trade deficit would be financed by a capital inflow.

POLICY DILEMMAS: INTERNAL AND EXTERNAL BALANCE

The potential for capital flows to finance a current account deficit is extremely important. Countries frequently face policy dilemmas, in which a policy designed to deal with one problem worsens another problem. In particular, there is sometimes a conflict between the goals of external and internal balance.

External balance exists when the balance of payments is close to balance. Otherwise, the central bank is either losing reserves—which it cannot keep on doing—or

---

[14]"Unlimited" is a very strong word. Capital flows are very large compared to the American economy, so the Fed needs to watch them carefully when changing interest rates. For other countries, capital flows can be so large in comparison to their economy that the word "unlimited" really is appropriate.

[15]When capital mobility is perfect, the domestic and foreign interest rates cannot get out of line, so in equilibrium we will find that $i = i_f$; however, we write the capital flows equation with i potentially not equal to i_f in order to demonstrate the forces at work—including potentially massive capital flows—that produce equilibrium.

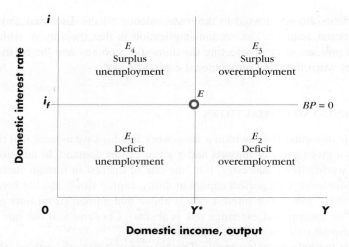

FIGURE 12-4   INTERNAL AND EXTERNAL BALANCE UNDER FIXED EXCHANGE RATES.

gaining reserves—which it does not want to do forever.[16] *Internal balance* exists when output is at the full employment level.

In Figure 12-4 we show the schedule $BP = 0$, derived from equation (8), along which we have balance-of-payments equilibrium. Our key assumption—perfect capital mobility—forces the $BP = 0$ line to be horizontal. Only at a level of interest rates equal to that of rates abroad can we have external balance: If domestic interest rates are higher, there is a vast capital account and overall surplus; if they are below foreign rates, there is an unlimited deficit.

Thus, $BP = 0$ must be flat at the level of world interest rates. Points above the $BP = 0$ schedule correspond to a surplus, and points below to a deficit. We have also drawn, in Figure 12-4, the full employment output level, Y^*. Point E is the only point at which both internal balance and external balance are achieved. Point E_1, for example, corresponds to a case of unemployment and a balance-of-payments deficit. Point E_2, by contrast, is a case of deficit and overemployment.

We can talk about policy dilemmas in terms of points in the four quadrants of Figure 12-4. For instance, at point E_1, there is a deficit in the balance of payments, as well as unemployment. An expansionary monetary policy would deal with the unemployment problem but worsen the balance of payments, thus apparently presenting a dilemma for the policymaker. The presence of interest-sensitive capital flows suggests the solution to the dilemma: If the country can find a way of raising the interest rate, it would obtain financing for the trade deficit.

That means that both monetary and fiscal policies would have to be used to achieve external and internal balance simultaneously. Each point in Figure 12-4 can be viewed

---

[16]However, some governments (e.g., Taiwan) do seem to want to have very large current account surpluses in order to be able to run capital account deficits that allow them to buy large amounts of foreign assets.

as an intersection of the *IS* and *LM* curves. Each curve has to be shifted, but how? How the adjustment takes place depends critically on the exchange rate regime.

We are now ready to extend the analysis of output determination to the open economy with perfect capital mobility. In the next section we assume the exchange rate is fixed. In Section 12-6 we consider output determination with flexible exchange rates.

12-5

THE MUNDELL-FLEMING MODEL: PERFECT CAPITAL MOBILITY UNDER FIXED EXCHANGE RATES

The analysis extending the standard *IS-LM* model to the open economy under perfect capital mobility has a special name, the *Mundell-Fleming model.* Nobel laureate Robert Mundell, now a professor at Columbia University, and the late Marcus Fleming, who was a researcher at the International Monetary Fund, developed this analysis in the 1960s, well before flexible exchange rates came into operation.[17] Although later research has refined their analysis, the initial Mundell-Fleming formulation discussed here remains essentially intact as a way of understanding how policies work under high capital mobility.

Under perfect capital mobility, the slightest interest differential provokes infinite capital flows. It follows that with perfect capital mobility, central banks cannot conduct an independent monetary policy under fixed exchange rates. To see why, suppose a country wishes to raise interest rates. It tightens monetary policy, and interest rates rise. Immediately, portfolio holders worldwide shift their wealth to take advantage of the new rate. As a result of the huge capital inflow, the balance of payments shows a gigantic surplus; foreigners try to buy domestic assets, tending to cause the exchange rate to appreciate and forcing the central bank to intervene to hold the exchange rate constant. It buys the foreign money, in exchange for domestic money. This intervention causes the home money stock to increase. As a result, the initial monetary contraction is reversed. The process comes to an end when home interest rates have been pushed back down to the initial level.

In other words, a small interest differential moves enough money in or out of the country to completely swamp available central bank reserves. The only way to keep the exchange rate from falling is for the monetary authority to back off from the interest rate differential.

The conclusion is this: **Under fixed exchange rates and perfect capital mobility, a country cannot pursue an independent monetary policy.**[18] **Interest rates cannot move out of line with those prevailing in the world market. Any attempt at**

---

[17]Mundell's work on international macroeconomics has been extraordinarily important. The adventurous student should certainly consult his two books: *International Economics* (New York: Macmillan, 1967) and *Monetary Theory* (Pacific Palisades, CA: Goodyear, 1971). You can view a video of Mundell's Nobel Prize lecture at www.nobel.se/economics/laureates/1999/mundell-lecture.html.

[18]"Fixed exchange rates and perfect capital mobility" is a pretty good description of much of the industrialized world from the early 1960s through 1973—except for the United States. The U.S. economy was then so much larger than others that the United States was able to conduct a relatively, but not completely, independent monetary policy.

BOX 12-2   Two Pieces of the Rate of Return—Two Policy Moves

In a world of perfect, or even near perfect, capital mobility, financial investments flow wherever the rate of return is highest and in the process equalize foreign and domestic yields. Computing the yield on a domestic investment is simple—it's simply the interest rate. To compute the yield on an investment made abroad, we have to take account of the possibility that the exchange rate will change between the time we make the investment and the time we repatriate our money.

Suppose that the dollar/euro exchange rate is initially 90 cents and that exchange rates remain fixed for a year. Take $1,000, convert it into €1,111.11 (1,000/.90), and invest in Europe. If the euro interest rate is 5 percent, then after a year the investment will have grown into €1,166.67, which converted back into dollars will bring $1,050 (1,166.67 × .90). So with fixed exchange rates, the foreign rate of return is just the foreign interest rate.

Now assume instead that exchange rates float and that at the end of the year the euro is worth 93 cents. When the euros are exchanged at the end of the year they bring $1,085 (1,166.67 × .93). The total return is 8.5 percent, the sum roughly of the 5 percent interest and the 3.33 percent appreciation of the euro.

So there are two pieces to the foreign rate of return: the interest rate and the appreciation of the foreign currency. In a world of perfect capital mobility, domestic and foreign rates of return must be equal.

If exchange rates are fixed, then the interest rates must do the equalizing so domestic and world interest rates must be the same. The central bank *cannot* change the interest rate. Effectively, the *LM* curve is horizontal: Fiscal policy is potent and there is no monetary policy.

If exchange rates float then the exchange rates do the rate of return equalizing, allowing foreign and domestic interest rates to decouple. But exchange rate changes move net exports and therefore the *IS* curve. Monetary policy is potent and there is no fiscal policy.

So remembering which part of the rate of return does the heavy lifting on equilibrating, interest rate or exchange rate, tells you which policy, fiscal or monetary, carries a punch.

independent monetary policy leads to capital flows and a need to intervene until interest rates are back in line with those in the world market.

Table 12-4 shows the steps in the argument. The commitment to a fixed rate involves step 5. With the exchange rate tending to appreciate because foreigners are trying to buy the domestic currency, the central bank has to provide the domestic currency. Just as in an open market operation the central bank buys and sells bonds for money, so in intervention in the foreign exchange market the monetary authority buys

TABLE 12-4 Payments Imbalances, Intervention, and the Money Supply with Fixed Exchange Rates and Perfect Capital Mobility

1. Tightening of money.
2. Increased interest rates.
3. Capital inflow, payments surplus.
4. Pressure for currency appreciation.
5. Intervention by selling home money and buying foreign money.
6. Monetary expansion due to intervention lowers interest rate.
7. Back to initial interest rates, money stock, and payments balance.

and sells foreign money (yen, euros, or Canadian dollars) for domestic money. Thus, the money supply is linked to the balance of payments. Surpluses imply *automatic* monetary expansion; deficits imply monetary contraction.

MONETARY EXPANSION

It is worthwhile looking at this point in terms of the open economy *IS-LM* model. In Figure 12-5 we show the *IS* and *LM* schedules as well as the *BP* = 0 schedule, which now, because of perfect capital mobility, is a horizontal line. Only at a level of interest rates equal to those abroad, $i = i_f$, can the country have payments balance. At any other interest rate, capital flows are so massive that the balance of payments cannot be in equilibrium, and the central bank has to intervene to maintain the exchange rate. This intervention shifts the *LM* schedule.

Consider specifically a monetary expansion that starts from point *E*. The *LM* schedule shifts down and to the right, and the economy moves to point *E'*. But at *E'* there is a large payments deficit and hence pressure for the exchange rate to depreciate. The central bank must intervene, selling foreign money and receiving domestic money in exchange. The supply of domestic money therefore declines. As a result, the *LM*

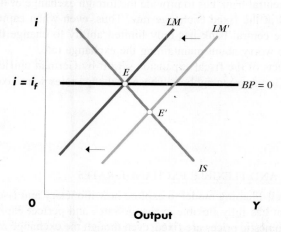

FIGURE 12-5 MONETARY EXPANSION UNDER FIXED RATES AND PERFECT CAPITAL MOBILITY.

schedule shifts back up and to the left. The process continues until the initial equilibrium at E is restored.

Indeed, with perfect capital mobility the economy never even gets to point E'. The response of capital flows is so large and rapid that the central bank is forced to reverse the initial expansion of the money stock as soon as it attempts it. Conversely, any attempt to contract the money stock would immediately lead to vast reserve losses, forcing an expansion of the money stock and a return to the initial equilibrium.

FISCAL EXPANSION

While monetary policy is essentially infeasible, fiscal expansion under fixed exchange rates with perfect capital mobility is, by contrast, extremely effective. We describe the effects in terms of the *IS-LM* model, but we do not draw the diagram, leaving that for one of the end-of-chapter problems.

With the money supply initially unchanged, a fiscal expansion moves the *IS* curve up and to the right, tending to increase both the interest rate and the level of output. The higher interest rate sets off a capital inflow that would lead the exchange rate to appreciate. To maintain the exchange rate, the central bank *has* to expand the money supply, shifting the *LM* curve to the right, thus increasing income further. Equilibrium is restored when the money supply has increased enough to drive the interest rate back to its original level, $i = i_f$. In this case, with an endogenous money supply, the interest rate is effectively fixed, and the simple Keynesian multiplier of Chapter 9 applies for a fiscal expansion.

THE ENDOGENOUS MONEY STOCK

Although the assumption of perfect capital mobility is extreme, it is a useful benchmark case that in the end is not too far from reality for many countries. The essential point is that **the commitment to maintain a fixed exchange rate makes the money stock endogenous** because the central bank has to provide the foreign exchange or domestic money that is demanded at the fixed exchange rate. Thus, even when capital mobility is less than perfect, the central bank has only limited ability to change the money supply without having to worry about maintaining the exchange rate.

Box 12-3 describes the effects of the fiscal expansion set off by German unification, and the consequences for Germany's neighbors whose exchange rates were fixed against the deutsche mark.

12-6

PERFECT CAPITAL MOBILITY AND FLEXIBLE EXCHANGE RATES

In this section we use the Mundell-Fleming model to explore how monetary and fiscal policy works in an economy that has fully flexible exchange rates and perfect capital mobility. We assume here that domestic prices are fixed, even though the exchange rate

BOX 12-3   German Unification and External Problems

In fall 1989, the Berlin Wall came down and soon the unification of West and East Germany was under way. The West German government began transferring large amounts of resources to East Germany. The fiscal program included massive investment in East Germany's infrastructure, investment in industry, and an extensive income support program for the unemployed and for those working in loss-making firms.

The large fiscal expansion helped moderate the economic collapse in East Germany. But it came at the expense of a large budget deficit. The expansionary fiscal policy brought with it a deterioration of the current account, higher interest rates, and an appreciation of the deutsche mark, as the Mundell-Fleming model predicts.

While Germany had been a net lender in world markets, starting in 1991 there was a deficit in the current account. German resources were being redirected from supplying the world market to reconstructing East Germany.

The German fiscal expansion had undesirable side effects on Germany's European trading partners, with whom Germany had a fixed exchange rate. In West Germany the economy overheated since demand from the East fell mostly on West German goods. In response to the overheating, the Bundesbank tightened monetary policy, raising interest rates sharply.

At the time of reunification, European countries still had their own currencies. Countries like France or Italy in principle faced the choice of devaluing within the European monetary system or allowing their interest rates to increase along with German interest rates. Because they valued stable exchange rates, they defended their currencies by raising interest rates to match those in Germany. Without the benefit of a fiscal expansion, as had occurred in Germany, their economies slowed down sharply. Germany's trading partners kept urging the Bundesbank to cut interest rates, but the Bundesbank argued that it had to keep on fighting inflation. The episode makes the point that fixed exchange rates are hard to maintain when countries' policies go in opposite directions or when they face disturbances that are not the same for everyone.

TABLE 1	German Unification (Percent of GNP)			
	1989	1990	1991	1992
Current account	4.8	3.3	−1.1	−1.1
Budget deficit	−0.1	2.1	3.3	2.8
Interest rate	7.1	8.5	9.2	9.5

Source: OECD, *Economic Outlook*, December 1995.

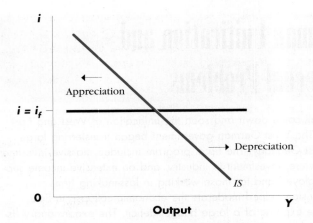

FIGURE 12-6   THE EFFECT OF EXCHANGE RATES ON AGGREGATE DEMAND.

is flexible. In Chapter 19 we examine how flexible exchange rates work when domestic prices are flexible.[19]

Under fully flexible exchange rates the central bank does not intervene in the market for foreign exchange. The exchange rate must adjust to clear the market so that the demand for and supply of foreign exchange balance. Without central bank intervention, therefore, the balance of payments must be equal to zero.

Under fully flexible exchange rates the absence of intervention implies a zero balance of payments. Any current account deficit must be financed by private capital inflows: A current account surplus is balanced by capital outflows. Adjustments in the exchange rate ensure that the sum of the current and capital accounts is zero.

A second implication of fully flexible exchange rates is that the central bank can set the money supply at will. Since there is no obligation to intervene, there is no longer any automatic link between the balance of payments and the money supply.

Perfect capital mobility implies that there is only one interest rate at which the balance of payments will balance:[20]

$$i = i_f \qquad (9)$$

At any other interest rate, capital flows are so large that the balance of payments cannot be zero. We show this in Figure 12-6 by the line $i = i_f$.

[19]The reason it is not misleading to examine the behavior of a system with flexible exchange rates and fixed domestic prices is that, in practice, exchange rates change much more quickly than do prices in most industrialized countries. The analysis of this section would not apply in cases in which the nominal exchange rate changes and domestic prices rise in the same proportion, so the real exchange rate is unchanged.

[20]Equation (9) assumes that investors do not expect the exchange rate to change. Otherwise, nominal interest rates differ among countries by an amount that reflects expected changes in the exchange rate, in a way to be described in Chap. 19.

From equation (7) we know that the real exchange rate is a determinant of aggregate demand and, therefore, that changes in the real exchange rate shift the *IS* schedule. Given prices P and P_f, a depreciation makes the home country more competitive, improves net exports, and hence shifts the *IS* schedule to the right. Conversely, a real appreciation means our goods become relatively more expensive; hence the trade balance worsens and demand for domestic goods declines, so the *IS* schedule shifts to the left.

The arrows in Figure 12-6 link the movement of aggregate demand to the interest rate. If the home interest rate were higher than i_f, capital inflows would cause currency appreciation. At any point above the $i = i_f$ schedule, the exchange rate is appreciating, our goods are becoming relatively more expensive, and aggregate demand is falling. Thus, the *IS* schedule will be shifting to the left. Conversely, any point below the $i = i_f$ schedule corresponds to depreciation, improving competitiveness, and increasing aggregate demand. The *IS* schedule will therefore be shifting to the right. We now see how various disturbances affect output and the exchange rate.

ADJUSTMENT TO A REAL DISTURBANCE

Using our model, represented by equations (7), (8), and (9), we want to know how various changes affect the level of output, the interest rate, and the exchange rate. The first change we look at is an exogenous rise in the world demand for our goods, or an increase in exports.

Starting from an initial equilibrium at point E in Figure 12-7, we see that the increase in foreign demand implies an excess demand for our goods. At the initial interest rate, exchange rate, and output level, demand for our goods now exceeds the

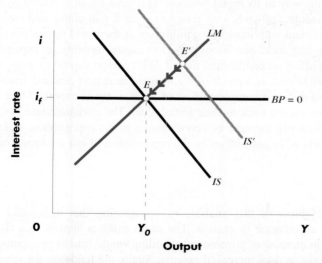

FIGURE 12-7   EFFECTS OF AN INCREASE IN THE DEMAND FOR EXPORTS.

available supply. For goods market equilibrium at the initial interest rate and exchange rate, we require a higher level of output. Accordingly, the *IS* schedule shifts out and to the right, to *IS'*.

Now consider for a moment point *E'*, at which the goods and money markets clear. Here output has increased to meet the increased demand. The rise in income has increased money demand and thus raised equilibrium interest rates. But point *E'* is not an equilibrium, because the balance of payments is not in equilibrium. In fact, we would not reach point *E'* at all. The tendency for the economy to move in that direction, as we now show, will bring about an exchange rate appreciation that will take us all the way back to the initial equilibrium at *E*.

THE ADJUSTMENT PROCESS

Suppose, then, that the increase in foreign demand takes place and that, in response, there is a tendency for output and income to increase. The induced increase in money demand will raise interest rates and thus bring us out of line with international interest rates. The resulting capital inflows immediately put pressure on the exchange rate. The capital inflows cause our currency to appreciate.

The exchange appreciation means, of course, that import prices fall and domestic goods become relatively more expensive. Demand shifts away from domestic goods, and net exports decline. In terms of Figure 12-7, the appreciation implies that the *IS* schedule shifts back from *IS'* to the left. Next, we have to ask how far the exchange appreciation will go and to what extent it will dampen the expansionary effect of increased net exports.

The exchange rate will keep appreciating as long as our interest rate exceeds the world level. This implies that the exchange appreciation must continue until the *IS* schedule has shifted back all the way to its initial position. This adjustment is shown by the arrows along the *LM* schedule. Only when we return to point *E* will output and income have reached a level consistent with monetary equilibrium at the world rate of interest.

We have now shown that under conditions of perfect capital mobility, an expansion in exports has no lasting effect on equilibrium output. With perfect capital mobility the tendency for interest rates to rise, as a result of the increase in export demand, leads to currency appreciation and thus to a complete offset of the increase in exports. Once we return to point *E*, net exports are back to their initial level. The exchange rate has, of course, appreciated. Imports will increase as a consequence of the appreciation, and the initial expansion in exports is, in part, offset by the appreciation of our exchange rate.

FISCAL POLICY

We can extend the usefulness of this analysis by recognizing that it is valid for disturbances other than an increase in exports. The same analysis applies to a fiscal expansion. A tax cut or an increase in government spending would lead to an expansion in demand in the same way as does increased exports. Again, the tendency for interest rates to rise leads to appreciation and therefore to a fall in exports and increased imports.

There is, accordingly, complete crowding out. The crowding out takes place not, as in Chapter 11, because higher interest rates reduce investment but because the exchange appreciation reduces net exports.

   The important lesson here is that real disturbances to demand do not affect equilibrium output under flexible rates with perfect capital mobility. We can drive the lesson home by comparing a fiscal expansion under flexible rates with the results we derived for the fixed rate case. In the previous section, we showed that with a fixed exchange rate, fiscal expansion under conditions of capital mobility is highly effective in raising equilibrium output. For flexible rates, by contrast, a fiscal expansion does not change equilibrium output. Instead, it produces an offsetting exchange rate appreciation and a shift in the composition of domestic demand toward foreign goods and away from domestic goods.

   This analysis helps in understanding developments in the U.S. economy in the early 1980s, when a fiscal expansion was accompanied by a current account deficit.

ADJUSTMENT TO A CHANGE IN THE MONEY STOCK

We now analyze a change in the money stock and show that it leads, under flexible exchange rates, to an increase in income and a depreciation of the exchange rate. Using Figure 12-8, we start from an initial position at point E and consider an increase in the nominal quantity of money, $\overline{M}$. Since prices are given, we have an increase in the real money stock, $\overline{M}/\overline{P}$. At E there will be an excess supply of real balances. To restore equilibrium, interest rates would have to be lower or income would have to be larger. Accordingly, the LM schedule shifts down and to the right to LM'.

   We ask once again whether the economy is in equilibrium at point E'. At E', the goods and money markets are in equilibrium (at the initial exchange rate), but interest

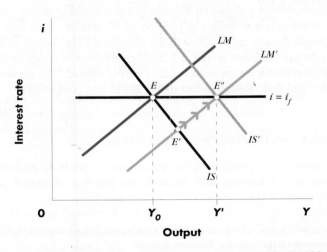

FIGURE 12-8   EFFECTS OF AN INCREASE IN THE MONEY STOCK.

rates have fallen below the world level. Capital outflows therefore put pressure on the exchange rate, leading to a depreciation. The exchange depreciation caused by the capital outflows leads import prices to increase, domestic goods become more competitive, and the demand for our output expands. The *IS* curve shifts out and to the right, and it continues doing so until exchange depreciation has raised demand and output to the level indicated by point E''. Only at E'' do we have goods market and money market equilibrium compatible with the world rate of interest. Consequently, there is no further tendency for exchange rates and relative prices, and hence demand, to change.[21]

We have now shown that a monetary expansion leads to an increase in output and a depreciation of the exchange rate under flexible rates. One way of thinking about this result is that with $\overline{P}$ fixed, an increase in $\overline{M}$ increases $\overline{M}/P$. The demand for real balances (L) is, from Chapter 10, equal to $L(i, Y)$. Since i cannot differ from the world rate of interest, Y has to rise to equate the demand for money to the supply. The exchange depreciation raises net exports, and the increase in net exports, in turn, sustains the higher level of output and employment. One interesting implication of our analysis, then, is the proposition that monetary expansion improves the current account through the induced depreciation.

How do our results compare with those in a fixed exchange rate world? **Under fixed rates, the monetary authorities cannot control the nominal money stock,** and an attempt to expand money will merely lead to reserve losses and a reversal of the increase in the money stock. Under flexible rates, by contrast, the central bank does not intervene, and so the money stock increase is *not* reversed in the foreign exchange market. The depreciation and expansion in output actually do take place, given the assumed fixed prices. **The fact that the central bank *can* control the money stock under flexible rates is a key aspect of that exchange rate system.**

Table 12-5 shows estimates of the quantitative impact of U.S. fiscal and monetary expansions on GNP in the United States and abroad, under flexible exchange rates. The table reports the percentage change in GNP over the first 2 years (on average) in response to two experiments. One is a sustained increase in government spending equal to 5 percent of GNP. The other is a monetary expansion of 10 percent. Note that, as expected, U.S. GNP expands in each case (although the estimated fiscal policy multiplier is relatively small). In line with our model, a U.S. fiscal expansion raises foreign output. By contrast, a U.S. monetary expansion reduces output abroad. The reason is that the dollar depreciates and that makes the rest of the world less competitive.

BEGGAR-THY-NEIGHBOR POLICY AND COMPETITIVE DEPRECIATION

We have shown that a monetary expansion in the home country leads to exchange depreciation, an increase in net exports, and therefore an increase in output and

---

[21]In the problem set at the end of this chapter, we ask you to show that the current account improves between E' and E'', even though the increased level of income increases imports.

TABLE 12-5	Effects of U.S. Policy Actions	
	(Percent Increase in GNP)	
	FISCAL EXPANSION*	MONETARY EXPANSION†
United States	2.7	5.3
Japan	0.4	−0.6
Germany	0.5	−0.8

*A 5 percent of GNP increase in government spending.

†A 10 percent increase in the money supply target.

Source: Paul Masson et al., "Multimod Mark II: A Revised and Extended Model," IMF occasional paper 71, 1990, tables 9 and 10.

employment. But our increased net exports correspond to a deterioration in the trade balance abroad. The domestic depreciation shifts demand from foreign goods toward domestic goods. Abroad, output and employment decline. It is for this reason that a depreciation-induced change in the trade balance has been called a *beggar-thy-neighbor policy*—it is a way of exporting unemployment or of creating domestic employment at the expense of the rest of the world.

Recognition that exchange depreciation is mainly a way of shifting demand from one country to another, rather than changing the level of world demand, is important. It implies that exchange rate adjustment can be a useful policy when countries find themselves in different stages of the business cycle—for example, one in a boom (with overemployment) and the other in a recession. In that event, a depreciation by the country experiencing a recession would shift world demand in its direction and thus work to reduce divergence from full employment in each country.

By contrast, when countries' business cycles are highly synchronized, such as in the 1930s or in the aftermath of the oil shock of 1973, exchange rate movements will not contribute much toward worldwide full employment. If total world demand is at the wrong level, exchange rate movements do not correct the level of aggregate demand but essentially affect only the allocation of a *given* world demand among countries.

Similarly, exchange rate changes within a group of countries experiencing similar shocks can only move demand among them and have a beggar-thy-neighbor quality. This is one of the reasons Europeans adopted a monetary union.

Nevertheless, from the point of view of an individual country, exchange depreciation works to attract world demand and raise domestic output. If every country tried to depreciate to attract world demand, we would have *competitive depreciation* and a shifting around of world demand rather than an increase in the worldwide level of spending. And if everyone depreciated to roughly the same extent, we would end up with exchange rates about where they started. Coordinated monetary and fiscal policies rather than depreciations are needed to increase demand and output in each country when worldwide aggregate demand is at the wrong level.

SUMMARY

1. The balance-of-payments accounts are a record of the international transactions of the economy. The current account records trade in goods and services as well as transfer payments. The capital account records purchases and sales of assets. Any transaction that gives rise to a payment by a U.S. resident is a deficit item for the United States.

2. The overall balance-of-payments surplus is the sum of the current and capital accounts surpluses. If the overall balance is in deficit, we have to make more payments to foreigners than they make to us. The foreign currency for making these payments is supplied by central banks.

3. Under fixed exchange rates, the central bank holds constant the price of foreign currencies in terms of the domestic currency. It does this by buying and selling foreign exchange at the fixed exchange rate. It has to keep reserves of foreign currency for that purpose.

4. Under floating, or flexible, exchange rates, the exchange rate may change from moment to moment. In a system of clean floating, the exchange rate is determined by supply and demand without central bank intervention. Under dirty floating, the central bank intervenes by buying and selling foreign exchange in an attempt to influence but not fix the exchange rate.

5. The introduction of trade in goods means that some of the demand for our output comes from abroad and that some spending by our residents is on foreign goods. The demand for our goods depends on the real exchange rate as well as on the levels of income at home and abroad. A real depreciation or increase in foreign income increases net exports and shifts the *IS* curve out to the right. There is equilibrium in the goods market when the demand for domestically produced goods is equal to the output of those goods.

6. The introduction of capital flows points to the effects of monetary and fiscal policy on the balance of payments through interest rate effects on capital flows. An increase in the domestic interest rate relative to the world interest rate leads to a capital inflow that can finance a current account deficit.

7. When capital mobility is perfect, interest rates in the home country cannot diverge from those abroad. This has major implications for the effects of monetary and fiscal policy under fixed and floating exchange rates. These effects are summarized in Table 12-6.

TABLE 12-6	Effects of Monetary and Fiscal Policy under Perfect Capital Mobility	
POLICY	FIXED EXCHANGE RATES	FLEXIBLE EXCHANGE RATES
Monetary expansion	No output change; reserve losses equal to money increase	Output expansion; trade balance improves; exchange depreciation
Fiscal expansion	Output expansion; trade balance worsens	No output change; reduced net exports; exchange appreciation

8. Under fixed exchange rates and perfect capital mobility, monetary policy is powerless to affect output. Any attempt to reduce the domestic interest rate by increasing the money stock would lead to a huge outflow of capital, tending to cause a depreciation which the central bank would then have to offset by buying domestic money in exchange for foreign money. This reduces the domestic money stock until it returns to its original level. Under fixed exchange rates with capital mobility, the central bank cannot run an independent monetary policy.

9. Fiscal policy is highly effective under fixed exchange rates with complete capital mobility. A fiscal expansion tends to raise the interest rate, thereby leading the central bank to increase the money stock to keep the exchange rate constant, reinforcing the expansionary fiscal effect.

10. Under floating rates, monetary policy is highly effective and fiscal policy is ineffective in changing output. A monetary expansion leads to depreciation, increased exports, and increased output. Fiscal expansion, however, causes an appreciation and completely crowds out net exports.

11. If an economy with floating rates finds itself with unemployment, the central bank can intervene to depreciate the exchange rate and increase net exports and thus aggregate demand. Such policies are known as beggar-thy-neighbor policies because the increase in demand for domestic output comes at the expense of demand for foreign output.

KEY TERMS

balance of payments	external balance	nominal exchange rate
balance-of-payments surplus	finance	open economies
beggar-thy-neighbor policy	fixed exchange rate system	perfect capital mobility
capital account	flexible (floating) exchange	purchasing power parity
clean floating	rate system	(PPP)
competitive depreciation	globalization	real exchange rate
convergence	interest differential	repercussion effects
currency appreciation	internal balance	reserves
currency depreciation	intervention	revaluation
current account	managed (dirty) floating	trade
devaluation	marginal propensity to	trade balance
euro	import	
European Monetary Union	Mundell-Fleming model	
(EMU)	net investment income	

PROBLEMS

Conceptual

1. It is sometimes said that a central bank is a necessary element for a balance-of-payments deficit. What is the explanation for this argument?

2.* Consider a country that is in a position of full employment and balanced trade. The exchange rate is fixed, and capital is not mobile. Which of the following types of disturbance

*An asterisk denotes a more difficult problem.

can be remedied with standard aggregate demand tools of stabilization? Indicate in each case the impact on external and internal balance as well as the appropriate policy response.

  a. A loss of export markets.

  b. A reduction in saving and a corresponding increase in demand for domestic goods.

  c. An increase in government spending.

  d. A shift in demand from imports to domestic goods.

  e. A reduction in imports with a corresponding increase in saving.

3. Explain how and why monetary policy retains its effectiveness when there is perfect mobility of capital.

4. a. If the dollar–pound exchange rate rises, has the dollar depreciated or appreciated?

  b. What has happened to the pound?

5. What is the difference between depreciation and devaluation?

6. Explain the purchasing power parity theory of the long-run behavior of the exchange rate. Indicate whether there are any circumstances under which you would *not* expect the PPP relationship to hold.

7. Why do economists care whether or not PPP holds?

8. When is a country in external balance? Internal balance? Should either or both of these be policy goals?

9. According to the Mundell-Fleming model, when exchange rates are fixed and capital is perfectly mobile, will fiscal or monetary policy be more successful? Explain.

10. Your country is in recession. You feel that a policy of exchange rate depreciation will stimulate aggregate demand and bring the country out of the recession.

  a. What can be done to trigger this depreciation?

  b. How might other countries react?

  c. When would this be a beggar-thy-neighbor policy?

Technical

1. Assume that capital is perfectly mobile, the price level is fixed, and the exchange rate is flexible. Now let the government increase purchases. Explain first why the equilibrium levels of output and the interest rate are unaffected. Then show whether the current account improves or worsens as a result of the increased government purchases of goods and services.

2. In 1990–1992 Finland fell into serious difficulties. The collapse of exports to the Soviet Union and a dramatic fall in the prices of pulp and paper—important export items—led to both a recession and a current account deficit. What adjustment policies would you recommend for such a case?

3. Suppose you expect the pound to depreciate by 6 percent over the next year. Assume that the U.S. interest rate is 4 percent. What interest rate would be needed on pound securities, such as government bonds, for you to be willing to buy those securities with your dollars today and then sell them in a year in exchange for dollars?

4. Illustrate, graphically, the effects of a fiscal expansion when capital is mobile and both prices and exchange rates are fixed. Over what horizon is the assumption of fixed prices a valid one? Explain.

5. What is the effect of a fiscal expansion on output and interest rates when exchange rates are fixed and capital is perfectly mobile? Show this rigorously, using the model developed in Section 12-5.

6.* This question is concerned with the repercussion effects of a domestic expansion once we recognize that, as a consequence, output abroad will expand. Suppose that at home there is an increase in autonomous spending, $\Delta \overline{A}$, that falls entirely on domestic goods. (Assume constant interest rates throughout this problem.)

   a. What is the effect on income, disregarding repercussion effects? What is the impact on our imports? Denote the increase in imports by ΔQ.

   b. Using the result for the increase in imports, consider what happens abroad. Our increase in imports means that foreign countries experience an increase in their exports and therefore an increase in the demand for their goods. In response, their output expands. Assuming the foreign marginal propensity to save is s^* and the foreign propensity to import is m^*, by how much will a foreign country's income expand as a result of an increase in its exports?

   c. Now combine the pieces by writing the familiar equation for equilibrium in the domestic goods market: Change in supply, ΔY, equals the total change in demand, $\Delta \overline{A} + \Delta X - m\Delta Y + (1 - s)\Delta Y$, or

   $$\Delta Y = \frac{\Delta \overline{A} + \Delta X}{s + m}$$

   Noting that our increase in exports, ΔX, is equal to foreigners' increase in imports, we can replace ΔX with the answer to part (b) to obtain a general expression for the multiplier with repercussions.

   d. Substitute your answer to part (b) in the formula for the change in our exports, $\Delta X = m^*\Delta Y^*$.

   e. Calculate the complete change in our income, including repercussion effects. Now compare your result with the case in which repercussion effects are omitted. What difference do repercussion effects make? Is our income expansion larger or smaller with repercussion effects?

   f. Consider the trade balance effect of a domestic expansion with and without repercussion effects. Is the trade deficit larger or smaller once repercussion effects are taken into account?

Empirical

1. Go to www.economagic.com and do a search for "Exchange rate." Find two countries that had a fixed exchange rate for a period sometimes during the last 20 years. *Hint:* Choose one of the developing countries (e.g., Malaysia, Thailand).

2. The textbook states that under perfect capital mobility, interest rates in the home country cannot diverge from those abroad. In this exercise you will take a look at interest rates in the United States and the European Union.

   a. Go to www.economagic.com. Under "Browse by Source, Federal Reserve Board of Governors" choose the heading "Interest rates." Select the variable "3-Year Treasury Constant Maturity Rate," and get the data since 1994.

b. Go back to "Browse by Source," scroll down and select the heading "Central Bank of Europe." Click on "Government Bond Yields," and select the variable "EU 3-year government bond yield."

c. Make a graph that includes the two 3-year interest rates on government bonds, one for the United States and one for the European Union. Use EXCEL or the built-in graphing facilities at www.economagic.com. Visually, what is the relationship between the two variables? Can you conclude something about the degree of capital mobility between the United States and the European Union?

PART 4

Behavioral Foundations

CHAPTER 13

Consumption and Saving

CHAPTER HIGHLIGHTS

- Consumption is a large but relatively stable fraction of GDP.

- Modern theories of consumption behavior link lifetime consumption to lifetime income. These theories suggest that the marginal propensity to consume out of transitory income should be small.

- Empirical evidence suggests that both modern theories and simple Keynesian "psychological rule-of-thumb" models contribute to explaining consumption.

- The saving rate in the United States is lower than the saving rate in many other countries.

Consumption accounts for more than 60 percent of aggregate demand, more than all other sectors combined. Fluctuations in consumption are proportionately smaller than fluctuations in GDP. These two facts—that consumption makes up a large fraction of GDP and that it is relatively stable—give the focus for this chapter.

We seek to understand what drives consumption, and we particularly wish to understand the dynamic link between consumption and income. In Chapter 9 we modeled consumption as a simple function of current income. Here we study several more advanced theories of consumption. The central finding is that lifetime consumption is linked to lifetime income, but the link between *this* year's consumption and *this* year's income is fairly weak.

The debate about different consumption theories can be viewed as a debate over whether the marginal propensity to consume (*MPC*) is large or small. Early Keynesian "psychological rule-of-thumb" models suggested a high *MPC,* while modern theories based on rational consumer decisions sometimes indicate a very low *MPC*. In introductory macromodels, the marginal propensity to consume, c, directly determines "the multiplier," $1/(1 - c)$. Even in more sophisticated models, a high *MPC* causes a large multiplier. The modern theories discussed below assign different values to the marginal propensity to consume out of income changes expected to persist for different lengths of time. The *MPC* out of income expected to be permanent is high, just as in earlier models, but the *MPC* out of transitory income is close to zero.

Before plunging into the theory and data of modern consumption models, let's look at a quick-and-dirty model to illustrate the central point of modern consumption theory—and to illustrate the pitfalls too. Suppose your entire future consists of two periods: "now" and "later." "Now" is this coming year, and "later" is the rest of your life, let's say the following 99 years. If you earn Y_{now} this year and Y_{later} each year thereafter, earnings over your lifetime will total $Y_{now} + 99 \times Y_{later}$. Suppose too that your goal is to maintain a constant standard of living. No feast or famine for you! If you are to consume C each year, then lifetime spending will be $100 \times C$. Spreading lifetime income over lifetime consumption gives the quick-and-dirty consumption function

$$C = \frac{Y_{now} + 99 \times Y_{later}}{100}$$

If your income were to rise $1,000 for this year ($Y_{now}$ only), you can see that consumption would rise by only $10/year. The short-run marginal propensity to consume would be only .01, because the remainder of the extra income would be saved to support future consumption. In contrast, if your income were to rise $1,000 now and forever (both Y_{now} and Y_{later}), your consumption would rise by the full $1,000 and so the long-run marginal propensity would be 1.

Our quick-and-dirty model illustrates the key ideas of modern consumption theory, but you've probably already thought of several reasons to be less than satisfied with this simple story. In this chapter we explore the strengths and the weaknesses of modern consumption theory. We begin with a look at the data.

Figures 13-1 to 13-3 tell the story of the underlying concepts of this chapter. Figure 13-1 plots both changes in per capita consumption and changes in per capita

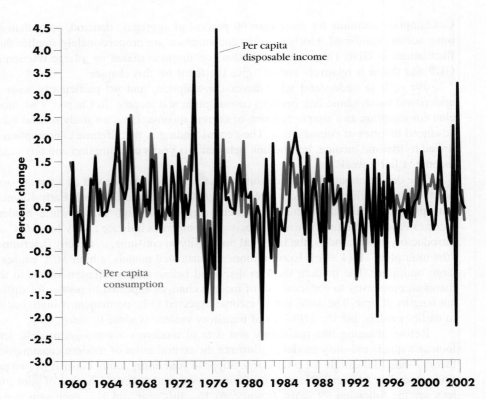

FIGURE 13-1   CHANGES IN REAL PER CAPITA CONSUMPTION AND DISPOSABLE INCOME, 1959–2002.

Changes in per capita disposable income and changes in per capita consumption are closely related, although the latter is less volatile than the former. Consumption does not respond much to positive or negative income spikes (short-term swings in income). (Source: Bureau of Economic Analysis.)

disposable income.[1] Income swings that last 5 or 10 years have roughly matching consumption swings. But consumption doesn't respond much to income spikes—1975, 1993, and 2001 are examples. Long-term income swings generate changes in consumption, but short-term spikes don't; in other words, the long-run *MPC* is high, but the short-run *MPC* is low.

Figure 13-2 compares consumption this quarter with consumption the previous quarter. The formula for the line drawn through the scatter diagram is $C_t = \$22.75 + 1.004 C_{t-1}$. So consumption this quarter is almost perfectly predicted by consumption

[1] Consumption accounts are broken down into nondurables (e.g., food), services (e.g., haircuts), and durables (e.g., refrigerators). The consumption theory we study and the data we show apply to nondurables and services. Durable-goods "consumption" is in large part a form of *investment* on the part of a household, but it is not treated as investment in the national income accounts.

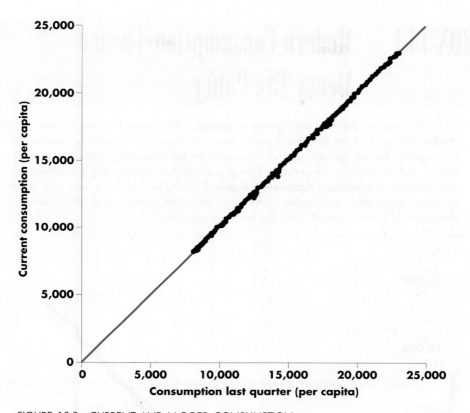

FIGURE 13-2   CURRENT AND LAGGED CONSUMPTION.

Consumption is almost perfectly predicted by consumption the previous period plus an allowance for growth. (Source: Bureau of Economic Analysis.)

last quarter plus a small allowance for growth. In Section 13-2 we will see that this relation is an outcome of the link between current consumption and expected future income.

Modern consumption theory needs to explain Figures 13-1 and 13-2. Early Keynesian theories, looking at the kind of data shown in Figure 13-3, had current consumption and current income moving in lockstep without trying to separate temporary versus permanent changes in income.[2] In previous chapters we assumed that consumption (C) is determined by disposable income (YD) in the simple linear relation

$$C = \overline{C} + cYD \qquad 0 < c < 1 \tag{1}$$

The estimated values for the parameters for the line in Figure 13-3 are $\overline{C} = -753$ and $c = .94$. In other words, the traditional, measured consumption function is $C = -753 + .94YD$, and the measured value of the *MPC*, .94, is quite high.

---

[2]For reasons of tradition, the consumption measurement for Fig. 13-3 includes durable goods as well as non-durables and services.

BOX 13-1   Modern Consumption Theory Meets Tax Policy

In 1968, President Johnson and Congress passed a temporary (1-year) income tax sur-charge. The goal at the time was to cool down an economy temporarily overheated by spending for the Vietnam war. A temporary tax for temporary overheating sounds logical. But the modern consumption theory predicts that a temporary tax increase, and therefore a temporary decrease in disposable income, will have very little effect on consumption and therefore very little effect on aggregate demand. The modern consumption theory worked—and the tax increase didn't.

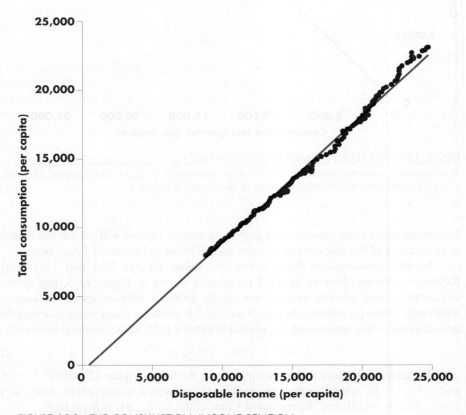

FIGURE 13-3   THE CONSUMPTION–INCOME RELATION.

There is a close relation, in practice, between consumption spending and disposable income. Consumption rises on average by 94 cents for each additional dollar of disposable income. (Source: Bureau of Economic Analysis.)

We begin by presenting modern theory and then turn to modern empirical evidence. The life-cycle and permanent income theories do well at explaining Figures 13-1 and 13-2, but empirical evidence, examined below, indicates that the traditional view depicted in Figure 13-3 is still useful and that there is much merit in the earlier, psychological rule-of-thumb theories.

13-1

THE LIFE-CYCLE–PERMANENT-INCOME THEORY OF CONSUMPTION AND SAVING

Modern consumption theory emphasizes lifetime decision making. Originally, the *life-cycle* hypothesis emphasized choices about how to maintain a stable standard of living in the face of changes in income over the course of life, while *permanent income* theory focused on forecasting the level of income available to a consumer over a lifetime. Today, these two theories have largely merged.

LIFE-CYCLE THEORY

The consumption function [equation (1)] assumes that individuals' consumption behavior in a given period is related to their income in that period. **The *life-cycle* hypothesis views individuals, instead, as planning their consumption and savings behavior over long periods with the intention of allocating their consumption in the best possible way over their entire lifetimes.** Instead of relying on a single value (based on a psychological rule of thumb) for the marginal propensity to consume, life-cycle theory (based on maximizing behavior) implies different marginal propensities to consume out of permanent income, transitory income, and wealth. The key assumption is that most people choose stable lifestyles—not, in general, saving furiously in one period to have a huge spending spree in the next but, rather, consuming at about the same level in every period. In its simplest form, the assumption is that individuals try to consume the same amount each year.

A numerical example illustrates the theory: Suppose that a person starts life at age 20, plans to work until 65, and will die at 80 and that annual labor income, YL, is $30,000. Lifetime resources are annual income times years of working life ($WL = 65 - 20 = 45$)—in this example, $30,000 \times 45 = $1,350,000.[3] Spreading lifetime resources over the number of years of life ($NL = 80 - 20 = 60$) allows for annual consumption of $C = $1,350,000/60 = $22,500$. The general formula is

$$C = \frac{WL}{NL} \times YL$$

So the marginal propensity to consume is WL/NL. Figure 13-4 illustrates the pattern of consumption and saving. (Note that once we have a theory of consumption, we also have a theory of saving, since saving is just income minus consumption.)

[3]Note that as a simplification we ignore the effect of interest earned on saving.

BOX 13-2   Linking Demography and Consumption

Life-cycle theory helps link consumption and savings behavior to demographic consid-erations, especially to the age distribution of the population. Note that the marginal propensity to consume out of permanent income, WL/NL, changes with age. In the text example, the MPC out of permanent income at age 20 is 45/60. As a person ages, both the number of working years and the number of years of life decline. By age 50, for example, the MPC would have declined to 15/30. (The exact argument holds only for labor income, since WL isn't relevant to income from investments.) The MPC out of transitory income would rise from 1/60 at age 20 to 1/30 at age 50.

   The economy is a mix of people of many different ages and life expectancies, so the MPC for the economy is a mix of corresponding MPCs. As a result, economies with different age mixtures have different overall marginal propensities to save and consume.

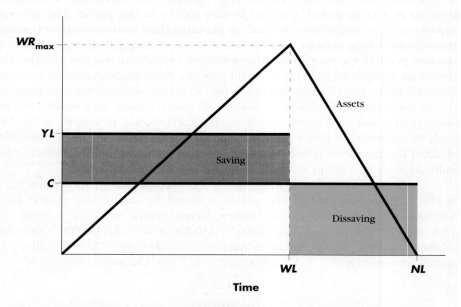

FIGURE 13-4   LIFETIME INCOME, CONSUMPTION, SAVING, AND WEALTH IN THE LIFE-CYCLE MODEL.

Consumption is constant throughout lifetime. During the working life, lasting WL years, the individual saves, accumulating assets. At the end of the working life, the individual begins to live off these assets, dissaving for the remaining years (NL − WL) of life such that assets equal exactly zero at the end of life.

BOX 13-3   Life-Cycle Consumption and Permanent-Income Theory: Why Can't Economists Ever Agree?

Modern consumption theory is due largely to Franco Modigliani of MIT (life-cycle theory) and Milton Friedman of the University of Chicago (permanent-income theory), both of whom have won Nobel Prizes. Modigliani is a leading Keynesian, and Friedman is the "father of modern monetarism." Their theories are quite similar. (So much so that economists frequently call the combination the life-cycle–permanent-income hypothesis, abbreviated *LC-PIH*.) Like much of good macroeconomics, both theories pay careful attention to microeconomic foundations. While the theories differed in their developmental stage, the two have largely merged and today are largely accepted by all economists.

The history of these theories offers an important methodological lesson. Economists seem to derive enjoyment from disagreeing with one another. This is a good thing, because progress comes from examining disputes, not from singing as a chorus. As disputes are resolved, the frontier moves on. What people often don't see is that this process leads economists to agree on 90 percent of how the economy works, even while still fiercely contesting the frontiers of the science.

Continuing with the numerical example, we can compute marginal propensities to consume by considering variations in the income stream. Suppose income were to rise permanently by $3,000 per year. The extra $3,000 times 45 working years spread over 60 years of life would increase annual consumption by $3,000 $\times$ (45/60) = $2,250. In other words, the *marginal propensity to consume out of permanent income* would be $WL/NL = 45/60 = .75$. In contrast, suppose income were to rise by $3,000 but only in 1 year. The extra $3,000 spread over 60 years would increase annual consumption by $3,000 $\times$ (1/60) = $50. In other words, the *marginal propensity to consume out of transitory income* would be $1/NL = 1/60 \approx .017$. While the exact examples are slightly contrived, the clear message is that the **MPC** out of **permanent income** is large and the **MPC** out of **transitory income** is small, fairly close to zero.

The life-cycle theory implies that the marginal propensity to consume out of wealth should equal the *MPC* out of transitory income and, therefore, be very small. The reasoning is that spending out of wealth, like spending out of transitory income, is spread out over the remaining years of life. The *MPC* out of wealth is used to link changes in the value of assets to current consumption. For example, an increase in the

BOX 13-4   Durable-Goods Consumption

The LC-PIH makes sense for consumption of nondurables and services, things from which we derive pleasure around the time of purchase. Durable goods, such as cars, refrigerators, and stereos, provide a stream of utility long after the purchase. The LC-PIH model explains the stream of utility, not the expenditure pattern. The theory of durable-goods purchases is really the theory of investment applied to households instead of firms. This has two implications for durable-goods expenditures. First, they are not smoothed out the way purchases of nondurables and services are. Second, durable-goods purchases are quite sensitive to interest rates, at least in countries like the United States and Canada, where consumer finance is readily available. Automobiles and household appliances are examples of goods that respond positively to swings in GDP and negatively to interest rates. In 2001, zero percent financing contributed to record car sales in the United States.

value of the stock market will increase current consumption. There is some evidence that wealthier people have a somewhat lower marginal propensity to consume out of income.[4] This is one of the ways that there is a link from income distribution back to macroeconomic policy, as the suggestion is sometimes made that shifting income to less wealthy families will increase overall consumption and stimulate the economy.

PERMANENT-INCOME THEORY

Like the life-cycle hypothesis, the permanent-income theory of consumption argues that consumption is related not to current income but to a longer-term estimate of income, which Milton Friedman, who introduced the theory, calls "permanent income." Friedman provides a simple example: Consider a person who is paid or receives income only once a week, on Fridays. We do not expect that person to consume only on Friday, with zero consumption on the other days of the week. People prefer a smooth consumption flow rather than plenty today and scarcity tomorrow or yesterday.

The idea that consumption spending is geared to long-term, or average or permanent, income is appealing and essentially the same as the life-cycle theory. *Permanent income* **is the steady rate of expenditure a person could maintain for the rest of his or her life, given the present level of wealth and the income earned now and in the future.**

[4]Karen E. Dynan, Jonathan S. Skinner, and Stephen P. Zeldes, "Do the Rich Save More?" NBER working paper no. W7906, September 2000.

BOX 13-5   Misleading-Introspection Alert!

Tonight, the good economics fairy will surprise you with ten $100 bills—an event that will surely not happen more than once in your life! How will you spend this windfall? According to the LC-PIH, you should adjust your consumption by buying something like one extra can of soda pop every week for the rest of your life. In case this wasn't the first thing that popped into your mind, how do some alternatives stack up to the theory? Suppose, being a thrifty sort, you choose to pay back part of your student loan. Colloquially, we'd call this "spending," but in economic terms paying off a debt is a form of saving. So this fits the theory perfectly. Suppose, being more of a spendthrift, you decide to buy a really nice television. You'll really be buying the ability to watch shows over the next several years (see Box 13-4), so this too fits the theory.

In its simplest form the theory argues that consumption is proportional to permanent income:

$$C = cYP \tag{2}$$

where YP is permanent (disposable) income.

To think about the measurement of permanent income, imagine someone trying to figure out what her permanent income is. The person has a current level of income and has formed some idea of the level of consumption she can maintain for the rest of her life. Now income goes up. The person has to decide whether the increase is permanent or merely transitory or temporary. In any particular case, an individual may know whether an increase is permanent or transitory. An associate professor who is promoted to professor and given a raise will think that the increase in income is permanent; a worker who has exceptionally high overtime in a given year will likely regard that year's increased income as transitory. But in general a person is not likely to be so sure whether a change is permanent or transitory. A good Christmas bonus might be due to a change in your employer's compensation scheme (permanent) or it might signal that your firm had an unusually good year (transitory). The difference matters because transitory income is assumed not to have any substantial effect on consumption. (Note that the weak link between consumption and transitory income parallels the worked-out example, above, for the *MPC* out of transitory income.)

According to the LC-PIH, consumption should be *smoother* than income because spending out of transitory income is spread over many years. Figure 13-1 shows that this prediction is largely correct. In particular, the really large up-and-down spikes in income generate only modest consumption response. (The traditional consumption function, in contrast, predicts that income spikes should be matched by consumption spikes.)

13-2

CONSUMPTION UNDER UNCERTAINTY: THE MODERN APPROACH

If permanent income were known exactly, then according to the LC-PIH, consumption would never change.[5] The modern version of the LC-PIH emphasizes the link between income uncertainty and changes in consumption and takes a more formal approach to consumer maximization. According to this newer version, changes in consumption arise from *surprise* changes in income. Absent income surprises, consumption this period should be the same as consumption last period. In Figure 13-2 we saw that this prediction is well supported by the data.

◆ OPTIONAL ◆

The modern approach to the LC-PIH begins by formally stating the lifetime utility maximization problem of a representative consumer. In a particular period, a consumer enjoys utility from consumption in that period, $u(C_t)$. *Lifetime utility* is the sum of period-by-period utilities, and the *lifetime budget constraint* equates the sum of period-by-period consumption with lifetime resources:[6]

$$\text{Lifetime utility} = u(C_t) + u(C_{t+1}) + \ldots + u(C_{T-1}) + u(C_T)$$
$$\text{subject to } C_t + C_{t+1} + \ldots + C_{T-1} + C_T \tag{3}$$
$$= \text{wealth} + YL_t + YL_{t+1} + \ldots + YL_{T-1} + YL_T$$

Consumers choose consumption each period to maximize lifetime utility subject to total lifetime consumption equaling lifetime resources. The optimal choice is the consumption path that equates the *marginal utility of consumption* across periods, $MU(C_{t+1}) = MU(C_t)$, and so on. Why? Consider the alternative: If marginal utility were a little higher in period t than in period $t + 1$, lifetime utility could be increased by shifting consumption into t from $t + 1$ because the gain from the former would outweigh the gain from the latter. (By definition, marginal utility is the increase in utility from a small increase in consumption.)

Now add considerations of uncertainty. The consumer cannot actually implement an equate-marginal-utilities rule because future marginal utility, $MU(C_{t+1})$, is uncertain at time t. The consumer *can* equate marginal utility today with her best guess of

---

[5]If a consumer knew total lifetime resources in advance, she could figure out once and for all how to spread consumption evenly. However, saying that "consumption would never change" is not quite right, because the statement ignores the effects of impatience and the financial return to saving. See footnote 6.

[6](*Optional*) Equation (3) leaves out two factors. People prefer to consume now rather than later, so a high rate of time preference, represented by the parameter δ, moves consumption earlier. Counteracting this effect, deferred spending accrues interest at rate r, allowing greater consumption if one is patient. Measuring both δ and r in percent per period, a more fully specified version of equation (3) is

$$\text{Lifetime utility} = u(C_t) + (1 + \delta)^{-1}u(C_{t+1}) + \ldots + (1 + \delta)^{t-T}u(C_T)$$
$$\text{subject to } C_t + (1 + r)^{-1}C_{t+1} + \ldots + (1 + r)^{t-T}C_T$$
$$= \text{wealth} + YL_t + (1 + r)^{-1}YL_{t+1} + \ldots + (1 + r)^{t-T}YL_T$$

marginal utility at time $t + 1$, so the modified rule is to equate today's marginal utility with the expected value of tomorrow's marginal utility, $E[MU(C_{t+1})] = MU(C_t)$.[7]

Marginal utility functions aren't observable, but in this simple case the functions will be equal only if their arguments are equal, so the rule can be rewritten as $E(C_{t+1}) = C_t$. Expected values aren't observable either, but in the late 1970s Robert Hall realized that rational expectations theory could be applied to the problem—and in so doing, he revolutionized macroeconometrics.[8] Observed consumption can be written as expected consumption plus a surprise, $C_{t+1} = E(C_{t+1})$ + surprise. According to rational expectations theory, the surprise is truly random and unpredictable. Combining this rational expectations formula with the equate-expected-consumption rule, $E(C_{t+1}) = C_t$, leads to Hall's famous *random-walk model:*[9]

$$C_{t+1} = C_t + \epsilon$$

which states that consumption tomorrow should equal consumption today plus a truly random error, $\epsilon = C_{t+1} - C_t$. Can such a strong implication of the LC-PIH possibly hold in the real world? Look again at Figure 13-2, which plots one period's consumption against the previous period's. The model appears to work nearly perfectly.[10] The random-walk model predicts that the line relating C_{t+1} to C_t should have an intercept of zero and a slope of 1. The actual equation has an intercept of $23 (compared to a mean consumption of $14,500) and a slope of 1.004, so these predictions of the random-walk model fail only in the third decimal place.

THE LC-PIH: THE TRADITIONAL MODEL STRIKES BACK

Based in rational consumer behavior, the LC-PIH is very attractive to economists. However, empirical evidence suggests that both the traditional rule-of-thumb consumption function and the LC-PIH contribute to explaining consumption behavior.[11] The actual behavior of consumption exhibits both *excess sensitivity* and *excess smoothness*. The former means that consumption responds too strongly to predictable changes in

---

[7]*(Optional)* To fully account for the rate of time preference and the interest rate, the equate-expected-marginal-utilities rule needs to be modified to read

$$E[MU(C_{t+1})] = \left(\frac{1 + \delta}{1 + r}\right) MU(C_t)$$

[8]Robert E. Hall, "Stochastic Implications of the Life Cycle–Permanent Income Hypothesis: Theory and Evidence," *Journal of Political Economy,* December 1978.

[9]At the time of Hall's discovery, everyone "knew" that consumption adjusted with long lags. Hall himself initially expected to *disprove* the LC-PIH. The random-walk model was so outlandish that Hall was the subject of much ribbing and good-natured abuse from his colleagues and his students—until everyone realized that he had found exactly the right approach to the problem.

[10]For those curious about formal statistical measures, 99.97 percent of the variance of C_{t+1} in Fig. 13-2 is explained by C_t. (In the language of statistics, $R^2 = .9997$.)

[11]The first crack in the LC-PIH wall was discovered by one of Hall's students, now a professor at the University of California–San Diego, Marjorie Flavin. See her article, "The Adjustment of Consumption to Changing Expectations about Future Income," *Journal of Political Economy,* October 1981.

income; the latter, that it responds too little to surprise changes in income.[12] John Campbell and Greg Mankiw have developed a clever way of combining the LC-PIH and the traditional consumption function in order to test for excess sensitivity.[13] According to the LC-PIH, the change in consumption equals the surprise element, ϵ, so $\Delta C_{\text{LC-PIH}} = \epsilon$. According to the traditional theory, $C = \overline{C} + cYD$, so $\Delta C_{\text{trad}} = c\Delta YD$. If λ percent of the population behaves in accordance with the traditional model and the remaining $(1 - \lambda)$ follow the LC-PIH, the total change in consumption is

$$\Delta C = \lambda \Delta C_{\text{trad}} + (1 - \lambda)\Delta C_{\text{LC-PIH}} = \lambda c \Delta YD + (1 - \lambda)\epsilon$$

Empirically estimating this equation yields

$$\Delta C = .523 \Delta YD$$

suggesting that half of consumption behavior is explained by current income rather than permanent income.[14]

LIQUIDITY CONSTRAINTS AND MYOPIA

Why might a theory so elegant as the LC-PIH miss explaining so much of consumption behavior? Two explanations are *liquidity constraints* and *myopia*. The first argues that when permanent income is higher than current income, consumers are unable to borrow to consume at the higher level predicted by the LC-PIH. The second suggests that consumers simply aren't as forward-looking as the LC-PIH suggests.

 A liquidity constraint exists when a consumer cannot borrow to sustain current consumption in the expectation of higher future income. Students in particular should appreciate the possibility that liquidity constraints exist. Most students can look forward to a much higher income in the future than they receive as students. The life-cycle theory holds that they should be consuming on the basis of their lifetime incomes, which means they should be spending much more than they currently earn. To do that, they would have to borrow. They can borrow to some extent, through student loan plans. But it is entirely possible that they cannot borrow enough to support consumption at its permanent level.

Such students are liquidity-constrained. When they leave college and take jobs, their incomes will rise and their consumption will rise, too. According to the life-cycle theory, consumption should not rise much when income rises, as long as the increase in income was expected. In fact, because the liquidity constraint is relieved, consumption

---

[12]To see how this works in a formal model, see David Romer, *Advanced Macroeconomics* (New York: McGraw-Hill, 1996), chap. 7.

[13]John Y. Campbell and N. Gregory Mankiw, "Consumption, Income, and Interest Rates: Reinterpreting the Time Series Evidence," *NBER Macroeconomics Annual,* 1989. For earlier evidence on the same topic, see Robert E. Hall and Frederic S. Mishkin, "The Sensitivity of Consumption to Transitory Income: Estimates from Panel Data on Households," *Econometrica,* March 1982. A contrary view is presented in Joseph DeJuan and John Seater, "The Permanent Income Hypothesis: Evidence from the Consumer Expenditure Survey," *Journal of Monetary Economics,* April 1999.

[14]Campbell and Mankiw, "Consumption, Income, and Interest Rates."

will rise a lot when income rises. Thus, consumption will be more closely related to *current* income than is implied by the LC-PIH. Similarly, individuals who cannot borrow when their incomes decline temporarily would be liquidity-constrained.[15]

The alternative explanation for the sensitivity of consumption to current income—that consumers are myopic—is hard to distinguish in practice from the liquidity constraints hypothesis. For instance, David Wilcox of the Federal Reserve Board of Governors has shown that the announcement that social security benefits will be increased (which always happens at least 6 weeks before the change) does not lead to a change in consumption *until the benefit increases are actually paid*.[16] Once the increased benefits are paid, recipients certainly do adjust spending—primarily on durables. The delay could be either because recipients do not have the assets to enable them to adjust spending before they receive higher payments (liquidity constraints), or because they fail to pay attention to the announcements (myopia), or perhaps because they do not believe the announcements.

UNCERTAINTY AND BUFFER-STOCK SAVING

The life-cycle hypothesis is that people save largely to finance retirement. However, additional savings goals also matter. The evidence on bequests suggests that some saving is done to provide inheritances for children. There is also a growing amount of evidence to support the view that some saving is *precautionary*, undertaken to guard against rainy days. In other words, savings are used as a *buffer stock*, added to when times are good in order to maintain consumption when times are bad.

One piece of evidence for these other motives is that old people rarely actually dissave. They tend to live off the income (e.g., interest and dividends) from their wealth—not to draw down wealth, as predicted by the LC-PIH. One explanation is that the older they are, the more they fear having to pay large bills for medical care and, therefore, the more reluctant they are to spend. Evidence from surveys of consumers, who were asked why they are saving, also indicates that saving is undertaken to meet emergency needs.

This evidence is consistent with a version of the life-cycle model in which uncertainty about future income and future needs is explicitly included. Recent work by Christopher Carroll uses these ideas to explain why the LC-PIH may be off the mark for the typical

[15]Estimates of the importance of liquidity constraints in the United States are presented in Marjorie Flavin, "Excess Sensitivity of Consumption to Current Income: Liquidity Constraints or Myopia?" *Canadian Journal of Economics,* February 1985. See also David B. Gross and Nicholas S. Souleles, "Do Liquidity Constraints and Interest Rates Matter for Consumer Behavior? Evidence from Credit Card Data," NBER working paper no. W8314, June 2001. Even in developing countries, where the paucity of financial institutions makes borrowing difficult for the typical consumer, people try to smooth out their consumption in the face of income fluctuations. See the articles by Anne Case, Robert M. Townsend, Jonathan Morduch, and Timothy Besley in "Symposium on Consumption Smoothing in Developing Countries," *Journal of Economic Perspectives,* Summer 1995.

[16]David W. Wilcox, "Social Security Benefits, Consumption Expenditure, and the Life Cycle Hypothesis," *Journal of Political Economy,* April 1989.

consumer.[17] Income fluctuations create considerable downside risk for the consumer, because the pain caused by a large drop in spending is greater than the pleasure caused by an equal-size increase in spending. One way consumers can avoid having to cut their consumption sharply in bad times is to save up a buffer stock of assets, which they can draw on in emergencies. On the other hand, most consumers are impatient; they would prefer to spend now rather than save for the future. Under these conditions, consumers will have a "target" wealth level. The target will be the point where impatience exactly balances the precautionary (or buffer-stock) saving motive. If the wealth is below the target, the precautionary saving motive will be stronger than impatience and the consumer will try to build up wealth toward the target; if wealth is above the target, impatience will be stronger than caution and the consumer will dissave. These effects lead to a much higher *MPC* than would be predicted by the standard LC-PIH model.

There is some evidence that consumers act as buffer stock agents when young, accumulating assets to protect against risk. Somewhere around age 40, savings behavior is more focused on retirement and the traditional LC-PIH works well.[18]

13-3

FURTHER ASPECTS OF CONSUMPTION BEHAVIOR

CONSUMPTION AND THE STOCK MARKET

We've mentioned earlier that the marginal propensity to consume out of wealth—stock market holdings being one part of wealth—is small. One recent estimate is that for households with moderate security holdings, a dollar increase in the value of stocks leads to an increase in consumption of between 5 cents and 15 cents, although most estimates are much lower.[19] But the value of stocks has been very volatile in recent years. In 1997 the value of stocks listed on the New York Stock Exchange (NYSE) rose about 1.5 trillion dollars. A 5 percent marginal propensity to consume would have increased consumption by $75 billion. In 1997 consumption was about $5,500 billion, so this would be a large increase. In the first 7 months of 2002 the value of the NYSE fell by more than $1.5 trillion, but consumption rose fairly strongly over this period. The lesson seems to be that the stock market matters for consumption, but that the magnitude of the relation is hard to pin down.

---

[17]See C. Carroll, "Buffer-Stock Saving and the Life Cycle/Permanent Income Hypothesis," *Quarterly Journal of Economics,* February 1997. Carroll writes, "It seems plausible that many consumers ensure that retirement is taken care of by joining a pension plan, buy a house, and then subject the post-pension-plan, post-mortgage-payment income and consumption streams to buffer-stock saving rules."

[18]Jonathan A. Parker and Pierre-Olivier Gourinchas, "Consumption over the Life Cycle," *Econometrica* 70, no. 1 (January 2002).

[19]Karen E. Dynan and Dean M. Maki, "Does Stock Market Wealth Matter for Consumption?" Board of Governors FEDS discussion paper no. 2001-23, May 2001. See also Karl E. Case, Robert J. Shiller, and John M. Quigley, "Comparing Wealth Effects: The Stock Market versus the Housing Market," NBER working paper no. W8606, November 2001.

CONSUMPTION, SAVING, AND INTEREST RATES

Anyone who saves receives a return in the form of interest or of dividends and capital gains (an increase in the price) on stocks. It seems, then, that the natural way to raise saving is to raise the return available to savers. Think of someone saving and receiving an interest rate of 5 percent each year for each dollar saved. Surely an increase in the rate to, say, 10 percent would make that person save more. This thinking has at times influenced tax policy in the United States. For instance, the interest received on savings in individual retirement accounts is exempt from the payment of taxes. This means the return received by the saver is higher than it would be if the return were taxed.

But should we really expect an increase in the interest rate to increase saving? It is true that when the interest rate rises, saving is made more attractive. But it is also made less necessary. Consider someone who has decided to save an amount that will ensure that $10,000 per year will be available for retirement. Suppose the interest rate is now 5 percent, and the person is saving $1,000 per year. Now let the interest rate rise to 10 percent. With such a high interest rate, the individual needs to save less to provide the given $10,000 per year during retirement. It may be possible to provide the same retirement income by saving only about $650 a year. Thus, an increase in the interest rate might reduce saving.[20]

What do the facts show? Does saving rise when the interest rate increases because every dollar of saving generates a higher return? Or does saving fall because there is less need to save to provide a given level of future income? The answers from the data are ambiguous. Many researchers have examined this question, but few have found strong positive effects of interest rate increases on saving. Typically, research suggests that the effects of interest rates on saving are small and hard to find.[21]

THE BARRO-RICARDO PROBLEM

Does the size of the deficit matter? That is, given the size of government spending, does it matter whether sufficient taxes are levied to pay for what we spend? The traditional aggregate supply–aggregate demand model gives a clear answer: Lower taxes mean higher aggregate demand, higher interest rates, more crowding out, and less investment for the future. New classical economists, led by Robert Barro,[22] give a surprisingly different answer: Deficits don't matter. The logic behind this answer follows directly from the LC-PIH and goes as follows: Suppose first that government spending increases $100 per family and that taxes also increase $100. Each family has $100 less

---

[20]These offsetting factors are called *substitution* and *income* effects. The substitution effect means that higher interest rates make consumption later more attractive. The offsetting income effect is that higher interest rates raise permanent income and encourage more consumption now.

[21]The best-known study finding positive interest rate effects is that by Michael Boskin, chairman of the President's Council of Economic Advisers from 1989 to 1993. See his "Taxation, Saving, and the Rate of Interest," *Journal of Political Economy,* part 2, April 1978. For more typical negative results, see Campbell and Mankiw, "Consumption, Income, and Interest Rates."

[22]See Robert Barro, "The Neoclassical Approach to Fiscal Policy," in R. Barro (ed.), *Modern Business Cycle Theory* (Cambridge, MA: Harvard University Press, 1989).

BOX 13-6   Consumption and Interest— The Micro Theory

The *Fisher diagram* is the classic microeconomic explanation of why an increase in the rate of interest can lead to either an increase or decrease in current consumption. Figures 1 and 2 both illustrate a two-period consumption choice with consumption now on the horizontal axis and consumption later on the vertical axis. In each figure the

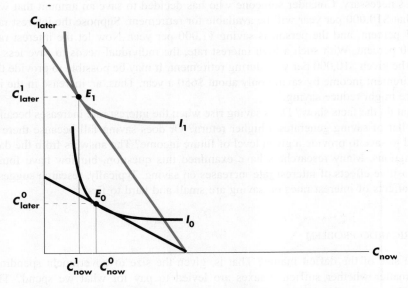

FIGURE 1   CONSUMPTION FALLS IN THE CLASSIC FISHER DIAGRAM.

in lifetime resources to allocate and makes choices to reduce lifetime spending accordingly. Suppose, instead, that the government had raised spending $100 per family but had left taxes unchanged and borrowed the $100. Just as in the first case, the "representative family" has $100 less in allocable resources *today,* but now it is because the family has loaned the money to the government. Since the family is in the same financial position in this $100-deficit case as it would be in the zero-deficit case, the family will make the same decisions. The deficit doesn't matter.

There is one *apparent* difference in the $100-deficit case: The family now owns a $100 government bond. However, the family also realizes that at the time its bond comes due, the government will find it has to raise taxes to pay off the principal and

black line is the budget line $C_{later} = [1 + r^0](Y_{now} - C_{now})$ for interest rate r^0. The green budget line, $C_{later} = [1 + r^1](Y_{now} - C_{now})$, shows that at a higher interest rate, $r^1 > r^0$, you get a better return in terms of deferred consumption for each dollar saved now.

In each figure the curved lines are indifference curves between spending now and later. The point where the budget line is tangent to the indifference curve (i.e., point E_0) determines the values of consumption now and later. Figures 1 and 2 are identical, except that the shapes of the indifference curves are slightly different. In Figure 1 the *substitution effect* dominates the *income effect* and current consumption falls with an increase in the interest rate. The income effect dominates in Figure 2, so current consumption rises.

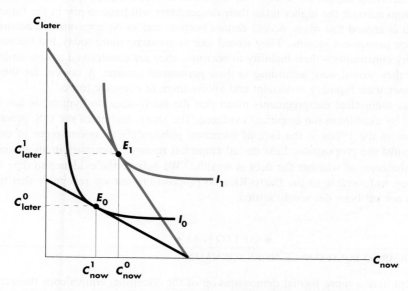

FIGURE 2   CONSUMPTION RISES IN THE CLASSIC FISHER DIAGRAM.

interest due on the bonds it issued to finance the deficit. So ownership of the bond does not affect the family's decisions because the value of the bond is exactly offset by the value of its implicit future tax liability.

The issue raised by this argument is sometimes posed as the question, "Are government bonds net wealth?" The question goes back at least to the classical English economist David Ricardo. Renewed by Robert Barro,[23] it is known as the *Barro-Ricardo*

[23]The original article is Robert Barro, "Are Government Bonds Net Wealth?" *Journal of Political Economy,* December 1974. See also, by the same author, "The Ricardian Approach to Budget Deficits," *Journal of Economic Perspectives,* Spring 1989. Theoretical challenges to the Barro-Ricardo view include Olivier Blanchard, "Debts, Deficits and Finite Horizons," *Journal of Political Economy,* April 1985; and Douglas Bernheim, "A Neoclassical Perspective on Budget Deficits," *Journal of Economic Perspectives,* Spring 1989.

equivalence proposition, or *Ricardian equivalence.* The proposition is that debt financing by bond issue merely postpones taxation and therefore, in many instances, is strictly equivalent to current taxation. (Incidentally, after raising this as a theoretical possibility, Ricardo rejected its practical significance.)

The strict Barro-Ricardo proposition that government bonds are not net wealth turns on the argument that people realize their bonds will have to be paid off with future increases in taxes. If so, an increase in the budget deficit unaccompanied by cuts in government spending should lead to an increase in saving that precisely matches the deficit.

There are two main theoretical objections to the Barro-Ricardo proposition. First, given that people have finite lifetimes, different people will pay off the debt than those who are receiving the tax cut today. This argument assumes that people now alive do not take into account the higher taxes their descendants will have to pay in the future. Second, it is argued that many people cannot borrow, and so do not consume according to their permanent income. They would like to consume more today, but because of liquidity constraints—their inability to borrow—they are constrained to consuming less than they would want according to their permanent income. A tax cut for these people eases their liquidity constraint and allows them to consume more.[24]

These theoretical disagreements mean that the Barro-Ricardo hypothesis has to be settled by examining the empirical evidence. The sharp decline of the U.S. private saving rate in the 1980s in the face of increased public deficits is one piece of evidence against the proposition. Less casual empirical research continues in an attempt to settle the issue of whether the debt is wealth.[25] We believe the evidence to date is, on balance, unfavorable to the Barro-Ricardo proposition, but we recognize that the issue has not yet been decisively settled.

◆ OPTIONAL ◆

BARRO-RICARDO EQUIVALENCE MORE FORMALLY

We present here a more formal demonstration of the Ricardian equivalence theorem. The demonstration emphasizes that the theorem relies on the absence of liquidity constraints and the presence of an *operational bequest motive,* that is, parents' desire to leave a bequest to their children. To make the example concrete, suppose a father and son, Alan and Larry, consume C_{Alan} and C_{Larry}, respectively. We look at the father's decision problem about how to allocate resources between his own consumption and a bequest, B, to Larry. Larry's utility depends on his own consumption. Alan's utility depends on his own consumption and on Larry's welfare. Let T be the amount of taxes Alan pays.

---

[24]Barro himself pointed out another qualification to the equivalence proposition. Changes in marginal tax rates change tax-induced distortions in private decision making. Deficits that allow low tax rates today at the expense of high tax rates in the future may create greater overall distortion than would a constant-over-time medium tax rate.

[25]See, for example, Joseph Altonji, Fumio Hayashi, and Laurence Kotlikoff, "Parental Altruism and Inter Vivos Transfers: Theory and Evidence," *Journal of Political Economy,* December 1997.

The key to the effect of deficit financing lies in writing out Alan and Larry's budget constraints. Larry's consumption equals his income plus the value of the bequest:

$$C_{\text{Larry}} = Y_{\text{Larry}} + B \tag{4}$$

Alan leaves a bequest equal to his saving plus accrued interest. Saving equals disposable income, income less taxes, minus his consumption:

$$B = (1 + r)[(Y - T) - C_{\text{Alan}}] \tag{5}$$

Alan chooses consumption, C_{Alan}, to maximize his utility consistent with his budget constraint, trading off his own consumption against the pleasure he gets from knowing Larry's utility rises with the extra consumption a bequest allows.[26]

Suppose now that rather than impose a tax on the current generation, the government practices deficit finance, borrowing the amount L, $L = T$, and promising to pay off the loan with interest, $(1 + r)L$, by imposing a tax, $(1 + r)T$, in the future. Larry's consumption will be reduced by the taxes he must pay:

$$C_{\text{Larry}} = [Y_{\text{Larry}} - (1 + r)T] + B \tag{6}$$

Alan now leaves a bequest that includes the principal and interest repayment on his loan to the government. Because he pays no taxes, his disposable income has risen, but in addition to consuming, he uses some of his money to make a loan to the government:

$$B = (1 + r)[Y - (L + C_{\text{Alan}})] + (1 + r)L \tag{7}$$

The question to be answered is, How does Alan's consumption choice under deficit spending compare to the choice he made under the tax-as-you-go system above? Can Alan still follow the same plan? Yes! Alan can set consumption at the same level by taking the money previously paid in taxes and lending it to the government. This allows Alan to increase his bequest by the eventual proceeds from the loan repayment, $(1 + r)L$. The increase in the bequest will provide Larry with just enough extra funds to pay *his* extra taxes, while leaving C_{Larry} unchanged. Thus, Alan and Larry will have the same consumption levels as before. All that has happened is that Alan has increased his private saving, in the form of the loan to the government, by just enough to offset the decrease in public saving, in the form of the increased deficit.

There is an implicit assumption in this analysis that the intergenerational bequest motive is operative—meaning that Alan *wants* to leave money to Larry. If he doesn't, then deficit finance allows Alan to spend more and leave a tax bill for Larry.

INTERNATIONAL DIFFERENCES IN SAVING RATES

For decades, the U.S. saving rate was lower than that in other major countries. As Table 13-1 shows, in the 1990s the U.S. saving rate was still much below that in Japan, but not too different from that of some of our other major economic partners.

---

[26]If one can imagine that Larry might also have an interest in intergenerational transfers and plan himself to leave a bequest, we get a more sophisticated argument that Alan gets pleasure out of Larry's happiness, which is due in part to money left to grandchildren—and future generations.

TABLE 13-1   Government and Private Gross Saving Rates, 1990s*
(Percent)

	UNITED STATES	JAPAN	GERMANY	UNITED KINGDOM	CANADA
Gross national saving	16.5	31.0	21.9	15.7	17.5
Government saving	−2.9	−2.6	−2.6	−3.7	−4.4
Private saving	19.4	33.6	24.5	19.4	21.9

*All data are gross saving relative to GDP.

Source: *OECD*, Economic Outlook.

It is useful to look at the different sectors of the economy that save. We start by looking at *government* and *private saving*.[27]

Gross national saving = government saving + private saving

The government saves when it spends less than it receives, that is, when it runs a budget surplus.

Next we look at the difference between *business* and *personal saving* in the United States:

Private saving = business saving + personal saving

Business saving consists of retained earnings, that amount of profits not paid out to the owners of the business. A business saves when it does not pay income to its owners but, rather, keeps those funds to plow back into the business.

The fact that business saving is much larger than personal saving in the United States (see Table 13-2) has not received the attention it should. That is partly because,

TABLE 13-2   Composition of U.S. Saving, 1987 and 2002*

	1987	2002
Gross national saving rate	17.1	15.1
Government saving	−0.6	−0.2
Gross business saving	12.3	12.5
Household saving	5.3	2.8

*All ratios are sectoral saving as a percentage of GDP.

Source: Bureau of Economic Analysis.

[27]The government sector in Table 13-1 consists of federal, state, and local governments. All three levels need to be included for a valid comparison. In the United States, deficit spending is largely limited to the federal level, as most state constitutions prohibit borrowing (except for capital projects). In other nations arrangements for local versus national finance differ. Canadian provinces, for example, sometimes run very large deficits.

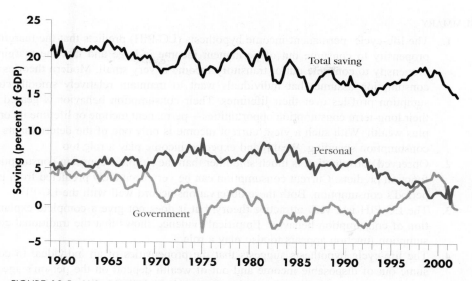

FIGURE 13-5   U.S. SAVING AS A PERCENT OF GDP, 1959–2002.

The diagram shows personal saving, government saving, and total U.S. saving. Total saving includes government saving, personal saving, and business saving. (Source: Bureau of Economic Analysis.)

for a long time, it seemed that households treated business saving as if it were being done on their behalf—that is, they "pierced the corporate veil"—and reduced their own saving exactly enough to offset any increased business saving. The more recent evidence is that households reduce their saving by only about 50 cents for every extra dollar of saving done by business.[28]

Personal saving in the United States trended up in the early postwar period but drifted sharply downward in the 1980s and 1990s (Figure 13-5). In the late 1990s, personal saving as a fraction of GDP declined precipitously for reasons that are not yet clear.[29] At the same time, government saving became positive as the federal budget went from deficit to surplus for the first time in decades.

So why does the United States save less than other countries? Demographic factors such as a large senior-citizen population account for some of the difference. It is also easier to borrow in the United States than in most other countries. In many countries, people have to save in order to make major purchases, such as a house or a car, whereas in the United States they can borrow for that purpose.

These factors do not fully account for international differences in saving rates. Some economists argue that there may simply be differences in national attitudes toward saving, but most still hope to find economic explanations for those underlying attitudes.

[28]James Poterba, "Tax Policy and Corporate Savings," *Brookings Papers on Economic Activity* 2 (1987).

[29]Jonathan A. Parker, "Spendthrift in America? On Two Decades of Decline in the U.S. Saving Rate," *NBER Macroeconomics Annual*, 1999.

SUMMARY

1. The life-cycle–permanent-income hypothesis (LC-PIH) predicts that the marginal propensity to consume out of permanent income is large and that the marginal propensity to consume out of transitory income is very small. Modern theories of consumption assume that individuals want to maintain relatively smooth consumption profiles over their lifetimes. Their consumption behavior is geared to their long-term consumption opportunities—permanent income or lifetime income plus wealth. With such a view, current income is only one of the determinants of consumption spending. Wealth and expected income play a role too.

2. Observed consumption is much smoother than the simple Keynesian consumption function predicts. Current consumption can be very accurately predicted from last period's consumption. Both these observations accord well with the LC-PIH.

3. The LC-PIH is a very attractive theory, but it does not give a complete explanation of consumption behavior. Empirical evidence shows that the traditional consumption function appears to also play a role.

4. The life-cycle hypothesis suggests that the propensities of an individual to consume out of disposable income and out of wealth depend on the person's age. It implies that saving is high (low) when income is high (low) relative to lifetime average income. It also suggests that aggregate saving depends on the growth rate of the economy and on such variables as the age distribution of the population.

5. The rate of consumption, and thus of saving, could in principle be affected by the interest rate. But the evidence, for the most part, shows little effect of interest rates on saving.

6. The Barro-Ricardo equivalence proposition notes that debt represents future taxes. It asserts that debt-financed tax cuts will not have any effect on consumption or aggregate demand.

7. The U.S. saving rate is very low by international standards. Most private saving in the United States is done by the business sector.

KEY TERMS

Barro-Ricardo equivalence proposition (Ricardian equivalence)	government saving	myopia
	life-cycle hypothesis	operational bequest motive
	lifetime budget constraint	permanent income
buffer stock	lifetime utility	personal saving
business saving	liquidity constraints	private saving
excess sensitivity	marginal utility of	random-walk model of
excess smoothness	consumption	consumption

PROBLEMS

Conceptual

1. The text implies that the ratio of consumption to accumulated saving declines over time until retirement.
   a. Why? What assumption about consumption behavior leads to this result?
   b. What happens to this ratio after retirement?

2. **a.** Suppose you earn just as much as your neighbor but are in much better health and expect to live longer than she does. Would you consume more or less than she does? Why? Derive your answer using the equation from the text, $C = (WL/NL) \times YL$.

    b. According to the life-cycle hypothesis, what would be the effect of the social security system on your average propensity to consume out of (disposable) income? Is the credibility of the social security system an issue here?

3. In terms of the permanent-income hypothesis, would you consume more of your Christmas bonus if (*a*) you knew there would be a bonus every year, or (*b*) this was the only year the bonus would be given?

4. Explain why successful gamblers (and thieves) might be expected to live very well even in years when they don't do well at all.

5. What are the similarities between the life-cycle and the permanent-income hypotheses? Do they differ in their approaches to explaining why the long-run *MPC* is greater than the short-run *MPC*?

6. The United States, during the 1980s, found its rate of personal saving to be particularly low. It also, during that time, had a demographic blip—the baby-boomer generation, then in its late twenties to early thirties.

    a. Does the life-cycle hypothesis suggest a reason that these two facts might be connected?

    b. What does this hypothesis suggest we should see as this generation ages?

7. Rank the following marginal propensities to consume:

    a. Marginal propensity to consume out of permanent income.

    b. Marginal propensity to consume out of transitory income.

    c. Marginal propensity to consume out of permanent income when consumers are liquidity-constrained.

    d. Marginal propensity to consume out of transitory income when consumers are liquidity-constrained.

8. What is a random walk? How is Hall's random-walk model of consumption related to the life-cycle and permanent-income hypotheses?

9. What are the problems of excess sensitivity and excess smoothness? Does their existence disprove or invalidate the LC-PIH? Explain.

10. What assumption(s) regarding consumers' knowledge and behavior in the life-cycle–permanent-income hypothesis do we need to change in order for it to explain the presence of precautionary, or buffer-stock, saving? Do these assumptions, in your opinion, bring the model closer to or further from the world as you know it?

11. **a.** Explain why the interest rate might affect saving.

    b. Has this relationship been confirmed empirically?

12. **a.** In the Barro-Ricardo view, does it make any difference whether the government pays for its expenditures by raising taxes or issuing debt?

    b. Why?

    c. What are the two main theoretical objections to the Barro-Ricardo view?

Technical

1. Suppose that permanent income is calculated as the average of income over the past 5 years; that is,

$$YP = 1/5(Y + Y_{-1} + Y_{-2} + Y_{-3} + Y_{-4}) \tag{P1}$$

Suppose further that consumption is given by $C = .9YP$.

a. If you have earned $20,000 per year for the past 10 years, what is your permanent income?

b. Suppose that next year (period $t + 1$) you earn $30,000. What is your new YP?

c. What is your consumption this year and next year?

d. What is your short-run marginal propensity to consume? Long-run MPC?

e. Assuming you continue to earn $30,000 starting in period $t + 1$, graph the value of your permanent income in each period, using equation (P1).

2. The graph below shows the lifetime earnings profile of a person who lives for four periods and earns incomes of $30, $60, and $90 in the first three periods of the life cycle. There are no earnings during retirement. Assume that the interest rate is 0.

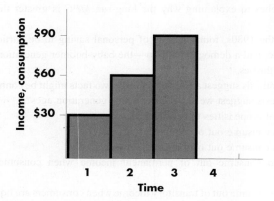

a. Determine the level of consumption, compatible with the budget constraint, for someone who wants an even consumption profile throughout the life cycle. Indicate in which periods the person saves and dissaves and in what amounts.

b. Assume now that, contrary to part (**a**), there is no possibility of borrowing. The credit markets are closed to the individual. Under this assumption, what is the flow of consumption the individual will pick over the life cycle? In providing an answer, continue to assume that, if possible, an even flow of consumption is preferred. (*Note:* You are assuming here that there are liquidity constraints.)

c. Assume next that the person described in part (**b**) receives an increase in wealth, or nonlabor income. The increase in wealth is equal to $13. How will that wealth be allocated over the life cycle with and without access to the credit market? How would your answer differ if the increase in wealth were $23?

3. Suppose that 70 percent of a country's population, as a consequence of liquidity constraints, behaves in accordance with the traditional model of consumption and thus consumes, every period, a given fraction of its disposable income. The other 30 percent of the population behaves in accordance with the LC-PIH.

a. If the MPC in the traditional model is .8 and disposable income changes by $10 million (you may assume that this change is due entirely to a change in transitory income), by how much will consumption change?

    b. What if 70 percent of the population behaves in accordance with the LC-PIH, and 30 percent behaves in accordance with the traditional model?

    c. What if 100 percent of the population behaves in accordance with the LC-PIH?

4. Suppose the real interest rate has increased from 2 to 4 percent.

    a. What will happen to the opportunity cost of consuming a set of goods today, as opposed to tomorrow? Explain how this will affect the fraction of income you choose to save.

    b. Now suppose that you save only to finance your retirement and that your goal is to have $1 million tucked away by the time you're 70. Explain how your rate of saving will respond to the rise in the interest rate in *this* context.

    c. Can you make a prediction regarding the net effect of this increase in r on the rate of saving? Why, or why not?

5. Let's say that your goal is to raise the rate of saving in the United States by 3 percentage points. What are the various ways you could accomplish this? Which of your solutions do you favor?

Empirical

1. Go to www.economagic.com and do a search for "saving rate." Using the built-in graphing facilities, make a graph for the U.S. personal saving rate over the last 40 years. Is the personal saving rate pretty stable over time? When did the personal saving rate start to fall in the United States?

CHAPTER 14

Investment Spending

CHAPTER HIGHLIGHTS

- Investment is the most volatile sector of aggregate demand.

- The demand for capital depends on interest rates, output, and taxes.

- Investment reflects the adjustment of the existing capital stock to the current demand for capital.

- Investment spending is the primary link from monetary policy to aggregate demand.

Investment links the present to the future. Investment links the money markets to goods markets. And investment fluctuations drive much of the business cycle. Following are some salient points about the investment sector:

- Investment spending is very volatile and thus responsible for much of the fluctuation of GDP across the business cycle.
- Investment spending is a primary link through which interest rates, and therefore monetary policy, affect the economy. Tax policies affecting investment, under the control of Congress and the president, are important tools of fiscal policy.
- On the supply side, investment over long periods determines the size of the stock of capital and thus helps determine long-run growth.

In this chapter we study how investment depends on interest rates and income. Recall from Chapter 10 that these relations are principal determinants of the slope of the *IS* curve. We also see how government policy can increase or decrease investment, thus shifting the *IS* curve and increasing or decreasing aggregate demand.

Figure 14-1 illustrates the volatility of investment by comparing U.S. GDP (left scale) and investment (right scale). Investment averages about 14 percent of GDP, but it is relatively very volatile. (Note that the left and right scales differ by a ratio of 5 to 1.) Dips in total output are associated with much larger proportional dips in investment.

The theory of investment is the theory of the demand for capital. We develop the theory carefully in Section 14-1, and then in Section 14-2 we apply the theory to *business*

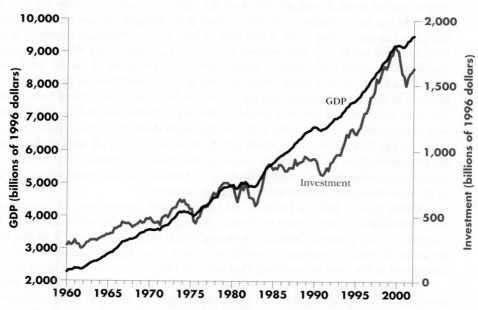

FIGURE 14-1   RELATIONSHIP OF PRIVATE INVESTMENT TO GDP, 1959–2002.

Investment averages about 14 percent of GDP, but it is relatively very volatile. (Source: Bureau of Economic Analysis.)

BOX 14-1   Why Investment Is Volatile— The Back-of-an-Envelope Explanation

Following along with the bathtub metaphor we can easily rough out expected magnitudes for changes in investment. In the United States, private capital is roughly 2.5 years' GDP. Investment is about one-sixth of GDP. So the stock of capital is approximately 15 years' worth of investment. If the demand for capital were to drop 1 percent, the investment-GDP ratio would have to drop from around 16 percent of GDP to around 13.5 percent to satisfy the drop within 1 year. Put differently, a 1 percent drop in the capital stock is produced by a 15 percent drop in annual investment flow.

fixed investment, residential investment, and *inventory investment.* First, though, you should understand that the dynamics of investment and capital are driven by a "stylized fact": The *flow of investment* is quite small compared to the *stock of capital.*

Stocks and flows are inevitably explained with a bathtub metaphor, with the level of the bathwater playing the role of the stock of capital and the flow from the spigot being analogous to the flow of investment. Businesses and individuals decide on the desired capital stock (how high they want the bathwater) and then invest (turn up the faucet) to top up the capital stock from where it is today (the height of the bathwater right now) to the desired level. A key fact, at least for the American economy, is that the size of the tub is very large relative to the flow from the spigot. At typical rates of investment it would take about 15 years' flow to fill the stock of capital to its usual level. As a result, even a pretty small increase in the desired level of capital turns the investment faucet to full open, and a pretty small decrease in the desired level of capital shuts investment down to a dribble. This large-stock-to-small-flow fact explains why investment is such a volatile sector of aggregate demand. It also explains why investment has little effect on aggregate supply in the short run: Full open or shut down, the investment flow is just a ripple on the capital stock. Of course, over the long run investment flow entirely determines the height of the capital stock and is therefore one of the most important determinants of aggregate supply.

Before getting down to business, we have to clarify terminology. In common usage, "investment" often refers to *buying* existing financial or physical assets. For example, we say someone "invests" in stocks, bonds, or a house when he or she buys the asset. In macroeconomics, "investment" has a more narrow, technical meaning: **Investment is the flow of spending that adds to the physi   stock of capital.**

In Section 14-1 we emphasize two elements: the demand for capital, and investment as a flow that adjusts the level of the *capital stock.* **Capital is a *stock,* the given dollar value of all the buildings, machines, and inventories at a point in time.** Both GDP and investment refer to spending *flows.* Investment is the amount spent by businesses to *add* to the stock of capital over a given period.

BOX 14-2   Investment: Gross, Net, and More Inclusive Concepts

The distinction between *gross* and *net* investment is essential even though the difference, depreciation, is hard to measure. Again using the bathtub metaphor, the flow from the faucet is gross investment and the water down the drain is depreciation. The difference between inflow and outflow (gross investment less depreciation) is net investment. Aggregate supply depends on net investment, since in the long run net investment determines the capital stock. Aggregate demand, in contrast, depends on gross investment— a job building an additional machine or building a replacement machine is still a job.

Depreciation is more than just the physical wear and tear that results from use and age. A piece of capital may become economically obsolete, for instance, because input prices change—as gas-guzzlers became obsolete when oil prices increased. Economic depreciation may be much more rapid than physical depreciation. Technological obsolescence may also cause rapid economic depreciation. This is particularly true of computers, for which quality improvements have been dramatic.

The rate of depreciation depends on the type of capital. For example, structures have a useful life of decades, while office equipment has a life of only a few years. This has an important implication: If investment shifts toward capital goods with a short life (e.g., computers), then those goods make up a larger share of the capital stock and, as a result, the overall rate of depreciation will rise. This is what happened in the United States starting in the 1980s.

Although it is traditional, the focus on private sector additions to the capital stock in this chapter takes a too-restricted view of investment in two respects. First, it ignores *government investment*. As anyone who attends a public school or travels on the public highways can tell, government investment also contributes to economic productivity. There has been much recent work on the productivity of government capital, and there is no question that government investment should be included in aggregate investment. Estimates are that the government capital stock is about 15 to 20 percent of the private capital stock; therefore, the U.S. capital stock and investment are 15 to 20 percent larger than the magnitudes discussed in this chapter.

Second, individuals invest not only in physical capital but also in *human capital*, in increasing the productive capacity of people, through schooling and training. The late Robert Eisner of Northwestern University estimated that the stock of human capital in the United States is almost as large as the stock of physical capital.* There is much evidence that this investment, like that in physical capital, yields a positive real return; indeed, the return on human capital typically exceeds that on physical capital.

In thinking about investment as spending that increases future productivity, we should look beyond just private sector gross investment.

*See Eisner's comprehensive work, *Total Incomes System of Accounts* (Chicago: University of Chicago Press, 1989).

14-1

THE STOCK DEMAND FOR CAPITAL AND THE FLOW OF INVESTMENT

Businesses and consumers demand a stock of capital in the form of machines and homes, but the supply of capital can be thought of as a fixed stock at a point in time. When the demand exceeds the existing stock, a flow of investment in the form of new machines and new home construction starts to fill the gap. We work through a formal analysis of the demand for capital in this section. But we start with a familiar example, the market for private homes, in order to build intuition.[1]

The stock of existing owner-occupied homes is very large compared to the number of new homes built in any given year. The number of new homes varies greatly with economic conditions but is never more than a few percent of the existing housing stock—if only because of the limited number of rough carpenters, finish carpenters, plumbers, electricians, and so on. The demand for private homes depends primarily on three factors: income, mortgage interest rates, and taxes. When income rises, more families buy first homes or trade up to larger ones. Since a home is a long-term investment, families look ahead, increasing their demand for housing when they expect high incomes to persist. Housing demand is extraordinarily sensitive to mortgage interest rates. Since mortgage payments are almost entirely comprised of interest, a small rise in interest rates can cause a big drop in housing demand. Finally, owner-occupied housing benefits from a variety of preferential tax treatments (in the United States). The tax rules don't change very often, but when they do change housing demand can change in a big way.

Suppose mortgage rates drop. The monthly cost of homeownership drops and the demand for housing rises. There isn't any way to make new homes appear overnight, so the initial reaction is an increase in the price of existing homes. The higher prices give builders the incentive to start new projects—which comprise the flow of new housing investment. Over time, enough homes are built to satisfy the new higher level of demand, and housing prices and new housing investment drop back toward their original levels. (Since the stock of housing would now be larger, there will now be more homes around to wear out. The home repair and remodel business will be permanently greater. In other words, housing depreciation increases, so gross housing investment will have increased permanently even if net housing investment returns to its original level.)

Two results from this informal analysis apply to investment more generally. First, investment is a principal conduit of monetary policy into the goods markets. Interest rates are a prime determinant of the cost of owning capital. Loose monetary policy lowers interest rates, lessens the cost of owning capital, and increases the demand for capital. Second, fiscal policy in the form of lower taxes on capital can directly increase investment.

As we move into the formal analysis you may find it helpful to refer back to two familiar concepts. In what follows, the "price of capital" is a generalization of the price of a house, and the "rental cost of capital" generalizes the example of "monthly mortgage payment."

---

[1] Familiar? Yes, if you live in the United States or Canada, where ownership of individual homes is very high. Perhaps less familiar in very capitalist Hong Kong, where over half the housing units are supplied by the government.

THE DESIRED CAPITAL STOCK: OVERVIEW

Firms use capital, along with labor, to produce goods and services for sale. Their goal is, of course, to maximize profits. In deciding how much capital to use in production, firms have to balance the contribution that more capital makes to their revenues against the cost of using more capital. The *marginal product of capital* **is the increase in output produced by using 1 more unit of capital in production. The** *rental (user) cost of capital* **is the cost of using 1 more unit of capital in production.** (Note that both concepts are *flows*.) Whether a firm actually buys its own capital or leases it, the rental cost is the right measure of the *opportunity cost*.[2] As long as the value of the marginal product of capital is above the rental cost, it pays the firm to add to its capital stock. Thus, the firm will keep investing until the value of the output produced by adding 1 more unit of capital is equal to the cost of using that capital—the rental cost of capital.

To derive the rental cost of capital, we think of the firm as financing the purchase of the capital by borrowing, at an interest rate i. In the presence of inflation, the nominal dollar value of capital rises over time, so the real cost of using capital over a year is the nominal interest payment less the nominal capital gain. At the time that a firm makes an investment, the nominal interest rate is known, but the inflation rate over the *coming* year is not. So the firm must base its decision on the *expected inflation rate, π^e*. In other words, the real cost of borrowing is the *expected real interest rate, $r = i - \pi^e$*. Of course, capital also wears out over time, so the cost of depreciation must be added. A conventional assumption is that depreciation is d percent per year. Thus, the complete formula for rental cost is $rc = r + d = i - \pi^e + d$. (Taxes matter too. They're discussed below.)

Firms desire to add capital until the marginal return to the last unit added drops to the rental cost of capital. *Diminishing marginal product* of capital means that the *marginal* product of capital drops as capital is increased. Figure 14-2 shows a *marginal-product-of-capital schedule*. A high rental cost can be justified only by a high marginal product. So an increase of the rental cost from rc_0 to rc_1 decreases the desired capital stock from K_0^* to K_1^*.

An increase in the size of the economy moves the entire marginal-product-of-capital schedule to the right, as in Figure 14-3. The rightward shift increases the demand for capital at any given rental cost.

The general relationship among the desired capital stock, K^*, the rental cost of capital, rc, and the level of output is given by

$$K^* = g(rc, Y) \tag{1}$$

where an increase in the rental cost decreases K^* and an increase in GDP increases K^*.

Expected Output

Equation (1) shows that the desired capital stock depends on the level of output. But that must be the level of output for some future period, during which the capital will be in production. For some investments the future time at which the output will be

[2]Even if the firm finances the investment out of profits it has made in the past—retained earnings—it should still think of the interest rate as the basic cost of using the new capital, since it could have lent those funds and earned interest on them or paid them out as dividends to shareholders.

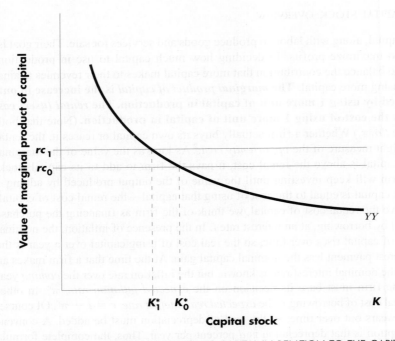

FIGURE 14-2 MARGINAL PRODUCT OF CAPITAL IN RELATION TO THE CAPITAL STOCK.
Given the marginal-product-of-capital schedule, a higher rental cost of capital corresponds to a lower desired capital stock.

produced is a matter of months or only weeks. For other investments, such as power stations, the future time at which the output will be produced is years away.

This suggests that the notion of permanent income (in this case, permanent output) introduced in Chapter 13 is relevant to investment as well as consumption. The demand for capital, which depends on the normal or permanent level of output, thus depends on expectations of future output levels rather than the current level of output. However, current output is likely to affect expectations of permanent output.

Taxes and the Rental Cost of Capital

In addition to interest and depreciation, the rental cost of capital is affected by taxes. The two main tax variables are the corporate income tax and the investment tax credit. The corporate income tax is essentially a proportional tax on profits; that is, the firm pays a proportion, say, t, of its profits in taxes. Since the mid-1980s the corporate tax rate in the United States has been 34 percent, down from 46 percent in the early 1980s. The higher the corporate income tax, the higher the cost of capital.[3]

---

[3]To the extent that corporate capital is financed by borrowing, deductions on interest payments roughly cancel profits earned from the capital, making the corporate income tax rate pretty much irrelevant. In practice, firms use considerable equity financing and high corporate income tax rates do raise the cost of capital.

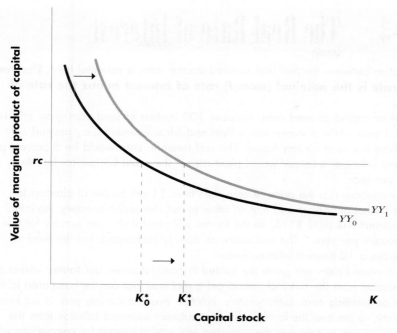

FIGURE 14-3   SHIFT OF THE MARGINAL-PRODUCT SCHEDULE.

An increase in the size of the economy shifts the marginal-product schedule to the right, increasing the desired capital stock at any given rental cost.

The second tool of investment tax policy, the investment tax credit, was in place in the United States for most of the period 1962–1986 but was discontinued in 1986. It allowed firms to deduct from their taxes a fraction, say, 10 percent, of their investment expenditures in each year. Thus, a firm spending $1 million for investment purposes in a given year could deduct 10 percent of the $1 million, or $100,000, from the taxes it would otherwise have to pay the federal government. The investment tax credit reduces the price of a capital good to the firm, since the Treasury returns to the firm a proportion of the cost of each capital good. The investment tax credit therefore reduces the rental cost of capital.

The Effects of Fiscal and Monetary Policy on the Desired Capital Stock

Equation (1) states that the desired capital stock increases when the expected level of output rises and when the rental cost of capital falls. The rental cost of capital, in turn, falls when the real interest rate and the rate of depreciation fall and when the investment tax credit rises. An increase in the corporate tax rate is likely, through the equity route, to reduce the desired capital stock.

The major significance of these results is that they imply that monetary and fiscal policy affect the desired capital stock. Fiscal policy exerts an effect through both the corporate tax rate and the investment tax credit.

BOX 14-3   The Real Rate of Interest

The distinction between the *real* and *nominal* interest rates is essential here. **The *real* interest rate is the nominal (stated) rate of interest minus the rate of inflation.**

Think of capital as seed corn. Suppose 100 bushels of seed corn grow into 105 bushels in 1 year's time if strewn into a field and left unattended (i.e., pretend corn grows without the need for any labor). The real return to corn would be 5 percent per year. Absent inflation, a farmer would plant corn if she could borrow for less than 5 percent per year.

Now suppose that the price of corn rises from $1 per bushel at planting to $1.10 per bushel at harvest and that all other prices rise proportionally. An initial $100 investment will yield $115, so the farmer will plant if she can borrow for less than 15 percent per year.* The *real* return on corn is unchanged, but the nominal return includes a 10 percent inflation factor.

Since interest rates are generally quoted in nominal terms, our farmer wishes to subtract inflation from the nominal rate to get a real rate that can be compared to the real return on planting corn. Unfortunately, inflation over the coming year is not known with certainty, so the best the farmer can do is subtract expected inflation from the nominal interest rate to calculate the *expected real* rate of interest for comparison with the return on corn.

The real rate of interest is

$$r = i - \pi^e$$

which states that the real rate of interest is the nominal interest rate minus the expected rate of inflation.

The nominal rate can be a very misleading guide to the cost of borrowing. If the expected rate of inflation is zero and the nominal interest rate is 5 percent, the real interest rate is 5 percent. By contrast, if the nominal interest rate is 10 percent and the expected inflation rate is 10 percent, the real interest rate is zero. Other things equal, the desired capital stock in this example would be higher with the nominal interest rate of 10 percent than with the nominal rate of 5 percent.

Investment spending tends to be higher when the rental cost of capital is lower. But because of the distinction between real and nominal interest rates, that is *not* the same as saying that investment tends to be higher when the nominal rate of interest is lower.

*Note that 105 × $1.10 actually equals $115.50. Technically, when we approximate 15.5 percent by 15 percent, we are ignoring a second-order term.

Fiscal policy also affects capital demand by its overall effects on the position of the *IS* curve and thus on the interest rate. A high-tax–low-government-spending policy keeps the real interest rate low and encourages the demand for capital. A low-tax–high-government-spending policy that produces large deficits raises the real interest rate and discourages the demand for capital.

BOX 14-4   The Demand for Capital: A Cobb-Douglas Example

The generic formula for the production function is $Y = AF(K, N)$. If you prefer to follow the discussion with a specific formula, you can use the *Cobb-Douglas production function,* $Y = AK^\theta N^{1-\theta}$, which, with $\theta \approx .25$, gives a very good approximation to the production function in the United States. Using the Cobb-Douglas, the marginal product of capital is $MPK = \theta AK^{\theta-1}N^{1-\theta} = \theta A(K/N)^{-(1-\theta)} = \theta Y/K$. We find the demand-for-capital function by setting marginal product equal to rental cost, $\theta Y/K = rc$, and solving for K. So for the Cobb-Douglas production function, the demand for capital can be written $K^* = g(rc, Y) = \theta Y/rc$.

Monetary policy affects capital demand by affecting the market interest rate. A lowering of the nominal interest rate by the Federal Reserve (given the expected inflation rate) induces firms to desire more capital. This expansion in capital demand, in turn, will affect investment spending.

The Stock Market and the Cost of Capital

Rather than borrowing, a firm can also raise the financing it needs to pay for its investment by selling shares, or equity. The people buying the shares expect to earn a return from dividends or, if the firm is successful, from the increase in the market value of their shares—that is, *capital gains*—or both.

When its share price is high, a company can raise a lot of money by selling relatively few shares. When stock prices are low, the firm has to sell more shares to raise a given amount of money. The owners of the firm, the existing shareholders, will be more willing to have the firm sell shares to raise new money if it has to sell few shares to do so, that is, if the price is high. Thus, we expect corporations to be more willing to sell equity to finance investment when the stock market is high than when it is low. That is why a booming stock market is good for investment.

The q Theory of Investment   The *q theory of investment* emphasizes this connection between investment and the stock market. The price of a share in a company is the price of a claim on the capital in the company. The managers of the company can, then, be thought of as responding to the price of the stock by producing more new capital—that is, investing—when the price of shares is high and as producing less new capital or not investing at all when the price of shares is low.

What is q?[4] It is an estimate of the value the stock market places on a firm's assets relative to the cost of producing those assets. In its simplest form, q is the ratio of the market value of a firm to the replacement cost of capital. When the ratio is

---

[4]You will often see q referred to as "Tobin's q." The late Nobel Prize winner James Tobin first put forth this way of connecting the stock market and investment.

BOX 14-5   Temporary Investment Tax Credit Carries a Big Punch

It's natural to think that permanent changes to fiscal policy have bigger impacts than do temporary changes. But the temporary investment tax credit provides an interesting counterexample. Imagine that, faced with a recession, the government decided to provide an investment tax credit. What is the effect of a temporary, as contrasted with permanent, investment tax credit?

Suppose, as a firm manager, you were told you could get a 10 percent tax credit, *but only this year*. You would rush all your near-future capital spending plans into the current year. So a temporary credit gives a big boost to current investment. (Of course, the next few years might see substantially decreased investment, as the capital spending pipeline had been emptied.) In this way, a temporary investment tax credit can be a particularly effective policy tool for boosting current investment spending. Unfortunately, governments are rarely able to so finely time tax changes.

high, firms will want to produce more assets, so investment will be rapid. In fact, the most simple version of this theory has a stronger prediction than "high q means high investment." Whenever q is greater than 1, a firm should add physical capital because for each dollar's worth of new machinery, the firm can sell stock for q dollars and pocket a profit $q - 1$. This implies a flood of investment whenever $q > 1$. In reality, adjustment costs (discussed below) make such a flood inefficient, so investment rises moderately with q.

FROM DESIRED CAPITAL STOCK TO INVESTMENT

Figure 14-4 illustrates an increase in the demand for the stock of capital by a rightward shift of the demand for capital schedule. At the initial capital stock, K_0, the price of capital is just high enough to generate enough investment, I_0 in panel (*b*), to replace depreciating capital. In the long run, the supply of new capital is very elastic, so eventually the increase in demand will be met without much change in price. In the short run, the price rises to P_1, increasing the investment flow to I_1. Implicitly, the unit of measurement in panel (*a*) is units of capital, so the shift from K_0 to K_1 might mean from 100 Boeing 747s to 150. The unit of measure meant in panel (*b*) is units of capital per period of time. The increased investment, moving from I_0 to I_1, would correspond to 11 new planes per year versus 10 new planes per year. Note that investment at rate I_1 needn't close the capital gap in a single period. The horizontal scales in panels (*a*) and (*b*) are not commensurable.

Why doesn't investment rise to instantaneously close the gap between the desired and existing capital stock? In two words, "adjustment costs." For one thing, the factors

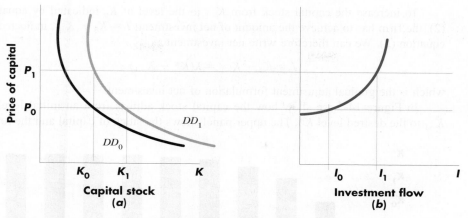

FIGURE 14-4   DEMAND FOR CAPITAL STOCK AND FLOW OF INVESTMENT.

Panel (a) shows an increase in demand for the capital stock raising prices from P_0 to P_1 in the short run and raising the capital stock from K_0 to K_1 in the long run. Panel (b) shows the corresponding increase in investment flow.

of production used to produce new capital are often themselves in limited short-run supply. (When the Seattle area experienced a major construction boom in 1999, skilled electricians were working 10-hour days, 7 days a week.) And many kinds of production just can't be sped up at any price, at least not in the short run.[5]

Capital Stock Adjustment

There are a number of hypotheses about the speed at which firms plan to adjust their capital stock over time; we single out the flexible accelerator model.[6] The basic notion behind this model is that **the larger the gap between the existing capital stock and the desired capital stock, the more rapid a firm's rate of investment.**

According to the flexible accelerator model, firms plan to close a fraction, λ, of the gap between the desired and actual capital stocks each period. Denote the capital stock at the end of the last period by K_{-1}. The gap between the desired and actual capital stocks is $(K^* - K_{-1})$. The firm plans to add to last period's capital stock K_{-1} a fraction λ of the gap $(K^* - K_{-1})$ so that the actual capital stock at the end of the current period K_0 will be

$$K_0 = K_{-1} + \lambda(K^* - K_{-1}) \qquad (2)$$

---

[5]There is a very old joke about an efficiency expert who decides that 9 months is too long for a pregnancy and figures that if he assigns two women to the job he should be able to get the job done in 4.5 months. For a more economic approach, see Russell Cooper and John Haltiwanger, "On the Nature of Capital Adjustment Costs," NBER working paper no. W7925, September 2000.

[6]The flexible accelerator model can be given a rigorous justification as a response to adjustment costs, but we don't pursue this avenue.

To increase the capital stock from K_{-1} to the level of K_0 indicated by equation (2), the firm has to achieve the amount of net investment, $I \equiv K_0 - K_{-1}$, indicated by equation (2). We can therefore write net investment as

$$I = K_0 - K_{-1} = \lambda(K^* - K_{-1}) \tag{3}$$

which is the gradual adjustment formulation of net investment.

In Figure 14-5 we show how the capital stock adjusts from an initial level of K_{-1} to the desired level K^*. The upper panel shows the stock of capital and the lower

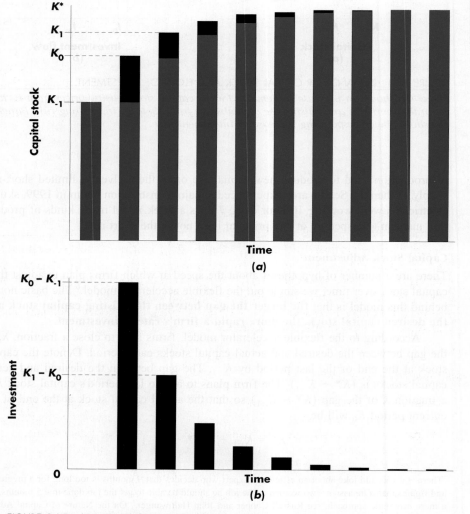

FIGURE 14-5   ADJUSTMENT OF THE CAPITAL STOCK.

If the desired capital stock changes, the capital stock adjusts to the new desired level over time, with investment in each period determined by the speed-of-adjustment parameter, λ.

shows the corresponding flow of investment. The assumed speed of adjustment is $\lambda = .5$.

Starting from K_{-1}, one-half the gap between target capital and current actual capital is made up in every period. First-period net investment is therefore $.5(K^* - K_{-1})$. In the second period, investment will be one-half the previous period's rate, since the gap has been reduced by half. Investment continues until the actual capital stock reaches the level of target capital. The larger λ is, the faster the gap is reduced.

In equation (3), we have reached our goal of deriving an investment function that shows current investment spending determined by the desired stock of capital, K^*, and the actual stock of capital, K_{-1}. Any factor that increases the desired capital stock increases the rate of investment. Therefore, an increase in expected output, a reduction in the real interest rate, or an increase in the investment tax credit will each increase the rate of investment. The flexible accelerator demonstrates that investment contains aspects of *dynamic behavior*—that is, behavior that depends on values of economic variables in periods other than the current period. Empirical evidence shows that the dynamics of the flexible accelerator are somewhat too rigid—for example, investment takes about 2 years to peak after a change in capital demand—but the basic principle of gradual adjustment is clear.

14-2

INVESTMENT SUBSECTORS—BUSINESS FIXED, RESIDENTIAL, AND INVENTORY

Figure 14-6 demonstrates the volatility of each of the three investment subsectors: *business fixed investment, residential investment,* and *inventory investment.* Fluctuations are on the order of several percent of GDP. Business fixed investment is the largest of the three, but all three subsectors undergo swings that are substantial fractions of swings in GDP. Inventory investment is considerably smaller than the other two portions, but as you can see, it is particularly volatile.

BUSINESS FIXED INVESTMENT

Figure 14-6 shows fixed investment as a share of GDP. In a recession or shortly before, the share of investment in GDP falls sharply; then investment begins to rise as the recovery gets under way. The cyclical relationships extend much further back in history. For instance, gross investment fell to less than 4 percent of GDP in the Great Depression years 1932 and 1933.

The Timing of Investment

Credit Rationing and Internal Sources of Finance   Table 14-1 shows the sources of manufacturing firms' funding in the United States during the period 1970–1984. The predominance of retained earnings as a source of financing stands out. Firms of all

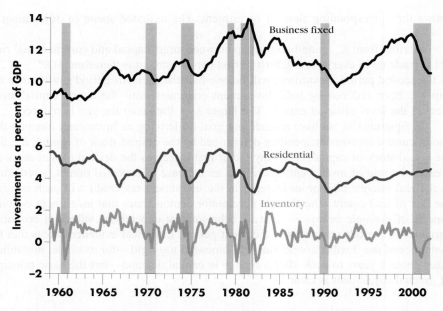

FIGURE 14-6   COMPONENTS OF INVESTMENT AS A PERCENTAGE OF GDP, 1959–2002.
The three different types of investment are shown: residential investment, business fixed investment, and inventory investment. The latter is very small and sometimes negative, but it is also relatively very volatile. (Source: Bureau of Economic Analysis.)

sizes use outside funding from banks, bond markets, and equity only to a limited extent.[7] Instead, they rely on retained earnings, profits that they do not pay out to stockholders, to finance investment. As the last column of the table shows, retained earnings exceeds 50 percent of earnings for all firms and is relatively most important for the smallest firms.

What do these facts mean for the investment decision? They suggest that there is a close link between the earnings of firms and their investment decisions. If firms cannot readily obtain funding from outside sources when they need it, the amount of assets they have on hand will affect their ability to invest. This would mean that the state of a firm's balance sheet, and not just the cost of capital, is a financial determinant of investment decisions.

Box 14-6 describes the important phenomenon of *credit rationing,* which occurs when individuals cannot borrow even though they are willing to do so at the existing interest rates. There are good reasons for credit rationing, all stemming from the risk that the borrower will not repay the lender, for instance, because the borrower goes bankrupt. These arguments suggest that credit rationing is more likely for small firms

[7]Equity funding is excluded from the table, but independent evidence, noted in the article by Fazzari, Hubbard, and Petersen (cited in Table 14-1) shows that it provides very little financing for firms, especially small ones.

TABLE 14-1 Sources of Funds, U.S. Manufacturing Firms, 1970–1984

	SOURCE OF FUNDS, % OF TOTAL*				
FIRM SIZE	SHORT-TERM BANK DEBT	LONG-TERM BANK DEBT	OTHER LONG-TERM BANK DEBT	RETAINED EARNINGS	PERCENT OF LONG-TERM DEBT FROM BANKS	AVERAGE RETENTION RATIO, %
All firms	0.6	8.4	19.0	71.1	29.6	60
Asset class						
Under $10 million	5.1	12.8	6.2	75.9	67.3	79
Over $1 billion	−0.6	4.8	27.9	67.9	14.7	52

*Minus sign indicates that firms have net assets (rather than liabilities) in this category.

Source: Steven M. Fazzari, R. Glenn Hubbard, and Bruce C. Petersen, "Financing Constraints and Corporate Investment," *Brookings Papers on Economic Activity* 1 (1988).

without an established reputation than for large firms with a track record. The fact that the retention ratio in Table 14-1 declines with firm size is consistent with this implication. These data, as well as the experience of firms that want to borrow, are consistent with the assumption that firms are rationed in their access to funding.[8]

Under such conditions, firms' investment decisions will be affected not only by the interest rate but also by the amount of funds the firms have saved out of past earnings and by their current profits. The cost of capital must still affect the investment decision, because firms that retain earnings have to consider the alternative of holding financial assets and earning interest rather than investing in plant and equipment. There is indeed evidence that the rate of investment is affected by the volume of retained earnings and by profits, as well as by the cost of capital.

In the early 1990s, in the aftermath of severe banking problems due to losses in real estate, credit rationing was held responsible for the slow—despite low short-term interest rates—rate of investment in the United States. Banks were lending very little, especially to small- and medium-size firms. The problem was especially severe in depressed regions, because small businesses can only borrow locally, from banks, but banks in a depressed region are especially unwilling to lend.

Irreversibility and the Timing of Investment Decisions   Beneath the stock-demand-for-capital-leads-to-investment-flow model lies the idea that capital is "putty-putty." Goods are in a malleable form that can be transformed into capital by investment and then easily transformed back into general goods. Much capital is better described as "putty-clay." Once capital is built, it can't be used for much except its original purpose.

[8]See Stephen D. Oliner and Glenn D. Rudebusch, "Is There a Broad Credit Channel for Monetary Policy?" Federal Reserve Bank of San Francisco *Economic Review* 1 (1996), for evidence showing that internal sources of funds are especially important for small firms and especially important in downturns.

BOX 14-6   Credit Rationing

In the *IS-LM* model, interest rates are the only channel of transmission between financial markets and aggregate demand. Credit rationing is an important additional channel of transmission of monetary policy.* **Credit rationing takes place when lenders limit the amount individuals can borrow, even though the borrowers are willing to pay the going interest rate on their loans.**

Credit rationing can occur for two different reasons. First, a lender often cannot tell whether a particular customer (or the project the customer is financing) is good or bad. A bad customer will default on the loan and not repay it. Given the risk of default, the obvious answer seems to be to raise the interest rate.

However, raising interest rates works the wrong way: Honest or conservative customers are deterred from borrowing because they realize their investments are not profitable at higher interest rates. But customers who are reckless or dishonest will borrow because they do not in any case expect to pay if the project turns out badly. However carefully they try to evaluate their customers, the lenders cannot altogether escape this problem. The answer is to limit the amount lent to any one customer. Most customers get broadly the same interest rate (with some adjustments), but the amount of credit they are allowed is rationed, according to both the kind of security the customer can offer and the prospects for the economy.

When times are good, banks lend cheerfully because they believe that the average customer will not default. When the economy turns down, credit rationing intensifies—and this may happen even though interest rates decline.

Credit rationing provides another channel for monetary policy. If lenders perceive that the Fed is shifting to restraint and higher interest rates to cool down the economy, lenders fearing a slowdown will tighten credit. Conversely, if they believe policy is expansionary and times will be good, they ease credit, via both lower interest rates and expanded credit rationing.[†]

A second type of credit rationing can occur when the central bank imposes credit limits on commercial banks and other lenders. Banks are then not allowed to expand their loans during a given period by more than, say, 5 percent or even less. Such a credit limit can bring a boom to an abrupt end. A striking example occurred in the United States in early 1980. Concerned with the risk of double-digit inflation, the Fed clamped on credit controls. In no time the economy fell into a recession, with output falling at an annual rate of 9 percent.

Credit controls thus are an emergency brake for the central bank. They work, but they do so in a very blunt way. For that reason, their use is very infrequent and remains reserved for occasions when dramatic, fast effects are desired.

*For a comprehensive survey on credit rationing, see Dwight Jaffee and Joseph Stiglitz, "Credit Rationing" in Ben Friedman and Frank Hahn (eds.), *Handbook of Monetary Economics* (Amsterdam: North-Holland, 1990).

[†]Frederick Mishkin provides a readable introduction to the transmission mechanism between monetary policy and the private economy in "Symposium on the Monetary Transmission Mechanism," *Journal of Economic Perspectives,* Fall 1995. In the same issue, see also John B. Taylor, "The Monetary Transmission Mechanism: An Empirical Framework," Ben S. Bernanke and Mark Gertler, "Inside the Black Box: The Credit Channel of Monetary Policy Transmission," and Allan H. Meltzer, "Monetary, Credit (and Other) Transmission Processes: A Monetarist Perspective."

A warehouse (putty-putty) may have high-valued alternative uses as a factory or an office building. A jetliner (putty-clay) isn't of much use except for flying. The essence of putty-clay investment is that it is *irreversible*. An irreversible investment will be executed not when it becomes merely profitable but, rather, when it does not pay to wait for any further improvement in profitability.[9]

◆ O P T I O N A L ◆

The Business Investment Decision: The View from the Trenches

Businesspeople making investment decisions typically use *discounted cash flow analysis*.[10] The principles of discounting are described in Chapter 17. Consider a businessperson deciding whether to build and equip a new factory. The first step is to figure out how much it will cost to get the factory into working order and how much revenue the factory will bring in each year after it starts operation.

For simplicity, consider a very short lived project, one that costs $100 to set up in the first year and then generates $50 in revenue (after paying for labor and raw materials) in the second year and a further $80 in the third year. By the end of the third year the factory has disintegrated.

Should the project be undertaken? Discounted cash flow analysis says that the revenues received in later years should be *discounted* to the present in order to calculate their present value. If the interest rate is 10 percent, $110 a year from now is worth the same as $100 now. (See Chapter 17 for a more extended discussion.) Why? Because if $100 is lent out today at 10 percent, a year from now the lender will end up with $110. To calculate the value of the project, the firm calculates the project's present discounted value at the interest rate at which it can borrow. If the present value is positive, the project is undertaken.

Suppose that the relevant interest rate is 12 percent. The calculation of the present discounted value of the investment project is shown in Table 14-2. The $50 received in year 2 is worth only $44.65 today: $1 a year from now is worth $1/1.12 = 0.893 today, and so $50 a year from now is worth $44.65. The present value of the $80 received in year 3 is calculated similarly. The table shows that the present value of the net revenue received from the project is positive ($8.41); thus, the firm should undertake the project.

Note that if the interest rate had been much higher—say, 18 percent—the decision would have been *not* to undertake the investment. We thus see that **the higher the interest rate, the less likely the firm will be to undertake any given investment project.**

---

[9]This statement is based on a sophisticated argument in terms of financial option theory. See Robert Pindyck, "Irreversible Investment, Capacity and Choice and the Value of the Firm," *American Economic Review*, December 1988; and Avinash K. Dixit and Robert S. Pindyck, *Investment under Uncertainty* (Princeton, NJ: Princeton University Press, 1993).

[10]Discounted cash flow analysis and the rental-cost-equals-marginal-product-of-capital models are simply different ways of thinking about the same decision process. You will sometimes hear businesspeople discussing what we call the marginal product of capital as the "internal rate of return."

TABLE 14-2 Discounted Cash Flow Analysis and Present Value
(Dollars)

	YEAR 1	YEAR 2	YEAR 3	PRESENT DISCOUNTED VALUE
Cash or revenue	−100	+50	+80	
Present value of $1	1	1/1.12 = 0.893	1/1.12^2 = 0.797	
Present value of costs or revenue	−100	50 × 0.893 = 44.65	80 × 0.797 = 63.76	−100 + 44.65 + 63.76 = 8.41

At any time, each firm has an array of possible investment projects and estimates of the costs and revenues from those projects. Depending on the level of the interest rate, the firm will want to undertake some of the projects and not undertake others. Adding the investment demands of all the firms in the economy, we obtain the total demand for investment in the economy at each interest rate.

RESIDENTIAL INVESTMENT

Figure 14-7 shows residential investment spending as a percentage of GDP, together with the nominal mortgage interest rate. Residential investment is low when mortgage interest rates are high, and it declines in all recessions.

Residential investment consists of the building of single-family and multifamily dwellings, which we call *housing* for short. Housing is distinguished as an asset by its long life. Consequently, investment in housing in any one year tends to be a very small proportion—about 3 percent—of the existing stock of housing. The theory of residential investment starts by considering the demand for the existing *stock* of housing.

The demand for the housing stock depends on the net real return obtained by owning housing. The gross return—before taking costs into account—consists either of rent, if the housing is rented out, or of the implicit return that the homeowner receives by living in the home plus capital gains arising from increases in the value of the housing. In turn, the costs of owning the housing consist of interest costs, typically the mortgage interest rate, plus any real estate taxes and depreciation. These costs are deducted from the gross return and, after tax adjustments, constitute the net return. An increase in the net return on housing, caused, for example, by a reduction in the mortgage interest rate, makes housing a more attractive form in which to hold wealth.

MONETARY POLICY AND HOUSING INVESTMENT

Monetary policy has powerful effects on housing investment. Part of the reason is that most houses are purchased with mortgages. Since the 1930s, a mortgage in the United

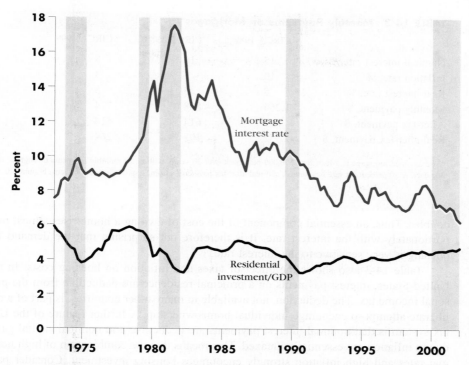

FIGURE 14-7   RESIDENTIAL INVESTMENT AND MORTGAGE INTEREST RATES, 1973–2002.

Residential investment spending as a percentage of GDP is low when nominal mortgage rates are high. Residential investment declines in recessions. (Source: Bureau of Economic Analysis and www.economagic.com.)

States has typically been a debt instrument of very long maturity, 20 to 30 years, with fixed monthly repayments until maturity.[11]

Monetary policy has powerful effects on housing investment because the demand for housing is sensitive to the interest rate. There is sensitivity to both the *real* and the *nominal* interest rates. The reason for this sensitivity can be seen in Table 14-3, which shows the monthly payment that has to be made by someone borrowing $100,000 through a conventional mortgage at different interest rates. All these interest rates have existed at some time during the last 20 years: 10 percent at the end of the 1970s and end of the 1980s, 15 percent in 1981 and 1982, and 8 percent at the end of 1999. The monthly repayment by the borrower approximately doubles when the interest rate

[11]Adjustable rate mortgages (ARMs) were introduced in the United States in the 1970s. The interest rate on such mortgages is adjusted in accordance with some reference rate, such as the 1-year Treasury-bill rate. Both fixed rate mortgages and ARMs are now used to finance housing. Arrangements for housing finance differ significantly across countries. Five-year renewable mortgages are common in Canada. In Japan and Korea, home buyers (and family) provide more housing funding than is common in the United States.

TABLE 14-3   Monthly Payments on Mortgages*

	CIRCA 1982	CIRCA 1988	CIRCA 1999
Nominal interest rate, %	15	10	8
Inflation rate, %	10	5	3
Real interest rate, %	5	5	5
Monthly payment, $	1,264	878	774
After-tax payment, $	885	614	514
Real after-tax payment, $	52	198	264

*The assumed mortgage is a loan for $100,000 paid back over 30 years, with equal monthly payments throughout the 30 years. A 30 percent tax rate is assumed, and real after-tax payments assume capital gains are effectively untaxed.

doubles. Thus, an essential component of the cost of owning a home rises almost proportionately with the interest rate. It is therefore not surprising that the demand for housing is very sensitive to the interest rate.

Table 14-3 also shows the effect of taxes and inflation on housing costs. In the United States, interest payments on a principal residence are deductible from the personal income tax. The deduction, not available in many other countries, is part of a deliberate attempt to encourage individual homeownership. A further feature of the U.S. tax system is that nominal interest payments are deductible and nominal capital gains due to inflation are essentially untaxed. This means that the combination of high nominal rates and high inflation strongly encourages housing investment. Consider payments on a $100,000 mortgage when the nominal interest rate is 15 percent and the inflation rate is 10 percent. Annual interest is approximately $15,000. For a homeowner in the 30 percent marginal tax bracket, the mortgage interest deduction is $4,500, so the after-tax interest cost is approximately $10,500. But at 10 percent inflation, this cost is offset by a $10,000 increase in the nominal value of the house. In effect, the real cost of capital for the house is nearly zero.

Despite this analysis, high nominal interest rates do discourage homeownership because of two kinds of liquidity effects. First, the homeowner has to make the full nominal payments up front and receives the offsetting capital gain far in the future. Second, banks use rules of thumb to qualify mortgage applicants (e.g., that payments can be no more than 28 percent of income) that don't adjust very much in periods of high inflation. Both these liquidity effects depend on the nominal, not real, interest rate.

INVENTORY INVESTMENT

Inventories consist of raw materials, goods in the process of production, and completed goods held by firms in anticipation of the products' sale. The ratio of manufacturing inventories to sales in the United States historically has been in the range of 13 to 17 percent. Adoption of *just-in time* manufacturing techniques has led to today's lower ratio of about 11.5 percent, as indicated in Figure 14-8.

FIGURE 14-8   RATIO OF MANUFACTURING INVENTORIES TO SALES.

(*Source: U.S. Census Bureau, Current Industrial Reports.*)

Firms hold inventories for several reasons:

- Sellers hold inventories to meet future demand for goods, because goods cannot be instantly manufactured or obtained to meet demand.
- Inventories are held because it is less costly for a firm to order goods less frequently in large quantities than to order small quantities frequently—just as the average householder finds it is useful to keep several days' worth of groceries in the house to avoid having to visit the supermarket daily.
- Producers may hold inventories as a way of smoothing their production. Since it is costly to keep changing the level of output on a production line, producers may produce at a relatively steady rate even when demand fluctuates, building up inventories when demand is low and drawing them down when demand is high.
- Some inventories are held as an unavoidable part of the production process. There is an inventory of meat and sawdust inside the sausage machine during the manufacture of sausage, for example.

Firms have a desired ratio of inventories to final sales that depends on economic variables. The smaller the cost of ordering new goods and the greater the speed with which such goods arrive, the smaller the inventory-sales ratio. The inventory-sales ratio may also depend on the level of sales, with the ratio falling with sales because there is relatively less uncertainty about sales as sales increase.

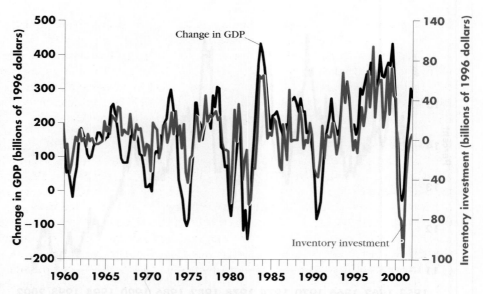

FIGURE 14-9   CHANGE IN GDP AND THE LEVEL OF INVENTORY INVESTMENT.
(Source: Bureau of Economic Analysis.)

Finally, there is the *interest rate*. Since firms carry inventories over time, the firms must tie up resources in order to buy and hold the inventories. There is an interest cost involved in such inventory holding, and the desired inventory-sales ratio should be expected to fall with increases in the interest rate.

The Accelerator Model

All these considerations notwithstanding, inventory investment can be explained surprisingly well with the simple *accelerator model*. **The accelerator model asserts that investment spending is proportional to the change in output and is not affected by the cost of capital,** $I = \alpha(Y - Y_{-1})$.[12] Figure 14-9 compares inventory investment to the change in GDP. Much, but not all, inventory investment can be explained this way. The connection of the *level* of inventory investment to the *change* in output is an important channel adding to the overall volatility of the economy.

Anticipated versus Unanticipated Inventory Investment

Inventory investment **takes place when firms increase their inventories.** The central aspect of inventory investment lies in the distinction between anticipated (desired) and unanticipated (undesired) investment. Inventory investment could be high in two circumstances. First, if sales are unexpectedly low, firms would find unsold inventories accumulating on their shelves; that constitutes unanticipated inventory investment.

---

[12]The accelerator model is actually a special case of the flexible accelerator. (The former came first.) To see this, ignore the role of the rental cost and set $\lambda = 1$ in the formula for the flexible accelerator.

Second, inventory investment could be high because firms plan to build up inventories; that is anticipated or desired investment.

The two circumstances obviously have very different implications for the behavior of aggregate demand. Unanticipated inventory investment is a result of unexpectedly low aggregate demand. By contrast, planned inventory investment adds to aggregate demand. Thus rapid accumulation of inventories could be associated with either rapidly declining aggregate demand or rapidly increasing aggregate demand.

Inventories in the Business Cycle

Inventory investment fluctuates proportionately more in the business cycle than any other component of aggregate demand. In every post-World War II recession in the United States there has been a decline in inventory investment between peak and trough. As a recession develops, demand slows down and firms add involuntarily to the stock of inventories. Thus, the inventory-sales ratio rises. Then production is cut, and firms meet demand by selling goods from inventories. At the end of every recession, firms were reducing their inventories, meaning that inventory investment was negative in the final quarter of every recession.

The role of inventories in the business cycle is a result of a combination of unanticipated and anticipated inventory change. Figure 14-10 illustrates the combination using data from the deep recession at the start of the 1980s. Before the 1981–1982 recession began, GDP increased rapidly, recovering from the previous recession. That meant firms were running down their inventories. From the beginning of 1981, firms began to accumulate inventories, as output exceeded their sales. Firms were probably anticipating high sales in the future and decided to build up their stocks of goods for future sale. Thus, there was *intended* inventory accumulation.

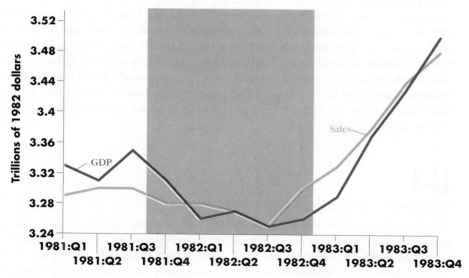

FIGURE 14-10   SALES AND OUTPUT IN RECESSION AND RECOVERY, 1981–1983.
The shaded area marks the period of recession. (Source: Bureau of Economic Analysis.)

Final sales turned down at the beginning of 1981, but GDP stayed high until the third quarter. Thus, the first half of 1981 was a period of *unintentional* inventory accumulation. Then firms realized their inventories were too high, and they cut production to get them back in line. In the first quarter of 1982, firms cut output way back and finally were successfully and *intentionally* reducing their inventories; hence, in that quarter sales exceeded output. This stage, in which output falls sharply as firms intentionally cut back production to get inventories back in line, has been typical in post-World War II recessions. Finally, inventories were built up *intentionally* as the recovery got under way in 1983.

To understand the *inventory cycle,* consider the case of a hypothetical automobile dealer who sells, say, thirty cars per month and holds an average of 1 month's sales—namely, thirty cars—in inventory. As long as sales stay steady at thirty cars per month, the dealer will be ordering thirty cars each month from the factory. Now suppose sales drop to twenty-five cars per month, and it takes the dealer 2 months to respond to the change. During those 2 months inventory will have climbed to forty cars. In the future, the dealer will want an inventory of only twenty-five cars on hand. Thus, when responding to the fall in demand, the dealer cuts the order from the factory from thirty cars to ten in the third month to get the inventory back to 1 month's sales. After the desired inventory-sales ratio has been restored, the order will be twenty-five cars per month. We see in this extreme case how the drop in demand of five cars, instead of leading to a simple drop in car output of five cars per month, causes a drop in output of twenty cars in 1 month, followed by the longer-run drop in output of five cars per month.

Just-in-Time Inventory Management   If inventories could be kept more closely in line with sales, or aggregate demand, fluctuations in inventory investment and in GDP would be reduced. As business methods are improving all the time, the hope is often expressed that new methods of management will enable firms to keep tighter control over their inventories and thus that the prospects for steadier growth can be improved. *Just-in-time inventory management* techniques, imported from Japan, emphasize the synchronization of suppliers and users of materials, thereby allowing firms to operate with small inventories, so production is "lean" in inventories. These improved methods help account for the downward trend in inventories. Indeed, in the 1990–1991 and 2001–? recessions, the inventory–final sales ratio increased very little, much less than in previous recessions.

14-3

INVESTMENT AND AGGREGATE SUPPLY

Investment is an important component of aggregate demand. Investment also increases capital, increasing the productive capacity of the economy. Does investment matter for aggregate supply? In the short run, no it doesn't. In the long run, yes it does. A little back-of-the-envelope arithmetic can help us make sense of this apparent contradiction.

We saw in Box 14-1 that a year's worth of investment is typically about 1/15 of the capital stock. Suppose someone found a policy to increase investment by 25 percent more than it would have otherwise grown. (The historical record suggests no one has come up with an idea nearly this effective—but hope springs eternal!) Over the course of a year, the effect of the policy would be to increase capital by about 1/60 extra, or about 1.6 percent. Looking back at what we learned about growth accounting in Chapter 3 [look back at equation (2)], this would translate into an increase in GDP of about 4/10 of 1 percent. The notion that short-run policy might increase investment by 25 percent is probably outlandish. The short-run supply-side effect of any realistic policy will probably be too small to measure.

So claims of stimulating investment in hope of a short-run supply-side effect are probably silly. *But* increasing investment may be among the most important tools for creating long-term prosperity. The effect of modest annual increases in the capital stock can cumulate to be quite large over long periods. We can see evidence by looking at the very high rates of investment as countries move into modern development with very high rates of growth sustained for considerable periods.

INVESTMENT AROUND THE WORLD

One reason that high-growth countries *are* high-growth countries is because they devote a substantial fraction of their output to investment. Table 14-4 shows the ratio of gross fixed capital formation to GDP for several countries. The investment ratios are determined by both the demand for capital, as studied in this chapter, and the supply of savings.

Table 14-4 suggests that high rates of investment occur in rapidly growing countries but not necessarily in countries that have already become very wealthy. In both 1975 and 2001, the United States and Canada were wealthy countries with moderate growth rates. In 1975, Japan was a moderately well off country with a high growth rate. Over this period, both Singapore and Korea grew very rapidly, due in part to their high rates of investment, but had not yet reached the income levels of the United States. In 1975, the three poor countries shown, Bangladesh, Ethiopia, and Ghana, had investment

TABLE 14-4	Ratio of Investment to Output (Percent)	
COUNTRY	1975	2001
United States	18.2	19.5
Canada	24.4	19.8
Japan	32.5	25.8
Korea	26.8	27.1
Singapore	35.1	29.2
Bangladesh	5.5	24.1
Ethiopia	10.5	17.6*
Ghana	11.6	23.7†

*For 1998.

†For 1997.

Source: *International Financial Statistics Yearbook* 2002; ratio of gross fixed capital formation to GDP.

rates too low to support rapid growth. By 2001, although all three countries remained relatively poor, their investment rates had picked up considerably.

The relatively low rates of investment in the United States and Canada, compared with their international competitors, are a source of long-run concern to policymakers.

SUMMARY

1. Investment is spending that adds to the capital stock. Investment usually constitutes about 14 percent of aggregate demand in the United States, but fluctuations in investment account for a large share of business cycle movements in GDP. We analyze investment in three categories: business fixed investment, residential investment, and inventory investment.

2. The neoclassical theory of business fixed investment sees the rate of investment being determined by the speed with which firms adjust their capital stocks toward the desired level. The desired capital stock is bigger the larger the *expected* output the firm plans to produce and the smaller the rental or user cost of capital.

3. The real interest rate is the nominal (stated) interest rate minus the inflation rate.

4. The rental cost of capital is higher the higher the real interest rate, the lower the price of the firm's stock, and the higher the depreciation rate of capital. Taxes also affect the rental cost of capital, in particular through the investment tax credit. The investment tax credit is, in effect, a government subsidy for investment.

5. In practice, firms decide how much to invest using discounted cash flow analysis. This analysis gives answers that are consistent with those of the neoclassical approach.

6. The flexible accelerator model of investment illustrates a special case of the gradual adjustment model of investment.

7. Because credit is rationed, firms' investment decisions are affected also by the state of their balance sheets, and thus by the amount of earnings they have retained.

8. Empirical results show that business fixed investment responds with long lags to changes in output. The accelerator model, which does not take into account changes in the rental cost of capital, does almost as good a job of explaining investment as the more sophisticated neoclassical model.

9. The theory of housing investment starts from the demand for the *stock* of housing. Demand is affected by wealth, the interest rates available on alternative investments, and the mortgage rate. The price of housing is determined by the interaction of the stock demand and the fixed stock supply of housing available at any given time. The rate of housing investment is determined by the rate at which builders supply housing at the going price.

10. Housing investment is affected by monetary policy because housing demand is sensitive to the mortgage interest rate (real and nominal). Credit availability also plays a role.

11. Monetary policy and fiscal policy both affect investment, particularly business fixed investment and housing investment. The effects take place through changes in real (and nominal, in the case of housing) interest rates and through tax incentives for investment.

12. There are substantial lags in the adjustment of investment spending to changes in output and other determinants of investment. Such lags are likely to increase fluctuations in GDP.

13. Inventory investment fluctuates proportionately more than any other class of investment. Firms have a desired inventory-to-sales ratio. The ratio may get out of line if sales are unexpectedly high or low, and then firms change their production levels to adjust inventories. For instance, when aggregate demand falls at the beginning of a recession, inventories build up. Then when firms cut back production, output falls even more than did aggregate demand. This is the inventory cycle.

KEY TERMS

accelerator model	dynamic behavior	just-in-time inventory
business fixed investment	expected inflation rate	management
capital gains	expected real interest rate	marginal product of capital
capital stock	flexible accelerator	opportunity cost
credit rationing	model	q theory of investment
diminishing marginal	flow of investment	real interest rates
product	inventory cycle	rental (user) cost of capital
discounted cash flow	inventory investment	residential investment
analysis	investment	

PROBLEMS

Conceptual

1. If an economy has achieved its desired capital stock and wishes merely to maintain it, should any investment occur? If not, why not? If so, how much?

2. What effect has the recent shift toward investment in high-tech capital goods had on the rate of depreciation? Do you think there is a rate of depreciation associated with the stock of human capital?

3. If a firm invests out of retained profits rather than borrowed funds, will its investment decisions still be affected by the changes in the interest rate? Explain.

4. The model of business fixed investment studied in Section 14-1 examines the benefits and costs to firms of owning capital goods. Its basic conclusion is that firms will increase their capital stock as long as the marginal product of their capital exceeds the marginal cost. What is Tobin's q, and how does it relate to the model in 14-1?

5. According to the description of business fixed investment in this chapter, how would you expect a firm's investment decisions to be affected by a sudden increase in the demand for its product? What factors would determine the speed of its reaction?

6. The number of small firms in the U.S. economy has grown substantially over the last decade. If small firms do, indeed, encounter more credit rationing than large firms, what effect might this have on output fluctuations (business cycles) in the United States?

7. **a.** Give at least two reasons why higher profits may increase the rate of investment.
   b. Explain why lenders may ration the quantity of credit rather than merely charge higher interest rates to more risky borrowers.

8. **a.** Explain why the housing market usually prospers when the (real) mortgage rates are low.

   b. In some states, usury laws prohibit (nominal) mortgage rates in excess of a legal maximum. Explain how this could lead to an exception to the conclusion in (**a**).

9. What is the relationship between the accelerator model of inventory investment and the flexible accelerator model of capital accumulation?

10. Can changes in inventories predict movements in the business cycle? Why does it matter whether these changes are planned or unplanned?

11. In the 1990–1991 recession, the inventory-sales ratio did not rise appreciably. How do you explain this fact?

12. Why should (or shouldn't) policymakers be concerned about the relatively low levels of U.S. investment that have prevailed in the last decade?

13. In Chapter 5 you learned that when the aggregate supply curve is vertical, monetary policy has no effect on the real interest rate. Give two reasons why monetary policy might still affect investment even if it does not affect the interest rate.

Technical

1. Describe how a car rental agency would calculate the price at which it rents cars, and relate your description to the equation for rental cost given in the text.

2. The cash flows for an investment project are listed below. The firm will invest if the present value of the cash flows is positive.

Year 1	Year 2	Year 3
−200	100	120

   Should the firm undertake this project:
   a. If the interest rate is 5 percent?
   b. If the interest rate is 10 percent?

3. Suppose that an explicitly temporary tax credit is enacted. The tax credit is at the rate of 10 percent and lasts only 1 year.

   a. What is the effect of this tax measure on investment in the long run (say, after 4 or 5 years)?

   b. What is the effect in the current year and in the following year?

   c. How would your answers in (**a**) and (**b**) differ if the tax credit were permanent?

4. **a.** Explain how final sales and output can differ.

   b. In Figure 14-10, point out periods of planned and unplanned inventory investment and drawing down.

   c. During a period of slow but steady growth, how would you expect final sales and output to be related? Explain. Draw a hypothetical figure like Figure 14-10 for such a period.

5. Given the following information, calculate Tobin's q statistic: Let's suppose that a company has 1 million outstanding shares of stock, each valued at $25. Let us suppose also that the replacement cost of its physical capital stock is $18 million.

   a. Should this firm invest (net) in more physical capital?

   b. Would your answer change if the replacement cost of its physical capital stock at this time was $25 million? $28 million?

6. (*Optional*) For this question use the Cobb-Douglas production function and the corresponding desired capital stock given by $K^* = g(rc, Y) = \theta Y/rc$. Assume that $\theta = .3$, $Y = \$5$ trillion, and $rc = .12$.
    a. Calculate the desired capital stock, K^*.
    b. Now suppose that Y is expected to rise to $6 trillion. What is the corresponding desired capital stock?
    c. Suppose that the capital stock was at the desired level before the change in income was expected. Suppose further that $\lambda = .4$ in the gradual adjustment model of investment. What will the rate of investment be in the first year after expected income changes? In the second year?
    d. Does your answer in (**c**) refer to gross or net investment?
7. From 1947 through 1991, the average annual return to holding common stocks was 7 percent while the average annual percentage growth in business fixed investment was 3.5 percent. From 1992 through 1999, the average annual return to holding common stocks was 16 percent and the average annual percentage growth in business fixed investment was 8 percent. How would q theory link these changes?

Empirical

1. We have seen that investment spending constitutes about 14 percent of aggregate demand (GDP) in the United States. Are other countries consistently investing more than 14 percent of their output?
    a. Go to www.economagic.com. Under "Browse by Source," choose the heading "Central Bank of Europe." Choose the link "EU GDP and Components at Constant Prices," and download data for the following three variables: GDP, gross fixed capital formation (just a different name for investment), and change in inventories.
    b. Calculate the share of investment in GDP ($I/GDP \times 100$). On average, what is the share of investment spending in aggregate demand in the European Union?
    c. Figure 14-9 illustrates the relationship between changes in GDP and inventory investment in the United States. Replicate Figure 14-9 for European Union data.
2. Figure 14-7 illustrates the relationship between mortgage interest rates and the share of residential investment in GDP. Another way of looking at the same relationship is to take housing starts instead of the share of residential investment.
    a. Go to www.economagic.com. Under "Browse by Source," "Federal Reserve Board of Governors," choose the heading "Interest Rates." Scroll down the page and download the variable "30-Year Conventional Mortgages—Federal Home Loan Mortgage Corporation." Under "Browse by Source," "Census Bureau," choose the heading "Housing Starts." Under the heading "Housing Starts, Seasonally Adjusted at Annual Rates," select the variable "Total."
    b. Using EXCEL or the built-in graphing facilities at www.economagic.com, create a graph that includes both the mortgage interest rates and the housing starts. Visually, what is the relationship between these two variables?

CHAPTER 15

The Demand for Money

CHAPTER HIGHLIGHTS

- Money is whatever asset is used in transactions. This varies over time and place.

- Money demand is a demand for *real balances,* the number of dollars divided by the price level.

- The demand for money rises with higher income and falls with higher interest rates.

What is "money" and why does anyone want it?

This question is less frivolous than it appears, because economists use the term "money" in a special technical sense. By "money" we mean the medium of exchange, the stuff you use to pay for things—cash, for example. In colloquial use, "money" sometimes means "income" ("I made a lot of money last year") or "wealth" ("That guy has a lot of money"). **When economists speak of the "demand for money," we are asking about the stock of assets held as cash, checking accounts, and closely related assets, specifically *not* generic wealth or income.** Our interest is in why consumers and firms hold money as opposed to an asset with a higher rate of return. The interaction between the demand for money and the supply of money provides the link through which the monetary authority, the Federal Reserve in the United States, affects output and prices.

Money **is the means of payment or medium of exchange.** More informally, money is whatever is generally accepted in exchange. In the past, seashells or cocoa or gold coins served as money in different places. In the United States, *M*1, consisting of currency plus checkable deposits, comes closest to defining the means of payment. At the end of 2002, *M*1 was about $4,190 per person. There is lively debate concerning whether a broader group of monetary assets—*M*2, or even *M*3 (both discussed below and standing at about $20,080 and $29,480 per person, respectively)—might better meet the definition of money in a modern payments system.

Which assets constitute money? Discussions of the meaning of money are fluid for a simple reason: In the past, money was the means of payment generally accepted in exchange, but it also had the characteristic that it did not pay interest. Thus, the sum of currency and demand deposits (which did not earn interest in the United States) was the accepted definition of money for a long time. This aggregate is now known as *M*1. In the course of the 1980s, however, a widening range of interest-bearing assets also became checkable. That has forced an ongoing review on where to draw the line between assets that form part of our definition of money and those that are just financial assets and not money proper. The issue is important not only conceptually but also for the evaluation of which monetary aggregate the Fed should try to control.

Recall that aggregate demand rises when money supply increases faster than money demand—with a concomitant rise in output or the price level. When the demand for money rises the *LM* curve shifts left, reducing aggregate demand unless the monetary authority recognizes the increase in time to push up the money supply by an equal amount. Understanding money demand, and how various factors affect that demand, is therefore a first step in setting a target for the monetary authority. And while it's easy in setting out macro theory to simply have an asset labeled *M*, we'll see in this chapter that measuring and understanding money in the complex, many-asset world in which we live is considerably more difficult.

15-1

COMPONENTS OF THE MONEY STOCK

There is a vast array of financial assets in any economy, from currency to complicated claims on other financial assets. Which part of these assets is called money? In the

BOX 15-1   Components of the Monetary Aggregates

We briefly describe here the components of the monetary aggregates.

1. *Currency:* Consists of coins and notes in circulation.*
2. *Demand deposits:* Non-interest-bearing checking accounts at commercial banks, excluding deposits of other banks, the government, and foreign governments.
3. *Traveler's checks:* Only those checks issued by nonbanks (such as American Express). Traveler's checks issued by banks are included in demand deposits.
4. *Other checkable deposits:* Interest-earning checking accounts, with a variety of legal arrangements and marketing names.

$$M1 = (1) + (2) + (3) + (4)$$

5. *Money market mutual fund (MMMF) shares:* Interest-earning checkable deposits in mutual funds that invest in short-term assets. Some MMMF shares are held by institutions; these are excluded from $M2$ but included in $M3$.
6. *Money market deposit accounts (MMDAs):* MMMFs run by banks, with the advantage that they are insured up to $100,000. They were introduced at the end of 1982 to allow banks to compete with MMMFs.
7. *Savings deposits:* Deposits at banks and other thrift institutions that are not transferable by check and are often recorded in a separate passbook kept by the depositor.

United States, there are four main monetary aggregates: currency, $M1$, $M2$, $M3$, and L. Box 15-1 describes the components of the different measures of money.

$M1$ comprises those claims that can be used *directly, instantly,* and *without restrictions* to make payments. These claims are *liquid.* **An asset is liquid if it can immediately, conveniently, and cheaply be used for making payments.** $M1$ corresponds most closely to the traditional definition of money as the means of payment. $M2$ includes, in addition, claims that are not instantly liquid—withdrawal of time deposits, for example, may require notice to the depository institution; money market mutual funds may set a minimum on the size of checks drawn on an account. But with these qualifications, these additional claims also fall into a broader category of money. In $M3$ we include items that most people never see, namely, large negotiable deposits and repurchase agreements. These are held primarily by corporations but also by wealthy individuals. Finally, L includes several liquid assets that are close substitutes for, but that are not themselves, money.

As we move from the top to the bottom of the list in Box 15-1, the liquidity of the assets decreases, while their interest yield increases. Currency earns zero interest, checking accounts earn less than money market deposit accounts, and so on. This is a

8. *Small time deposits:* Interest-bearing deposits with a specific maturity date. Before that date they can be used only if a penalty is paid. "Small" means less than $100,000.

$$M2 = M1 + (5) + (6) + (7) + (8)$$

9. *Repurchase agreements (RPs):* Transactions in which a bank borrows from a non-bank customer. The bank sells a security (e.g., a Treasury bill) to the customer today and promises to buy it back at a fixed price tomorrow. That way the bank gets to use the amount borrowed for a day.

10. *Eurodollars:* Deposits that pay interest and mature the next day, held in overseas, typically Caribbean, branches of U.S. banks.

11. *Large-denomination time deposits:* Interest-earning deposits of more than $100,000 de-nomination. The total excludes amounts held by MMMFs or MMDAs (and some other in-stitutions) to make sure the same asset is not counted twice in the monetary aggregates.

12. *Institutional holdings of MMMFs.*

$$M3 = M2 + (9) + (10) + (11) + (12)$$

13. *Savings bonds:* U.S. government bonds, typically sold to small savers.

14. *Banker's acceptances:* Orders to pay a specific amount at a specific time that are obligations of banks. They arise largely in international trade.

15. *Commercial paper:* Short-term liabilities of corporations.

16. *Short-term Treasury securities:* Securities issued by the U.S. Treasury that have less than 12 months to maturity.

$$L = M3 + (13) + (14) + (15) + (16)$$

*A picture tour of the history of American currency can be found at www.frbsf.org/currency.

Source: *Federal Reserve Bulletin,* which reports the data and definition in each monthly issue.

---

typical economic tradeoff—in order to get more liquidity, asset holders have to give up yield.

M2 AND OTHER MONETARY AGGREGATES

All the assets described in Box 15-1 are to some extent substitutes for one another, and there is therefore no clear point at which to draw the line in defining money. *M2* adds to *M1* assets that are close to being usable as a medium of exchange. The largest part of *M2* consists of savings and small (less than $100,000) time deposits at banks and thrift institutions. These can be used with little difficulty for making payments. In the case of a savings deposit, the bank has to be notified to transfer funds from the savings deposit to a checking account; for time deposits, it is in principle necessary to wait until the time deposit matures or else to pay an interest penalty.

The second-largest category of assets in *M2* consists of money market mutual funds and deposit accounts. A money market mutual fund (MMMF) invests its assets in short-term interest-bearing securities, such as negotiable certificates of deposit (CDs) and Treasury bills.[1] MMMFs pay interest and permit the owner of the account to write checks against the account. Money market deposit accounts (MMDAs) are MMMFs held in commercial banks. A limited number of checks can be written against MMDAs each month. Obviously, MMDAs and MMMFs are close to being checkable deposits— but they also serve as financial investments.

Until 1987, $M1$ was the most closely watched money stock, both because it comes closest to the theoretical definition of money as a medium of exchange and because its demand function was reasonably stable. But after the demand for $M1$ became difficult to predict,[2] many economists, including those at the Federal Reserve Board, began to pay more attention to the behavior of $M2$. Since the early 1990s, the behavior of $M2$ has also become unpredictable, and $M3$ is not much better. Unpredictability of the demand for the monetary aggregates complicates the task of monetary policy, as we shall see in Chapter 16.

FINANCIAL INNOVATION

Changes in the definitions of the monetary aggregates followed financial innovations, frequently a result of attempts to get around government regulations. For instance, thrifts, which pay interest on deposits and had been forbidden to have checkable accounts, invented negotiable order of withdrawal (NOW) accounts as a way of getting around the prohibition. A NOW looks and smells like a check but is not, legally speaking, a check. Similarly, money market mutual funds were invented only in 1973. Until 1982, banks were not allowed to issue money market deposit accounts, but as soon as they were permitted to do so, there was a rapid inflow of such deposits to banks: MMDA deposits rose from zero in November 1982 to $320 billion in March 1983.

Clearly, there is no unique set of assets that will always constitute the money supply, nor are present definitions beyond question. For instance, there is a question of whether credit cards should be regarded as a means of making payment. And there are even arguments for using a *less* broad definition than $M1$—for example, should $1,000 bills, which are not easily used to buy groceries, be included? What is certain is that over the course of time, the particular assets that serve as a medium of exchange, or means of payment, will change further, and so will the definitions of the monetary aggregates.

 # 15-2

THE FUNCTIONS OF MONEY

Money is so widely used that we rarely step back to think how remarkable a device it is. It is impossible to imagine a modern economy operating without the use of money or something very much like it. **In a mythical barter economy in which there is no money,**

---

[1] Negotiable CDs are liabilities of the banks that can be bought and sold in the open market like other securities. Typically, they come in large denominations of $100,000 or more.

[2] Yoshihisa Baba, David Hendry, and Ross Starr provide a detailed investigation of the instability of $M1$ in "The Demand for $M1$ in the U.S.A., 1960–1988," *Review of Economic Studies,* January 1992.

BOX 15-2   Who's Got the Cash?

A 1995 survey of cash holdings of U.S. households, undertaken for the Federal Reserve System, showed that the average amount of currency held per person surveyed then was about $100.* At that time, total currency outstanding divided by population was $1,375. Thus, the vast majority of the currency outstanding is not held by U.S. households—or at least they do not admit to holding it. Some currency is held by legitimate businesses, but large amounts must be held to finance illegal activities, particularly drug-related ones, or are held outside the United States. In many countries undergoing severe financial distress, U.S. currency circulates in preference to local currency.

Since 1990, there has been a dramatic upswing in the proportion of U.S. currency held outside the United States. Richard Porter and Ruth Judson estimate that over $8 billion per year in currency now flows abroad.

*Richard D. Porter and Ruth A. Judson, "The Location of U.S. Currency: How Much Is Abroad?" *Federal Reserve Bulletin,* October 1996.

every transaction has to involve an exchange of goods (and/or services) on both sides of the transaction. The examples of the difficulties of barter are endless. The economist wanting a haircut would have to find a barber wanting to listen to a lecture on economics; the actor wanting a suit would have to find a tailor wanting to watch a performance; and so on. Without a medium of exchange, modern economies could not operate. **Money, as a *medium of exchange,* makes it unnecessary for there to be a "double coincidence of wants,"** such as the barber and economist bumping into each other at just the right time.

There are four traditional functions of money, of which medium of exchange is the first.[3] The other three are store of value, unit of account, and standard of deferred payment. These stand on a different footing from the medium-of-exchange function.

A *store of value* **is an asset that maintains value over time.** Thus, an individual holding a store of value can use that asset to make purchases at a future date. If an asset were not a store of value, it would not be used as a medium of exchange. Imagine trying to use ice cream as money in the absence of refrigerators. There would hardly ever be a good reason for anyone to give up goods for money (ice cream) if the money were sure to melt within the next few minutes. To be useful as money, an asset must be a store of value, but there are many stores of value other than money—such as bonds, stocks, and houses.

The *unit of account* **is the unit in which prices are quoted and books kept.** Prices are quoted in dollars and cents, and dollars and cents are the units in which the money stock is measured. Usually, the money unit is also the unit of account, but that is not essential. In many high-inflation countries, dollars become the unit of account even though the local money continues to serve as the medium of exchange.

---

[3]For the classic statement of the functions of money, see W. S. Jevons, *Money and the Mechanism of Exchange* (London: Kegan Paul, 1875).

Finally, as a *standard of deferred payment,* money units are used in long-term transactions, such as loans. The amount that has to be paid back in 5 or 10 years is specified in dollars and cents. Dollars and cents are acting as the standard of deferred payment. Once again, though, it is not essential that the standard of deferred payment be the money unit. For example, the final payment of a loan may be related to the behavior of the price level, rather than being fixed in dollars and cents. This is known as an indexed loan. The last two of the four functions of money are, accordingly, functions that money *usually* performs but not functions that it *necessarily* performs. And the store-of-value function is one that many assets perform.

There is one final point we want to reemphasize: **Money is whatever is generally accepted in exchange.** In the past an astounding variety of monies have been used: simple commodities such as seashells, then metals, pieces of paper representing claims on gold or silver, pieces of paper that are claims only on other pieces of paper, and then paper and electronic entries in banks' accounts.[4] However magnificently a piece of paper may be engraved, it is not money if it is not accepted in payment. And however unusual the material of which it is made, anything that is generally accepted in payment is money. There is thus an inherent circularity in the acceptance of money. **Money is accepted in payment only because of the belief that it will later also be accepted in payment by others.**

15-3

THE DEMAND FOR MONEY: THEORY

In this section we review the three major motives underlying the demand for money, and we concentrate on the effects of changes in income and the interest rate on money demand. Before we take up the discussion, we must make an essential point about money demand: **The demand for money is a demand for *real balances.*** In other words, people hold money for its purchasing power, for the amount of goods they can buy with it. They are not concerned with their *nominal* money holdings, that is, the number of dollar bills they hold. Two implications follow:

1. *Real* money demand is unchanged when the price level increases, and *all* real variables, such as the interest rate, real income, and real wealth, remain unchanged.
2. Equivalently, *nominal* money demand increases in proportion to the increase in the price level, given the real variables just specified.

In other words, we are interested in a money demand function which tells us the demand for real balances, M/P, not nominal balances, M. There is a special name for the behavior described here. **An individual is free from *money illusion* if a change in the level of prices, holding all real variables constant, leaves the person's real behavior, including real money demand, unchanged.**[5]

---

[4]See Glyn Davies, *A History of Money from Ancient Times to the Present* (Aberystwyth: University of Wales Press, 1994).

[5]Mixing economics and psychology, Eldar Shafir, Peter Diamond, and Amos Tversky describe fun experiments about money illusion in "Money Illusion," *Quarterly Journal of Economics,* May 1997.

The theories we are about to review correspond to Keynes's famous three motives for holding money:[6]

- The *transactions motive,* which is the demand for money arising from the use of money in making regular payments
- The *precautionary motive,* which is the demand for money to meet unforeseen contingencies
- The *speculative motive,* which arises from uncertainties about the money value of other assets that an individual can hold

In discussing the transactions and precautionary motives, we are mainly discussing $M1$, whereas the speculative motive refers more to $M2$ or $M3$, as we shall see.[7]

These theories of money demand **are built around a tradeoff between the benefits of holding more money versus the interest costs of doing so.** Money ($M1$, that is, currency and some checkable deposits) generally earns no interest or less interest than other assets. The higher the interest loss from holding a dollar of money, the less money we expect the individual to hold. In practice, we can measure the cost of holding money as the difference between the interest rate paid on money (perhaps zero) and the interest rate paid on the most nearly comparable other asset, such as a savings deposit or, for corporations, a certificate of deposit or commercial paper. **The interest rate on money is referred to as the *own rate of interest,* and the *opportunity cost* of holding money is equal to the difference between the yield on other assets and the own rate.**

TRANSACTIONS DEMAND

The transactions demand for money arises from the lack of synchronization of receipts and disbursements. In other words, you aren't likely to get paid at the exact instant you need to make a payment, so between paychecks you keep some money around in order to buy stuff. In this section we examine a simple model of how much money an individual will hold to make purchases.

The tradeoff here is between the amount of interest an individual forgoes by holding money and the costs and inconveniences of holding a small amount of money. To make the problem concrete, consider someone who is paid, say, $1,800 each month. Assume the person spends the $1,800 evenly over the course of the month, at the rate of $60 per day. Now at one extreme, the individual could simply leave the $1,800 in cash and spend it at the rate of $60 per day. Alternatively, on the first day of the month the individual could take $60 to spend that day and put the remaining $1,740 in a

---

[6]J. M. Keynes, *The General Theory of Employment, Interest and Money* (New York: Macmillan, 1936), chap. 13.

[7]Although we examine the demand for money by looking at the three motives for holding it, we cannot separate a particular person's money holdings, say, $500, into three neat piles of, say, $200, $200, and $100, each being held from a different motive. Money being held to satisfy one motive is always available for another use. The person holding unusually large balances for speculative reasons also has those balances available to meet an unexpected emergency, so they serve, too, as precautionary balances. All three motives influence an individual's holdings of money.

BOX 15-3   A Back-of-the-Envelope Calculation Using Income Elasticity

You are now the monetary authority of the small country of Baumol-Tobania. Real growth reliably averages 3 percent per year. How fast should you increase the money supply to stabilize the price level?

According to equation (1), 3 percent growth in GDP raises money demand 1.5 percent per year. If you increase the nominal money supply by the same 1.5 percent, real money supply and demand will stay in balance with a constant price level. If you had thought the income elasticity was 1 instead of ½ you would have created money at 3 percent per year, in the erroneous belief that money demand was rising 3 percent per year, leading to a small but steady inflation.

daily-interest savings account. Then every morning the person could go to the bank and withdraw that day's $60 from the savings account. By the end of the month the depositor would have earned interest on the money retained each day in the savings account. That would be the *benefit* of keeping the money holdings down as low as $60 at the beginning of each day. The *cost* of keeping money holdings down is simply the cost and inconvenience of the trips to the bank to withdraw the daily $60.

The greater the number of trips to the bank, the larger the amount earning interest in the savings account. With one trip—everything taken as cash on the first day—no interest is earned. The cash balance falls smoothly from $1,800 on the first day to $0 at the end of the month for an average balance of ($1,800 − $0)/2 = $900, forgoing interest of $i \times$ $900. For two trips, the cash balance falls from $1,800/2 to zero at midmonth and then repeats, for an average cash balance of ($1,800/2 − $0)/2 = $450. We show in the appendix to this chapter that this generalizes so that starting with income Y, if n trips are made, the average cash balance is $Y/2n$. If each trip costs tc, the combined cost of trips plus forgone interest is $(n \times tc) + i \times (Y/2n)$. Choosing n to minimize costs and computing the implied average money holdings leads to the famous square-root Baumol-Tobin formula for the demand for money:[8]

$$\frac{M}{P} = \sqrt{\frac{tc \times Y}{2i}} \tag{1}$$

---

[8]The theory has quite general applicability for determining optimal inventories of goods as well as money. This inventory-theoretical approach to the demand for money is associated with the names of William Baumol and James Tobin: William Baumol, "The Transactions Demand for Cash: An Inventory Theoretic Approach," *Quarterly Journal of Economics,* November 1952; James Tobin, "The Interest Elasticity of Transactions Demand for Cash," *Review of Economics and Statistics,* August 1956.

Equation (1) shows that the demand for money decreases with the interest rate and increases with the cost of transacting. Money demand increases with income, but less than proportionately. This point is sometimes put in different words by saying that there are *economies of scale* in cash management.

Equation (1) makes two very strong predictions: The income elasticity of money demand is ½, and the interest elasticity is $-½$.[9] Empirical evidence supports the signs of these predictions but suggests that the income elasticity is somewhat closer to 1 and that the interest elasticity is somewhat closer to zero.

THE PRECAUTIONARY MOTIVE

In discussing the transactions demand for money, we focused on transactions costs and ignored uncertainty. In this section, we concentrate on the demand for money that arises because people are uncertain about the payments they might want, or have, to make.[10] Realistically, an individual does not know precisely what payments she will be receiving in the next few weeks and what payments will have to be made. The person might decide to have a hot fudge sundae, or need to take a cab in the rain, or have to pay for a prescription. If the person does not have money with which to pay, she will incur a loss.

The more money an individual holds, the less likely he or she is to incur the costs of illiquidity (that is, not having money immediately available). But the more money the person holds, the more interest he or she is giving up. We are back to a tradeoff similar to that examined in relation to the transactions demand. The added consideration is that greater uncertainty about receipts and expenditures increases the demand for money.

Technology and the structure of the financial system are important determinants of precautionary demand. In times of danger, families may keep hidden hordes of cash in case they need to flee. In contrast, in much of the developed world credit cards, debit cards, and smart cards reduce precautionary demand.

THE SPECULATIVE DEMAND FOR MONEY

The transactions demand and the precautionary demand for money emphasize the medium-of-exchange function of money, for each refers to the need to have money on hand to make payments. Each theory is most relevant to the $M1$ definition of money, though the precautionary demand could certainly explain some of the holding of savings accounts and other relatively liquid assets that are part of $M2$. Now we move over to the store-of-value function of money and concentrate on the role of money in the investment portfolio of an individual.

---

[9]Meaning that if income rises 1 percent, money demand should rise 1/2 of 1 percent, and so forth. Be careful about the definition of percentage change with interest rates. If the interest rate goes from 10 percent per year to 10.5 percent per year, it has gone up by 5 percent of its original level, so money demand should drop by 2.5 percent.

[10]See Edward H. Whalen, "A Rationalization of the Precautionary Demand for Cash," *Quarterly Journal of Economics,* May 1966.

An individual who has wealth has to hold that wealth in specific assets. Those assets make up a *portfolio*. One would think an investor would want to hold the asset that provides the highest returns. However, given that the return on most assets is uncertain, it is unwise to hold the entire portfolio in a single *risky asset*. You may have a hot tip that a certain stock will surely double within the next 2 years, but you would be wise to recognize that hot tips are far from infallible. The typical investor will want to hold some amount of a safe asset as insurance against capital losses on assets whose prices change in an uncertain manner. Money is a safe asset in that its nominal value is known with certainty.[11] In a famous article, James Tobin argued that money would be held as the safe asset in the portfolios of investors.[12] The title of the article, "Liquidity Preference as Behavior towards Risk," explains the essential notion. In this framework, the demand for money—the safest asset—depends on the expected yields as well as on the riskiness of the yields on other assets. Tobin showed that an increase in the expected return on other assets—an increase in the opportunity cost of holding money (that is, the return lost by holding money)—lowers money demand. By contrast, an increase in the riskiness of the returns on other assets increases money demand.

An investor's aversion to risk certainly generates a demand for a safe asset. However, that asset is not likely to be $M1$. From the viewpoint of the yield and risks of holding money, it is clear that time or savings deposits or MMDAs have the same risks as currency or checkable deposits. However, the former generally pay a higher yield. Given that the risks are the same, and with the yields on time and savings deposits higher than those on currency and demand deposits, portfolio diversification explains the demand for assets such as time and savings deposits, which are part of $M2$, better than the demand for $M1$.

15-4

EMPIRICAL EVIDENCE

This section examines the empirical evidence—the studies made using actual data—on the demand for money. We know from Chapter 10 that the *interest elasticity* of the demand for money plays an important role in determining the effectiveness of monetary and fiscal policies. We showed in Section 15-3 that there are good theoretical reasons for believing that the demand for real balances should depend on the interest rate. The empirical evidence supports that view. Empirical studies have established that the demand for money is negatively related to the interest rate.

---

[11]Of course, when the rate of inflation is uncertain, the real value of money is also uncertain, and money is no longer a safe asset. Even so, the uncertainties about the values of equity are so much larger than the uncertainties about the rate of inflation that money can be treated as a relatively safe asset (countries at risk of hyperinflation excepted).

[12]James Tobin, "Liquidity Preference as Behavior towards Risk," *Review of Economic Studies,* February 1958.

The theory of money demand also predicts that the demand for money should depend on the level of income. The response of the demand for money to the level of income, as measured by the *income elasticity* of money demand, is also important from a policy viewpoint. As we shall see below, the income elasticity of money demand provides a guide for the Fed as to how fast to increase the money supply in order to support a given rate of GDP growth without changing the interest rate.

LAGGED ADJUSTMENT

The empirical work on the demand for money has introduced one complication that we did not study in the theoretical section—that the demand for money adjusts to changes in income and interest rates *with a lag*. When the level of income or the interest rate changes, there is first only a small change in the demand for money. Then, over the course of time, the change in the demand for money increases, slowly building up to its full long-run change.

There are two basic reasons for these lags. First, there are costs of adjusting money holdings; second, money holders' expectations are slow to adjust. The costs of adjustment include the costs of figuring out the new best way to manage money and the cost of opening up a new type of account if that is needed. On the expectations side, if people believe that a given change in the interest rate is temporary, they may be unwilling to make a major change in their money holdings. As time passes and it becomes clearer that the change is not transitory, they are willing to make a larger adjustment.

EMPIRICAL RESULTS FOR M1 DEMAND

Estimates of the response of $M1$ demand to income and interest rate changes are reported in Table 15-1.[13] In the short run (one quarter), the elasticity of demand with respect to real income is .11. This means that a 1 percent increase in real income raises money demand by .11 percent, which is considerably less than proportionately. The table shows that an increase in interest rates reduces money demand. The short-run interest responses are quite small. A 1 percentage point increase in the Treasury bill rate reduces the demand for money by only .8 percent.

The long-run responses exceed the short-run responses by a factor of 5, as Table 15-1 shows. The long-run real income elasticity is .53, meaning that in the long run the increase in real money demand occurring as a result of a given increase in real income is only .53 percent as large as the proportional increase in income. Real money demand thus rises less than proportionately to the rise in real income. A 1 percentage

[13]Laurence Ball, "Short-Run Money Demand," NBER working paper no. W9235, October 2002. For a summary of earlier work on money demand, see Stephen Goldfeld and Daniel Sichel, "The Demand for Money," in B. M. Friedman and F. H. Hahn (eds.), *Handbook of Monetary Economics,* vol. 1 (Amsterdam: North-Holland, 1990), chap. 8.

TABLE 15-1   Response of Real *M*1 Money Demand

	INCOME ELASTICITY	INTEREST RATE SEMI-ELASTICITY
Short run	.109	−.008
Long run	.532	−.040

Source: Laurence Ball, "Short-Run Money Demand," NBER working paper no. W9235, October 2002; and authors' calculations.

point increase in the Treasury bill rate reduces money demand by 4 percent in the long run.

Empirical work thus establishes four essential properties of money demand:

- The demand for real money balances responds negatively to the rate of interest. An increase in interest rates reduces the demand for money.
- The demand for money increases with the level of real income.
- The short-run responsiveness of money demand to changes in interest rates and income is considerably less than the long-run response. The long-run responses are estimated to be about 5 times the size of the short-run responses.
- The demand for nominal money balances is proportional to the price level. There is no money illusion; in other words, the demand for money is a demand for *real* balances.

In the past, the demand for real money balances was considered one of the best understood and most highly stable equations in the U.S. macroeconomy, and indeed in other countries too. Since then, *M*1 demand has been shifting and has not yet settled down to the extent that there is agreement on the empirically correct form of the money demand function. However, there is general agreement on the fact that money demand is affected primarily by income and interest rates.

*M*2 MONEY DEMAND

Innovation in the financial system has made it easier to move back and forth between *M*1 and other assets. For example, automatic teller machines typically allow cash withdrawals from savings accounts. We would say that savings accounts are now better substitutes for *M*1 than they were in the past. When money flows between savings accounts and cash, as an example, *M*1 changes but *M*2 does not. For this reason, financial innovation has made the demand for *M*2 more stable than the demand for *M*1.[14]

We would expect real money demand to depend negatively on the opportunity cost of holding *M*2, the difference between a market interest rate, such as the Treasury bill

[14]See Robert Hetzel and Yash Mehra, "The Behavior of Money Demand in the 1980s," *Journal of Money, Credit and Banking,* November 1989; and R. W. Hafer and Dennis Jansen, "The Demand for Money in the United States: Evidence from Cointegration Tests," *Journal of Money, Credit and Banking,* May 1991.

BOX 15-4   Money Demand and High Inflation

The demand for real balances depends on the alternative cost of holding money. That cost is normally measured by the yield on alternative assets, say, Treasury bills, commercial paper, or money market funds. But there is another margin of substitution. Rather than holding their wealth in financial assets, households or firms can also hold real assets: stocks of food or houses or machinery. This margin of substitution is particularly important in countries in which inflation is very high and capital markets do not function well. In that case it is quite possible that the return on holding goods can even be higher than that on financial assets.

Consider a household deciding whether to hold $100 in currency or a demand deposit or to hold its wealth in the form of groceries on the shelf. The advantage of holding groceries is that, unlike money, they maintain their real value. Rather than having the purchasing power of money balances eroded by inflation, the household gets rid of money, buying goods and thus avoiding a loss.

This *flight out of money* occurs systematically when inflation rates become high. In a famous study of hyperinflations (defined in the study as inflation rates of more than 50 percent *per month*), Phillip Cagan of Columbia University found large changes in real balances taking place as inflation increased.* In the most famous hyperinflation, that in Germany in 1922–1923, the quantity of real balances at the height of the hyperinflation had fallen to one-twentieth of its preinflation level. The increased cost of holding money leads to a reduction in real money demand and, with it, to changes in the public's payment habits as everybody tries to pass money on like a hot potato.

In well-developed capital markets, interest rates will reflect expectations of inflation, and hence it will not make much difference whether we measure the alternative cost of holding money by interest rates or inflation rates. But when capital markets are not free because interest rates are regulated or have ceilings, it is often appropriate to use inflation, not interest, rates as the measure of the alternative cost. Franco Modigliani has offered the following rule of thumb: The right measure of the opportunity cost of holding money is the higher of the two, interest rates or inflation.

*Phillip Cagan, "The Monetary Dynamics of Hyperinflation," in Milton Friedman (ed.), *Studies in the Quantity Theory of Money* (Chicago: University of Chicago Press, 1956).

rate, and a weighted average of the interest rates paid on various kinds of deposits constituting *M*2. We also expect real *M*2 money demand to depend positively on the level of income.

These hypotheses are, indeed, confirmed by the empirical evidence. An estimate with quarterly data for the period 1953–1991 yields the elasticities shown in Table 15-2. The table confirms that the elasticity with respect to the opportunity cost is negative. The short-run elasticities are smaller than the long-run elasticities.

TABLE 15-2	Elasticities of Real *M*2 Money Demand, 1953–1991	
	Y	OPPORTUNITY COST*
Short run	.39	−.017
Long run	.98	−.08

*Six-month commercial paper rate less own rate on *M*2.

Source: Yash P. Mehra, "The Stability of the *M*2 Demand Function: Evidence from an Error-Correction Model," *Journal of Money, Credit, and Banking,* August 1993.

The long-run income elasticity of *M*2 is clearly positive and is approximately equal to unity. This implies that, other things equal, the ratio of real balances, measured by *M*2, to real GNP will remain constant over time.

 # 15-5

THE INCOME VELOCITY OF MONEY

The *income velocity of money* is the number of times the stock of money is turned over per year in financing the annual flow of income. It is equal to the ratio of nominal GDP to the nominal money stock. Thus, in 2002 GDP was about $10,446 billion, the *M*2 money stock averaged $5,620 billion, and *M*2 velocity was therefore about 2. The average dollar of *M*2 money balances financed $2 of spending on final goods and services, or the public held an average of 50 cents of *M*2 per dollar of income.

Income velocity (from now on, we shall refer to "velocity" rather than "income velocity")[15] is defined as

$$V \equiv \frac{P \times Y}{M} = \frac{Y}{M/P} \tag{2}$$

that is, the ratio of nominal income to the nominal money stock or, equivalently, the ratio of real income to real balances.

The concept of velocity is important largely because it is a convenient way of talking about money demand. Let the demand for real balances be written $M/P = L(i, Y)$. Substituting into equation (2), velocity can be rewritten as $V = Y/L(i, Y)$. This is especially convenient if money demand is proportional to income, as is roughly true for long-run *M*2 demand, so money demand can be written as $L(i, Y) = Y \times l(i)$. In this case equation (2)

[15]Why do we say "income velocity" and not plain "velocity"? There is another concept, transactions velocity, which is the ratio of *total transactions* to money balances. Total transactions far exceed GDP for two reasons. First, many transactions involving the sale and purchase of assets do not contribute to GDP. Second, a particular item in final output typically generates total spending on it that exceeds the contribution of that item to GDP. For instance, a dollar's worth of wheat generates transactions as it leaves the farm, as it is sold by the miller, and so forth. Transactions velocity is thus higher than income velocity.

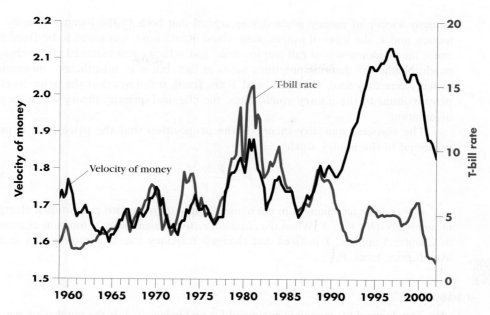

FIGURE 15-1   VELOCITY OF MONEY (LEFT SCALE) AND TREASURY BILL RATES (RIGHT SCALE).
(*Source: www.economagic.com.*)

is simply $V = 1/l(i)$, so velocity is a quick way to summarize the effect of interest rates on money demand—remembering that high velocity means low money demand.[16]

Figure 15-1 shows $M2$ velocity (left scale) and the Treasury bill interest rate (right scale). $M2$ velocity is relatively stable—the left-hand scale is only between 1.5 and 2.2 over a 40-year period—and velocity has a strong tendency to rise and fall with market interest rates.

Figure 15-1 also shows that in the last decade $M2$ velocity has become much less stable than in the past. When the monetary aggregates all become relatively unstable, the monetary authority should use the interest rate rather than the money supply as the direct operating target. In the next chapter we'll see why this is so.

THE QUANTITY THEORY

The *quantity theory of money,* which we met in Chapter 5, provides a very simple way to organize thinking about the relation between money, prices, and output:

$$M \times V = P \times Y \qquad (3)$$

Equation (3) is the famous *quantity equation,* linking the price level and the level of output to the money stock. The quantity equation became the *classical*

---

[16]In fact, while academic economists use velocity and money demand more or less interchangeably, Wall Street tends to focus directly on velocity.

quantity theory of money when it was argued that both V, the income velocity of money, and Y, the level of output, were fixed. Real output was taken to be fixed because the economy was at full employment, and velocity was assumed not to change much. Neither of these assumptions holds in fact, but it is, nonetheless, interesting to see where they lead. **If both V and Y are fixed, it follows that the price level is proportional to the money stock.** Thus, the classical quantity theory was a theory of inflation.

The classical quantity theory is the proposition that the price level is proportional to the money stock:

$$P = \frac{V \times M}{Y} \tag{3a}$$

If V is constant, changes in the money supply translate into proportional changes in *nominal GDP*, $P \times Y$. When the *classical case* (vertical) supply function examined in Chapter 5 applies, Y is fixed and changes in money translate into changes in the overall price level, P.

SUMMARY

1. The demand for money is a demand for real balances. It is the purchasing power, not the number of dollar bills, that matters to holders of money.
2. The money supply, $M1$, is made up of currency and checkable deposits. A broader measure, $M2$, also includes savings and time deposits at depository institutions as well as some other interest-bearing assets.
3. The chief characteristic of money is that it serves as a means of payment. The three classic reasons to hold money are for transactions purposes ($M1$) and for precautionary ($M1$ and $M2$) and speculative reasons ($M2$ and $M3$).
4. Decisions to hold money are based on a tradeoff between the liquidity of money and the opportunity cost of holding it when other assets have a higher yield.
5. The inventory-theoretic approach shows that an individual will hold a stock of real balances that varies inversely with the interest rate but increases with the level of real income and the cost of transactions. According to the inventory approach, the income elasticity of money demand is less than unity, implying that there are economies of scale.
6. Uncertainty about payments and receipts in combination with transactions costs gives rise to a precautionary demand for money. Precautionary money holdings are higher the greater the variability of net disbursements, the higher the cost of illiquidity, and the lower the interest rate.
7. Some assets that are in $M2$ form part of an optimal portfolio because they are less risky than other assets—their nominal value is constant. Because they earn interest, assets such as savings or time deposits and MMMF shares dominate currency and demand deposits for portfolio diversification purposes.
8. The empirical evidence provides support for a negative interest elasticity of money demand and a positive income elasticity. Because of lags, short-run elasticities are much smaller than long-run elasticities.

9. The demand function for $M1$ started showing instability in the mid-1970s. The demand function for $M2$ appears to be somewhat more stable, showing a unit income elasticity, a positive elasticity with respect to the own rate, and a negative elasticity with respect to the commercial paper rate.

10. The income velocity of money is defined as the ratio of income to money or the rate of turnover of money. The behavior of velocity is closely tied to the demand for money, so an increase in the opportunity cost of holding money leads to an increase in velocity.

11. The velocity of $M2$ was roughly constant for many years. The constancy is a reflection of small changes in the opportunity cost of holding money and of a unit income elasticity of demand for $M2$. In recent years, $M2$ velocity has varied considerably.

12. Inflation implies that money loses purchasing power, and inflation thus creates a cost of holding money. The higher the rate of inflation, the lower the amount of real balances that will be held. Hyperinflations provide striking support for this prediction. Under conditions of very high expected inflation, money demand falls dramatically relative to income. Velocity rises as people use less money in relation to income.

KEY TERMS

classical quantity theory	$M3$	quantity theory of money
flight out of money	medium of exchange	real balances
income elasticity	money	risky asset
income velocity of money	money illusion	speculative motive
interest elasticity	opportunity cost	standard of deferred
L	own rate of interest	payment
liquid (assets)	portfolio	store of value
$M1$	precautionary motive	transactions motive
$M2$	quantity equation	unit of account

PROBLEMS

Conceptual

1. What is money, and why does anyone want it?

2. To what extent would it be possible to design a society in which there was no money? What would the problems be? Could currency at least be eliminated? How? (Lest all this seem too unworldly, you should know that some people are beginning to talk of a "cashless economy" in this century.)

3. Do you think credit card credit limits should be counted in the money stock? Why or why not?

4. Discuss the various factors that go into an individual's decision regarding how many traveler's checks to take on a vacation.

5. Explain the concept of the opportunity cost of holding money.

6. The demand for nominal balances rises with the price level. At the same time, inflation causes the real demand to fall. Explain how these two assertions can both be correct.

7. "Muggers favor deflation." Comment.

Technical

1. Evaluate the effects of the following changes on the demand for $M1$ and $M2$. Which of the functions of money do they relate to?
   a. "Instant-cash" machines that allow 24-hour withdrawals from savings accounts at banks.
   b. The employment of more tellers at your bank.
   c. An increase in inflationary expectations.
   d. Widespread acceptance of credit cards.
   e. Fear of an imminent collapse of the government.
   f. A rise in the interest rate on time deposits.
   g. The rise of e-commerce.
2. a. Is velocity high or low relative to trend during recessions? Why?
   b. How can the Fed influence velocity?

The next two questions are related to the material in the appendix.

3.* The transactions demand-for-money model can also be applied to firms. Suppose a firm sells steadily during the month and has to pay its workers at the end of the month. Explain how the firm would determine its money holdings.

4.* a. Determine the optimal strategy for cash management for a person who earns $1,600 per month, can earn .5 percent interest per month in a savings account, and has a transaction cost of $1. (*Hint:* Integer constraints matter here.)
   b. What is the individual's average cash balance?
   c. Suppose income rises to $1,800. By what percentage does the individual's demand for money change?

Empirical

1. The chapter reviewed the different measures of money stock ($M1$, $M2$, and $M3$). You can use any of these money stock measures in order to determine the velocity of money. What is the relationship between $M1$ velocity, $M2$ velocity, and $M3$ velocity? Which is the largest and which is the smallest? Go to www.economagic.com. Under "Most Requested Series," take a look at these three alternative velocity measures in order to confirm the answer you got for the previous question.

2. Is there today in real terms more U.S. currency outstanding per capita than 30 years ago? To answer this question, go to www.economagic.com and get the data in order to fill in the first three columns of the table. To get the currency data, under "Browse by Source," choose the link to the "Federal Reserve, St. Louis." Click on "U.S. monetary data," and select "Currency Component of Money Stock Figure; SA." You can get U.S. population and CPI data from the "Most Requested Series" page.

	CURRENCY ($ BILLION)	U.S. POPULATION (THOUSANDS)	CPI (1982–84 = 100)	PER CAPITA REAL CURRENCY
December 1972				
December 2002				

*An asterisk denotes a more difficult problem.

◆ OPTIONAL ◆

APPENDIX: THE BAUMOL-TOBIN TRANSACTIONS DEMAND MODEL

The assumptions of the Baumol-Tobin transactions demand are set out in the text and summarized here. An individual receives a payment, Y, at the beginning of each month and spends it at an even pace during the month. He or she can earn interest at the rate i per month by holding money in a savings account (equivalently, bonds). There is a cost of tc per transaction for moving between bonds and money. We denote by n the number of transactions per month between bonds and money, and we assume, for convenience, that monthly income is paid into the savings account or paid in the form of bonds.

The individual minimizes the cost of money management during the month. Those costs consist of the transactions cost, $(n \times tc)$, plus the interest forgone by holding money instead of bonds during the month. The interest cost is $(i \times M)$, where M is the average holdings of money during the month.

M, the average holdings of money, depends on n, the number of transactions. Suppose that each time the individual makes a transaction, she transfers amount Z from bonds into money.[17] If the individual makes n equal-size withdrawals during the month, the size of each transfer is $Y/2n$, since a total of Y has to be transferred. Thus,

$$nZ = Y \tag{A1}$$

Now, how is the *average* cash balance related to n? Figure 15A-1 helps answer the question. In Figure 15A-1a ($n = 1$), the average cash balance held during the month is $Y/2 = Z/2$, since the cash balance starts at Y and runs down in a straight line to zero.[18] In the case of Figure

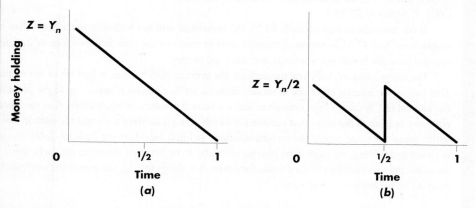

FIGURE 15A-1   AMOUNT OF CASH HELD BY THE PUBLIC RELATED TO NUMBER OF TRANSACTIONS.

---

[17]With simple interest being paid on the savings account, the individual's transactions between bonds and cash should be evenly spaced over the month.

[18]The average cash balance is the average of the amount of cash the individual holds at each moment during the month. For instance, if the balance held is $400 for 3 days and zero for the rest of the month, the average cash balance would be $40, or one-tenth (3 days ÷ 30 days) of the month times $400.

15A-1b ($n = 2$), the average cash balance for the first half of the month is $Y/4 = Z/2$, and the average cash balance for the second half of the month is also $Z/2$. Thus, the average cash balance for the entire month is $Y/4 = Z/2$. In general, the average cash balance is $Z/2$, as you might want to confirm by drawing diagrams similar to Figure 15A-1 for $n = 3$ or other values of n. Using equation (A1), it follows that the average cash balance is $Y/2n$.

The total cost of cash management is, accordingly,

$$\text{Total cost} = (n \times tc) + \frac{iY}{2n} \tag{A2}$$

The optimum number of transactions is found by minimizing total cost with respect to n.[19] That implies

$$n^* = \sqrt{\frac{iY}{2tc}} \tag{A3}$$

where n^* is the optimal number of transactions. As we should expect, the individual makes more transactions the higher the interest rate, the higher the income, and the lower the transactions cost.

The Baumol-Tobin result, equation (1) in the text, is obtained using equation (A3) and the fact that $M/P = Y/2n$.

In addition to deriving the square-root formula, we want also to show why for many people, it is optimal to make only one transaction between bonds and money. Consider the example in the text of an individual who receives \$1,800 per month. Suppose that the interest rate on deposits is as high as .5 percent per month. The individual cannot avoid making one initial transaction, since income is paid into the savings account to start with. Does it pay to make a second transaction? For $n = 2$, the average cash balance is \$1,800/2n = \$450, so interest earned would be (.005 × \$450) = \$2.25.

If the transaction cost exceeds \$2.25, the individual will not bother to make more than one transaction. And \$2.25 is not an outrageous cost in terms of the time and nuisance of making a transfer between bonds (or a savings account) and money.

For anyone making only one transaction, the average cash balance is half his or her income. That means the interest elasticity of money demand for that person is zero—up to the point that the interest rate becomes high enough to make a second transaction worthwhile. And the income elasticity is 1, up to the point that income rises high enough to make a second transaction worthwhile. Since for some people the income elasticity is 1 and for others the Baumol-Tobin formula is closer to applying, we expect the income elasticity to be between ½ and 1; similarly, since for some the interest elasticity is zero while for others it is closer to −½, we expect the interest elasticity to be between −½ and zero.

---

[19]If you can handle calculus, derive equation (A3) by minimizing the total cost with respect to n in equation (A2).

CHAPTER 16

The Fed, Money, and Credit

CHAPTER HIGHLIGHTS

- The Federal Reserve provides the monetary base (bank reserves and currency) upon which the money supply (currency and deposits) is built.

- The primary tool for controlling the money supply is open market purchases, purchases of bonds paid for with newly printed money.

- The Federal Reserve chooses both intermediate and ultimate targets. The key consideration in choosing targets is uncertainty about different kinds of economic shocks.

In the recession of 2001, the Fed cut interest rates repeatedly as can be seen in Figure 16-1. In his semiannual monetary policy report to the Congress, Federal Reserve chairman Alan Greenspan affirmed that

> By aggressively easing the stance of monetary policy, the Federal Reserve has moved to support demand and, we trust, help lay the groundwork for the economy to achieve maximum sustainable growth. Our accelerated action reflected the pronounced downshift in economic activity, which was accentuated by the especially prompt and synchronous adjustment of production by businesses utilizing the faster flow of information coming from the adoption of new technologies. A rapid and sizable easing was made possible by reasonably well-anchored inflation expectations, which helped to keep underlying inflation at a modest rate, and by the prospect that inflation would remain contained as resource utilization eased and energy prices backed down.[1]

Should the Fed have cut interest rates more rapidly? Could the Fed have made *M*2 grow faster if it had wanted to? And what precisely does the Fed do to cut interest rates?

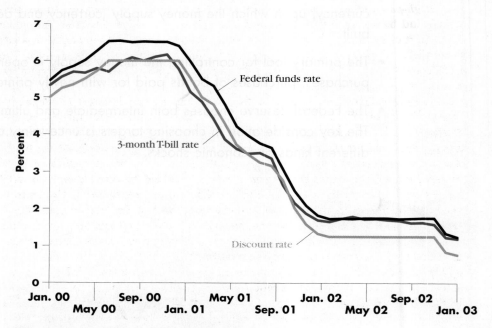

FIGURE 16-1   U.S. INTEREST RATES, 2000–2002.

(Source: Federal Reserve Economic Data.)

[1]Testimony of Alan Greenspan before the Committee on Financial Services, U.S. House of Representatives, July 18, 2001.

16-1

MONEY STOCK DETERMINATION: THE MONEY MULTIPLIER

The money supply consists mostly of deposits at banks,[2] which the Fed does not control directly. In this section we develop the details of the process by which the money supply is determined, and particularly the role of the Fed. The key concept to understand is *fractional reserve banking*. In a world in which only gold coins were money and in which the king reserved to himself the right to mint coins, the money supply would equal the number of coins minted. Contrast this with a futuristic cashless society in which all payments are made by electronic transfers through banks and in which the law requires (here's where the "fractional reserve" part comes in) banks to hold gold coins equal to 20 percent of their outstanding deposits. In this latter case, the money available to the public would be 5 times the number of gold coins (coins/.20). The coins would not be used as money. Rather, the coins would form a "base" supporting deposits available through the banking system. The real money supply is determined by a blend of these two fictional systems.

High-powered money (or the monetary base) consists of currency (notes and coins) and banks' deposits at the Fed. The part of the currency held by the public forms part of the money supply. The currency in bank vaults and the banks' deposits at the Fed are used as reserves backing individual and business deposits at banks. The Fed's control over the monetary base is the main route through which it determines the money supply.

The Federal Reserve has direct control over high-powered money, H. We are interested in the supply of money, M. The two are linked by the money multiplier, *mm*. Before going into details, we want to think briefly about the relationship between the money stock and the stock of high-powered money (see Figure 16-2). At the top of the figure we show the stock of money. At the bottom we show the stock of high-powered money, also called the *monetary base*. As we said, money and high-powered money are related by the *money multiplier*. **The money multiplier is the ratio of the stock of money to the stock of high-powered money.** The money multiplier is larger than 1. It is clear from the diagram that the larger deposits are as a fraction of the money stock, the larger the multiplier is. That is true because currency uses up a dollar of high-powered money per dollar of money. Deposits, by contrast, use up only a fraction of a dollar of high-powered money (in reserves) per dollar of money stock. For instance, if the reserve ratio is 10 percent, every dollar of the money stock in the form of deposits uses up only 10 cents of high-powered money. Equivalently, each dollar of high-powered money held as bank reserves can support $10 of deposits.

For simplicity, ignore the distinction between various kinds of deposits (and thus the distinction between different Ms) and consider the money supply process as if there

---

[2]We refer to all deposit-taking institutions, including savings and loan associations, mutual savings banks, and credit unions, as "banks."

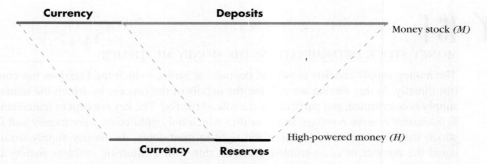

FIGURE 16-2   RELATIONSHIP BETWEEN HIGH-POWERED MONEY AND THE MONEY STOCK.

were only a uniform class of deposits, D. Using this simplification, the money supply consists of currency, CU, plus deposits:

$$M = CU + D \tag{1}$$

High-powered money consists of currency plus reserves:

$$H = CU + \text{reserves} \tag{2}$$

We summarize the behavior of the public, the banks, and the Fed in the money supply process by three variables: the *currency-deposit ratio, cu* ≡ *CU/D*; the *reserve ratio, re* ≡ reserves/D; and the stock of high-powered money. Rewrite equations (1) and (2) as $M = (cu + 1)D$ and $H = (cu + re)D$. In this way we can express the money supply in terms of its principal determinants, re, cu, and H:

$$M = \frac{1 + cu}{re + cu} H \equiv mm \times H \tag{3}$$

where *mm* is the money multiplier given by

$$mm \equiv \frac{1 + cu}{re + cu}$$

- The money multiplier is larger the smaller the reserve ratio, *re*.
- The money multiplier is larger the smaller the currency-deposit ratio, *cu*. That is because the smaller the *cu*, the smaller the proportion of the high-powered money stock that is being used as currency (which translates high-powered money only one-for-one into money) and the larger the proportion that is available to be reserves (which translates much more than one-for-one into money).

We turn now to the determinants of the reserve-deposit and currency-deposit ratios.

BOX 16-1   Deposit Insurance and Bank Runs

Many banks failed in the 1930s; that is, they were unable to meet the demands of their depositors for cash. If you have a deposit in a failed bank, you cannot "get your money out." Anyone who believes his or her bank may run out of cash will rush to the bank to try to withdraw money before the other depositors. **A *run on a bank* occurs when depositors rush to try to withdraw cash because they believe others will also try to do so.** There may be good reasons for the running investors to worry about the bank's safety, but it is even possible that a run on a fundamentally sound bank may occur precisely because its depositors believe that a run on the bank is likely to occur.*

Bank runs have both microeconomic and macroeconomic effects. The former takes the form of *disintermediation*. Having lost deposits, banks are no longer able to make loans to support business investment and purchases of private homes. The latter takes the form of an increase in the currency-deposit ratio, *cu*, and, therefore, a drop in the money multiplier. Unless the central bank offsets this by increasing the monetary base, the macroeconomic effect is a drop in the money supply.

The massive bank failures of the 1930s, as a consequence of runs on banks, gave rise to an important institutional reform, the creation of the *Federal Deposit Insurance Corporation (FDIC)*. That institution insures bank deposits, so depositors get paid even if a bank fails. That means there is no reason to worry about losing your money if your bank fails; as a result, bank runs have been rare since the 1930s.† Bank failures virtually disappeared between 1940 and 1979, but in the 1980s they became a more serious problem. Still, the scale today is much less than in the early 1930s, and—because of the FDIC—the economic consequences are much less serious now.

*The notion of self-justifying runs on banks has both intuitive appeal and historical support. It has been formalized in an ingenious but very difficult article by Douglas Diamond and Philip Dybvig, "Bank Runs, Deposit Insurance and Liquidity," *Journal of Political Economy*, June 1983. A less technical example appears in the movie *It's a Wonderful Life*, with Jimmy Stewart.

†In the 1980s there were runs on thrift institutions in Ohio and Rhode Island whose deposits were not covered by federal insurance.

THE CURRENCY-DEPOSIT RATIO

The payment habits of the public determine how much currency is held relative to deposits. The currency-deposit ratio is affected by the cost and convenience of obtaining cash; for instance, if there is a cash machine nearby, individuals will on average carry less cash with them because the costs of running out are lower. The currency-deposit ratio has a strong seasonal pattern, being highest around Christmas.

THE RESERVE-DEPOSIT RATIO

Bank reserves consist of deposits banks hold at the Fed and "vault cash," notes and coin held by banks. In the absence of regulation, banks would hold reserves to meet (1) the demands of their customers for cash and (2) payments their customers make by checks that are deposited in other banks. However, in the United States banks hold reserves primarily because the Federal Reserve requires them to. In addition to these *required reserves,* banks hold some *excess reserves* in order to meet unexpected withdrawals. Because reserves earn no interest, banks try to minimize excess reserves. When market interest rates are high, banks try especially hard to keep excess reserves to a minimum. So while *re* is mostly determined by regulation,[3] high interest rates do to a limited extent reduce *re*.

Banks have to keep reserves in the form of notes and coin because their customers have a right to currency on demand. They keep accounts at the Fed mainly to make payments among themselves. Thus, when I pay you with a check drawn on my bank account, which you deposit in your bank, my bank makes the payment by transferring money from its account at the Fed to your bank's account at the Fed.[4] Banks can also use their deposits at the Fed to obtain cash; the Fed sends the cash over in an armored truck on request.

16-2
THE INSTRUMENTS OF MONETARY CONTROL

The Federal Reserve has three instruments for controlling the money supply: *open market operations,* the *discount rate,* and the *required-reserve ratio.* As a practical matter, open market operations are nearly always the tool of choice.

AN OPEN MARKET PURCHASE

The method by which the Fed most often changes the stock of high-powered money is an open market operation.[5] We examine the mechanics of an *open market purchase,* an operation in which the Fed buys, say $1 million of government bonds from a private individual. An open market purchase *increases* the monetary base.

The accounting for the Fed's purchase is shown in Table 16-1. The Fed's ownership of government securities rises by $1 million, which is shown in the "Government securities" entry on the assets side of the balance sheet. How does the Fed pay for the

---

[3]This is so in the United States. In Canada and the United Kingdom, for example, reserve requirements are not set by regulation.

[4]Many banks, particularly small ones, hold their reserves in the form of deposits at other banks. These *interbank deposits* serve the same function as reserves but are not included in the U.S. measure of reserves. They are excluded from the definitions of the money stock.

[5]A very nice description of the hard details of open market operations is given in M. A. Akhtar, "Understanding Open Market Operations," Federal Reserve Bank of New York *Review,* 1997.

TABLE 16-1 Effects of an Open Market Purchase on the Fed Balance Sheet
(Millions of Dollars)

ASSETS		LIABILITIES	
Government securities	+1	Currency	0
All other assets	0	Bank deposits at Fed	+1
Monetary base (sources)	+1	Monetary base (uses)	+1

bond? It writes a check on itself. In return for the bond, the seller receives a check instructing the Fed to pay (the seller) $1 million. The seller takes the check to his or her bank, which credits the depositor with the $1 million and then deposits the check at the Fed. That bank has an account at the Fed; the account is credited with $1 million, and the "Bank deposits at Fed" entry on the liabilities side of the balance sheet rises by $1 million. The commercial bank has just increased its reserves by $1 million, which are held in the first instance as a deposit at the Fed.

The only unexpected part of the story is that the Fed can pay for the securities it bought by giving the seller a check on itself. The eventual owner of the check then has a deposit at the Fed. That deposit can be used to make payments to other banks, or it can be exchanged for currency. Just as the ordinary deposit holder at a bank can obtain currency in exchange for deposits, the bank deposit holder at the Fed can acquire currency in exchange for its deposits. When the Fed pays for the bond by writing a check on itself, it creates high-powered money with a stroke of the pen. The striking result is that **the Fed can create high-powered money at will merely by buying assets, such as government bonds, and paying for them with its own liabilities.**

THE FED BALANCE SHEET

Table 16-2 and 16-3 show two ways of looking at the balance sheets of the Federal Reserve system. Table 16-2 shows the principal assets and liabilities of the Fed: government bonds and currency. Table 16-3 shows the monetary base and two different ways of looking at reserves. Most reserves are required, and only a small fraction is borrowed at the discount window.

TABLE 16-2 Main Assets and Liabilities of All Federal Reserve Banks, January 1, 2003
(Billions of Dollars)

ASSETS (SOURCES)		LIABILITIES (USES)	
Gold and special drawing rights certificate account	$ 13.24	Federal Reserve notes	$654.27
Total U.S. government securities and loans	629.41	Total deposits	22.54

Source: Federal Reserve Board, *Factors Affecting Reserve Balances*, January 2, 2003.

TABLE 16-3	Aggregate Reserves of Depository Institutions and the Monetary Base, December 2002 (Billions of Dollars)	
Reserves of depository institutions	$ 40.07	
Required reserves	38.08	
Excess reserves	1.99	
Reserves of depository institutions	40.07	
Nonborrowed reserves	39.99	
Borrowed reserves	0.08	
Monetary base	680.33	
Vault cash in excess of required reserves	13.36	
Currency	626.90	
Reserves	40.07	

Source: Federal Reserve Board, *Aggregate Reserves of Depository Institutions and the Monetary Base; Money Stock Measures,* January 23, 2003.

FOREIGN EXCHANGE AND THE BASE

The Fed sometimes buys or sells foreign currencies in an attempt to affect exchange rates. These purchases and sales of foreign exchange—*foreign exchange market intervention*—affect the base. Note from the balance sheet that if the central bank buys gold[6] or foreign exchange, there is a corresponding increase in high-powered money, as the Fed pays with its own liabilities for the gold or foreign exchange that is purchased. Thus, foreign exchange market operations affect the base.[7] However, the Fed frequently pairs foreign exchange purchases with offsetting open market operations precisely to avoid changing the base. Such offset purchases are said to be "sterilized." (For further discussion, see Chapter 19.)

LOANS AND DISCOUNTS

A bank that runs short of reserves can borrow to make good the deficiency. It may borrow either from the Fed or from other banks that have spare reserves. The cost of borrowing from the Fed is the *discount rate*. **The discount rate is the interest rate charged by the Fed to banks that borrow from it to meet temporary needs for reserves.** The discount rate is the explicit cost of Fed borrowing, but there is also an implicit cost, since the Fed frowns on banks that try to borrow from it too often.

---

[6]The Fed's 2002 holdings of gold were about $11.0 billion, valued at $42 an ounce. The market value of the gold is much higher, since the market price of gold is far above $42 per ounce. In the problem set, you are asked to show how the balance sheet would be affected if the Fed decided to value its gold at the free-market price.

[7]Details of this impact may be complicated by the fact, which we do not pursue, that the Fed and the Treasury usually collaborate in foreign exchange intervention.

BOX 16-2   The Fed as Lender of Last Resort

An important function assigned to central banks since the nineteenth century is to act as "lender of last resort." When financial panic threatens the collapse of the financial system, swift action by the central bank can restore confidence and avoid a systemwide run on financial intermediaries, a freezing of credit lines, or, worse, a widespread calling in of loans. The Fed does act in this role whenever major financial institutions go under or whenever there is a serious risk of instability, as when the stock market fell 20 percent on one day in the October 1987 collapse.

The need for a lender of last resort emerges from the following consideration: The credit system is by its very nature *illiquid*, though not *insolvent*—various debtors can repay their loans given time but cannot do so on demand. But many liabilities, for example, bank deposits or large CDs of banks and corporations, have very short maturities. If all creditors ask for their assets, many of the debtors would not be able to pay and would have to default.

Now imagine that a major financial institution, say First Bank of Nowhere (First, for short) has payment difficulties. Other financial institutions may well have lent to First and will want to recover their money before anyone else. A bank run starts. Other financial institutions are aware that *some* institutions have lent to First, cannot recover their loans, and are therefore vulnerable themselves, as are their creditors in turn. There arises a general uncertainty as to who lent to whom and who is in trouble because someone (or many) in the many layers of credit and intermediation cannot meet redemption demands. As a result, *all* credit freezes; nobody wants to lend to anyone because everyone is afraid of being pulled into the default. But if nobody wants to lend, short-term credit lines cannot be rolled over, and many institutions become illiquid. The process deteriorates in a 1930s-style financial collapse as assets are liquidated to recover liquidity.

The Fed enters in such a situation by *isolating* the center of the storm, guaranteeing the liabilities of the individual financial institution (beyond the guarantees of the FDIC). The guarantee assures everybody that third parties will not suffer losses and hence not become a risk.* Thus, the lender-of-last-resort function prevents spillover effects to the credit market of individual payment difficulties. But the function also comes into its own when there is a marketwide problem. Walter Bagehot (1826–1877) in his famous 1873 book, *Lombard Street*, gave the classic prescription: *"During crisis discount freely!"*

Milton Friedman and Anna Schwartz, in their *A Monetary History of the United States*, blamed the Fed for not responding to the systemwide problems induced by the stock market crash of 1929, thus violating Bagehot's prescription. But during the stock market crash of 1987, the lesson had been learned. Fed chairman Alan Greenspan did not hesitate. He announced that the Fed stood behind the banking system. The Fed immediately reduced interest rates, providing much needed liquidity that would help stem the risk of a credit collapse.

*Knowing that the Fed stands ready to bail them out in case of trouble, bank managers have an incentive to take too many risks. To discourage such behavior, the Fed often fires bank managers and eliminates stockholder equity when bailing out a bank.

The cost of borrowing from other banks is the *federal funds rate*. **Federal funds are reserves that some banks have in excess and others need.** The federal funds rate varies together with other market rates and can be affected by the Fed. Figure 16-3 shows three interest rates: the three-month Treasury bill rate, the federal funds rate, and the discount rate. You can see that in the big picture, all the rates move closely together. To a banker of course, the remaining small differences represent opportunities to make money.

The Fed provides high-powered money to banks that need it temporarily by lending to them at the discount rate. Banks' willingness to borrow from the Fed is affected by the discount rate, which accordingly influences the volume of borrowing. Since borrowed reserves are also part of high-powered money, the Fed's discount rate has some effect on the monetary base. However, the real role of the discount rate is as a signaling mechanism of Fed intentions. When the Fed increases the discount rate, banks and financial markets take this as a signal that the Fed intends to reduce the money supply and increase market interest rates.

What happens when the Fed raises interest rates and does *not* increase the discount rate? Banks have an incentive to borrow more from the Fed, since the banks can then relend the funds at the higher interest rate. Historically, the Fed frequently changed the discount rate along with market interest rates to prevent "profiteering" of this sort. But then the Fed needed to convince the market that the change in the discount rate was *not* intended to send a signal. In 2002 the Fed changed the operation of the discount window so that the discount rate would automatically float up and down as the Fed's target for the federal funds rate changed. The discount rate is set higher—initially 1 percentage point higher—than the Fed funds rate.

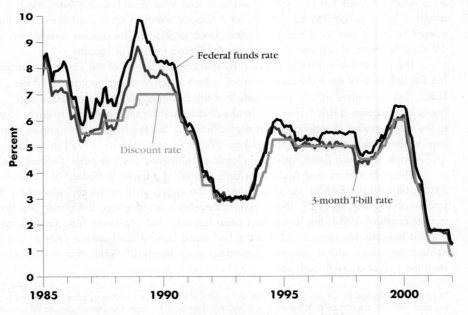

FIGURE 16-3   THE THREE MAJOR U.S. INTEREST RATES, 1985–2002.

(Source: Federal Reserve Economic Data.)

BOX 16-3   The Discount Rate Is <u>Not</u> Itself a Component of a Bank's Cost of Funds

It is often thought that banks obtain funds primarily from the Fed and that, as a result, changes in the discount rate directly change the banks' cost of funds. Changes in the discount rate sometimes affect market interest rates through the money supply mechanism, but the amount banks borrow from the Fed is completely trivial as a component of costs. For example, at the beginning of 2002 borrowing from the Fed equaled about 1/1,000 of 1 percent of loans and securities at commercial banks.

Discount rate changes serve two principal functions: (1) They signal the Fed's intentions; (2) they affect the free-market federal funds rate.

In some countries other than the United States, the central bank is a more significant source of funds for the banking system.

THE RESERVE RATIO

Looking at the money multiplier in equation (3), it is easy to see that the Fed can increase the money supply by reducing the required-reserve ratio. However, this has not been done in recent years. Reserves pay no interest, and so are a kind of interest-free loan from banks to the Fed—a sort of implicit tax. Therefore, changes in reserve requirements have undesirable side effects on bank profits.

FINANCING FEDERAL DEFICITS

The U.S. Treasury maintains an account at the Fed and makes payments to the public by writing checks on its Fed account. The relationship between the Fed and the Treasury helps clarify the financing of government budget deficits.

Budget deficits can be financed by the Treasury's borrowing from the public. In that case, the Treasury sells bonds to the public. The public pays for the bonds with checks, which the Treasury deposits in an account it holds in a commercial bank, thereby making sure it does not affect the stock of high-powered money. When the Treasury uses the proceeds of the bond sales to make a payment, it moves the money into its Fed account just before making the payment. As a result, the monetary base is not affected by the Treasury's deficit financing, except for the short time between which the Treasury moves the money into its Fed account and then pays it out.

Alternatively, the Treasury can finance its deficit by borrowing from the Fed. It is simplest to think of the Treasury's selling a bond to the Fed instead of to the public. When the bond is sold, the Fed's holdings of government securities increase and, simultaneously, Treasury deposits (a liability of the Fed) rise. But then when the Treasury uses the borrowed money to make a payment, the stock of high-powered money rises.

Accordingly, when a budget deficit is financed by the Treasury's borrowing from the Fed, the stock of high-powered money is increased.

We often talk of central bank financing of government deficits as financing through the printing of money. Typically, the deficit is not literally financed by the central bank through the printing of money, but central bank financing increases the stock of high-powered money, which comes to much the same thing.

In some countries the central bank automatically finances the treasury and may be subordinated to the treasury. In the United States, by contrast, the Federal Reserve answers to Congress and is not legally obliged to finance government deficits by buying bonds. Thus, it still retains its ability to control the stock of high-powered money even when the Treasury is running a budget deficit.

16-3

THE MONEY MULTIPLIER AND BANK LOANS

We now present an alternative way of describing the workings of the money multiplier by showing how adjustments by banks and the public following an increase in the monetary base produce a multiple expansion of the money stock.

A Fed open market purchase increases the monetary base. To start with, the increase in the base shows up as an increase in bank reserves. This is because the Fed pays for the securities by writing a check on itself, which the seller of the securities deposits in his or her bank account. The bank in turn presents the check for collection to the Fed and will be credited with an increase in its reserve position at the Fed.

The bank in which the original check was deposited now has a reserve ratio that is too high. Its reserves and deposits have gone up by the same amount. Therefore, its ratio of reserves to deposits has risen. To reduce the ratio of reserves to deposits, it increases its lending.

When the bank makes a loan, the person receiving the loan gets a bank deposit. At this stage, when the bank makes a loan, **the money supply has risen by more than the amount of the open market operation.** The person who sold the security to the Fed has increased his or her holdings of money by the value of the bonds sold. The person receiving the loan has a new bank deposit and thus the process has already generated a multiple expansion of the money stock.

In the subsequent adjustment, part of the increase in high-powered money finds its way into the public's holdings of currency and part serves as the basis for an expansion of lending by the banking system. When banks lend, they do so by crediting the deposits of their loan customers with the loan. Banks therefore create money whenever they make loans.

The expansion of loans, and hence money, continues until the reserve-deposit ratio has fallen to the desired level and the public again has achieved its desired currency-deposit ratio. The money multiplier summarizes the total expansion of money created by a dollar increase in the monetary base.

16-4

CONTROL OF THE MONEY STOCK AND CONTROL OF THE INTEREST RATE

We make a simple but important point in this section: **The Fed cannot simultaneously set both the interest rate and the stock of money at any given target levels that it may choose.**

Figure 16-4 illustrates this point. Suppose that the Fed, for some reason, wants to set the interest rate at a level i^* and the money stock at a level M^* and that the demand-for-money function is as shown by LL. The Fed can move the money supply function around, but it cannot move the money demand function around. It can set only the combinations of the interest rate and the money supply that lie along LL. At interest rate i^*, it can have money supply $M_0/\bar{P}$. At target money supply $M^*/\bar{P}$, it can have interest rate i_0. But it cannot have both $M^*/\bar{P}$ and i^*.

The point is sometimes put more dramatically, as follows: When the Fed decides to set the interest rate at some given level and keep it fixed—a policy known as *pegging the interest rate*—it loses control over the money supply. If the money demand curve were to shift, the Fed would have to supply whatever amount of money was demanded at the pegged interest rate.

The Fed in its day-to-day operations can more accurately control interest rates than the money stock. The Fed buys and sells government securities through its *open market*

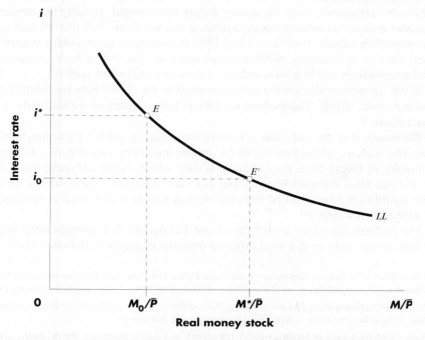

FIGURE 16-4   RELATIONSHIP BETWEEN THE REAL MONEY STOCK AND INTEREST RATES.

desk at the New York Fed every day. If it wants to raise the price of government securities (lower the interest rate), it can buy the securities at that price. If it wants to reduce the price of government securities (raise the interest rate), it can sell a sufficient amount of securities from its large portfolio. Thus, on a day-to-day basis, the Fed can determine the market interest rate quite accurately.[8]

These are *technical* reasons why the Fed cannot hit the target stock of money exactly even if it wants to. But over a slightly longer period, the Fed can determine the money supply fairly accurately. As data on the behavior of the money stock and the money multiplier become available, the Fed can make midcourse corrections to its setting of the base. For example, if the Fed were aiming for monetary growth of 5 percent over a given period, it might start the base growing at 5 percent. If it found halfway into the period that the multiplier had been falling, and the money stock therefore growing by less than 5 percent, the Fed would step up the growth rate of the base to compensate.

The main reasons the Fed does not hit its money growth targets are not technical but, rather, have to do with its having both interest rate *and* money stock targets, and as we have seen in this section, it cannot hit them both at the same time.

 ## 16-5

MONEY STOCK AND INTEREST RATE TARGETS

Over the period since the 1950s, the emphasis the Fed has placed on controlling the interest rate versus controlling the money supply has changed. Initially the emphasis was almost entirely on interest rates—indeed, it was not until 1959 that the Fed even began to publish money stock data. Until 1982 the emphasis on monetary targets increased more or less steadily. Since then the emphasis has shifted back increasingly toward interest rates and to a more eclectic approach to monetary policy.[9]

In this section we discuss the issues involved in the choice between interest rate and money stock targets. The analysis we present here is based on a classic article by William Poole.[10]

We assume that the Fed's aim is to have the economy reach a particular level of output. The analysis, which uses the *IS-LM* model, applies to a short period such as 3 to 9 months. In Figure 16-5, the *LM* curve labeled *LM(M)* is the *LM* curve that exists when the Fed fixes the money stock. The *LM* curve labeled *LM(i)* describes money market equilibrium when the Fed fixes the interest rate. It is horizontal at the chosen level of the interest rate, i^*.

The problem for policy is that the *IS* and *LM* curves shift unpredictably. When they shift, output ends up at a level different from the target level. In Figure 16-5*a* we

[8]For a description of techniques of monetary control, see Daniel Thornton, "The Borrowed-Reserves Operating Procedure: Theory and Evidence," Federal Reserve Bank of St. Louis *Review,* January–February 1988.

[9]See Ann-Marie Meulendyke, "A Review of Federal Reserve Policy Targets and Operating Guides in Recent Decades," Federal Reserve Bank of New York *Quarterly Review,* Autumn 1988.

[10]W. Poole, "Optimal Choice of Monetary Policy Instruments in a Simple Stochastic Macro Model," *Quarterly Journal of Economics,* May 1970.

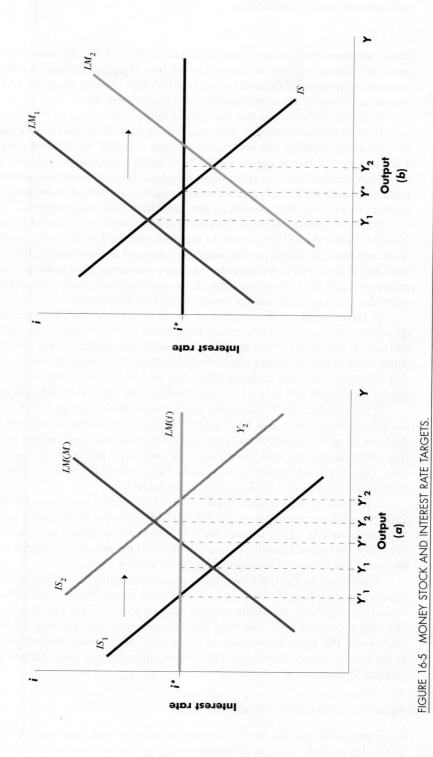

FIGURE 16-5 MONEY STOCK AND INTEREST RATE TARGETS.

show two alternative positions for the *IS* curve: IS_1 and IS_2. We assume that the Fed does not know in advance which will be the true *IS* curve: The position depends, for instance, on investment demand, which is difficult to predict. The Fed's aim is to have income come out as close as possible to the target level, Y^*.

In Figure 16-5*a* we see that the level of output stays closer to Y^* if the *LM* curve is *LM(M)*. In that case the level of output will be Y_1 if the *IS* curve is IS_1 and Y_2 if the *IS* curve is IS_2. If policy had kept the interest rate constant, we would in each case have a level of income that is further from Y^*: Y'_1 instead of Y_1, and Y'_2 instead of Y_2.

Thus, we have our first conclusion: **If output deviates from its equilibrium level mainly because the *IS* curve shifts about, output is stabilized by keeping the money stock constant. The Fed should, in this case, have monetary targets.**

We can see from Figure 16-5*a* why it is more stabilizing to keep M rather than i constant. When the *IS* curve shifts to the right and the *LM(M)* curve applies, the interest rate rises, thereby reducing investment demand and moderating the effect of the shift. But if the *LM(i)* curve applies, there is no resistance from monetary policy to the effects of the *IS* shift. Monetary policy is thus automatically stabilizing in Figure 16-5*a* when the *IS* curve shifts and the money stock is held constant.

In Figure 16-5*b* we assume that the *IS* curve is stable. Now the uncertainty about the effects of monetary policy results from shifts in the *LM* curve. Assuming that the Fed can fix the money stock, the *LM* curve shifts because the money demand function shifts. When it sets the money stock, the Fed does not know what the interest rate will be. The *LM* curve could end up being either LM_1 or LM_2. Alternatively, the Fed could simply fix the interest rate at level i^*. That would ensure that the level of output is Y^*.

If the Fed were to fix the money stock, output could be either Y_1 or Y_2. If it fixes the interest rate, output will be Y^*. Thus, we have our second conclusion: **If output deviates from its equilibrium level mainly because the demand-for-money function shifts about, the Fed should operate monetary policy by fixing the interest rate.** That way it automatically neutralizes the effects of the shifts in money demand. In this case the Fed should have interest rate targets.

The Poole analysis helps explain why the Fed stopped specifying $M1$ targets from 1987 on, while continuing to target $M2$ (and $M3$ and total nonfinancial debt). The increasing instability of the demand for $M1$ limited its usefulness as a monetary target. Similarly, the unpredictability of the growth of all the monetary aggregates in the last few years has led to the increasing weight on interest rates.

In practice, the Federal Reserve sets its short-term targets in terms of interest rates, specifically, the federal funds rate. The Federal Open Market Committee (FOMC) typically meets every six weeks and announces a federal funds rate target, although in turbulent times the FOMC can meet more frequently or even set rates following a teleconference. But while the immediate target is an interest rate, the Fed looks carefully at the money supply, output, unemployment, inflation, and other factors in deciding whether to raise or lower its target.

THE SHORT RUN AND THE LONG RUN

It is important to note that the Poole argument discusses Fed targeting over short periods. The Fed is *not* to be thought of as announcing or desiring that the interest rate will be, say, 8 percent forever. Rather, the Fed should readjust its targets in light of the changing behavior of the economy: The target interest rate might be 5 percent at the bottom of a recession and 15 percent when the economy is overheating. Similarly, the money growth targets could also be adjusted in response to the state of the economy.

Monetarist proponents of money stock targeting might agree with the technical details of the Poole analysis but still argue that it is a mistake to target interest rates rather than money. They argue that increases in the money stock lead eventually to inflation and that the only way to avoid inflation in the long run is by keeping money growth moderate. The problem with focusing on interest rates, they suggest, is that while the Fed keeps its eye on interest rates, the growth rate of money and the inflation rate often tend to increase.[11] This argument appears to fit the facts of the 1960s and 1970s well.

However, that experience has led the Fed to watch inflationary trends very closely and to tighten policy when inflation threatens. That experience, and the monetarist analysis, has also led the Fed to set monetary targets for itself and, when it misses the targets, to appraise carefully the reasons why. At the same time, it pays attention to interest rates in case its monetary targets lead in the short run to recession or inflation if there are shifts in money demand.

 # 16-6

MONEY, CREDIT, AND INTEREST RATES

The Fed targets not only *M*2 and *M*3 but also the increase in the total *debt* of the nonfinancial sectors, that is, the debt of the government, households, and firms other than financial firms. Their debt is equal to the *credit* (lending) that has been extended to them. Thus, the Fed can also be described as having *credit targets.*

Why? In the first instance, this is a very old approach of the Fed, which had credit targets in the 1950s. The Fed returned to them in 1982 in part because of econometric evidence, presented by Benjamin Friedman of Harvard, showing that there was a tighter link between the volume of debt and GNP than between money and nominal GNP.[12]

At a fundamental level, proponents of the credit view, such as Federal Reserve governor Ben Bernanke and Mark Gertler of New York University, argue for the importance of the extent of financial intermediation—the volume of lending and borrowing through financial institutions—in the economy. Financial intermediation occurs when financial institutions channel funds from savers to investors, as banks do when they lend funds deposited with them to borrowers who want to invest. Bernanke's research suggests that a large part of the decline in output in the Great Depression was the result of the breakdown of the financial system and the collapse in the quantity of

---

[11]Another argument for money targeting arises from the distinction between real and nominal interest rates. The nominal interest rate can rise because inflation is expected. If the Fed fights this increase in the nominal rate by increasing the money stock, it is only feeding the inflation. We examined this argument in Chap. 8.

[12]B. Friedman, "The Roles of Money and Credit in Macroeconomic Analysis," in James Tobin (ed.), *Macroeconomics, Prices, and Quantities* (Washington, DC: The Brookings Institution, 1983).

BOX 16-4   Money Growth, Interest Rates, and Credit in the 1990—1991 Recession

In the 1990–1991 recession, fiscal policy was completely immobilized by the size of the budget deficit. The burden of dealing with the recession therefore fell on monetary policy, which ran into severe difficulties as banks appeared unwilling to lend and the different monetary aggregates grew at very different rates.

The starting point for the 1990–1991 recession was the gradually rising inflation rate at the end of the 1980s. From a low of 1.9 percent in 1986, the CPI inflation rate reached 4.8 percent in 1989. With the unemployment rate in 1989 at 5.2 percent, perhaps even below the natural rate, the Fed's main concern was to fight inflation.

The main indicators of monetary policy showed a tightening in 1989 (see Table 1). The most visible sign was the rise in the Treasury bill rate from an average of 6.7 percent in 1988 to 8.1 percent in 1989; in addition, the growth rate of each

TABLE 1   Monetary Policy 1988–1992
(Percent per Annum)

	1988	1989	1990	1991	1992
Growth rate of $M1$	4.9	0.9	4.0	8.7	14.2
Growth rate of $M2$	5.5	5.1	3.5	3.0	2.3
Growth rate of $M3$	6.6	3.5	1.3	1.4	0.4
Growth rate of debt	9.3	8.0	6.8	4.2	4.3
Growth rate of bank loans	9.1	7.7	4.4	−0.1	−0.3
Treasury bill rate	6.7	8.1	7.5	5.4	3.8
10-year bond rate	8.9	8.5	8.6	7.9	7.3
Real GDP growth	3.9	2.5	1.0	−0.7	2.1
Inflation (GDP deflator)	3.9	4.4	4.1	3.7	2.5

Note: Money growth rates for 1989–1992 are for December relative to previous December; interest rates are averages for the period shown.

Source: DRI/McGraw-Hill.

credit, rather than the decline in the quantity of money.[13] The slow growth of credit in 1989–1991 has also been blamed for the 1990–1991 recession (see Box 16-4).

[13]Ben Bernanke, "Non-Monetary Effects of the Financial Crisis in the Propagation of the Great Depression," *American Economic Review,* June 1983. See, too, Ben Friedman, "Monetary Policy without Quantity Variables," *American Economic Review,* May 1988; and Anil Kashyap, Jeremy Stein, and David Wilcox, "Monetary Policy and Credit Conditions: Evidence from the Composition of External Finance," *American Economic Review,* March 1993. For more recent work on the operation of the credit channel, see Stephen D. Oliner and Glenn D. Rudebusch, "Is There a Broad Credit Channel for Monetary Policy?" Federal Reserve Bank of San Francisco *Economic Review* 1 (1996).

of the monetary aggregates and of debt declined between 1988 and 1989—though M1 growth virtually collapsed while M2 fell very little. The Fed entered 1990 with inflation on its mind, viewing the 2.5 percent GDP growth in 1989 as being at about the sustainable rate.

The recession dates from July 1990, before the Iraqi invasion of Kuwait. We know now that GDP fell in both the third and fourth quarters of 1990, though the third-quarter decline showed up only in revised data in July 1992. But the Fed, then preoccupied with the question of how to deal with the 40 percent rise in the price of oil that followed the Iraqi invasion, held its interest rates constant through the end of the year. Then, as the recession continued, the Fed kept reducing the interest rate, very slowly through 1991, always concerned not to go too far in case it reignited inflation.

At the end of 1991, with the recession probably already over, the data again began to show signs of weakening production and output. There was much talk of a double-dip recession. This time the Fed moved decisively, cutting the discount rate from 4.5 to 3.5 percent. Treasury bill rates moved to their lowest level in 20 years, and then as growth continued sluggish, they fell to their lowest level in 30 years. Interestingly though, long-term interest rates were very slow to come down, as can be seen by looking at the 10-year bond rate in Table 1. The explanation is that markets believed that inflation would soon return.

It is striking that in the 1990–1992 period, the Fed conducted monetary policy almost entirely with reference to interest rates. The reason can be seen in Table 1: The growth rates of the different monetary aggregates diverged wildly.

There was one other special feature of the recession: the view that credit was unusually difficult to get. Even before the recession began, business executives and policy makers were complaining about the difficulty of getting loans. The credit crunch—the reluctance of banks and thrifts to lend—seemed to worsen as the recession continued. The volume of bank loans declined in the recession, confirming the existence of the problem.*

Why was there a crunch? Bank regulators, worried about bank failures, were tightening their standards, trying to make sure the banks did not make bad loans. Banks, in response, tended to move to safety, holding government securities rather than making loans to businesses.

*Ben Bernanke and Cara Lown, "The Credit Crunch," *Brookings Papers on Economic Activity* 2 (1991). See also the special issue on the credit slowdown published by the Federal Reserve Bank of New York *Quarterly Review*, Spring 1993.

Proponents of the central role of credit also argue that *credit rationing* makes interest rates an unreliable indicator of monetary policy. **Credit is rationed when individuals cannot borrow as much as they want at the going interest rate.** Credit is rationed because lenders fear that borrowers who are willing to borrow may not be able to repay. But if credit is rationed at a given interest rate, that interest rate does not fully describe the impact of monetary policy on investment and aggregate demand. Proponents of the credit view argue that the Fed should focus directly on the volume of credit to see what impact monetary policy is having on demand.

16-7

WHICH TARGETS FOR THE FED?

We are now ready to set monetary policy in a broader perspective by discussing the targets of monetary policy. There are three points to note before we get down to the details:

1.   A key distinction is between *ultimate targets* of policy and *intermediate targets*. Ultimate targets are variables such as the inflation rate and the unemployment rate (or real output) whose behavior matters. The interest rate or the rate of growth of money or credit are intermediate targets of policy—targets the Fed aims at so that it can hit the ultimate targets more accurately. The discount rate, open market operations, and reserve requirements are the *instruments* the Fed has with which to hit the targets.[14]

2.   It matters how often the intermediate targets are reset. For instance, if the Fed were to commit itself to 5.5 percent money growth over a period of several years, it would have to be sure that the velocity of money was not going to change unpredictably; otherwise, the actual level of GDP would be far different from the targeted level. If the money target were reset more often, as velocity changed, the Fed could come closer to hitting its ultimate targets.

3.   The need for targeting arises from a lack of knowledge. If the Fed had the right ultimate goals and knew exactly how the economy worked, it could do whatever was needed to keep the economy as close to its ultimate targets as possible.[15]

Intermediate targets give the Fed something concrete and specific to aim for in the next year. That enables the Fed itself to focus on what it should be doing. It also helps the private sector know what to expect. If the Fed announces and will stick to its targets, firms and consumers have a better idea of what monetary policy will be.

Another benefit of specifying targets for monetary policy is that the Fed can then be held *accountable* for its actions. It has a job to do. By announcing targets, the Fed makes it possible for outsiders to discuss whether it is aiming in the right direction and then later to judge whether it succeeded in its aims.

The ideal intermediate target is a variable that the Fed can control exactly and that, at the same time, has an exact relationship with the ultimate targets of policy. For instance, if the ultimate target could be expressed as some particular level of nominal GDP, and if the money multiplier and velocity were both constant, the Fed could hit its ultimate target by having the money base as its intermediate target.

In practice, life is not so simple. Rather, **in choosing intermediate targets, the Fed has to trade off between those targets it can control exactly and those targets that are most closely related to its ultimate targets.**

---

[14]See Benjamin Friedman, "Targets and Indicators of Monetary Policy," in B. Friedman and F. Hahn (eds.), *Handbook of Monetary Economics* (Amsterdam: North-Holland, 1991).

[15]See the discussions of lags and of multiplier uncertainty in Chap. 8.

SUMMARY

1. The stock of money is determined by the Fed through its control of the monetary base (high-powered money); by the public, through its preferred currency-deposit ratio; and by the banks, through their preferred reserve-holding behavior.

2. The money stock is larger than the stock of high-powered money because part of the money stock consists of bank deposits, against which the banks hold less than 1 dollar of reserves per dollar of deposits.

3. The money multiplier is the ratio of the money stock to high-powered money. It is larger the smaller the reserve-deposit ratio and the smaller the currency-deposit ratio.

4. The Fed creates high-powered money in open market purchases when it buys assets (e.g., Treasury bills, gold, foreign exchange) by creating liabilities on its balance sheet. These purchases increase banks' reserves held at the Fed and lead, through the multiplier process, to an increase in the money stock which is larger than the increase in high-powered money.

5. The money multiplier builds up through an adjustment process in which banks make loans (or buy securities) because deposits have increased their reserves above desired levels.

6. The Fed has three basic policy instruments: open market operations, the discount rate, and required reserves for depository institutions.

7. The Fed cannot control both the interest rate and the money stock exactly. It can only choose combinations of the interest rate and money stock that are consistent with the demand-for-money function.

8. The Fed operates monetary policy by specifying target ranges for both the money stock and the interest rate. In order to hit its target level of output, the Fed should concentrate on its money targets if the *IS* curve is unstable or shifts about a great deal. It should concentrate on interest rate targets if the money demand function is the major source of instability in the economy.

9. The Fed targets not only *M*2 and *M*3 and interest rates but also total nonfinancial debt, or the volume of credit, in the economy.

KEY TERMS

credit	foreign exchange market	open market purchase
credit rationing	intervention	pegging the interest rate
credit targets	fractional reserve banking	required reserves
currency-deposit ratio	high-powered money	required-reserve ratio
discount rate	instruments	reserve ratio
disintermediation	intermediate targets	run on a bank
excess reserves	monetary base	ultimate targets
Federal Deposit Insurance	money multiplier	
Corporation (FDIC)	open market desk	
federal funds rate	open market operations	

PROBLEMS

Conceptual

1. The Fed wants to increase the money supply. What are the main instruments available to it, and how can each, specifically, increase the money supply? (*Hint:* There are three.)
2. Can the Fed affect the currency-deposit ratio?
3. Under what circumstances should the Fed conduct monetary policy by targeting mainly *(a)* interest rates or *(b)* the money stock?
4. a. What is a bank run?
   b. Why might one occur?
   c. If the Fed took no action in the face of a bank run, what would be the effects on the money supply and on the money multiplier?
   d. How does the existence of the FDIC help prevent this problem?
5. a. Why does the Fed not stick more closely to its target paths for money?
   b. What are the dangers of targeting nominal interest rates?
6. Categorize each of the following as either an ultimate or intermediate target or an instrument of monetary policy:
   a. Nominal GDP
   b. The discount rate
   c. The monetary base
   d. *M*1
   e. The Treasury bill rate
   f. The unemployment rate
7. What might be the danger in using interest rates as targets for monetary policy when credit rationing is taking place?
8. Why might the Fed choose intermediate targets for its monetary policy, as opposed to directly pursuing its ultimate targets? What are the benefits and the dangers of using these intermediate targets?

Technical

1. Show how an open market sale affects the Fed's balance sheet and also the balance sheet of the commercial bank of the purchaser of the bond sold by the Fed.
2. When the Fed buys or sells gold or foreign exchange, it automatically offsets, or *sterilizes,* the impact of these operations on the monetary base by compensating open market operations. What it does is to buy gold and at the same time sell bonds from its portfolio. Show the effects on the Fed balance sheet of a purchase of gold and a corresponding sterilization through an open market sale.
3. A proposal for "100 percent banking" involves a reserve-deposit ratio of unity. Such a scheme has been proposed for the United States in order to enhance the Fed's control over the money supply.
   a. Indicate why such a scheme would help monetary control.
   b. Indicate what bank balance sheets would look like under this scheme.
   c. Under 100 percent banking, how would banking remain profitable?
4. You, as chair of the Fed (congratulations), are considering whether the monetary base or the interest rate should be used as a target. What information do you need to have to make an informed decision? When would each be a good (or bad!) choice?

Empirical

1. Go to www.federalreserve.gov/FOMC/default.htm, the official website of the Federal Open Market Committee (FOMC) of the Federal Reserve Board. Scroll down the page and choose the link to one of the most recent statements from FOMC meetings. What are the factors cited in this statement that determined the FOMC's decision of changing (or keeping constant) its target for the federal funds rate?

2. Box 16-4 and Table 1 investigate U.S. monetary policy during the 1990–1991 recession. In this exercise you will take a look at the monetary policy conducted by the Federal Reserve during the 2001–? recession (hopefully, by the time the textbook is published you will know what the end date for the recession was). Go to www.economagic.com and get the data that is needed in order to fill out the following table. You can get the money stock measures, annual real GDP growth, GDP deflator, and the 3-month Treasury bill rate from "Most Requested Series." For the debt data, scroll down the page and choose the link to "Department of the Treasury: US Public Debt." For the loan data, under "Browse by Source," choose the link "Federal Reserve, St. Louis." Click on "US Commercial Banking Data," and choose the variable "Commercial and Industrial Loans at all Commercial Banks." Compare your table with Table 1 in Box 16-4.

	1999	2000	2001	2002	2003
Growth rate of $M1$					
Growth rate of $M2$					
Growth rate of $M3$					
Growth rate of debt					
Growth rate of bank loans					
Treasury bill rate (3-month)					
10-year bond rate (Treasury)					
Real GDP growth					
Inflation (GDP deflator)					

Note: Money, debt, and bank loans growth rates are for December to December; interest rates are averages for each year.

CHAPTER 17

Financial Markets and Asset Prices

CHAPTER HIGHLIGHTS

- We can understand how the returns on two different investments are related by asking what sort of returns would make investors willing to hold both.

- The term structure of interest explains how long-term interest rates relate to short-term interest rates.

- In a well-functioning stock market, stock price changes are largely unpredictable.

- Changes in exchange rates can be explained in part as reflecting international differences in interest rates.

Financial markets link the macroeconomy and government policy directly to the lives of everyday people. Changes in interest rates affect our ability to finance a home or a car. The movements of the stock market determine the value of pensions for many people. The rates of return in financial markets also feed back into the goods markets by affecting the levels of investment and consumption. In this chapter we examine the behavior of three important financial markets: the bond market, the stock market, and the foreign exchange market. In each case the analysis begins with two ideas:

- **Markets are forward-looking.**
- **Key relations depend on the idea of *arbitrage:* In equilibrium, prices must make investors equally willing to buy or sell an asset; any other price will place everyone on only one side of the market.**

17-1

INTEREST RATES: LONG AND SHORT TERM

Through much of the text we represent interest rates with the single symbol i, as if there were only one interest rate in the economy. In fact, since an interest rate summarizes the promised repayment terms on a bond or loan, interest rates differ according to the creditworthiness of the issuer, tax treatments, and other factors. The factor of greatest interest here is the length of time the interest rate covers—the *term* of the bond. The Federal Reserve directly manipulates very short term interest rates (moving the *LM* curve), but investment (along the *IS* curve) depends on longer-term rates.

The interest rate on a 10-year bond is usually, but not always, greater than the interest rate on a 1-year bond. **The relation between interest rates of different *maturities* is called the *term structure of interest*.**

Figure 17-1 shows interest rates for U.S. Treasury securities with maturities from 3 months to 30 years. Three patterns emerge. First, interest rates of different maturities mostly go up and down together. Rates were all relatively high in 1981 and low in 2002. Second, the gap between long-term rates and short-term rates varies. In 1989 the interest rate on 30-year bonds and the interest rate on 3-month Treasury bills were about equal, but in January 2002 the 30-year rate was about 4 percentage points higher. Third, long-term rates are usually higher than short-term rates. Between 1980 and January 2002 the 30-year rate averaged about 2.0 percentage points more than the 3-month rate. The theory of the term structure explains these three patterns.

As a concrete example, let's examine the relation between the 1-year rate and the 3-year rate. Pretend that today's date is January 1, 2010. On the financial page of "today's" newspaper you can read the current 1-year rate, $_1i_{2010}$; that is the rate on money lent at the beginning of the year 2010 to be repaid at the beginning of 2011. You can also read the current 3-year rate covering a bond to be repaid at the beginning of the year 2013, $_3i_{2010}$. (The "frontscripts" indicate the length of the investment and the subscripts in their usual spot indicate the date the investment is made.) You have the option of making a 3-year investment today and earning $_3i_{2010}$ each year or of investing

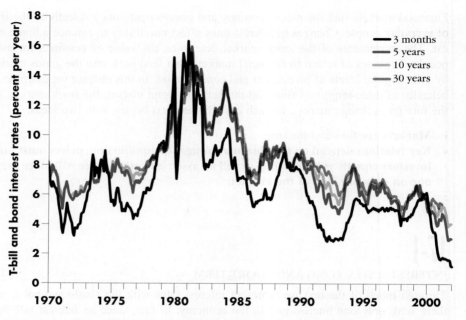

FIGURE 17-1 INTEREST RATES ON TREASURY BILLS AND BONDS, 1970–2002.
(Source: Federal Reserve Economic Data.)

for 1 year, reinvesting for another year at the rate prevailing at the beginning of 2011, and then reinvesting for a final year at the rate prevailing in 2012. Figure 17-2 illustrates the two alternatives.

If all the rates shown in Figure 17-2 were known in advance, the total return from one 3-year investment would have to equal the return from the series of three 1-year investments. If the total returns were not equal, everyone would choose the alternative with the higher return, completely abandoning the other path. For both long-term and short-term investments to coexist when the rates of return are known in advance, the total

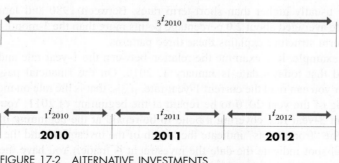

FIGURE 17-2 ALTERNATIVE INVESTMENTS.

BOX 17-1   Compound Interest

$100 invested at 5 percent earns $5 the first year and in the second year earns . . . ? No, not another $5, but $5 additional interest on the principal plus 5 percent of the interest earned the first year ($5 × 0.05 = $0.25), for a second-year total of $5.25. Interest on money invested for multiple periods compounds. Thus, $100 invested at 5 percent grows to $100 × 1.05 = $105.00 after 1 year and ($100 × 1.05) × 1.05 = $110.25 after 2 years. In general, an amount P invested at rate i for t years grows to $P(1 + i)^t$.

Because interest rates multiply rather than add, our term structure equation should really rely on geometric rather than arithmetic averages. Under certainty, a more accurate version of the term structure equation given in the text is $(1 + {}_3i_{2010})^3 = (1 + {}_1i_{2010})(1 + {}_1i_{2011})(1 + {}_1i_{2012})$. For example, if the three short-term interest rates were 5, 10, and 15 percent, the exact 3-year rate would be 9.924 percent, rather than 10 percent. You can see that this difference doesn't matter for understanding the term structure but would be worth paying attention to if you were investing hundreds of millions of dollars.

returns from long and short investments must be equal. This argument illustrates the idea of *arbitrage:* 3 years of returns at the 3-year rate must equal the total of three single-year returns, ${}_3i_{2010} + {}_3i_{2010} + {}_3i_{2010} = {}_1i_{2010} + {}_1i_{2011} + {}_1i_{2012}$. Note that the subscripts on the 3-year rate all indicate that this is the rate agreed to at the beginning of 2010.

We can rewrite the arbitrage condition as ${}_3i_{2010} = ({}_1i_{2010} + {}_1i_{2011} + {}_1i_{2012})/3$. This brings us to our first simple model of the term structure: **The long-term interest rate equals the average of current and future short-term interest rates.** (But see Box 17-1.)

The only problem with this theory is that at the beginning of the year 2010 we can't know either ${}_1i_{2011}$ or ${}_1i_{2012}$ with certainty, although we can make an educated guess. Uncertainty about future short-term rates necessitates two modifications to our simple theory. First, today's long-term rate depends on the current short-term rate and the *expected* future short-term rates. Second, uncertainty implies risk, and long-term investments command a *term premium, PR,* to compensate for this risk. Putting these into our example, we would write the term structure equation as

$$ {}_3i_{2010} = \frac{{}_1i_{2010} + {}_1i^e_{2011} + {}_1i^e_{2012}}{3} + PR \qquad (1) $$

where the e superscripts indicate the expectation of the future short-term interest rate. Written this way, equation (1) shows the *expectations theory of the term structure.* Term premiums vary over time but are generally higher for longer-term rates. The higher-term premiums in part reflect the higher risk associated (for reasons discussed below) with the greater price volatility of longer-term bonds. Table 17-1 shows average term premiums based on the interest rates shown in Figure 17-1.

TABLE 17-1	Average Term Premiums above 3-Month Treasury Bill, 1970–2002
TERM	PREMIUM
3 months	—
6 months	0.14
1 year	0.67
2 years	1.04
3 years	1.15
5 years	1.37
7 years	1.53
10 years	1.59
30 years	1.92

Source: Federal Reserve Economic Data.

THE YIELD CURVE

Interest rates for different maturities are shown on the *yield curve,* a snapshot of the opportunities available on a particular day. Figure 17-3 shows two such yield curves, one for January 2002 and one for January 1981. Because long rates are generally higher than short rates, the yield curve usually rises with maturity, as it did in January 2002. Occasionally, the yield curve slopes down, meaning that short rates are above long rates. The expectations theory of the term structure implies that a downward-sloping yield curve means that financial markets expect interest rates to fall. (Since the long rate is an average of current and future short rates, the long rate can be below the current short rate only if future short rates are expected to be below the current short rate.)

A downward-sloping yield curve is often, but not always, a recessionary signal.[1] It signals that the market anticipates a coming drop in interest rates. Low interest rates are often, but not always, associated with a drop in aggregate demand through a leftward shift of the *IS* curve.

BOND PRICES AND YIELDS

Bond prices are inversely related to interest rates. If a bond is to pay $100 a year from now and has an interest rate i, then its price, P, must be such that $P(1 + i) = 100$ or $P = 100/(1 + i)$. For example, a $100 bond will have a 5 percent yield if its price is $95.24 \, [\$95.24 = \$100/(1 + 0.05)]$.

[1]Michael Deuker presents evidence for this in "Strengthening the Case for the Yield Curve as a Predictor of U.S. Recessions," Federal Reserve Bank of St. Louis *Review,* March–April 1997. See also Marcelle Chauvet and Simon Potter, "Forecasting Recessions Using the Yield Curve," University of California working paper, June 2001.

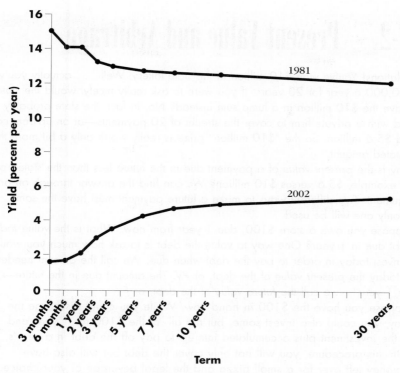

FIGURE 17-3   COMPARISON OF TWO YIELD CURVES.
(*Source: Federal Reserve Economic Data.*)

Most bonds in the United States make a periodic payment called a *coupon* (because once upon a time there were actual coupons that had to be clipped and mailed in to receive payment) and then return the bond's *face value* at maturity. For example, a bond priced at $100 with a $5 coupon at the end of year 1 and again at the end of year 2, plus a $100 return of principal at the end of year 2, would have a 5 percent yield: $100 × (1.05)^2 = $5 × (1.05) + $5 + $100. When a bond price equals its face value, the bond is said to trade "at par."

In order to see how changes in market interest rates affect bond prices, suppose that an instant after you bought the bond just described the market interest rate rose from 5 to 10 percent. In order to sell the bond, you would have to lower the price sufficiently to compensate the buyer for receiving $5 coupons instead of the $10 available with a brand-new bond: $P × (1.10)^2 = $5 × (1.10) + $5 + 100, or $P = $91.32. The longer the remaining term of the bond, the greater the required change in the price to compensate for a change in the interest rate. For this reason, long-term bonds are subject to considerable price fluctuations. The same interest rate change applied to a 30-year bond would drop the bond's price to $52.87.

BOX 17-2   Present Value and Arbitrage

Congratulations! You've won $10 million in the state lottery. Well . . . actually you've won $500,000 a year for 20 years. If you were to ask really nicely, would the state let you have the $10 million in a lump sum instead? No. In fact, the state probably contracted with a private firm to cover the stream of 20 payments—at an up-front cost of around $5.6 million. So the "$10 million" prize is really worth only a bit more than half the stated amount.

Why is the *present value* of a payment due in the future less than the stated payment, for example, $5.6 versus $10 million? We can find the answer through an arbitrage argument: Two different ways to make a future payment must have the same value or only one will be used.

Suppose you owe a store $100, due 1 year from now. What is the value *today* of the debt due in 1 year? One way to value the debt is to ask how much you would need to invest today in order to pay the debt when due. We call the amount needed to invest today the *present value* of the debt, or *PV*. The amount due in the future—"$100 in 1 year"—we call the *future value* of the debt, or *FV*.

Suppose you have the $100 in hand now. While you could discharge the debt today, you could also invest some, but not all, of the $100 for 1 year and then use the investment plus accumulated interest to pay off the debt in a year's time. With this procedure, you will not only cover the debt but will also have enough money left over for a small pizza and the legal beverage of your choice. The amount you need to invest is less than *FV* since part of the debt will be covered by accumulated interest. Since *FV*-in-a-year and *PV*-today-plus-interest both discharge the debt, they must have the same value: $FV = PV + i \times PV$. We can turn this around to figure out the present value of a future debt, that is, how much needs to be set aside today:

$$PV = \frac{FV}{1 + i}$$

The same argument can be extended to payments due more than 1 year in the future. For a debt due in 2 years we have $PV = FV/(1 + i)^2$, and for a debt due in T years we have $PV = FV/(1 + i)^T$. If you owe FV_1 due in 1 year and FV_2 due in 2 years, then to cover both debts, you would need to set aside

$$PV = \frac{FV_1}{(1 + i)^1} + \frac{FV_2}{(1 + i)^2}$$

By the way, another common name for "present value" is *net present value*, or *NPV*.

BOX 17-3　The Math of Net Present Value, Prices, and Yield

Formally, the price of a bond equals the *net present value (NPV)* of coupons plus face value at current interest rates. If a bond makes *T* annual coupon payments and returns face value *F* at the end of year *T*, its price must be

$$P = \frac{c}{1+i} + \frac{c}{(1+i)^2} + \ldots + \frac{c}{(1+i)^T} + \frac{F}{(1+i)^T}$$

Using an algebraic theorem about geometric series, this can be rewritten

$$P = \frac{c}{i}\left[1 - \frac{1}{(1+i)^T}\right] + \frac{F}{(1+i)^T}$$

Note two useful facts: First, if $i = c/P$, then $P = F$. For example, a bond with a $100 face value and a $5 coupon is, unsurprisingly, worth $100 when the interest rate is 5 percent. Second, the formula for a bond that lasts forever, called a *consol* or a *perpetuity*, is simply $P = c/i$. A very long term bond with a $5 coupon is worth $100 when the interest rate is 5 percent, but the price drops to $50 if the interest rate rises to 10 percent. Consols exist in Canada and the United Kingdom, but they are rarely traded in the United States. However, the consol formula gives a reasonable approximation to the pricing of common long-term bonds such as 30-year U.S. government bonds.

 ## 17-2

THE RANDOM WALK OF STOCK PRICES

Surely, one of the best-established facts in economics is that changes in stock prices are essentially unpredictable. And just as surely, this fact is one of the least believed and most disliked. After all, one objective of the study of economics is the ability to explain and predict market behavior. What we show in this section is that it is exactly the fact that the stock market is well understood that makes stock price changes hard to predict.

Figure 17-4 plots an index of Canadian stock prices against the same prices lagged 1 month.[2] The central stylized fact of the plot is that the data are tightly scattered around

---

[2]Actually, the plot shows the natural logarithm of the price.

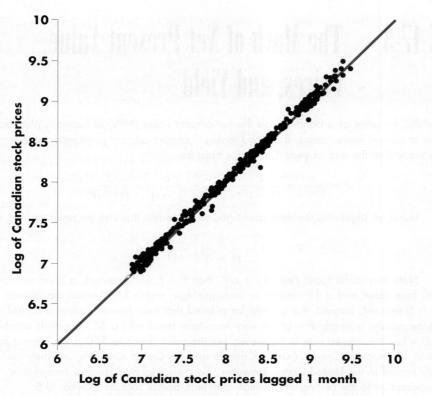

FIGURE 17-4   RELATIONSHIP OF CANADIAN STOCK PRICES TO THEIR PAST VALUES, 1970–2002.

(Source: Datastream.)

a 45° line that intersects the vertical axis a smidgen above the point (0, 0). We can write the equation for the 45° line as $P_{t+1} \approx P_t + \epsilon$ or, to account for the small vertical displacement, as

$$P_{t+1} = a + P_t + \epsilon \qquad (2)$$

where a is quite small and represents the expected return to holding stocks. In either formulation ϵ represents the surprise change in the stock price.

Why should an innocuous equation like (2) be so controversial?[3] First, equation (2) implies that aside from the very small a component, the change in the stock price, $\Delta P = a + \epsilon$, is unpredictable. Second, equation (2) states that following a shock, stock prices *do not* have a tendency to return to a "normal" level. Rather, changes to stock prices are independent over time. If stocks did well last month, they are no more likely

---

[3]"Controversial" is a funny term here. Economists *all* agree that equation (2) gives an excellent description of the behavior of major stock markets.

to either do well or do poorly this month than at any other time. The process described by equation (2) is called a *random walk*.[4] A random walk is a sign of market efficiency. Using just two assumptions, we can show that a random walk is just what we should expect from a well-functioning market:

• The price of a stock is the net present value of expected dividends.
• New information changes expectations of future dividends but only by surprise, since if it's not a surprise, it's not *new* information.

Suppose that at date t we expect to start receiving dividends in k periods at levels d_{t+k}, d_{t+k+1}, d_{t+k+2}, and so on. The stock price at date t will equal the net present value of these expected dividends, discounted at a rate r. (The discount rate r will be higher than the interest rate on Treasury bills in order to compensate for the riskiness of stock investment.) We can write the relation as

$$P_t = \frac{d_{t+k}}{(1+r)^k} + \frac{d_{t+k+1}}{(1+r)^{k+1}} + \frac{d_{t+k+2}}{(1+r)^{k+2}} + \cdots \qquad (3)$$

At date $t+1$ the same relation will apply, but with dividends discounted by one less interest factor since it will be closer to their receipt:

$$P_{t+1} = \frac{d_{t+1+(k-1)}}{(1+r)^{k-1}} + \frac{d_{t+1+(k)}}{(1+r)^k} + \frac{d_{t+1+(k+1)}}{(1+r)^{k+1}} + \cdots \qquad (4)$$

Multiply both sides of equation (3) by $(1+r)$ to make the right-hand side look just like the right-hand side of equation (4). For example, the first term becomes

$$\frac{d_{t+k}}{(1+r)^k} \times (1+r) = \frac{d_{t+k}}{(1+r)^k} \times \frac{1}{(1+r)^{-1}} = \frac{d_{t+k}}{(1+r)^{k-1}} = \frac{d_{t+1+(k-1)}}{(1+r)^{k-1}}$$

Equating P_{t+1} with P_t times $(1+r)$ we have

$$P_{t+1} = (1+r)P_t \qquad (5)$$

In practice, our expectations of future dividends are likely to change between periods t and $t+1$, so the effect of this news must be added to equation (5), as in

$$P_{t+1} = (1+r)P_t + \epsilon \qquad (6)$$

which is pretty much what Figure 17-4 shows.[5]

Not all stock markets are "efficient" in the sense of the market following a random walk, but the really major markets do follow random walks. Figure 17-5 shows the same picture of tomorrow's price versus today's as does Figure 17-4, only for U.S. rather than Canadian data.

[4]The classic—and readable—book on the subject is Burton Malkiel's *A Random Walk Down Wall Street: Updated for the 1990s Investor* (New York: Norton 1991).

[5]More precisely we could write $P_{t+1} = (1+r)P_t \times \epsilon$ and then, taking logarithms of both sides, write $\ln P_{t+1} = \ln(1+r) + \ln P_t + \ln \epsilon$. The log of P is what's actually shown in Figs. 17-4 and 17-5. Note that the "small intercept," a, should approximately equal the expected return to stocks, r.

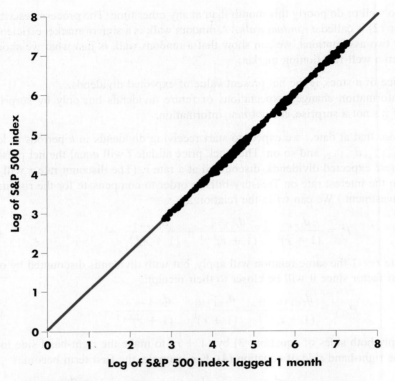

FIGURE 17-5   RELATIONSHIP OF S&P 500 INDEX TO PAST VALUES.

The diagram shows the close correspondence of the index to its value from the previous month. (Source: www.economagic.com.)

Figure 17-5 is based on the Standard & Poor's (S&P) 500 index, an index of the stocks of 500 large companies in the U.S. stock market. The equation behind the line in Figure 17-5, estimated using monthly data from 1950 through 2002, is

$$\ln P_{t+1} = .011 + .999 \ln P_t$$

which corresponds extraordinarily well with the theoretical prediction.

Theory and data are in agreement, but is it *really* true that stock returns are unpredictable? The answer is no, yes, and no.

Figure 17-6 shows a plot of the 3-month Treasury bill interest rate shown in Figure 17-1, along with the return to the S&P 500. The return to the stock market is extraordinarily volatile compared to interest rates, but it is also substantially higher on average. So the first "no" is because the return is predictably higher *on average* than the return on less volatile investments. Similarly, some classes of stocks are riskier than others and so have predictably higher returns. The "yes" is because while mean return is higher, the timing of swings is unpredictable, as random-walk theory predicts.

BOX 17-4   Linking the Bond Market and Stock Market

The stock market is heavily influenced by long-term interest rates, as stock prices fall when interest rates rise. One easy way to understand the connection is to pretend that a stock is expected to pay a dividend, d, forever, making the stock much like a consol. The present value formula in equation (3) would simplify to $P = d/r$. A very small change in r will cause a very large change in P.

As an example, a rise in long-term interest rates from 5 to 5.05 percent would be enough to drop the entire stock market 1 percent in this formulation. A .05 interest rate change is—outside financial markets—too small to notice. A 1 percent drop in the stock market is certainly large enough to make the headlines of the business section of the newspaper.

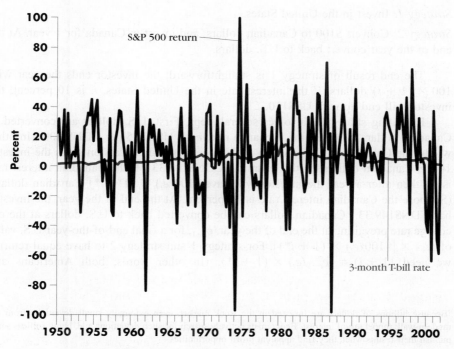

FIGURE 17-6   COMPARISON OF TREASURY BILL RATE TO S&P 500 INDEX, 1950–2002.
(*Source: www.economagic.com; and Federal Reserve Economic Data.*)

The final "no" arises because there are findings of return predictability, particularly over very short (weeks) and very long (decades) periods.[6] Nonetheless, the random-walk model is probably a $99\,^{44}\!/_{100}$ percent accurate description of stock market behavior.

During the 1990s the United States saw an unprecedented run-up in stock prices. But as the millennium turned, the market fell sharply. As we saw in Chapter 13, the value of the stock market can have a considerable effect on the macroeconomy. Some observers sharply criticized the Fed for not having raised interest rates early on to "burst the bubble" in the stock market and thus prevent the subsequent drop. But Fed governors sensibly replied that they are in no better position than anyone else to be sure that the stock market is "too high"—and that in any event the Fed's job is to manage unemployment and inflation, not the stock market.

 # 17-3

EXCHANGE RATES AND INTEREST RATES

Arbitrage arguments also link exchange rate changes to international interest rate differentials. Consider the following two investment strategies for an American wishing to invest $100 for 1 year:[7]

Strategy 1: Invest in the United States.

Strategy 2: Convert $100 to Canadian dollars, and invest in Canada for 1 year. At the end of the year convert back to U.S. dollars.

The end result of strategy 1 is straightforward; the investor ends the year with $100 \times (1 + i)$ dollars. If the interest rate in the United States, i, is 10 percent, the investor will end up with US$110.

Executing strategy 2 involves several steps. First, U.S. dollars are converted to Canadian dollars. Suppose the exchange rate, e_t, is US$0.75 per CDN$1.00. (In other words, the Canadian dollar is worth 75 U.S. cents.) The conversion gives the investor $100/e_t$ Canadian dollars (in this example, CDN$133.33). If the Canadian interest rate is i^*, then after a year the investor will have $(100/e_t) \times (1 + i^*)$ Canadian dollars. (Suppose the Canadian interest rate is 12 percent. At the end of the year, the investor has CDN$149.33.) Canadian dollars can be converted back to U.S. dollars at the exchange rate prevailing at the end of the year, e_{t+1}, for a final end-of-the-year U.S. value of $e_{t+1} \times [(100/e_t) \times (1 + i^*)]$. For strategy 1 and strategy 2 to have equal returns, we need $(1 + i) = (e_{t+1}/e_t) \times (1 + i^*)$. (In other words, both Americans and

---

[6]Because billions of dollars are invested in the stock market, even extremely small deviations from the random-walk model are of interest. Economists actively search for such deviations and, being selfless sorts, publish their results when they find apparent profit opportunities.

[7]Remember that neither of these are investment in the $C + I + G + NX$ sense.

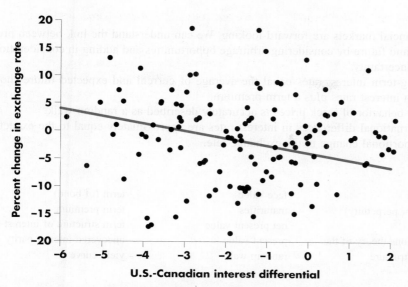

FIGURE 17-7   RELATIONSHIP OF THE CHANGE IN THE U.S.-CANADIAN EXCHANGE RATE TO U.S.-CANADIAN INTEREST RATE DIFFERENTIALS.

(Source: www.economagic.com; Bank of Canada and Federal Reserve Economic Data.)

Canadians should have invested only in Canada if $e_{t+1} > .737$ or only in the United States if $e_{t+1} < .737$.) This relation can be closely approximated by

$$\frac{e_{t+1} - e_t}{e_t} = i - i^* \qquad (7)$$

which is sometimes called *uncovered interest parity*—"uncovered" because e_{t+1} is not known with certainty at the time the investment is made. However, e_{t+1} should turn out to be higher than the prediction in equation (7) about half the time and lower about half the time. Since there is an inherent risk, equation (7) may not hold exactly, even on average.

The vertical axis in Figure 17-7 shows changes in the Canadian dollar—the horizontal axis shows interest rate differentials.[8] Unsurprisingly, e_{t+1} is frequently much higher or much lower than might have been expected at time t. During the period shown, the exchange rate change averaged .13 percent per year more than the U.S.-Canadian interest rate differential. The relation between interest rate differentials and exchange rate changes is roughly, but not perfectly, as predicted. Uncovered interest parity provides a good first approximation to the data we see in the world.

---

[8]More precisely, the vertical is 400 times the percentage change in e at 90-day intervals and the horizontal axis is the difference in the U.S. and Canadian 3-month interest rate.

SUMMARY

1. Financial markets are forward-looking. We can understand the link between present and future by considering arbitrage opportunities and adding in considerations of uncertainty.
2. Long-term interest rates equal the average of current and expected future short-term interest rates plus a term premium.
3. The behavior of stock prices is accurately described as a random walk.
4. International differences in interest rates are approximately equal to the expected proportional change in the exchange rate.

KEY TERMS

arbitrage	face value	term (of bond)
consol (or perpetuity)	maturities	term premium
coupon	net present value	term structure of interest
expectations theory of the	present value	uncovered interest parity
term structure	random walk	yield curve

PROBLEMS

Conceptual

1. What role do financial markets play in the economy? Why do we, as macroeconomists, study them?
2. What is arbitrage? What makes the concept of arbitrage so central to our understanding of financial markets?
3.* Suppose you observe that short-term interest rates are higher than long-term interest rates.
    a. What expectations must people have regarding future interest rates?
    b. Why might the above relationship signal a recession? Why might it not?
    c. What will the yield curve for this problem look like?
4. Why is the fact that stock prices follow a random walk a signal of stock market efficiency? What would have to be true if stock prices did not follow a random walk?
5. We saw in Section 17-2 that stock prices reflect expectations regarding the future dividend payments of firms and the future direction of interest rates. Given this, why might stock prices be a good predictor of recessions?
6. Explain why an increase in U.S. interest rates relative to Canadian interest rates would affect the U.S.-Canadian dollar exchange rate.

Technical

1. a. What is the relationship between the rates of interest on a 10-year bond and on the series of 1-year bonds covering the same period? Assume, for the moment, that all interest rates are known in advance, so there is no uncertainty.
    b. Suppose the interest rate on the 10-year bond is 12 percent and that the interest rates on 1-year bonds, for the next 10 years, are expected to remain at 10 percent. What must the term premium be on the 10-year bond?

*An asterisk denotes a more difficult problem.

2. **a.** Suppose a 10-year bond is to be issued at par, so its price is equal to its $100 face value. Suppose also that the prevailing rate of interest on the bond is 10 percent. How big would the bond's coupon have to be to induce people to hold it?

    b. Now suppose that, just after this bond has been issued [its coupon is now fixed at the rate you found in part (**a**)], interest rates on all 10-year bonds fall to 5 percent. What will happen to the bond's price? If you happened to be holding this bond, would this help you, hurt you, or not affect you at all?

3.* Suppose that Japanese interest rates increase 5 percentage points and those in the United States remain fixed. What will happen to the relative value of this period's versus next period's dollar-yen exchange rate? [*Hint:* Use equation (7).]

4. Since 1992, the average return to holding U.S. common stocks has been 11 percent, which is much higher than the average return experienced from the end of World War II through 1991. Given the model of stock price determination discussed in this chapter, what do such high returns imply about the market's expectations regarding the future profitability of U.S. firms?

Empirical

1. Figure 17-1 presents the evolution of long- and short-term interest rates on U.S. Treasury bills and bonds. The graph illustrates that long-term interest rates are usually higher than short-term rates. Go to www.economagic.com and examine if the same thing is true for interest rates on European Union or Australian Treasury bonds. Under "Browse by Source," choose the link to "Australia" or "Central Bank of Europe."

2. Figures 17-4 and 17-5 present the relationship of Canadian and U.S. stock prices to their past values, illustrating the random walk of stock prices. Does this relationship hold for Australian stock prices? Go to www.economagic.com, and under "Browse by Source," choose the heading "Australia." Choose the category "Share Markets," and copy the variable "ASX: 200" into an EXCEL spreadsheet. Calculate the natural logarithm of this variable [using the function *ln()*] and create a scatterplot that has the log of Australian stock prices lagged 1 month on the X axis, and the log of Australian stock prices on the Y axis. Does your graph look like the ones in Figures 17-4 and 17-5?

PART 5

Big Events, International Adjustments, and Advanced Topics

CHAPTER 18

Big Events: The Economics of Depression, Hyperinflation, and Deficits

CHAPTER HIGHLIGHTS

- Modern macroeconomics grew out of the Great Depression.

- Money and inflation are tightly linked during high inflations.

- Large budget deficits typically play a role in the extensive money creation that generates hyperinflations.

- After years of massive budget deficits in the United States, the budget balance turned to a large but temporary surplus at the end of the twentieth century.

- We ask whether the social security system will crash in the twenty-first century.

Great events shape both the economy and the study of economics. The study of macroeconomics in particular grows out of economic experiences—especially traumatic experiences. In the Great Depression one-fourth of the labor force in the United States was out looking for work. During the twentieth century many countries experienced hyperinflations in which prices doubled every month. Over the last part of the twentieth century the budget balance in the United States swung from massive deficit back to surplus and then early in this century, back to deficit. And looking at a possible future catastrophe, we ask whether the social security system will survive or crash in the twenty-first century.

18-1

THE GREAT DEPRESSION: THE FACTS

The *Great Depression* shaped many institutions in the economy, including the Federal Reserve and modern macroeconomics.[1] The essential facts about the Depression are shown in Table 18-1.

The best-known event of the Great Depression is the stock market crash. Between September 1929 and June 1932, the market fell by 85 percent, which means that stocks worth $1,000 at the stock market peak were worth only $150 at the bottom of the market in 1932. The Depression and the stock market crash are popularly thought of as almost the same thing. In fact, the economy started turning down in August 1929, before the stock market crash, and continued falling until 1933.

Between 1929 and 1933, GNP fell by nearly 30 percent and the unemployment rate rose from 3 to 25 percent. Until early 1931, the economy was suffering from a very severe depression, but not one that was out of the range of the experience of the previous century.[2] It was in the period from early 1931 until Franklin Roosevelt became president in March 1933 that the Depression became "Great." More than anything else, the Great Depression is remembered for the mass unemployment that it brought. During the 10 years 1931 to 1940, the unemployment rate averaged 18.8 percent, ranging between a low of 14.3 percent in 1937 and a high of 24.9 percent in 1933.[3] By contrast, the post-World War II high, reached in 1982, was under 11 percent.

---

[1] A nice historical perspective is given in J. Bradford De Long, "Keynesianism, Pennsylvania Avenue Style: Some Economic Consequences of the Employment Act of 1946," *Journal of Economic Perspectives,* Summer 1996.

[2] The classic work by Milton Friedman and Anna J. Schwartz, *A Monetary History of the United States, 1867–1960* (Princeton, NJ: Princeton University Press, 1963), gives a very detailed account of the Great Depression, comparing it with other recessions and emphasizing the role of the Fed.

[3] Michael Darby, "Three-and-a-Half Million U.S. Employees Have Been Mislaid: Or, an Explanation of Unemployment, 1934–1941," *Journal of Political Economy,* February 1976. Darby argues that unemployment has been mismeasured after 1933 because those on government work relief programs are counted as unemployed. Adjusted for those individuals, the unemployment rate falls rapidly from 20.6 percent in 1933 to below 10 percent in 1936. See also Thomas Mayer, "Money and the Great Depression: A Critique of Professor Temin's Thesis," *Explorations in Economic History,* April 1978; and Karl Brunner (ed.), *The Great Depression Revisited* (Boston: Martinus Nijhoff, 1981).

TABLE 18-1 Economic Statistics of the Great Depression (see back endsheet)

	(1)	(2)	(3)	(4)	(5)	(6)	(7)	(8)	(9)	(10)
YEAR	GNP, 1992 $, BILLIONS	I/GNP, %	G, 1992 $, BILLIONS	UN-EMPLOY-MENT RATE, %	CPI, 1929 = 100	COM-MERCIAL PAPER RATE, %	AAA RATE, %	STOCK MARKET INDEX*	M1, 1929 = 100	FULL-EMPLOY-MENT SURPLUS/Y*, %†
1929	938.1	17.8	121.9	3.2	100.0	5.9	4.7	83.1	100.0	−0.8
1930	850.2	13.5	133.0	8.7	97.4	3.6	4.6	67.2	96.2	−1.4
1931	784.9	9.0	137.7	15.9	88.7	2.6	4.6	43.6	89.4	−3.1
1932	676.1	3.5	131.2	23.6	79.7	2.7	5.0	22.1	78.0	−0.9
1933	662.1	3.8	127.6	24.9	75.4	1.7	4.5	28.6	73.5	1.6
1934	713.7	5.5	145.2	21.7	78.0	1.0	4.0	31.4	81.4	0.2
1935	777.4	9.2	148.5	20.1	80.1	0.8	3.6	33.9	96.6	−0.1
1936	882.7	10.9	174.4	16.9	80.9	0.8	3.2	49.4	110.6	−1.1
1937	923.5	12.8	167.8	14.3	83.3	0.9	3.3	49.2	114.8	1.8
1938	885.7	8.1	182.7	19.0	82.3	0.8	3.2	36.7	115.9	0.6
1939	953.0	10.5	190.2	17.2	81.0	0.6	3.0	38.5	127.3	−0.1

*Stock market index is Standard & Poor's composite index, which includes 500 stocks; September 1929 = 100.

†Y* denotes full-employment output.

Source: Cols. 1, 2, 3: U.S. Department of Commerce, *The National Income and Product Accounts of the United States, 1929–1974*. Col. 4: Revised Bureau of Labor Statistics data taken from Michael Darby, "Three-and-a-Half Million U.S. Employees Have Been Mislaid: Or, an Explanation of Unemployment, 1934–1941," *Journal of Political Economy*, February 1976. Cols. 5, 6, 7: *Economic Report of the President*, 1957. Col. 8: Standard & Poor's Statistical Service, *Security Price Index Record*, 1978. Col. 9: Milton Friedman and Anna J. Schwartz, *A Monetary History of the United States, 1867–1960* (Princeton, NJ: Princeton University Press, 1963), table A1, col. 7. Col. 10: E. Cary Brown, "Fiscal Policy in the Thirties: A Reappraisal," *American Economic Review*, December 1956, table 1, cols. 3, 5, and 19.

Investment collapsed in the Great Depression; indeed, net investment was negative from 1931 to 1935. The consumer price index fell nearly 25 percent from 1929 to 1933.

In the recovery, from 1933 to 1937, real GNP grew at a rapid annual rate of nearly 9 percent, but even that did not get the unemployment rate down to normal levels. Then, in 1937–1938 there was a major recession within the Depression, pushing the unemployment rate back up to nearly 20 percent. In the second half of the decade, short-term interest rates, such as the commercial paper rate, were near zero.

ECONOMIC POLICY

What was economic policy during this period? The money stock had already declined nearly 4 percent from 1929 to 1930, and then it fell rapidly in 1931 and 1932 and continued falling through April 1933.

The fall in the money stock was in part the result of large-scale bank failures. Banks failed because they did not have the reserves with which to meet customers' cash withdrawals,[4] and in failing they destroyed deposits and hence reduced the money

[4]We discussed bank runs in Chap. 16.

TABLE 18-2   Government Spending and Revenue, 1929–1939
(Percent)

	TOTAL GOVERNMENT*		FEDERAL GOVERNMENT		
	(1)	(2)	(3)	(4)	(5)
YEAR	EXPEN-DITURE/ GNP	ACTUAL SURPLUS/ GNP	EXPEN-DITURE/ GNP	ACTUAL SURPLUS/ GNP	TOTAL GOVERNMENT:* FULL-EMPLOYMENT SURPLUS/Y*†
1929	10.0	1.0	2.5	1.2	−0.8
1930	12.3	−0.3	3.1	0.3	−1.4
1931	16.4	−3.8	5.5	−2.8	−3.1
1932	18.3	−3.1	5.5	−2.6	−0.9
1933	19.2	−2.5	7.2	−2.3	1.6
1934	19.8	−3.7	9.8	−4.4	0.2
1935	18.6	−2.8	9.0	−3.6	−0.1
1936	19.5	−3.8	10.5	−4.4	−1.1
1937	16.6	0.3	8.2	0.4	1.8
1938	19.8	−2.1	10.2	−2.5	0.6
1939	19.4	−2.4	9.8	−2.4	−0.1

*Includes federal, state, and local.

†Y* denotes full-employment output.

Source: Cols. 1, 2, 3, 4: *Economic Report of the President,* 1972, tables B1 and B70. Col. 5: E. Cary Brown, "Fiscal Policy in the Thirties: A Reappraisal," *American Economic Review,* December 1956, table 1, cols. 3, 5, and 19.

stock. But the failures went further in reducing the money stock, because they led to a loss of confidence on the part of depositors and hence to an increase in the desired currency-deposit ratio. Furthermore, banks that had not yet failed adjusted to the possibility of a run by increasing reserve holdings relative to deposits. The rise in the currency-deposit ratio and the reserve-deposit ratio reduced the money multiplier and hence sharply contracted the money stock.

The Fed took very few steps to offset the fall in the money supply. For a few months in 1932 it did undertake a program of open market purchases, but otherwise seemed to acquiesce in bank closings and certainly failed to act vigorously to prevent the collapse of the financial system.[5]

Fiscal policy, too, was weak. The natural impulse of politicians then was to balance the budget in times of trouble, and both major presidential candidates campaigned on balanced-budget platforms in 1932. In fact, as Table 18-2 shows, the federal government ran large deficits, particularly for that time, averaging 2.6 percent of GNP from 1931 to 1933 and even more later. (But these deficits are lower as a percentage of GNP than those in the early 1990s.) The belief in budget balancing was more than rhetoric, however, for state and local governments raised taxes to match their expenditures, as did the federal government, particularly in 1932 and 1933. President Roosevelt tried seriously to balance the budget—he was no Keynesian. The full-employment surplus

[5]Friedman and Schwartz (*A Monetary History*) speculate on the reasons for the Fed's inaction; the whodunit or who didn't do it on pages 407–419 of their book is fascinating.

BOX 18-1   Black Tuesday and Black Monday

On Tuesday, October 29, 1929, the New York stock market crashed, with the Dow Jones Average falling by 12 percent. The "Great Crash" has remained fixed in the popular mind as the genesis of the Great Depression.

The crash of 1987, on Monday, October 19, was far worse in terms of the stock market. On that day the Dow dropped 22.6 percent. The next day, stock markets around the world also fell sharply. But perhaps those who learn from history are blessed not to repeat it. In 1987, the Fed and other central banks acted instantly, promising to flood the market with unlimited liquidity if necessary to prevent a panic. (The Fed allowed the federal funds rate—the interest rate on 1-day loans—to drop massively, from 7.56 percent on the 19th to 6.87 on the 20th and then to 6.50 percent on the 21st.) After a few jittery days, investors and the general public regained confidence and both the stock market and the economy continued to prosper.

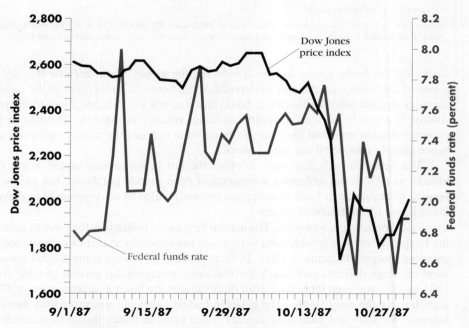

FIGURE 1   THE DOW JONES INDUSTRIAL AVERAGE AND THE INTEREST RATE ON FEDERAL FUNDS, SEPTEMBER AND OCTOBER 1987.

(Source: Datastream International.)

shows fiscal policy (combined state, local, and federal) to have been most expansionary in 1931 and to have moved to a more contractionary level from 1932 to 1934. In fact, the full-employment surplus was positive in 1933 and 1934, despite the actual deficits. Of course, the concept of the full-employment surplus had not yet been invented in the 1930s.

Economic activity recovered in the period from 1933 to 1937, with fiscal policy becoming more expansionary and the money stock growing rapidly. The growth of the money stock was based on an inflow of gold from Europe. This provided high-powered money for the monetary system. It was in the 1930s that the Fed acquired most of its current holdings of gold.

INSTITUTIONAL CHANGE

The period from 1933 to 1937 also saw substantial legislative and administrative action—the *New Deal*—from the Roosevelt administration. The Fed was reorganized, and the Federal Deposit Insurance Corporation (FDIC) was established to insure deposits and supervise banks. A number of regulatory agencies were also created, most notably the Securities and Exchange Commission, which regulates the securities industry. Its purpose was to prevent speculative excesses that were thought to be largely responsible for the stock market crash.

The Social Security Administration was set up so that the elderly would not have to rely on their own savings to ensure themselves a minimally adequate standard of living in retirement. By the mid-1990s, such social welfare payments would be the biggest single item in the federal budget. The Roosevelt administration also believed that the route to recovery lay in increasing wages and prices, so it encouraged trade unionization, as well as price-raising and price-fixing schemes by business, through the National Recovery Administration.

INTERNATIONAL ASPECTS

The Great Depression was virtually worldwide. To some extent, this was the result of the collapse of the international financial system.[6] It resulted, too, from the mutual adoption by many countries (including the United States) of high-tariff policies, which were intended to keep out foreign goods in order to protect domestic producers.

The policies were called "beggar-thy-neighbor" strategies (see Chapter 12) since they attempted to "export" unemployment by improving one country's trade position and hence demand for its goods at the expense of its trading partners. And, of course, if each country keeps out foreign goods, the volume of world trade declines, providing a contractionary influence on the world economy. Table 18-3 documents the decline in *world* production and in world trade.

---

[6]This aspect of the Depression is emphasized by Charles Kindleberger, *The World in Depression, 1929–1939* (Berkeley: University of California Press, 1986); and Gottfried Haberler, *The World Economy, Money and the Great Depression* (Washington, DC: American Enterprise Institute, 1976).

TABLE 18-3	World Production and Trade, 1929–1935 (1929 = 100)			
	1929	1932	1933	1935
Production	100	69	78	95
Trade				
Volume	100	75	76	82
Price	100	53	47	42

Source: League of Nations, *World Economic Survey, 1935/36.*

Almost every country suffered a deep recession in the 1930s, but some countries did better than the United States. Sweden began an expansionary policy in the early 1930s and reduced its unemployment relatively quickly in the second half of the decade. Britain's economy suffered high unemployment in both the 1920s and the 1930s. In 1931, Britain went off the gold standard and the ensuing devaluation of the pound sterling set the stage for at least some improvement. Germany grew rapidly after Hitler came to power and expanded government spending. China escaped the recession until after 1931, essentially because it had a floating exchange rate.[7]

In 1939, real GNP in the United States rose above its 1929 level for the first time in the decade. But it was not until 1942, after the United States formally entered World War II, that the unemployment rate finally fell below 5 percent.

18-2

THE GREAT DEPRESSION: THE ISSUES AND IDEAS

The Depression was the greatest economic crisis the Western world had experienced. In the 1930s, by contrast with the 1990s, it was the economy of the Soviet Union that was booming while Western economies seemed to be collapsing. The questions of what caused the Great Depression, whether it could have been avoided, and whether it could happen again have therefore to be taken seriously.

The classical economics of the time had no well-developed theory that would explain persistent unemployment nor any policy prescriptions to solve the problem. Many economists then did, in fact, recommend government spending as a way of reducing unemployment, but they had no macroeconomic theory by which to justify their recommendations.

Keynes wrote his great work, *The General Theory of Employment, Interest and Money,* in the 1930s, after Britain had suffered during the 1920s from a decade of

[7]A particularly valuable source on the international experience is Barry Eichengreen, *Golden Fetters* (New York: Oxford University Press, 1992). The central thesis of this book is that adherence to the gold standard forced countries into deflation and only after gold was abandoned could recovery start. The devaluation of sterling in 1931 is also discussed in Alec Cairncross and Barry Eichengreen, *Sterling in Decline* (Oxford, England: Basil Blackwell, 1983).

double-digit unemployment and while the United States was in the depths of its Depression. He was fully aware of the seriousness of the issues. As the late Don Patinkin of the Hebrew University put it:

> the period was one of fear and darkness as the Western world struggled with the greatest depression that it had known. . . . [T]here was a definite feeling that by attempting to achieve a scientific understanding of the phenomenon of mass unemployment, one was not only making an intellectual contribution, but was also dealing with a critical problem that endangered the very existence of Western civilization.[8]

Keynesian theory explained what had happened, what could have been done to prevent the Depression, and what could be done to prevent future depressions. The explanation soon became accepted by most macroeconomists, in the process described as the *Keynesian revolution,* even though the Keynesian revolution did not have much impact on economic policymaking in the United States until the 1960s.

THE KEYNESIAN EXPLANATION

The essence of the Keynesian explanation of the Great Depression is contained in the simple aggregate demand model. Growth in the 1920s, in this view, was based on the mass production of the automobile and radio and was fueled by a housing boom. The collapse of growth in the 1930s resulted from the drying up of investment opportunities and a downward shift in investment demand. The collapse of investment, shown in Table 18-1, fits in with this picture. Some researchers also believe there was a downward shift in the consumption function in 1930.[9] Poor fiscal policy, as reflected in the perverse behavior of the full-employment surplus from 1931 to 1933, shares the blame, particularly for making the Depression worse.

It was also widely believed that the experience of the Depression showed that the private economy was inherently unstable—that recessions could begin spontaneously as a result of self-fulfilling prophecy. The experience of the 1930s was, implicitly or explicitly, the basis for the belief that an active stabilization policy was needed to maintain good economic performance.

The Keynesian model not only offered an explanation of what had happened but also suggested policy measures that could have been taken to prevent the Depression and that could be used to prevent future depressions. Vigorous use of countercyclical fiscal policy was the preferred method for reducing cyclical fluctuations. If a recession ever showed signs of deteriorating into a depression, the cure would be to cut taxes and increase government spending. And those policies would, too, have prevented the Depression from being as deep as it was.

---

[8]Don Patinkin, "The Process of Writing *The General Theory:* A Critical Survey," in Don Patinkin and J. Clark Leith (eds.), *Keynes, Cambridge and the General Theory* (Toronto: University of Toronto Press, 1978), p. 3. For a biography of Keynes, see D. E. Moggridge, *John Maynard Keynes* (New York: Macmillan, 1990).

[9]Peter Temin, *Did Monetary Forces Cause the Great Depression?* (New York: Norton, 1976).

What about monetary factors in the Depression? The Fed argued in the 1930s that there was little it could have done to prevent the Depression, because interest rates were already as low as they could possibly go. A variety of sayings of the type "You can't push on a string" were used to explain that further reductions in interest rates would have had no effect if there was no demand for investment. Investment demand was thought to be very unresponsive to the rate of interest—implying a very steep *IS* curve. At the same time, the *LM* curve was believed to be quite flat, though not necessarily reaching the extreme of a liquidity trap. In this situation, monetary expansion would be relatively ineffective in stimulating demand and output.

There is nothing in the *IS-LM* model developed in Chapter 10 that suggests that fiscal policy is more useful than monetary policy for stabilization of the economy. Nonetheless, it is true that until the 1950s, Keynesians tended to give more emphasis to fiscal than to monetary policy.

THE MONETARIST CHALLENGE

The Keynesian emphasis on fiscal policy, and its downplaying of the role of money, was challenged by Milton Friedman and his coworkers during the 1950s.[10] They emphasized the role of monetary policy in determining the behavior of both output and prices.

If monetary policy was to be given an important role, though, it was necessary to dispose of the view that monetary policy had been tried in the Great Depression and had failed. In other words, the idea that you can't push on a string had to be challenged.

The view that monetary policy in the 1930s had been impotent was attacked in 1963 by Friedman and Schwartz in their *Monetary History*. They argued that the Depression, far from showing that money does not matter, "is in fact a tragic testimonial to the importance of monetary factors."[11] They argued, with skill and style, that the failure of the Fed to prevent bank failures and the decline of the money stock from the end of 1930 to 1933 was largely responsible for the recession's being as serious as it was. This monetary view, in turn, came close to being accepted as the orthodox explanation of the Depression.[12]

SYNTHESIS

Both the Keynesian and the monetarist explanations of the Great Depression fit the facts, and both provide answers to the questions of why it happened and how to prevent it from happening again. Both inept fiscal and inept monetary policies made the Great Depression severe. If there had been prompt, strong, expansive monetary and fiscal policy, the economy would have suffered a recession but not the trauma it did.

[10]See, in particular, Milton Friedman (ed.), *Studies in the Quantity Theory of Money* (Chicago: University of Chicago Press, 1956).

[11]Friedman and Schwartz, *A Monetary History*, p. 300.

[12]Ben Bernanke, in "Nonmonetary Effects of the Financial Crisis in the Propagation of the Great Depression," *American Economic Review*, June 1983, takes issue with the monetary view, arguing instead that the destruction of the financial system made it difficult for borrowers to obtain funds needed for investment. However, there is no conflict between that argument and the view that more decisive monetary policy by the Fed in 1930 and 1931 would have mitigated the Depression.

There is general agreement that the Great Depression could not happen today, except, of course, in the event of truly perverse government policy. But that is less likely now than it was then. For one thing, we have history to help us avoid its repetition. Taxes would not again be raised in the middle of a depression, nor would attempts be made to balance the budget. The Fed would seek actively to keep the money supply from falling and not allow bank failures to reduce the money stock.[13] In addition, the government now has a much larger role in the economy than it did then, and automatic stabilizers, including the income tax and unemployment insurance, reduce the size of the multiplier and hence the impact of demand shocks on output.

If, as we argue, there is no inherent conflict between the Keynesian and monetarist explanations of the Great Depression, why has there been controversy over its causes? The reason is that the 1930s are seen as the period that set the stage for massive government intervention in the economy. Those opposed to an active role for government have to explain away the debacle of the economy in the 1930s. If the Depression occurred because of, and not despite, the government (particularly the Fed), the case for an active government role in economic stabilization is weakened. Further, the 1930s are a period in which the economy behaved in such an extreme way that competing theories have to be subjected to the test of whether they can explain that period.

18-3

MONEY AND INFLATION IN ORDINARY BUSINESS CYCLES

Some people believe that money growth and inflation go hand in hand in a very simpleminded way. While money growth is very important in explaining inflation, there's more to the story. At least there's more to the story in ordinary times. That's the message of this section. Later in this chapter we examine hyperinflations—where money growth *is* the dominant player.

Our study of money demand and the long-run aggregate supply curve has shown the following:

- A sustained increase in the growth rate of money will, in the long run when all adjustments have taken place, lead to an equal increase in the rate of inflation. In the long run, the inflation rate is equal to the growth rate of money adjusted for trend growth in real income.
- A sustained increase in money growth will have no long-run effects on the level of output: There is no long-run tradeoff between inflation and output.

This is consistent with the monetarist claim that inflation is caused by money growth, *in the long run.*[14] But as one moves away from the long run, disturbances other than changes in the money stock—such as supply shocks—affect inflation and, conversely, changes in the money stock do have real effects.

[13]See Federal Reserve Board Governor Ben Bernanke's statement in Box 11-1.

[14]See, for instance, Milton Friedman, "Monetarism in Rhetoric and Practice," Bank of Japan *Monetary and Economic Studies,* October 1983.

In examining the links between inflation and money growth, it is convenient to use the *quantity theory of money*. As a reminder, the quantity theory relates the level of nominal income (PY), the money stock (M), and the velocity of money (V):

$$MV = PY \tag{1}$$

Recall that the *velocity of money* is the number of times the money stock turns over each year in financing payments made to purchase the economy's output.

The quantity equation can also be written in terms of the percentage change over time of each of the four terms in equation (1):

$$m + v = \pi + y \tag{2}$$

Putting the inflation rate on the left, we obtain the central result:

$$\pi = m - y + v \tag{3}$$

where m is money growth, v is the percentage change in velocity, π is the inflation rate, and y is the growth rate of output.

Equation (3) can be used to account for the sources of inflation, that is, for what part is due to velocity changes or to money growth or to output growth. The monetarist claim that inflation is predominantly a monetary phenomenon implies that velocity and output changes are small.

Now we turn to the data. Figure 18-1 shows annual $M2$ growth and the inflation rate of the GDP deflator for the United States. We see that the inflation rate and the growth rate of money have broadly moved together. Both trend upward until the late 1970s and trend downward from sometime in the 1980s to the present. But the relationship is *very* rough, with large gaps between the growth lines that persist for several years. As equation (3) shows, that means that changes in output growth or velocity, or both, were affecting inflation.

In Table 18-4 we examine the link between money growth and inflation over longer periods, specifically decades, and also adjust for growth in output. The growth adjustment is made by subtracting the growth rate of output from the growth of money, as implied by equation (3).[15]

In Table 18-4, inflation is closely related to the growth rate of $M2$.[16] For example, in the 1960s money growth less real growth was 2.6 percent and actual inflation averaged 2.4 percent, not far off the mark. Likewise, for the 1970s equation (3) predicts 6.2 percent whereas actual inflation was 6.6 percent. And the same close forecast is evident once more in the 1980s, with a predicted inflation rate of 4.9 percent versus an actual rate of 4.7 percent. But during the 1990s the $M2$/inflation relation seemed to have largely broken down.

---

[15]In making this adjustment for output growth, we are assuming that velocity is not systematically related to income. That means we are assuming a unit income elasticity of money demand (see Chap. 15). In general, the inflation rate is equal to money growth minus the product of the income elasticity of money demand and the growth rate of output.

[16]In Chap. 15 we saw that the demand for real money balances ($M2$) has a long-run income elasticity of about unity. Thus, the long-run relationship between $M2$ growth and inflation should be approximately 1:1 except for changes in velocity unrelated to income growth.

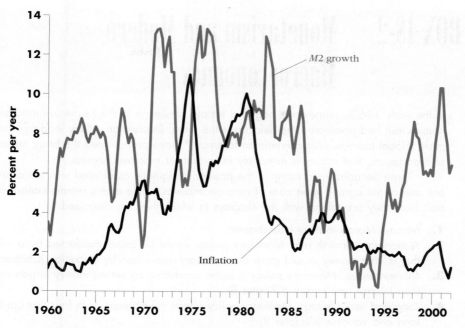

FIGURE 18-1   MONEY GROWTH AND INFLATION, 1960–2002.

Money growth is based on M2 and inflation on the GDP deflator. (Source: Federal Reserve Economic Data.)

The relationship between money growth and inflation is much looser for *M*1. This is a reflection of the instability of *M*1 money demand, especially in the 1980s. To obtain a stable relationship between money growth and inflation, we need a stable real money demand or, equivalently, stable velocity.

Historical and International Trends

In the United States, the *M*2 money-inflation link has not always been as tight as it was in the past three decades. In the end-of-chapter problems we provide data for decadal

TABLE 18-4	Money, Inflation, and Output Growth				
	(Percent per Year)				
	*M*1	*M*2	GDP GROWTH	*M*2 − GDP GROWTH	INFLATION*
1960–1969	3.7	7.0	4.4	2.6	2.4
1970–1979	6.4	9.5	3.3	6.2	6.6
1980–1989	7.8	8.0	3.1	4.9	4.7
1990–1999	3.7	4.0	3.0	1.0	2.3
1960–1999	5.4	7.2	3.5	3.7	4.0

*Based on the GDP deflator.

Source: Haver Analytics Macroeconomic Database.

BOX 18-2   Monetarism and Modern Macroeconomics

In the early 1960s, monetarists began a serious challenge to the Keynesian macroeconomics that had dominated the field since the Great Depression. Many leading economists, Nobel laureate Milton Friedman foremost,* have propounded the basic message of monetarism, that money is extremely important for macroeconomics.

Three decades later, many of the positions originally associated with monetarism are part of the agreed-upon core of macroeconomics, while others remain controversial. Here they are, along with the chapters in which they are discussed:

1. *Money.* Money matters (this chapter).
2. *A monetary growth rule.* Monetary policy would be better conducted by a rule—that is, that money should grow at a constant rate—than by discretion (Chapter 8).
3. *Money targets.* Monetary policy is better conducted by setting money targets rather than interest rate targets (Chapter 8).
4. *Long and variable lags.* Monetary policy affects the economy with lags that are both long and variable (Chapter 8).

There are two other monetarist positions that should be noted:

5. *The inherent stability of the private sector.* Monetarists argue that the private sector is inherently stable and that most disturbances to the economy are caused by mistaken

averages in the period 1860–1989 and ask you to investigate the money-inflation link for that period. There are clearly some outliers, for example, the 1890s, when money growth (adjusted for real income growth) was high but prices were falling.

International data, shown in Table 18-5, give the same impression as the data for the United States: Generally, higher growth rates of money (adjusted for output growth) are associated with higher inflation, but the relationship is not 1:1. For some countries, such as the United Kingdom, inflation is well below the "predicted" rate (the growth rate of money minus output growth), while for others, such as Italy, the converse is true. Once again the reasons the relationship is not exact include shifts in money demand, perhaps caused by financial deregulation, changes in interest rates that affect velocity, and income elasticities of money demand that are different from unity.[17]

---

[17]Definitions of monetary aggregates differ substantially among countries. The term "money" in Table 18-5 describes the closest aggregate corresponding to $M2$ in the United States.

government policy. They believe that less government is better than more and that governments have an inherent tendency to grow. (Some of these issues are discussed later in this chapter.)

6. *Flexible exchange rates.* In the 1950s Milton Friedman was the outstanding proponent of the view that exchange rates should be flexible rather than fixed. Although this view is not necessarily monetarist—in the sense that it is independent of the argument that money matters—most monetarists (along with many other macroeconomists) accept it, regarding the exchange rate as just another price that markets should be free to set and that governments are likely to get wrong. In practice, more and more countries have adopted flexible exchange rate systems (Chapter 19).

Where does the profession come out on the issues? As Nobel laureate Franco Modigliani of MIT has said, "We are all monetarists now," in the sense that we all believe that *some* stock of money has major impacts on the economy, that sustained rapid money growth leads to inflation, and that inflation cannot be kept low unless money growth is low. While other monetarist positions are generally more controversial, there is no question that monetarism has had major successes, including the adoption of money growth targets in the 1980s in many countries—a success that turned out to be temporary, as some of the countries that adopted money growth targets have now abandoned them in the light of the instability of money demand.

*For an account of Friedman's views, see his *Money Mischief* (New York: Harcourt Brace Jovanovich, 1992). Among the prominent monetarists are Anna J. Schwartz of the National Bureau of Economic Research, Friedman's coauthor of (among other books and articles) the magisterial *A Monetary History of the United States, 1867–1960* (Princeton, NJ: Princeton University Press, 1963), and the late Karl Brunner of the University of Rochester, Allan Meltzer and Bennett McCallum of Carnegie-Mellon, Phillip Cagan of Columbia University, David Laidler and Michael Parkin of the University of Western Ontario, William Poole of the St. Louis Fed, and many leading economists around the world.

TABLE 18-5	**Money and Inflation in International Perspective, 1960–2001** (Percent per Year)			
	MONEY GROWTH*	OUTPUT GROWTH	PREDICTED INFLATION	ACTUAL INFLATION
Canada	10.2	3.8	6.4	4.6
United States	7.7	3.4	4.3	4.4
Japan	11.0	4.9	6.2	4.3
Germany	8.2	3.0	5.2	3.1
France†	6.3	2.1	4.2	5.3
Italy‡	10.5	2.2	8.2	9.6
United Kingdom	12.8	2.5	10.2	6.6

*$M1$ plus quasi-money.

†For 1978–1998 only, previous or later data being unavailable for broad monetary aggregates.

‡For 1975–1998 only, previous or later data being unavailable for broad monetary aggregates.

Source: IMF, *International Financial Statistics*, 2002.

Summary: Is Inflation a Monetary Phenomenon?

The answer to the question of whether inflation is a monetary phenomenon *in the long run* is yes. No major inflation can take place without rapid money growth, and rapid money growth will cause rapid inflation. Further, any policy that determinedly keeps the growth rate of money low will lead eventually to a low rate of inflation.

18-4
HYPERINFLATION

Although there is no precise definition of the rate of inflation that deserves the star ranking of *hyperinflation* rather than "high inflation," a working definition is that a country is in hyperinflation when its annual inflation rate reaches 1,000 percent per annum.[18] Table 18-6 shows recent extreme inflation experiences.[19] Note that in the 1990s many Latin American countries successfully stabilized the inflation rate at nonhyperinflationary levels. In contrast, several of the countries emerging out of the former Eastern bloc saw very high rates of inflation.

In a hyperinflationary economy, inflation is so pervasive and such a problem that it completely dominates daily economic life. People spend significant amounts of resources minimizing the inflationary damage. They have to shop often so as to get to

TABLE 18-6   Recent High-Inflation Experiences
(Percent per Year)

	1985	1990	1991	1992	1993	1994	1995	1996	1997	1998	1999	2000	2001
Argentina	672	2,314	172	25	11	4	3	0	1	1	−1	−1	−1
Bolivia	11,750	17	21	12	9	8	10	12	5	8	2	5	2
Brazil	226	2,948	433	952	1,928	2,076	66	16	7	3	5	7	7
Israel	305	17	19	12	11	12	10	11	9	5	5	1	1
Mexico	58	27	23	16	10	7	35	34	21	16	17	10	6
Nicaragua	219	7,485	2,945	24	20	7	11	12	9	13	11	—	—
Peru	163	7,482	410	74	49	24	11	12	9	7	3	4	2
Romania	—	—	231	211	255	137	32	39	155	59	46	46	34
Russia	—	—	—	—	875	308	197	48	15	28	86	21	21
Ukraine	—	—	—	—	4,735	891	377	80	16	11	23	—	—

Source: IMF, *International Financial Statistics,* 2002.

---

[18]When inflation becomes very high, it is reckoned in terms of *monthly* rates, not inflation per year. The power of compound interest is apparent when we look at the correspondence between monthly inflation rates and the same rate annualized. For example, a 20 percent inflation per month corresponds to an annualized rate of 791 percent.

[19]Hyperinflation is not a contemporary invention. Extreme experience with inflation can be found in history. See Edwin Seligman, *Currency Inflation and Public Debts: An Historical Sketch* (New York: Equitable Trust Company, 1921). There was a wave in the 1920s, notably in Austria, Hungary, Germany, and Poland, and again in the 1940s. The most famous experience is that in Germany in the 1920s; see Steven Webb, *Hyperinflation and Stabilization in Weimar Germany* (Oxford, England: Oxford University Press, 1989.)

the stores before the prices go up; their main concern in saving or investing is how to protect themselves against inflation; they reduce holdings of real balances to a remarkable extent to avoid the inflation tax but have to compensate by going to the bank more often—daily or hourly instead of weekly, for example—to get currency. Wages are paid very often—at the end of the German hyperinflation, several times a day.

It seems difficult to believe that countries can function for any length of time with inflation rates of several hundred percent or more. In fact, they do not function well, and sooner or later they will stabilize a high inflation simply because the economy turns chaotic. Thus, Israel successfully stabilized in 1985, as did Bolivia (see Box 18-3). However, such experiences do not seem to prevent other countries from entering hyperinflations.[20] Although true hyperinflations have been rare since 1947, there have been many instances of 100 percent annual inflation rates. (Bad enough!) Such high inflations are frequently associated with high deficits.[21]

DEFICITS AND HYPERINFLATION

The proximate cause of hyperinflation is always massive growth in the money supply. But it is also true that the hyperinflationary economies all suffered from large budget deficits. In several cases the origin of the budget deficit was wartime spending, which generated large national debts and also destroyed the tax-gathering apparatus of the country.

But there is a two-way interaction between budget deficits and inflation. Large budget deficits can lead to rapid inflation by causing governments to print money to finance the deficit. In turn, high inflation increases the measured deficit. There are two main mechanisms through which inflation increases budget deficits: tax collection effects and increases in nominal payments on the national debt.

As the inflation rate rises, the real revenue raised from taxation falls. The reason is that there are lags in both the calculation and payment of taxes. Suppose, to take an

---

[20]The classic hyperinflations have taken place in the aftermath of wars or the breakup of empires. The most famous of all—though not the most rapid—was the German hyperinflation of 1922–1923. The average inflation rate during the hyperinflation was 322 percent *per month*. The highest rate of inflation was in October 1923, just before the end of the hyperinflation, when prices rose by over 29,000 percent. In dollars that means that something that cost $1 at the beginning of the month would have cost $290 at the end of the month. The most rapid hyperinflation was that in Hungary at the end of World War II: The *average* rate of inflation from August 1945 to July 1946 was 19,800 percent per month, and the maximum monthly rate was 41.9 quadrillion percent. (At least, so we think. The price level rose 41.9×10^{15} percent in July 1946.) Data are from Phillip Cagan, "The Monetary Dynamics of Hyperinflation," in Milton Friedman (ed.), *Studies in the Quantity Theory of Money* (Chicago: University of Chicago Press, 1956). This classic paper contains data on seven hyperinflations. For additional historical perspective, see Forrest H. Capie (ed.), *Major Inflations in History* (Brookfield, VT: Edgar Elger, 1991).

Keynes, in a masterful description of the hyperinflation process in Austria after World War II, tells of how people would order two beers at a time because the beer grew stale at a rate slower than that at which the price was rising. [See John Maynard Keynes, *A Tract on Monetary Reform* (New York: Macmillan, 1923), which remains one of the most readable accounts of inflation.] The story is also told of a woman who carried her (almost worthless) currency in a basket and found that when she set it down for a moment, the basket was stolen but the money left behind.

[21]Stanley Fischer, Ratna Sahay, and Carlos A. Vegh, "Modern Hyper- and High Inflations," *Journal of Economic Literature,* September 2002.

BOX 18-3   Bolivian Hyperinflation and Stabilization

In the 1920s, Europe experienced hyperinflation, and the experience is reviewed in an important paper by Thomas Sargent.* Latin America followed in the 1980s. In 1985 Bolivia experienced a full-fledged hyperinflation, as can be seen in Figure 1. At the peak, in mid-1985, inflation was, at an annual rate, 35,000 percent!

There were three main reasons for the Bolivian hyperinflation. First, like other Latin American countries, Bolivia had overborrowed in the 1970s. When, in the early 1980s, interest rates increased in world markets, it could no longer service its debt by taking out new loans for the purpose of paying the interest on the old loans. But without borrowing, the country did not have the budgetary resources to service the debt. The attempt to do so strained the budget and led to high rates of money creation. Second, commodity prices, especially of tin, fell sharply. For Bolivia this meant a large fall in real income and in revenues for the government. Third, substantial political instability led to capital flight. The combination of factors set off an inflationary spiral that forced increasing depreciation

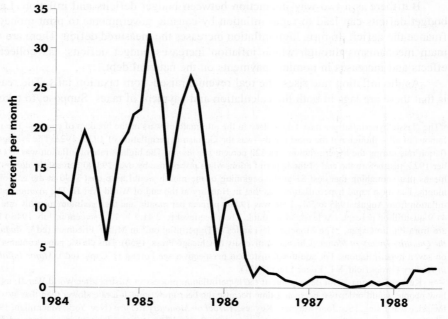

FIGURE 1   BOLIVIAN HYPERINFLATION, 1984–1988.

(Source: Banco Central de Bolivia.)

*See Thomas Sargent, "The End of Four Big Inflations," in R. Hall (ed.), *Inflation* (Chicago: University of Chicago Press, 1982).

TABLE 1 The Bolivian Hyperinflation

	1980–1983	1984	1985	1986
Budget deficit*	11.9	26.5	10.8	3.0
Tax collection†	6.7	2.3	3.1	6.6
Inflation	123.0	1,282.0	11,750.0	276.0

*Percent of GDP.

†Percent per year.

Source: World Bank and Banco Central de Bolivia.

of the currency and opened an ever-wider gap between government outlays and revenues. Tax collection dropped sharply by more than half, as can be seen in Table 1.

By 1984–1985 the government was attempting to finance nearly 25 percent of GNP with money creation. But, of course, by this time the demand for real balances had fallen to negligible levels because of the hyperinflation. It took ever-larger rates of inflation to finance the ever-growing deficit.

In August–September 1985 a new government came into power and, in a short time, imposed a drastic stabilization plan, sometimes described as "shock therapy." By stopping external debt service and raising taxes, the drain in the budget was brought under control; money creation was reduced from the extreme rates of the past years; and the exchange rate was stabilized. Within half a year the inflation rate had come down to less than 50 percent. Moreover, because the decrease in the budget deficit was maintained and reinforced, the gain in disinflation continued; by 1989, inflation rates had fallen to less than 10 percent per year.

The Bolivian stabilization is a good example of how a sharp turn toward fiscal stabilization can stop a major inflation.† But there should be no illusion about the costs. As a result of austerity (and of poor export prices), Bolivian per capita income in 1989 was 35 percent less than it had been 10 years earlier, at its peak. Inflation had been brought under control, but confidence was not sufficient to bring back growth on a significant scale.

While Bolivia succeeded in controlling inflation, inflation was exploding in several other Latin American countries. An important question for these countries was whether *heterodox* programs, combining wage-price controls with the *orthodox* medicine of fiscal austerity, would reduce the costs of stabilization. The stabilization attempts, undertaken several times in 1985–1989 in Argentina and Brazil, were long on price controls and short on fiscal contraction. As might have been predicted, wage-price controls without fiscal and monetary reform were ineffective.‡

†See Juan A. Morales, "Inflation Stabilization in Bolivia," in M. Bruno et al. (eds.), *Inflation Stabilization* (Cambridge, MA: MIT Press, 1988); and J. Sachs, "The Bolivian Hyperinflation and Stabilization," *American Economic Review*, May 1987.

‡See E. Helpman and L. Leiderman, "Stabilization in High Inflation Countries: Analytical Foundations of Recent Experience," *Carnegie-Rochester Conference Series on Public Policy* 28 (1988); M. Kiguel and N. Liviatan, "Inflationary Rigidities and Orthodox Stabilization Policies: Lessons from Latin America," *World Bank Economic Review* 3 (1988); M. Blejer and N. Liviatan, "Fighting Hyperinflation," *IMF Staff Papers*, September 1987; and Bruno et al. (eds.), *Lessons from Stabilization and Its Aftermath* (Cambridge, MA: MIT Press, 1991).

extreme example, that people pay taxes on April 15 on the income they earned the previous year. Consider someone who earned $50,000 last year and has a tax bill of $10,000 due on April 15. If prices have in the meantime gone up by a factor of 10, as they might in hyperinflation, the real value of the taxes is only one-tenth of what it should be. The budget deficit can rapidly get out of hand.[22]

The measured budget deficit includes the interest payments on the national debt. Since the nominal interest rate tends to rise when inflation increases, higher inflation generally increases the *nominal* interest payments that are made by the government, and the measured deficit therefore increases. Accordingly, economists in high-inflation countries often calculate the *inflation-adjusted deficit:*

$$\text{Inflation-adjusted deficit} = \text{total deficit} - (\text{inflation rate} \times \text{national debt}) \quad (4)$$

The inflation adjustment removes that component of interest payments on the debt that is attributed directly to inflation, and gives a more accurate picture of what the budget situation would be at a very low inflation rate than does the actual deficit.

STOPPING HYPERINFLATIONS

All hyperinflations come to an end. The dislocation of the economy becomes too great for the public to bear, and the government finds a way of reforming its budget process. Often a new money is introduced, and the tax system is reformed. Typically, too, the exchange rate of the new money is pegged to that of a foreign currency in order to provide an anchor for prices and expectations. Frequently, there are unsuccessful attempts at stabilization before the final success.

The presence of so many destabilizing factors in inflation, particularly the collapse of the tax system as the inflation proceeds, together with an economy that is extremely dislocated by inflation, raises the fascinating possibility that a coordinated attack on inflation may stop the inflation with relatively little unemployment cost. Monetary, fiscal, and exchange rate policies are combined with income policies in this *heterodox approach to stabilization.* This approach was used in Argentina and Israel in 1985 and in Brazil in 1986, when the governments froze wages and prices. That stopped the inflation at a single blow.

The Israeli stabilization succeeded, while the Argentinean and Brazilian did not. The difference, as noted above, was fiscal policy. The Israelis corrected their fiscal deficit, whereas the two others did not. Wage and price controls alone cannot keep inflation in check if the underlying fundamentals of fiscal and monetary policy are not consistent with low inflation.[23]

---

[22]This impact of inflation on the real value of tax revenues is called the *Tanzi-Olivera effect,* so named after two economists who independently documented it, Vito Tanzi of the IMF and Julio Olivera of the University of Buenos Aires.

[23]One more important feature of the stabilizations should be brought out: *Money growth rates following stabilization are very high.* Why? Because as people expect less inflation, nominal interest rates decline and the demand for real balances rises. With the demand for real balances increasing, the government can create more money without creating inflation. Thus, at the beginning of a successful stabilization there may be a bonus for the government: It can temporarily finance part of the deficit through the printing of money, without renewing inflation. But it certainly cannot do so for very long periods without reigniting inflation.

INFLATIONS, HYPERINFLATIONS, AND CREDIBILITY

Inflation is determined by fundamentals—shifts in aggregate demand relative to aggregate supply. In hyperinflations money growth dominates all other fundamentals. But people's expectations about the future also play a role. A belief that policy has changed will by itself drive down the expected rate of inflation and for that reason cause the short-run Phillips curve to shift down. Thus, a *credible policy* earns a *credibility bonus* in the fight against inflation.

Throughout the period of disinflation in the United States, starting with the Fed's change in policy in October 1979, there was strong emphasis on the credibility of policy. Some proponents of rational expectations even believed that if policy could only be made credible, it would be possible to disinflate practically without causing any recession at all.[24]

The argument went like this: The expectations-augmented aggregate supply curve is

$$\pi = \pi^e + \lambda(Y - Y^*) \tag{5}$$

If the policy is credible, people adjust their expectations of inflation when a new, lower money growth rate is observed, and the short-run aggregate supply curve therefore moves down immediately. Accordingly, if policy is credible and if expectations are rational, the economy can move immediately to a new long-run equilibrium when there is a change in policy. **In other words, if policy is credible, π can be reduced by lowering π^e while suffering less from low $(Y - Y^*)$.**

The experience of the United States in the early 1980s—the worst recession since the Great Depression—casts doubt on the relevance of this optimistic scenario; even more so does the experience of Britain in the same period, when the unmistakably tough-minded Thatcher government was pursuing a resolute anti-inflationary policy but still reached a 13 percent unemployment rate.

There are two possible reasons the simple credibility–rational expectations argument does not work. First, credibility may be very difficult to obtain; second, the economy has, at any time, an overhang of past contracts embodying past expectations, and the contract renegotiations take time. Thus, because of *inflationary inertia,* a rapid return to lower inflation in economies experiencing inflation rates in the 10 to 20 percent range is unlikely.

It is easiest to change the inflation rate when there are no long-term contracts that embody the ongoing inflation—for instance, by building in high rates of wage increase for the next several years—in the economy. There will be very few such contracts if inflation is high, for instance, in a hyperinflation. Under such conditions, negotiators will not want to sign an agreement in nominal terms because they will be gambling too much on the future behavior of the price level. Long-term nominal contracts disappear, and wages and prices are frequently reset. In these circumstances, a credible policy will have rapid effects. But such rapid success cannot be expected in an economy in which the structure of contracts has not yet been destroyed by extreme inflation.

---

[24]See John Fender, *Inflation* (Ann Arbor: University of Michigan Press, 1990); and Dean Croushore, "What Are the Costs of Disinflation?" Federal Reserve Bank of Philadelphia *Business Review,* May–June 1992. For views on credibility from both central bankers and macroeconomists, see Alan S. Blinder, "Central Bank Credibility: Why Do We Care? How Do We Build It?" NBER working paper no. W7161, June 1999.

BOX 18-4   The Rational Expectations School, Monetarism, and Hyperinflation

The *rational expectations school* in macroeconomics accepts many monetarist positions, including a preference for rules and the belief that government intervention usually makes the situation worse. Indeed, many of the leaders of the rational expectations school were students of Friedman. Some, including Robert Lucas, studied under Friedman at the University of Chicago; others, such as Robert Barro and Thomas Sargent, studied his works while they were graduate students at other universities.

Rational expectations views include

1. The market-clearing rational expectations approach to the Phillips curve (Chapter 20).
2. Rational expectations as a theory of expectations (Chapters 6 and 20).
3. An emphasis on the credibility of policymakers (Chapter 8 and this chapter).
4. A preference for policymaking rules rather than discretion (Chapter 8).

Most of these views can be seen as extensions of the monetarist approach. However, the monetarist and rational expectations schools differ on one key issue: Whereas monetarists, like Keynesians, see the economy as reacting to disturbances and policy changes slowly and with long and variable lags and are willing to allow the possibility that markets may not clear, the rational expectations school generally insists that markets clear rapidly. (In the simplest case, monetarists think monetary policy has real effects for several quarters to several years; the rational expectations school does not.) Obviously, we do not share the latter view, nor does much of the

It remains true, though, that whatever the structure of contracts, the more credible a policy that aims to disinflate the economy is, the more successful that policy will be.

DISINFLATION AND THE SACRIFICE RATIO

Inflation reduction almost always costs a recession, but what exactly is the tradeoff? How much output is lost through different methods of disinflation, such as cold turkey and gradualism? Discussion of the costs of disinflation makes extensive use of the concept of the *sacrifice ratio*.[25] **The sacrifice ratio is the ratio of the cumulative percentage loss of GDP (as a result of a disinflation policy) to the reduction in inflation that is actually achieved.**

Thus, suppose a policy reduces the inflation rate from 10 to 4 percent over a 3-year period, at the cost of levels of output that are 10 percent below potential in the first year, 8 percent below potential in the second year, and 6 percent below potential in the

---

[25]See Chap. 7 for more on the sacrifice ratio.

profession. However, the rational expectations approach to expectations is wid
shared. So is the emphasis on the *credibility* of policymakers.

Though the rational expectations approach started influencing macroeconom
theory in the early 1970s, the single most influential article in the macroeconomic policy debate was Thomas Sargent's "The Ends of Four Big Inflations."* In this article,
written while the United States was suffering from double-digit inflation, Sargent argued that the major European hyperinflations had, as a result of a *credible* reform of
monetary and fiscal policy, ended rapidly and at very little cost in terms of forgone
output. By implication, he suggested that the United States could do the same.

Critics of this view argue that it was one thing to end a hyperinflation in an
economy that had broken down and another to end an inflation that was just barely in
the double digits. In any event, the United States ended its inflation only after the deep
recession of 1981–1982. Further research has shown that even the European hyperinflations did not end costlessly.†

All experience suggests that credibility is difficult to earn and difficult to keep
and that the structure of contracts that exist in an economy has to be taken into account in analyzing the effects of policy changes. Thus, while we do not doubt that
credibility is an important aspect of policymaking, we believe that its role has been
exaggerated by proponents of rational expectations, and we are suspicious of policy
arguments in which credibility is the main reason for pursuing a policy that otherwise
makes little economic sense.

*In Robert E. Hall (ed.), *Inflation: Causes and Effects* (Chicago: University of Chicago Press, 1982). For a general overview of twentieth-century hyperinflations, see Perre Siklos (ed.), *Great Inflations of the 20th Century* (Brookfield, VT: Edgar Elger, 1995), in particular the article by Carlo Vegh, "Stopping High Inflation."

†See Elmus Wicker, "Terminating Hyperinflation in the Dismembered Habsburg Monarchy," *American Economic
Review,* June 1986; see also the articles on modern high inflations in Michael Bruno et al. (eds.), *Lessons of Economic Stabilization and Its Aftermath* (Cambridge, MA: MIT Press, 1991).

third year. The total loss of GDP is 24 percent (10 + 8 + 6), the reduction in inflation is 6 percent (10 − 4), and the sacrifice ratio is 4.

Before the disinflation of the 1980s, economists estimated sacrifice ratios that
would apply if a disinflation program were undertaken. Estimates ranged between 5
and 10. The Reagan-Volcker disinflation and recession shocked the economy with high
unemployment but succeeded in reducing inflation. Laurence Ball estimates that the
sacrifice ratio was 1.83—well below then-existing estimates.[26] The fact that the sacrifice ratio was low suggests that the economy benefited from the credible position of
the Fed chairman and the president as inflation fighters.

Credibility always plays a role in stopping hyperinflations. Symbolic gestures can
play a part. For example, countries frequently rename their currency and change the
design of paper money. Usually something more tangible is required. Governments
often have to drastically reduce spending. In poor countries this can be especially painful

[26]Laurence Ball, "How Costly Is Disinflation? The Historical Evidence," Federal Reserve Bank of Philadelphia *Business Review,* November–December 1993.

if food subsidies are cut. Sometimes governments peg their exchange rate to another, more stable, currency (the U.S. dollar for example). Governments even sometimes yield control of the money supply process to guarantee that they will not resume profligate use of the printing press.

18-5
DEFICITS, MONEY GROWTH, AND THE INFLATION TAX

We have seen that a sustained increase in money growth ultimately translates into increased inflation. But that still leaves the question of what determines the money growth rate. A frequent argument is that money growth is the result of government budget deficits. In this section we examine several possible relationships between the budget deficit and inflation in both ordinary times and during hyperinflations.

THE GOVERNMENT'S BUDGET CONSTRAINT

The federal government as a whole, consisting of the Treasury plus the Fed, can finance its budget deficit in two ways. It can either sell bonds or "print money." **The Fed "prints money" when it increases the stock of high-powered money, typically through open market purchases that buy up part of the debt that the Treasury is selling.**

The *government budget constraint* is

$$\text{Budget deficit} = \text{sales of bonds} + \text{increase in money base} \qquad (6)$$

There are two types of possible links between budget deficits and money growth. First, in the short run, an increase in the deficit caused by expansionary fiscal policy will tend to raise nominal and real interest rates. If the Fed is targeting interest rates in any way, it may increase the growth rate of money in an attempt to keep the interest rate from rising. Second, the government may deliberately be increasing the stock of money as a means of financing itself over the long term.

We examine first the short-run links between money and deficits that come from central bank policy and then the use of money printing as a means of financing government budgets. Finally, we link the short- and long-run aspects.

THE FED'S DILEMMA

The Fed is said to *monetize* deficits whenever it purchases a part of the debt sold by the Treasury to finance the deficit. In the United States the monetary authorities enjoy independence from the Treasury and therefore can choose whether to monetize or not.[27]

---

[27]In other countries the central bank may enjoy much less independence; for instance, it might be under the control of the Treasury, and then it may simply be ordered to finance part or all of the deficit by creating high-powered money. It is noteworthy that the Maastricht Accord strictly prohibits the new European Central Bank from financing government deficits.

The Fed faces a dilemma in deciding whether to monetize a deficit. If it does not finance the deficit, the fiscal expansion, not being accompanied by accommodating monetary policy, raises interest rates and thus crowds out private expenditure. There is accordingly a temptation for the Fed to prevent crowding out by buying securities, thereby increasing the money supply and hence allowing an expansion in income without a rise in interest rates.

But such a policy of accommodation, or *monetization,* runs a risk. If the economy is near full employment, the monetization feeds inflation. If, however, the economy is in a deep recession, there is no reason to shy away from accommodating a fiscal expansion with higher money growth.

In any particular case, the Fed has to judge whether to pursue an accommodating monetary policy or whether to stay with an unchanged monetary target or even offset a fiscal expansion by a tightening of monetary policy.

THE U.S. EVIDENCE

A number of studies have tried to determine how the Fed reacts to deficits in practice. The question here is whether there is a systematic link between monetary policy and the budget. Specifically, does the Fed allow money growth to rise when the budget deficit increases?

Figure 18-2 shows a scatterplot of the change in the growth rate of the monetary base and the change in the budget deficit (expressed as a percent of GDP).[28] There is no notable pattern of accommodation.

More sophisticated empirical work provides some evidence that the Fed does react in the direction of accommodation, monetizing deficits at least in part. But the evidence is not conclusive because it is difficult to know whether the Fed is reacting to the deficit itself or to other macroeconomic variables, specifically unemployment and the rate of inflation.[29]

THE INFLATION TAX

In discussing monetization of deficits in the United States, we paid no attention to the fact that financing government spending through the creation of high-powered money is an alternative to explicit taxation. For the United States, and for most of the industrialized economies, the creation of high-powered money is a fairly minor source of revenue. Other governments can—and some do—obtain significant amounts of resources year after year by printing money, that is, by increasing high-powered money. **This source of revenue is sometimes known as *seigniorage,* which is the government's ability to raise revenue through its right to create money.**

---

[28]The monetary base is the relevant aggregate because the deficit can be financed either by the sale of bonds or by the creation of high-powered money (or monetary base).

[29]See Alan Blinder, "On the Monetization of Deficits," in Laurence Meyer, *The Economic Consequences of Government Deficits* (Norwell, MA: Kluwer-Hijhoff, 1983); Gerald Dwyer, "Federal Deficits, Interest Rates and Monetary Policy," *Journal of Money, Credit and Banking,* November 1985; and Douglas Joines, "Deficits and Money Growth in the United States: 1872–1983," *Journal of Monetary Economics,* November 1985.

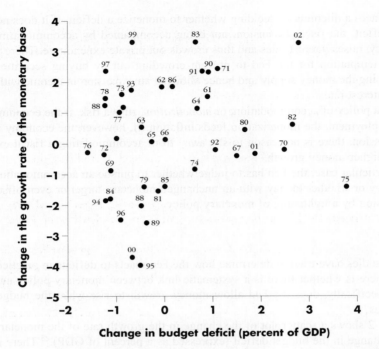

FIGURE 18-2   CHANGE IN MONEY GROWTH AND CHANGE IN THE BUDGET DEFICIT, 1960–2002.

The budget deficit is expressed as a percentage of GDP. (Source: Bureau of Economic Analysis and Federal Reserve Economic Data.)

When the government finances a deficit by creating money, it in effect keeps print-ing money, period after period, that it uses to pay for the goods and services it buys. This money is absorbed by the public. But why would the public choose to increase its holdings of nominal money balances period after period?

The only reason, real income growth aside, for the public's adding to its holdings of nominal money balances would be to offset the effects of inflation. Assuming there is no real income growth, in the long run the public will hold a constant level of *real* balances. But if prices are rising, the purchasing power of a given stock of *nominal* balances is falling. To maintain the real value of its money balances constant, the pub-lic has to be adding to its stock of nominal balances at a rate that will exactly offset the effects of inflation.

When the public is adding to its stock of nominal balances in order to offset the effects of inflation on holdings of real balances, it is using part of its income to increase holdings of nominal money. Suppose a person has to add, say, $300 to a bank account just to maintain the real value of his or her money holdings. That $300 is not available for spending. The person seems to be saving $300 in the form of money holdings, but

BOX 18-5   Real Balances and Inflation

A sustained increase in money growth and in inflation ultimately leads to a reduction in the real money stock.

Here is a very important result that might seem a bit puzzling: Increased *nominal* money growth reduces the long-run *real* money stock. Conversely, reduced nominal money growth raises the long-run real money stock. The reason is that higher inflation raises the nominal interest rate and hence raises the opportunity cost of holding money. Hence, money holders will reduce the amount of real balances they choose to hold. This reduction in real balances is an important part of the adjustment process to an increase in money growth. It means that, **on average, in the period of adjustment to an increase in money growth, prices must rise faster than money.**

Higher money growth means higher inflation in the long run, and therefore higher interest rates and lower real money balances, $\overline{M}/P$. For $\overline{M}/P$ to drop, P must at some point grow faster than M grows. During this transition, inflation is higher than the long-run inflation rate. Empirically, this extra "transitional" inflation can be quite high.

in fact all that person is doing is preventing his or her wealth from decreasing as a result of inflation.

Inflation acts just like a tax because people are forced to spend less than their income and pay the difference to the government in exchange for extra money.[30] The government thus can spend more resources, and the public less, just as if the government had raised taxes to finance extra spending. **When the government finances its deficit by issuing money, which the public adds to its holdings of nominal balances to maintain the real value of money balances constant, we say the government is financing itself through the *inflation tax*.**[31]

How much revenue can the government collect through the inflation tax? The amount of revenue produced is the product of the tax rate (the inflation rate) and the object of taxation (the real monetary base):

$$\text{Inflation tax revenue} = \text{inflation rate} \times \text{real money base} \tag{7}$$

---

[30]There is one complication in this analysis. As noted above, the amount that is received by the government is the increase in the stock of *high-powered* money, because the Fed is buying Treasury debt with high-powered money. But the public is increasing its holdings of both bank deposits and currency, and thus part of the increase in the public's holdings of money does not go to the government to finance the deficit. This complication in no way changes the essence of the analysis.

[31]Inflation is often referred to as the "cruelest tax." This refers not to the above analysis of the inflation tax but, rather, to the redistribution of wealth and income associated particularly with unanticipated inflation, which was discussed in Chap. 7.

TABLE 18-7   Inflation and Inflation Tax, 1983–1988
(Percent)

| | AVERAGE 1983–1988 | | |
COUNTRY	INFLATION TAX, % OF GDP	ANNUAL INFLATION RATE	PEAK-YEAR INFLATION TAX, % OF GDP
Argentina	3.7	359	5.2
Bolivia	3.5	1,797	7.2
Brazil	3.5	341	4.3
Chile	0.9	21	1.1
Colombia	1.9	22	2.0
Mexico	2.6	87	3.5
Peru	4.7	382	4.5

Source: M. Selowsky, "Preconditions Necessary for the Recovery of Latin America's Growth," World Bank, June 1989 (mimeographed).

Table 18-7 shows data on the inflation tax for Latin American countries in the 1983–1988 period.[32] Clearly the amounts are very significant, as are the inflation rates at which these amounts of revenue are obtained by the government.

The amount of revenue the government can raise through the inflation tax is shown by curve *AA* in Figure 18-3. When the inflation rate is zero, the government gets no revenue from inflation.[33] As the inflation rate rises, the amount of inflation tax received by the government increases. But, of course, as the inflation rate rises, people reduce their real holdings of the money base—because the base is becoming increasingly costly to hold. Individuals hold less currency, and banks hold as few excess reserves as possible. Eventually, the real monetary base falls so much that the total amount of inflation tax revenue received by the government falls. That starts to happen at point *C* and signifies that there is a maximum amount of revenue the government can raise through the inflation tax; the maximum is shown as amount *IR** in the figure. There is a corresponding inflation rate, denoted π^*: the inflation rate at which the inflation tax is at its maximum.[34]

Suppose that in Figure 18-3, the economy is initially in a situation where there is no deficit and no printing of money. Inflation is zero and the economy is at point 0 in the figure. Now the government cuts taxes and finances the deficit by printing money. We assume that the deficit is equal to amount *IR'* in Figure 18-3, and thus it can be financed

[32]Hyperinflation has been a frequent plague for much of Latin America. For more information on both the monetary and real sides of Latin American economies, see Eliana Cardoso and Ann Helwege, *Latin America's Economy: Diversity, Trends, and Conflicts* (Cambridge, MA: MIT Press, 1995).

[33]When the economy is growing, the government obtains some revenue from seigniorage even if there is no inflation. That is because when the demand for the real monetary base is growing, the government can create some base without producing inflation.

[34]Miguel A. Keguel and Pablo Andres Neumeyer, in "Seigniorage and Inflation: The Case of Argentina," *Journal of Money, Credit and Banking,* August 1995, consider whether Argentina went past the revenue-maximizing point in the 1980s. They estimate that the revenue-maximizing inflation rate was in the range of 20 to 30 percent per month. With the exception of spring 1989, inflation in Argentina was generally below these levels.

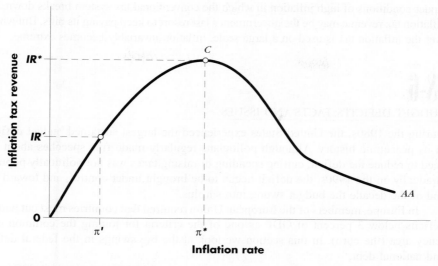

FIGURE 18-3 THE INFLATION TAX.

entirely through the inflation tax. Money growth is permanently increased, and inflation in the long run moves to the rate π', corresponding to the inflation tax revenue IR'.

INFLATION TAX REVENUE

The amounts of inflation tax revenue obtained in the high-inflation developing countries in Table 18-7 are very large. In the more industrialized economies, in which the real money base is small relative to the size of the economy, the government obtains only small amounts of inflation tax revenue. For instance, in the United States the base is about 6 percent of GDP. At a 5 percent inflation rate the government would, from equation (7), be collecting about .3 percent of GDP in inflation tax revenue. That is not a trivial amount, but it is not a major source of government revenue either.[35] It is hard to believe that the inflation rate in the United States is set with the revenue aspects of inflation as the main criterion. Rather, the Fed and the administration choose policies to influence the inflation rate on the basis of an analysis of the costs and benefits of inflation, along the lines presented in Chapter 7.

In countries in which the banking system is less developed and in which people therefore hold large amounts of currency, the government obtains more revenue from inflation and is more likely to give much weight to the revenue aspects of inflation in setting policy.

---

[35]A measure of seigniorage different from the value of the printing of high-powered money is sometimes used in the United States. It is the value of the interest payments the Fed earns on its portfolio. Since the Fed's securities were obtained through open market purchases that increased the high-powered money stock, this is a measure of how much interest the Treasury saves (since the Fed pays its profits to the Treasury) as a result of *previous* Fed money printing. The printing of high-powered money is a measure of the *current* command over resources obtained as a result of money printing this period.

Under conditions of high inflation in which the conventional tax system breaks down, the inflation tax revenue may be the government's last resort to keep paying its bills. But whenever the inflation tax is used on a large scale, inflation invariably becomes extreme.

18-6
BUDGET DEFICITS: FACTS AND ISSUES

During the 1980s, the United States experienced the largest sustained budget deficits in its peacetime history. Although politicians regularly made fine speeches about the need to reduce the deficit, cutting spending or raising taxes was not politically popular. Gradually, in the 1990s, the deficit began to be brought under control, and toward the end of the decade the budget swung into surplus.

In Europe, members of the European Union required that countries must cut budget deficits below 3 percent of GDP as one of the criteria for joining the common currency area (the euro). In this section we look at the big swings in the federal deficit and national debt.

First, we will review the facts about the composition of and trends in U.S. government spending and revenues, the deficit and the public debt. Historically, the United States ran large deficits during wartime and slowly paid off the deficits while at peace.

OUTLAYS

Table 18-8 shows the outlays of the federal government since 1962. The table introduces some special terminology. There is a distinction between *mandatory* and *discretionary outlays.* The former are outlays that are made under *entitlement programs,* for which the law specifies that a person meeting certain requirements is automatically entitled to receive payments. Examples of entitlement programs are Medicaid and social security. Discretionary spending, by contrast, is governed by the congressional appropriation process and includes, for example, defense expenditures and foreign aid.

TABLE 18-8	**Federal Government Outlays** (Percent of GDP; Fiscal Years; Period Average)				
	1962–1969	1970–1979	1980–1989	1990–1999	2000–2002
National defense	8.6	5.9	5.8	4.1	3.2
Entitlements and other mandatory spending	6.2	9.4	10.8	11.2	11.0
Nondefense discretionary spending	3.9	4.5	4.1	3.5	3.5
Net interest	1.3	1.5	2.8	3.0	2.0
Total outlays*	18.8	20.0	22.2	20.7	18.8

*Column totals do not match total outlays because "offsetting receipts" and deposit insurance figures are excluded.

Source: Congressional Budget Office, *The Budget and Economic Outlook: Fiscal Years 2003–2013,* January 2003.

TABLE 18-9   Sources of Federal Revenue
(Percent of GDP; Fiscal Years; Period Average)

	1962–1969	1970–1979	1980–1989	1990–1999	2000–2002
Individual income tax	7.8	8.1	8.4	8.4	9.5
Corporate income tax	3.8	2.7	1.7	1.9	1.7
Social insurance taxes and contributions	3.5	5.0	6.3	6.6	6.8
Other*	2.7	2.1	1.8	1.6	1.5
Total revenue	17.8	17.9	18.2	18.6	19.5

*Includes excise (sales) taxes, estate and gift taxes, custom duties, and miscellaneous receipts.

Source: Congressional Budget Office, *The Budget and Economic Outlook: Fiscal Years 2003–2013*, January 2003.

Three points stand out in Table 18-8. First, defense expenditures have declined significantly as a fraction of GDP. Second, entitlement programs have nearly doubled. Third, interest payments by the government have become an important part of government outlays. The share of federal interest payments in GDP has doubled over the past 40 years.

Government spending consists of *purchases* of goods and services and *transfer payments*.[36] By the year 2001, only one-third of federal government outlays (less than 10 percent of GDP) represented spending on goods and services, while transfer payments accounted for two-thirds.

RECEIPTS

Most of the federal government's revenues come from taxes. The sources of revenue and the total are shown in Table 18-9. The revenue sources are self-explanatory, except perhaps for social insurance taxes. These are taxes on wages paid by employers and by wage earners.

Total federal government revenue as a share of GDP has changed very little over the past 40 years. However, there has been a shift in the sources of revenue. Social security taxes and contributions have become a substantially higher source of revenue, corporate income taxes have declined by more than half, and personal income taxes have remained mostly unchanged.

MEASURING THE DEFICIT

Government Assets

The U.S. government traditionally kept its books in a most bizarre fashion. It measured the deficit by simply subtracting current revenues from current spending, as if the government had heard neither of capital acquisition nor of depreciation. So in the years

---

[36]Purchases are a component of aggregate demand—the G term in $Y = C + I + G$—whereas transfer payments affect aggregate demand indirectly, via changes in disposable income.

that Grand Coulee Dam was built, the government added the construction cost to those years' deficits.[37] It is important to recognize that the government has assets as well as debts. The real capital—Grand Coulee Dam—acquired by the government should be treated as an offset against the debt issued to pay for its construction.

In public discussions it is often forgotten that government spending is not all consumption or transfers. The late Robert Eisner of Northwestern University strongly emphasized this point in presenting government balance sheets in which both government debts and assets are listed.[38] For example, in 1990 the federal government owned reproducible assets (valued at replacement cost) of $834 billion but had debts of $2,687 billion. Thus, the government had a net debt of $1,853 billion, far less than the size the official debt numbers would suggest. If additional adjustment were made for holdings of land, the net debtor position would be even lower.[39] However, these adjustments do not change the conclusion that the deficit was relatively larger in the 80s than in past periods of peace.

Interest Payments versus the Primary Deficit

Measuring the federal deficit is complicated by the fact that most of the deficit can be accounted for by interest payments on the national debt. So most of the deficit represents not the excess of current spending over revenues but the legacy of past deficits. We distinguish between two components of the budget deficit: the *primary* (or *noninterest*) *deficit* and interest payments on the public debt:

$$\text{Total deficit} \equiv \text{primary deficit} + \text{interest payments} \qquad (8)$$

The primary deficit (or surplus) represents all government outlays, except interest payments, minus all government revenue. The primary deficit is also called the noninterest deficit.

The black line in Figure 18-4 shows the primary deficit. The primary deficit clearly was higher in the 1980s and the early 1990s than it was during the 1960s, but the increase is less striking than is the increase in the overall deficit.

When interest payments are large, as they are in the United States, proper measurement of the deficit is complicated by the distinction between real and nominal interest rates. Since the nominal interest rate equals the real interest rate plus inflation, interest payments on the debt can be divided into real payments and payments due to inflation. The latter do not cost the government anything in real terms, because they are exactly offset by the decrease in the real value of the nominal debt.[40] During periods

---

[37]*Economic Report of the President,* February 1996, Box 2–3; "Preview of the Comprehensive Revision of the National Income and Product Accounts: Recognition of Government Investment and Incorporation of a New Methodology for Calculating Depreciation," *Survey of Current Business,* September 1995; "Improved Estimates of the National Income and Product Accounts for 1959–1995: Results of the Comprehensive Revision," *Survey of Current Business,* January–February 1996.

[38]See Robert Eisner, *How Real Is the Federal Deficit?* (New York: Free Press, 1986); and "Budget Deficits: Rhetoric and Reality," *Journal of Economic Perspectives,* Spring 1989.

[39]See the data series on the economy's capital stock in *Survey of Current Business,* January 1992.

[40]See Mario Blejer and Adrienne Cheasty, "The Measurement of Fiscal Deficits: Analytical and Methodological Issues," *Journal of Economic Literature,* December 1991.

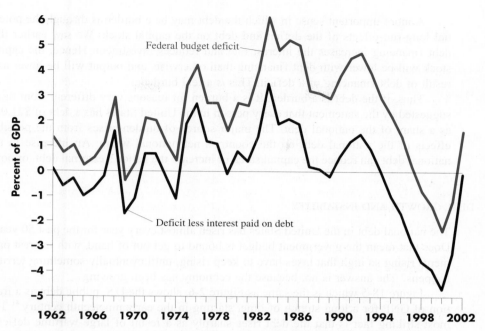

FIGURE 18-4   U.S. BUDGET DEFICITS WITH AND WITHOUT INTEREST PAID ON DEBT, 1962–2002.

(*Source: Congressional Budget Office,* The Budget and Economic Outlook: Fiscal Years 2003 – 2013, *January 2003.*)

of high inflation most of the interest payments are offset by inflation. Even during periods of low inflation, nearly half the interest payments may be offset in this way.

THE BURDEN OF THE DEBT

As deficits continue, the national debt piles up. The U.S. (gross) federal debt at the beginning of 2002 exceeded $6 trillion, enough to get anyone worried. In per capita terms, the national *debt* amounts to about $21,000 per person. Do we actually have to pay off this debt? It is the notion that every person in the country owes a large debt that makes the existence of the debt seem so serious.

By and large, we owe the national debt to ourselves. Each individual shares in the obligation to repay the public debt, but many individuals own the national debt in the form of Treasury bonds held directly or indirectly through financial intermediaries. As a first step, one could think of the liability of future taxes to repay the debt as canceling out the asset that the debt represents to the individuals who hold claims on the government. In this case, the debt would not be a net burden on society. However, this argument is limited by the fact that a large portion of the debt is owned by foreigners. The portion of the debt owned by foreigners does represent a future tax burden to be borne by U.S. taxpayers.

A more important sense in which the debt may be a burden is through the potential long-run effects of the deficit and debt on the capital stock. We saw earlier that debt financing increases the interest rate and reduces investment. Hence, the capital stock will be lower with debt financing than otherwise, and output will be lower as a result of debt financing of a deficit. This *is* a real burden.

Thus, if the debt is a burden, it is a burden for reasons very different from those suggested by the statement that every person in the United States has a debt of $21,000 as a share of the national debt. The major source of burden arises from the possible effects of the national debt on the country's net national worth: An increase in the national debt can reduce the capital stock or increase the nation's external debt, or both.

DEBT, GROWTH, AND INSTABILITY

The national debt in the United States has risen almost every year for the past 50 years. Does that mean the government budget is bound to get out of hand, with interest payments rising so high that taxes have to keep rising, until eventually something terrible happens? The answer is no, because the economy has been growing.

Figure 18-5 which is the same as Figure 2-6, shows the U.S. public debt as a fraction of GNP for a long stretch of time, starting in the early nineteenth century.[41] The most striking fact is that the debt rises sharply as a result of large wartime deficits. Then, in each postwar period, it declines. Over most of the period from World War II to 1974, the debt-income ratio was falling even though the debt itself was rising as the result of budget deficits.

How could this happen? It is helpful to look at the definition of the *debt-income ratio:*

$$\text{Debt ratio} = \frac{\text{debt}}{PY} \qquad (9)$$

where PY represents nominal GDP. The ratio of debt to GDP falls when nominal GDP grows more rapidly than the debt. To see this point, it is useful to look separately at the numerator and denominator of the debt-GDP ratio. The numerator, the debt, grows because of deficits. The denominator, nominal GDP, grows as a result of both inflation and real GDP growth.

Why is it useful to look at the ratio of debt to income rather than at the absolute value of the debt? The reason is that GDP is a measure of the size of the economy, and the debt-GDP ratio is thus a measure of the magnitude of the debt relative to the size of the economy. A national debt of $6 trillion would have been overwhelming in 1929 when U.S. GDP was about $100 billion: Even if the interest rate had been only 1 percent, the government would have had to raise 50 percent of GDP in taxes to pay interest on the debt. But when GDP is $10 trillion, a $6 trillion debt is large—but certainly not overwhelming.

---

[41]Since GNP and GDP are almost the same for the United States, it does not make a difference whether we discuss the debt-to-GNP or debt-to-GDP ratio. Only debt-GNP data are available for earlier years.

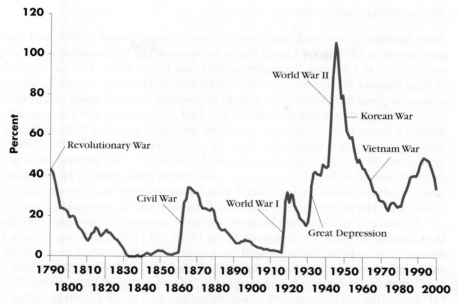

FIGURE 18-5   THE U.S. DEBT-TO-INCOME RATIO IN HISTORICAL PERSPECTIVE.
(Source: Congressional Budget Office.)

GENERATIONAL ACCOUNTING

There is no hard-and-fast economic principle that describes what is fair and not fair in allocating burdens among generations. Nonetheless, politicians and nonpoliticians have strong views on how burdens should be shared across generations. Such decisions have, of course, to be based on an accounting of just how much current policies impose burdens on different generations. *Intergenerational accounting* **evaluates the costs and benefits of the entire fiscal (tax and spending) system for various age groups in society.**

Laurence Kotlikoff of Boston University has made a systematic estimate of the intergenerational redistribution involved in U.S. fiscal policies. He came up with a stark and controversial finding:[42]

> The big winners from fiscal policy in the 1980s were Americans over forty at the time. Americans under forty were hurt by the policies. Young women were particularly hard hit by the decline in real welfare benefits and the rise in excise taxation.

As the last sentence of the quote suggests, Kotlikoff arrived at his unexpected conclusion by taking into account not only the future tax burdens imposed by the growing debt but also the burdens and benefits different generations derive from government tax and spending programs.

---

[42]Laurence Kotlikoff, *Generational Accounting* (New York: Free Press, 1992), p. 184.

THE SIZE-OF-GOVERNMENT DEBATE

There has been a worldwide trend over the last 40 years toward an increased share of government in GDP. In the United States, government (all levels) outlays were 23 percent of GDP in 1960 and 30 percent in 2002 (see Figure 18-6). This increase reflects in large measure the broadening of government social programs, especially the growth of transfer programs. Since 1981, growth in spending has been under sharp attack.

How large should the government be? That is, of course, a difficult question to answer. Clearly, some government programs are widely regarded as desirable; for instance, relatively few dispute the need for an adequate national defense. Other programs, such as social security, also command wide support, though just how large such programs should be is controversial. To conservatives government is far too large, and hence the deficit—and the pressures it puts on interest rates and financial stability—is desirable. Deficit pressure, in this view, is the best way to get spending cuts.

In practice, of course, the issue of how much government spending there should be is handled by the political process. In the 1930s and in the 1960s, the rules and traditions of fiscal policy were changed by activist government policy in pursuit of full employment and widening social objectives. Today many believe that things have gone too far and need to be brought under control by a return to "sound fiscal policy." The fiscal revolt reflects a disagreement in society on how best to use resources. At the same

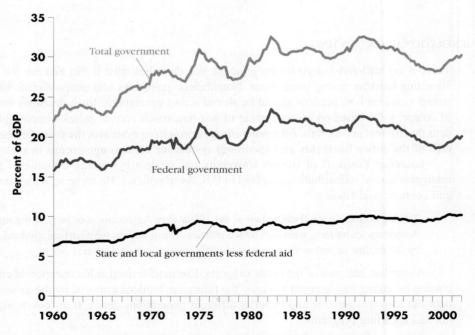

FIGURE 18-6   GOVERNMENT SPENDING AS A PERCENTAGE OF GDP, 1960–2002.

(Source: Bureau of Economic Analysis.)

time, there is a strand of thinking that calls for a resumption of government activity from infrastructure to education. The debate is not over, and the acute fiscal problem is bound to keep the difficult tradeoffs involved at the forefront of the discussion.

 # 18-7

SOCIAL SECURITY

The typical American pays more to the federal government in social security taxes than in income tax. Most of the people reading this textbook can expect to make large contributions to the social security system, while wondering whether the system will have enough funds to pay them pensions after they retire. In this section we consider two aspects of the social security system: intergenerational transfers and economic efficiency. The key to understanding both is that in most countries, and certainly in the United States, social security is a *pay-as-you-go system,* whereby taxes on the currently working generation are used to fund payments to retirees.[43]

SOCIAL SECURITY AS AN INTERGENERATIONAL TRANSFER

A pay-as-you-go social security system may transfer resources from the young to the old for three reasons: (1) because of population growth, (2) because of real income growth, and (3) because of the political process. We deal with each in turn. As a benchmark, we ask first what would benefits and payments look like in a no-resource-transfer system?

Suppose the typical person works and makes contributions to the social security system from age 26 through 65 and receives benefits from age 66 through 75. Since there are 40 years of work for 10 years of retirement, there will be four active contributors for each active beneficiary.[44] This means that the social security system budget will balance if each beneficiary receives the payments of four workers. And, since each worker pays in for 4 times the number of years she receives benefits, over a lifetime her contributions and benefits will balance.

Intergenerational Transfers because of Population Growth

Growing populations have a higher ratio of young to old than do stable populations. The higher ratio arises simply because each succeeding generation is larger than the one before it. For example, if population growth is 2 percent a year, the ratio of the working-age to retirement-age population in the example above will be 7 to 1 instead of 4 to 1. Thus, the benefit-contribution ratio can be much higher in a growing population than in a stable population.

---

[43]"Pay as you go" is a bit of an oversimplification. Currently, taxes exceed payments in the United States, so the balance in the Social Security Trust Fund is rising. However, obligations to pay future benefits are larger than the fund balance. Under current law, social security will run out of money in 2042.

[44]We pick a round number, four, for purposes of illustration. Real social security systems have more complicated rules for computing taxes and benefits.

TABLE 18-10	The Ratio of Working-Age Population to Retirement-Age Population						
YEAR	CANADA	FRANCE	GERMANY	ITALY	JAPAN	UNITED KINGDOM	UNITED STATES
1960	7.7	5.3	6.3	7.5	10.5	5.6	6.5
1990	5.9	4.7	4.5	4.7	5.8	4.3	5.3
2010	4.7	4.1	2.8	3.9	3.4	4.5	5.3
2030	3.5	3.3	3.0	3.4	3.0	3.9	4.9
2040	2.6	2.6	2.1	2.4	2.6	3.0	3.1

Source: Patricia S. Pollard, "How Will Demographics Affect Social Security," Federal Reserve Bank of St. Louis *International Economic Trends,* August 1996, based on OECD data.

Taking advantage of population growth to increase the benefit-contribution ratio is understandably politically attractive. The problem with such a setup is that one day population growth may end. To maintain expected benefits, contributions by the working generations will have to increase drastically. (In the example we've been using, contributions would have to nearly double, increasing by a ratio of 7 to 4.) This is exactly what has happened as most of the world's industrialized countries have moved toward zero population growth (ZPG).

Table 18-10 gives projections of the working-age to retirement-age population for seven industrialized countries. You can see that in the future in all these countries pay-as-you-go social security will have to either increase contributions from each worker or cut benefits to each retiree.[45]

Intergenerational Transfers because of Income Growth

Younger generations have a higher standard of living than older generations that is simply due to economic growth.[46] Suppose that contributions are set at a certain percentage of income, rather than a fixed dollar level. In a pay-as-you-go system, retired workers receive benefits higher than their own contributions because the source of the contributions is the higher income of the younger generation. At reasonable levels of productivity growth, this effect allows benefits to be much higher than would otherwise be possible. If long-run economic growth were to falter, the system would collapse. But as long as economic growth continues, each generation can count on receiving extra benefits based on the productivity of the young.

Intergenerational Transfers because of the Political Process

Social security systems are in trouble in many countries. Put simply, social security has been set up to pay out more in benefits than can be supported by the level of

[45]For projections on the effect of possible social security reforms in the major industrial countries, see "Fiscal Challenges Facing Industrial Countries," *World Economic Outlook* (International Monetary Fund), May 1996.

[46]Not every member of every generation is better off than his or her parents, of course. For example, in the United States today, young workers with low levels of education generally have a standard of living no higher than that of their parents.

contributions, even considering population and income growth. This worked to the advantage of early recipients, but, the day of reckoning having arrived, young people today can expect to receive a far lower benefit per dollar of contribution than did their parents. This situation has a political, rather than purely economic, explanation. Older people vote more than younger people, and current generations can vote for benefit programs without consulting the not-yet-born generations who will be required to pay for them. Older generations are, at least sometimes, in a position to enforce intergenerational transfers through the political system.

SOCIAL SECURITY AND ECONOMIC EFFICIENCY

There is a strong economic argument in favor of a social security system. As a society, there is a minimal standard of living we find acceptable for the elderly. Social security is a roundabout way of forcing everyone to undertake at least some saving for old age. Without a social security system, we would have to choose between seeing some of the elderly go hungry and having younger generations support older generations who had insufficient savings.

Unfortunately, in a pay-as-you-go system, society as a whole does not save for the future. Since contributions are immediately disbursed, no productive capital is created. (The so-called Social Security Trust Fund consists of IOUs from one generation to another. Unlike private pension plans, it isn't backed by any real investment.) So while social security forces some people to "save" who otherwise would not, it also reduces the effectiveness of investment by those who would have saved anyway by a remarkable amount.

In a pay-as-you-go system, $100 in contributions produces $100 in benefits. In our pay-in-40-year/take-out-10-year example, a worker would pay in $25 per year to sustain a $100 per year benefit level. Contrast this return with the compound return on real investment. At 5 percent interest, $25 per year in contributions sustains a $391 per year benefit level.[47] The difference between the $391 per year and the $100 per year benefit level is the economic cost of society's forgoing productive investment.[48]

Social security contributions almost certainly do not crowd out private (productive) retirement savings one-for-one. But each dollar of private saving that is displaced significantly reduces the size of society's nest egg.

POLICY RESPONSES

Finding a "fix" for social security is a hot political problem. Avoiding a crunch in the future requires making hard decisions today—and political systems are not good at

---

[47]This calculation is sensitive to the real interest rate used in the calculation. We use 5 percent per year, a number commonly used by universities in computing a rate at which endowments may be drawn on. At 2 percent annual interest, the benefit would be $168; at 8 percent the benefit would be $965.

[48]You can also think of the efficiency argument in terms of the effect of lower saving reducing economic growth and lowering very long run output. We studied this point in Chaps. 3 and 4.

making current sacrifices for future benefits. Reforms are being considered to attack both the insolvency and the inefficiency aspects of social security.[49] The solution to insolvency necessarily requires increasing taxes or cutting benefits, at least indirectly. Suggested reforms include[50]

- Increase the age at which one becomes eligible for benefits.
- Tax all benefits received in excess of contributions.
- Reduce cost-of-living increases by changing the way inflation is measured.[51]

Suggested reforms to reduce the inefficiency associated with pay-as-you-go social security involve investing part of the Social Security Trust Fund in productive investments rather than government IOUs.[52] Two specific suggestions are

- Invest part of the trust fund in a wide variety of stocks and corporate bonds.
- Allow individuals to substitute investment in private retirement accounts in place of part of their social security contributions.

Investments in the private sector earn higher returns than investments in the government bonds which now back the social security system. Thus, allowing productive investment also helps solve the insolvency problem.

WILL SOCIAL SECURITY CRASH?

Untouched, the current system will run dry in about 40 years—well before most current college students retire. No one seriously expects social security to disappear; the political system won't allow that. The greater question, in the United States and elsewhere, is how to find a reform that pays the debts already incurred with minimal collateral damage to the supply of capital into productive investments.

[49]For readable-but-technical articles on social security reform, see Edward Gramlich, "Different Approaches for Dealing with Social Security," Olivia S. Mitchell and Stephen P. Zeldes, "Social Security Privatization: A Structural Analysis," Laurence J. Kotlikoff, "Privatizing Social Security at Home and Abroad," and Sylvester J. Schieber and John B. Shoven, "Social Security Reform: Around the World in 80 Ways," all in *American Economic Association Papers and Proceedings,* May 1996. Several quite readable articles appear in "Reforming Social Security in Theory and Practice," Federal Reserve Bank of St. Louis *Review,* March–April 1998. A careful look at the ins and outs of privatization of social security appears in John Geanakoplos, Olivia Mitchell, and Stephen Zeldes, "Would a Privatized Social Security System Really Pay a Higher Rate of Return?" Yale working paper, September 1999.

[50]Suggestions for reforms, some of which have been implemented, have been made by a series of study commissions. Doubtlessly, new commissions and new ideas will continue to appear. As an example of some of the difficulties reformers face, look at the headline story about the Advisory Council on Social Security, "Panel in Discord on the Financing of Social Security: A Baby-Boom Shortage," *New York Times,* December 8, 1996.

[51]As we discussed in Chap. 2, there is good reason to believe current statistics overstate the true inflation rate.

[52]See Edward M. Gramlich, "Different Approaches for Dealing with Social Security," and Peter A. Diamond, "Proposals to Restructure Social Security," both in *Journal of Economic Perspectives,* Summer 1996.

SUMMARY

1. The Great Depression shaped both modern macroeconomics and many of the economy's institutions. The extremely high unemployment and the length of the Depression led to the view that the private economy was unstable and that government intervention was needed to maintain high employment levels.

2. Keynesian economics succeeded because it seemed to explain the causes of the Great Depression—a collapse of investment demand—and because it pointed to expansionary fiscal policy as a means of preventing future depressions.

3. In the U.S. economy, broad trends in money growth and in inflation do coincide. Money growth does affect inflation, but the effects occur with a lag that is not very precise. In the short term, inflation is affected by other than monetary shocks, for example, fiscal policy changes and supply shocks.

4. When fiscal policy turns expansionary, the Fed has to decide whether to monetize the deficit, printing money in order to prevent a rise in interest rates and crowding out; to keep the growth rate of money constant; or even to tighten monetary policy. If the government monetizes the deficit, it runs the risk of increasing the inflation rate. The evidence on deficit monetization in the United States remains ambiguous.

5. Inflation is a tax on real balances. To keep constant the purchasing power of holdings of money in the face of rising prices, a person has to add to nominal balances. In this fashion resources are transferred from money holders to money issuers, specifically the government.

6. Hyperinflations have generally taken place in the aftermath of wars. Large budget deficits are typical in hyperinflations. Governments can use the inflation tax to finance deficits to a limited extent, but if too large a deficit has to be financed, inflation explodes.

7. There is a two-way interaction between inflation and budget deficits. Higher deficits tend to cause higher inflation, since they are typically financed in part by money printing. As well, higher inflation causes higher deficits, by reducing the real value of tax collection. Higher nominal interest rates raise the measured deficit by increasing the value of nominal interest payments in the budget. The inflation-corrected deficit adjusts for this effect.

8. Money growth rates are very high following a successful inflation stabilization, as people increase their holdings of real balances.

9. Central bank independence is one avenue democracies use to add to the credibility of policy and to help mitigate the problem of dynamic inconsistency.

10. Federal government expenditures are financed through taxes and borrowing.

11. Federal government receipts come chiefly from the individual income tax and from social insurance taxes and contributions. The share of the last category has increased rapidly in the postwar period, especially since the 1960s.

12. Federal government expenditures are chiefly for defense and transfer payments to individuals. The share of defense in federal expenditure has fallen over the past 30 years, while the shares of transfers and interest have risen.

13. The debt-income ratio rises if the growth rate of debt—determined by interest payments and the primary deficit—exceeds the growth rate of nominal income.

---

14. Social security is financed on a pay-as-you-go system. Social security systems around the world have become vulnerable as population growth has slowed.

15. To the extent social security displaces private saving and investment, the productive capital stock is substantially reduced.

KEY TERMS

burden of the debt
credibility bonus
credible policy
debt-income ratio
discretionary outlays
entitlement programs
government budget constraint
government purchases
Great Depression

heterodox approach to stabilization
hyperinflation
inflation tax
inflation-adjusted deficit
inflationary inertia
intergenerational accounting
Keynesian revolution
mandatory outlays
monetization

New Deal
pay-as-you-go (social security) system
primary (or noninterest) deficit
quantity theory of money
sacrifice ratio
seigniorage
transfer payments
velocity of money

PROBLEMS

Conceptual

1. a. What do "Keynesians" believe caused the Great Depression?
   b. What do "monetarists" believe caused the Great Depression?
   c. Are these explanations mutually exclusive?
   d. Why are macroeconomists so interested in explaining the causes of the Great Depression?
2. Is inflation a monetary phenomenon? Be sure to distinguish, in your answer, between the long run and the short run.
3. a. Evaluate the strengths and weaknesses of gradual versus cold-turkey strategies of inflation reduction.
   b. Why is the credibility of anti-inflationary policy important?
4. Are budget deficits a problem? Why or why not?
5. When should, and shouldn't, the Fed monetize deficits?
6. How can inflation create government revenue?
7. At the height of the German hyperinflation, the government was covering only 1 percent of its spending with taxes.
   a. How could the German government have financed the remaining 99 percent of its spending?
   b. Explain how, after the end of hyperinflation, it was possible for the nominal money stock in Germany to increase by a factor of nearly 20 without restarting the inflation.
8.* The classic hyperinflations have occurred in the aftermath of wars or major social upheavals. What factors lay behind the high rates of Russian inflation in the early 1990s?
9. a. To what extent do we need to worry about the component of our total deficit that consists of interest payments on the public debt? (*Hint:* Ask yourself how much of this component is a real cost to the government.)

*An asterisk denotes a more difficult problem.

   b. To what extent do we need to worry about the national debt? In what way or ways is it a burden on society?

10. Should we require that the budget be balanced? Discuss.

11. Why is it more useful to look at the ratio of debt to GDP than at the absolute value of the debt?

12. German unification involved massive expenditures for infrastructure in the east, as well as transfer payments to many former East Germans. Should such expenditures have been financed by (a) money creation because of their transitory, exceptional nature, (b) debt, or (c) taxes? Justify your answer.

13. **a.** Why might a pay-as-you-go social security system transfer resources from the young to the old?

   b. What are the consequences of such a system on economic efficiency?

   c.* Are there other ways to structure a social security system that might alleviate some of the problems associated with this one? Explain.

Technical

1. It is sometimes said that the Great Depression would have been a severe recession if it had stopped in 1931 but would not have been the calamity it was.

   a. From Table 18-1 calculate the rate at which GNP was falling from 1929 to 1931.

   b. How does that rate compare with the rate at which real GDP fell during the 1990–1991 recession?

   c. Do you agree with the first sentence in this question? Explain.

2. Using Table 18-2, explain why concentration on the actual budget deficit might have given a misleading impression of fiscal policy at some stages between 1929 and 1933.

3. Suppose the money base is 10 percent of GDP. Suppose also that the government is considering raising the inflation rate from 0 to 10 percent per annum and believes that doing so will increase government revenue by 1 percent of GDP. Explain why the government must be overestimating the revenue it will receive from the resulting inflation tax.

4. Calculate the inflation-adjusted deficit when the national debt is 30 percent of GDP, the inflation rate is 7 percent per annum, and the total budget deficit is 4 percent of GDP.

5. Table 18-11 shows the growth rate of $M2$, the rate of inflation, and the rate of growth in output for the United States in decade averages, starting with the 1870s. Discuss the extent to which money growth, adjusted for output growth, helps explain inflation in recent U.S. history.

6. Table 18-8 shows how the U.S. government's spending has changed over the last several decades.

   a. Calculate how much total spending as a percentage of GDP has increased since the 1960s.

   b. In the 1960s (due largely to spending for the war in Vietnam) defense spending was the single largest component of total outlays. What has been the largest component since then?

   c. What types of outlays does the table suggest are responsible for growth in total spending since the 1960s?

7. Table 18-9 shows how the U.S. government's income has changed over the last several decades.

   a. Calculate how much total revenues have increased since the 1960s.

   b. The individual income tax was the largest component of federal revenue in the 1960s and remains the largest today. The second-largest component has changed dramatically, however. What was it in the 1960s, and what has it been since?

TABLE 18-11	Money, Output and Inflation		
	MONEY GROWTH, %*	OUTPUT GROWTH, %†	INFLATION, %†
1870–1879	2.3	5.5	−3.0
1880–1889	6.6	1.4	−1.1
1890–1899	5.0	3.7	−2.2
1900–1909	7.3	4.0	1.9
1910–1919	9.8	3.5	6.6
1920–1929	3.3	4.2	2.2
1930–1939	0.8	1.5	−1.9
1940–1949	11.5	3.4	5.6
1950–1959	3.8	3.3	2.5
1960–1969	7.1	4.0	2.7
1970–1979	9.8	2.8	7.1
1980–1989	8.0	2.6	5.4
1990–1999	4.0	3.0	2.3

*Money refers to $M2$.

†Inflation refers to the GNP deflator.

Source: Data for 1870 to 1959 are from Milton Friedman and Anna Schwartz, *Monetary Trends in the United States and the United Kingdom* (Chicago: University of Chicago Press, 1982); data for 1960 to 1989 are from DRI/McGraw-Hill; data for 1990 to 1999 are from www.economagic.com.

c. What types of income does the table suggest are responsible for growth in total revenues as a percentage of GDP since the 1960s?

8. Use the data in Tables 18-8 and 18-9 to find an estimate of the U.S. budget deficit as a percentage of GDP during each of the decades represented. How much has it increased since the 1960s?

9. If the growth rate of output averaged roughly 4 percent a year and the growth rate of the national debt averaged 5 percent, what would happen to the ratio of debt to GDP over time? Why?

Empirical

1. Tables 18-8 and 18-9 investigate the distribution of outlays and the sources of revenue for the U.S. federal government. One of the main trends one can notice is a considerable reduction in national defense expenditures. While national defense constituted about 45 percent of federal outlays in the period 1962–1969, by 2000–2002 national defense only represented about 17 percent of federal outlays. Is a similar trend taking place in Australia as well? Go to www.economagic.com, and under "Browse by Source," choose the heading "Australia." Click on "Commonwealth Government Finance," and take a look at Australian defense expenditures versus total expenses.

2. Go to www.economagic.com and take a look at the Australian Commonwealth Government's expenditures for social security and welfare. You can do a search for "Social Security and Welfare" and get the data. Transform the data to annual by using the option "Annual totals." Did Australian GDP grow faster than expenditures on social security and welfare?

CHAPTER 19

International Adjustment and Interdependence

CHAPTER HIGHLIGHTS

- National economies are linked through trade flows, exchange rates, and interest rates.

- Failure to keep exchange rates in line with prices ultimately leads to a devaluation crisis.

- The monetary approach to the balance of payments emphasizes the connection between the domestic money supply and the balance of payments.

International economic issues are increasingly prominent on the macroeconomic scene. Countries are interdependent: Booms or recessions in one country spill over to other countries through trade flows, and changes in interest rates in any major country cause immediate exchange or interest rate movements in other countries.

For example, spring 1997 saw the beginning of an economic crisis in Asia. One nation after another was forced to devalue its currency. Banks were shut down and unemployment soared. On the Hong Kong stock market the Heng Seng index dropped nearly a quarter of its value in a four-day period in October. Both troubled and fundamentally sound Asian economies were swept up in the contagion. For months, fears rose of a worldwide economic depression. Fortunately, the crisis did not spread to the rest of the world and by the end of the 1990s most Asian economies were on the mend.[1]

We introduced the basic facts and models of international linkages in Chapter 12. Now we explore the issues of international interdependence further. In the first three sections of this chapter we discuss aspects of the mechanisms through which a country with a fixed exchange rate adjusts to balance-of-payments problems. This discussion helps clarify current international economic issues even though exchange rates among the dollar, yen, and other major currencies have been flexible since 1973; the fixed exchange rate mechanisms remain relevant because some smaller countries still operate with fixed exchange rates. In addition, an understanding of the adjustment mechanisms that operate under fixed exchange rates helps in grasping the operation of flexible exchange rates.

In the rest of the chapter we take up aspects of the behavior of the current flexible exchange rate system.[2]

19-1

ADJUSTMENT UNDER FIXED EXCHANGE RATES

Adjustment to a balance-of-payments problem can be achieved in two ways. One is to change economic policy; the second is through *automatic adjustment mechanisms*. There are two automatic mechanisms: Payments imbalances affect the money supply and hence spending, and unemployment affects wages and prices and thereby competitiveness. Policy measures, by contrast, include monetary and fiscal policy, and also tariffs or devaluation.

THE ROLE OF PRICES IN THE OPEN ECONOMY

We start the analysis by bringing prices explicitly into our analysis of the open economy. In Chapter 12 we assumed that the price level was constant. With fixed prices and a

---

[1]An excellent chronology of the Asian crises can be found at http://faculty.washington.edu/karyiu/Asia/manuscri.htm.

[2]For an extensive review of work on both theory and evidence, see Mark Taylor, "The Economics of Exchange Rates," *Journal of Economic Literature,* March 1995.

given exchange rate, the *real* exchange rate is also fixed. Recall the definition of the real exchange rate:

$$R = \frac{eP_f}{P} \qquad (1)$$

Here e is the nominal exchange rate, P_f the foreign price level, and P the domestic price level. We now abandon the assumption of a fixed domestic price level but, for the time being, take the exchange rate and foreign prices as given.

How does the openness of the economy affect the aggregate demand curve? In the closed economy version of the model, aggregate demand declines when the price level rises: A higher price level implies lower real balances, higher interest rates, and lower spending. In an open economy with a fixed exchange rate, an increase in the price level reduces demand for an additional reason: An increase in our prices makes our goods less competitive with (more expensive relative to) foreign-produced goods. Given the exchange rate, when the prices of goods produced at home rise, our goods become more expensive for foreigners to buy and their goods become *relatively* cheaper for us to buy. An increase in our price level thus shifts demand away from our goods toward imports and also reduces exports.

In Figure 19-1 we show the downward-sloping demand schedule for our goods, *AD*. Demand is equal to aggregate spending by domestic residents plus net exports, or $AD \equiv A + NX$, and now there are two reasons for the aggregate demand curve to slope down.

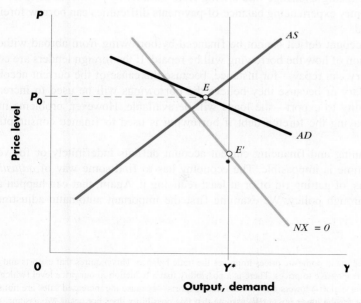

FIGURE 19-1   OPEN ECONOMY EQUILIBRIUM WITH PRICE ADJUSTMENT.

The demand for domestic goods, *AD*, is drawn for a given level of foreign prices, a given nominal money supply, given fiscal policy, and an exchange rate that is fixed. An increase in the nominal money stock shifts the schedule upward, as does expansionary fiscal policy. We show, too, the short-run aggregate supply schedule, *AS*, and the full-employment level of output, *Y**. Initial equilibrium is at point *E*, at which we have unemployment.

Next we look at the trade balance equilibrium schedule, *NX* = 0. An increase in our income raises imports and worsens the trade balance. To restore trade balance equilibrium, domestic prices would have to be lower. This would make the home country more competitive, raise exports, and reduce imports. Thus, we show the trade balance equilibrium schedule as downward-sloping.[3] We assume that it is steeper than the demand schedule for domestic goods. The schedule is drawn for a given level of prices abroad.

FINANCING AND ADJUSTMENT

At point *E* the home country has a trade deficit. Our prices are too high or our income is too high to have exports balance imports. To achieve trade balance equilibrium, we would have to become more competitive, thus exporting more and importing less. Alternatively, we could reduce our level of income in order to reduce import spending.

What does a country with a current account deficit, like that at *E*, do? In a fixed exchange rate system, it is possible for the central bank to use its reserves to finance temporary imbalances of payments—that is, to meet the excess demand for foreign currency at the existing exchange rate arising from *balance-of-payments deficits*. Alternatively, a country experiencing balance-of-payments difficulties can borrow foreign currencies abroad.

A current account deficit cannot be financed by borrowing from abroad without raising the question of how the borrowing will be repaid. If the foreign lenders are convinced the country can repay—for instance, because the cause of the current account deficit is temporary or because they believe the borrowings will be used to increase the country's ability to export—the loans will be available. However, problems may well arise in repaying the foreign debt if borrowing is used to finance consumption spending.

But maintaining and financing current account deficits indefinitely or for very long periods of time is impossible. The economy has to find some way of *adjusting* the deficit, that is, of getting rid of or at least reducing it. Again, that can happen automatically or through policy. We examine first the important automatic adjustment mechanisms.

---

[3]We assume that a decline in domestic prices improves the trade balance. This requires that exports and imports be sufficiently responsive to prices. There is a possibility that a reduction in our price level (which reduces the prices of our exports) lowers our revenue from exports—because the increased sales are not sufficient to compensate for the lower prices. We assume that this possibility does not occur. We assume, too, that import spending does not depend on the interest rate.

AUTOMATIC ADJUSTMENT

First we look at the aggregate demand side. When a country runs a balance-of-payments deficit, the demand for foreign exchange is by definition larger than the amount being supplied by the private markets, and the central bank has to sell the difference. When the central bank sells foreign exchange, it reduces domestic high-powered money and therefore the money stock—unless it sterilizes its foreign exchange intervention by buying bonds as it sells foreign exchange. (We discuss sterilization later in this chapter.) Ruling out that possibility, the deficit at point E implies that the central bank is pegging the exchange rate, selling foreign exchange to keep the exchange rate from depreciating, and reducing the domestic money stock. It follows immediately that over time the aggregate demand schedule (which is drawn for a given money supply) will be shifting downward and to the left.

Turning now to the aggregate supply side, point E in Figure 19-1 is also a point of unemployment. Unemployment leads to declines in wages and costs, which are reflected in a downward-shifting aggregate supply schedule. Over time, therefore, the short-run equilibrium point, E, moves downward as both demand and supply schedules shift (not shown). The points of short-run equilibrium move in the direction of point E', and the process will continue until that point is reached. (The approach may be cyclical, but that is not of major interest here.)

Once point E' is reached, the country has automatically achieved long-run equilibrium. Because the trade balance is in equilibrium, there is no pressure on the exchange rate and therefore no need for exchange market intervention, so there are no further changes in the money supply. On the supply side, wages and costs are constant, so the supply schedule is not shifting. Thus, at E' the country has successfully and automatically adjusted to the initial balance-of-payments deficit: It has achieved trade balance equilibrium combined with full employment.

This is the *classical adjustment process*. It relies on price adjustments and an adjustment in the money supply based on the trade balance. The adjustment process "works," *but* it may take a very long time and require a very long recession.[4] The alternative to waiting for the automatic adjustment mechanisms to do the whole job is to make explicit policy changes to move the economy more rapidly toward balance.

POLICIES TO RESTORE BALANCE: EXPENDITURE SWITCHING AND REDUCING

Because of their side effects, policies to restore external balance must generally be combined with policies to achieve full employment: Policies to create employment will typically worsen the external balance, and policies to create a trade surplus will affect employment. **In general it is necessary to combine** *expenditure-switching policies,* **which shift demand between domestic and imported goods, and** *expenditure-reducing* **(or** *expenditure-increasing) policies* **in order to cope with the two targets of** *internal*

---

[4]Olivier Blanchard and Pierre-Alain Muet, in "Competitiveness through Disinflation: An Assessment of French Macro Policy," *Economic Policy,* April 1993, show that it took France almost a decade to achieve such an adjustment, starting in 1983.

BOX 19-1   Why Are Devaluations So Often Delayed?

Countries that have fixed their exchange rates often delay devaluing until they have no choice—and when they reach that point, the government is perceived to have suffered a major defeat. This was certainly the case in Mexico in 1994; earlier it was the case in the United Kingdom and Italy, which were forced to devalue in 1992. In late 2001 Argentina had held the peso fixed one to one to the U.S. dollar for a decade, but by the end of February 2002 the Argentine peso was worth less than 33 cents.

Why do countries wait too long? First, the economic reasons: For a devaluation to be effective, for it to reduce the balance-of-payments deficit, it has to make imported goods more expensive so that domestic residents buy fewer of them. When Mexico devalued, American candies (and many more important imports) became more expensive, and the living standards of Mexicans fell accordingly. But it is not only the prices of imports that rise; so do the prices of goods that use imported raw materials in their production.

Devaluations are unpopular because they reduce the domestic standard of living. In addition, the increases in prices of imports sometimes set off more general price rises, or inflation, which is also unpopular.

There is another reason that governments often delay devaluations too long. Devaluations are in many ways self-fulfilling prophecies: The expectation that a country will devalue increases the probability that it will do so.* Why? Because if you expect the currency to devalue (e.g., if you expect the value of the peso to fall from 3.5 to the dollar to 6 to the dollar), you will buy dollars as soon as possible for only 3.5 pesos, expecting that you will later make a profit in pesos by selling the dollars at a higher (peso) price. But as you buy dollars, you deplete the country's peso reserves and make it harder to maintain the exchange rate. Accordingly, especially when the public begins to fear that a devaluation is likely, government officials often make stirring statements to the effect that there will under no circumstances be a devaluation. For a while that may reassure the public and thus help prevent the devaluation. But when devaluation becomes necessary, the government officials look foolish and defeated—and that is another reason they delay too long.

*See Paul Krugman, "Self-Fulfilling Currency Crises," *NBER Macro Annual*, 1996; and Norbert Funke, "Vulnerability of Fixed Exchange Rate Regimes: The Role of Fundamentals," *OECD Economic Studies* 26 (1996).

---

balance and *external balance.* This point is of general importance and continues to apply when we take account of capital flows and other phenomena omitted in this section.

One method of adjusting a current account deficit is by imposing *tariffs*—taxes on imports. However, tariffs cannot be freely used to adjust the balance of trade, partly because there are international organizations and agreements such as the *World Trade*

Organization (WTO) and the *International Monetary Fund (IMF)* that outlaw, or at least frown on, the use of tariffs. Tariffs have generally fallen in the post-World War II period as the industrialized world has moved to desirably freer trade between countries.

Another way of adjusting a current account deficit is to use policies to reduce aggregate demand. These are expenditure-reducing policies. In this regard, it is worth repeating that a trade deficit reflects an excess of expenditure over income. The identities in Chapter 2 imply that

$$NX \equiv Y - (C + I + G) \tag{2}$$

where *NX* is the trade surplus and *I* is investment. Thus, a balance-of-trade deficit can be reduced by reducing spending $(C + I + G)$ relative to income (Y) through restrictive monetary and/or fiscal policy.

The link between the external deficit and budget deficits is shown in equation $(2a)$:[5]

$$NX \equiv (S - I) + [TA - (G + TR)] \tag{2a}$$

where *S* denotes *private* saving and $TA - (G + TR)$ is the government budget surplus. Equation $(2a)$ shows an immediate relation between the budget and the external balance. If saving and investment were constant, then changes in the budget would translate, one for one, into changes in the external balance; budget cutting would bring about equal changes in the external deficit. But budget cutting will affect saving and investment, and therefore we need a more complete model to explain how budget cuts affect the external balance.

Devaluation

The unemployment that typically accompanies automatic adjustment and the desirability of free trade, which argues against the use of tariffs, both suggest the need for an alternative policy for restoring internal and external balance. The major policy instrument for dealing with payments deficits is *devaluation,* which usually has to be combined with restrictive monetary or fiscal policy, or both. A devaluation is an increase in the domestic currency price of foreign exchange. Given the nominal prices in two countries, devaluation increases the relative price of imported goods in the devaluing country and reduces the relative price of exports from the devaluing country. Devaluation is primarily an expenditure switching policy.

How does a devaluation work? Consider first the special case of a country that has been in full employment with balance-of-trade equilibrium and is at point *E* in Figure 19-2. Now let there be an exogenous decline in export earnings, so the $NX = 0$ schedule shifts to the left to $NX' = 0$. With a lower demand for exports and with a fixed exchange rate, output would decline. The *AD* schedule moves to the left as a result of the fall in exports. The lower level of income reduces imports but not enough to make up for the loss of export revenue. The net effects are therefore unemployment and a trade deficit.

The automatic adjustment mechanism would work, but slowly, to restore equilibrium. Alternatively, the country can devalue its currency. This has the obvious advantage

[5]To derive equation $(2a)$, we combine equation (2) with the accounting identities $Y \equiv YD + (TA - TR)$ and $YD \equiv C + S$.

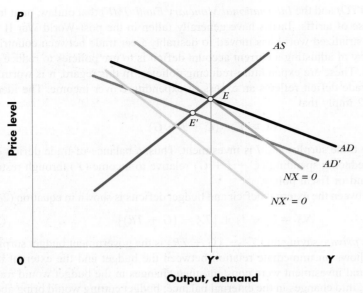

FIGURE 19-2   EFFECTS OF A LOSS OF EXPORT REVENUE.

that it does not require a protracted recession to reduce domestic costs. The adjustment is done by the stroke of a pen—a devaluation of the currency. Why would a devaluation achieve the adjustment? *Given* prices of foreign goods in terms of foreign currency (e.g., the yen prices of Japanese goods), a devaluation raises the relative price of foreign goods. Imports fall, and exports rise.

The case we have just considered is special, however, in one important respect. The economy was initially in balance-of-trade equilibrium at full employment. The disturbance to the economy took place in the trade account. Accordingly, if we could move the $NX' = 0$ locus back to the full-employment level of income—as we could with a devaluation—both internal and external balance would be attained. Put differently, the reason there was unemployment in Figure 19-2 was the reduction in exports and consequent external balance problem. Both problems could thus be cured through devaluation.

In general, though, a country cannot secure both external and internal balance following a disturbance by using just one instrument of policy. A general rule of policy making is that we need to use as many policy instruments as we have policy targets.

Finally, a comment on the role of the exchange rate in a fixed rate system: In a fixed rate system, the exchange rate is an *instrument of policy*. The central bank can change the exchange rate for policy purposes, devaluing when the current account looks as though it will be in for a prolonged deficit. In a system of clean floating, by contrast, the exchange rate moves freely to equilibrate the balance of payments. In a system of dirty floating, the central bank attempts to manipulate the exchange rate while not committing itself to any given rate. The dirty floating system is thus intermediate between a fixed rate system and a clean floating system.

EXCHANGE RATES AND PRICES

A devaluation that takes place when domestic and foreign prices are constant will succeed in reducing the relative price of a country's goods and will thus improve the trade balance. However, the price level typically changes along with the exchange rate. The essential issue when a country devalues is whether it can achieve a *real devaluation*. **A country achieves a real devaluation when a devaluation reduces the price of the country's own goods relative to the price of foreign goods.**

Recalling the definition of the real exchange rate, eP_f/P, and taking the foreign price level (P_f) as given, **a real devaluation occurs when e/P rises, or when the exchange rate increases by more than the price level.**

We use Figure 19-3, and the example of Mexico, to illustrate the problem of securing a real devaluation. Let $P_{U.S.}$ be the price level in the United States, P the Mexican price level, and e Mexico's exchange rate, that is, the number of pesos per dollar. (So the analysis treats Mexico as the home country and the United States as "abroad.") Mexico's competitiveness then is measured by U.S. prices relative to Mexican prices, both measured in dollars: $P_{U.S.}/(P/e) = (eP_{U.S.}/P)$. We assume that the U.S. price level is given and show P/e, the Mexican price level measured in dollars, on the vertical axis in Figure 19-3. For a given U.S. price level, a rise in Mexican dollar prices (P/e) worsens Mexico's net exports. Accordingly, points to the right of $NX = 0$ correspond to deficits.

Consider now the problem of adjustment to external shocks. Suppose that an oil price fall in world markets reduces Mexico's export earnings at each price level and

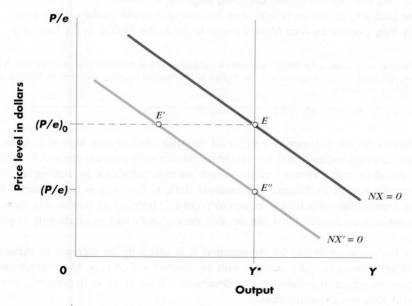

FIGURE 19-3   COMPETITIVENESS AND ADJUSTMENT.
An adverse external shock can be shown as a leftward shift of the NX schedule.

BOX 19-2   Mexico's External Balance

In the 1980s Mexico went through a deep crisis. The country had borrowed too much in world markets and under the pressure of high world interest rates in the early 1980s found it impossible to service its external debt. Borrowing abroad became impossible from one day to the next. Mexico had to rebuild its economy, starting by depreciating its currency, reducing import tariffs and quotas, privatizing state-owned firms, and reducing government regulation of the economy. By the end of the 1980s these reforms bore fruit: The Mexican economy was growing again.*

With the return of growth and especially with a domestic investment boom, the current account worsened sharply. There was no trouble financing the current account deficit, because foreign firms and investors were investing heavily in Mexico. The question that arose was whether the Mexican government should allow the deficit to continue and even grow or, rather, cut the deficit by devaluation and a reduction in domestic spending. Table 1 shows how large the Mexican capital account surplus was. Much of the surplus went to the Mexican private sector. But capital inflows far exceeded the borrowings of Mexican private residents. A large part of the inflow was bought by the Mexican central bank, to add to its foreign exchange reserves. Such a situation is possible when, as in the Mexican case, the rest of the world decides that a country has outstanding profit opportunities and, as a result, invests in that country's stock market or in high-yield government bonds. Mexico in 1990–1992 offered that attraction and thus had no trouble attracting large capital flows.

The problem, of course, is that when borrowing in world markets is too easy, a country may overborrow—as Mexico certainly did in the 1970s. In the face of a

*On the Mexican experience in the 1980s, see Pedro Aspe, *Economic Transformation: The Mexican Way* (Cambridge, MA: MIT Press, 1993). An annual account is given in *The Mexican Economy*, published by Mexico's central bank, Banco de Mexico.

thus creates a deficit. (Mexico is a major oil exporter.) Initially we were at E, with internal and external balance, and now external balance only prevails along $NX' = 0$.

In the short run a country might absorb an external shock by staying at point E, borrowing abroad to finance the external deficit. But that is not possible forever; the country has somehow to return to point E''. It could do that slowly, through the automatic mechanisms. Or it can devalue the currency and move directly to point E''.

But the devaluation can be frustrated if it is offset by an increase in domestic prices. What matters is that a country with an external deficit (say, Mexico) succeeds in reducing its prices in dollars, P/e. If devaluation leads to a rise in domestic prices, there is no gain in competitiveness.

Mexico undertook exchange rate devaluations in 1976, 1982, 1985–1986, and 1994 that sharply reduced the dollar prices of Mexican goods. But the gains in competitiveness

TABLE 1   Mexico's External Balance
(Millions of U.S. Dollars)

	1989	1990	1991
Current account	−6,050	−7,114	−13,283
Trade balance	−404	−882	−6,930
Capital account	6,050	7,114	13,283
Private*	5,654	3,881	5,777
Decrease in reserves	396	3,233	7,506

*Including errors and omissions.

current account deficit of almost $20 billion in 1992, that question emerged once again. Was it not a more prudent policy choice to say no to foreign investors, reduce demand by a tightening of fiscal policy, and perhaps even devalue the peso to make Mexican goods more competitive in world trade and imports more expensive in Mexico?

Countries rarely adjust early because tightening policy before that step becomes inevitable is politically difficult. That is what happened in 1982. A crisis emerged when foreign lenders and investors lost confidence in Mexico and were no longer willing to buy Mexican assets and when the Mexican private sector sent its capital abroad. A huge financing gap emerged. For a while the central bank met the financing gap by running down its reserves. Ultimately, the process ended in a major devaluation and a deep recession. Many observers in 1992 were conscious of just how destructive it would be to go through the same cycle once more.

The argument against doing so was that devaluation would be disruptive to confidence in capital markets and to the attempt to reduce inflation. Moreover, it was argued, the deficit in the current account primarily reflected a high level of Mexican investment, which would generate the revenues with which to pay off the borrowing. In a few years, it was argued, the deficit would go down, and in the meantime it could be financed without grave risk. *A good story, but for how long?*

---

did not last after the first three of these four devaluations. Inflation in Mexico soon raised prices relative to the exchange rate; by 1992 the *real* exchange rate was less than it had been in 1987. Failure to keep exchange rates in line with prices—that is, to maintain competitiveness—ultimately results in devaluation crises, as happened in December 1994.[6] In Boxes 19-2 and 19-3 we discuss Mexican adjustment.[7]

[6]See Paul Krugman, *Currencies and Crises* (Cambridge, MA: MIT Press, 1992); and Pierre-Richard Agenor, Jagdeep Bhandari, and Robert Flood, "Speculative Attacks and Models of Balance of Payments Crises," *IMF Staff Papers,* June 1992. The problem of postponed adjustment is not peculiar to developing countries, as the European currency crisis of 1992 in countries including Italy, Finland, and the United Kingdom demonstrates.

[7]For more on the Mexican peso crisis, see the January–February 1996 issue of the Federal Reserve Bank of Atlanta *Economic Review.* For more on currency management, see Robert Bartley, "Mexico's Money Theorists Need a Tip from Hong Kong," and David Malpass, "Currency Stability on the March," both in *The Wall Street Journal,* December 20, 1996.

BOX 19-3   Balance-of-Payments Crises Are Pretty Well Understood

We have intentionally left Box 19-2 untouched from the 6th edition. Except for italicizing the last sentence, *"A good story, but for how long?"* According to our notes, the text has essentially been unchanged since October 14, 1992.

In 1994 and 1995, Mexico underwent the exchange rate drop foreseen in a previous edition of this text. The exchange rate began to fall early in 1994. Starting in December 1994, shortly after a new president took office in Mexico City, the peso went into free fall. The peso recovered slightly, assisted by massive American and IMF loans (since repaid) and then fell further through 1995.*

While predicting the precise timing or even the depth of an exchange rate crisis is difficult, the need for a policy change—voluntary or market-driven—was both predictable and predicted.

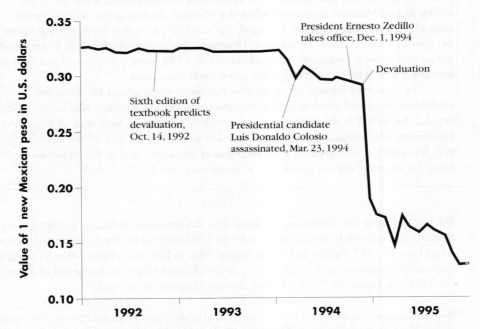

FIGURE 1   VALUE OF THE MEXICAN PESO, 1992–1996.

(Source: DRI/McGraw-Hill Macroeconomic Database.)

*To learn more about what happened in the Mexican crisis and why, see Jeffrey Sachs, Aaron Tornell, and Andrés Velasco, "The Collapse of the Mexican Peso: What Have We Learned?" *Economic Policy*, April 1996.

BOX 19-4   Debt Crises Are Not a New Phenomenon

The loans from the creditor country begin with a modest amount and proceed crescendo. They are likely to be made in exceptionally large amounts toward the culminating stage of a period of activity and speculative upswing, and during that stage become larger from month to month so long as the upswing continues. With the advent of a crisis, they are at once cut down sharply, even cease entirely. . . . A sudden reversal takes place in the debtor country's international balance sheet; it feels the consequences abruptly, in an immediate need of increased remittances to the creditor country, in a strain on its banks, high rates of discount, falling prices. And this train of events may ensue not only once.

—Harvard economist Frank Taussig writing on speculation and repeated debt crises . . . in 1927!

Source: Frank Taussig, *International Trade* (New York: MacMillan, 1927), p. 130.

Crawling Peg Exchange Rates

When a country experiences inflation above the rate of its trading partners, holding the exchange rate fixed would imply a steady loss in competitiveness. In order to avoid the widening deficits, many countries follow a *crawling peg* exchange rate policy. **Under a crawling peg exchange rate policy, the exchange rate is depreciated at a rate roughly equal to the inflation differential between the country and its trading partners.** The idea of a crawling peg is to maintain the *real* exchange rate, $R = P_f/(P/e)$, constant by raising e at the same rate as (P/P_f) is rising.

It is clear from Figure 19-4 that for lengthy periods, for example, in 1989–1992, Mexico failed to offset the impact of its inflation on competitiveness. The exchange rate was not depreciated fast enough to maintain the real exchange rate. As a result, competitiveness fell and foreign exchange problems remained.

Countries are often and easily tempted to use the exchange rate to slow inflation. When the exchange rate is held constant, the prices of imports stay constant (assuming foreign prices are not rising), and therefore the prices of some of the goods that enter the consumer price index are not increasing. This slows inflation. But the reduction in inflation is bought by steadily reducing competitiveness. Often such a strategy ultimately brings about a foreign exchange crisis. In the end, inflation has to be stopped by monetary and fiscal policy; exchange rate policy is at best a supplementary tool—at times a very valuable one,[8] but it cannot do most of the work in disinflation.

---

[8] For example, as discussed in Chap. 18, when it is necessary to stop an extreme inflation.

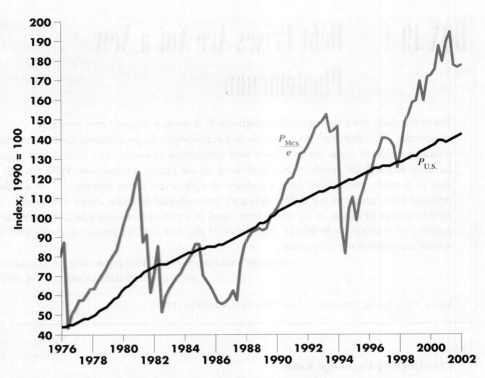

FIGURE 19-4   DOLLAR PRICE LEVELS: UNITED STATES AND MEXICO, 1976–2002.
(*Source: IMF, International Financial Statistics, 2002.*)

19-2

EXCHANGE RATE CHANGES AND TRADE ADJUSTMENT: EMPIRICAL ISSUES

In this section we take up two important empirical issues related to the possibility of adjusting current account imbalances by changes in the exchange rate.[9] The first is whether nominal devaluations do usually succeed in achieving real devaluations or whether, as Figure 19-4 suggests, that may be unusual.

The second issue is whether changes in relative prices, if they occur, do improve the current account. We have explicitly assumed here that a decline in the relative price of our goods improves the current account. But a perverse reaction is possible. When import prices rise, import demand may not decline sufficiently to compensate for the higher prices of imports, and thus total import spending (price times quantity) may actually increase. We turn our attention now to these two issues.

[9]For a comprehensive survey on the response of trade flows, see P. Hooper and J. Marquez, "Exchange Rates, Prices and External Adjustment in the United States and Japan," in Peter Kenen (ed.), *Understanding Interdependence: The Macroeconomics of the Open Economy* (Princeton, NJ: Princeton University Press, 1995).

EXCHANGE RATES AND RELATIVE PRICE ADJUSTMENT

In studying the flexible wage-price model, we assumed that wages and prices adjust to achieve full employment. But in practice prices are based on labor cost or wages. Now suppose that wages are inflexible in real terms, because labor wants to maintain the purchasing power of wages. This may be reflected in the formal indexation of wages to the consumer price index, or it may be the outcome of the bargaining between firms and workers. In such a world, changes in the cost of living triggered by a devaluation would lead to changes in money wages, which would feed back into prices, which could offset the effects of the nominal devaluation.

A process in which changes in prices feed back into wages and from there into prices is a *wage-price spiral* that may produce considerable volatility in the price level. Small disturbances can set off quite large changes in the price level. Suppose, first, that the real wage is fixed in terms of the consumer price index, which includes both domestic goods and imports, so changes in the consumer price index are fully passed on into wages. Assume, second, that changes in wages are fully passed on into increased domestic prices.

Now suppose that the country has to devalue to try to restore the trade balance. The devaluation raises import prices and thereby raises consumer prices. To maintain the real wage, workers demand higher money wages, which firms grant and pass on by raising prices. Where are we after the process ends? Real wages are constant, which means wages and the price level (a weighted average of the prices of domestic and imported goods) have risen in the same proportion; wage increases have been fully passed on, which means that real wages *in terms of domestic output* are also unchanged. The two results imply that relative prices are unchanged and that *the nominal devaluation has had no effect on the real exchange rate.*

Of course, this is not the whole story, because we have to ask how the higher price level affects aggregate demand. If the government did not increase the money stock, the higher prices reduce real balances and aggregate demand; with income down, the current account improves. The spiral will take place only if, when wages rise, the government raises the money stock so as not to create unemployment. Hence, in this context of a devaluation, it is crucial that the central bank not accommodate nominal price increases if it wants to achieve a real devaluation.

A second context in which the idea of *sticky real wages* (wages that are difficult to change) is important is that of real disturbances. Suppose our export demand declines permanently because of, say, the introduction of superior technology abroad. To return to full employment, the relative price of our goods must fall to encourage foreign demand. But how can the relative price fall? If we devalue, and workers succeed in restoring their real wages, and prices are marked up on wages, there will be no change in the relative price of our goods. Then the only way to reduce the real wage would be protracted unemployment.

The empirical question, then, is, How flexible are real wages? That is, to an important extent, a question of institutional arrangements. In small, open economies with substantial cost-of-living indexation in wage agreements, it may indeed be very difficult to change real wages and relative prices through exchange rate changes. In general, countries that devalue have to use restrictive aggregate demand policies to make sure that induced increases in prices do not simply undo the real effects of the nominal devaluation.

RELATIVE PRICES AND THE TRADE BALANCE: THE J CURVE

We come now to the second issue, the effect of changes in relative prices on the trade balance and the possibility that a depreciation *worsens* the trade balance. To make this point clear, we write out the trade balance, measured in terms of domestic goods, as

$$NX = X - \frac{eP_f}{P}Q \tag{3}$$

where X denotes the foreign demand for our goods or exports and Q denotes our own import quantity. The term $(eP_f/P)Q$ thus measures the *value* of our imports in terms of domestic goods.

Suppose that we now have an exchange depreciation and that, in the first instance, domestic and foreign prices, P and P_f, are unchanged. Then the relative price of imports, eP_f/P, rises. This leads to two effects. First, if the physical *volume* of imports does not change, their *value* measured in domestic currency unambiguously increases because of the higher price. This means higher import spending (measured in terms of the domestic currency) and thus a worsening of the trade balance. This is the source for the potentially perverse response of the trade balance to exchange depreciation.

However, there are two *volume* responses that run in the opposite direction: Exports should rise because our goods are now cheaper for foreigners to buy, and the volume of imports should decline because imports are more expensive.

The question, then, is whether the volume effects on imports and exports are sufficiently strong to outweigh the price effect, that is, whether depreciation raises or lowers net exports. The empirical evidence on this question is quite strong and shows the following result:[10] **The short-term volume effects, say, within a year, are quite small and thus do not outweigh the price effect. The long-term volume effects, by contrast, are quite substantial, and certainly enough to make the trade balance respond in the normal fashion to a relative price change.**

Why does this pattern of responses take place? First, the low short-term and high longer-term volume effects result from the length of time consumers and producers take to adjust to changes in relative prices. Some of these adjustments may be instantaneous, but it is clear that tourism patterns, for example, may take 6 months to a year to adjust and that relocation of production internationally in response to changes in relative costs and prices may take years. A case in point is increased foreign direct investment in the United States—say, Toyota's moving from Japan to California. In the long term, such direct investment leads to reduced imports by the United States, and thus to an improved trade balance, but such an adjustment takes years, not weeks or months.

The lag in the adjustment of trade flows to changes in relative prices is thus quite plausible. What do these lags imply about the impact of relative price changes on the trade balance? Suppose that at a particular time, starting with a deficit, we have a

---

[10]See Tamin Bayoumi, "Estimating Trade Equations from Aggregate Bilateral Data," International Monetary Fund working paper 1999/74, and Paul Krugman, "The J-Curve, the Fire Sale and the Hard Landing," *American Economic Review,* May 1989.

depreciation that raises the relative price of imports. The short-term effects result primarily from increased import prices with very little offsetting volume effects. Therefore, the trade balance initially worsens. Over time, as trade volume adjusts to the changed relative prices, exports rise and import volume progressively declines. The volume effects come to dominate, and in the long run the trade balance shows an improvement. This pattern of adjustment is referred to as the *J-curve effect,* because diagrammatically the response of the trade balance looks like a "J."

The J-curve effect could be seen in the behavior of the U.S. current account after 1985. Despite a rapid depreciation of the dollar starting in February 1985, the current account continued to worsen for the next year. But the current account began to improve in 1987 and continued improving in 1988.

The medium-term problem of sticky real wages and the J-curve effect provides important clues for the interpretation of macroeconomic experiences across countries, particularly in showing why depreciations typically do not lead to improvements in the current account in the short term.

Hysteresis Effects of Overvaluation

A further complication has been suggested in the aftermath of the large and persistent overvaluation of the dollar in 1980–1985, namely, *hysteresis* effects. Such effects are present, in the case of the exchange rate, when a change in the exchange rate that is later exactly reversed nonetheless leaves a long-term impact on the trade account. In the early 1980s, the U.S. dollar was very strong. This put U.S. firms at a sharp disadvantage in world trade and in the U.S. market. The dollar prices of imports declined, and in foreign markets, U.S. firms lost out because their relative prices increased.

These are the normal effects of a currency appreciation. The hysteresis argument is that when exchange rate changes are very large and long-lasting, they will lead to a relatively permanent change in trade patterns.[11] Once foreign firms have become established in the United States and consumers have become accustomed to their goods, even a reversal of the exchange rate to the initial level will not be enough to enable U.S. firms to recapture their share of the market. Similarly, when U.S. firms have lost foreign market share and even left some foreign markets entirely, going back to the initial exchange rate will not be enough to bring U.S. firms back. To return to the initial trade pattern, exchange rates would have to overshoot in the opposite direction, making it profitable to incur the costs of starting up export operations and competing with foreign firms that supply imports.

The evidence on these hysteresis effects remains tentative, but the idea is certainly plausible. The continued higher share of imports into the U.S. market and the failure of the U.S. external balance to correct itself fully, even after the 1985–1988 depreciation brought the real exchange rate back close to its 1980 level, support the idea that the damage of overvaluation may be a lasting one.

---

[11]See Richard Baldwin and Paul Krugman, "Persistent Trade Effects of Large Exchange Rate Shocks," *Quarterly Journal of Economics,* November 1989; and by the same authors, "The Persistence of the U.S. Trade Deficit," *Brookings Papers on Economic Activity* (1987).

19-3

THE MONETARY APPROACH TO THE BALANCE OF PAYMENTS

It is frequently suggested that external balance problems are monetary in nature and that, in particular, balance-of-payments deficits are a reflection of an excessive money supply.

There is a simple first answer to that suggestion. It is obviously true that, for any given balance-of-payments deficit, a sufficient contraction of the money stock will restore external balance. The reason is that a monetary contraction, by raising interest rates and reducing spending, reduces income and therefore imports. It is equally true that this result could be achieved by tight fiscal policy, and so there is nothing especially monetary about this interpretation of remedies for external imbalance.

A more sophisticated interpretation of the problem recognizes the links among the balance-of-payments deficit, foreign exchange market intervention, and the money supply in a fixed exchange rate system. The automatic mechanism is for a sale of foreign exchange—as arises in the case of a balance-of-payments deficit—to reduce the stock of high-powered money and hence the money stock. In a surplus country the central bank increases the outstanding stock of high-powered money when it buys foreign exchange, thereby expanding the money stock. Given this link between the money supply and the external balance, it is obvious that this adjustment process must ultimately lead to the right money stock so that external payments will be in balance. This is the adjustment process discussed in Section 19-1.

STERILIZATION

The only way the automatic adjustment process can be suspended is through *sterilization* operations. Central banks frequently offset, or sterilize, the impact of foreign exchange market intervention on the money supply through open market operations. Thus, a deficit country that is selling foreign exchange and correspondingly reducing its money supply may offset this reduction by open market purchases of bonds that restore the money supply.[12]

With sterilization, persistent external deficits are possible because the link between the external imbalance and the equilibrating changes in the money stock is broken. It is in this sense that persistent external deficits are a monetary phenomenon: By sterilizing, the central bank actively maintains the stock of money too high for external balance.

---

[12]*Currency boards,* such as those set up in Lithuania, Bulgaria, and Estonia, fix their country's exchange rate and permit high-powered money to be created only if it is fully backed by holdings of foreign currency. Currency boards amount to a fixed exchange rate system strictly without sterilization. Because sterilization is ruled out, adjustment is automatic, though of course not painless. Excellent references on currency boards include Steve Hanke and K. Schuler, *Currency Boards for Developing Countries* (San Francisco: International Center for Economic Growth, 1994); and Anna Schwartz, "Currency Boards: Their Past, Present, and Possible Future Role," *Carnegie-Rochester Conference on Public Policy,* December 1993.

THE MONETARY APPROACH AND THE IMF

The emphasis on monetary considerations in the interpretation of external balance problems is called the *monetary approach to the balance of payments.*[13] The monetary approach has been used extensively by the IMF in its analysis and design of economic policies for countries in balance-of-payments trouble. We give the flavor of the approach by describing typical IMF procedure in analyzing a balance-of-payments problem.

We start with the balance sheet of the monetary authority, usually the central bank, as in Table 19-1. The monetary authority's liabilities are high-powered money. But on the asset side it can hold both foreign assets—including foreign exchange reserves, gold, and claims on other central banks or governments—and domestic assets, or *domestic credit.* Domestic credit consists of the monetary authority's holdings of claims on the public sector—government debt—and on the private sector—usually loans to banks.

From the balance sheet identity, we have

$$\Delta NFA = \Delta H - \Delta DC \tag{4}$$

where ΔNFA denotes the change in net foreign assets, ΔH the change in high-powered money, and ΔDC the change in the central bank's extension of domestic credit. In words, the change in the central bank's holdings of foreign assets is equal to the change in the stock of high-powered money minus the change in domestic credit.

The important point about equation (4) is that ΔNFA is the balance of payments: Official reserve transactions, which are all that ΔNFA is, are equal to the balance of payments.

The first step in developing a monetary-approach type of stabilization policy package is to decide on a balance-of-payments target, ΔNFA^*. The IMF asks how much of a deficit the country can afford and then suggests policies to make the projected deficit no larger. The target is based largely on the availability of loans and credit from abroad and the possibility of drawing down existing reserves or the need to add revenues.

The next step is to ask how much the demand for money in the country will increase. The planned changes in the stock of high-powered money, ΔH^*, will have to be just sufficient to produce, via the money multiplier process, the right increases in the stock of money to meet the expected increase in demand. Then, given ΔNFA^* and ΔH^*, equation (4) tells the monetary authority how much domestic credit it can extend consistent with its balance-of-payments target and expected growth in money demand. Typically, a stabilization plan drawn up by the IMF will include a suggested limit on the expansion of domestic credit.

The limit provides a ceiling on domestic credit expansion. The adoption of a *domestic credit ceiling* helps the central bank avoid the temptation of expanding its loans to the government or private sector in the face of rising interest rates or government budget deficits.

---

[13]For a collection of essays on this topic, see Jacob Frenkel and Harry G. Johnson (eds.), *The Monetary Approach to the Balance of Payments* (London: Allen & Unwin, 1976). See also IMF, *The Monetary Approach to the Balance of Payments* (Washington, DC: International Monetary Fund, 1977); and Nadeem Haque, Kajal Lahiri, and Peter Montiel, "A Macroeconometric Model for Developing Countries," *IMF Staff Papers,* September 1990.

TABLE 19-1 **Balance Sheet of the Monetary Authorities**	
ASSETS	LIABILITIES
Net foreign assets (*NFA*)	High-powered money (*H*)
Domestic credit (*DC*)	

HOW DOES IT WORK?

The simplicity of equation (4) raises an obvious question. Since all it takes to improve the balance of payments is a reduction in the rate of domestic credit expansion, why not balance payments immediately and always? To answer this question, we need to understand the channels through which the curtailment of domestic credit improves the balance of payments.

Controlling domestic credit means operating tight monetary policy. Consider an economy that is growing and has some inflation, so demand for nominal balances is rising. If domestic credit expansion is slowed, an excess demand for money develops. This, in turn, causes interest rates to rise and spending to decline. The increase in interest rates leads to a balance-of-payments improvement. That is, the monetary approach as used by the IMF relies on restrictive monetary policy to control the balance of payments. There is, though, a subtle difference between domestic credit ceilings and ordinary tight money. In an open economy with fixed exchange rates, the money stock is endogenous. The central bank cannot control the money stock, since it has to meet whatever demand arises for foreign currency. But it can make "money" tight by reducing the growth of domestic credit. That will imply that the only source of money growth becomes an increase in foreign exchange reserves or foreign borrowing. The economy has to go through enough of a recession or rise in interest rates to generate a balance-of-payments surplus.

The use of domestic credit ceilings is a crude but easy-to-understand policy to improve the balance of payments. The simplicity of the conceptual framework, and the apparent definiteness of the policy recommendations to which it leads, frequently makes it the best policy tool available, particularly if dramatic action is needed and the credibility of the government's policies needs to be restored.

THE MONETARY APPROACH AND DEPRECIATION

Proponents of the monetary approach have argued that depreciation of the exchange rate cannot improve the balance of payments except in the short run. The argument is that in the short run the depreciation does improve a country's competitive position and that this very fact gives rise to a trade surplus and therefore to an increase in the money stock. Over the course of time, the rising money supply raises aggregate demand and therefore prices until the economy returns to full employment and external balance. Devaluation thus exerts only a transitory effect on the economy, which lasts as long as prices and the money supply have not yet increased to match fully the higher import prices.

The analysis of the monetary approach is entirely correct in its insistence on a longer-run perspective in which, under fixed exchange rates, prices and the money stock adjust and the economy achieves internal and external balance. It is also correct in arguing that monetary or domestic credit restraint will improve the balance of payments. Typically, the tight money policy produced by slow domestic credit growth produces a recession.

The monetary approach is misdirected when it suggests that exchange rate policy cannot, even in the short run, affect a country's competitive position. More important, exchange rate changes frequently arise from a position of deficit and unemployment. In that case, a devaluation can be used to speed up the adjustment process.

We return now to the world of flexible exchange rates.[14]

19-4

FLEXIBLE EXCHANGE RATES, MONEY, AND PRICES

In studying flexible exchange rates, we assume, as in Chapter 12, that capital is perfectly mobile. The only difference from that earlier treatment is that now prices are allowed to change. We examine how output, the exchange rate, and prices respond to monetary and fiscal policies and how that response evolves over time. Our starting point is a discussion of the adjustment of prices and the exchange rate to the state of the economy.

THE ADJUSTMENT PROCESS

Figure 19-5 shows the interest rate and output, with full employment at Y^*. The assumption of perfect international capital mobility is reflected in the horizontal BB schedule. Only at an interest rate $i = i_f$ will the balance of payments be in equilibrium. If the interest rate were higher, there would be net inflows of capital. Conversely, with a lower domestic interest rate, capital would flow out and the balance of payments would turn toward a deficit position.

We make two strategic assumptions to describe the adjustment process: First, prices are rising whenever output exceeds the full-employment level. Second, because capital is highly mobile, the interest rate in Figure 19-5 is always moving toward the BB schedule—our interest rate cannot diverge far from that in the rest of the world.

There is a complicated set of adjustments in the background as the economy moves toward BB. For instance, say there is a monetary expansion that causes a decline in interest rates. Capital flows out, which means that people try to sell our currency to buy foreign currencies. Our currency depreciates, exports and income increase, money demand rises, and so do interest rates, thus moving us back toward BB. This mechanism works in reverse if domestic interest rates tend to rise because of a monetary tightening or fiscal expansion.

---

[14]See Ronald MacDonald and Mark Taylor, "Exchange Rate Economics: A Survey," *IMF Staff Papers*, March 1992, for a broad discussion of models of exchange rate determination and the empirical evidence.

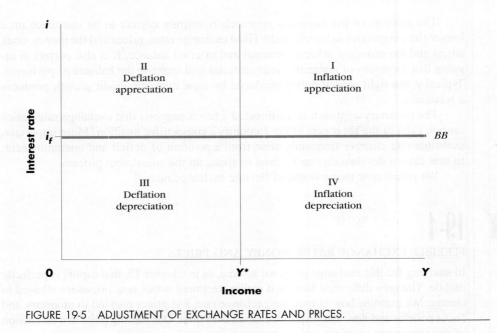

FIGURE 19-5   ADJUSTMENT OF EXCHANGE RATES AND PRICES.

With these assumptions we can study the adjustment process using Figure 19-5. Anywhere to the right of Y^*, prices are rising; to the left, prices are falling. Points above BB lead to capital inflows and appreciation; points below, to capital outflows and depreciation. Moreover, with extremely high capital mobility, the exchange rate will adjust very rapidly, so we are always close to or on the BB schedule.

A MONETARY EXPANSION: SHORT- AND LONG-RUN EFFECTS

With given prices a monetary expansion under flexible rates and perfect capital mobility leads to depreciation and increased income. We ask how that result is modified once we take adjustments in prices into account. The answer is that the output adjustment is now only transitory. In the long run a monetary expansion leads to an exchange depreciation and to higher prices with no change in competitiveness.

In Figure 19-6 we start at point E with full employment, a payments balance, monetary equilibrium, and equilibrium in the domestic goods market. Now a monetary expansion takes place and shifts the LM schedule to LM'. The new goods and money market equilibrium at E' involves an interest rate below the world level, and therefore the exchange rate immediately depreciates, raising home competitiveness and thus shifting the IS schedule to IS'. The economy moves rapidly from E via E' to E''. Output has risen, the exchange rate has depreciated, and the economy has thereby gained in external competitiveness. But that is not the end of the story.

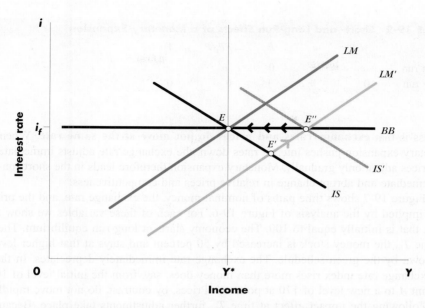

FIGURE 19-6   SHORT- AND LONG-RUN EFFECTS OF A MONETARY EXPANSION.

At E'' output is above the full-employment level. Prices are therefore rising, and that implies that real balances are falling. As the real money stock, M/P, declines because of rising prices, the LM schedule starts shifting to the left. Interest rates tend to rise, capital tends to flow in, and the resulting appreciation leads now to a decline in competitiveness that also shifts the IS schedule back toward the initial equilibrium. Both the IS and LM schedules thus move back toward point E. The process continues until point E is reached again.

What adjustments have taken place once the economy is back to point E? At point E, interest rates have returned to their initial level and so have relative prices, eP_f/P. In moving from E to E' the exchange rate depreciated immediately, ahead of the rise in prices. But when prices increased and real balances fell, some of that depreciation was reversed. Over the whole adjustment process, prices and exchange rates rose in the same proportion, leaving relative prices, eP_f/P, and therefore aggregate demand unchanged. In the long run, money was therefore *entirely neutral*. Table 19-2 summarizes these results. By the end of the adjustment process, nominal money, prices, and the exchange rate have all increased in the same proportion, so the real money stock and relative prices—including the real exchange rate—are unchanged.

EXCHANGE RATE OVERSHOOTING

The analysis of monetary policy under flexible exchange rates, given above, leads to an important insight about the adjustment process. The important feature of the adjustment

TABLE 19-2   Short- and Long-Run Effects of a Monetary Expansion

	M/P	e	P	EP_f/P	Y
Short run	+	+	0	+	+
Long run	0	+	+	0	0

process is that **exchange rates and prices do not move at the same rate.** When a monetary expansion pushes interest rates down, the exchange rate adjusts immediately but prices adjust only gradually. Monetary expansion therefore leads in the short run to an immediate and abrupt change in relative prices and competitiveness.

Figure 19-7 shows time paths of nominal money, the exchange rate, and the price level implied by the analysis of Figure 19-6. For each of these variables we show an index that is initially equal to 100. The economy starts at long-run equilibrium. Then, at time T_0, the money stock is increased by 50 percent and stays at that higher level, as shown by the green schedule. The exchange rate immediately depreciates. In fact, the exchange rate index rises more than money does, say, from the initial level of 100 at point A to a new level of 170 at point A'. Prices, by contrast, do not move rapidly.

Following the impact effect at time T_0, further adjustments take place. Because the gain in competitiveness at time T_0 has raised output above potential, there is now inflation. Prices are rising and, at the same time, the exchange rate is appreciating, thus undoing part of the initial, sharp depreciation. Over time, prices rise to match the

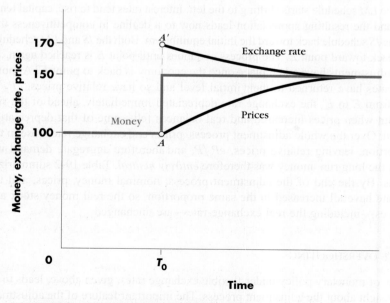

FIGURE 19-7   EXCHANGE RATE OVERSHOOTING.

increase in money, and the exchange rate will also match the higher level of money and prices. In the long run, real variables are unchanged. The adjustment pattern for the *exchange rate* seen in Figure 19-7 involves *overshooting*. **The exchange rate overshoots its new equilibrium level when, in response to a disturbance, it first moves *beyond* the equilibrium it ultimately will reach and then gradually returns to the long-run equilibrium position.** Overshooting means that changes in monetary policy produce large changes in exchange rates.

Those who believe that exchange rate overshooting introduces an undesirable instability into the economy argue that governments should intervene in foreign exchange markets to avoid large, excessive exchange rate fluctuations. The sharp dollar appreciation in 1980–1985 strongly reinforced the call for such intervention. In 1985 the major countries agreed in principle that they would intervene to try to prevent exchange rate instability. The agreement notwithstanding, major exchange rate movements continue to occur. For instance, in 1995 the yen reached an exchange rate of 80 yen to the dollar. The major industrial countries agreed that the yen was overvalued and should depreciate. This declaration, and intervention by the Bank of Japan, moved the exchange rate to 110 yen to the dollar within a year. Similarly, between March 2002 and March 2003, the $/€ (€ = euro) exchange rate changed from $.87 to $1.10, i.e., the U.S. dollar lost a little over 25 percent of its value relative to the euro within a year. Accordingly, although the current flexible rate system emerged because the Bretton Woods system of fixed rates broke down in 1973,[15] it is not viewed as the last word, and reform of the international monetary system is always on the agenda.

PURCHASING POWER PARITY (PPP)

In the preceding analysis, the exchange rate rose by precisely the right amount to offset the effects of domestic inflation on the real exchange rate. That is, the exchange depreciation maintained the *purchasing power* of our goods in terms of foreign goods between the initial and the final equilibrium points.

An important view of the determinants of the exchange rate is the theory that exchange rates move primarily as a result of differences in price-level behavior between the two countries in such a way as to maintain the terms of trade constant. This is the *purchasing power parity (PPP)* theory. **The purchasing power parity theory of the exchange rate argues that exchange rate movements primarily reflect differences in inflation rates between countries.** Examining the real exchange rate, eP_f/P, the theory maintains the following: When P_f or P changes, e changes in such a way as to maintain eP_f/P constant.[16]

PPP is a plausible description of the trend behavior of exchange rates, especially when inflation differentials between countries are large. In particular, we have seen that

---

[15]This is the system of fixed exchange rates that prevailed from the end of World War II to 1973, so called because it was designed, in 1944, in a major international conference held in Bretton Woods, New Hampshire.

[16]Assuming, of course, that the initial level of the real exchange rate had equated purchasing power between the two countries.

the PPP relationship does hold in the case of an increase in the money stock. If price-level movements are caused by monetary changes—as they are likely to be if the inflation rate is high—we should expect PPP relationships to hold in the long term.

But qualifications are necessary. First, even a monetary disturbance affects the real exchange rate in the short run. Exchange rates tend to move quite rapidly relative to prices, and thus in the short term of a quarter or a year we should not be at all surprised to see substantial deviations of exchange rates from the rates implied by PPP even if the exchange rate change is caused by monetary policy.

The second important qualification concerns the role of nonmonetary disturbances in affecting exchange rates. For example, we saw that an increase in exports leads to currency appreciation at unchanged domestic prices. This example illustrates that, over time, adjustments to *real* disturbances will affect the *equilibrium* real exchange rate. In the longer run, exchange rates and prices do *not* necessarily move together, as they do in a world where all disturbances are monetary. On the contrary, we may have changes in relative prices, which run counter to the purchasing power parity view of exchange rates.

Consider Figure 19-8, which shows that the real exchange rate between the U.S. dollar and Canadian dollar ($eP_{Can}/P_{U.S.}$) fluctuates a great deal over time. The figure also shows the nominal exchange rate. According to PPP, when the exchange rate index changes, the real exchange rate should not—because the exchange rate should be

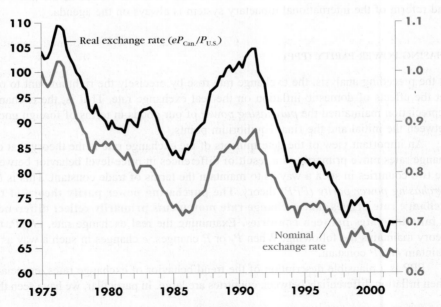

FIGURE 19-8   THE REAL AND NOMINAL EXCHANGE RATE, CANADA AND THE UNITED STATES, 1975–2002.

Note the different scales of the axes. The left axis shows the real exchange rate, indexed to 1990 = 100. The right axis shows the number of U.S. dollars per Canadian dollar. (Source: IMF, International Financial Statistics, *2002.)*

TABLE 19-3 Unit Labor Costs in Manufacturing
(Dollar Index, 1992 = 100)

	UNITED STATES	GERMANY	JAPAN	CANADA
1960	—	10.4	11.0	32.9
1970	—	17.1	15.5	36.0
1980	78.8	59.6	51.8	67.4
1985	87.3	41.7	50.3	69.8
1990	93.7	87.3	83.8	98.0
1995	94.8	115.5	131.7	83.0
2000	91.7	76.9	100.4	78.2
2001	91.4	76.2	93.6	79.2

Source: Bureau of Labor Statistics, www.bls.gov.

moving only because relative price levels change. However, the real exchange rate clearly moves roughly in parallel with the nominal exchange rate, showing that PPP does not hold in the case of Canada and the United States over the period since 1976. Nor is PPP a good description of the behavior of exchange rates among the major currencies over any recent period.

EXTERNAL COMPETITIVENESS

PPP measures are closely related to the behavior of a country's competitiveness in external trade. A decline in a country's relative price level makes the country's goods relatively cheaper and thus more competitive. In Table 19-3 we show unit labor costs in manufacturing measured in U.S. dollars for several countries.

The data make it clear that nominal exchange rates affect unit labor costs in dollars. In 1985, when the dollar peaked, Germany and Japan had very low costs in dollars compared, say, to 1990, by which time the dollar had weakened considerably. Thus, **nominal exchange rate movements clearly affect competitiveness.**

19-5

INTEREST DIFFERENTIALS AND EXCHANGE RATE EXPECTATIONS

A cornerstone of our theoretical model of exchange rate determination was international capital mobility. In particular, we argued that with capital markets sufficiently integrated, we would expect interest rates to be equated across countries. How does this assumption stand up to the facts?[17] In Figure 19-9 we show the U.S. federal funds rate and the money market rate in Germany. Obviously, these rates are not equal. How do we square this fact with our theory?

[17]On capital mobility, see Jeffrey Frankel, "International Capital Mobility: A Review," *American Economic Review,* May 1991.

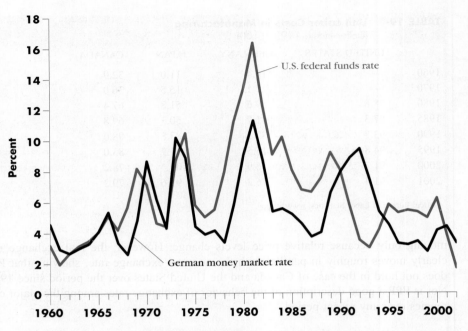

FIGURE 19-9   THE U.S. FEDERAL FUNDS RATE AND GERMAN MONEY MARKET RATE, 1960–2001.

(*Source: IMF*, International Financial Statistics, *2002.*)

EXCHANGE RATE EXPECTATIONS

Our theoretical analysis was based on the assumption that capital flows internationally in response to nominal interest differentials. For example, if domestic interest rates were 6 percent and foreign rates were 10 percent, we would, according to the earlier sections, expect a capital outflow.

However, such a theory is incomplete in a world in which exchange rates can, do, and are expected to change.[18] For example, consider a situation in which the euro is expected to depreciate by 5 percent over the next year relative to the dollar. With a 5 percent euro depreciation, the return *in dollars* of investing in Europe is only 5 percent (= 10 percent − 5 percent). The natural preference is to invest in American bonds, even though the U.S. interest rate is below the European rate.

It is clear, therefore, that we must extend our discussion of interest rate equalization to incorporate expectations of exchange rate changes. Anyone who invests in domestic bonds earns the interest rate *i*. Alternatively, by investing in foreign bonds, the investor earns the interest rate on foreign bonds, i_f, *plus* whatever she earns from the

---

[18]You may wish to review the material in Chap. 17, "Financial Markets and Asset Prices."

appreciation of the foreign currency. The total return on foreign bonds, measured in our currency, is then

$$\text{Return on foreign bonds (in terms of domestic currency)} = i_f + \Delta e/e \qquad (5)$$

Of course, since the investor does not know at the time she makes a decision by how much the exchange rate will change, the term $\Delta e/e$ in equation (5) should be interpreted as the *expected* change in the exchange rate.

The introduction of exchange rate expectations modifies our equation for the balance of payments. Now capital flows are governed by the difference between our interest rate and the foreign rate adjusted for expected depreciation: $i - i_f - \Delta e/e$. An increase in foreign interest rates or an expectation of depreciation, given our interest rates, would lead to a capital outflow. Conversely, a rise in our rates or an expectation of appreciation would bring about a capital inflow. We thus write the balance of payments as

$$BP = NX\left(Y, \frac{eP_f}{P}\right) + CF\left(i - i_f - \frac{\Delta e}{e}\right) \qquad (6)$$

The adjustment for exchange rate expectations thus accounts for international differences in interest rates that persist even when capital is freely mobile among countries. **When capital is completely mobile, we expect interest rates to be equalized, after adjusting for expected depreciation:**

$$i = i_f + \Delta e/e \qquad (6a)$$

Expected depreciation helps account for differences in interest rates among low- and high-inflation countries. When the inflation rate in a country is high, its exchange rate is expected to depreciate. In addition, the Fisher relationship suggests that the nominal interest rate in that country will be high.[19] Thus, high-inflation countries tend to have high interest rates and depreciating currencies. This is an international extension of the Fisher equation, which relies on PPP to argue that inflation differentials internationally are matched by depreciation. Our long-term relation, then, is

$$\text{Inflation differential} \cong \text{interest differential} \cong \text{depreciation rate} \qquad (7)$$

The $\cong$ means "approximately equal to." The relation is only approximate because exchange rates can move independently of prices and also because obstacles to capital flows may create long-term interest differentials.

SPECULATIVE CAPITAL FLOWS

Changes in exchange rate expectations can affect the actual exchange rate as well as the domestic interest rate and output. The point is made with the help of Figure 19-10, which assumes perfect capital mobility, as specified in equation (6a). Here the *BB* schedule is drawn for a given foreign interest rate and a given expected rate of change of the exchange rate, say, zero.

[19]The Fisher relationship states that the nominal interest rate equals the expected real interest rate plus expected inflation, $i = r + \pi^e$.

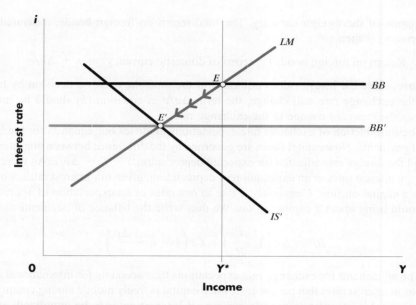

FIGURE 19-10 RESPONSE TO AN EXPECTED APPRECIATION OF CURRENCY.

Suppose that we start in full equilibrium at point E and that the market develops the expectation that the home currency will appreciate. This implies that even with a lower home interest rate, domestic assets are attractive, and so the BB schedule shifts downward by the amount of expected appreciation.

Point E is no longer an equilibrium, given the shift of the BB schedule to BB', but rather a position of surplus with large-scale capital inflows motivated by the anticipation of appreciation. The surplus at E causes the exchange rate to start appreciating, and we move in a southwesterly direction, as indicated by the arrow. The speculative attack causes appreciation, a loss in competitiveness, and, consequently, falling output and employment. Thus the expectation of an exchange rate appreciation is a *self-fulfilling expectation*.

This analysis confirms that exchange rate expectations, through their impact on capital flows and thus on actual exchange rates, are a potential source of disturbance to macroeconomic equilibrium—something that policymakers who try to fix exchange rates when capital is fully mobile keep having to learn.

19-6
EXCHANGE RATE FLUCTUATIONS AND INTERDEPENDENCE

In the 1960s there was growing dissatisfaction with fixed exchange rates. The Bretton Woods system put in place at the end of World War II was called a "crisis system" because from time to time exchange rates would get out of line and expectations of exchange rate changes would mobilize massive capital flows that often precipitated the exchange rate changes that speculators expected. Is the system of flexible rates among the major currencies of the period since 1973 better? Is it less crisis-prone, and does it provide a better framework for macroeconomic stability? Before providing answers, we look briefly at how flexibly the system has, in fact, operated.

FOREIGN EXCHANGE MARKET INTERVENTION

When exchange rates are fully flexible, the government takes no action in the foreign exchange market. It stays out of the foreign exchange market, whatever happens to the exchange rate. Such a system is almost unheard of, although the United States rarely intervenes in the foreign exchange markets. More commonly, governments intervene in the foreign exchange market to a lesser or greater extent. *Foreign exchange market intervention* **occurs when a government buys or sells foreign exchange in an attempt to influence the exchange rate.**

The extent to which governments intervene in the foreign exchange markets varies substantially. They may try only to offset short-term fluctuations and buy or sell foreign exchange to maintain "orderly markets." But they also may try to keep an overvalued exchange rate from depreciating or an undervalued exchange rate from appreciating. *Dirty* (as opposed to clean) *floating* is the practice of using substantial intervention to try to maintain an exchange rate against the pressure of market forces.

For almost the entire period since 1973, exchange rate floating has been of the dirty variety. Governments have from time to time intervened on a very large scale. This leads naturally to the question of why a government would try to resist market forces to prevent an appreciation or a depreciation of the currency.

WHY GOVERNMENTS INTERVENE

Central banks intervene to affect exchange rates for several reasons.[20] Probably the main reason is the belief that many capital flows represent merely unstable expectations and that the induced movements in exchange rates cause unnecessary changes in domestic output. The second reason for intervention is a central bank's attempt to move the real exchange rate in order to affect trade flows. The third reason arises from the effects of the exchange rate on domestic inflation. Central banks sometimes intervene in the exchange market to prevent the exchange rate from depreciating, with the aim of preventing import prices from rising and thereby helping to slow inflation.

The basic argument for intervention (dirty floating) is that the central bank can intervene to smooth out fluctuations in exchange rates. The only—and overwhelming— objection to this argument is that there is no simple way of telling an erratic movement

[20]Some academic critics oppose intervention. See, for instance, Milton Friedman, "Deja Vu in Currency Markets," *The Wall Street Journal,* September 22, 1992. Paul Volcker and Toyoo Gyohten, two prominent practitioners of intervention, discuss its merits in *Changing Fortunes: The World's Money and the Threat to American Leadership* (New York: Random House, 1992).

from a trend movement. How can we tell whether a current appreciation in the exchange rate is merely the result of a disturbance that will soon reverse itself or is the beginning of a trend movement in the exchange rate? There is no way of telling at the time a change occurs, although with the benefit of hindsight one can see which exchange rate movements were later reversed.

There is one circumstance under which central bank intervention might be desirable. It is clear from our earlier analysis that one of the key determinants of exchange rate behavior is expectations of economic policy. It may sometimes be possible to make it clear that there has been a change in policy only by intervening in the foreign exchange market. This is a case of putting your money where your mouth is.

STERILIZED VERSUS NONSTERILIZED INTERVENTION

In discussing intervention, it is important also to ask whether it works. For instance, does it make any difference to the exchange rate if the Bank of Japan sells $1 billion from its foreign currency reserves?

To judge the effectiveness of intervention, we must distinguish between *sterilized* and *nonsterilized intervention*. (Sterilization operations were discussed earlier in this chapter.) In the case of sterilized intervention, a central bank, say, buys foreign exchange, issuing domestic money. But then the increase in home money is reversed by an open market sale of securities. In the sterilized intervention case, therefore, the home money supply is kept unchanged. In the case of nonsterilization, by contrast, there is a change in the money stock equal to the amount of intervention.

It is widely agreed that nonsterilized intervention, because it changes the money supply, will affect exchange rates. There is widespread skepticism, however, about the effectiveness of sterilized intervention. In 1978–1979 the U.S. dollar was depreciating in currency markets even though there was intervention on a massive scale. But that intervention was carefully sterilized. Only in late 1979, when the dollar depreciation began to alarm the Fed, did a change in policy take place. Monetary policy was tightened, and immediately the dollar depreciation was stopped and soon massively reversed.

That episode, and other evidence, strongly suggests the effectiveness of nonsterilized intervention and of intervention that is backed by credible policies. The earlier failure of sterilized intervention suggested that only unsterilized intervention could affect the exchange rate. But a more recent episode gives cause for rethinking that issue.

The very large appreciation of the dollar from 1980 to 1985, described in Box 19-5, was a major concern to policymakers in the United States, Europe, and Japan. Many policymakers thought that the markets had pushed the dollar too high and that only speculative forces were keeping it up. In September 1985 the finance ministers of the "Group of Five" (the United States, Japan, Germany, France, and the United Kingdom) announced their view that the dollar was too high, and their central banks went into action to sell dollars in order to drive the rate down. The dollar responded quickly, suggesting that concerted action can affect the exchange rate even if there is no obvious change in

TABLE 19-4 Monetary and Fiscal Policy Effects with Interdependence

	U.S. MONETARY CONTRACTION		U.S. FISCAL EXPANSION	
	UNITED STATES	REST OF THE WORLD	UNITED STATES	REST OF THE WORLD
Exchange rate	$ appreciates		$ appreciates	
Output	−	+	+	+
Inflation	−	+	−	+

monetary policy. Such action is certainly not guaranteed to work, but it could work if there is widespread speculation in the markets about the future course of policy and if announcements and intervention suggest that future policy will try to move the exchange rate in a particular direction. By contrast, if policymakers are unwilling to use interest rates to defend their currency, as was the case in the United Kingdom in September 1992, even a $30 billion intervention cannot help the exchange rate.

INTERDEPENDENCE

It used to be argued that under flexible exchange rates countries could pursue their own national economic policies—monetary and fiscal policy and the inflation rate—without having to worry about the balance of payments. That is certainly correct, but it is also misleading. There are important linkages between countries *whatever the exchange rate regime*.[21]

These *spillover*, or *interdependence*, *effects* have been at the center of the discussion about flexible exchange rates. For instance, suppose the United States tightens monetary policy. As discussed earlier, U.S. interest rates rise and that attracts capital flows from abroad. The dollar appreciates, and foreign currencies depreciate. Table 19-4 shows the effects in other countries.

The U.S. appreciation implies a loss in competitiveness. World demand shifts from U.S. goods to those produced by our competitors. Therefore, at home, output and employment decline. Abroad, our competitors benefit from the depreciation of their currency. They become more competitive, and therefore output and employment abroad expand. Our monetary tightening thus tends to promote employment gains abroad, which come, of course, at the expense of our own employment.

There are also spillover effects through prices. When our currency appreciates, import prices in dollars fall. Therefore, our inflation tends to decline quite rapidly when there is a sharp dollar appreciation. But abroad the opposite occurs. Foreign currencies depreciate,

[21]On interdependence, see Ralph C. Bryant et al., "Domestic and Cross-Border Consequences of U.S. Macroeconomic Policies," International Finance discussion paper 344, Board of Governors of the Federal Reserve System, March 1989; Jeffrey Shaffer, "What the U.S. Current Account Deficit Has Meant for Other OECD Countries," *OECD Studies,* Spring 1988; and Paul Masson et al., "Multimod Mark II: A Revised and Extended Model," IMF occasional paper 71, 1990.

BOX 19-5   Unsustainable Deficits and the Dollar Bubble

In the early 1980s there was very little concern about U.S. current account deficits. Following the 1982 world recession, the U.S. economy was growing much faster than others, and a deficit in the current account was seen as a by-product of a strong expansion. But increasingly the strong dollar added to the deficit by eroding U.S. competitiveness (see Figure 1).

By 1985 an ever-larger deficit and an ever-stronger dollar started raising questions: If the dollar remained at its 1985 level, would the deficit ever go away? And if the deficit did not decline, would the United States soon become a net foreign debtor and then, year after year, have to go increasingly into debt? And if debt and the interest that had to be paid on the debt were to grow for a long period, would that be consistent with a strong dollar?

THE DOLLAR AS A BUBBLE

The extreme rise of the dollar and the large deficit in 1985 led to the conclusion that the dollar was overvalued. Dollar depreciation on a major scale would have to take place at some time in order to trim the deficit and thus slow down the rate of increase in foreign indebtedness. But if a major dollar depreciation was inevitable, why were the foreign exchange markets still pushing the dollar up? If the foreign exchange markets anticipated a major dollar decline, traders would be quick to buy other currencies, trying to avoid being caught when the dollar fell. The attempt by everybody to sell would therefore bring about a very rapid alignment of the dollar.

Even as the discussion of an unsustainable dollar emerged, the dollar actually started its post-1985 decline. But that left unanswered the question of why it had risen so much in the first place. Explanations of tight U.S. monetary policy and fiscal expansion went some way in explaining the rise of the dollar, but that could not be the whole story; the timing did not match, since monetary policy had started easing already in fall 1982.

Some observers concluded that the dollar peak of 1985 had been a *speculative bubble*, a departure of the dollar from the level justified by the fundamental factors

and therefore prices in those currencies tend to increase. Inflation abroad thus rises. Foreigners might welcome an increase in employment as a side effect of our monetary policy, but they certainly could do without the inflation that comes from currency depreciation.

In the same way, U.S. fiscal policies exert effects abroad. A U.S. fiscal expansion, such as the one in the 1980–1985 period, will lead to dollar appreciation and a loss in competitiveness. The direct increase in our spending and the deterioration in

FIGURE 1   THE U.S. CURRENT ACCOUNT AS A PERCENTAGE OF GDP, 1970–2002.
(Source: Bureau of Economic Analysis.)

that should determine its value: interest rates, the current account, and expected future current accounts. Once the bubble had burst, in part because of central bank cooperation in intervention, the dollar declined for 2 years to reach more realistic levels. The discussion of whether asset markets and, in particular, the foreign exchange market are or are not rational continues unresolved.*

---

*See Jeffrey Frankel and Ken Froot, "Using Survey Data to Test Standard Propositions Regarding Exchange Rate Expectations," *American Economic Review*, March 1987. Exchange rate expectations, and their rationality, are reviewed in Takatoshi Ito, "Foreign Exchange Rate Expectations: Micro Survey Data," *American Economic Review*, June 1990; Shinji Takagi, "Exchange Rate Expectations," *IMF Staff Papers*, March 1991; and Ken Froot and Richard Thaler, "Anomalies: Foreign Exchange," *Journal of Economic Perspectives*, Summer 1990.

---

our competitiveness are the channels through which our expansion is shared abroad. When the United States has a fiscal expansion, the rest of the world shares via increased exports.

Table 19-4 also shows the effects of monetary and fiscal policy on inflation. Because fiscal expansion leads to appreciation, the decline in import prices helps reduce inflation in the expanding country. But abroad import prices will rise, and that means inflation will be increased. These impacts of exchange rate movements on inflation were important factors in changing inflation rates in industrial countries in the 1980–1985 period.

Policymakers abroad therefore must decide whether to accept the higher-employment–higher-inflation effects of our policies or whether they should change their own policies. If inflation is already a problem abroad, or if the rest of the world is highly averse to inflation, the policy response abroad to this *imported inflation* may well be to tighten money. If the dollar appreciation was caused by a tightening of U.S. monetary policy, it will also cause a monetary contraction abroad if foreign countries decide to fight imported inflation. That means our monetary tightening touches off worldwide tightening. This was substantially what happened in the worldwide recession of 1981–1982.

POLICY SYNCHRONIZATION

The large changes in exchange rates that occur when policies are not fully synchronized between countries pose a major threat to free trade. When import prices fall by 20 or 30 percent because of a currency appreciation, large shifts in demand will occur. Domestic workers become unemployed, and they have no trouble seeing that it is foreigners who gain the jobs they just lost. Accordingly, there will be pressure for protection—tariffs or quotas—to keep out imports that are "artificially cheap" due to the currency appreciation. In the United States in 2001 repeated calls for protection in the steel and other industries reflected in part the high value of the dollar and the corresponding low cost of imports.

The experience of the last 20 years offers an unambiguous answer to the question of whether flexible exchange rates isolate countries from shocks that originate abroad. Under flexible exchange rates there is as much or more interdependence as there is under fixed rates. Moreover, because exchange rates are so flexible and so ready to respond to policies (good or bad), macroeconomic management does not become easier. Further, to the extent that exchange rate overshooting causes sharp changes in competitiveness, it leads to protectionist sentiment.

On all counts then, flexible rates are far from being a perfect system. But there is no better system, for the Bretton Woods system collapsed. Therefore, we can ask only whether, through international coordination of interests and policies, we can make the system work better than it has in the recent past. Although the leaders of the major industrial countries have repeatedly recognized their interdependence and agreed to work toward more coordinated policies, there have been no major institutional changes to ensure coordination of economic policies.[22]

---

[22]See Jacob A. Frenkel, Morris Goldstein, and Paul Masson, "Characteristics of a Successful Exchange Rate System," IMF occasional paper 82, July 1991; and Morris Goldstein, Peter Isard, Paul Masson, and Mark Taylor, "Policy Issues in the Evolving International Monetary System," IMF occasional paper 96, June 1992.

19-7

THE CHOICE OF EXCHANGE RATE REGIMES

In the aftermath of the Asian crisis the question of the best exchange rate regime—fixed or floating—came up once again. The immediate issue was the contribution to the crisis of the large swing in the dollar-yen exchange rate. Many Asian economies had their currencies pegged to the dollar. As a result, when the dollar appreciated strongly, these currencies also strengthened—and that proved a disaster for current accounts and financial stability. It was a short step from there to a financial crisis. Should exchange rates between the major currencies—dollar, yen, euro—be fixed, float freely, or fluctuate in a more limited way in target zones?[23]

Emerging economies, too, must ask whether they should have fixed rates on the dollar, yen, or euro. If so, should the rates be "fixed until further notice" or fixed in a really hard way by either a currency board or outright use of a key money (i.e., *dollarization*)? Or should their rates fluctuate freely so that defending the currency is just not part of the agenda? Fixing the rates begs the question of how to avoid crises; allowing flexible rates begs the question of how to forestall huge volatility. In this section we present some of the pros and cons on this wide-open debate.

TARGET ZONES

Target zones allow exchange rates to float within limited bands and provide for government intervention if the exchange rate passes outside the band. Proponents of target zones argue that wide swings in exchange rates, far away from fundamental equilibrium exchange rates, distort trade flows and risk financial crises. To avoid the inconvenience and, worse, dramatic risks, they argue for limits to the extent of fluctuation: Governments should undertake to set limits of, say, 10 or 15 percent on either side of the fundamental equilibrium exchange rate and to keep rates from going any further. The proponents argue that these limits would give markets enough play and that anything more would signal that a market had lost touch with reality and, ultimately, would experience a hard landing.

Opponents make two points: First, where does one look for an equilibrium exchange rate other than in the market itself? Studies of equilibrium rates come with sharply divergent estimates; hence there is no starting point for a discussion. Table 19-5 shows one estimate of fundamental equilibrium exchange rates for the year 2000. Note that the range of estimates for the "equilibrium" exchange rate is itself as wide as a target zone.

---

[23]For further discussion see B. Eichengreen, *Toward a New International Financial Architecture* (Washington, DC: Institute of International Economics, 1999). For the emerging market issues, see International Monetary Fund, *Exchange Rate Regimes* (1999). See too the very eclectic piece by J. Frankel, "No Single Exchange Rate Regime Is Right for All Countries or at All Times," *Essays in International Finance* 215, International Finance section, Princeton University, 1999.

TABLE 19-5   Actual and Fundamental Equilibrium Exchange Rates (FEER)
(Foreign Currency/$U.S.)

	FEER (2000)	ACTUAL (EARLY 2000)
Japan	77–95	109
Germany	1.35–1.65	1.99
Canada	1.40–1.72	1.44

Source: Fundamental equilibrium exchange rate estimates come from S. Wren-Lewis and R. Driver, *Real Exchange Rates for the Year 2000*. Institute for International Economics, Washington, DC, 2000.

Second, how does one enforce the target zones? It is one thing to say governments should cooperate to make it happen. But consider the situation in early 2000, when the dollar was far stronger than the equilibrium rates in Table 19-5. Should the United States in the midst of a superboom lower interest rates to reduce the attractiveness of U.S. assets? Or should Japan, on the edge of a recession, raise rates? Surely neither is a likely option. Although the discussion of target zones stays alive, don't expect governments to edge in that direction.

AD HOC JOINT INTERVENTION

A much less structured way of limiting exchange rate fluctuations is ad hoc joint intervention. Suppose rates have gone far away from their historical average, such as the dollar in 1985 or the yen in 1996. Then governments with good timing can enter the market when it is known to be very thin (4:00 Friday afternoon in New York) and buy a huge amount of the depreciated currency. They may succeed driving up its price in a major way, forcing short sellers to liquidate their positions in distress and creating a huge momentum of reversal. This *can* work, but the yen episode in the spring of 1996 provides a dire warning: Intervention was tried twice, but both attempts failed because markets could not be convinced that intervention alone was enough. Only in August, with the exchange rate at an extreme of 80 yen to the dollar, did joint U.S.-Japanese intervention finally work. Intervention is an instrument that can help at what already might be a turning point; it is not an instrument for convincing a market that holds strong views of its own.

DOLLARIZATION AND CURRENCY BOARDS

In the late-nineteenth and early-twentieth centuries most countries adopted a gold standard. Central banking was simple: At times of a balance-of-payments deficit the central bank would lose gold, automatically reducing the domestic money supply, raising interest rates, and bringing in capital flows while cutting spending and the trade deficit. Conversely, with a surplus, interest rates would fall, which would bring about capital outflows, a rise in spending, and a reduced trade surplus. There was, accordingly, an *automatic* adjustment mechanism—one without central bank discretion.

Why would a nation choose to forgo discretionary policy? Consider the case of Argentina, with fifty-five central bank presidents in as many years, more than ten monies in succession, and a hyperinflation to boot. Not surprisingly, Argentina chose in the 1990s to have a *currency board*. A currency board provides local currency with 100 percent backing in foreign reserves. As a result, there is no discretion for the central bank, no money printing to finance budget deficits, and never again a devaluation. In essence, Argentine monetary policy was set during the 1990s by the Federal Reserve in Washington. Except that, as a sovereign nation, Argentina could always abandon the currency board if its fixed exchange rate became unsustainable. And this is exactly what Argentina did when it let its currency float (see Figure 19-11).

There is one more stop on the way to hard money: Dollarize. Do away with domestic money altogether and adopt the dollar (or the euro, or the yen) as the national money. That was done for instance, by Ecuador in 2000 and El Salvador in 2001. In a world where governments still value sovereignty and its symbols, that is swallowing a lot. But increasingly countries understand that national politicized central banking is dramatically costly.

Currency boards are no panacea—especially not in countries where every institution from public finance to property rights malfunctions—but they can be one powerful pillar for creating a functioning economy. In economies that are mostly functional, currency boards can be a powerful extra force for enhancing credibility of policies and thus advancing integration in the world economy.

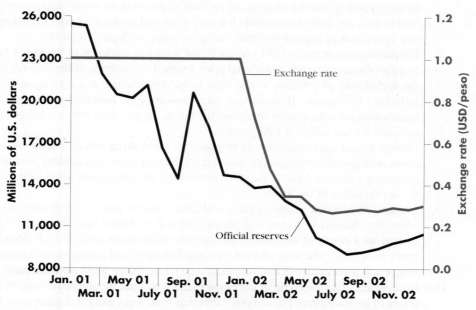

FIGURE 19-11   OFFICIAL RESERVES AND THE EXCHANGE RATE IN ARGENTINA.
(*Source: IMF*, International Financial Statistics, *2002*.)

SUMMARY

1. A monetary expansion in the long run increases the price level and the exchange rate, keeping real balances and the terms of trade constant. In the short run, though, the monetary expansion increases the level of output and reduces the interest rate, depreciating the exchange rate. The exchange rate overshoots its new equilibrium level.

2. External imbalances can be financed in the short term. In the long run they call for adjustment. Adjustment of the external balance calls for expenditure-reducing and expenditure-switching policies. The former change the level of spending; the latter affect the composition of spending between domestic goods and imports and exports.

3. Under fixed exchange rates, the automatic adjustment mechanism works through prices and money. Unemployment leads to a decline in prices, a gain in competitiveness, increased net exports, and a gain in employment. Money responds to trade imbalances, affecting the level of interest rates, spending, and hence the payments deficit.

4. Because trade flows respond only gradually to a change in the real exchange rate, we observe a J curve: A real depreciation will worsen the trade balance in the short run but then will gradually improve it in later years as volume effects dominate.

5. The monetary approach to the balance of payments draws attention to the fact that a payments deficit is always a reflection of a monetary disequilibrium and is always self-correcting. But the correction mechanism, because it involves unemployment, may be excessively painful compared with policy actions such as devaluation.

6. Exchange rate overshooting results from the rapid response of exchange rates to monetary policy and the sluggish adjustment of prices. A monetary expansion will lead to an immediate depreciation but only a gradual increase in prices. Exchange rate overshooting implies that real exchange rates are highly volatile.

7. Purchasing power parity (PPP) refers to the long-run tendency of exchange rates to offset divergent trends in national price levels. The currency of the country with the higher rate of inflation would tend to be depreciating at a rate equal to the inflation differential. If exchange rates follow PPP, nominal exchange rate movements have no effects on competitiveness. In the short run, exchange rates certainly do not follow a PPP pattern.

8. Capital moves internationally in response to yield differentials, taking into account anticipated exchange rate movements. Interest rates in a country with a depreciating currency have to be sufficiently high to compensate asset holders for the depreciation of the assets.

9. Changes in nominal exchange rates will affect relative prices only if there are no offsetting changes in wages and prices. The real exchange rate, $R = eP_f/P$, can change as a result of nominal exchange rate movements only if P_f/P does not move in a fully offsetting manner. Among industrialized countries stickiness of wages and prices ensures that real exchange rates change when nominal rates do.

10. Governments can intervene in exchange markets to limit the impact on output and prices of exchange rate fluctuations stemming from asset market disturbances. But intervention is problematic when the authorities cannot determine whether the exchange rate is moving on account of fundamentals or for purely speculative reasons.

11. Even under flexible exchange rates economies are closely tied to one another. A monetary expansion at home will lead to unemployment and disinflation abroad. A fiscal expansion will cause an expansion abroad along with inflation. These interdependence effects make a case for coordinating policies.

12. Nations choose between fixed and floating exchange rates. They also can choose different institutional arrangements, including target zones, currency boards, and dollarization, which allow for a varying amount of discretion by policymakers.

KEY TERMS

automatic adjustment mechanisms	external balance	self-fulfilling expectation
balance-of-payments deficit	foreign exchange market intervention	speculative bubble
classical adjustment process	hysteresis	spillover (interdependence) effects
crawling peg	internal balance	sterilization
currency board	International Monetary Fund (IMF)	sterilized intervention
devaluation	J-curve effect	sticky real wages
dollarization	monetary approach to the balance of payments	tariff
domestic credit		target zones
domestic credit ceiling	neutrality of money	wage-price spiral
exchange rate overshooting	nonsterilized intervention	World Trade Organization (WTO)
expenditure-reducing (-increasing) policies	purchasing power parity (PPP)	
expenditure-switching policies	real devaluation	

PROBLEMS

Conceptual

1. In relation to external imbalance, a distinction is frequently made between imbalances that should be "adjusted" and those that should be "financed." Give examples of disturbances that give rise, respectively, to imbalances that require adjustment and those that should more appropriately be financed.

2. Should countries intervene to stabilize the exchange rate?

3. What is a wage-price spiral, and how can a devaluation start one? Is it something undesirable? Explain. How can a wage-price spiral be avoided?

4. What is a target-zone arrangement? What are the benefits and costs of participating in one?

5. It is a consequence of our model of (flexible) exchange rate determination that, when capital markets are sufficiently integrated, interest rates across countries must be equated. Clearly, however, there *are* differences across countries. How can we reconcile this fact with our theory?

6. Equation (7) in Section 19-5 tells us that inflation differentials, interest differentials, and depreciation rates are all *approximately equal*. Why are they only approximately, as opposed to exactly, equal?

7. In the early 1970s, the United States moved from a system of fixed exchange rates to a system of floating ones. Is the current flexible system less crisis-prone, or does it provide a better framework for macroeconomic stability? Discuss.

8. Discuss the lures and dangers in exchange market intervention when exchange rates are flexible. Do you think such intervention is a good idea?

9. Is the importance of spillover effects larger or smaller under flexible exchange rates, as opposed to fixed ones? Is macroeconomic management easier under one regime than the other?

Technical

1. Assume that there is perfect mobility of capital. How does the imposition of a tariff affect the exchange rate, output, and the current account? (*Hint:* Given the exchange rate, the tariff reduces our demand for imports.)

2. Use the central bank balance sheet to show how a balance-of-payments deficit affects the stock of high-powered money under fixed exchange rates. Show, too, how sterilization operations are reflected in the central bank's balance sheet.

3. Consider a world with some capital mobility; the home country's capital account improves as domestic interest rates rise relative to the world rate of interest. Initially, the home country is in internal and external balance. (Draw the *IS*, *LM*, and *BB* schedules.) Assume now that the rate of interest abroad increases.
   a. Show the effect of the foreign interest rate increase on the *BB* schedule.
   b. What policy response would immediately restore internal and external balance?
   c. If the authorities took no action, what would be the adjustment process along the lines described by the monetary approach to the balance of payments?

4. Suppose your country's exports were to permanently increase. Explain how income, price adjustments, and adjustments to the real money supply would interact to lead it back to full employment and external balance.

5. What are the short- and long-term volume effects of an exchange depreciation? Does empirical evidence suggest that they are of sufficient size to outweigh price effects and therefore improve the trade balance?

6. Show, graphically, the short- and long-run effects of a monetary expansion when both exchange rates and prices are flexible and capital is perfectly mobile. What happens during the period of adjustment from the short to the long run?

7.* Consult *The Wall Street Journal* or some other newspaper that lists foreign exchange rates on its financial pages. For some countries, such as Britain and Japan, you should find futures prices listed. A futures price is the price to be paid today to receive 1 unit of the foreign currency in the future. A 30-day futures price for the pound sterling, say, is the price paid today to receive 1 pound 30 days from now. Explain why the futures prices are not generally equal to the spot price—the price paid today to receive the foreign currency today. See whether you can explain the difference between the relationship of spot and futures prices for the pound and yen, respectively.

---

*An asterisk denotes a more difficult problem.

Empirical

1. Figure 19-8 presents the evolution of real and nominal exchange rates for Canada and the United States. Obtain a similar graph for real and nominal exchange rates in Germany and the United States.

   a. Go to www.economagic.com and download monthly data over the period 1982–1997 for

   Consumer price index in Germany: Under "Browse by Source," "Bureau of Labor Statistics," choose the heading "International Employment and Prices." Scroll down the list and choose the variable "Germany: Consumer Price Index; All Items; NSA."

   Consumer price index in the United States: You can get this data from the "Most Requested Series" link.

   Exchange rate between the DM and the US$: Under "Browse by Source," choose the heading "Federal Reserve, St. Louis." Choose the heading "US Exchange Rate Data," and download data for "Exchange Rate: German Marks to one U.S. Dollar."

   b. Calculate the real exchange rate between Germany and the United States using the formula

   $$R = \frac{XR_{DM/\$} \times CPI_{U.S.}}{CPI_{GER}}$$

   c. Create a graph that includes both the real and the nominal exchange rate. Do the two variables move together?

CHAPTER 20

Advanced Topics

CHAPTER HIGHLIGHTS

- We discuss four ideas that have revolutionized macroeconomics. Each idea has changed the way we think about the macroeconomy, but each also remains controversial.

- In a rational expectations model, people form expectations that are consistent with the way the economy operates. Anticipated monetary policy has no real effects in the short run or the long run.

- The random walk theory of GDP argues that most shifts in output are permanent, as opposed to transitory booms and recessions, and that changes in aggregate demand are much less important than changes in aggregate supply.

- Real business cycle theory argues that money is very unimportant and that economic fluctuations are due largely to changes in technology.

- The New Keynesian models of price stickiness offer new "microfoundations," explaining why the price level does not always adjust quickly to changes in the money supply.

This chapter offers advanced material presenting the revolution in macroeconomics that has developed over the last 30 years. These ideas are exciting and controversial. When introduced, each seemed as if it would forever change macroeconomics in both teaching and practice. Some of the dramatic impact has failed to materialize, in part because empirical support for these challenging ideas has not been as full and convincing as had been hoped by their proponents. What's more, the ideas in part contradict each other—as well as the traditional aggregate supply–aggregate demand model. Even so, the impact of these concepts on both research and policy has been revolutionary. And while the ideas continue to be contested, each remains an active component of the economics research agenda.

We look at four theories in this chapter:

- Rational expectations.
- The random walk of GDP.
- Real business cycle theory.
- New Keynesian models of price stickiness.

These models yield contrasting conclusions about the conduct of monetary policy, but they are alike in their emphasis on the importance of consistency between macroeconomic and microeconomic theory.

These theories are at the forefront of research, and their exposition is necessarily more technical than is most of the text. For this reason, we begin with an informal overview.

 # 20-1

AN OVERVIEW OF THE NEW MACROECONOMICS

RATIONAL EXPECTATIONS EQUILIBRIUM MODELS

In a *rational expectations equilibrium* model, markets clear and there is nothing systematic that monetary policy can do to affect output or unemployment. The rational expectations approach is most closely associated with Nobel laureate Robert Lucas of the University of Chicago.

The term "rational expectations equilibrium" identifies two key features of this approach. First, it places weight on the role of expectations—specifically, *rational* expectations. Economic agents do not know the future with certainty and therefore have to base their plans and decisions, including price setting, on their forecasts or expectations of the future. If these expectations are made in a rational fashion, agents use all available information as well as possible to come out with the best forecasts. Second, the rational expectations model insists on *equilibrium:* Markets clear immediately. Phenomena such as insider-outsider effects simply do not come into play.

The full neoclassical theory of aggregate supply asserts that unemployment is always at the natural rate, output is always at the full-employment level, and any unemployment is purely frictional. Changes in the price level—for example, as a result of an increase in the money stock—leave output and employment unchanged. Money wages will rise, but since the real wage is unchanged, neither the quantity of labor supplied nor that demanded will change. The analysis of the classical case in Chapter 5 applies in full: Neither monetary nor fiscal policy changes will have any systematic effect on output. The rational expectations equilibrium approach, first presented in "the Lucas model," offers a qualified departure from that conclusion.

Lucas presents a neoclassical model with one changed assumption: Some people do not know the aggregate price level but do know the nominal (dollar) wage or price at which they can buy and sell. For instance, at a given moment in time, a worker knows that the going nominal wage rate is $12 per hour but does not know the aggregate price level, and thus does not know the real wage (the nominal wage divided by the price level, equal to the amount of goods the wage will buy). Suppose all nominal prices and wages rise in proportion. The real wage is unchanged, but if workers do not realize that prices have also risen, they will think that the real wage has risen and will supply more labor, so output will rise.

We turn now to the *rational expectations* aspect of this approach. How are firms and workers to form expectations of the price level? **The rational expectations approach assumes that people use all relevant information in forming expectations of economic variables.** In particular, it assumes that workers and firms will think through the economic mechanisms underlying the determination of the actual price level and then use the implied value of the actual price level as the expected price level.

Households' and firms' best guess is that full employment will prevail, although they recognize that this guess may be wrong in either direction. The expected price level, p^e, will be the price level consistent with full employment, or price level which equates aggregate demand and supply, that is, $AS = AD$. The central implication of the rational expectations approach is that people may not always get forecasts right but they do not make *systematic* errors.

We are now ready to see the central implication of the Lucas approach, namely, the differential reaction of the economy to anticipated versus unanticipated changes in the money supply. In response to an anticipated change in the money supply, agents will expect an equiproportionate change in the price level. Both p and p^e will change in proportion to the change in the money supply, the real money supply will remain unchanged, and the economy will remain at full employment. In contrast, an unanticipated change in money will have its full AS–AD effect—precisely because an unanticipated change will not affect p^e. Of course, agents will discover any change in the money supply relatively quickly, so even unanticipated changes will have real effects only in the very short run.

Policy Irrelevance

At first sight, the Lucas model seems to be almost the same as the classical model: Both models predict *policy irrelevance*—that neither monetary nor fiscal policy can affect the equilibrium level of income in the long run. The Lucas model is more interesting than the classical model, though, because it allows at least *transitory* deviations from full employment. However, these transitory deviations are the result of expectational errors, and they last only as long as the errors last—and that cannot be very long.

Moreover, there is no room for monetary policy in this world of rational expectations and market clearing. Suppose agents believe that the price level is lower than it actually is. The government need simply announce the correct statistics, and the market will, by itself, immediately go back to full employment. There is no need for accommodating monetary or fiscal policy to hasten the return to full employment. Thus, policy does not matter. In fact, in some versions of this approach, policy responses are problematic because they make it more complicated for economic agents to determine exactly what is happening in the economy and how best to adjust to it. This is a radically different perspective from a Keynesian world, where policy offers relief from unemployment.[1]

THE RANDOM WALK OF GDP

Are fluctuations in output mainly transitory or mainly permanent? If fluctuations are primarily permanent, changes in aggregate demand—the heart of Keynesian macroeconomics—must be of relatively little importance. The logic is as follows: (1) According to the *AS–AD* model, the effect of aggregate demand shocks wears off with time because the long-run aggregate supply curve is vertical. (2) Therefore, if the effect of shocks is permanent, their source must be something other than aggregate demand.

This argument was first advanced by Charles Nelson and Charles Plosser, who presented careful statistical evidence in favor of the dominant role of permanent shocks.[2] Nelson and Plosser's work does not suggest that the *AS–AD* model is theoretically flawed, but it does argue that the aggregate demand side is simply not very important. Their work serves as the inspiration for much of the real business cycle literature, discussed below.

The idea that changes in output are permanent is sometimes described by saying that GDP follows a *random walk,* meaning that, having wandered up or down, GDP has no tendency to return to trend. This contrasts with the implicit model in the text. We think of the path of output over time as following a growth trend, explained largely by technological improvement and capital accumulation, plus a business cycle of transitory fluctuations, explained by our *AS–AD* model. Since the fluctuations are transitory, output in our model tends to revert to the growth trend.

Inevitably, there has been a counterreaction to the random-walk argument. The evidence is clear that large permanent changes to output are important, but a number of economists have argued that these permanent changes are infrequent and that in between such changes aggregate demand is the primary source of fluctuations.

---

[1] For an important dissent from the "New Classical" view by a Nobel laureate, see George Akerlof, "Behavioral Macroeconomics and Macroeconomic Behavior," *American Economic Review,* June 2002.

[2] Charles R. Nelson and Charles I. Plosser, "Trends and Random Walks in Macroeconomic Time Series: Some Evidence and Implications," *Journal of Monetary Economics,* September 1982.

REAL BUSINESS CYCLE THEORY

Equilibrium *real business cycle (RBC) theory* asserts that fluctuations in output
and employment are the result of a variety of real shocks that hit the economy,
with markets adjusting rapidly and remaining always in equilibrium.[3] Real business cycle theory is the natural outgrowth of the theoretical implication of the rational
expectations approach—that anticipated monetary policy has no real effect—and of
the empirical implication of random-walk theory—that aggregate demand shocks are
not an important source of fluctuations.[4]

   With monetary causes of the business cycle assumed out of the way, real business
cycle theory is left with two tasks. The first is to explain the shocks, or disturbances,
that hit the economy, causing fluctuations in the first place. The second is to explain
the *propagation mechanisms*. A propagation mechanism is a mechanism through
which a disturbance is spread through the economy. In particular, the aim is to explain why shocks to the economy seem to have long-lived effects. We start with propagation mechanisms.

Propagation Mechanisms

The propagation mechanism that is most associated with equilibrium business cycles
is the *intertemporal substitution of leisure*. Any theory of the business cycle has to explain why people work more at some times than at others: During booms employment
is high and jobs are easy to find; during recessions employment is lower and jobs are
hard to find. A simple, but unsatisfactory, equilibrium explanation would be that people voluntarily supply more labor in response to a higher wage. (Remember that the
equilibrium approach requires that people be on their supply and demand curves at all
times.) However, the empirical evidence does not support this explanation. The elasticity of the labor supply with respect to the real wage is very small, and the real wage
changes very little over the business cycle.

   RBC models explain large movements in output with small movements in wages
as follows: There is a high elasticity of labor supply in response to *temporary* changes
in the wage. Or, as the argument is put, people are very willing to substitute leisure

---

[3]To read more about the real business cycle approach, see Jordi Gali, "Technology, Employment, and the
Business Cycle: Do Technology Shocks Explain Aggregate Fluctuations?" *American Economic Review*,
March 1999; S. Rao Aiyagari, "On the Contribution of Technology Shocks to Business Cycles," Federal Re-
serve Bank of Minneapolis *Quarterly Review*, Winter 1994; and Mark W. Watson, "Measures of Fit for
Calibrated Models," *Journal of Political Economy*, December 1993. For a forceful negative view of real business cycle theory, see Lawrence Summers, "Some Skeptical Observations on Real Business Cycle Theory,"
Federal Reserve Bank of Minneapolis *Quarterly Review*, Fall 1986. See also Charles Plosser, "Understanding Real Business Cycles," and N. Gregory Mankiw, "Real Business Cycles: A New Keynesian Perspective,"
both in *Journal of Economic Perspectives*, Summer 1989.

[4]Real business cycle theory also has some methodological differences from other areas of macroeconomics
with regard to the best way to identify underlying economic parameters. For a methodological and historical perspective on some of these differences, see Robert G. King, "Quantitative Theory and Econometrics,"
Federal Reserve Bank of Richmond *Economic Quarterly*, Summer 1995. For a somewhat more eclectic view
on methodology in empirical macroeconomics, see Christopher A. Sims, "Macroeconomics and Methodology," *Journal of Economic Perspectives*, Winter 1996.

intertemporally. The argument is that people care about their total work effort but care very little about *when* they work. Suppose that within a 2-year period they plan to work 4,000 hours at the going wage (50 weeks each year at 40 hours a week). If wages are equal in the 2 years, they would work 2,000 hours each year. But if wages were just 2 percent higher in one year than the other, they might prefer to work, say, 2,200 hours in one year, forgoing vacations and working overtime, and 1,800 hours in the other. By substituting between years, they work the same total amount but earn more total income. Note that the intertemporal substitution of leisure does not mean that the labor supply is sensitive to *permanent* changes in wages. If the wage rises, and will stay higher, there is nothing to be gained by working more this period than next. So it is quite possible for the response of labor supply to a permanent change in wages to be very small, even though the response to a temporary wage change is large.

This intertemporal substitution of leisure is clearly capable of generating large movements in the amount of work done in response to small shifts in wages—and thus could account for large output effects in the cycle accompanied by small changes in wages. However, there has not been strong empirical support for this view.

Disturbances

The mechanisms that propagate business cycles are set in motion by events or *disturbances* that change the equilibrium levels of output and employment in individual markets and the economy as a whole. The most important disturbances isolated by equilibrium business cycle theorists are shocks to *productivity,* or supply shocks, and shocks to *government spending*. **A *productivity shock* changes the level of output produced by given amounts of inputs.** Changes in the weather and new methods of production are examples. Suppose there is a temporary favorable productivity shock this period. Individuals will want to work harder to take advantage of the higher productivity. In working more this period, they raise output. They also invest more, thus spreading the productivity shock into future periods by raising the stock of capital. If the effect of the intertemporal substitution of leisure is strong, even a small productivity shock could have a relatively large effect on output.

Real business cycle theory has been, and continues to be, a major area of research for many macroeconomists. However, proponents of this view have been less successful at converting the rest of the profession to their view than they had once hoped. In part, this is because the evidence for the importance of money seems persuasive. Most policymakers continue to rely on the *AS–AD* model we have studied throughout the book.

NEW KEYNESIAN MODELS OF PRICE STICKINESS

The models described above are all in the equilibrium–market-clearing tradition. These models have become important in part because of their merits but also in part because economists have found rational decision making and market clearing to be a sound guiding principle. However, these models are inconsistent with the aggregate supply–aggregate demand behavior that many economists believe characterizes the real world. *New Keynesians* **accept the premise of individual rational behavior but develop**

models in which markets do not quickly reach the full classical equilibrium and prices do not always adjust to changes in the money supply.[5]

We focus on a particular model of *price stickiness* developed by Greg Mankiw, and closely related work by George Akerlof and Janet Yellen. Suppose that the money supply increases. According to equilibrium theories, firms should all increase prices proportionately. But suppose there is a small cost, a *menu cost,* of actually making the price change. Might firms choose to leave their price at its old—now "wrong"—value? The traditional answer is no, because the benefit of getting the price right surely outweighs any very small cost of changing it.

Under *imperfect competition* the losses to a firm from having the "wrong" price may be a very small fraction of the value to society of having the correct price. This suggests that menu costs can be quite small compared to fluctuations in output but still be large enough that no single firm is willing to incur the costs and change prices. So an increase in the nominal money supply may leave prices unchanged, and the resulting increase in real money increases output.

We turn now to more detailed—and more technically challenging—considerations of these ideas.

20-2
THE RATIONAL EXPECTATIONS REVOLUTION

In this section we work through a basic rational expectations model in several steps. First, we give a simplified version of our *AS–AD* model and solve it with exogenously given price expectations. We show that, except by coincidence, the price predicted by the model will be inconsistent with the price that people expected. We turn then to a perfect-foresight model—a model in which we assume that people use the model's own predictions to form their price expectations. Finally, we change the perfect-foresight assumption to the weaker assumption of rational expectations, where agents do use the model to form price expectations but do so with only partial information. In both the perfect-foresight and rational expectations models, anticipated monetary policy will have no real effects. This is a direct consequence of the fact that actual and expected prices are consistent with one another and that the expectations-augmented Phillips curve asserts that deviations of unemployment from the natural rate are tied to the difference between realized inflation and expected inflation.

In each step of the model's development, you should focus on the link between the specification of expectations and the monetary policy multiplier. In the simplified

[5]For overviews of this literature, see Jean-Pascal Bénassy, "Classical and Keynesian Features in Macroeconomic Models with Imperfect Competition," Huw D. Dixon and Neil Rankin, "Imperfect Competition and Macroeconomics: A Survey," and Richard Startz, "Notes on Imperfect Competition and New Keynesian Economics," all in Huw D. Dixon and Neil Rankin (eds.), *The New Macroeconomics: Imperfect Markets and Policy Effectiveness* (Cambridge, England: Cambridge University Press, 1995). See also Robert J. Gordon, "What Is New Keynesian Economics?" *Journal of Economic Literature* 28 (1990); and Jacquim Silvestre, "The Market-Power Foundations of Macroeconomic Policy," *Journal of Economic Literature* 31 (1993). See footnote 33 for more readings.

AS–AD model with exogenous expectations, the monetary policy multiplier is relatively large. In the perfect-foresight model, where expectations adjust perfectly, the monetary policy multiplier is *zero*. Finally, the rational expectations model combines the assumptions of the *AS–AD* and perfect-foresight models. Expectations adjust perfectly with respect to anticipated changes in the money supply, but not at all to unanticipated changes; the monetary policy multiplier is zero with respect to anticipated changes in the money supply and relatively large with respect to unanticipated changes.

A SIMPLE AGGREGATE SUPPLY–AGGREGATE DEMAND MODEL

We begin with a simplified version of the aggregate supply–aggregate demand model, stripping out much of the detail developed in earlier chapters. We begin by specifying a simple aggregate demand schedule:

$$AD: \quad m + v = p + y \tag{1}$$

Equation (1) is the *quantity theory equation: m* is (the log of) the money supply; *v* is "velocity" and is assumed to be constant; *p* is the price level; and *y* is GDP.[6]

We next specify a simple short-run aggregate supply curve, one that emphasizes the role of price expectations:

$$p = p^e + \lambda(y - y^*) \tag{2}$$

where *p* is again the price level, p^e is the *expected* price level, *y* is again GDP, and *y** is potential GDP. The parameter λ gives the slope of the aggregate supply curve. If λ is large, an increase in output above potential output causes a steep rise in prices above what had been expected. If λ is small, the short-run response of prices to output is small.

The aggregate demand and aggregate supply equations can be combined to solve for output [equation (3)] and prices [equation (4)] in terms of the money supply and other variables:[7]

$$y = \frac{1}{1+\lambda}m + \frac{1}{1+\lambda}(v - p^e) + \frac{\lambda}{1+\lambda}y^* \tag{3}$$

$$p = \frac{\lambda}{1+\lambda}(m + v - y^*) + \frac{1}{1+\lambda}p^e \tag{4}$$

[6]We employ here a quite technical, but quite useful, "trick." Equation (1), and the equations that follow, are written using the natural logarithms of the indicated variables. The quantity equation is usually written $MV = PY$, where *M* is the money supply, *P* is the price level, and so on. We use lowercase letters to represent logarithms, so $m = \ln(M)$, and so on. Thus, we get to equation (1) by writing $\ln(MV) = \ln(PY) \Rightarrow \ln M + \ln V = \ln P + \ln Y \Rightarrow m + v = p + y$. Using logarithms has the advantage that a change in *m* can be interpreted as the *percentage* change in *M*. Having said all this, if you aren't comfortable with logarithms, no noticeable harm will be done if you just think of *m* as the money supply. Note that we call *m* "the money supply" in the text without continually qualifying the definition by saying "the logarithm of."

[7]If you want to work through the algebra yourself, a useful first step is to rewrite equation (1) with price on the left, as in $p = m + v - y$. Use this expression to substitute out for the price level in equation (2), giving an equation with *y* on both sides, $m + v - y = p^e + \lambda(y - y^*)$. Collecting terms and solving for output gives equation (3). Putting equation (3) back into $p = m + v - y$ and solving for the price level gives equation (4).

Together, equations (3) and (4) tell us the equilibrium output and prices in our model economy. If the money supply rises 1 percent, output rises $1/(1 + \lambda)$ percent and prices rise $\lambda/(1 + \lambda)$ percent. To be concrete, suppose λ is $\frac{1}{2}$; then a 1 percent increase in the money supply causes a $\frac{2}{3}$ percent increase in output and a $\frac{1}{3}$ percent increase in the price level.

Now we use equations (3) and (4) to illustrate the standard approach to making an economic "forecast." (Be warned that this forecast will be subject to the Lucas critique, below.) For our fabricated example, suppose that λ equals $\frac{1}{2}$ and the values for the money supply, velocity, and potential GDP are $m = 2$, $v = 3$, $y^* = 4$, respectively. Most particularly, we assume that *agents in the economy expect* the price level to be $p^e = 5$. *What do you expect the price level to be?* What do you expect output to be? Try working out the answers for yourself. Our answers appear in the next paragraph.

Plugging the values given into equation (3), we find output is $y = 1\frac{1}{3} = \frac{2}{3}(2) + \frac{2}{3}(3 - 5) + \frac{1}{3}(4)$. From equation (4) we expect the price to be $p = 3\frac{2}{3} = \frac{1}{3}(2 + 3 - 4) + \frac{2}{3}(5)$.

So the prediction from our model is that we expect the price to be $3\frac{2}{3}$, taking as an input to the model that the expected price is 5! Shouldn't rational agents, who have a great deal at stake, make forecasts that are consistent with the way the economy (represented here by our simple model) actually operates? **This is the essence of the *Lucas critique:* The standard aggregate supply–aggregate demand model assumes that economic agents make predictions for the economy that are inconsistent with the predictions the model itself makes.**

Suppose that economic decision makers accept our forecast and change their expectation of the price level to $p^e = 3\frac{2}{3}$. Reworking equations (3) and (4) would then lead to predicting $y = 2\frac{2}{9} = \frac{2}{3}(2) + \frac{2}{3}(3 - 3\frac{2}{3}) + \frac{1}{3}(4)$ and $p = 2\frac{7}{9} = \frac{1}{3}(2 + 3 - 4) + \frac{2}{3}(3\frac{2}{3})$. Now the expected price we put into the model and the price predicted by the model are closer, but they're still not the same. Modifying the model so that the predicted value of p and the input value p^e are equal leads to the idea of a perfect-foresight model.

A PERFECT-FORESIGHT MODEL

We now assume that agents *do* use the *AS–AD* model to forecast prices and that they have all the information necessary to make the forecast. Agents are said to have *perfect foresight*. Rather than assuming p^e is given from outside the model, we assume agents use the model itself to compute p^e. In other words, agents compute p based on m, v, p^e, and so forth. Agents then set their predicted price at $p^e = p$. Since p itself depends on p^e, the two must be solved for simultaneously.

Assume that our model correctly describes the economy, so economic decision makers use equation (4) to *predict prices and compute p^e*. Then setting $p^e = p$:

$$p^e = p = \frac{\lambda}{1 + \lambda}(m + v - y^*) + \frac{1}{1 + \lambda}p^e \qquad (5)$$

Collecting terms containing p^e,[8] we can rearrange equation (5) to give the perfect-foresight forecast and solution for the price level and the corresponding solution for output:

$$p^e = p = m + v - y^* \tag{6}$$

$$y = y^* \tag{7}$$

The perfect-foresight predictions in equations (6) and (7) are quite different from the original *AS–AD* predictions embodied in equations (4) and (3). The latter assume *exogenously* given price expectations; the former assume that price expectations are formed *endogenously* and, specifically, that expectation formation is consistent with the predictions of the model.

The switch to such consistently formed expectations has dramatic implications for the effectiveness of monetary policy. According to equation (4), a 1 percent increase in the money supply increases prices by $\lambda/(1 + \lambda)$ percent, but **under perfect foresight a 1 percent increase in the money supply leads to exactly a 1 percent increase in the price level.** According to equation (3), a 1 percent increase in the money supply increases output by $1/(1 + \lambda)$ percent, but **under perfect foresight a 1 percent increase in the money supply leads to no increase at all in output.** Notice that these perfect-foresight short-run results are the same as the long-run *AS–AD* results. Under perfect foresight, prices rise not only as a direct result of the increase in the money supply but also because of the increase in price expectations. This extra boost raises prices just enough to completely offset the increase in the money supply.

Under perfect foresight, monetary policy is neutral in the short run as well as in the long run.

A perfect-foresight model has two important shortcomings. First, it requires that economic decision makers know everything about the economy. Second, it implies that the economy is always at full employment.[9] Neither of these shortcomings is really critical, as we will see when we consider a rational expectations model in the next section.

A RATIONAL EXPECTATIONS MODEL

A *rational expectations model* assumes that agents make the best use of whatever information is available to them and that expectations are formed in a manner consistent with the way the economy actually operates. A rational expectations model is much like a perfect-foresight model in which some of the key variables are uncertain. To illustrate, suppose that before the money supply is known, economic decision makers expect the money supply to equal m^e. If the money supply actually turns out to be m, we can define the difference between the agents' expectation and the actual money supply,

$$\epsilon_m = m - m^e$$

---

[8]Write $p^e\left(1 - \dfrac{1}{1 + \lambda}\right) = \dfrac{\lambda}{1 + \lambda}(m + v - y^*)$, and then multiply through by $1 + \lambda$.

[9]You can see in equation (2) that $p^e = p$ implies $y = y^*$.

as the agents' money forecast error. (Analogously, suppose agents expect potential output to be y^{*e}. Since potential output is actually y^*, the agents' potential output forecast error is $\epsilon_{y^*} = y^* - y^{*e}$.) **We show below that the monetary policy multiplier with respect to *anticipated* money, m^e, is zero, just as in the perfect-foresight model. The monetary policy multiplier with respect to *unanticipated* money, ϵ_m, is positive, just as in the *AS–AD* model.**

The forecast errors in a particular quarter may be either positive (the money supply, for instance, turned out to be larger than anticipated) or negative (the money supply turned out to be smaller than anticipated), but **on average rational forecast errors equal zero.** The argument here is straightforward. Suppose ϵ_m averaged 7. In this case we could improve our forecasts by just raising every forecast m^e by 7. So while rational forecast errors may be either large or small, depending on the quality of information available, they average zero. Another way to express this is $(\epsilon_m)^e = 0$.

We next ask what the price level will be in equilibrium. We begin by repeating equation (4) but substituting $m^e + \epsilon_m$ for m and $y^{*e} + \epsilon_{y^*}$ for y^*:

$$p = \frac{\lambda}{1 + \lambda}\left[\left(m^e + \epsilon_m\right) + v - \left(y^{*e} + \epsilon_{y^*}\right)\right] + \frac{1}{1 + \lambda}p^e \tag{8}$$

We assume that agents form their expectations, p^e, on the basis of the price forecast in equation (8). However, we recognize that forecasts are based only on the information the agents have:[10]

$$p^e = \frac{\lambda}{1 + \lambda}(m^e + v - y^{*e}) + \frac{1}{1 + \lambda}p^e \tag{9}$$

Simplifying equation (9) gives

$$p^e = m^e + v - y^{*e} \tag{10}$$

Notice that the expected price under rational expectations, in equation (10), is the same as that under perfect foresight, in equation (6), except that it is based only on the limited information available to those making the forecast: m^e rather than m, for example. The equilibrium solutions for price and output are[11]

$$y = y^{*e} + \frac{1}{1 + \lambda}\epsilon_m + \frac{\lambda}{1 + \lambda}\epsilon_{y^*} \tag{11}$$

$$p = m^e + v - y^{*e} + \frac{\lambda}{1 + \lambda}(\epsilon_m - \epsilon_{y^*}) \tag{12}$$

---

[10]The expectation of ϵ_m, for instance, is zero, and the expectation of m^e is m^e. We assume, for simplicity of illustration, that v and λ are known exactly.

[11]If you're working out the algebra for yourself, replace p^e in the price-level equation, (8), with the value from equation (10) to find

$$p = \frac{\lambda}{1 + \lambda}\left[\left(m^e + \epsilon_m\right) + v - \left(y^{*e} + \epsilon_{y^*}\right)\right] + \frac{1}{1 + \lambda}\left(m^e + v - y^{*e}\right)$$

Simplify and make the analogous substitutions for output in equation (3) to derive equations (11) and (12).

BOX 20-1 Rational Expectations Forecast Errors Are Unpredictable

Rational expectations differs from perfect foresight in that rational expectations forecasts are imperfect. They may be too high or too low, although the forecast is right on average. Rational expectations forecasts make the best use of the information available to the agents making the forecasts. As a consequence, the best guess of the forecast error, based on the information available when the forecast is made, is zero.

Suppose agents forecast p to be p^e. The forecast error, ϵ, is the difference between the realized value of p and the forecast:

$$\epsilon = p - p^e$$

It's straightforward to show that the expected value of the forecast error, call it ϵ^e, is zero. The expected forecast error is the difference between the average value of p and the average value of p^e. But these two are equal on average, precisely because agents adjust p^e to make them equal on average. If p^e were higher on average than p, agents could improve their guesses just by lowering p^e.

What is the effect of an increase in the money supply under rational expectations? The question must now be broken down into two parts: What is the effect of an anticipated increase in the money supply? What is the effect of an unanticipated increase in the money supply?

From examination of equation (11), we see that **under rational expectations an anticipated increase in money supply has no effect at all on output but an unanticipated increase in the money supply increases output,** by $1/(1 + \lambda)$. Notice that anticipated changes operate just as predicted by the perfect-foresight model above and that unanticipated changes operate just as predicted by our initial, exogenous price expectation, *AS–AD* model. In effect, anticipated monetary policy is neutral; unanticipated policy has its full *AS–AD* effects.

You should use equations (11) and (12) to check the effects of supply shocks (y^{*e} and ϵ_{y*}) on the price level to see that these also behave as in the perfect-foresight model when anticipated and as in the *AS–AD* model when unanticipated.

THE RATIONAL EXPECTATIONS EQUILIBRIUM APPROACH: EMPIRICAL EVIDENCE

The rational expectations model has the very strong prediction that anticipated monetary policy should have no effect on output. Early studies seemed consistent with this view,

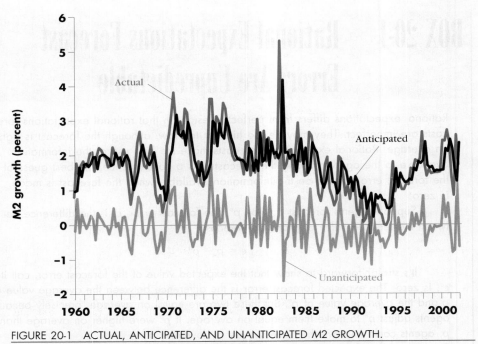

FIGURE 20-1   ACTUAL, ANTICIPATED, AND UNANTICIPATED *M2* GROWTH.

(Source: DRI/McGraw-Hill Macroeconomic Database; and authors' calculations.)

finding evidence that only unanticipated changes in the money stock increase output.[12] However, these results did not stand up to further testing.[13]

We give here the flavor of these empirical tests. We wish to ask whether anticipated money growth increases output, as the *AS–AD* model predicts, or whether there is no effect, as suggested by rational expectations models. The test involves two steps. First, we have to estimate anticipated money growth. Second, we compare anticipated money growth to changes in output.

Figure 20-1 shows quarterly *M2* growth from 1960 through 2002 in green. The actual growth rate is split into anticipated growth, in black, and unanticipated growth, in gray. In other words, we show three lines: $m = m^e + \epsilon_m$. Anticipated money growth is a statistical forecast based on the preceding four quarters of money growth.[14]

---

[12]See, for instance, Robert Barro, "Unanticipated Money, Output, and the Price Level in the United States," *Journal of Political Economy,* August 1978.

[13]Two influential, if difficult, articles are John Boschen and Herschel Grossman, "Tests of Equilibrium Macroeconomics with Contemporaneous Monetary Data," *Journal of Monetary Economics,* November 1982, and Frederic Mishkin, "Does Anticipated Monetary Policy Matter? An Econometric Investigation," *Journal of Political Economy,* February 1982.

[14]For the statistically curious, the forecast is based on a least-squares regression of *M2* growth on four lags of *M2* growth.

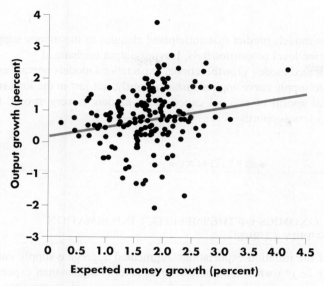

FIGURE 20-2   EXPECTED MONEY GROWTH AND GROWTH OF OUTPUT.
(Source: DRI/McGraw-Hill Macroeconomic Database; Bureau of Economic Analysis; and authors' calculations.)

Unanticipated growth is the difference between the forecast and the growth that actually occurred.

We plot output growth against our estimate of anticipated money growth in Figure 20-2, showing also the line that best fits the data. Two aspects of Figure 20-2 are salient: (1) Anticipated money growth by no means explains all output growth (many of the data points are far from the line); and (2) there is a strong positive relation between anticipated money growth and output growth (the line slopes upward). The estimated relation between output growth and anticipated money growth is

$$\Delta y = .18 + .36\Delta m^e \qquad (13)$$

suggesting that a 1 percent increase in money growth leads to about a .4 percent increase in output growth.[15]

Thus, the statistical evidence is not very supportive of a strict interpretation of the rational expectations model. This view is bolstered by careful historical research on Federal Reserve records: Christina Romer and David Romer found six episodes of shifts in monetary policy that were intended to lower inflation, and they found that each such instance of contractionary monetary policy was followed by a recession.[16]

---

[15]Again, for the statistically curious, the *t* statistic of the coefficient in equation (13) is 3.4.

[16]Christina D. Romer and David H. Romer, "Does Monetary Policy Matter? A New Test in the Spirit of Friedman and Schwartz," *NBER Macroeconomics Annual*, 1989.

RECAP

- Rational expectations models predict that anticipated changes to the money supply change the overall price level proportionately, leaving output unchanged.
- With respect to anticipated money growth, rational expectations models operate as if the long-run aggregate supply curve applied instantaneously, not just in the long run.
- While the intellectual appeal of rational expectations models is very strong, the empirical evidence is less supportive.

◆ O P T I O N A L ◆

 ## 20-3

THE MICROECONOMICS OF THE IMPERFECT INFORMATION AGGREGATE SUPPLY CURVE[17]

An important feature of the inflation-expectations-augmented aggregate supply curve is that output is high ($y > y^*$) when the nominal price level is higher than expected ($p > p^e$). This feature plays a central role in both the aggregate supply–aggregate demand model of Chapter 5 and the rational expectations model just presented. In this section we examine Lucas's *imperfect-information model* of the aggregate supply curve.[18]

Why does output sometimes rise when the overall price level rises? Lucas's answer is that firms usually observe prices only in their own market. A high price might be due to high demand, or it might just reflect an increase in the overall price level. In the former case, the firm would like to increase production; in the latter case, the price change should be neutral and production should be unchanged. But information is imperfect: When the firm sees a high price for its product, it doesn't know whether the cause is high demand or high overall prices. The firm, rationally, acts as if each cause were partially responsible and raises production a small amount. At the aggregate level, an unanticipated overall price increase is "misinterpreted" by every firm as a possible signal of higher demand, so the overall price increase leads to increased output. Within the Lucas model, this connection gives us the Phillips curve relation we see in real-world data. We turn now to a simplified version of Lucas's original model.

Suppose the economy is composed of distinct markets—Lucas originally suggested a parable in which each market was on an isolated island. Inhabitants of each island produce goods and then meet at a central location to trade. People on island i are

---

[17]This section and Sec. 20-5 are by far the most technically difficult in the book. Be warned!

[18]See Robert E. Lucas, Jr., "Expectations and the Neutrality of Money," *Journal of Economic Theory,* April 1972. Also see Edmund S. Phelps, "Introduction," in Edmund S. Phelps et al., *Microeconomic Foundations of Employment and Inflation Theory* (New York: Norton, 1970).

We strip many of the details from Lucas's original presentation. For a more thorough presentation, see David Romer, *Advanced Macroeconomics* (New York: McGraw-Hill, 1995), chap. 6.

willing to work longer hours when the output from their island is expected to fetch a price, p_i, which is high relative to the overall price level in the economy, p. The supply of output produced on island i would be

$$y_i = \alpha(p_i - p) \tag{14}$$

if island i's inhabitants knew the overall price level.[19] We assume, instead, that they have to make a guess as to the overall price level. Call this guess the expectation of the price level given the information available on island i, $E(p|\text{island } i)$, so the supply is

$$y_i = \alpha[p_i - E(p|\text{island } i)] \tag{15}$$

The price that will be paid for goods produced on island i depends on the overall price level p and on a demand shock specific to the particular kind of goods made on island i, z_i. We suppose the inhabitants of the island know their local price, p_i, but observe neither the demand shock nor the overall price level. They must therefore infer the overall price level from p_i. High p_i might mean that z_i is high *or* that p is high. So when the inhabitants observe a high p_i, they increase their estimate of p, but not by too much, because sometimes high p_i is due to high z_i and normal levels of p. The best guess of p is

$$E(p|p_i) = k_0 + \frac{1}{a}\beta p_i, \qquad 0 < \beta < 1 \tag{16}$$

where $E(p|p_i)$ indicates that the only information used in making a guess is the local price,[20] and a is a constant reflecting the slopes of the supply and demand curves.[21] If most changes in local prices, p_i, are due to changes in the overall price level, p, then β will be close to 1; if most changes are due to local demand shocks, z_i, then β will be close to zero.[22] **The value of β is the key to the slope of the aggregate supply curve—we see below that if $\beta = 1$, the aggregate supply curve will be vertical.**
   We can use equation (16) to express supply as

$$y_i = \alpha\left[p_i - \left(k_0 + \frac{1}{a}\beta p_i\right)\right] = \alpha\left[\left(1 - \frac{\beta}{a}\right)p_i - k_0\right] \tag{17}$$

Demand for the product of island i depends on aggregate GDP, y, on the demand shock for the product of the island, z_i, and on the relative price of the island's product, $p_i - p$. That is,

$$y_i = y + z_i - \gamma(p_i - p) \tag{18}$$

---

[19]As before, lowercase y and p really represent logarithms of output and price. Nothing of any importance rests on this point.

[20]Since we don't permit the islanders any aggregate information, we must be implicitly assuming the anticipated inflation rate is zero.

[21]The intercept k_0 is not of any particular interest. It appears for technical reasons.

[22]Engineers will recognize this as a signal extraction problem where p is the signal and z_i is the noise; β will be close to 1 if there is a high signal-to-noise ratio.

BOX 20-2   A Visual Example of Forming an Expectation

Expectations formation plays a key role in the derivation of the imperfect-information aggregate supply curve. Equation (16) can be derived algebraically by using statistical theory, but we present here a more visual approach. Figure 1 shows three possible relations between observed p_i and the rational guess $E(p)$. Suppose the value of p_i contains no information about p. As shown on the gray horizontal line, a rational person would guess p independently of the value of p_i. (This is the $\beta = 0$ case.) If all movements in p_i were due to movements in p, the best guess would be along the black 45° line. (This is the $\beta = 1$ case.) With imperfect information, as shown in green, the optimal guess lies partway between the no-information and the perfect-information cases.

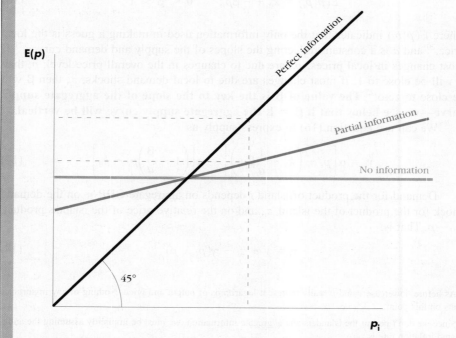

FIGURE 1   VISUAL EXAMPLE OF FORMING AN EXPECTATION.

The equilibrium price on an island is found by equating supply [equation (17)] and demand [equation (18)]:

$$\alpha\left[\left(1 - \frac{\beta}{a}\right)p_i - k_0\right] = y + z_i - \gamma(p_i - p) \tag{19}$$

Equation (19) gives the equilibrium relation between shocks, prices, and output for a particular island. But any one island is *representative* of the economy as a whole. Islands differ from one another because of idiosyncratic shocks, but the aggregate economy is just the average of the economies on the individual islands. Specifically, this means that aggregate output y is the average of the y_i's, that the overall price level p is the average of the p_i's, and that the z_i's average out to zero. If we average both sides of equation (19), we get

$$y = \alpha\left[\left(1 - \frac{\beta}{a}\right)p - k_0\right] \tag{20}$$

Equation (20) is the aggregate supply curve for the economy. With some further algebra, we can show that $a = 1$,[23] so the final expression for the aggregate supply curve is

$$p = \frac{1}{\alpha(1 - \beta)} \times (y + \alpha k_0) \tag{21}$$

The slope of the aggregate supply curve depends on both the slope of individual supply curves, α, and the relative importance of aggregate versus idiosyncratic shocks, β. If shocks to the overall price level play a dominant role, β will be close to 1 and the aggregate supply curve will be relatively steep. Thus, when most price shocks are attributed to changes in the overall price level, price shocks will be largely neutral, with little effect on output.

RECAP

- Agents forecast the overall price level on the basis of imperfect information. Agents are uncertain whether a price increase in an individual market is due to increased aggregate demand or to increased market-specific demand. As a result, increases in market-specific prices are attributed partially to increases in the overall price level and partially to increases in real demand.
- Unanticipated increases in the overall price level, p, generate partial increases in the anticipated price level, p^e, and partial increases in output, y. The positive associations between increases in p and y become the Phillips curve that we see in the data.

[23]If you want to do the algebra, use equation (20) to substitute for y in equation (19). Collect terms and simplify to show that

$$p_i = \frac{1}{\gamma + (1 - \beta)\alpha}z_i + p.$$

The generic expression for p_i is $p_i = a_0 + a_1 z_i + ap$, and the implicit coefficient of p in the expression just given shows that $a = 1$.

20-4

THE RANDOM WALK OF GDP: DOES AGGREGATE DEMAND MATTER, OR IS IT ALL AGGREGATE SUPPLY?

In the orthodox model of the economy the business cycle is presented as fluctuations of GDP around a smooth trendline. These fluctuations last from a few quarters to several years. Shocks to aggregate demand are presumed to be the primary cause of these transitory fluctuations. In 1982, Charles Nelson and Charles Plosser offered a challenge by suggesting that the trend is not so smooth but, rather, is subject to large and frequent shocks that have a permanent effect on the level of GDP.[24] If the Nelson and Plosser view is correct, aggregate demand shocks—which are transitory—are less important than aggregate supply shocks—which may be permanent.

Think of output as composed of a *trend,* or *secular, component,* perhaps the result of the growth processes discussed in Chapters 3 and 4, and a *cyclical component,* representing perhaps the business cycle. Figure 20-3 presents a stylized view of trend growth and fluctuations around the trend. In studying business cycles, we are interested in the fluctuations. So the first step in most studies of the economy is to create a *stationary* picture of the economy, that is, to *detrend* the data. Nelson and Plosser showed that the method used to model the trend plays a critical role in identifying shocks.

TWO EQUIVALENT REPRESENTATIONS OF TREND AND SHOCK

Suppose the trend in y can be represented by a literal time trend, as in

$$y_t = \alpha + \beta t \tag{22}$$

Equation (22) states that y rises by β in each time period. By subtracting $y_{t-1} = \alpha + \beta(t-1)$ from each side of equation (22), we get

$$y_t - y_{t-1} = [\alpha + \beta t] - [\alpha + \beta(t-1)] \tag{23}$$

or

$$y_t = y_{t-1} + \beta \quad or \quad \Delta y_t = \beta \tag{24}$$

where Δy_t is defined as $y_t - y_{t-1}$. Equation (24) also states that y rises by β in each time period.

[24]Christian J. Murray and Charles R. Nelson, "The Uncertain Trend in U.S. GDP," *Journal of Monetary Economics,* August 2000; Charles R. Nelson and Charles I. Plosser, "Trends and Random Walks in Macroeconomic Time Series: Some Evidence and Implications," *Journal of Monetary Economics,* September 1982. See also Stephen Beveridge and Charles R. Nelson, "A New Approach to Decomposition of Economic Time Series into Permanent and Transitory Components with Particular Attention to Measurement of the Business Cycle," *Journal of Monetary Economics,* March 1981; and John H. Cochrane, "How Big Is the Random Walk in GNP?" *Journal of Political Economy,* October 1988.

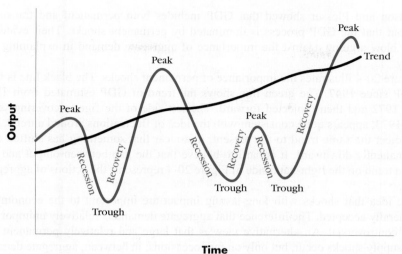

FIGURE 20-3   THE BUSINESS CYCLE.

IS THE EFFECT OF SHOCKS PERMANENT OR TRANSITORY?

Equations (22) and (24) are precisely equivalent to one another. But suppose we add an output shock, u_t, to equation (22) or to equation (24)? If we add the shock to equation (22), we have

$$y_t = \alpha + \beta t + u_t \quad \text{or} \quad \Delta y_t = \beta + u_t - u_{t-1} \tag{25}$$

If we, instead, add the shock to equation (24), we have

$$y_t = y_{t-1} + \beta + u_t \quad \text{or} \quad y_t = \alpha + \beta t + u_t + u_{t-1} + u_{t-2} + \ldots + u_0 \tag{26}$$

According to equation (25), the effect of a shock lasts one period, or, said differently, shocks to the change in y reverse themselves after one period. In sharp contrast, according to equation (26), the effect of a shock on the level of y is permanent, or, said differently, shocks to y accumulate over time. A variable that behaves as described by equation (25), that can be made stationary by taking out a time trend, is called *trend stationary*. A variable that behaves as described by equation (26), that can be made stationary by differencing, is called *difference stationary*. A difference-stationary process is dominated by permanent shocks; a trend-stationary process is dominated by transitory shocks.

Whether GDP is better described by equation (25) or by equation (26) sounds at first like a question of arcane statistical interest only. But the distinction strikes to the heart of the relevance of aggregate demand theory. According to the *AS–AD* model, business cycles caused by aggregate demand fluctuations are relatively short-lived, a matter of a few quarters or, at most, a few years. In contrast, shocks to aggregate supply might be permanent if they derived from permanent productivity improvements.

Nelson and Plosser showed that GDP includes both permanent and transitory shocks but that the GDP process is dominated by permanent shocks. Their evidence struck a blow arguing against the importance of aggregate demand in explaining the economy.

Figure 20-4 illustrates the importance of permanent shocks. The black line is U.S. real GDP since 1947. The green line shows the trend of GDP estimated from 1947 through 1972 and then projected forward. The left side of the figure, covering years prior to 1973, appears quite consistent with the idea of fluctuations around a trend. But if we project the same trend to the present, it is clear that something has shifted output permanently downward. It is hard to believe that the gap between output and the projected trend on the right-hand side of Figure 20-4 represents the actions of aggregate demand.

The idea that shocks with long-lasting impact are important to the economy is now generally accepted. The inference that aggregate demand is relatively unimportant remains controversial. An alternative view is that large and relatively permanent aggregate supply shocks occur, but only on rare occasions; in between, aggregate demand

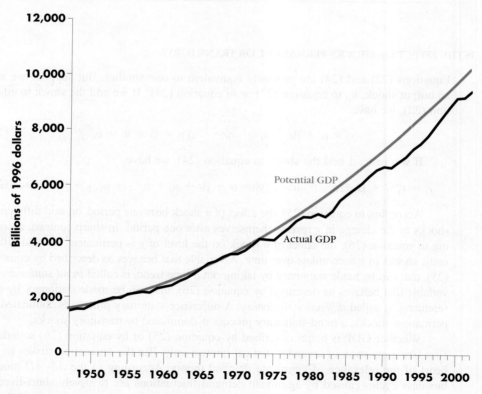

FIGURE 20-4   ACTUAL AND POTENTIAL GDP.

(*Source: Bureau of Economic Analysis, www.bea.gov; and authors' calculations.*)

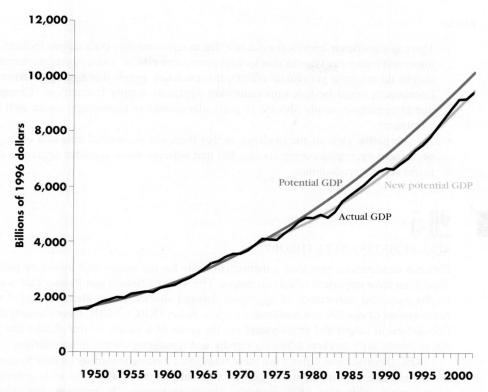

FIGURE 20-5   ACTUAL AND POTENTIAL GDP AND THE NEW POTENTIAL GDP.

Note that the newly calculated potential GDP is closer to the actual GDP than the original forecast. (Source: Bureau of Economic Analysis, www.bea.gov; and authors' calculations.)

shocks dominate. Pierre Perron is the original exponent of this point of view.[25] Perron argues that while there are occasional permanent breaks in trend, within decades-long subperiods the economy does have important short-run fluctuations around trend. In Figure 20-5, we estimate separate trends for output before 1973 and after 1973. Within each subperiod, output appears to be well modeled as transitory fluctuations around trend. This view of the world argues that there are large, permanent, but infrequent, aggregate supply shocks and that, in between these shocks, aggregate demand shocks dominate year-to-year fluctuations.

Because the dispute between believers in difference stationary and believers in *trend stationary with breaks* rests on measurements of long-lasting phenomena, the dispute can't be easily settled by statistical analysis of the relatively short data periods currently available. The importance of aggregate demand shocks is likely to remain a controversial area.

---

[25]Evidence for this view is given in an influential, but difficult, article by Pierre Perron, "The Great Crash, the Oil Shock and the Unit Root Hypothesis," *Econometrica,* November 1989.

RECAP

- There is significant empirical evidence that macroeconomic fluctuations include an important component due to shocks with permanent effects. Since aggregate demand shocks do not have permanent effects, this evidence argues that aggregate demand fluctuations could be less important than aggregate supply fluctuations. Changes due to aggregate supply shocks, in particular shocks to technology, could well be permanent.
- An alternative view of the evidence is that there are occasional episodes of large, permanent aggregate supply shocks, but that between these episodes aggregate demand shocks predominate.

20-5

REAL BUSINESS CYCLE THEORY

Rational expectations provided a theoretical basis for the notion that monetary policy should not have important effects on output. The work of Nelson and Plosser cast doubt on the empirical importance of aggregate demand shocks. These ideas supported the development of *equilibrium real business cycle theory* (RBC).[26] RBC theory asserts that fluctuations in output and employment are the result of a variety of real shocks that hit the economy, with markets adjusting rapidly and remaining always in equilibrium.

RBC theorists also differ from more traditional macroeconomists on how to measure the economic *parameters* that govern a model's behavior. RBC theorists generally prefer using *calibration* or *quantitative theory* techniques. In practice, this means choosing a small number of parameters that are crucial to the behavior of a model and estimating the value of each parameter from microeconomic studies, rather than from the macroeconomic data itself. We explore here a very simple RBC model that focuses attention on a single parameter, the *intertemporal elasticity of substitution of labor*.

A SIMPLE REAL BUSINESS CYCLE MODEL

Real business cycle theorists create models in which firms choose optimal investment and hiring plans and individuals make optimal consumption and labor supply choices—all choices being made in a dynamic, uncertain environment. The resulting models are technically complex. In fact, they can be solved only by use of relatively sophisticated mathematics combined with computer simulation. We present here a simple model that gives the flavor of real business cycle models and focuses on the question of the intertemporal substitution of labor. In this simple model, the firm buys labor and produces output in each of the many periods. A representative worker sells her labor and buys consumption goods each period. If she wishes, the worker can save her consumption goods for another period.[27]

[26]See footnote 3 for further readings.

[27]The pattern of capital investment and shifts in interest rates play important roles in real business models. We are omitting both in the interest of simplicity.

Each period, the representative firm buys labor L_t and uses it to produce output Y_t according to the production function

$$Y_t = a_t L_t \tag{27}$$

where a_t is the marginal product of labor in period t. (Looking ahead, we know the real wage rate will end up equaling a_t because in a competitive market the real wage rate equals the marginal product of labor.) Changes in the marginal product of labor are the source of real shocks in this simple model.

The representative worker has up to $\bar{L}$ hours available to sell in each period. The worker's leisure is $\bar{L}$ hours less the time she sells, so leisure equals $\bar{L} - L_t$. Each period the representative worker receives utility from leisure and from consumption, C_t. We assume that the worker's utility function in a given period can be expressed as[28]

$$U(C_t, \bar{L} - L_t) = C_t^{\gamma}(\bar{L} - L_t)^{\beta} \tag{28}$$

The worker's lifetime budget constraint states that the sum of lifetime consumption must equal the sum of lifetime earnings:[29]

$$C_t + C_{t+1} + C_{t+2} + \ldots = w_t L_t + w_{t+1} L_{t+1} + w_{t+2} L_{t+2} + \ldots \tag{29}$$

where w_t is the real wage rate in period t. The worker chooses consumption and leisure each period in amounts that will maximize the sum of lifetime utility subject to the budget constraint in equation (29).

It will prove helpful to note that the marginal utility of leisure is

$$MU_{\text{leisure}} = \beta C_t^{\gamma}(\bar{L} - L_t)^{\beta - 1} = \frac{\beta U_t}{\bar{L} - L_t} \tag{30}$$

How do we find the worker's optimal tradeoff defining her intertemporal substitution of leisure? If the worker reduces leisure 1 hour this period, she earns w_t more, which permits her to add w_t/w_{t+1} hours of leisure the following period. It follows that the marginal utility of leisure this period must equal w_t/w_{t+1} times the marginal utility of leisure next period:

$$MU_{\text{leisure}_t} = (w_t/w_{t+1}) \times MU_{\text{leisure}_{t+1}} \tag{31}$$

Equating the values of the marginal utilities of present and future leisure—using equation (30) twice in equation (31)—gives us the worker's intertemporal substitution of leisure:

$$\frac{\bar{L} - L_t}{\bar{L} - L_{t+1}} = \left(\frac{w_{t+1}}{w_t}\right)^{\frac{1-\gamma}{1-\gamma-\beta}} \tag{32}$$

Equation (32) tells us that if the wage in period $t + 1$ increases 1 percent while the wage in other periods remains constant, leisure in period $t + 1$ will fall by $(1 - \gamma)/(1 - \gamma - \beta)$. Depending on the values of β and γ, leisure might be very responsive or quite unresponsive to temporary changes in the wage rate.

---

[28]We assume that γ and β are both positive.

[29]Note again that we are implicitly assuming a zero interest rate.

Our model needs to be consistent with the empirical observation that *permanent* wage changes have little effect on labor supply. We can check this by computing the long-run response of leisure to a permanent wage change. Suppose the wage were constant over time, say, w^*. In this case, consumption and labor supply would also be constant over time, say, C^* and L^*. From the budget constraint [equation (29)], it must be true that $C^* = w^*L^*$. Combine this with the worker's *consumption-leisure tradeoff,* $\bar{L} - L_t = (\beta/\gamma)(C_t/w_t)$ to derive the long-run labor supply, and we find

$$\bar{L} - L^* = \frac{(\beta/\gamma)(w^*L^*)}{w^*} \quad or \quad L^* = \frac{\gamma}{\beta + \gamma}\bar{L} \qquad (33)$$

Equation (33) shows that the long-run response of labor to the wage rate is zero, since w^* drops out of equation (33) entirely. So in this aspect our model is in accord with the facts.[30]

Consider now the effect of intertemporal substitution of labor as a *propagation mechanism.* Suppose there is a transitory technology shock in period t and thus the marginal product of labor rises by $\%\Delta a$. We know that the wage rate equals the marginal product of labor, so the wage rate will increase along with the increase in a. The total change in output will be

$$\%\Delta Y = \%\Delta a + \%\Delta L \qquad (34)$$

The propagation mechanism is the "extra kick" to output $\%\Delta L$. We know from equation (32) that leisure will decrease by $[(1 - \gamma)/(1 - \gamma - \beta)] \times \%\Delta a$. Since leisure hours are roughly three times labor hours,[31] the percentage increase in labor should be approximately $\%\Delta L = 3 \times [(1 - \gamma)/(1 - \gamma - \beta)] \times \%\Delta a$. The total change in output will be

$$\%\Delta Y = \left(1 + 3 \times \frac{1 - \gamma}{1 - \gamma - \beta}\right) \times \%\Delta a \qquad (35)$$

The parameters β and γ are examples of what are called *deep parameters* in the real business cycle literature. RBC theorists argue that our models should depend on the parameters that describe the preferences of consumer-workers and the parameters that describe the production function of firms. These parameters can be identified from microeconomic studies. In our very simple model, if $\beta + \gamma$ is close to 1, the intertemporal substitution of leisure will be very strong and the propagation mechanism in equation (35) will translate relatively small technology shocks into much larger output shocks. In contrast, if the intertemporal substitution of leisure is weak, this propagation mechanism will be relatively unimportant. The empirical evidence, based on microeconomic data, favors the view that intertemporal substitution is relatively weak.[32]

---

[30]Empirically, the long-run supply of labor is slightly backward-bending. In the long run, higher wages reduce labor supply somewhat as people prefer to spend some of their higher income on increased leisure.

[31]Suppose one works 2,000 out of $8,760 = 24 \times 365$ hours.

[32]See Joseph Altonji, "Intertemporal Substitution in Labor Supply: Evidence from Micro Data," *Journal of Political Economy,* June 1986; and David Card, "Intertemporal Labor Supply: An Assessment," NBER working paper no. W3602, January 1991.

RECAP

- Real business cycle theory models the macroeconomy through the optimizing decisions about work and consumption made by individuals and the optimizing decisions about production made by firms. The model presented above is a simple version of the dynamic models deployed by RBC theorists.
- Real business cycle theory minimizes the role of nominal fluctuations and money.
- RBC theorists try to identify deep parameters that can be measured in microeconomic studies. The elasticity of the intertemporal substitution of leisure is a key example. The conclusions from the measurement of such parameters are not always favorable to the RBC models.

20-6

A NEW KEYNESIAN MODEL OF STICKY NOMINAL PRICES

The introduction of rational expectations theory and real business cycle theory constituted a *New Classical* revolution against the Keynesian orthodoxy of the aggregate supply–aggregate demand model. New Classical theories are grounded in rational, maximizing behavior, characteristics that economists, by training, greatly prefer. On the other hand, these theories leave little or no role for the kind of sluggish nominal price adjustment that Keynesian economists believe they see in the real economy. Beginning in the mid-1980s, and continuing today, a *New Keynesian* counterrevolution has arisen. New Keynesian models try to play by the intellectual rules of the New Classicists— that is, reflect rational, maximizing behavior—while still giving *AS–AD*-like results.

New Keynesian models generally rely on an assumption of imperfect competition. Under perfect competition, the individual actions of firms and consumers lead society to an "efficient" equilibrium. But under imperfect competition, individual decisions need not lead to efficient social outcomes. New Keynesian models explain how individually rational decisions under imperfect competition lead to socially undesirable booms and busts. In this section we examine one New Keynesian model, Mankiw's model of nominal price stickiness. Mankiw's model explains why individual, imperfectly competitive firms might leave nominal prices unchanged ("sticky") in the face of a change in the nominal money supply.

The intellectual problem that Mankiw faced is that according to economic theory, *nominal* prices are just measures based on an arbitrary unit of account. Microeconomic theory makes clear that only *relative* prices matter. In fact, microeconomic theory makes a very clear prediction related to the neutrality of money. Suppose that the economy initially has money supply $\overline{M}$ and that, through the supply and demand process, it reaches equilibrium with prices p_1, p_2, p_3, and so forth, for an average price level p. Now suppose that the money supply is $2\overline{M}$ instead. Microeconomic theory predicts that markets will reach the identical equilibria as previously, this time with prices $2p_1$, $2p_2$, $2p_3$, and an average price level $2p$. Nothing *real* has changed. The real money supply remains $2\overline{M}/2p = \overline{M}/p$, and the ratio of prices in any pair of markets, say, markets 1 and 3, remains unchanged, $2p_1/2p_3 = p_1/p_3$. So the Keynesians faced the question of how to reconcile rational, microeconomically justified economic theory with the idea that the nominal price level might not immediately reflect changes in the nominal money supply.

The beginning of the answer lay in recognizing that setting and changing prices is itself an economic activity. Firms will change prices only when the benefits from the price change outweigh the costs. On the surface, this seems a reasonable explanation for leaving prices unchanged in the face of a change in the money supply. The problem with this argument is that the cost of changing prices is surely very small and swings in the economy are on the order of several percent of GDP. It would seem that the benefits of a price change would nearly always outweigh the cost.

In 1985, Greg Mankiw and George Akerlof and Janet Yellen solved this conundrum by using very basic microeconomic theory to show that the *private* benefits of changing a price can be much smaller than the *social* benefits if there is substantial monopoly power in the economy.[33] Firms base their decisions on the private benefit only, so it is possible that in the face of changed demand each firm will decide to hold constant the price it charges, even though the social benefit of changing the price outweighs the social cost. We present a simplified version of Mankiw's analysis.

Suppose the production side of the economy consists of many small firms, each with some element of monopoly power in its own market. Indexing the markets by i, we can write the demand facing firm i as

$$Y_i = \left(\frac{P_i}{P}\right)^{-\epsilon} \frac{M}{P} \tag{36}$$

where P_i is the price charged by firm i, P is the overall price level, and $\epsilon\,(\epsilon > 1)$ is the elasticity of demand. Suppose that labor is the only input, the marginal product of labor is a, and the nominal wage is W. A monopolist sets its price as a markup over costs. Since marginal cost is W/a, the firm will charge[34]

$$P_i = \left(\frac{\epsilon}{\epsilon - 1}\right)\frac{W}{a} \tag{37}$$

and the firm's nominal profit will be

$$\left(P_i - \frac{W}{a}\right)Y_i \tag{38}$$

To provide a base of comparison for looking at sticky prices, we first ask what happens in the neoclassical model when the money supply increases by, say, 2 percent.

---

[33]N. Gregory Mankiw, "Small Menu Costs and Large Business Cycles: A Macroeconomic Model of Monopoly," *Quarterly Journal of Economics,* May 1985; George A. Akerlof and Janet L. Yellen, "A Near Rational Model of the Business Cycle, with Wage and Price Inertia," *Quarterly Journal of Economics,* Supplement, 1985. These and a number of related articles are reprinted in N. Gregory Mankiw and David Romer (eds.), *New Keynesian Economics* (Cambridge, MA: MIT Press, 1991). For an overview, see Laurence Ball and N. Gregory Mankiw, "A Sticky-Price Manifesto," *Carnegie-Rochester Conference Series on Public Policy,* December 1994.

[34]Equation (37) can be derived from solving the monopolist's profit maximization problem. If you have had an intermediate microeconomics course, you may have seen the formula there.

Since money is neutral in a neoclassical model, we know that all nominal prices and wages will rise by 2 percent. We see that both the left and the right sides of equation (37) rise by 2 percent. Since M, P, and all the P_i's rise by 2 percent, real demand in equation (36) is unchanged. From equation (38), nominal profits rise 2 percent, but since overall prices have risen, real profits are unchanged. So everything in our model is consistent with the neutrality of money.

Suppose now that each firm has to undertake a small expenditure, z, called a "menu cost," if it raises its price. Each firm will compare the cost of maintaining its now "too low" price with the potential increase in profit if it raises prices 2 percent. Mankiw showed that the potential profit can be very small—literally "second order"—when two conditions hold:

- If the deviation between optimal price and existing price is small, the profit opportunity is *very* small.
- If the elasticity of firm demand is low, profit is relatively less sensitive to getting the price exactly right.

As an example, Figure 20-6 shows profit losses, measured as a percentage of optimal output, on the vertical axis and the percentage deviation of price from optimal price on the horizontal axis. The black line shows profit losses for a modestly monopolistic firm (as it happens, one with a demand elasticity of 20). Suppose the firm's current price is 2 percent below optimal. Then, reading across on the black line, we

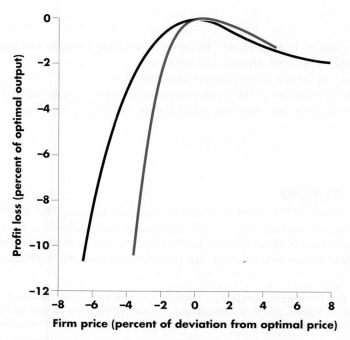

FIGURE 20-6   MANKIW'S BREAKTHROUGH.

see that the firm is forgoing potential profit equal to .5 percent of output. If the menu cost is more than this, the firm will leave its price unchanged. Since other firms face similar choices, they too leave prices unchanged. The net effect is that all nominal prices remain fixed, the overall price level remains fixed, the real money supply increases, and aggregate demand rises along with the real money supply. From equation (36), we see that the real money supply (M/P) and output will rise 2 percent. Note that the 2 percent gain in societal output is 4 times the privately forgone firm profits.

The key to the New Keynesian breakthrough is the assumption that firms face a downward-sloping demand curve. In a perfectly competitive market, every firm faces a horizontal (infinitely elastic) demand curve, even though the demand curve for the market as a whole can have an arbitrary slope. If the demand curve facing an individual firm is horizontal, or nearly so, a small deviation of price from the optimal price causes a huge swing in demand and a correspondingly huge swing in profits. So in a competitive market, the private profit from getting prices right always outweighs a small menu cost.[35] In contrast, with a downward-sloping demand curve facing each firm, a small menu cost may well be bigger than potential profit changes.

This work provides a rigorous microeconomic justification for nominal price stickiness. Since New Classical economists attack the rigor of the underpinnings of Keynesian models, such justification is a key piece of the Keynesian response to rational expectations and real business cycle models. Not everyone agrees on the empirical significance of the formulation by Mankiw and by Akerlof and Yellen, but the work is certainly a milestone in the New Keynesian counterrevolution.

RECAP

- The New Keynesians try to build models based on maximizing behavior that result in aggregate supply–aggregate demand-like behavior.
- Most New Keynesian models rely on imperfect competition.
- Prices can be sticky, even though the menu costs of adjustment are quite small, because the increased profit from resetting prices is even smaller.

 ## 20-7

BRINGING IT ALL TOGETHER

Much remains unsettled at the frontier of macroeconomic science. The theories presented by equilibrium theorists and by New Keynesians have undeniable appeal, but the empirical relevance of these theories is less clear. Similarly, many advocates of real business cycle theory now acknowledge the importance of sticky prices. To

---

[35]The green line in Fig. 20-6 shows potential profits for a relatively more competitive firm. The same 2 percent mispricing here costs more than 2 percent of output, about 4 times the cost in the less competitive, black case. By manipulating the elasticity, ϵ, one can make the contrast between the black and green lines as large or small as desired.

some extent there has begun to be a partial convergence of the theories studied in this chapter. A new set of *stochastic dynamic general equilibrium* (SDGE) models has been developed. The models take real business cycle models and add sticky prices while retaining rational expectations. The results of these models are sometimes surprisingly Keynesian.

Part of the beauty of macroeconomics as a science is the interplay between theory, empirical work, and policy. Macroeconomists with very different viewpoints and economic philosophies interact and work quite hard to listen to one another. As a result, our understanding of the real macroeconomy is ever changing and improving.

SUMMARY

1. Modern theories emphasize the consistency of macroeconomic and microeconomic theories.
2. The rational expectations approach emphasizes the consistency of public expectations about the behavior of the economy.
3. Rational forecasts make errors, but not predictable ones.
4. The rational expectations approach suggests that anticipated monetary policy is neutral even in the short run.
5. An imperfect-information approach will explain a short-run upward-sloping aggregate supply curve, but one in which the tradeoff between output and inflation cannot be exploited through anticipated monetary policy.
6. The random-walk model of output suggests that economic fluctuations are highly persistent—and therefore not due to changes in aggregate demand.
7. The real business cycle approach builds models of a dynamic economy in which real shocks are propagated. These models minimize the role of the monetary sector.
8. New Keynesian models attempt to reintegrate aggregate demand, especially sticky prices, with solid microeconomic foundations.

KEY TERMS

cyclical component (of GDP)
deep parameters
difference stationary
imperfect competition
imperfect-information model
intertemporal substitution of leisure
Lucas critique

menu cost
New Classical economics
New Keynesian economics parameters
perfect foresight
policy irrelevance
price stickiness
productivity shock
propagation mechanism
random walk (of GDP)

rational expectations
rational expectations equilibrium
real business cycle (RBC) theory
trend (secular) component (of GDP)
trend stationary
trend stationary with breaks

PROBLEMS

Conceptual

1. This chapter covers four broad classes of research—rational expectations theory, random walk in output, real business cycle theory, and models that endeavor to explain why output can diverge, in the short run, from its full-employment level. To what extent do these models complement or contradict each other? Discuss.

2.* What are rational expectations? How do rational expectations differ from perfect foresight? Is monetary policy neutral under both assumptions?

3. Describe a propagation mechanism used in real business cycle theory. Explain, briefly, how it works.

4.* What are the similarities and differences between Mankiw's menu-cost model of aggregate supply and Lucas's imperfect-information one? Classify each as New Keynesian or New Classical.

5.* What is the key assumption in Mankiw's menu-cost model of aggregate supply?

6.* What are deep parameters, in the sense used by proponents of real business cycle theory?

7.* In Lucas's imperfect-information model of aggregate supply, when will aggregate shocks (shocks to the economy at large, rather than to particular regions or markets) have the strongest effect on output? Explain.

8.* **a.** What is the difference between trend-stationary and difference-stationary processes?

   b. Why is this an important distinction, and how does our belief regarding which of these best characterizes output affect our forecasting strategy?

   c. Perron suggested that output might best be characterized as trend stationary with breaks. How does this help resolve the question of the importance of shocks to aggregate demand?

Technical

1.* **a.** Use equations (3) and (4) to forecast both the price level and the level of output that result from the simple *AS–AD* model of Section 20-2. You may assume that the slope of the aggregate supply curve is 2/3; that the values of the money supply, velocity, and potential GDP are 9, 8, and 7, respectively; and that the expected price level is 5.

   b. Evaluate your forecast in light of the Lucas critique.

   c. How does this forecast differ from that which would result from a perfect-foresight model?

   d. Is this forecast better or worse? Explain.

2.* Use equations (11) and (12) to check the effects of anticipated and unanticipated supply shocks on the level of output. Show that they behave as they would in a perfect-foresight model when anticipated and as they would in the standard *AS–AD* model when unanticipated.

3. Does empirical evidence support the rational expectations result that anticipated monetary policy should have no effect on output? Explain.

4.**a. Suppose, in the simple RBC model developed in Section 20-5, that $\gamma = .35$ and $\beta = .05$. How much of an output increase will result from a 10 percent increase in the marginal product of labor, given these parameter values? [*Hint:* Use equation (35).]

   b. Would there be strong intertemporal substitution of leisure in using the parameters given in part (**a**)? Why or why not?

5.* **a.** What does empirical evidence suggest regarding the extent to which people substitute leisure over time?

*One asterisk denotes a more difficult problem. Two asterisks means the problem is *really* hard.

b. What does this suggest regarding the role of intertemporal substitution in propagating shocks throughout the economy and regarding the ability of small technology shocks to generate large output shocks?

6.* This question relates to expectations formation in the Lucas imperfect-information model of aggregate supply.

a. If $\alpha = 1$ and $\beta = .75$, what is the expected change in the overall price level when local prices, p_i, rise to 4 times their original level? [*Hint:* Use equation (19).]

b. If α (the slope of the "local" supply function) is 1/2 for a particular region, by how much will output increase in the region as a result of this increase in its local prices?

c. How would this result change if β were .25 instead of .75, and what would it mean for β to have such a small value?

d. What if β were 1?

Empirical

1.**The subsection "The Rational Expectations Equilibrium Approach: Empirical Evidence" investigates the rational expectations hypothesis for the United States. Do the same analysis for Australia.

a. Go to www.economagic.com, and under "Browse by Source," choose the heading "Australia." Download data for "*M*3 SA" and "Total Real GDP."

b. Calculate the growth rate of *M*3 as $[\ln(M3) - \ln(M3_{-1})] \times 100$. Calculate the anticipated growth rate of *M*3 by regressing the growth rate of *M*3 on a constant and four lags. Make a graph that includes the actual, anticipated, and unanticipated growth rate of *M*3. Comment.

c. Calculate the quarter-to-quarter growth rate in real GDP as

$$[\ln(RGDP) - \ln(RGDP_{-1})] \times 100$$

Make a scatterplot that has the anticipated growth rate of *M*3 on the X axis and the growth rate of output on the Y axis. Comment.

GLOSSARY

A

absolute convergence   Tendency of both the levels and growth rates of output in different countries to approach each other over time and for their steady-state values to be the same.

accelerator model   Asserts that investment spending is proportional to the change in output, and is not affected by the cost of capital; describes the behavior of inventory investment surprisingly well.

accommodating policy   Use of policy to offset a shock. For example, increase in money supply to prevent increase in interest rate resulting from outward shift in *IS* curve. See also *accommodation of supply shocks*.

accommodation of supply shocks   Use of demand-side policies to prevent GDP from falling in response to a temporary drop in aggregate supply.

action lag   Period between the time a policy is decided on and the time it is implemented.

activist policies   Policies that respond to the current state of the economy and try to stabilize output.

activist rules   Rules that have countercyclical features.

adjustable rate mortgage (ARM)   A home loan in which the interest rate changes in line with current market interest rates.

adjusted GNP   Series that tries to correct for the inclusion of welfare-reducing "goods" in GNP and for its inability to capture quality improvements; a measure of welfare.

adverse supply shock   Inward shift in the aggregate supply curve. The increase in the price of oil that resulted from the OPEC oil embargo of the early 1970s is a classic example.

aggregate demand   Sum of the values of all of the final goods purchased in an economy.

aggregate demand (*AD*) curve   Relationship between the amount of goods and services people wish to purchase and the price level.

aggregate demand schedule   Synonym for aggregate demand curve.

aggregate supply (*AS*) curve   Relationship between the amount of final goods and services produced in an economy and the price level.

aggregate supply–aggregate demand model   Uniquely determines price level and level of output at which the economy is in equilibrium.

anticipated inflation   Inflation that people expect.

anticipatory monetary policy   Monetary policy adopted in response to problems (i.e., inflationary pressure) that are expected to arise in the future.

appreciation   Increase in the value of the domestic currency relative the currencies of other countries. Used when exchange rates are flexible.

arbitrage   Buying/selling assets to take advantage of differences in returns.

augmented Phillips curve   Phillips curve that includes inflationary expectations as a determinant of the inflation rate.

automatic adjustment mechanisms   Mechanisms that automatically act to eliminate balance-of-payments problems.

automatic stabilizer   Policy that reduces the impact of an economic shock without requiring case-by-case intervention. Proportional income taxes and unemployment insurance are examples.

B

balance of payments   Measures the net flow of currency into the country from abroad.

balance-of-payments deficit   Occurs when more money is leaving the country than is entering it.

balance-of-payments surplus   Occurs when more money is entering the country than is leaving it.

balanced budget multiplier   Increase in output that results from equal increases in taxes and government purchases.

Barro-Ricardo equivalence proposition   See *Ricardian equivalence*.

beggar-thy-neighbor policy   Attempt to increase domestic output at the expense of the output of other countries.

Board of Governors of the Federal Reserve   A government agency that oversees regional Federal Reserve Banks, has sole authority over changes in reserve requirements, and forms a part of the Federal Open Market Committee (FOMC). Its chair has traditionally had the power to determine U.S. monetary policy.

bubble   See *speculative bubble*.

budget constraint   Limit to the amount of money an individual, a firm, or the government can spend. An individual's purchases might be constrained by his or her income (or wealth).

budget deficit   The difference between the amount of money the government spends and the revenue that it receives in the form of taxes.

budget surplus   Opposite of *budget deficit*.

buffer-stock saving   Excess consumer savings used to maintain consumption when income is lower than usual (saving for a rainy day).

Bundesbank   Germany's central bank, now part of the European System of Central Banks (ESCB).

burden of the debt   Each individual's share of the national debt.

business cycle   Pattern of expansion and contraction of the economy.

business fixed investment Annual increase in machinery, equipment, and structures used in production.

business saving Saving by firms; profits not paid out to owners/stockholders.

C

capital account Net flow of dollars into the country resulting from the acquisition of domestic assets by foreigners.

capital gains The amount an asset appreciates in value over time.

capital stock The amount of capital available for use in the economy.

capital-labor ratio The amount of capital available for use by each worker; the capital stock divided by the labor supply.

central bank Bank that has control over the money supply. In the United States, the Federal Reserve. In Europe, the European Central Bank.

certainty-equivalence policy A policy made under the assumption that there is no uncertainty regarding future events.

classical adjustment process Process by which the economy automatically moves towards internal and external balance.

classical aggregate supply curve Vertical *AS* curve; output equals potential output.

classical case Vertical *LM* curve; case in which money demand is completely insensitive to changes in the real interest rate.

classical quantity theory See *quantity theory of money.*

clean floating Flexible exchange rate system in which the central bank does not intervene in foreign exchange markets. Contrast *dirty floating.*

Cobb-Douglas production function Production function with constant returns to scale, constant elasticity of output, and unit elasticity of substitution between input factors.

COLA See *cost-of-living adjustment.*

cold-turkey strategy Strategy of moving immediately to the desired target rather than trying to spread the cost of adjustment out over time.

competitive depreciation Occurs when one country allows its currency to depreciate in order to improve its trade balance, hurting another country; a series of retaliatory depreciations.

composition of output Relative amounts of consumption, investment, and government purchases that make up GDP.

conditional convergence Tendency of growth rates of output in different countries to approach each other over time. Contrast *absolute convergence.*

consol (or perpetuity) An asset that pays a fixed amount (coupon) each period forever.

consumer durables Consumer goods that yield services over a period of time; washing machines are an example.

consumer price index (CPI) Fixed-weight price index that measures the cost of the goods purchased by the typical urban family.

consumer spending Spending by consumers.

consumption function Equation relating consumption to disposable income.

convergence See *conditional* and *absolute convergence.*

cost-of-living adjustment (COLA)   Indexes wages to the inflation rate.

coupon   Periodic payment made to the holders of a bond.

crawling peg   Exchange rate policy; exchange rate is devalued at a rate roughly equal to the inflation differential between a country and its trading partners.

credibility   The degree to which the public believes that the government will implement its announced policies.

credibility bonus   The extra reduction in inflation due directly to the public's belief in the central bank's commitment to fighting inflation.

credible policy   Policy that people believe their government will follow.

credit rationing   Limiting the amount of money that individuals can borrow at the prevailing interest rate.

credit targeting   Using monetary policy to achieve a particular level of debt.

crowding out   Reduction in some component of aggregate demand—usually investment—that results from an increase in government spending.

currency appreciation, or depreciation   See *appreciation* and *depreciation*.

currency board   The requirement that a specific amount of foreign currency must back up each unit of domestic currency that is printed.

currency-deposit ratio   Ratio of the currency to bank deposits; a primary determinant of the money multiplier.

current account   Net flow of dollars into the country resulting from the sale of domestic goods and services, and from net transfers from abroad.

cyclical component of GDP   Fluctuations of output around its trend; the output gap.

cyclical deficit   Portion of the budget deficit that results from business cycle fluctuations. Contrast *structural deficit*.

cyclical unemployment   Unemployment resulting from business cycle fluctuations.

D

debt-income ratio   Ratio of national debt to GDP.

decision lag   Period of time required to decide on the proper response to a macroeconomic shock.

deep parameters   Parameters that describe the preferences of individuals and the production of firms, and that can be identified from microeconomic studies.

deflation   Rate at which the price level falls, in percentage terms; opposite of *inflation*.

demand for real balances   Quantity of real money balances people wish to hold.

demand shock   A shock that causes the *AD* curve to shift.

demand-side policy   Policy that causes the aggregate demand curve to shift.

depreciation   Decrease in the value of the domestic currency relative to the currencies of other countries; used when exchange rates are flexible.

depreciation   Rate at which the capital stock wears out.

desired capital stock   Capital stock that maximizes profits.

devaluation   Decrease in the value of the domestic currency relative to the currencies of other countries; used when exchange rates are fixed.

difference stationary   Temporary shocks to a variable permanently affect its level. A random walk is an example of a difference stationary process.

diminishing marginal product A characteristic of a production function whereby the marginal product of a factor falls as the amount of the factor increases while all other factors are held constant.

dirty floating Flexible exchange rate system in which the central bank intervenes in foreign exchange markets in order to affect the short-run value of its currency. Contrast *clean floating*.

discount rate Interest rate charged by the Fed to banks that borrow money from it.

discounted cash flow analysis Method of determining the present value of cash to be received in the future.

discrete lag Time that passes before an effect is felt. Contrast *distributed lag*.

discretionary outlays Portion of the federal budget under immediate annual congressional control. Contrast *entitlement programs*.

disintermediation Withdrawal of deposits from financial intermediaries when interest rates rise above the regulated ceiling rates on time deposits.

disposable income Income available for a household to spend; total income less taxes plus transfers.

dissaving Negative saving; borrowing/spending out of accumulated wealth.

distributed lag Time that passes while an effect gradually accumulates. Contrast *discrete lag*.

distributional consequences of unemployment The costs of unemployment (recession) are borne very unevenly, namely by those people who lose their job.

diversification of policy instruments Simultaneous use of different policy instruments.

dollarization Replacement of a domestic currency with another country's currency for example, the U.S. dollar.

domestic credit The monetary authority's holdings of claims on the public sector—government debt—and on the private sector—usually loans to banks.

domestic credit ceiling A limit on domestic credit expansion, often suggested by the IMF as part of a stabilization plan.

durable goods Goods that yield services over a period of time. See *consumer durables*.

dynamic behavior Behavior that depends on values of economic variables in periods other than the current period.

dynamic inconsistency Tendency of optimal policy to be different at different points in time.

dynamic programming A way of solving a problem by working backward through time; choices made at one point in time anticipate choices that will need to be made later.

dynamic scoring The process of incorporating the macroeconomic effects of a tax change into the revenue estimates.

E

econometric model Model used to make quantitative economic predictions.

efficiency wage theory Theory suggesting that wages might be set above the market clearing rate in order to motivate workers; a possible explanation for wage rigidity, labor market disequilibrium.

employed person   A person who has a job. An employed person is defined by the Bureau of Labor Statistics as one who during the reference week (the week including the 12th of the month), (*a*) did any work at all (at least 1 hour) as paid employees, worked in their own business, profession, or on their own farm, or worked 15 hours or more as unpaid workers in an enterprise operated by a member of the family, and (*b*) all those who were not working but who had jobs or businesses from which they were temporarily absent because of vacation, illness, bad weather, childcare problems, maternity or paternity leave, labor-management dispute, job training, or other family or personal reasons, whether or not they were paid for he time off or were seeking other jobs.

employment stability   Low rate of job layoff, turnover.

endogenous growth   Steady-state output growth determined by endogenous variables, for example, the saving rate.

endogenous variable   Variable that is determined within a particular model (whose value is affected by the values of other variables).

entitlement programs   Programs that transfer money from the government to individuals; social security, unemployment insurance, and Temporary Assistance for Neady Families (TANF) are examples.

equilibrium level of output   Level of output at which aggregate supply equals aggregate demand.

equity   Share of ownership in a company; claim to a fraction of its profits.

euro   The common currency of the European Monetary Union.

European Exchange Rate Mechanism (ERM)   Agreement between a number of European countries to loosely fix their exchange rates, allowing them to fluctuate only in a narrow band.

European Monetary Union (EMU)   The countries that have signed the Maastricht Treaty and adopted a common currency, the euro. Box 12-1 in the textbook reviews the status of this union.

excess reserves   Reserves held by banks over and above the level required by the Federal Reserve.

excess sensitivity   When one variable's response to changes in another is larger than theory predicts. Consumption, for example, is said to exhibit excess sensitivity; it changes more in response to predictable income changes than the life-cycle–permanent-income theory suggests.

excess smoothness   When one variable's response to changes in another is smaller than theory predicts. Consumption, for example, exhibits excess smoothness; it changes by a smaller amount than the life-cycle–permanent-income theory suggests in response to unexpected changes in income.

exchange rate   Price of foreign currency per unit of domestic currency.

exchange rate overshooting   Movement of the exchange rate past its target. Adjustment of exchange rates toward long-run equilibrium is frequently accompanied by a move, in the medium run, of the exchange rate past its final position.

exogenous variable   Variable that is determined outside a particular model (whose value is independent of the values of a model's other variables).

expansion   See *recovery*.

expectations theory of the term structure   States that long-term interest rates are equal to the average of current and expected future short-term interest rates, plus a term premium.

expectations-augmented Phillips curve   See *augmented Phillips curve*.

expected inflation rate   The inflation rate expected in the future by workers and firms.

expected real interest rate   The real cost of borrowing, or the real return on a deposit. $r^e = i - \pi^e$

expenditure-reducing (increasing) policies   Policies aimed at offsetting the effects of expenditure-switching policy.

expenditure-switching policies   Policies aimed at increasing purchases of domestic goods and decreasing purchases of imported goods.

experience rating   Setting the unemployment insurance tax higher for firms whose employees have high unemployment rates.

external balance   Occurs when the balance of payments is neither in surplus nor in deficit; when the current account and the capital account exactly offset each other.

external deficit   Balance-of-payments deficit.

F

face value   The amount that a bond pays its holder on expiration. The market value of a bond will equal its face value when the market interest rate is equal to the coupon rate on the bond.

factor payments   Payments made to factors of production; wages paid to labor are an example.

factor shares   Portion of national income paid to each productive input.

factors of production   Inputs to production; capital, labor, and natural resources are examples.

favorable supply shock   An economic disturbance which shifts the aggregate supply outward, implying firms are willing to produce more at any given price level.

Fed   Short for Federal Reserve.

Federal Deposit Insurance Corporation (FDIC)   Government agency that insures deposits of most commercial banks and mutual savings banks to a maximum of $100,000.

federal funds rate   The cost to a bank of borrowing from other banks.

Federal Open Market Committee (FOMC)   Oversees open market operations, sets monetary targets. Made up of the Board of Governors of the Federal Reserve System, the president of the New York Federal Reserve Bank, and the presidents of four other regional banks on a rotating basis.

Federal Reserve   The central bank of the United States. See *Federal Reserve System*.

Federal Reserve System   Consists of twelve Federal Reserve Banks, each representing its own district, all overseen by the Board of Governors of the Federal Reserve System.

final goods   Goods that are sold to firms, the public, or the government for any purpose other than use as an input to production; all goods excluding intermediate ones.

finance   The sale/purchase of assets.

fine tuning   Continuous attempts to stabilize the economy in the face of small disturbances.

fiscal accommodation   Fiscal response to a supply shock; prevents it from affecting output.

fiscal policy   Government policy with respect to government purchases, transfer payments, and the tax structure.

fiscal policy multiplier   Increase in aggregate demand for a $1 increase in government purchases (or other changes in autonomous demand).

Fisher relationship   Tendency of inflation and nominal interest rates to move together.

Fisher equation $i = r + \pi^e$

fixed exchange rate system   A system in which exchange rates are determined by governments and central banks rather than the free market, and maintained through foreign exchange market intervention.

flexible accelerator model   Asserts that firms plan their investment to close a fraction of the gap between their actual capital stock and their desired capital stock; a result is that firms with a larger gap between their actual and desired capital stocks accumulate capital more quickly than other firms.

flexible (floating) exchange rate system   A system in which exchange rates are allowed to fluctuate with the forces of supply and demand. See also *clean floating* and *dirty floating*.

flight out of money   Tendency of people to hold goods rather than assets during periods of high inflation.

flow of investment   The amount of spending per unit of time, usually per quarter or year, that adds to the physical stock of capital.

flow variable   A variable that is measured in rates per unit time rather than levels. Contrast *stock variable*.

foreign exchange market intervention   The sale/purchase of currency in foreign exchange markets for the express purpose of increasing or decreasing the value of the domestic currency. Carried out by a country's central bank.

fractional reserve banking   Banks are only required to keep a fraction of their deposits in the form of cash, or cash equivalents.

frequency of unemployment   The average number of times, per period, that workers become unemployed.

frictional unemployment   Unemployment associated with the movement of workers in and out of jobs in "normal" times.

full-employment budget surplus   What the budget surplus would be (hypothetically) with existing fiscal policy if the economy were at full employment.

full-employment output   See *potential output*.

G

GDP deflator   Measure of the price level obtained by dividing nominal GDP by real GDP.

GDP gap   Difference between actual GDP and potential GDP. See *output gap*.

GDP per capita   GDP per person.

globalization   Notion that the world is moving toward a single global economy.

golden-rule capital stock   The steady-state level of capital that provides the most consumption each period. When the capital stock is at the golden-rule level, the marginal product of capital is equal to the rate of depreciation plus the rate of population growth (and, when there is growth in technology, the rate of technological progress).

goods market equilibrium schedule   See *IS curve*.

government budget constraint   A limit that says the government can finance its deficits only by selling bonds (accumulating debt) or by increasing the monetary base.

government budget deficit   Excess of government expenditure over government revenue.

government expenditure   Total government spending; includes both government purchases and transfers.

government purchases   Government spending on goods and services. Contrast *government expenditure*.

government saving   Saving by the government; the difference between the revenues taken in (i.e., from taxes) and the money used/given away (i.e., transfer payments, interest payments on the national debt).

gradualism   Policy strategy of moving toward a desired target slowly.

Great Depression   A historical period of very low output and very high unemployment that occurred during the years 1929–1941 in the United States. A number of other countries also experienced severe depressions during this period.

gross domestic product (GDP)   Measure of all final goods and services produced within the country in 1 year. Real GDP measured in units of constant value. Nominal GDP measured in dollars.

gross investment   Total investment; flow into the capital stock.

gross national product (GNP)   Measure of the value of all final goods and services produced by domestically owned factors of production.

gross private domestic investment   The total amount of investment spending by businesses and firms located within a country.

growth accounting   The theory of measurement of the sources of economic growth.

growth accounting equation   The equation that summarizes the relationship between input growth and output growth.

growth rate   Rate at which a variable increases in value; percentage change in the level of a variable.

growth theory   Tries to explain why output grows over time and to identify the factors that affect its growth rate.

H

heterodox approach to stabilization   Coordinated use of monetary, fiscal, and exchange rate policies accompanied by wage and price controls.

high-powered money   Currency (notes and coins) and banks' deposits at the Fed; also called the *monetary base*.

human capital   Education and training of individuals to increase productivity.

hyperinflation   Very rapid price increase, sometimes defined as over 1,000 percent per year.

hysteresis   Occurs when temporary fluctuations in one variable have permanent effects on another. See also *unemployment hysteresis*.

I

imperfect competition   Form of competition in which firms have market power—can choose, to some extent, the price at which they will sell the goods they produce.

imperfect information   Incomplete information. Forecasts based on imperfect information will be less than fully accurate, though not necessarily biased.

income elasticity of money   Amount that demand for real money balances changes, in percentage terms, when income increases by 1 percent.

income velocity of money   Ratio of income to the money stock.

incomes policies   Attempts to reduce inflation by wage or price controls.

increasing returns to scale   When, in a production function, doubling all of the inputs to the production process more than doubles output.

indexation   Automatic adjustment of prices and wages according to inflation rate.

indexed debt   Debt in which interest payments are adjusted upward each year to account for inflation.

indicators   Economic variables that signal us as to whether we are getting close to our desired targets.

inflation   Percentage rate of increase in the general price level.

inflation differential   Difference between domestic and foreign rates of inflation.

inflation targeting   Using monetary and fiscal policy to achieve a particular inflation rate.

inflation tax   Revenue gained by the government because of inflation's devaluation of money holdings.

inflation-adjusted deficit   Measure of the budget deficit that adjusts for effects of inflation; specifically, the correction reduces the measured budget deficit by the capital gain on nominal bonds.

inflationary inertia   The tendency of inflation rates to only decrease slowly over time.

inside lag   Period between the time a disturbance occurs and the time action is taken.

insider-outsider model   Predicts that wages will remain above the market-clearing level because those who are unemployed do not sit at the bargaining table.

instruments   The tools policymakers manipulate directly to affect the economy.

interest differential   Difference between rates of interest paid in different countries for the same asset, or in the same country for different assets.

interest elasticity of money   Percentage change in the demand for real money balances resulting from a 1 percent increase in the interest rate.

intergenerational accounting   Evaluates the costs and benefits of taxes and spending for various age groups in society.

intermediate goods   Goods used to produce other goods or services; flour purchased by bakers is an example.

intermediate targets Policy targets used for control rather than because of their inherent interest. For example, the money supply might be an intermediate target in the attempt to ultimately control inflation. Contrast *ultimate targets.*

internal balance Occurs when output equals potential output.

International Monetary Fund (IMF) International organization created to promote international monetary cooperation; makes its resources temporarily available, under stringent conditions, to member countries experiencing balance-of-payments problems.

international trade The exchange of goods and services between countries.

intertemporal substitution of leisure The extent to which temporarily high real wages cause workers to work harder today and enjoy more leisure tomorrow.

intervention Sales or purchases of foreign exchange by the central bank in order to stabilize exchange rates.

inventory cycle Response of inventory investment to changes in sales that causes further changes in aggregate demand.

inventory investment Increase in the stock of goods on hands.

investment Purchase of new capital, principally by the business sector.

investment subsidy Government payment of part of the cost of private investment.

investment tax credit Tax credit given to firms when they reinvest their earnings.

IS **curve** Shows all of the combinations of the real interest rate and the level of output for which the goods market is in equilibrium ($Y = C + I + G + NX$).

IS-LM **model** Interaction of *IS* and *LM* curves determines the real interest rate and the level of income for a given price level, for which both goods and money markets are in equilibrium.

J

J-curve effect Observation that when a currency depreciates, the value of net exports rises temporarily, and then falls.

just-in-time inventory management Inventory management strategy; firms hold inventories for as short a time as possible by sending goods out as soon as they are produced, and ordering parts only as they are needed.

K

Keynesian aggregate supply curve Horizontal aggregate supply curve.

L

L The broadest definition of money considered by the Federal Reserve.

labor force Consists of people who are working and people who are actively looking for work.

labor market turnover The frequency with which workers change jobs in an economy.

layoff   A suspension without pay lasting or expected to last more than 7 consecutive days, initiated by the employer without prejudice to the worker.

life-cycle hypothesis   Consumption theory emphasizing that consumers consume and save out of total life income and plan to provide for retirement.

lifetime budget constraint   Limits amount of money we can spend over our lifetimes; the total amount of money that we earn/inherit/find on the street over our lifetimes.

lifetime utility   The total benefit we derive from consumption (and whatever other activities we value) over our lifetimes.

liquid assets   Assets that can be easily and quickly converted into the unit of account (dollars in the United States). Easily used to make transactions.

liquidity   A measure of the ability to make funds available on short notice.

liquidity constraint   Limitations on ability to borrow in order to finance consumption plans.

liquidity trap   Horizontal *LM* curve due to extreme interest sensitivity of money demand.

LM curve   Shows all of the combinations of the real interest rate and the level of output for which the demand for real money balances equals the supply of real money balances. Drawn for a given price level.

long run   In *AS–AD* analysis, period of time long enough for prices to clear all markets so that output is equal to potential output, but short enough for potential output to be fixed.

loss function   A rule used to evaluate the success of a policy. It measures the damage done when the policy misses its target.

Lucas (econometric policy evaluation) critique   Points out that many macroeconomic models assume that expectations are given by a particular function, when that function can change.

M

M1   Currency plus checkable deposits.

M2   *M*1 plus small time and savings deposits, overnight repurchase agreements (RPs) and eurodollars, and money market funds.

M3   *M*2 plus other liquid assets.

Maastricht Treaty   Treaty that created a common European currency and central bank.

managed (dirty) floating   Flexible exchange rate system in which central banks intervene in exchange markets to moderate short-run fluctuations in exchange rates.

mandatory outlays   Spending made under entitlement programs.

marginal loss function   Measures the change in the loss function from a small change in the policy instrument.

marginal product of capital (*MPK*)   Increment to output obtained by adding one unit of capital, with other factor inputs held constant.

marginal product of labor (*MPL*)   Increment to output obtained by adding one unit of labor, with other factor inputs held constant.

marginal propensity to consume   Increase in consumption for each $1 increase in disposable income.

marginal propensity to import   The increase in the demand for imports that results from a 1-unit increase in domestic income.

marginal propensity to save   Increase in savings for each $1 increase in disposable income. Equals 1 minus the marginal propensity to consume.

marginal utility of consumption   The increase in utility from consuming an additional unit of some good.

market share   The fraction of a market's sales made by a firm, or by firms from a particular country.

maturity (or term) of bond   Length of time until a bond expires.

medium of exchange   One of the roles of money; asset used to make payments.

menu cost   Small cost incurred when the nominal price of a good is changed; for example, the cost for a restaurant of reprinting its menus when it raises/lowers its prices.

misery index   Index used by political analysts to measure people's unhappiness with the dual problems of inflation and unemployment; the sum of inflation and unemployment.

monetary accommodation   Use of monetary policy to stabilize interest rates during active fiscal policy operations; also the use of monetary policy to prevent a supply shock from affecting output.

monetary approach to the balance of payments   Emphasizes monetary causes of balance-of-payments problems.

monetary base   See *high-powered money.*

monetary policy multiplier   Increase in aggregate demand for $1 increase in the money supply.

monetary-base targeting   Using monetary policy to keep the monetary base at a particular level.

monetization   See *monetizing budget deficits.*

monetizing budget deficits   Purchase of government debt by the Federal Reserve, thus indirectly funding the deficit by printing money.

money (money stock)   Assets that can be used for making immediate payment.

money illusion   Belief that the numbers used to express prices have significance— that changes in the nominal price of a good are meaningful in and of themselves.

money market equilibrium schedule   See *LM curve.*

money multiplier   Ratio of money stock to the monetary base.

multiplier   Increase in endogenous variable for each $1 increase in exogenous variable; particularly, increase in GDP for each $1 increase in government purchases.

multiplier uncertainty   Uncertainty about effects of policy changes due to uncertainty about value of fiscal policy multiplier, monetary policy multiplier, and so on.

Mundell-Fleming model   Model first proposed by Robert Mundell and Marcus Fleming that explores economy with flexible exchange rates and perfect capital mobility.

myopia   Shortsightedness by households regarding future income streams.

N

national income   Total payments to factors of production; net national product minus indirect taxes.

national income accounting identity $Y \equiv C + I + G + NX.$

natural rate of unemployment   Rate of unemployment at which the flows into and out of the unemployment pool balance; also the point on the augmented Phillips curve at which expected inflation equals actual inflation.

neoclassical growth theory   Theory that asserts that the growth rate of output is determined by exogenous technological growth.

net domestic product (NDP)   GDP minus allowance for depreciation of capital.

net exports   Exports minus imports.

net investment   Gross investment less depreciation; measures the increase in the capital stock each period.

net investment income   The interest and profits that result from foreign assets held by domestic residents less the income foreigners earn on the domestic assets *they* own.

net present value   Same as present value; amount today that is equivalent to a future payment—the amount of money that, invested at the market interest rate, would generate that amount of money.

neutrality of money   Proposition that equiproportional changes in the money stock and prices leave the economy unaffected.

New Classical economics   Belief that the private economy is inherently efficient and that the government ought not to attempt to stabilize output and unemployment.

New Deal   Slogan for Franklin D. Roosevelt's economic policy reforms.

New Economics   Economic policy of the Kennedy-Johnson years, emphasizing the use of Keynesian theory to maintain full employment.

New Keynesian economics   Models whose basis is rational behavior and conclude that the economy is not inherently efficient and that, at times, the government ought to stabilize output and unemployment.

nominal exchange rate   The price of one currency in terms of another.

nominal GDP   Value of all final goods and services produced in the economy; not adjusted for inflation.

nominal GDP targeting   Using monetary policy to achieve a certain level of GDP, or to achieve a particular rate of growth of GDP.

nominal interest rate   Expresses the payment in current dollars on a loan or other investment (over and above principal repayment) in terms of an annual percentage.

nominal money supply   Nominal value of bills and coins in circulation; says nothing about the amount that these bills and coins can purchase.

nonsterilized intervention   Occurs when the central bank does not use monetary policy to offset the effect of foreign exchange market intervention on the domestic money supply. Contrast *sterilized intervention.*

O

Okun's law   Empirical law relating GDP growth to changes in unemployment; named for its discoverer, the late Arthur Okun.

OPEC   Organization of Petroleum Exporting Countries, an international oil cartel.

open economy   An economy that trades goods, services, and assets with other countries.

open market desk   The facility at the New York Fed through which the Fed buys and sells government securities on the secondary market on a daily basis.

open market operation   Federal Reserve purchase or sale of Treasury bills in exchange for money.

open market purchase   An operation in which the Fed buys government bonds on the secondary market. Contrast *open market sale.*

open market sale   An operation in which the Fed sells government bonds on the secondary market.

operational bequest motive   A reason for saving; desire to leave some of one's money behind for descendants, friends, or charity.

opportunity cost   What is forgone to take an action. For example, one opportunity cost of attending college is the lost wages the student could be earning in a full-time job.

optimal   Best.

output gap   Difference between actual GDP and potential GDP.

outside lag   Time required for a policy change to take effect.

own rate of interest   The interest rate paid on money (often zero).

P

parameter   Type of exogenous variable; gives a function its specific form. The parameter θ in the function $K^\theta L^{1-\theta}$ is an example.

pay-as-you-go social security system   Social security system in which payments to retirees are made with funds provided, not by their social security taxes, but by the social security taxes paid by the working population.

pegging the interest rate   The practice of using monetary policy to keep the interest rate near a target level.

perfect capital mobility   Capital is perfectly mobile when it has the ability to move instantly, and with a minimum of transactions costs, across national borders in search of the highest return.

perfect foresight   Assumption that people know the future value of all relevant variables, or that their expectations are always correct.

perfectly/imperfectly anticipated inflation   The extent to which people have perfect foresight with regards to the inflation rate.

permanent-income theory   Says that people form expectations of their future income and choose how much to consume based on those as well as their current income.

personal saving   Saving by individuals and families.

Phillips curve   Relation between inflation and unemployment; in a sense, a dynamic version of the aggregate supply curve.

policy irrelevance   Refers to the inability of monetary or fiscal policy to affect output in rational expectations equilibrium models.

policy mix   Combination of fiscal and monetary policy to achieve both *internal* and *external* balance.

policy variable   An exogenous variable whose value is determined by government policy.

political business cycle theory Theory that politicians deliberately manipulate the economy to produce an economic boom at election time.

portfolio The mix of assets someone owns.

portfolio disequilibrium Occurs when people are holding more of some asset (i.e., money) at the prevailing interest rate than they wish to.

portfolio of policy instruments The range of policy instruments available to the policymaker.

potential GDP See *potential output*.

potential output Output that is produced when all factors are fully employed.

precautionary motive A reason people hold money; they do not know how much they'll need to spend.

present value See *net present value*.

price stickiness When prices are unable to adjust quickly enough to keep markets in equilibrium.

primary (or noninterest) deficit The budget deficit except for interest payments.

private saving Saving by individuals, by families, and by firms; saving by everyone other than the government.

producer price index (PPI) Price index based on a market basket of goods used in production. The PPI replaced the wholesale price index (WPI).

production function Technological relation showing how much output can be produced for a given combination of inputs.

productivity shock Change in technology that affects workers' productivity. See also *supply shock*.

propagation mechanism Mechanism by which current economic shocks cause fluctuations in the future, for example, intertemporal substitution of leisure.

purchasing power parity (PPP) Theory of exchange rate determination arguing that the exchange rate adjusts to maintain equal purchasing power of foreign and domestic currency.

Q

q **theory of investment** Investment theory emphasizing that investment will be high when assets are valuable relative to their reproduction cost. The ratio of asset value to cost is called *q*.

quantity equation Money times velocity equals price times quantity ($M \times V = P \times Y$).

quantity theory of money Theory of money demand emphasizing the relation of nominal income to nominal money. Sometimes used to mean a vertical *LM* curve.

R

random walk A variable in which changes over time are unpredictable.

random walk of GDP Theory that suggests most shocks to output have permanent effects—that supply shocks play a more important role in explaining business cycle fluctuations than demand shocks.

random-walk model of consumption Model that suggests consumption should follow a random walk. Because consumption is supposedly based on expected future income as well as current income, changes in consumption should not be predictable.

rational expectations Theory of expectations formation in which expectations are based on all available information about the underlying economic variable; frequently associated with New Classical macroeconomics.

rational expectations equilibrium model A model in which expectations are formed rationally, and markets are always in equilibrium.

real balances Real value of the money stock (number of dollars divided by the price level).

real business cycle (RBC) theory Theory that recessions and booms are due primarily to shocks in real activity, such as supply shocks, rather than to changes in monetary factors.

real devaluation A decline in the purchasing power of the dollar relative to other currencies.

real exchange rate Purchasing power of foreign currency relative to the U.S. dollar.

real GDP A measure of output; adjusts the value of final goods and services to reflect changes in the price level.

real GDP targeting Using monetary and fiscal policy to achieve a particular rate of real GDP growth.

real interest rate Return on an investment measured in dollars of constant value; roughly equal to the difference between the nominal interest rate and the rate of inflation.

real money balances See *real balances*.

real money supply Real value of the bills and coins in circulation; equal to the nominal money supply divided by the price level.

recognition lag Period between the time a disturbance occurs and the time policymakers discover the disturbance.

recovery A sustained period of rising real income.

rental (user) cost of capital Cost of using a dollar's worth of capital for a given unit of time, usually a year.

repercussion effects Feedback of domestic economic changes through foreign economies and back into the domestic economy.

replacement ratio The ratio of after-tax income while unemployed to after-tax income while employed.

reporting effects Changes in the measurement of some variable due to a change in the number of people who claim to be in a certain group; unemployment can appear to rise, for example, when more people register for unemployment benefits.

required-reserve ratio Fraction of a bank's deposits that it is required to keep on reserve.

required reserves The amount of reserves a bank is required to keep at the central bank.

reservation wage The lowest wage an individual is willing to accept; if you were offered a job that paid a wage lower than your reservation wage, you would turn it down.

reserve ratio   Ratio of bank reserves to bank deposits; a primary determinant of the money multiplier.

reserves   Part of a bank's deposit kept at the Fed, or in its vaults; money that a bank keeps on hand instead of lending out.

residential investment   Investment in housing.

revaluation   Increase in the value of the domestic currency relative to the currencies of other countries. Used when exchange rates are fixed.

Ricardian (or Barro-Ricardo) equivalence   Under Barro-Ricardo equivalence, there is no difference between taxes and the accumulation of debt; debt is thought to be the same as future taxes.

risky asset   Asset whose future payoff is uncertain.

rules versus discretion   The issue of whether or not monetary and fiscal authorities should conduct policy in accordance with preannounced rules.

run on a bank   A rapid withdrawal of deposits from a bank. This can result in the forced sale of a bank's illiquid assets at fire-sale prices, causing the bank, even if healthy, to fail.

S

sacrifice ratio   During a period of anti-inflation policy, the ratio of cumulative GDP lost to reduction in the inflation rate.

saving   Money that is not spent.

scatterplot   A graph made up of a number of unconnected points on an X-Y plane.

search unemployment   Unemployment that exists because people have quit one job to search for another.

seigniorage   Revenue derived from the government's ability to print money.

self-fulfilling expectations   Expectations that cause a variable to change in the expected manner; if enough people expect a currency to depreciate, capital flows generated by their expectations will cause it to do so.

short run   A period of time short enough that markets are unable to clear, so that output can deviate from potential output.

social infrastructure   All the institutions and government policies that determine the economic environment.

Solow residual   A measure of total factor productivity; change in the level of production that cannot be accounted for by changes in factor inputs.

speculative bubble   Occurs when the value of a variable departs from the level that the factors that determine its value suggest; when people argue that a stock is over- or undervalued, they are suggesting that such a bubble exists.

speculative motive   A reason people hold money; although the return on holding money is small, people hold it because it reduces the risk associated with their portfolio of assets.

speed of price adjustment   Amount of time that it takes prices to fully adjust so that all markets are in equilibrium and output equals potential output.

spell of unemployment   The amount of time that the average person spends in the unemployment pool.

spillover (interdependence) effects   Occur when policy changes or supply/demand shocks in one country affect output in another.

stable equilibrium   An equilibrium that draws nearby variables into itself; if a variable is moved slightly away from a stable equilibrium, it will return.

stagflation   Simultaneous inflation and recession.

staggered price adjustment   Occurs when firms set their prices or negotiate their contracts at different times.

standard of deferred payment   Asset normally used for making payments due at a later date.

steady-state equilibrium   State in which real (per capita) economic variables are constant.

sterilization   Open market purchase or sale by the Fed in order to offset effects of foreign exchange market intervention on the monetary base.

sterilized intervention   Occurs when the central bank uses monetary policy to offset the effect of foreign exchange market intervention on the domestic money supply.

sticky real wages   See *wage stickiness*.

stock of capital   See *capital stock*.

stock variable   A variable that is measured in levels rather than rates of change. Contrast *flow variable*.

store of value   Asset that maintains its value over time.

structural deficit   Deficit that would exist with current fiscal policy if the economy were at full employment. Formerly called "high-employment" or "full-employment" deficit. Contrast *cyclical deficit*.

supply shock   An economic disturbance whose first impact is a shift in the aggregate supply curve.

supply-side policy   Policy that causes the aggregate supply curve to shift.

T

target zone   A specified range to which central banks limit exchange rate fluctuations.

targets   Identified goals of policy.

tariff   A tax imposed on imported goods.

term of bond   See *maturity of bond*.

term premium   Premium paid holders of bonds for the risk associated with a particular maturity.

term structure of interest   The relationship between interest rates on bonds of different maturities.

total factor productivity   Rate at which productivity of inputs increases; measure of technological progress. See also *Solow residual*.

trade   See *international trade*.

trade balance   The net flow of dollars into the country due to sales of goods abroad.

transactions motive   A reason people hold money—they use it to purchase goods and services.

transfer payments   Money given by the government to individuals, not in exchange for goods or services; welfare payments are an example. See also *entitlement programs*.

transmission mechanism   Process by which monetary policy affects aggregate demand.

trend (secular) component of GDP   Potential output.

trend path of GDP   See *trend path of output*.

trend path of output   The path followed by potential output over time.

trend stationary   A variable is trend stationary when temporary shocks do *not* permanently affect its level. Changes in *AD*, for example, can only temporarily affect output. If changes in output were driven primarily by demand shocks, output would be trend stationary.

trend stationary with breaks   Trend stationary, but with a trend that sometimes changes.

U

ultimate targets   Policy targets of inherent interest. For example, the inflation rate might be an ultimate target. Contrast *intermediate targets*.

uncovered interest parity   Relationship between interest differentials and expected currency appreciation.

unemployed person   A person who does not have a job but is actively seeking one.

unemployment gap   The difference between the actual unemployment rate and the natural rate.

unemployment hysteresis   Theory that argues that recessions may permanently affect the natural rate of unemployment.

unemployment pool   Group of individuals in transition between jobs.

unemployment rate   The fraction of the labor force that is out of work and looking for a job or expecting a recall from a layoff.

unit of account   Asset in which prices are denoted.

unit labor cost   The total amount a firm pays to labor divided by the number of units produced.

unstable equilibrium   An equilibrium that pushes nearby variables away from itself; if a variable is moved slightly away from an unstable equilibrium, forces will push it even further away.

V

value added   Increase in value of output at a given stage of production. Equivalently, value of output minus cost of inputs.

velocity of money   The number of times the typical dollar changes hands during the year.

very long run   A period of decades or more, over which potential output is expected to grow.

W

wage-price spiral   A process in which changes in prices feed back into wages, and from there again into prices.

wage stickiness   When wages are unable to adjust quickly enough to clear the labor market.

World Trade Organization (WTO)   International organization that works out rules of trade between its member nations; created January 1, 1995, as a result of the Uruguay Round of the General Agreement on Tariffs and Trade (GATT).

Y

yield curve   Shows how interest rates change as bond maturities increase.

INDEX

Selected Historical Series on U.S. Gross Domestic Product and Related Series (Billions of chained 1996 dollars, except as noted)

YEAR	GDP (1996 DOLLARS)	GDP (CURRENT DOLLARS)	IMPLICIT PRICE DEFLATOR (1996 = 100)	PERSONAL CONSUMPTION EXPENDITURES	GROSS PRIVATE DOMESTIC INVESTMENT	GOVERNMENT CONSUMPTION EXPENDITURES AND GROSS INVESTMENT	EXPORTS	IMPORTS	DISPOSABLE PERSONAL INCOME	SAVINGS AS A % OF DISPOSABLE PERSONAL INCOME
1929	822.2	103.7	12.6	625.7	93.6	110.1	35.8	46.3	672.3	4.7
1930	751.5	91.3	12.1	592.3	62.5	121.3	29.6	40.3	629.3	4.3
1931	703.6	76.6	10.9	574.3	39.2	126.6	24.6	35.1	607.8	4.0
1932	611.8	58.8	9.6	523.0	11.8	122.4	19.3	29.2	526.5	−0.8
1933	603.3	56.4	9.3	511.0	17.5	118.0	19.4	30.4	510.7	−1.5
1934	668.3	66.0	9.9	546.9	31.6	133.0	21.5	31.0	560.3	1.2
1935	728.3	73.3	10.1	580.6	58.4	137.0	22.7	40.7	614.7	4.4
1936	822.5	83.7	10.2	639.6	74.9	158.9	23.9	40.2	692.2	6.4
1937	865.8	91.9	10.6	663.5	93.6	153.2	30.1	45.2	716.6	6.2
1938	835.6	86.1	10.3	652.6	61.9	164.6	29.8	35.2	675.9	2.2
1939	903.5	92.0	10.2	689.0	79.6	179.7	31.4	36.9	732.3	4.7
1940	980.7	101.3	10.3	724.9	110.9	182.4	35.7	37.8	781.1	5.9
1941	1148.8	126.7	11.0	776.7	135.4	303.0	36.7	46.5	899.0	12.4
1942	1360.0	161.8	11.9	758.3	71.6	711.1	24.1	42.2	1012.4	24.4
1943	1583.7	198.4	12.5	779.1	42.3	1059.9	20.1	53.2	1057.9	25.8
1944	1714.1	219.7	12.8	801.7	52.2	1195.6	21.6	55.7	1096.1	26.3
1945	1693.3	223.0	13.2	851.8	69.0	1041.0	30.5	59.2	1081.5	20.6
1946	1505.5	222.3	14.8	956.9	175.0	359.7	66.5	49.1	1074.4	10.1
1947	1495.1	244.4	16.3	976.4	168.6	307.1	75.9	46.6	1035.2	4.7
1948	1560.0	269.6	17.3	998.1	215.3	328.9	59.8	54.4	1090.0	7.3
1949	1550.9	267.7	17.3	1025.3	164.3	367.3	59.2	52.5	1095.6	5.2
1950	1686.6	294.3	17.4	1090.9	232.5	367.4	51.8	62.0	1192.7	7.2
1951	1815.1	339.5	18.7	1107.1	233.2	500.0	63.5	64.5	1227.0	8.5
1952	1887.3	358.6	19.0	1142.4	211.1	605.1	60.6	70.1	1266.8	8.5
1953	1973.9	379.9	19.2	1197.2	221.0	647.5	56.5	76.7	1327.5	8.2
1954	1960.5	381.1	19.4	1221.9	210.8	602.9	59.3	72.9	1344.0	7.5
1955	2099.5	415.2	19.8	1310.4	262.1	580.4	65.6	81.7	1433.8	6.9
1956	2141.1	438.0	20.5	1348.8	258.6	580.8	76.5	88.4	1502.3	8.4
1957	2183.9	461.5	21.1	1381.8	247.4	606.7	83.1	92.1	1539.5	8.4
1958	2162.8	467.9	21.6	1393.0	226.5	626.2	71.8	96.4	1553.7	8.5
1959	2319.0	507.4	21.9	1470.7	272.9	661.4	72.4	106.6	1623.8	7.6
1960	2376.7	527.4	22.2	1510.8	272.8	661.3	87.5	108.0	1664.8	7.2
1961	2432.0	545.7	22.4	1541.2	271.0	693.2	88.9	107.3	1720.0	8.3
1962	2578.9	586.5	22.7	1617.3	305.3	735.0	93.7	119.5	1803.5	8.3
1963	2690.4	618.7	23.0	1684.0	325.7	752.4	100.7	122.7	1871.5	7.8
1964	2846.5	664.4	23.3	1784.8	352.6	767.1	114.2	129.2	2006.9	8.8
1965	3028.5	720.1	23.8	1897.6	402.0	791.1	116.5	142.9	2131.0	8.6
1966	3227.5	789.3	24.5	2006.1	437.3	862.1	124.3	164.2	2244.6	8.3
1967	3308.3	834.1	25.2	2066.2	417.2	927.1	127.0	176.2	2340.5	9.4
1968	3466.1	911.5	26.3	2184.2	441.3	956.6	136.3	202.4	2448.2	8.4
1969	3571.4	985.3	27.6	2264.8	466.9	952.5	143.7	213.9	2524.3	7.8
1970	3578.0	1039.7	29.1	2317.5	436.2	931.1	159.3	223.1	2630.0	9.4
1971	3697.7	1128.6	30.5	2405.2	485.8	913.8	160.4	235.0	2745.3	10.0
1972	3898.4	1240.4	31.8	2550.5	543.0	914.9	173.5	261.3	2874.3	8.9
1973	4123.4	1385.5	33.6	2675.9	606.5	908.3	211.4	273.4	3072.3	10.5
1974	4099.0	1501.0	36.6	2653.7	561.7	924.8	231.6	267.2	3051.9	10.7
1975	4084.4	1635.2	40.0	2710.9	462.2	942.5	230.0	237.5	3108.5	10.6
1976	4311.7	1823.9	42.3	2868.9	555.5	943.3	243.6	284.0	3243.5	9.4
1977	4511.8	2031.4	45.0	2992.1	639.4	952.7	249.7	315.0	3360.7	8.7
1978	4760.6	2295.9	48.2	3124.7	713.0	982.2	275.9	342.3	3527.5	9.0
1979	4912.1	2566.4	52.2	3203.2	735.4	1001.1	302.4	347.9	3628.6	9.2
1980	4900.9	2795.6	57.0	3193.0	655.3	1020.9	334.8	324.8	3658.0	10.2
1981	5021.0	3131.3	62.4	3236.0	715.6	1030.0	338.6	333.4	3741.1	10.8
1982	4919.3	3259.2	66.3	3275.5	615.2	1046.0	314.6	329.2	3791.7	10.9
1983	5132.3	3534.9	68.9	3454.3	673.7	1081.0	306.9	370.7	3906.9	8.8
1984	5505.2	3932.7	71.4	3640.6	871.5	1118.4	332.6	461.0	4207.6	10.6
1985	5717.1	4213.0	73.7	3820.9	863.4	1190.5	341.6	490.7	4347.8	9.2
1986	5912.4	4452.9	75.3	3981.2	857.7	1255.2	366.8	531.9	4486.6	8.2
1987	6113.3	4742.5	77.6	4113.4	879.3	1292.5	408.0	564.2	4582.5	7.3
1988	6368.4	5108.3	80.2	4279.5	902.8	1307.5	473.5	585.6	4784.1	7.8
1989	6591.8	5489.1	83.3	4393.7	936.5	1343.5	529.4	608.8	4906.5	7.5
1990	6707.9	5803.2	86.5	4474.5	907.3	1387.3	575.7	632.2	5014.2	7.8
1991	6676.4	5986.2	89.7	4466.6	829.5	1403.4	613.2	629.0	5033.0	8.3
1992	6880.0	6318.9	91.8	4594.5	899.8	1410.0	651.0	670.8	5189.3	8.7
1993	7062.6	6642.3	94.0	4748.9	977.9	1398.8	672.7	731.8	5261.3	7.1
1994	7347.7	7054.3	96.0	4928.1	1107.0	1400.1	732.8	819.4	5397.2	6.1
1995	7543.8	7400.5	98.1	5075.6	1140.6	1406.4	808.2	886.6	5539.1	5.6
1996	7813.2	7813.2	100.0	5237.5	1242.7	1421.9	874.2	963.1	5677.7	4.8
1997	8159.5	8318.4	101.9	5423.9	1393.3	1455.4	981.5	1094.8	5854.5	4.2
1998	8508.9	8781.5	103.2	5683.7	1558.0	1483.3	1002.4	1223.5	6168.6	4.7
1999	8859.0	9274.3	104.7	5964.5	1660.5	1540.6	1036.3	1356.8	6328.4	2.6
2000	9191.4	9824.6	106.9	6223.9	1762.9	1582.5	1137.2	1536.0	6630.3	2.8
2001	9214.5	10082.2	109.4	6377.2	1574.6	1640.4	1076.1	1492.0	6748.0	2.3
2002	9439.9	10446.2	110.7	6576.0	1589.6	1712.8	1058.8	1547.4	7032.2	3.7

Source: *Bureau of Economic Analysis*, www.bea.gov/

Real Net Stock of U.S. Fixed Reproductible Tangible Wealth, 1929–2001

(Billions of chained 1996 dollars; yearend estimates)

YEAREND	TOTAL	FIXED PRIVATE CAPITAL	NONRESIDENTIAL	EQUIPMENT AND SOFTWARE	STRUCTURES	RESIDENTIAL	GOVERNMENT-OWNED FIXED CAPITAL	FEDERAL	STATE AND LOCAL	DURABLE GOODS OWNED BY CONSUMERS
		TOTAL	TOTAL				TOTAL			
1929	3604.2	3253.0	1658.2	266.3	1513.3	1589.7	462.6	81.1	404.1	147.2
1930	3672.0	3294.3	1687.0	268.7	1543.3	1601.0	488.7	81.6	431.7	149.7
1931	3695.3	3291.0	1678.5	260.6	1547.9	1606.6	515.8	83.4	459.4	147.7
1932	3678.4	3248.1	1644.7	244.5	1538.2	1599.4	537.7	86.0	479.7	141.3
1933	3646.6	3198.5	1606.7	230.1	1519.9	1590.5	552.7	91.5	489.1	135.2
1934	3640.2	3167.1	1582.2	222.4	1504.6	1585.7	572.3	99.0	501.4	131.4
1935	3653.0	3153.9	1569.6	221.0	1492.4	1587.3	593.3	109.2	512.1	130.7
1936	3705.9	3168.8	1575.5	227.7	1487.3	1594.5	627.3	119.0	537.7	134.1
1937	3767.4	3198.5	1595.7	238.5	1491.4	1604.2	655.8	127.9	557.7	139.1
1938	3805.5	3200.1	1589.0	237.1	1486.8	1613.9	688.0	136.3	582.4	139.3
1939	3864.9	3221.6	1589.8	238.8	1483.2	1635.7	724.9	143.9	612.8	143.8
1940	3936.9	3259.6	1600.8	247.9	1480.7	1663.2	758.0	155.8	634.8	151.1
1941	4089.5	3319.1	1629.5	262.6	1487.8	1693.0	848.1	227.3	646.8	156.0
1942	4348.0	3310.8	1617.7	259.6	1478.7	1698.7	1090.8	455.7	648.1	154.9
1943	4648.8	3286.1	1598.3	255.2	1463.4	1694.6	1391.0	754.6	642.4	150.8
1944	4901.0	3281.1	1598.3	261.6	1453.2	1689.0	1639.8	1008.3	635.4	145.9
1945	5009.1	3302.6	1624.5	282.1	1451.1	1684.2	1727.1	1101.9	630.1	144.3
1946	5000.6	3408.3	1683.6	311.6	1475.6	1729.4	1606.2	978.8	630.4	160.1
1947	5043.0	3545.4	1757.1	356.5	1496.0	1794.8	1503.5	866.4	638.1	182.0
1948	5123.5	3700.7	1834.0	398.8	1523.5	1873.1	1425.5	773.8	650.4	202.4
1949	5227.3	3824.6	1888.0	425.0	1548.9	1943.3	1401.3	726.8	672.1	224.6
1950	5382.0	3991.5	1953.1	454.8	1580.5	2045.8	1383.1	681.8	697.8	255.1
1951	5581.1	4136.9	2018.1	482.6	1615.2	2125.8	1438.1	710.0	724.4	272.7
1952	5788.8	4270.7	2075.6	505.8	1647.8	2202.5	1512.3	758.2	751.1	287.2
1953	6011.3	4416.1	2142.3	532.3	1686.0	2281.6	1592.6	808.9	781.1	308.5
1954	6223.2	4559.8	2199.7	550.4	1726.7	2368.8	1661.2	839.2	819.1	323.4
1955	6458.4	4735.0	2273.2	577.2	1772.5	2472.1	1718.7	854.5	861.1	349.6
1956	6685.1	4905.1	2353.5	603.4	1826.5	2562.6	1774.2	867.6	903.5	364.5
1957	6899.1	5063.7	2431.2	629.2	1878.5	2644.1	1830.7	878.2	949.1	381.3
1958	7089.8	5189.3	2477.7	637.3	1919.8	2725.6	1897.4	893.9	1000.1	384.2
1959	7333.5	5356.2	2537.6	653.7	1964.6	2835.4	1975.4	920.8	1051.8	398.2
1960	7566.5	5519.7	2606.1	672.8	2015.5	2933.1	2045.4	939.9	1102.8	411.1
1961	7806.0	5676.7	2669.4	687.9	2066.4	3030.0	2127.1	965.9	1158.5	418.8
1962	8073.0	5860.0	2746.3	711.4	2120.4	3138.2	2213.0	995.2	1215.8	435.3
1963	8361.1	6064.9	2829.1	739.9	2173.9	3263.3	2295.6	1015.2	1278.9	457.3
1964	8679.0	6299.5	2933.8	778.1	2237.6	3395.8	2378.7	1031.1	1346.9	484.4
1965	9032.8	6568.8	3076.6	834.5	2319.6	3520.1	2462.2	1042.2	1419.9	521.3
1966	9403.6	6843.1	3241.3	904.6	2406.2	3626.7	2558.4	1061.0	1497.6	563.1
1967	9753.2	7094.2	3388.3	964.6	2488.2	3725.2	2659.7	1080.1	1580.6	600.2
1968	10117.7	7365.1	3539.5	1027.3	2570.7	3843.8	2751.6	1086.3	1666.6	646.1
1969	10484.3	7652.6	3703.4	1097.4	2658.8	3965.8	2830.0	1086.2	1745.3	687.3
1970	10806.3	7910.3	3849.5	1154.8	2744.4	4074.7	2894.0	1080.9	1814.9	716.2
1971	11141.1	8194.5	3982.2	1205.1	2825.4	4227.3	2943.9	1065.8	1879.3	754.9
1972	11533.1	8531.5	4136.8	1273.5	2907.4	4411.4	3000.0	1062.9	1938.6	806.0
1973	11956.9	8909.8	4332.7	1371.1	3000.1	4593.1	3047.1	1052.1	1996.6	867.7
1974	12315.0	9220.4	4513.5	1462.3	3085.2	4720.6	3098.0	1045.4	2053.3	905.7
1975	12590.4	9443.5	4636.8	1517.0	3151.4	4819.1	3150.7	1042.8	2107.6	939.0
1976	12901.9	9707.8	4764.4	1577.1	3217.1	4955.6	3200.2	1040.4	2159.0	989.8
1977	13285.4	10048.2	4925.8	1663.6	3286.3	5135.6	3242.7	1039.0	2203.7	1050.9
1978	13738.9	10448.0	5131.9	1777.6	3371.4	5329.4	3295.0	1039.2	2256.0	1114.0
1979	14213.5	10861.0	5362.5	1899.7	3474.8	5509.4	3354.7	1043.6	2311.7	1166.0
1980	14605.5	11189.8	5568.6	1989.6	3588.9	5631.3	3416.3	1050.5	2366.0	1188.4
1981	14980.5	11510.3	5783.2	2074.1	3718.3	5734.7	3470.0	1060.9	2409.3	1210.8
1982	15264.5	11746.5	5947.9	2121.1	3838.0	5801.7	3518.1	1072.9	2445.0	1228.0
1983	15590.8	12019.1	6090.7	2173.4	3928.1	5931.7	3572.2	1091.4	2480.7	1275.9
1984	16042.1	12402.4	6309.5	2271.0	4048.3	6094.0	3641.3	1115.1	2526.0	1353.7
1985	16527.3	12800.6	6545.1	2365.9	4188.4	6254.6	3727.2	1147.3	2579.7	1446.0
1986	17004.1	13182.6	6735.2	2446.4	4296.9	6447.6	3821.5	1182.9	2638.7	1552.0
1987	17455.4	13537.4	6899.1	2505.8	4401.8	6638.1	3918.6	1220.8	2698.1	1647.5
1988	17898.2	13892.6	7071.4	2578.6	4500.6	6822.2	4006.3	1245.5	2761.1	1745.9
1989	18336.9	14242.9	7248.8	2657.7	4598.4	6993.3	4094.5	1267.9	2826.7	1835.0
1990	18754.3	14561.7	7418.6	2722.4	4703.4	7142.7	4192.6	1291.2	2901.1	1899.0
1991	19074.2	14789.7	7538.6	2769.7	4775.2	7251.7	4283.6	1307.9	2975.4	1914.8
1992	19402.7	15032.6	7648.4	2826.1	4828.2	7384.1	4370.9	1321.6	3048.4	1949.6
1993	19788.3	15344.8	7797.9	2915.0	4886.7	7546.4	4444.6	1326.8	3117.5	2009.5
1994	20205.7	15693.4	7973.6	3035.7	4939.2	7720.0	4511.8	1326.2	3185.5	2087.3
1995	20659.2	16075.1	8190.7	3183.0	5007.5	7884.7	4585.1	1325.9	3259.1	2169.7
1996	21188.9	16521.1	8447.5	3354.0	5093.5	8073.6	4667.7	1333.9	3333.8	2261.5
1997	21758.9	17010.2	8749.1	3554.6	5197.4	8260.9	4749.4	1329.0	3420.2	2368.7
1998	22405.1	17571.9	9099.7	3796.4	5314.1	8474.0	4834.8	1327.1	3506.5	2508.2
1999	23087.4	18155.1	9457.0	4044.6	5434.8	8702.5	4932.4	1327.9	3602.5	2685.5
2000	23801.5	18773.0	9849.0	4321.0	5567.2	8933.4	5028.6	1327.2	3698.2	2880.7
2001	24390.5	19266.9	10115.1	4479.9	5682.3	9161.9	5125.6	1327.2	3793.5	3082.2

Source: *Bureau of Economic Analysis,* www.bea.gov/

Selected International Macroeconomic Statistics

(yearend 2001), except as noted

COUNTRY	GDP PER CAPITA (PPP, U.S. DOLLARS)	INFLATION RATE (GDP DEFLATOR)	UNEMPLOYMENT RATE	EXPORTS—PERCENT OF GDP	EXCHANGE RATE (PER U.S. DOLLAR) AS OF DECEMBER 6th, 2002
Argentina	$12,000	4.0%	25.0%	10.8***	3.56 A. pesos
Australia	$24,000	4.3%	6.7%	19.9*	1.78 A. dollars
Austria	$27,000	2.6%	4.8%	45.1*	0.99 euros
Bangladesh	$1,750	5.8%	35.0%	15.4	57.36 takas
Brazil	$7,400	7.7%	6.4%	13.4	3.75 reals
Cambodia	$1,500	1.6%	2.8%	40.7	3,815.8 riels
Canada	$27,700	2.8%	7.2%	43.7*	1.56 C. dollars
China	$4,300	0.8%	10.0%	25.6	8.28 yuans
Croatia	$8,300	5.0%	23.0%	47.5	7.28 kunas
Denmark	$28,000	2.4%	5.3%	42.4***	7.36 D. kroner
Ethiopia	$700	6.8%	N.A.	15.1	8.36 birr
Finland	$25,800	2.6%	9.4%	42.7***	0.99 euros
France	$25,400	1.7%	8.9%	28.7***	0.99 euros
Germany	$26,200	2.4%	9.4%	33.4***	0.99 euros
Ghana	$1,980	25.0%	20.0%	52.2	8,328.19 cedis
Greece	$17,900	3.4%	11.0%	20.2*	0.99 euros
Haiti	$1,700	14.0%	60%*	12.5***	36.32 gourdes
Hong Kong, China	$25,000	−1.6%	5.2%	150.0***	7.80 H.K. dollars
Hungary	$12,000	9.2%	6.5%	62.5***	234.07 forints
India	$2,500	3.5%	4.4%	13.6	48.23 rupees
Israel	$20,000	1.1%	9.0%	40.0***	4.70 shekels
Italy	$24,300	2.7%	10.0%	28.4***	0.99 euros
Japan	$27,200	−0.6%	4.9%	10.0*	123.84 yen
Kenya	$1,000	3.3%	40.0%	26.6	79.65 shillings
Mexico	$9,000	6.5%	3.0%	27.6	10.21 M. pesos
Morocco	$3,700	1.0%	23%*	30.8	10.46 dirhams
Netherlands	$25,800	4.5%	2.4%	60.6*	0.99 euros
Nigeria	$840	14.9%	28%**	37.0*	127.66 nairas
Norway	$30,800	3.1%	3.6%	46.6***	7.22 N. kroners
Peru	$4,800	1.5%	9.0%	15.9	3.50 nuevos soles
Poland	$8,800	5.3%	16.7%	19.8	3.27 zlotych
Russia	$8,300	21.9%	8.7%	36.8	31.86 rubbles
Rwanda	$1,000	5.0%	N.A.	9.2	487.55 R. francs
South Africa	$9,400	5.8%	37.0%	27.8	9.21 rands
Spain	$18,900	3.8%	13.0%	29.9***	0.99 euros
Sweden	$24,700	2.7%	3.9%	47.4***	8.98 S. kroners
Switzerland	$31,100	1.0%	1.8%	42.1*	1.46 S. francs
Syrian Arab Republic	$3,200	0.3%	20%***	35.5	51.24 S. pounds
Thailand	$6,600	1.6%	3.9%	68.9	43.57 bahts
Uganda	$1,200	3.5%	N.A.	10.5	1,817.90 U. shillings
Ukraine	$4,200	12.0%	3.6%	56.7	5.30 hryvnias
United Arab Emirates	$21,100	4.5%	N.A.	N.A.	3.67 dirhams
United Kingdom	$24,700	1.8%	5.1%	27.2***	0.64 B. pounds
United States	$36,300	2.8%	5.0%	10.7*	1.00 U.S. dollar
Venezuela	$6,100	12.3%	14.1%	22.7	1318.39 bolivars
Vietnam	$2,100	−0.3%	25.0%	43.6****	15,311.00 dongs
Zimbabwe	$2,450	100.0%	60.0%	21.8	54.67 Z. dollars

*1999
**1992
***2000
****1997

Source: *CIA World Factbook,* www.cia.gov; *World Bank, World Development Indicators;* and *The Universal Currency Converter,* www.xe.net/ucc/.

Levels of GDP per Capita (Internationally Comparable 1990 dollars)

	1820	1870	1913	1950	1973	1998
Australia	1,528	3,801	5,505	7,493	12,759	20,390
Bangladesh	531	–	617	540	497	813
Brazil	670	740	839	1,672	3,882	5,459
Canada	893	1,620	4,213	7,437	13,838	20,559
China	600	530	552	439	839	3,117
Egypt	–	–	508	718	1,022	2,128
former USSR	689	943	1,488	2,834	6,058	3,893
Germany	1,058	1,821	3,648	3,881	11,966	17,799
Ghana	–	–	648	1,122	1,407	1,244
India	533	533	673	619	853	1,746
Japan	669	737	1,387	1,926	11,439	20,413
South Korea	–	–	948	770	2,841	12,152
United States	1,257	2,445	5,301	9,561	16,689	27,331

Source: Angus Maddison, *Monitoring the World Economy 1820–1992,* and *The World Economy: A Millennial Perspective* (Paris: Organization for Economic Cooperation and Development, 1995 and 2001.)

THE U.S. CURRENT ACCOUNT AS A PERCENTAGE OF GDP, 1970–2002.

(*Source: Bureau of Economic Analysis.*)

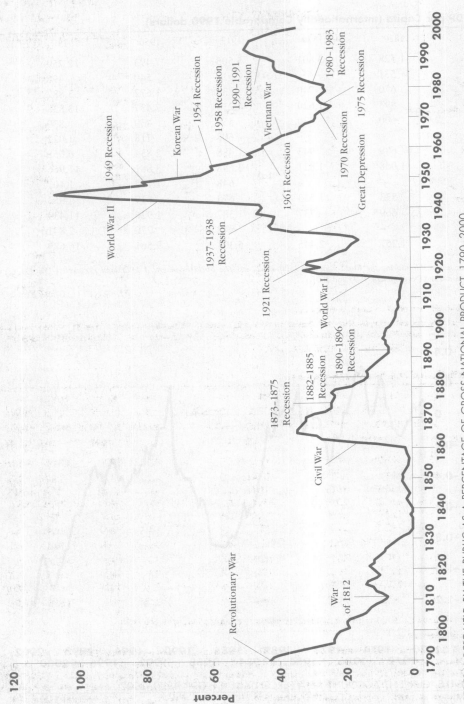

FEDERAL DEBT HELD BY THE PUBLIC AS A PERCENTAGE OF GROSS NATIONAL PRODUCT, 1790–2000.

(Source: Congressional Budget Office.)